COMMON CULTURE

Reading and Writing About American Popular Culture

FIFTH EDITION

Edited by

Michael Petracca
Madeleine Sorapure

University of California at Santa Barbara

D0061192

PEARSON
Prentice
Hall

Upper Saddle River, New Jersey 07458

Library of Congress Cataloging-in-Publication Data

Common culture : reading and writing about American popular culture / edited by
Michael Petracca, Madeleine Sorapure.— 5th ed.
    p. cm.
  Includes bibliographical references and index.
  ISBN-13: 978-0-13-220267-1 (pbk.)
  ISBN-10: 0-13-220267-0 (pbk.)
  1. Popular culture–United States. 2. United States–Social life and customs–1971-
3. United States–Civilization–1970- 4. Popular culture–Study and teaching–United States.
5. United States–Social life and customs–1971—Study and teaching. 6. United States–
Civilization–1970—Study and teaching. I. Petracca, Michael, 1947- II. Sorapure, Madeleine.
  E169.Z83C65 2007
  306.0973--dc22   2006007751

Editorial Director: Leah Jewell
Senior Acquisitions Editor: Brad Potthoff
Editorial Assistant: Tara Culliney
Executive Managing Editor: Ann Marie
  McCarthy
Production Liaison: Fran Russello
Senior Marketing Manager: Windley
  Morley
Marketing Assistant: Kara Pottle
Permissions Coordinator: Fred
  Courtright
Manufacturing Buyer: Mary Ann
  Gloriande
Cover Art Director: Jayne Conte
Cover Design: Bruce Kenselaar

Director, Image Resource Center:
  Melinda Reo
Manager, Rights and Permissions:
  Zina Arabia
Interior Image Specialist: Beth
  Boyd-Brenzel
Cover Image Specialist: Karen Sanatar
Image Permission Coordinator: Cynthia
  Vincenti
Photo Researcher: Kathy Ringrose
Composition/Full-Service Project
  Management: GGS Book Services
Printer/Binder: R.R. Donnelley &
  Sons Company
Cover Printer: Coral Graphic Services, Inc.

Cover art: Douglas Kirkland/CORBIS; (c) Michael A. Keller/Corbis; Andy Crawford
(c) Panasonic Corporation of North America (PNA), Courtesy of Blue Note Records, a
division of Capitol Records, Inc., Dorling Kindersley Images; Laima Druskis/Pearson
Education/PH College

For permission to use copyrighted material, grateful acknowledgment is made to the
copyright holders on pages 631-635, which are hereby made part of this copyright page.

Pearson Education LTD, London
Pearson Education Singapore, Pte. Ltd
Pearson Education, Canada, Ltd
Pearson Education–Japan
Pearson Education Australia PTY, Limited

Pearson Education North Asia Ltd
Pearson Educación de Mexico, S.A. de C.V.
Pearson Education Malaysia, Pte. Ltd
Pearson Education, Upper Saddle River,
  New Jersey

10 9 8 7 6 5 4 3
ISBN: 0-13-220267-0

For my sister, brave explorer of nerve pathways,
healer of wounded neckbones,
dedicated connoisseur of the half-hour sitcom.
—M.P.

For my daughter Sophia, from whom I will learn much about
popular culture (and much else) in the coming years.
—M.S.

Contents

7 Movies 521

Preface

When we started teaching composition courses that examined television, pop music, movies, and other media-generated artifacts, we looked for a text that would cover a full range of topics in the field of popular culture from a variety of theoretical perspectives. We discovered that no satisfactory text existed, and therefore we began putting together assignments and reading materials to meet our needs. From this compilation *Common Culture* emerged.

The more we've taught writing courses based on popular culture, the more convinced we've become that such courses are especially appealing for students and effective in improving their critical thinking, reading, and writing skills. Students come into the writing classroom already immersed in the culture of Britney, Benetton, Beastie Boys, and Barry Bonds. The advantage, then, is that we don't have to "sell" the subject matter of the course and can concentrate on the task at hand—namely, teaching students to think critically and to write clear and effective prose. Obviously, a course that panders to the lowest common denominator of students' taste would be a mindless, unproductive enterprise for all concerned. However, the underlying philosophy of a pop culture-based writing course is this: By reading, thinking, and writing about material they find inherently interesting, students develop their critical and analytical skills—skills which are, of course, crucial to their success in college.

Although students are already familiar with the many aspects of popular culture, few have directed sustained, critical thought to its influence or implications—that is, to what shopping malls might tell them about contemporary culture or to what they've actually learned from watching "Survivor." Because television shows, advertisements, and music videos, for example, are highly crafted artifacts, they are particularly susceptible to analysis; and because so much in contemporary culture is open to interpretation and controversy, students enjoy the opportunity to articulate and argue for their own interpretations of objects and institutions in the world around them.

Although popular culture is undeniably a sexy (or, at least, lively) subject, it has also, in the past decade, become accepted as a legitimate object of academic discourse. While some may contend that it's frivolous to write a dissertation on "Buffy the Vampire Slayer," most scholars recognize the importance of studying the artifacts and institutions of contemporary life. Popular culture is a rich field of study, drawing in researchers from a variety of disciplines. Because it is also a very inviting field of study for students, a textbook that addresses this subject in a comprehensive and challenging way will be especially appealing both to them and to their writing teachers.

Common Culture, Fifth Edition, contains an introductory chapter that walks students through one assignment—in this case, focusing on the Barbie doll—with step-by-step instruction in reading carefully and writing effectively. The chapters that follow open with a relevant and catchy cultural artifact (for example, a cartoon, an ad, an album cover) that leads into a reader-friendly, informative introduction; a selection of engaging essays on an issue of current interest in the field of pop culture; carefully constructed reading and discussion questions; and writing assignments after each reading and at the end of the chapter. This edition also contains sections on visual literacy and conducting research on popular culture, along with a selection of color and black & white images that students can analyze and enjoy.

Common Culture approaches the field of popular culture by dividing it into its constituent parts. The book contains chapters on advertising, television, music, technology, sports, and movies. Most of the chapters are divided into two parts: the first presents essays that address the topic generally, while the second offers essays that explore a specific aspect of the topic in depth. For example, in the chapter on advertising, the essays in the first group discuss theories and strategies of advertising, while later essays explore images of women in advertising.

We've purposely chosen readings that are accessible and thought-provoking, while avoiding those that are excessively theoretical or jargon-ridden. The 46 readings in this book, 24 of which are new to the fifth edition, have the added advantage of serving as good models for students' own writing; they demonstrate a range of rhetorical approaches, such as exposition, analysis, and argumentation, and they offer varying levels of sophistication and difficulty in terms of content and style. Similarly, the suggested discussion and writing topics, now including a "Thinking Rhetorically" prompt with each selection in the fifth edition, move from relatively basic concerns to tasks that require a greater degree of critical skill. Because of this range, instructors using *Common Culture* can easily adapt the book to meet the specific needs of their students.

SUPPLEMENTARY MATERIAL FOR INSTRUCTORS AND STUDENTS

For more details on these supplements, available for college adoptions, please contact your Prentice Hall representative.

Instructor's Manual

A comprehensive Instructor's Manual is available online and includes sample syllabi, teaching tips and other information. Please contact your Prentice Hall representative for access.

Companion Website™

A Companion Website™ to accompany *Common Culture* can be found at *www.prenhall.com/petracca*. This useful Website contains quizzes and objectives for each chapter, additional links, and research tools.

Writer's OneKey

Use Writer's OneKey to enhance your composition classes. Everything in one place on the Web for students and instructors, including:

- Personal tutoring available to students
- Paper review tool and research tools, including The *New York Times* archive
- Visual analysis exercises
- Mini-handbook
- And much more…

A subscription to Writer's OneKey can be packaged with each copy of this text by specifying ISBN 0-13-223599-4. See *www.prenhall.com/writersonekey* for details.

Prentice Hall Pocket Readers

Each reading in our pocket readers has withstood the test of time and teaching, making each the perfect companion for any writing course.

To order the student edition packaged with...

ARGUMENT: A Prentice Hall Pocket Reader, by Christy Desmet, Deborah
   Miller, and Kathy Houff, specify package ISBN 0-13-174664-2
LITERATURE: A Prentice Hall Pocket Reader, by Mary Balkun, specify
   package ISBN 0-13-174671-5
PATTERNS: A Prentice Hall Pocket Reader, by Dorothy Minor, specify
   package ISBN 0-13-3174668-5
THEMES: A Prentice Hall Pocket Reader, by Clyde Moneyhun, specify
   package ISBN 0-13-174670-7
PURPOSES: A Prentice Hall Pocket Reader, by Stephen Reid, specify
   package ISBN 0-13-174663-4
WRITING ACROSS THE CURRICULUM: A Prentice Hall Pocket Reader,
   by Stephen Brown, and PAPERS ACROSS THE CURRICULUM, by
   Judith Ferster, specify package ISBN 0-13-223598-6.

The New American Webster Handy College Dictionary

To order the student edition with a dictionary, specify package ISBN
0-13-174653-7.

The New American Roget's College Thesaurus

To order the student edition with a thesaurus, specify package ISBN
0-13-174667-7.

ACKNOWLEDGMENTS

As California instructors and therefore participants in the growth-and-
awareness movement, we'd like first to thank each other for never
straying from the path of psychic goodwill and harmony, and then to
thank the universe for raining beneficence and light upon this project.
And while on the subject of beneficence and light, we'd like to thank
our original editor, Nancy Perry, as well as Harriett Prentiss, who
helped us with the second edition, Vivian Garcia, who patiently shep-
herded us through the third, and Karen Schultz, who worked with us
on the fourth edition. We thank our current editorial team—Brad
Potthoff, Jennifer Conklin, and Tara Culliney—for their expert assistance with this edition.
     We also want to thank Muriel Zimmerman and Judith Kirscht,
former Directors of the Writing Program at UCSB, for lending moral

and intellectual support to the original project, and Susan McLeod, our current Director. Thanks also to Larry Behrens and Sheridan Blau for lending their expertise in the area of textbook publishing. Madeleine would like to thank Bob Samuels for his many delightful contributions to the cause of *Common Culture*. Michael would like to shower Jan Ingram with bonus megadollars for her unflagging support of this project and her inspiring devotion to reality television, but he will exercise his usual restraint and merely thank her. In addition, we extend our thanks to the following reviewers: Katherine Kessler, James Madison University; Karen L. Morris, Concordia University; Marisa Tomlinson, Irvine Valley College; Kevin J. Harty, La Salle University; Michael McKenna, SUNY Delhi; Vandana S. Gavaskar, Ohio State University; Crystal R. Gorham, University at Buffalo; Analicia C. Buentello, Estrella Mountain Community College; Tanya Cochran, Georgia State University.

Michael Petracca

Madeleine Sorapure

Reading and Writing About American Popular Culture

iPod.
CSI.
The Gap.
Caesar's Palace.
Tiger Woods.
Instant Messaging.
The Apprentice.
The World Series of Poker.
The Black Eyed Peas.

If any of these names and phrases sounds familiar—and it would be a great surprise if some didn't—it's because we spend our lives immersed in popular culture. There's no escaping it. Like hydrogen atoms and common-cold viruses, pop culture is everywhere. You absorb it at home watching television, listening to the stereo, or reading a magazine or newspaper; passing billboards or listening to the radio on the street; chatting over coffee at work or having a burger with friends; going out to movies and dance clubs, health spas, fast-food restaurants, shopping malls and sports arenas; even noticing the graffiti that glares out at you on building facades and highway overpasses.

In fact, unless you're isolated in a mountaintop cave, you can hardly avoid the influence of popular culture. Television, radio, newspapers, and magazines shape your ideas and behavior; like family, friends, and school, pop culture is part of your learning environment, supplying ready-made images, ideas, and patterns of behavior that you draw from, consciously or unconsciously, as you live your daily life. Exactly how you learn and just what you learn may not be all that certain, but it is undeniable that popular culture is one of your most powerful teachers.

One reason to study popular culture is that by paying closer attention to this daily bombardment of information you can think more critically about how it affects you and others. You may start by asking relatively simple questions—"Do I really need my breath to be 'Mentos fresh and full of life'?"—and work your way to far more significant ones—"How can we keep young women from starving themselves in their desire to conform to the images they see in advertisements?" Analyzing pop culture with a critical eye allows you to begin to free yourself from the manipulation of the media; it is an important step toward living an examined life.

WHAT IS POPULAR CULTURE?

What do we mean by popular culture? The term may at first seem contradictory. *Popular,* in its broadest sense, means "of the people," while we often associate *culture* with refinement and intellectual superiority, "the best which has been thought and said," as Matthew Arnold put it. We might ask how culture, traditionally reserved for the elite, the educated, and the upper class, can simultaneously belong to the common mass of humanity.

One way to resolve this seeming dilemma is to think of culture in an anthropological sense, as the distinct practices, artifacts, institutions, customs, and values of a particular social group. This is the way, for instance, that we distinguish the culture of the United States in the early twenty-first century from the culture of our great-grandparents or from that of societies in other times and places.

We can also define popular culture by distinguishing it from its counterparts: *high culture* and *folk culture.*

High culture consists of the artifacts traditionally considered worthy of study by university academics and other educated people: classical music by composers such as Beethoven and Brahms; "fine" art from the impressionists and expressionists; literature and philosophy written by the likes of Shakespeare and Sartre.

At the other end of the spectrum, folk culture refers to artifacts created by a specific community or ethnic group, usually a relatively isolated nontechnological society such as the pygmies of Africa's Ituri Forest or certain communities in our own Appalachian Mountains. While high culture is primarily preserved and studied in the academy, folk culture is generally transmitted through oral communication; both, however, place a high value on tradition, on artifacts produced in the past, and on the shared history of the community.

By contrast, popular culture encompasses the most immediate and contemporary elements in our lives—elements which are often subject to rapid changes in a highly technological world in which people are brought closer and closer by the ubiquitous mass media. Pop culture offers a common ground, as the most visible and pervasive level of culture in a given society. If the Metropolitan Opera House represents high culture, then Madison Square Garden represents pop. If the carefully crafted knives used in Asian cooking rely on a folk tradition, then the Veg-O-Matic is their pop counterpart.

Several other terms help us establish a working definition of popular culture. *Mass culture* refers to information we receive through print and electronic media. While mass culture is often denigrated as juvenile or "low," it has to be treated as an important component of popular culture by virtue of the immense size of its audience. The terms *subculture* and *counterculture,* on the other hand, suggest a desire to resist the pressures, implied or explicit, to conform to a common culture. Subcultures are specific segments of society outside the core of dominant culture. Minority groups in the United States might be called subcultures, just as certain groups such as artists, homosexuals, lawyers, or teenagers can be thought of as having cultural markers distinct from the broader culture. A counterculture, on the other hand, is a group or movement that defines itself specifically as opposing or subverting the dominant culture. Hippies of the 1960s and punk-rockers of the 1980s defined themselves as countercultural groups.

Although we may place ourselves in specific folk or high cultures, subcultures or countercultures, we are still aware of and immersed in the broader popular culture simply by virtue of living in society. As Edward Jay Whetmore notes,[1] "Popular culture represents a common denominator, something that cuts across most economic, social, and

---

[1]Whetmore, Edward Jay. *Mediamerica: Form, Content, and Consequence of Mass Communication.* Belmont, CA: Wadsworth, 1989.

educational barriers." If the notion of culture reflects a certain degree of social stratification and differentiation, then popular culture represents the elements of everyday life, the artifacts and institutions shared by a society, and a body of common knowledge.

Another distinguishing characteristic of popular culture is its transitory nature. New images appear on our TV screens, replacing the popular images of years or seasons before; new phrases supersede former favorites in our popular lexicon; unknown entertainers become celebrities overnight, while others fade just as quickly from the spotlight. Beyoncé takes the place of Britney, who took the place of Madonna, who took the place of Gidget. "The Bachelor" replaces" "Change of Heart," which replaced "Studs," which replaced "Singled Out," which took over from "The Dating Game"; the expression "Just do it!" was for the 1990s and 2000s what "Ring around the collar!" was for the 1970s.

Interestingly, if an icon of popular culture survives, it can often make the leap into high culture. For example, Wilkie Collins's nineteenth-century horror stories were read as avidly as Stephen King's novels are today. His works survive among today's elite audiences but are virtually unknown to most popular audiences. We might ask then, what of contemporary popular culture might survive beyond the immediate here and now and ultimately speak to future audiences at a higher, more specialized level?

What, then, is pop culture? Although it's notoriously difficult to define, some elements of a definition emerge from this discussion: pop culture is the shared knowledge and practices of a specific group at a specific time. Because of its commonality, pop culture both reflects and influences people's way of life; because it is linked to a specific time and place, pop culture is transitory, subject to change, and often an initiator of change.

WHY STUDY POPULAR CULTURE?

Though pop culture is increasingly accepted as a legitimate object of academic inquiry, educators still debate whether it should be studied. Some critics contend that it would be more valuable to study the products of high culture—Shakespeare rather than Spielberg, Eliot rather than Elvis. Their arguments often center on the issue of *quality,* as they assert that pop culture, transitory and often trendy, lacks the lasting value and strong artistic merit of high culture. Further, they argue that, because pop appeals to a mass audience rather than an educated elite, it is necessarily of low quality, no better than average. Although few critics of pop culture deny its pervasive influence, many argue that this influence should be considered negative, and they point to the violence and sexual explicitness of song lyrics, television programs, and movies, as well as to the triviality and downright foolishness of many popular trends. Pop culture debases us, these critics contend, turning us into passive recipients of low-quality goods, distracting us from higher pursuits.

It's important to note that very few proponents of pop culture—pop cultists, as Marshall Fishwick[2] calls them—take a wholesale, uncritical approach and approve all things popular. Many, for example, accept the argument that products with mass appeal are often qualitatively inferior to those intended for an educated, elite audience. However, pop cultists remind us that the gap between the two isn't always so wide; that the same basic activities of creation, refinement, and reception are involved in both popular and high culture; and that, as we've noted, the "popular" works of one era can become the "classics" of another.

Moreover, pop cultists argue for the validity of studying MTV, *The National Enquirer*, video games, and the Miss America Pageant because such mass phenomena serve as a kind of mirror in which we can discern much about ourselves. George Lipsitz,[3] for instance, suggests that "perhaps the most important facts about people have always been encoded within the ordinary and the commonplace." And as Ray Browne,[4] a noted scholar of pop culture, puts it, "Popular culture is a very important segment of our society. The contemporary scene is holding us up to ourselves to see; it can tell us who we are, what we are, and why."

We see reflected in pop culture certain standards and commonly held beliefs about beauty, success, love, or justice. We also see reflected there important social contradictions and conflicts—the tension between races, genders, or generations, for example. To find out about ourselves, then, we can turn to our own popular products and pastimes.

Another argument for studying popular culture focuses on the important influence it exerts on us. The media and other pop culture components are part of the fund of ideas and images that inform our daily activities, sometimes exerting a more compelling influence than family or friends, school or work. When we play sports, we mimic the

---

[2]Browne, Ray B., and Marshall Fishwick. *Symbiosis: Popular Culture and Other Fields.* Bowling Green, OH: Bowling Green University Press, 1988.

[3]Lipsitz, George. *Time Passages: Collective Memory and American Popular Culture.* Minneapolis: University of Minnesota Press, 1990.

[4]Browne, Ray B., and Marshall Fishwick. *Symbiosis: Popular Culture and Other Fields.* Bowling Green, OH: Bowling Green University Press, 1988.

gestures and movements of professional athletes; we learn to dance from the videos on MTV; we even name our children after popular television characters. More importantly, we discover role models; we learn lessons about villainy and heroism, love and relationships, acceptable and unacceptable behavior; we see interactions with people from other cultures. Even if popular culture is merely low-quality amusement or a means of escaping the demands of the "real" world, it delivers important messages that we may internalize and later act on— for better or for worse. We should examine and analyze pop culture, then, in order to assess—and sometimes resist—its influences.

The readings and assignments in *Common Culture* give you the chance to explore these issues and determine for yourself the role of popular culture in shaping society and in shaping you as an individual. The book includes chapters on important components of popular culture: advertising, television, music, technology, sports, and movies. You may already know quite a lot about some of these topics, and you may have relatively little interest in or exposure to others. Either way, as an engaged participant or a disinterested observer, you can bring your critical skills to bear on phenomena of the contemporary world. The readings and assignments encourage you to observe carefully, to question, and to construct and defend your own interpretations of some of the institutions and events, the beliefs and practices, the media and the messages in your everyday life.

Before beginning, we will look at methods of reading and writing that will help you participate fully and critically in reaching the goals of this book.

ACTIVE READING

We've discussed the importance of paying attention to the "common culture" that surrounds you in order to recognize its meanings and influences on your life. In this section, we present specific reading strategies that you can apply both to pop culture and to the essays in this book. Whether you're watching TV or reading an essay about TV, the habit of active, engaged interpretation will make the experience much more worthwhile. While you may have been encouraged to be an active reader of print material, the essays throughout this book also encourage you to be an active reader of the culture around you, including the images in which popular culture immerses you. We use the term "reading" here to apply to both texts and images, although in a later section we suggest specific strategies for reading and interpreting images.

There's a crucial difference between passively receiving and actively reading. Passively ingesting information requires very little effort or interest, and it gives very little in terms of reward or stimulation. Active reading demands more of your time, effort, and thought, but it is ultimately much more useful in helping you develop a better understanding of ideas.

Although reading a text or an image is generally a solitary activity, it helps to think of active reading as a discussion or dialogue with another person. You look and listen carefully; you compare what the person tells you to what you already know; you question statements that strike you as complicated, confusing, or incorrect; you identify ideas that are particularly interesting and important to you; you respond with ideas of your own. As a result of your active participation, you come away with new insights and a clearer sense of your own position. You may even be stimulated to seek out more information from other sources in order to clarify your thoughts.

When you read actively—whether printed texts or visual products of popular culture—you use very similar strategies, questioning and responding and speculating about what you're reading. You are no longer a disinterested bystander simply "listening in"; rather you are a participant who is energetically engaged with an author's ideas.

Strategies for Actively Reading a Text

There are a number of specific stages and strategies involved in active reading. In the **preparatory** stage you develop a general sense of what the essay will be about. In the **reading** stage, you begin the actual dialogue with the author by paying close attention to what he or she has written, identifying key points, responding to certain ideas, and asking questions. Next comes the **re-reading** stage, in which you go back through the essay to get a clear and firm understanding of what you've read. Finally, in the **reviewing** stage, you take time to draw conclusions, evaluate the author's position, and develop your own responses; often you'll want to go back to the essay and read certain sections even more carefully or to turn to other sources to help you formulate your response. In the actual practice of active reading, these four stages circle back on one another as well as spiral outward, prompting you to do further reading and exploration.

As you see, actively reading a text is quite different from passively receiving or consuming information. By reading actively, you'll be able to clarify and develop your own ideas and your responses to the influences operating on you in your everyday life. You can become a more proficient and accomplished writer, increasing the range and precision of your vocabulary, using different options for constructing sentences and paragraphs, creating different stylistic effects, and, in general, improving your "feel" for written language.

An Active Reading Casebook: Three Selections About Barbie

This section includes three reading selections—a poem and two essays about the Barbie doll—that demonstrate the strategies of active reading and suggest the kind of reading you'll be doing in later chapters. In the color insert at the center of the book, you will find two images of Barbie (p. CI-1) that you can interpret using strategies discussed in the "Reading Images" section.

We've chosen to begin with a look at Barbie because of her longevity, popularity, and cultural significance. Since her "birth" in 1959, Barbie has achieved celebrity status in United States culture and, indeed, worldwide. More than one billion Barbies have been sold in the last forty-five years, and Barbie products continue to bring in over a billion dollars every year for Mattel, Inc., her owner and America's biggest toy company. Placed head to toe, all of the Barbies and friends sold since 1959 would circle the earth three and a half times. Barbie lives in nearly every United States and Canadian household that includes children and in more than 140 other countries as well. In addition to her extensive accessories and her many friends (among them, her boyfriend, Ken, and her African American pal, Shani), Barbie has her own magazine and fan club and her own corps of press agents, advertising executives, and "personal secretaries" to answer her fan mail. Versace, Dolce & Gabana, Vera Wang, Gucci, Yves St. Laurent, and Bill Blass have designed clothes especially for her; Tiffany created a sterling silver version of Barbie; and New York City's Fifth Avenue became "Barbie Boulevard" to mark her twenty-fifth birthday.

For three decades, girls (and boys, too) have been playing with and learning from Barbie, and thus she serves as an important force in conveying cultural values and attitudes. Barbie's influence is undeniable, but opinions vary as to the quality of that influence on the children who play with her and on the adults they become. Barbie's critics argue that her influence has been largely detrimental, that her improbable measurements (36-18-33), her even more improbable hair, and her inexhaustible supply of clothes and accessories help perpetuate an inappropriate model of women's interests and lives. However, defenders argue that her influence has been positive, at least in part. They point out that Barbie has recently had careers such as corporate executive, airline pilot, medical doctor, animal rights activist, and even presidential candidate, offering girls a chance to envision themselves being successful in the working world. Although Barbie's wedding dress is one of her most popular outfits, she's never officially married Ken (or G.I. Joe), and she remains a single, independent career woman, providing, some observers say, an alternative to the view that women's primary roles are as wives and mothers.

You can see that Barbie has served as a symbolic reference point for broader debates about femininity and masculinity, about beauty and success, about consumerism and lifestyle in our culture. Barbie is a good example of the way elements of popular culture can be interpreted in order to reveal some fundamental aspects of our society.

While reading this background information on Barbie, you may be thinking of your own experience as a child playing with Barbie or with other dolls and toys, and speculating about their formative influence on you. If so, you've begun to prepare for reading, by orienting yourself to the topic, by exploring your own ideas and experiences, and by thinking about the issues at hand.

Preparing to Read   Let's turn now to our first selection, a poem about Barbie written by Hilary Tham. All the readings in this book are accompanied by headnotes, which briefly explain what the reading is about and give some background information on the author. In this sense, headnotes are like the front and back covers of many books, providing an overview of what will follow and serving as the place to begin thinking about the topic. Here is the headnote for the poem "Barbie's Shoes":

> Our first selection is a poem by Hilary Tham. Tham was born in Kelang, Malaysia, and currently lives in Virginia with her husband and three daughters. She teaches creative writing in high schools and has published several books of poetry, including *No Gods Today, Paper Boats, Bad Names for Women,* and *Tigerbone Wine.*

You can get an idea of what to expect from the poem both by reading the headnote and by recalling what you know about poetry in general. The headnote tells you that Hilary Tham is originally from Malaysia and now lives in the United States. You might conclude from this information that Tham brings a dual perspective to the Barbie doll and other features of United States pop culture. The headnote also points out that Tham has three daughters and teaches high school students. Before you read the poem, then, you might speculate on how being a mother and a teacher would influence Tham's thoughts about the Barbie doll.

Reading and Annotating   In the reading stage, one of the most useful strategies you can use is *annotating* the text. When you annotate you use a pencil or pen to mark key words and phrases in the text and to write questions and responses in the margins. You underline words that you need to look up in a dictionary and phrases that you find particularly interesting, forceful, important, questionable, or confusing.

You also record your reactions, thoughts, questions, and ideas in the margins. By annotating in this way, you keep track of what the author is saying and of what you're thinking as you read.

Here are one student's annotations of Tham's poem . . . but keep in mind that your annotation would probably identify different elements as particularly important.

Barbie's Shoes
HILARY THAM

I'm down in the (basement)   *Why the basement?*
  sorting Barbie's shoes.
    sequin pumps, satin courts,
    western boots, Reebok sneakers,   *Different shoes show*
    glass slippers, ice-skates, thongs.   *Barbie's many activities*
All will fit the dainty, forever arched
feet of any one Barbie: Sweet Spring
    Glitter-Eyed, Peaches and Cream,
    a Brazilian, Russian, Swiss, Hong Kong
    Hispanic or Mexican, Nigerian
    or Black Barbie. All are cast   *Barbies are different*
in the (same) mold, (same) rubbery,   *But also the same*
<u>impossible embodiment of male fantasy</u>
with carefully measured
    doses of melanin to make
      a Caucasian Barbie,
      Polynesian Barbie
      African-American Barbie.
Everyone knows that she is the (same)   *Barbie =*
Barbie and worthy of the American Dream   *American Dream*
House, the Corvette, opera gloves, a
hundred pairs of shoes to step into. If only
the differently colored men and women we know
could be like Barbie, <u>always smiling, eyes</u>
<u>wide with admiration, even when we yank</u>
<u>off an arm with a hard-to-take-off dress.</u>
Barbie's shoes, so easily lost, mismatched,   *Simile: Barbie's shoes*
useless; they end up, <u>like our prejudices,</u>   *are like our prejudices—*
in the basement, forgotten as spiders   *forgotten, but still there,*
sticking webs in our darkest corners,   *in the basement, like*
we are amazed we have them still.   *spider webs.*

Re-reading   After you read and annotate the poem, your task is to fully understand it and formulate your own response to it. Many students close the book after just the first reading without realizing that the next two stages, re-reading and reviewing, are crucial to discovering the significance of what they have read.

In the re-reading stage, you go back through the poem and the annotations in order to develop a good understanding of the writer's ideas. Then you begin to articulate those ideas—in your own words. Here's an example drawn from the earlier annotation of "Barbie Shoes."

> I'm really drawn to the simile in the last few lines: that Barbie's shoes are "like our prejudices, / in the basement, forgotten as spiders / sticking webs in our darkest corners, / we are amazed we have them still." Tham is saying that Barbie's shoes are more than just tiny plastic footwear. They represent prejudices which we think we've thrown away but in fact still have in our "basements" (our subconscious thoughts?). And by comparing these prejudices to spiders' webs "in our darkest corners," perhaps Tham is suggesting that our prejudices still "catch" things; they still operate in our lives even if we've forgotten them or don't see them.

With ideas like these as a starting point, you can go back through the entire poem and begin to formulate a response to other key ideas and phrases: the list of Barbie's shoes; the list of different nationalities and ethnicities of Barbie dolls; the idea that all Barbies are in some way the same; the suggestion that Barbie represents the American Dream. Re-reading like this will surely provoke further questions about the poem. For instance, why does Tham make a point of mentioning the many different types of Barbies? In what ways are these differences only superficial and unrealistic? And what does Tham mean when she writes, "If only / the differently colored men and women we know / could be like Barbie, always smiling, even when we yank / off an arm. . . ."? You know that Tham is being ironic since we don't generally yank arms off other people, but what point is she making in this comparison, and how does it relate to her ideas about prejudice?

These kinds of questions lead you to re-read the poem, clarifying your understanding and finding further meanings in it. After each essay in this book there are similar sorts of reading questions which will help you explore the ideas you've read about. We also encourage you to develop your own questions about what you read to focus your exploration on those points that you find most interesting, important, or controversial.

Reviewing After re-reading, questioning, and exploring the writer's ideas in detail, you should take time to summarize what you've learned. Here is a student's summary of her analysis of "Barbie's Shoes."

1. Tham suggests that Barbie's shoes are like prejudices (forgotten, seemingly lost, down in the basement, "useless" and "mismatched"); why can't we just throw them out? why are they still in the basement?
2. Why does Barbie have so many shoes?! Perhaps Tham is implying that we have an equal number of seemingly insignificant prejudices, one for every occasion, even.
3. Tham points out that there are many different kinds of Barbie dolls (Caucasian, Polynesian, African American) but all are "worthy of the American Dream House." In this sense Barbies are all the same. So does Barbie influence us to overlook the real differences in women's lives? We're not dolls, after all, and although we're all worthy of success and accomplishment, we don't all get the same chances.
4. Tham describes Barbie as the "impossible embodiment of male fantasy." How is this observation related to the rest of the poem? Could she be saying that this fantasy is related to prejudice?

Such questions and tentative answers can help you begin to formulate your own interpretation of and complete response to what you've read.

Reading Pop Cultural Criticism   In the previous discussion we used Hilary Tham's poem as our example because poetry can pack so much meaning into the space of relatively few words. In the chapters that follow you'll be reading not poems but rather articles, essays, and chapters of books, most of which fall into one of two categories. The first we might call *pop cultural criticism* and includes the kind of pieces written for general audiences of popular magazines and mass market books. Typically these reflect a particular social perspective, whether traditionalist or cutting edge, conservative or liberal, pro- or anticapitalist, and often they are written in response to a particular issue or phenomenon reported in the media.

The following piece by John Leo is an example of pop cultural criticism. As you read, practice the strategies that we've discussed. Begin by considering the headnote and what it suggests about Leo's perspective and purpose, then underline important passages in the essay and jot down your thoughts, responses, and questions in the margins.

The Indignation of Barbie
JOHN LEO

John Leo's "The Indignation of Barbie" was first published in U.S. News &
World Report *in 1992. Leo, a conservative journalist and social commentator,
writes about the controversy surrounding the talking Barbie doll produced by
Mattel in the early 1990s. Among Talking Barbie's repertoire of phrases was
"Math class is tough," viewed by some feminists and professional women as dis-
couraging girls from pursuing the subject. Here, Leo imagines a dialogue with
Barbie, in which the talking doll defends herself against charges that she's a
"prefeminist bimbo."*

Barbie will probably survive, but the truth is, she's in a lot of trouble. It
seems that the new Teen Talk Barbie, the first talking Barbie in 20 years,
has shocked many feminists with a loose-lipped comment about girls
and math. Each $25 doll speaks four of 270 programmed one-liners. In
one of those messages, Barbie says, "Math class is tough." This was a big
error. She should have said, "Math is particularly easy if you're a girl,
despite the heavy shackles of proven test bias and male patriarchal
oppression." 1

Because of this lapse from correctness, the head of the American
Association of University Women is severely peeved with Barbie, and
you can no longer invite both of them to the same party. Other feminists
and math teachers have weighed in with their own dudgeon. 2

Since this is Barbie's darkest hour, I placed a phone call out to
Mattel, Inc. in California to see how the famous long-haired, long-legged
forerunner of Ivana Trump was holding up. To my astonishment, they
put me right through to Barbie herself. 3

"Barbie, it's me," I said. As the father of three girls, I have shopped
for 35 to 40 Barbies over the years, including doctor Barbie, ballerina Barbie,
television news reporter Barbie, African-American Barbie, animal-rights
Barbie, and Barbie's shower, which takes two days to construct and
makes the average father feel like a bumbling voyeur. So I figured that
Barbie would know me. 4

Barbie spoke: "Do you want to go for a pizza? Let's go to the mall.
Do you have a crush on anyone? Teaching kids is great. Computers make
homework fun!" 5

In a flash I realized that Barbie was stonewalling. These were not
spontaneous comments at all. They were just the prerecorded messages
that she was forced to say, probably under pressure from those heartless,
controlling patriarchs at Mattel. 6

Subtle rebuttal. At the same time, I began to appreciate Barbie's
characteristic subtlety; by reminding me that she was recommending the
educational use of computers to young girls, she was, in effect, stoutly
rebutting the charge of antifeminist backlash among talking toys. I had to
admit it was pretty effective. 7

So I pleaded with her to speak honestly and clear her name. I heard a telltale rustle of satin, and then she spoke. "You're the one who took three days to put my shower together. That was ugly."   8

"Two days," I said, gently correcting the world-famous plastic figurine. I asked her about the harsh words of Sharon Schuster, the awfully upset head of the AAUW. Schuster had said, "The message is a negative one for girls, telling them they can't do well in math, and that perpetuates a stereotype."   9

"That's a crock," Barbie replied. "Just because a course is tough or challenging doesn't mean my girls can't do it. Weren't your daughters a little apprehensive about math?" I admitted that they were. "Well, how did they do?" "Top of the class," I replied brightly.   10

"Then tell Sharon Schuster to stop arguing with dolls and go get a life." Her remark was an amazement. This was not roller-skating Barbie or perfume-wearing Barbie. It was the real thing: in-your-face tough-talking Barbie.   11

"The first time I open my mouth after 20 years, and what happens? I get squelched by a bunch of women." At this point, I mentioned that my friend M. G. Lord, the syndicated columnist who is doing a book on Barbie, is firmly on her side. M. G. told me: "Math class *is* tough, but it doesn't mean you have to drop out and go to cosmetology school. These people are projecting a lot of fears onto Barbie."   12

Barbie was grateful. "Thank M. G. and tell her I look forward to her biography of me. And tell her that if she ever fails in life, she can always become head of the AAUW." That remark may have been a trifle sharp, I said. "Well," said Barbie, "I'm just tired of taking all this guff from women's groups. They're scapegoating the wrong girl. I'll match feminist credentials with any of them. I worked my way up from candy striper to doctor. I was a stewardess in the '60s, and now I'm a pilot. Ken is one of my flight attendants. You can buy me as Olympic athlete, astronaut and executive."   13

Barbie was on a roll now. I was writing furiously to keep up. "This summer they put out a presidential candidate Barbie, and two days later, Ross Perot withdrew. Figure it out," she said. "As far back as 1984, my ad slogan was, 'We girls can do anything.' I've done more than any other doll to turn girls into achievers, and still they treat me as a prefeminist bimbo. What's wrong with the women's movement?"   14

I knew enough not to touch that one. Besides, it's a very short column. But I was struck by her comment that Ken was now employed as a flight attendant. "Didn't he used to be a corporate executive?" I asked. "We're not voting for Bush again," she replied bitterly.   15

Then I heard a muffled side comment: "Ken! Be careful with those dishes." I said I felt bad about Ken's comedown, but Barbie brought me back to reality: "Remember," she said, "he's only an accessory." This was tough to take, but the issue was settled. Barbie is indeed a feminist. Over to you, Sharon Schuster.   16

As you first read Leo's essay, his technique of personifying the doll as an "in-your-face tough-talking Barbie" is most striking and allows him to humorously present a talking Barbie who seemingly speaks up for herself. In re-reading you can see even more clearly Leo's purpose: he uses Barbie's "voice" to offer his own defense of her influence and significance. Moreover, ultimately he is making fun of feminists "projecting a lot of fears onto Barbie," since she herself derisively asks, "What's wrong with the women's movement?" When Leo has Barbie "say" that she's "done more than any other doll to turn girls into achievers," it's clear that Leo himself agrees and feels that Barbie critics should lighten up.

As a reviewing activity, you might write down your thoughts about the following questions and discuss them with your group or class:

1. Do you agree that Barbie has "done more than any other doll to turn girls into achievers" (paragraph 14)?
2. Do you think Leo's use of humor contributes to the effect of his essay?
3. According to Leo, what is the relationship between Barbie and Ken? Do you agree with Leo's ideas?
4. If you could give speech to Barbie, what would you have her say?

Reading Academic Analysis   In addition to pop cultural criticism, this book provides essays on pop cultural phenomena written not for a general audience, but by academics primarily for other academics. Generally published in academic journals or in collections from scholarly presses, these essays often present the results of extensive research or provide a very close, detailed, and original analysis of the subject at hand. You may find them more difficult than the pieces of pop cultural criticism, but in many ways they are closer to the kind of writing that will be expected of you in many of your college courses.

Note that, while "objective" in tone, academic cultural analysis generally reflects a particular interpretive framework, which may be ideological (e.g., feminist or Marxist) or methodological (e.g., semiotic, structuralist, or quantitative) or some combination of the two. These frameworks will be discussed in more detail in the headnotes to individual readings.

The following excerpt from an essay by Marilyn Ferris Motz is an example of academic cultural analysis, written from a perspective that might be called "feminist-historical." As you read the headnote and the essay itself, apply the strategies we've discussed: familiarize yourself with Motz's view and with the topic as it's presented in the headnote; then read the essay carefully and make your own annotations in the text and in the margins.

"Seen Through Rose-Tinted Glasses":
The Barbie Doll in American Society
MARILYN FERRIS MOTZ

Originally published in a longer form in The Popular Culture Reader, *Marilyn Motz's "'Seen Through Rose-Tinted Glasses': The Barbie Doll in American Society," takes its title from a 1983 Barbie sticker album marketed by Mattel: "If you stay close to your friend Barbie, life will always be seen through rose-tinted glasses." In her essay, however, Motz suggests that Barbie has other messages for us and that the doll's influence is more problematic, especially for children. Pointing out that several generations of girls have learned cultural values and norms from playing with Barbie, Motz focuses on the fact that, although Barbie has changed through the years to keep up with changes in the "baby boom" generation, the doll and her accessories still convey an outdated image of women's circumstances and interests.*

A 1983 Barbie sticker album copyrighted by Mattel describes Barbie: 1

As beautiful as any model, she is also an excellent sportswoman. In fact, Barbie is seen as a typical young lady of the twentieth century, who knows how to appreciate beautiful things and, at the same time, live life to the fullest. To most girls, she appears as the ideal elder sister who manages to do all those wonderful things that they can only dream of. With her fashionable wardrobe and constant journeys to exciting places all over the world, the adventures of Barbie offer a glimpse of what they might achieve one day. If Barbie has a message at all for us, it is to ignore the gloomy outlook of others and concentrate on all those carefree days of youth. Whatever lies in store will come sooner or later. If you stay close to your friend Barbie, life will always be seen through rose-tinted glasses.

Most owners of Barbie dolls are girls between the ages of three and   2
eleven years of age. A Mattel survey shows that by the late 1960s, the median age for Barbie doll play had dropped from age ten to age six (Rakstis 30). Younger children find it difficult to manipulate the relatively small dolls, although Mattel created "My First Barbie," that ostensibly was easier for young children to handle and dress. Although some boys admit to playing with Ken, or even Barbie, Barbie doll play seems to be confined largely to girls.

Like all small figures and models, Barbie, at 11 1/2 inches high, has   3
the appeal of the miniature. Most people are fascinated with objects recreated on a smaller scale, whether they are model airplanes, electric trains, dollhouse furnishings, or doll clothes. Miniatures give us a sense

of control over our environment, a factor that is particularly important for children, to whom the real world is several sizes too large. In playing with a Barbie doll, a girl can control the action, can be omnipotent in a miniature world of her own creation.

When a girl plays with a baby doll, she becomes in her fantasy   4
the doll's mother. She talks directly to the doll, entering into the play as an actor in her own right. When playing with a Barbie doll, on the other hand, the girl usually "becomes" Barbie. She manipulates Barbie, Ken and the other dolls, speaking for them and moving them around a miniature environment in which she herself cannot participate. Through the Barbie doll, then, a pre-adolescent can engage in role-playing activities. She can imitate adult female behavior, dress and speech and can participate vicariously in dating and other social activities, thus allaying some of her anxieties by practicing the way she will act in various situations. In consultation with the friends with whom she plays, a girl can establish the limits of acceptable behavior for a young woman and explore the possibilities and consequences of exceeding those limits.

The girl playing with a Barbie doll can envision herself with a   5
mature female body. "Growing-Up Skipper," first produced in 1975, grew taller and developed small breasts when her arms were rotated, focusing attention on the bodily changes associated with puberty. Of course, until the end of puberty, girls do not know the ultimate size and shape their bodies will assume, factors they realize will affect the way others will view and treat them. Perhaps Barbie dolls assuage girls' curiosity over the appearance of the adult female body, of which many have only limited knowledge, and allay anxiety over their own impending bodily development.

Through Barbie's interaction with Ken, girls also can explore their   6
anxieties about future relationships with men. Even the least attractive and least popular girl can achieve, by "becoming" Barbie, instant popularity in a fantasy world. No matter how clumsy or impoverished she is in real life, she can ride a horse or lounge by the side of the pool in a world undisturbed by the presence of parents or other authority figures. The creator of the Barbie doll, Ruth Handler, claims that "these dolls become an extension of the girls. Through the doll each child dreams of what she would like to be" (Zinsser, "Barbie" 73). If Barbie does enable a girl to dream "of what she would like to be," then what dreams and goals does the doll encourage? With this question, some of the negative aspects of the Barbie doll emerge.

The clothes and other objects in Barbie's world lead the girl play-   7
ing with Barbie to stress Barbie's leisure activities and emphasize the importance of physical appearance. The shape of the doll, its clothes and the focus on dating activities present sexual attractiveness as a key to popularity and therefore to happiness. Finally, Barbie is a consumer. She demands product after product, and the packaging and advertising imply that Barbie, as well as her owner, can be made happy if only she wears the right clothes and owns the right products. Barbie conveys the

message that, as the saying goes, a woman can never be too rich or too thin. The Barbie doll did not create these attitudes. Nor will the doll insidiously instill these values in girls whose total upbringing emphasizes other factors. An individual girl can, of course, create with her own doll any sort of behavior and activities she chooses. Still, the products available for the doll tend to direct play along certain lines. Barbie represents an image, and a rather unflattering one, of American women. It is the extent to which this image fits our existing cultural expectations that explains the popularity of the Barbie doll. . . .

As an icon, Barbie not only reflects traditional, outdated roles for women; she and Ken also represent, in exaggerated form, characteristics of American society as a whole. Through playing with these dolls, children learn to act out in miniature the way they see adults behave in real life and in the media. The dolls themselves and the accessories provided for them direct this play, teaching children to consume and conform, to seek fun and popularity above all else.   8

Thorstein Veblen wrote in 1899 that America had become a nation of "conspicuous consumers." We buy objects, he wrote, not because we need them but because we want others to know we can afford them. We want our consumption to be conspicuous or obvious to others. The more useless the object, the more it reflects the excess wealth the owner can afford to waste. In the days before designer labels, Veblen wrote that changing fashions represent an opportunity for the affluent to show that they can afford to waste money by disposing of usable clothing and replacing it with new, faddish styles that will in turn be discarded after a few years or even months of wear (Veblen 60–131).   9

Sociologist David Riesman wrote in 1950 that Americans have become consumers whose social status is determined not only by what they can afford to buy but also by the degree to which their taste in objects of consumption conforms to that of their peers. Taste, in other words, becomes a matter of assessing the popularity of an item with others rather than judging on the basis of one's personal preference. Children, according to Riesman, undergo a process of "taste socialization," of learning to determine "with skill and sensitivity the probable tastes of the others" and then to adopt these tastes as their own. Riesman writes that "today the future occupation of all moppets is to be skilled consumers" (94, 96, 101). This skill lies not in selecting durable or useful products but in selecting popular, socially acceptable products that indicate the owner's conformity to standards of taste and knowledge of current fashion.   10

The Barbie doll teaches a child to conform to fashion in her consumption. She learns that each activity requires appropriate attire and that outfits that may at first glance appear to be interchangeable are slightly different from one another. In the real world, what seems to be a vast array of merchandise actually is a large collection of similar products. The consumer must make marginal distinctions between nearly identical products, many of which have different status values. The child playing with a Barbie doll learns to detect these nuances. Barbie's   11 clothes, for instance, come in three lines: a budget line, a medium-priced line, and a designer line. Consumption itself becomes an activity to be practiced. From 1959 to 1964, Mattel produced a "Suburban Shopper" outfit. In 1976 the "Fashion Plaza" appeared on the market. This store consisted of four departments connected by a moving escalator. As mass-produced clothing made fashion accessible to all classes of Americans, the Barbie doll was one of the means by which girls learned to make the subtle fashion distinctions that would guarantee the proper personal appearances.

Barbie must also keep pace with all the newest fashion and 12 leisure trends. Barbie's pony tail of 1959 gave way to a Jackie Kennedy style "Bubble-cut" in the early 1960s and to long straight hair in the 1970s. "Ken-A-Go-Go" of 1960s had a Beatle wig, guitar and micro-phone, while the "Now Look Ken" of the 1970s had shoulder-length hair and wore a leisure suit (Leavy 102). In the early 1970s Ken grew a detachable beard. In 1971 Mattel provided Barbie and Ken with a motorized stage on which to dance in their fringed clothes, while Barbie's athletic activities, limited to skiing, skating, fishing, skydiving and tennis in the 1960s, expanded to include backpacking, jogging, bicycling, gymnastics and sailing in the 1970s. On the shelves in the early 1980s were Western outfits, designer jeans, and Rocker Barbie dressed in neon colors and playing an electric guitar. In 1991 Rollerblade Barbie was introduced.

Barbie clearly is, and always has been, a conspicuous consumer. 13 Aside from her lavish wardrobe, Barbie has several houses complete with furnishings, a Ferrari and a '57 Chevy. She has at various times owned a yacht and several other boats as well as a painted van called the "Beach Bus." Through Barbie, families who cannot afford such luxury items in real life can compete in miniature. In her early years, Barbie owned a genuine mink coat. In the ultimate display of useless-ness, Barbie's dog once owned a corduroy velvet jacket, net tutu, hat, sunglasses and earmuffs. Barbie's creators deny that Barbie's life is devoted to consumption. "These things shouldn't be thought of as pos-sessions," according to Ruth Handler. "They are props that enable a child to get into play situations" (Zinsser 73). Whether possessions or props, however, the objects furnished with the Barbie doll help create play situ-ations, and those situations focus on consumption and leisure.

A perusal of the shelves of Barbie paraphernalia in the Midwest Toys 14 "R" Us store reveals not a single item of clothing suitable for an executive office. Mattel did produce a doctor's outfit (1973) and astronaut suit (1965 and 1986) for Barbie, but the clothes failed to sell. According to Mattel's marketing manager, "We only kept the doctor's uniform in the line as long as we did because public relations begged us to give them something they could point to as progress" in avoiding stereotyped roles for women (Leavy 102). In the 1960s, Mattel produced "all the elegant accessories" for the patio including a telephone, television, radio, fashion magazines and a pho-tograph of Barbie and Ken (Zinsser 72). The "Busy Barbie," created in 1972, had hands that could grasp objects and came equipped with a telephone, television, record player, "soda set" with two glasses and a travel case. Apparently Barbie kept busy only with leisure activities; she seems unable to grasp a book or a pen. When Barbie went to college in the 1970s, her "campus" consisted only of a dormitory room, soda shop (with phone booth), football stadium and drive-in movie (Zinsser 72). In the 1980s, Barbie traveled in her camper, rode her horse, played with her dog and cat, swam in her pool and lounged in her bubble bath (both with real water).

The Barbie doll of the 1980s presents a curiously mixed message. The   15
astronaut Barbie wore a pink space suit with puffed sleeves. The executive Barbie wore a hot pink suit and a broad-brimmed straw hat, and she carried a pink briefcase in which to keep her gold credit card. Lest girls think Barbie is all work and no play, the jacket could be removed, the pink and white spectator pumps replaced with high-heeled sandals, and the skirt reversed to form a spangled and frilly evening dress. Barbie may try her hand at high-status occupations, but her appearance does not suggest competence and professionalism. In a story in *Barbie* magazine (Summer 1985) Barbie is a journalist reporting on lost treasure in the Yucatan. She spends her time "catching some rays" and listening to music, however, while her dog discovers the lost treasure. Barbie is appropriately rewarded with a guest spot on a television talk show! Although Barbie is shown in a professional occupation and even has her own computer, her success is attributed to good luck rather than her own (nonexistent) efforts. She reaps the rewards of success without having had to work for it; indeed, it is her passivity and pleasure-seeking (could we even say laziness) that allows her dog to discover the gold. Even at work, Barbie leads a life of leisure.

Veblen wrote that America, unlike Europe, lacked a hereditary   16
aristocracy of families that were able to live on the interest produced by inherited wealth. In America, Veblen wrote, even the wealthiest men were self-made capitalists who earned their own livings. Since these men were too busy to enjoy leisure and spend money themselves, they delegated these tasks to their wives and daughters. By supporting a wife and daughters who earned no money but spent lavishly, a man could prove his financial success to his neighbors. Therefore, according to Veblen, affluent women were forced into the role of consumers, establishing the social status of the family by the clothes and other items they bought and the leisure activities in which they engaged (Veblen 44–131).

Fashions of the time, such as long skirts, immobilized women, mak-   17
ing it difficult for them to perform physical labor, while ideals of beauty that included soft pale hands and faces precluded manual work or outdoor activities for upper-class women. To confer status, Veblen writes, clothing "should not only be expensive, but it should also make plain to all observers that the wearer is not engaged in any kind of productive employment." According to Veblen, "the dress of women goes even farther than that of men in the way of demonstrating the wearer's abstinence from productive labor." The high heel, he notes, "makes any, even the simplest and most necessary manual work extremely difficult," and thus is a constant reminder that the woman is "the economic dependent of the

man—that, perhaps in a highly idealized sense, she still is the man's chattel" (Veblen 120–21, 129). . . .

Despite changes in the lives and expectations of real women, 18 Barbie remains essentially the woman described by Veblen in the 1890s, excluded from the world of work with its attendant sense of achievement, forced to live a life based on leisure activities, personal appearance, the accumulation of possessions and the search for popularity. While large numbers of women reject this role, Barbie embraces it. The Barbie doll serves as an icon that symbolically conveys to children and adults the measures of success in modern America: wealth, beauty, popularity and leisure.

Suggestions for Further Reading

Leavy, Jane. "Is There a Barbie Doll in Your Past?" *Ms.* Sept. 1979.
Riesman, David, Nathan Glazer, and Reual Denney. *The Lonely Crowd: A Study of the Changing American Character.* Garden City, NY: Doubleday Anchor, 1950.
Rakstis, Ted. "Debate in the Doll House." *Today's Health* Dec. 1970.
Veblen, Thorstein. The Theory of the Leisure Class. 1899. New York: Mentor, 1953.
Zinsser, William K. "Barbie Is a Million Dollar Doll." *Saturday Evening Post* 12 Dec. 1964: 72–73.

As you can see from Motz's essay, academic cultural analysis can present you with much information and many ideas to digest. A useful re-reading activity is to go through the text and highlight its main points by writing a one- or two-page summary of it. Then in the reviewing stage, you can use your summary to draw your own conclusions and formulate your own responses to the writer's ideas. To do so with Motz's essay, you might use the following questions as starting points:

1. In what ways do you think fashion dolls like Barbie provide a different play experience for children than "baby dolls"? Do you think one type of doll is "healthier" or more appropriate than the other?
2. To what extent do you think Thorstein Veblen's comments on status and consumerism in American society (paragraph 9) still apply today? Do you agree with Motz that Barbie contributes to the promotion of "conspicuous consumption"?
3. If Motz is right that Barbie represents an outdated and potentially detrimental image of women's lives, why do you think the doll continues to sell more and more successfully every year?
4. To what extent do you think that the values represented by Barbie—"wealth, beauty, popularity and leisure" (18)—are still central to success in America?

Ultimately, your goal as a reader in this course will most likely be to prepare yourself to complete specific writing assignments. In the "Writing Process" section, we will present the process one writing student went through in composing an essay requested in the following assignment:

> What do you see as the significance of the Barbie doll in contemporary American culture? How are your ideas related to those of Tham, Leo, and Motz in the selections presented here?

READING IMAGES

Before turning to this assignment, however, we will address strategies you can use to read images effectively. In many ways, the four-step process we just described for reading texts—Preparing to Read, Reading and Annotating, Re-reading, and Reviewing—applies to images as well. There are some differences, though, as we discuss below.

Preparing to Read

With both text and image, it is wise to begin by getting an idea of what to expect, a first impression. Just as you read the headnote in order to get an introduction to an essay or poem, so too can you read the information that surrounds the image. Next to a painting in a museum, for instance, you'll often find information about the work: the name of the artist, the dates he or she lived, the date the work was completed, the media used in the work (oils, watercolor, paper, etc.), the dimensions of the work.

But outside of a museum, images are often presented to you without this kind of helpful, orienting information. In these instances, which are of course far more common in the world of popular culture, an important strategy to prepare yourself before diving in to interpret the image is to look at the context in which the image occurs. Is it an advertisement you're being asked to analyze? If so, what magazine is the ad in? What is the typical audience of this magazine? On what page of the magazine is the ad found (in the expensive beginning pages or in the more modestly priced pages toward the end of the magazine)? Is it a Web site you're interpreting? If so, who is the author of the site? Who is its audience? What is the purpose of the site? When was the site last updated?

These questions of context can orient you in the same way that headnotes can: they give you a general sense of what to expect. Moreover, knowing the context, and especially the audience and purpose of an image, can guide your subsequent interpretation by helping you determine why certain features are present or absent in the image.

Finally in the "Preparing to Read" stage, you should think about your initial impressions of the image you're analyzing. What key features do you notice immediately? What mood or feeling does the image evoke in you? What immediate response do you have to the image?

Let's turn to a specific example and begin with the "Preparing to Read" process. Take a look at the image of Barbie at the top of page CI-1. As you can see from the information included below the image, the photographer is Aaron Goodman and the caption for the image is "Barbie and Ken Branding." This information gets you started on your analysis of the image, particularly with the idea of "branding" mentioned in the caption. The fact that the image is created by a photographer indicates, in this instance, that it is a composite of many photographs that generate a not-quite realistic image of Barbie and Ken in New York City's Times Square.

As you think about determining the audience and purpose of this image, you might consider the fact that it doesn't seem to be officially sponsored or endorsed by Mattel, Inc., Barbie's creator. We can assume that the primary purpose of the information and images generated by Mattel would be to promote its products. If you take a look at Barbie's official website (*http://barbie.everythinggirl.com/*), for example, you can assume that everything included there has the ultimate function of selling Barbie dolls to little girls and their parents. Aaron Goodman's image, by contrast, doesn't have this promotional purpose; rather, it is more likely to be driven by aesthetic goals or intended to deliver a critical interpretation of Barbie.

What's your first impression of this image? What strikes you as most immediately noticeable about it? We can put it in one word: brands! We count at least seventeen identifiable brand names and/or logos competing for space in this image. Let's move on now to the next step, in which you take a closer look at the details of the image and begin interpreting it.

Reading and Annotating

Unless you own the image that you're interpreting, it would probably be a good idea to refrain from annotating (that is, writing on it). You can get into some trouble doing this, particularly in places like the Metropolitan Museum of Art. Instead, annotating becomes a process of note taking, and reading becomes a process of looking. Put simply, look at the image and take notes.

But that's putting it too simply. What should you look at in an image, and what sort of notes should you take?

One of the major differences between text and image is that a text generally presents information in a sequential and linear manner; there's usually no question about where you should begin reading and, having read one word, it's not usually difficult to decide what word you should read next. With images (and here we're speaking only of still images and not videos, commercials, or other kinds of sequenced images), everything is presented simultaneously so that you can begin and end where you choose and your eyes can follow different paths through the image. Having said that, though, it's also the case that images often try to draw your attention to a certain place, a focus point. This focus point is often relevant in understanding the key messages of the image.

What is the focus point of the Barbie image? For us, it's Barbie herself. It seems fairly obvious that Barbie would be the key element in an image with the caption "Barbie and Ken Branding," but what details in the image can we find to support this claim? Here's where the qualities of *arrangement* and *dimension* come into play. The arrangement (or placement) of elements in the image clearly draws our attention to Barbie. Although the center is the key focus point in many images, in this case Barbie's placement closest to the viewer makes us notice her first. Dimension (or proportion) also draws our attention to Barbie because she is larger than any other object in the image. In fact, she's unnaturally large, as is Ken; it's difficult to imagine them cramming themselves into the taxicab that's right alongside them. So here again, evidence in the image supports a (fairly obvious) claim that the focus of the image is Barbie herself.

It's often helpful to imagine alternative arrangements and dimensions for images that you're analyzing in order to register the impact of the image as it is. For instance, what if the placement of Ken and Barbie were switched in this image? That would place Barbie in the center, but it would also make her significantly smaller than Ken, and perhaps would even suggest that she's tagging along after him or is subordinate to him. Envisioning this alternative, we can see all the more clearly that placement gives Barbie primary importance. In terms of dimension, what if Barbie and Ken were realistically sized? The taxi and car would become more important elements of the image, and the "Times Square" background might threaten to overwhelm them. As it is, Barbie and Ken are disproportionately large in order to draw attention to their significance in the image.

Continuing to look at the image and to take notes, we might next turn to the remarkable number of brand names and logos and try to determine why they're there and how they contribute to the meaning of the image. While the real Times Square certainly has many billboards and advertisements, a photograph of it wouldn't show so many legible, identifiable, and well placed brand names. Clearly, Aaron Goodman created this composite photograph with brands and branding in mind. But what is the relation between Barbie and all of the other brands in the image? The *perspective* of the image suggests that Barbie and Ken are in the forefront of a world composed almost entirely of consumer goods. Perspective is often a helpful category to use in analyzing images. The perspective essentially situates the viewer, defining the relation of the viewer to the image: are you positioned above or below the objects in the image? Are you on the outside looking in (implying perhaps that you're excluded or don't belong)? In this case, the perspective asks you to see Barbie and Ken first, and then to see brand names and consumerism all around them. Carrying her Coke, her Gap bag, and her American Express Card, Barbie is clearly in her element.

Re-reading

Having looked carefully at the image and taken notes on its focus, arrangement, dimension, and perspective, the next step is to articulate the ideas you've developed. Making statements about the image and writing down questions you have about it will compel you to look at it even more closely, clarifying your understanding and finding further meanings.

Based on the information discussed above, a general statement about the image might be that it promotes an idea of Barbie as a key player in an overwhelmingly consumerist world. Given the fact that many little girls play with Barbie, the image may be suggesting that Barbie initiates girls into this consumerist culture. Indeed, perhaps the image is implying that just as girls collect Barbie's clothes and accessories, grownups continue this collecting by buying other name brand products.

But some questions remain. For instance, what is the significance of the fact that the image evokes Times Square as its setting? What connotations does Times Square have for Barbie, for branding, and for consumerism? Concerning the *colors* and *contrasts* of elements in the image, why do red, white, and blue seem to be the predominant colors (along with yellow in the taxi and Kodak sign on the left side of the image)? How would the meaning of the image be changed if the colors were mostly browns, greens, or purples? Taken together with the Times Square reference, is the image suggesting a strong connection between Barbie, consumer brands, and the American lifestyle? Finally, the *medium* of the image can be an important component of its meaning. In this case, the composite photograph created by Goodman suggests both the realism of photography (which captures how people and places actually look) and the complete artificiality of this particular scene (with Barbie and Ken figured as real people walking in a distorted version of New York). In what ways might this interplay of reality and illusion be related to the meaning of the image?

Reviewing

So we've examined the image, taken notes, looked at the image again, asked questions, and formulated some ideas and some questions about it. In the final stage, take the time to summarize what you've learned. Perhaps you can do this in the form of a statement about what you think the image means, or perhaps it's more effective to write about what strategies the image uses to convey its messages. In either case, you'll be prepared if you're asked to write about the image, or to include an analysis of it with an analysis of a text.

Before concluding this section and turning to the writing process, take a look at the second Barbie image we've selected, at the bottom of page CI-1. Follow the same steps described above in reading this image:

1. Take a look at the explanatory information and decide on the context of the image. Who is its audience, and what is its purpose? Note your first impressions of the image.
2. Read the image by noting where your eyes are initially drawn; why is this focal point important to the message of the image? Note other important features of the image: color, dimension, contrast, perspective, arrangement, shape, and medium. What reasons can you determine for the choices the artist made in these areas?
3. Write down a statement or two that you think explains the meaning of the image, along with any questions you still have about it. Examine it carefully to see what elements you have previously missed.
4. Summarize what you think are the messages and strategies of this image.

We think that one of the most enjoyable parts of studying popular culture is gaining expertise in interpreting the images that bombard us everyday, from all angles, from many media. This composite photograph of Barbie gives us a lot to think about in terms of what the doll symbolizes for American culture.

At the end of the introductory chapter and scattered throughout *Common Culture,* you'll find more images upon which you can exercise your interpretative powers. They are drawn from magazines, posters, the Web, and other sources, and they comment on the themes of the chapters of this text: advertising, television, music, technology, sports, and movies. In a highly visual culture like ours, these images serve as "readings" that supplement and provide a different perspective on the more traditional reading materials in each chapter.

THE WRITING PROCESS

Frequently, when an instructor gives a writing assignment—for example, "Write an essay exploring the significance of the Barbie doll in contemporary American culture"—students experience a type of mini-panic: producing a focused, coherent, informative, and logically developed paper seems a monumental task. Some students may be overwhelmed by the many ideas swirling around in their heads, worrying they won't be able to put them into coherent order. Others may think they won't have enough to say about a given topic and complain, "How long does the paper have to be? How can I come up with four pages!"

However, there's really no reason to panic. Just as there are definable activities in the active process of reading, so the writing process can be broken down into four discrete stages: **prewriting, drafting, distancing,** and **revising.** Taking it a step at a time can make writing an essay a manageable and productive experience.

Prewriting

The first stage of the essay-writing process should be especially invigorating and stress-free, since at this point you don't have to worry about making your prose grammatically sound, logically organized, or convincing to a reader. All you have to do is write whatever comes into your head regarding your topic, so that you can discover the beginnings of ideas and phrasings that may be developed in the drafting stage and ultimately massaged into an acceptable form of academic writing.

There are a number of prewriting strategies writers use to generate ideas and happy turns of phrase. Experiment with all of these, in order to discover which of them "click" in terms of how you think and which help you most productively get your ideas down on paper. Most writers rely more heavily on one or two of these prewriting strategies, depending on their own styles and dispositions; it's a matter of individual preference. If you're a spontaneous, organic sort of person, for example, you might spend more time freewriting. On the other hand, if you have a more logical, mathematical mind, you might gravitate naturally to outlining and do very little freewriting. There's no right or wrong way to prewrite; it comes down to whatever works best for you. But what's best usually involves some combination of the three following techniques.

Freewriting   This prewriting strategy lets your mind wander, as minds will, while you record whatever occurs to you. Just write, write, write, with no judgment about the validity, usefulness, grammatical correctness, or literary merit of the words you're putting down. The only requirement is that you write nonstop, either on paper or a word processor, for a manageable period of time: say, fifteen minutes without a break.

Your freewriting can be open—that is, it can be pure, stream-of-consciousness writing in which you "stay in the present moment" and record every thought, sense impression, disturbing sound—or it can be focused on a specific topic, such as Barbie dolls. When freewriting in preparation for writing an essay, it's frequently helpful to keep in mind a central question, either one from your instructor's original topic assignment or one sparked by your own curiosity, so that your freewritten material will be useful when you start composing your actual essay. Here is a typical focused freewrite on the subject of Barbie dolls written by a student in response to the writing assignment quoted earlier:

> *Toys: what did you want as a child vs. what you were given? I don't know, but I wanted cars and ended up with Barbie Corvette. Brother got G.I. Joe, Tonka trucks, I got talking Barbie, Barbie play house, Corvette.*
>
> *B. served as model for ideal female figure, and now that ideal is depicted in magazines. I guess that represents a kind of perpetuation of this image: girls raised on Barbie → cycle continues w/images in the media. The I = ideal image of women in America seems to be let's see: white, flawless, flat nose, wide eyes, that kind of thing. Whatever, it's clear that Barbie creates unreal expectations for women.*
>
> *Yeah! her figure would be inhuman if a real person had it—they would probably die! If she puts on jogging shoes, Barbie stands sloped because she's*

designed for high heels . . . so it seems as though Barbie is clearly designed for display rather than real activity, let alone profession. Display.

 literature (written stuff) on Barbie packages—she's not interested in doctoring nurse, etc.; just having money, cars, looking good, taking trips etc. Re: tech—women think computers are "fun." Re: math—women supposedly aren't good at it. Barbie reinforces these stereotypes—and lots more—in girls
 Changes in society? discuss for concl.?

Clustering   Clustering is especially useful for discovering relationships between ideas, impressions, and facts. As a prewriting activity, it falls between freewriting and outlining, in that it's usually more focused than freewriting but less logically structured than an outline.

To prewrite by clustering, begin by writing a word or central phrase down in the center of a clean sheet of paper. In the case of the Barbie doll assignment, for example, you would probably start by writing "Barbie" in the middle of the page, and then drawing a circle around it. Having written and circled this central word or phrase, you can then jot down relevant facts, concrete examples, interesting ideas, and so on. Cluster these around the circled word, like this:

Frequently, one or more of your random jottings will serve as a new central word—as a jumping-off point for a new cluster of ideas. Later on, when you're drafting, you can use these clustered "nodes" as the basis for supporting paragraphs in the body of your essay.

Outlining   If you have a rough idea of what the main points of your paper will be, outlining is an extremely useful prewriting technique, in that it helps you plan the overall structure for your paper and often generates new ideas about your topic. There are several different types of outlines, most notably scratch, sentence, and topic outlines.

For a *scratch outline* you list your intended points in a very tentative order, one that may only reflect the fact that you don't yet know in what order you want to put your supporting ideas. A scratch outline might not even suggest which subordinating points are most important to developing your thesis. For this reason, scratch outlines are most useful early in the prewriting phase, as a means of generating ideas as well as beginning to organize your thoughts logically. In fact, if you have not yet arrived at a thesis for your paper, one may emerge in the process of listing all your main and subordinate points and then reviewing that list to discover which of those ideas is the most central and important.

As you think more about your essay and come up with new ideas and supporting evidence, you will almost certainly revise your scratch outline to make it more detailed and conventionally formatted with numbered and lettered headings and subheads. A *topic outline* presents items in key words or brief phrases, rather than sentences, and frequently features no indentation. A *sentence outline* is even more developed than a topic outline, in that it describes the listed items in complete sentences, each of which is essentially a subtopic for a supporting paragraph. In fact, sentence outlines, when fully developed, can contain most of the supporting information you're going to present in your essay, and can therefore be extremely useful tools during the prewriting process.

Developing her freewritten material about Barbie into an outline, our student writer sketched out the following:

I. *Introduction*
   A. *Discuss my own experience with toys while growing up: parents "let" me play with Tonka trucks, but they gave me a Barbie Corvette when I wanted a race car.*
   B. *Discuss social shaping of gender roles generally.*
   C. *Working Thesis: Significance of Barbie in American society is that although people say women have "come a long way" and that there are new expectations, this is not really true. If it were, Barbie, depicted as mere sexual, leisureseeking consumer, could not be accepted.*
II. *The media see that people—especially young ones—need role models, and manufacture products to fill the following needs.*
   A. *Childhood: Barbie.*
      1. *Barbie presents a totally unrealistic female body as a role model for young women.*

2. *This role-modeling is crucial in young women's psychological develop-ment, because little girls role-play with Barbie, taking her actions as their own.*

B. *Pre-teen: Models in Seventeen magazine.*

C. *Teen: Vogue and Mademoiselle.*

D. *Adult: Cosmopolitan, Victoria's Secret lingerie models, advertisements in mainstream magazines.*

III. *The popularity of Barbie depicts the entrenched nature of traditional female roles.*

A. *The change toward women's equality is not something that is deemed bene-ficial by everyone, such as the religious ultra-right.*

B. *People purchasing Barbie either:*

1. *don't see the image that's being perpetuated; or*

2. *respect those values and want to pass them on to their children.*

C. *Significance in popular culture of Barbie is that she illustrates inconsisten-cies between changing social roles (women and minorities) and the concepts we are teaching youngsters.*

D. *Although the makers of Barbie make a superficial attempt at updating her, Barbie depicts traditional women absorbed in leisure, consumption, and beauty.*

1. *Barbie completely reinforces old role expectations.*

2. *Barbie in the '90s can have a career (she has some doctor outfits, I think), but she isn't ever functional in that career. The emphasis is still on leisure.*

IV. *The Racial Issue*

A. *Barbie illustrates the assimilation of minorities; they lose part of their cul-ture, because Americans are supposed to belong to the "same mold."*

B. *In the '90s we say that we aren't prejudiced and that everyone should be accepted for who they are, but since the dominant culture is white, white men and women unconsciously (or in some cases consciously, I'm afraid) assume that others must take on white norms.*

V. *Conclusion*

A. *Bring it back around to my childhood play time and the necessity for parents to think about the sorts of toys they are giving their children, so that they don't reinforce and perpetuate these old patterns.*

You'll discover that this outline, while detailed, doesn't contain some of the points raised in the final essay's supporting paragraphs and that it includes a good deal of material that was not used in the final essay. The reason for this discrepancy is simple and illustrates a key point for you to remember about the writing process. As this writer began her essay, she discovered new points which she thought relevant to her thesis. At the same time, she realized that some of her outlined points were tangential and digressive rather than helpful in supporting her main point. She therefore cut some of those points, even though she thought they were valid and interesting ideas. That's one of the most painful but absolutely necessary tasks of the writer: getting rid of material which took some work to create and seems interesting and well written. If cutting some of your previously written material makes the final result better, then it's worth the sacrifice!

Drafting

Having generated a good amount of prewritten material and perhaps developed it into a detailed outline, your next task is to transform that material into an actual essay. Before proceeding with the drafting of your essay, however, it's a good idea first to consider your audience—your instructor only? Your instructor *and* your classmates? An imaginary editor or publisher? A third-grade student? Consider, too, the point you want to make about your topic to that audience. Unlike freewriting, which is by its nature often rambling and disjointed, essays succeed to the degree that they focus on a specific point and develop that point with illustrations and examples.

Thesis and Thesis Statement   The main point, the central assertion of your essay, is called a *thesis.* It helps to have a clear sense of your thesis before writing a paper. However, keep in mind that this isn't always necessary: some people use writing as a discovery process, and don't arrive at their thesis until they've completed a first draft. Generally, however, the process is easier if you have a thesis in mind—even one that's not yet fully formed or that's likely to change—before you begin drafting.

While the form of thesis statements may vary considerably, there are some qualities that separate effective thesis statements from vague or weak ones. First of all, your thesis statement should be inclusive but focused: that is, it should be broad enough to encompass your paper's main supporting ideas, but narrow enough to represent a concise explanation of your paper's main point that won't require you to write fifty pages to cover the topic adequately. Furthermore, you want your thesis statement to be a forceful assertion rather than a question or an ambiguous statement of purpose such as, "In this paper I am going to talk about Barbie dolls and their effect on society."

Much more effective, as you will see in the sample student paper that concludes this chapter, is a statement which takes a stand:

> This is certainly one of the more dangerous consequences of Barbie's popularity in our society: a seemingly innocent toy defines for young girls the sorts of career choices, clothing, and relationships that will be "proper" for them as grown-up women.

Notice how this statement gives an excellent sense of the thematic direction the paper will take: clearly, it will examine the relationship between Barbie dolls and gender role identification in contemporary America.

Opening Paragraphs   In most academic writing, you want to arrive at your thesis statement as quickly as possible, so that your reader will have a clear sense of your essay's purpose from the start. Many readers expect to find a thesis statement at the end of the introduction—generally the final sentence of the first or second paragraph. Effective introductions are often structured so as to lead up to the thesis statement: they draw the reader in by opening with an interesting specific point or question, a quotation, a brief anecdote, a controversial assertion—which serves to introduce the topic generally; a general overview then leads up to the specific statement of the thesis in the last sentence.

In the student essay on page 44, for example, observe how the writer begins with a personal reflection about Barbie. Her anecdote may strike a familiar chord with readers and therefore draw them into the topic. Having made the attempt to arouse her readers' interest in her opening paragraph, the writer moves more pointedly into the general topic, discussing briefly the possible social and psychological implications of her parents' gift choices. This discussion leads into her thesis statement, a focused assertion that concludes her second paragraph.

Keep in mind that many writers wait until they have written a first draft before they worry about an introduction. They simply lead off with a tentative thesis statement, then go back later to look for effective ways to lead up to that statement.

Supporting Paragraphs   As you draft the body of your paper, keep two main goals in mind. First, try to make sure that all your supporting paragraphs are aimed at developing your thesis, so that you maintain your focus and don't ramble off the topic. Second, work toward presenting your supporting ideas in logical order, and try to provide smooth transitions between points.

The order in which you choose to present your ideas depends in large part on your topic and purpose. When you are arguing for a particular position, you might begin with less important ideas and work toward a final, crucial point. In this way you can build a case that you "clinch" with your strongest piece of evidence. Other kinds of essays call for different structures. For example, an essay tracing the history of the Barbie doll and its effect on American culture would probably be structured chronologically, from the introduction of the toy to its present-day incarnations, since that would be the most natural way to develop the discussion.

The student essay at the end of this chapter moves from a personal reflection on the topic of Barbie (paragraph 1); to a thesis statement that asserts the point of the paper (2); to a transitional paragraph moving from the writer's childhood experiences and a more general discussion of Barbie's role in reinforcing gender-role stereotypes in other young girls (3); to an overview of how sociologists and historians critique the Barbie phenomenon (4); to an examination of whether Barbie has changed in response to evolving attitudes regarding women in society (5–7), the heart of the writer's argument; to a conclusion that frames the essay by returning to the original, personal example (8). Each new discussion seems to flow naturally into the next because the writer uses a transitional phrase or parallel language to link the first sentence in each paragraph to the end of the preceding paragraph.

Evidence   Using evidence effectively is the critical task in composing body paragraphs, because your essay will be convincing only to the degree that you make your arguments credible. Evidence can take many forms, from facts and figures you collect from library research to experiences you learn about in conversations with friends. While library research isn't necessary for every paper, it helps to include at least some "hard" facts and figures gathered from outside sources—journals, newspapers, textbooks—even if you're not writing a full-blown research paper. Frequently, gathering your evidence doesn't require scrolling through computer screens in your school's library; it could be accomplished by watching the six o'clock newscast or while reading the paper over breakfast.

Quotations from secondary sources are another common way of developing and supporting a point in a paragraph. Using another person's spoken or written words will lend your arguments a note of authenticity, especially when your source is a recognized authority in the field about which you're writing. A few points to remember when using quotations:

1. Generally, don't begin or end a supporting paragraph with a quotation. Articulate your point *in your own words* in the first sentence or two of the paragraph; *then* provide the quotation as a way of supporting your point. After the quotation, you might include another focusing sentence or two that analyzes the quotation and suggests how it relates to your point.
2. Keep your quotations brief. Overly lengthy quotations can make a paper difficult to read. You've probably read texts that nearly

put you to sleep because of their overuse of quotations. As a general rule, quote source material only when the precise phrasing is necessary to support your abstract points. Be careful not to allow cited passages to overpower your own assertions.

3. Remember that all of your secondary material—whether quoted or paraphrased—needs to be accurately attributed. Make sure to mention the source's name and include other information (such as the publication date or page number) as required by your instructor.

While quotations, facts, and figures are the most common ways of developing your supporting paragraphs with evidence, you can also use your imagination to come up with other means of substantiating your points. Design a questionnaire, hand it out to your friends, and compile the resulting data as evidence. Interview a local authority on your topic, make notes about the conversation, and draw upon these as evidence. Finally, be your own authority: use your own powers of reasoning to come up with logical arguments that convince your readers of the validity of your assertions.

This body paragraph from the student essay on Barbie provides a good example of a writer using evidence to support her points:

> As Motz observes later in her article, Barbie has changed to adjust to the transforming attitudes of society over time. Both her facial expressions and wardrobe have undergone subtle alterations: "The newer Barbie has a more friendly, open expression, with a hint of a smile, and her lip and eye make-up is muted" (226), and in recent years Barbie's wardrobe has expanded to include some career clothing in addition to her massive volume of recreational attire. This transition appears to represent a conscious effort on the part of Barbie's manufacturers to integrate the concept of women as important members of the work force, with traditional ideals already depicted by Barbie.

The paragraph begins with an assertion of the general point that Barbie has changed in some ways over the years to reflect changes in societal attitudes toward women. This point is then supported with a quotation from an expert, and the page number of the original source is noted parenthetically. (Note that page references in this student essay are from the complete original essay by Motz, published in *The Popular Culture Reader,* not from the excerpt of the Motz essay earlier in this chapter.) The point is further developed with evidence presented in the writer's own words. The paragraph concludes with a final sentence that summarizes the main point of the evidence presented in the previous sentences, keeps the paragraph focused on the essay's thesis that

Barbie perpetuates gender stereotypes, and sets the reader up for a transition into the next subtopic.

Obviously, all supporting paragraphs won't take this exact form; essays would be deadly boring if every paragraph looked the same. You'll encounter body paragraphs in professional essays that begin with quotations or end with quotations, for example. Just keep in mind that you want to *support* whatever general point you're making, so each paragraph should include a measure of specific, concrete evidence. The more you practice writing the more ways you'll discover to develop body paragraphs with illustrations, examples, and evidence.

Conclusions   You may have learned in high school English courses that an essay's conclusion should restate the main points made in the paper, so that the reader is left with a concise summary that leaves no doubt as to the paper's intention. This was an excellent suggestion for high school students, as it reinforced the notion of focusing an essay on a specific, concrete point. In college, however, you'll want to start developing a more sophisticated academic style. Conclusions to college-level essays should do more than merely repeat the paper's main points; they should leave the reader with something to think about.

Of course, what that *something* is depends on your topic, your audiences, and your purpose in writing. Sometimes it may be appropriate to move from an objective discussion of a topic to a more subjective reflection on it. For instance, in analyzing the social effects of Barbie dolls, you might end by reflecting on the doll's significance in your own life or by commenting ironically on feminist critics who in your view make too much of Barbie's influence. Other ways to conclude are providing a provocative quotation; offering a challenge for the future; asserting a forceful opinion; creating a striking image or memorable turn of phrase; or referring back to an image or idea in your introduction.

What you want to avoid is a bland and overly general conclusion along the lines of, "Thus, in conclusion, it would seem to this author that Barbie has had a great and wide-reaching impact on today's contemporary society." Note how the writer of the Barbie essay created a strong conclusion by first returning to the subject of her opening paragraph—her own childhood toys—and then leaving the reader with a relatively memorable final sentence offering a challenge for the future:

> Looking back at my childhood, I see my parents engaged in this same struggle. By surrounding me with toys that perpetuated both feminine and masculine roles, they achieved a kind of balance among the conflicting images in society. However, they also seemed to succumb to traditional social pressures by giving me that Barbie Corvette, when all I

wanted was a radio-controlled formula-one racer, like the one Emerson Fittipaldi drives. In a time when most parents agree that young girls should be encouraged to pursue their goals regardless of gender boundaries, their actions do not always reflect these ideals. Only when we demand that toys like Barbie no longer perpetuate stereotypes will this reform be complete.

Distancing

Distancing is the easiest part of the writing process because it involves doing nothing more than putting your first draft aside and giving yourself some emotional and intellectual distance from it. Pursue your daily activities, go to work or complete assignments for other classes, take a hike, throw a frisbee, polish your shoes, do anything but read over your draft . . . ideally for a day or two.

The reason to take the time to distance yourself is simple: you've been working hard on your essay and therefore have a strong personal investment in it. In order to revise effectively, you need to be able to see your essay dispassionately, almost as though someone else had written it. Stepping away from it for a day or two gives you the opportunity to approach your essay as an editor who has no compunction about changing, reordering, or completely cutting passages that don't work.

Also, the process of distancing allows your mind to work on the essay subconsciously even while you're going about your other non-writing activities. Frequently, during this distancing period, you'll find yourself coming up with new ideas that you can use to supplement your thesis as you revise.

Finally, factoring the process of distancing into the writing process will help you avoid the dread disease of all students: procrastination. Since you have to allot yourself enough time to write a draft *and* let it sit for a couple of days, you'll avoid a last-minute scramble for ideas and supporting material, and you'll have time to do a thorough revision.

One note of warning: Don't get so distanced from your draft that you forget to come back to it. If you do forget, all your prewriting and drafting will have gone to waste.

Revising

Many professional writers believe that revision is the most important stage in the writing process. Writers view the revision stage as an opportunity to clarify their ideas, to rearrange text so that the logical flow of their work is enhanced, to add new phrases or delete ones that don't work, to modify their thesis and change editorial direction . . . or, in some extreme cases, to throw the whole thing out and start over!

Just as with prewriting and drafting, many students dread revision because all the different issues that need to be considered make it appear to be a forbidding task. Most find it helpful to have a clear set of criteria with which to approach their first drafts. Following is such a checklist of questions, addressing specific issues of content, organization, and stylistics/mechanics. If you find that your answer is "no" to any one of these questions, then you need to rework your essay for improvement in that specific area.

Revision Checklist

Introduction
✔ Does the paper begin in a way that draws the reader into the paper while introducing the topic?

✔ Does the introduction provide some general overview that leads up to the thesis?

✔ Does the introduction end with a focused, assertive thesis in the form of a statement (not a question)?

Supporting Paragraphs and Conclusion
✔ Do your supporting paragraphs relate back to your thesis, so that the paper has a clear focus?

✔ Do your body paragraphs connect logically, with smooth transitions between them?

✔ Do your supporting paragraphs have a good balance between general points and specific, concrete evidence?

✔ If you've used secondary sources for your evidence, do you attribute them adequately to avoid any suspicion of plagiarism?

✔ If you've used quotations extensively, have you made sure your quoted material doesn't overpower your own writing?

✔ Does your last paragraph give your readers something to think about rather than merely restate what you've already said elsewhere in the essay?

Style and Mechanics
✔ Have you chosen your words aptly and sometimes inventively, avoiding clichés and overused phrases?

✔ Have you varied your sentence lengths effectively, thus helping create a pleasing prose rhythm?

✔ Have you proofread carefully, to catch any grammatical problems or spelling errors?

Make the minor changes or major overhauls required in your first draft. Then type or print out a second draft, and read it *out loud* to yourself, to catch any awkward or unnatural sounding passages, wordy sentences, grammatical glitches and so on. Reading your prose out loud may seem weird—especially to your roommates who can't help overhearing—but doing so helps you gain some new perspective on the piece of writing you have been so close to, and frequently highlights minor, sentence-level problems that you might otherwise overlook.

Writing Research on Popular Culture

A research essay focusing on popular culture follows the same steps as those presented in the previous discussion of essay writing in general—with a significant addition: the research essay focuses on a central hypothesis or research question, and it includes outside sources. For that reason, you might envision a slightly different sequence of activities for your writing process, one that moves according to the following stages:

- *Topic Selection:* Spend some time thinking about an issue that you actually are interested in, or want to know more about. Your teachers will sometimes give you relatively open-ended essay prompts, allowing you to select a research area with which you are familiar and/or interested. Even in those cases in which the teacher narrows the topic significantly—perhaps assigning an essay on the relationship between Barbie dolls and gender stereotyping, or between music lyrics and violence, for example—you still have a great deal of leeway in focusing the topic on elements of interest to you. In the music/violence example, you still have the freedom to select bands and lyrics you know well, and this will make your research much more well informed, while keeping the topic fresh and interesting to you.
- *Focus:* Narrow the topic as much as you can to ensure that your work will be thorough, focused and well supported with evidence. In the Barbie example at the end of this chapter, the author focused on childhood psychological development as it is affected by stereotype-perpetuating toys such as Barbie. Likewise, in the music/violence example, you might narrow the focus by restricting your research to certain types of popular music, such as punk or hip-hop, or to music by artists of a certain gender or ethnic population. The less global you make your topic, the less you will find yourself awash in volumes of disparate material as you develop your essay drafts.
- *Working Thesis:* Develop a preliminary research question or hypothesis related to your topic. This working thesis will

undoubtedly go through several refinements as you begin researching your topic, but it helps greatly to organize your research material if you begin with a concrete point of view, even if you change it later on, as you find more information on the topic. In the case of the student essay that follows, a research question might have been: do certain toys reinforce gender stereotyping in children? The working hypothesis would probably have supported the affirmative position. In the music/violence topic, a working thesis might be something such as: while many observers believe that lyrics in hip-hop music incite young people to violence, research demonstrates that there is no causal connection between listening to certain types of music and violent behavior. You would then proceed to the next step, to find material that supports (or disproves) this initial hypothesis.

- *Secondary Sources:* Find the most valuable materials written by other people on your chosen topic. As much as possible, include examples from a wide range of sources, including scholarly journals, books, popular literature (such as magazine and newspaper articles), and World Wide Web sites. Don't be daunted if you don't find materials from each of these source categories; in some cases, for example, a topic will be so new and fresh that there haven't been books written about it, and you may have to rely more on newspaper articles and Web sites.

- *Primary Sources:* If possible and applicable to your assignment, include some research conducted by yourself, such as interviews with professors who are experts on the topic you are examining, or even with friends and peers who can provide a "person-on-the-street" perspective to balance some of the more academic or journalistic perspectives found in your secondary sources.

- *Critical Reading:* To avoid becoming a passive receptor of someone else's obvious or popular conclusions, analyze your assembled source information to find its literal and implied meanings and to weigh the validity of the information it presents. At the same time, check the validity of your own previously held assumptions and beliefs; as much as possible, try to have an open mind about your topic, even if you have a working hypothesis you are developing. In the case of the above-described working thesis on the relationship between music and violence, you may find material that disproves your original hypothesis, suggesting that there is in fact a relationship between listening to music and acting violently. You may then want to revise your thesis to reflect the material you have found, if you think that information is valid. Feel free to use or reject discovered information based upon your critical analysis of it.

- *Documentation:* Finally, keep careful record of your sources so that you can attribute them accurately, using a bibliographic format appropriate to your research topic and approach. Keep in mind that any time you use source material to support your arguments in academic papers, it is necessary that you document that material. You accomplish this by using footnotes and/or parenthetical in-text citations in the body of your essay, along with bibliographies and/or Works Cited pages at the end of your essay. This academic convention accomplishes two purposes: first, it serves to acknowledge your having relied upon ideas and/or actual phrases from outside source material; and second, it allows readers to explore a paper's topic further, should they find the issues raised thought-provoking and worthy of pursuit.

  In academic settings the major systems of documentation—namely, APA, MLA, and CBE—share certain key characteristics. That is, they all furnish readers with uniform information about quoted or paraphrased material from books, journals, newspapers, Web sites, and so forth. While it may seem strange for such a multiplicity of documenting styles to exist, there actually is a good reason why there is not one single documentation format for all academic disciplines: the different documentation styles support the unique needs and preferences of certain academic communities. Social scientists cite their sources by author and date, because in the social sciences, broad articulations of concepts, refined through time, are paramount; APA format reflects this. By contrast, researchers working in humanities-related fields rely frequently upon direct quotations; the MLA format therefore furnishes page numbers rather than dates.

  If you have already selected a major, you will probably be writing most, if not all, of your essays for a certain discipline, such as English literature or psychology. While you will probably want to acquaint yourself to some degree with the basics of all the major citation formats, you will certainly want to learn, memorize, and practice with special diligence the documentation requirements of the area in which you will be majoring. All three of the above-mentioned professional organizations periodically issue revised guidelines for documentation, and if you want to be sure about the specific rules in your area of specialization, you might want to buy one of the following:

  MLA Handbook for Writers of Research Papers (5th edition, 1999)

  The Publication Manual of the American Psychological Association (5th edition, 2001)

> *The CBE* [Council of Biology Editors, recently changed to the Council of Science Editors] *Manual of Authors, Editors, and Publishers* (6th edition, 1994)
> *The Chicago Manual of Style* (14th edition, 1993)

Furthermore, there are numerous handbooks available, such as the *Prentice Hall Guide to Research: Documentation,* 4th edition, which provide detailed information on documentation in all of the disciplines. In the absence of such books, the following section gives features of the two most popular documentation styles, the MLA and the APA.

Modern Language Association Documentation Format

• Within the body of the text, all sources are cited within parentheses (known in the academic world as "in-text parenthetical citations"), using the author's name and the number of the page from which the source was derived. You should include an in-text citation any time you use another writer's ideas or phrasings within the text of your own paper, either by direct quotation or by paraphrase.

• At the end of the paper, sources are listed alphabetically, on a page or pages with the heading "Works Cited." In the Works Cited section, list book-derived citations using the following information, in this order: the author's name exactly as it appears on the book's title page, last name first; the title of the book, underlined; the place of publication followed by a colon; the publisher, followed by a comma; and the date of publication. A typical MLA-formatted book listing will look like this:

> Berger, Arthur Asa. <u>Television as an Instrument of Terror: Essays on Media, Popular Culture, and Everyday Life.</u> New Brunswick, N.J.: Transaction Books, 1980.

A typical MLA journal or magazine citation will contain six pieces of information: the author, listed last name first; the article's title in quotation marks; the journal's title underlined; the volume number followed by the issue number; the date of publication; and the article's page numbers. A typical MLA-formatted journal listing will appear in this way:

> Auerbach, Jeffrey. "Art, advertising, and the legacy of empire." <u>Journal of Popular Culture</u> 35, 4 (2002): 1–23.

For files acquired from the World Wide Web, give the author's name (if known), the full title of the work in quotation marks, the title of the complete work (if applicable) in italics, and the full HTTP address. For example:

> Brooke, Collin. "Perspective: Notes Toward the Remediation of Style." *Enculturation: Special Multi-journal Issue on Electronic Publication* 4.1 (Spring 2002): *http://enculturation.gmu.edu/4_1/style*

American Psychological Association Documentation Format

- Within the body of the text, all sources are cited within parentheses, using the author's name and the number of the page from which the source was derived, along with the year of publication. That latter bit of information—the publication date—is the important difference in parenthetical in-text citation format between the APA and MLA documentation styles.
- At the end of the paper, sources are listed alphabetically on a page or pages of reference materials. List book-derived citations using the following information, in order: the author's last name and initials for first name (and middle name if given), last name first; the year of publication in parentheses; the title of the book in italics with only the first word of the title capitalized; the place of publication followed by a colon; and the publisher, followed by a period. A typical APA-formatted book listing will look like this:

> Charyn, J. (1989). *Movieland: Hollywood and the great American dream culture.* New York: Putnam.

An APA-formatted journal or magazine citation will contain six pieces of information: the author's name; the date of publication; the article's title; the journal's title, italicized along with the volume number; and the article's page numbers. A typical APA-formatted journal listing will look like this:

> Banks, J. (1997). MTV and the globalization of popular culture. *Gazette, 59* (1), 43–44.

For electronic citations, give the author's name (if known), the date of publication or of the latest update, the full title of the work, a note in brackets identifying the source as one that is on-line, then a sentence starting with the word "Available" followed by a colon and the source's URL or HTTP address. For example,

> Cole, S. K. (1999). I am the eye, you are my victim: the pornographic ide-
> ology of music video. *Enculturation Magazine* [On-line serial].
> Available: *http://enculturation.gmu.edu/ 2_2/ cole/*

Of course, there are many other sources—newspapers, interviews, videos, e-mail conversations, just to name a few—that are omitted here for the sake of brevity, but that carry specific formatting requirements within the major documentation styles. You will undoubtedly want to refer to a handbook or a style sheet published by one of the national associations, should you be asked to write a more extensive research paper that includes the full range of source materials.

Sample Student Essay

The following essay demonstrates one way of approaching the assignment we presented earlier. As you read, note the essay's introductory paragraphs and thesis statement, the way body paragraphs are developed with illustrations and examples, the way it concludes without simply restating the writer's points, the writer's effective use of words and sentence structure, the ways in which it incorporates source material into the developing arguments, and the correct MLA documentation format. While this is not, strictly speaking, a research essay as described above, it does incorporate source material in the ways discussed above.

Role-Model Barbie: Now and Forever?
CAROLYN MUHLSTEIN

During my early childhood, my parents avoided placing gender bound-   1
aries on my play time. My brother and I both had Tonka trucks, and these
were driven by Barbie, Strawberry Shortcake, and GI Joe to my doll
house, or to condos built with my brother's Erector Set. However, as I got
older, the boundaries became more defined, and certain forms of play
became "inappropriate." For example, I remember asking for a remote
controlled car one Christmas, anticipating a powerful race car like the
ones driven at De Anza Days, the local community fair. Christmas morning waiting for me under the tree was a bright yellow Barbie Corvette. It
seemed as though my parents had decided that if I had to have a remote
controlled car, at least it could be a feminine Barbie one!

Although I was too young to realize it at the time, this gift repre- 2
sented a subtle shift in my parents' attitudes toward my gender-role
choices. Where before my folks seemed content to let me assume either
traditional "boy" or traditional "girl" roles in play, now they appeared to
be subtly directing me toward traditional female role-playing. This is certainly one of the more dangerous consequences of Barbie's popularity in
our society: a seemingly innocent toy defines for young girls the sorts of
career choices, clothing, and relationships that will be "proper" for them
as grown-up women.

Perhaps the Barbie Corvette was my parents' attempt to steer me 3
back toward more traditional feminine pursuits. Since her birth thirty-five
years ago, Barbie has been used by many parents to illustrate the "appropriate" role of a woman in society. During earlier decades, when women
were expected to remain at home, Barbie's lifestyle was extremely fitting.
Marilyn Ferris Motz writes that Barbie "represents so well the widespread
values of modern American society, devoting herself to the pursuit of happiness through leisure and material goods . . . teaching them [female chil-
dren] the skills by which their future success will be measured" (212).
Barbie, then, serves as a symbol of the woman's traditional role in our society, and she serves to reinforce those stereotypes in young girls.

Motz' opinion isn't an isolated one. In fact, the consensus among 4
sociologists, historians, and consumers is that Barbie represents a life of
lazy leisure and wealth. Her "forever arched feet" and face "always smiling, eyes wide with admiration" (Tham 180) allow for little more than
evenings on the town and strolls in the park. In addition, the accessories
Barbie is equipped with are almost all related to pursuits of mere pleasure. According to a Barbie sticker album created by Mattel:

Barbie is seen as a typical young lady of the twentieth century, who knows how
to appreciate beautiful things and, at the same time, live life to the fullest . . . with
her fashionable wardrobe and constant journeys to exciting places all over the
world, the adventures of Barbie offer a glimpse of what they [girls] might achieve
one day. (qtd. in Motz 218)

In this packaging "literature"—and in the countless other advertisements
and packaging materials that have emerged since Barbie's invention some
thirty years ago—the manufacturers exalt Barbie's materialism, her
appreciation of "beautiful things," fine clothing, and expensive trips as
positive personality traits: qualities which all normal, healthy girls in this
society should try to emulate, according to the traditional view.

As Motz observes later in her article, Barbie has changed to adjust 5
to the transforming attitudes of society over time. Both her facial expressions and wardrobe have undergone subtle alterations: "The newer
Barbie has a more friendly, open expression, with a hint of a smile, and
her lip and eye make-up is muted" (226), and in recent years Barbie's
wardrobe has expanded to include some career clothing in addition to
her massive volume of recreational attire. This transition appears to represent a conscious effort on the part of Barbie's manufacturers to

integrate the concept of women as important members of the work force, with traditional ideals already depicted by Barbie.

Unfortunately, a critical examination of today's Barbie doll 6 reveals that this so-called integration is actually a cynical, half-hearted attempt to satisfy the concerns of some people—especially those concerned with feminist issues. Sure, Barbie now has office attire, a doctor outfit, a nurse outfit, and a few other pieces of "career" clothing, but her image continues to center on leisure. As Motz observes, "Barbie may try her hand at high-status occupations, but her appearance does not suggest competence and professionalism" (230). Quite the opposite, in fact: there are few, and in some cases, no accessories with which a young girl might imagine a world of professional competence for Barbie. There are no Barbie hospitals and no Barbie doctor offices; instead, she has only mansions, boats, and fast cars. Furthermore, Barbie's arched feet make it impossible for her to stand in anything but heels, so a career as a doctor, an astronaut—or anything else that requires standing up for more than twenty minutes on a fashion runway— would be nearly impossible!

From these examples, it's clear that Barbie's manufacturers have 7 failed to reconcile the traditional image of women as sexual, leisure-seeking consumers with the view that women are assertive, career-oriented individuals, because their "revision" of the Barbie image is at best a token one. This failure to reconcile two opposing roles for Barbie parallels the same contradiction in contemporary society. By choice and necessity women are in the work force in large numbers, seeking equal pay and equal opportunities with men; yet the more traditional voices in our culture continue to perpetuate stereotyped images of women. If we believe that we are at a transitional point in the evolution toward real equality for women, then Barbie exemplifies this transitional stage perfectly.

Looking back at my childhood, I see my parents engaged in this 8 same struggle. By surrounding me with toys that perpetuated both feminine and masculine roles, they achieved a kind of balance among the conflicting images in society. However, they also seemed to succumb to traditional social pressures by giving me that Barbie Corvette, when all I wanted was a radio-controlled formula-one racer, like the one Emerson Fittipaldi drives. In a time when most parents agree that young girls should be encouraged to pursue their goals regardless of gender boundaries, their actions do not always reflect these ideals. Only when we demand that toys like Barbie no longer perpetuate stereotypes will this reform be complete.

References

Motz, Marilyn Ferris. "Through Rose-Tinted Glasses," in *Popular Culture: An Introductory Text*, eds. Jack Trachbar and Kevin Lause. Bowling Green, OH: Bowling Green University Press, 1992.

Tham, Hilary, "Barbie's Shoes," in *Mondo Barbie*, eds. Lucinda Ebersole and Richard Peabody. New York: St. Martin's Press, 1993.

Advertising

What you see above is a very simple advertisement for a Timex watch. A picture of the watch, a short statement, a tag with information about the watch and the familiar Timex slogan, some small print at the bottom: there doesn't seem to be much more to it than that. But appearances can be deceiving—and indeed, they often are in advertisements.

Let's take a closer look. The ad is centered on a simple statement: "If you think it's cool, it is." The longest word in the sentence is only five letters, reminding us of other familiar advertising slogans such as "Just do it" and "Coke is it." In addition to their quite basic vocabulary, these slogans share a certain quality of vagueness: the "it" in "Just do it," like the "it" in "Coke is it," are what semioticians might call "floating signifiers:" their meaning is open and flexible, determined substantially by the reader of the ad. The same can be said for the "it" in this Timex ad: does "it" refer only to the watch? If so, why doesn't the statement say, "If you think *this watch* is cool, it is"? Clearly, an all-encompassing word like "it" allows the statement to be about more than just the watch.

Even more interesting in this ad is the word "cool": what exactly is "cool"? It's a word that we all define differently, and Timex invites us here to take our own definition of "cool" and associate it with the watch. Whatever each of us thinks of as "cool," that's what this watch is. While vagueness usually leads to poor communication, you can see how it's used effectively here by the advertiser: "cool" tells us virtually nothing about the watch, but makes us feel good about it nonetheless. And of course, "cool" appeals to a certain audience: precisely the young, upscale, Generation X types who might be reading *Icon,* the glossy and expensive "thoughtstyle" magazine in which we found the ad. So, targeting a smaller audience, Timex can afford to be more specific than Coke can be when it claims to be "it." Still, the watch is "cool" rather than "groovy" (too old) or "rad" (too California-surfer). In that one word alone and in the way it's used, we can see the ad hard at work trying to make its product appealing to potential customers.

When we look at the entire sentence, we can also see a degree of complexity behind its seeming simplicity. Even if we accept that the word "it" refers only to the watch, the sentence invites two different interpretations:

1. "If you think this watch is cool, well, you're right, because it is."
2. "If you think this watch is cool, then it is (because you say it is)."

This is a fine difference, but an important one. The first way of reading the sentence suggests that the watch is naturally, essentially cool, and so the reader is to be congratulated on being perceptive enough to see coolness when he or she comes across it. In the second reading, the watch isn't naturally cool at all; it's the reader who decides that the watch is cool. Either way, the reader of the ad gets a compliment and perhaps an ego-boost: either he or she is cool enough to recognize a cool watch, or he or she has the power to determine coolness. The first option might appeal to a more insecure sort of reader, someone who fears that he or she can't distinguish cool from uncool. The second reading confirms the confidence of a more secure reader, someone who knows perfectly well what's cool and what isn't. In other words, the statement appeals simultaneously to both the "wanna-be cools" and the "already cools" who might be reading *Icon.*

Now you may think that we're reading too much into so simple an advertisement, especially considering the fact that we haven't gotten past the statement yet to consider other elements in the ad: all that white space, the strange information presented on the label (why do we need to know the date of the original design?), the Timex slogan at the bottom of the label. It's true that we're spending far more time interpreting this ad than most readers spend on it as they thumb through *Icon* looking for an interesting article to read. But we're not spending nearly as much time on the ad as its designers did. The fact is that nothing in this ad—or in any ad—is there by mistake; every detail is carefully chosen, every word carefully selected, every photograph carefully arranged. Advertisers know that readers usually spend only a few seconds glancing at ads as they page through a magazine; we drive quickly past billboards and use TV commercial minutes to grab food from the fridge. In those seconds that the advertisers have our attention, they need to make as strong a pitch as possible. All that we're doing with the Timex ad is speculating about each of the choices that the designers of the ad made in creating their pitch. In several writing and discussion assignments in this chapter, you'll be asked to do the same kind of analysis with ads that you select, and in readings in this chapter you'll see more detailed and complete analyses of ads that can serve, along with this mini-analysis of the Timex ad, as models for your own interpretations.

Keep in mind, too, that advertising agencies spend a great deal of time and money trying to understand the complex psychodynamics of their target audiences and then tailoring ads to appeal to those audiences. Even their simplest and most seemingly direct advertisements still carry subtly powerful messages—about "coolness" as well as about appropriate modes of behavior, standards of beauty and success, gender roles, and a variety of other markers for normalcy and status. In tailoring ads to appeal both to basic human impulses and to more culturally conditioned attitudes, they also ultimately reinforce and even engender such impulses and attitudes. So although advertisements like the one above seem to be thoroughly innocuous and unimportant, the argument of many pop culture critics is that they have quite an influence—perhaps all the more so because we think they're so bland and harmless.

Several readings in this chapter explain in further detail the ways in which we can be manipulated by advertising. Jib Fowles, for example, points out a variety of strategies advertisements use to appeal to our emotions even though we may think we are making product choices using our intellect. The readings in the second section of the chapter look at how advertising works to manipulate our notions of masculinity and femininity. You'll probably find that many advertisements, especially the ones in gender-specific magazines like *GQ* and *Vogue,* attempt to sell products by connecting them, however tenuously, to idealized and highly desirable images of masculinity and femininity: put bluntly, it's "buy this cologne (perfume) and you'll be the man (woman) you've always dreamed of being." No one really believes that, of course . . . at least not consciously. But these kinds of ads must

be working or else advertisers would find other, more effective strategies to make their products appealing to consumers.

Whatever your view of advertising, keep in mind as you read the
following sections that everything in advertisements—from sexy models to simple black and white pictures of watches—exist solely for three
well-calculated reasons: to sell, sell, and sell.

Approaches to Advertising

The Cult You're In

Kalle Lasn

We begin this chapter on advertising with an intriguing, lyrical, but quite bleak piece by one of advertising's most interesting critics, Kalle Lasn. Lasn is one of the founders of Adbusters Media Foundation, which publishes Adbusters magazine and coordinates such "culture jamming" campaigns as "TV Turn-Off Week," "Buy Nothing Day," and "Car Free Day" (http:// www.adbusters.org). The selection reprinted here comes from Lasn's book Culture Jam: The Uncooling of America.*

Through his book, magazine, Web site, and "culture jamming" campaigns, Lasn delivers a critique of contemporary consumer culture, focused in particular on advertising, the influence of mass media, and the power of large corporations. In Lasn's words, his movement is "about reclaiming democracy, returning this country to its citizens as citizens, not marketing targets or demographics. It's about being a skeptic and not letting advertising tell you what to think."

In the following article, Lasn describes a scenario in which advertising does tell us what to think, and even what to dream, exerting a profound and complete power over our lives as citizen-consumers. Whether this scenario is an accurate description of the present or a disturbing possibility for the future is for you to decide. **Before you read***, consider the title of this article: "The Cult You're In." What effect does it have to be told in this title that you're in a cult? What do you already know about cults that might influence your reaction to the title?*

A beeping truck, backing up in the alley, jolts you out of a scary dream—a mad midnight chase through a supermarket, ending with a savage beating at the hands of the Keebler elves. You sit up in a cold sweat, heart slamming in your chest. It was only a nightmare. Slowly, you reintegrate, remembering who and where you are. In your bed, in your little apartment, in the very town you grew up in.

It's a "This Is Your Life" moment—a time for mulling and stock-taking. You are still here. Just a few miles from the place you had your first kiss, got your first job (drive-through window at Wendy's), bought your first car ('73 Ford Torino), went nuts with the Wild Turkey on prom night and pulled that all-nighter at Kinko's, photocopying transcripts to send to the big schools back East.

Those big dreams of youth didn't quite pan out. You didn't get into Harvard, didn't get courted by the Bulls, didn't land a recording contract with EMI (or anyone else), didn't make a million by age

1

2

3

twenty-five. And so you scaled down your hopes of embarrassing riches to reasonable expectations of adequate comfort—the modest condo downtown, the Visa card, the Braun shaver, the one good Armani suit.

Even this more modest star proved out of reach. The state college   4
you graduated from left you with a $35,000 debt. The work you found hardly dented it: dreadful eight-to-six days in the circulation department of a bad lifestyle magazine. You learned to swallow hard and just do the job—until the cuts came and the junior people were cleared out with a week's severance pay and sober no-look nods from middle management. You began paying the rent with Visa advances. You got call-display to avoid the collection agency.

There remains only one thing no one has taken away, your only   5
real equity. And you intend to enjoy fully that Fiat rustmaster this weekend. You can't run from your problems, but you may as well drive. Road Trip. Three days to forget it all. Three days of living like an animal (in the best possible sense), alert to sights and sounds and smells: Howard Stern on the morning radio, Slumber Lodge pools along the I-14. "You may find yourself behind the wheel of a large automobile," sings David Byrne from a tape labeled "Road Tunes One." The Fiat is, of course, only large at heart. "You know what FIAT stands for?" Liv said when she first saw it. "Fix It Again, Tony." You knew then that this was a girl you could travel to the ends of the Earth with. Or at least to New York City.

The itinerary is set. You will order clam chowder from the   6
Soup Nazi, line up for standby Letterman tickets and wander around Times Square (Now cleaner! Safer!) with one eye on the Jumbotron. It's a place you've never been, though you live there in your mind. You will jog in Battery Park and sip Guinness at Michael's Pub on Monday night (Woody Allen's night), and you will dance with Liv in the Rainbow Room on her birthday. Ah Liv, who when you first saw her spraying Opium on her wrist at the cosmetics counter reminded you so much of Cindy Crawford—though of late she's put on a few pounds and now looks better when you close your eyes and imagine.   7

And so you'll drive. You'll fuel up with Ho Ho's and Pez and Evian and magazines and batteries for your Discman, and then you'll bury the pedal under your Converse All-Stars—like the ones Kurt Cobain died in. Wayfarers on, needle climbing and the unspoken understanding that you and Liv will conduct the conversation entirely in movie catchphrases.

"Mrs. Nixon would like you to pass the Doritos."   8
"You just keep thinking, Butch. That's what you're good at."   9
"It's over, Rock. Nothing on Earth's gonna save you now."   10

It occurs to you that you can't remember the last time Liv was just   11
Liv and you were just you. You light up a Metro, a designer cigarette so
obviously targeted at your demographic . . . which is why you steered
clear of them until one day you smoked one to be ironic, and now you
can't stop.

You'll come back home in a week. Or maybe you won't. Why   12
should you? What's there to come back *for*? On the other hand, why
should you stay?

A long time ago, without even realizing it, just about all of us were   13
recruited into a cult. At some indeterminate moment, maybe when we
were feeling particularly adrift or vulnerable, a cult member showed
up and made a beautiful presentation. "I believe I have something to
ease your pain." She made us feel welcome. We understood she was
offering us something to give life meaning. She was wearing Nike
sneakers and a Planet Hollywood cap.

Do you *feel* as if you're in a cult? Probably not. The atmosphere is   14
quite un-Moonielike. We're free to roam and recreate. No one seems to
be forcing us to do anything we don't want to do. In fact, we feel privileged to be here. The rules don't seem oppressive. But make no mistake: There are rules.

By consensus, cult members speak a kind of corporate Esperanto: 15
words and ideas sucked up from TV and advertising. We wear
uniforms—not white robes but, let's say, Tommy Hilfiger jackets or Air-
walk sneakers (it depends on our particular subsect). We have been
recruited into roles and behavior patterns *we did not consciously choose.*

Quite a few members ended up in the slacker camp. They're   16
bunked in spartan huts on the periphery, well away from the others.
There's no mistaking cult slackers for "downshifters"—those folks
who have *voluntarily* cashed out of their high-paying jobs and simpli-
fied their lives. Slackers are downshifters by necessity. They live fru-
gally because they are poor. (Underemployed and often overeducated,
they may never get out of the rent-and-loan-repayment cycle.)

There's really not much for the slackers to *do* from day to day. They   17
hang out, never asking, never telling, just offering intermittent wry
observations. They are postpolitical, postreligious. They don't define
themselves by who they vote for or pray to (these things are pretty much
prescribed in the cult anyway). They set themselves apart in the only
way cult members can: by what they choose to wear and drive and listen
to. The only things to which they confidently ascribe value are things
other people have already scouted, deemed worthy and embraced.

Cult members aren't really citizens. The notions of citizenship   18
and nationhood make little sense in this world. We're not fathers and
mothers and brothers: We're consumers. We care about sneakers, music

and Jeeps. The only *Life, Freedom, Wonder* and *Joy* in our lives are the brands on our supermarket shelves.

Are we happy? Not really. Cults promise a kind of boundless   19
contentment—punctuated by moments of bliss—but never quite deliver on that promise. They fill the void, but only with a different kind of void. Disillusionment eventually sets in—or it would if we were allowed to think much about it. Hence the first commandment of a cult: *Thou shalt not think.* Free thinking will break the trance and introduce competing perspectives. Which leads to doubt. Which leads to contemplation of the nearest exit.

How did all this happen in the first place? Why have we no mem-   20
ory of it? When were we recruited?

The first solicitations began when we were very young. If you   21
close your eyes and think back, you may remember some of them.

You are four years old, tugging on your mother's sleeve in the   22
supermarket. There are products down here at eye level that she cannot see. Cool products with cartoon faces on them. Toys familiar from Saturday morning television. You want them. She keeps pushing her cart. You cry. She doesn't understand.

You are eight. You have allowance money. You savor the buying   23
experience. A Coke here, a Snickers bar there. Each little fix means not just getting what you want, but *power.* For a few moments *you* are the center of attention. *You* call the shots. People smile and scurry around serving you.

Michael Jordan goes up on your bedroom door. He is your first   24
hero, throwing a glow around the first brand in your life—Nike. You wanna be like Mike.

Other heroes follow. Sometimes they contradict each other. Michael   25
Jackson drinks Pepsi but Michael Jordan drinks Coke. Who is the false prophet? Your friends reinforce the brandhunting. Wearing the same stuff and hearing the same music makes you a fraternity, united in soul and form.

You watch TV. It's your sanctuary. You feel neither loneliness nor   26
solitude here.

You enter the rebel years. You strut the malls, brandishing a Dr   27
Pepper can full of Scotch, which you drink right under the noses of the surveillance guards. One day you act drunk and trick them into "arresting" you—only this time it actually *is* soda in the can. You are immensely pleased with yourself.

You go to college, invest in a Powerbook, ride a Vespa scooter,   28
don Doc Martens. In your town, a new sports complex and performing arts center name themselves after a car manufacturer and a software company. You have moved so far into the consumer maze that you can smell the cheese.

After graduating you begin to make a little money, and it's quite   29
seductive. The more you have, the more you think about it.

You buy a house with three bathrooms. You park your BMW out-   30
side the double garage. When you grow depressed you go shopping.

The cult rituals spread themselves evenly over the calendar: 31
Christmas, Super Bowl, Easter, pay-per-view boxing match, summer
Olympics, Mother's Day, Father's Day, Thanksgiving, Halloween. Each
has its own imperatives—stuff you have to buy, things you have to do.

You're a lifer now. You're locked and loaded. On the go, trying to   32
generate more income to buy more things and then, feeling dissatisfied
but not quite sure why, setting your sights on even greater income and
more acquisitions. When "consumer confidence is down," spending is
"stagnant," the "retail sector" is "hurting" and "stingy consumers are
giving stores the blues," you do your bit for the economy. You are a star.

Always, always you have been free to dream. The motivational   33
speakers you watched on late-night TV preached that even the most
sorry schleppers can achieve their goals if they visualize daily and stay
committed. *Think and grow rich.*

Dreams, by definition, are supposed to be unique and imaginative.   34
Yet the bulk of the population is dreaming the same dream. It's a dream of
wealth, power, fame, plenty of sex and exciting recreational opportunities.

What does it mean when a whole culture dreams the same dream?   35

Examining the Text
1. What is the function of the story that opens this reading? What feelings does the story evoke in you?
2. What is the effect of all of the products and brand names that Lasn
includes in this article?
3. How does Lasn define the term "cult"? How is his definition different from (and similar to) the common usage of this word?
4. *Thinking rhetorically*: In this article, Lasn uses the rhetorical strategy
of direct address—that is, he uses the pronoun "you" and directly
addresses readers of the article. Why do you think Lasn uses this strategy?
What effect does it have on you as a reader? How does the strategy of
direct address contribute to (or detract from) Lasn's argument?

For Group Discussion
Discuss the characteristics of the cult that Lasn describes. Who are its
members (and nonmembers)? What are its rules? How are we initiated
into this cult? What are the cult's beliefs and rituals? How do we get
ourselves out of this cult? After discussing these questions, decide on
the extent to which you're persuaded by Lasn's argument that contemporary consumer culture is a kind of cult.

ƐƧC4ℜƐ C4ℜℾ1/1ℾɣ
BUY NOTHING DAY
NOVEMBER 29, 2002 WWW.ADBUSTERS.ORG

Writing Suggestion

Lasn ends his essay by asking, "What does it mean when a whole culture dreams the same dream?" Try writing a response to this question. What are the characteristics of this dream that Lasn claims are shared by the entire culture? Why is it a problem if everyone dreams the same dream? Alternately, you can take issue with the question itself, either by arguing that what it implies isn't true (in other words, that we each dream different dreams), or by arguing that it's perfectly acceptable if we all dream the same dream. Be sure to support any claims in your essay with specific evidence drawn from Lasn's argument as well as from your own experiences and observations.

You might consider using the black-and-white image above as one of the examples in your essay. This image, a poster for Adbuster's "Buy Nothing Day," graphically presents the problem Lasn discusses in "The Cult You're In," and it also points to a solution, of sorts. How might the image be used to bolster an argument either for or against Lasn's assertions?

Salespeak

Roy Fox

A colleague who shall remain nameless once suggested an intriguing way for teachers to supplement their generally meager salaries: we could have our classes sponsored. We live in an age where double plays in baseball are sponsored by Jiffy Lube, where pro football games include the "Taco Bell Halftime Report," and where our shirts, shorts, shoes, and even underwear are imprinted

*with product names and logos. Why shouldn't teachers take advantage of a lit-
tle corporate sponsorship? After all, we've got a captive audience of a very
desirable demographic group (that's you). For a few extra dollars, we could easily play an advertising jingle softly in the background before class starts; we
could say "This class is brought to you by Snapple!" at the beginning of class,
and distribute free samples as students leave at the end of class.*

*If this scenario seems strange to you, you're about to read an even
stranger scenario described by Roy Fox. Fox places us in a school of the future,
in which students attend classes in order to learn how to be good consumers.
They are inundated by advertisements, marketing pitches, and product-testing
at school, where they watch commercially sponsored lessons on TV, read
corporate-produced instructional materials, and shop at the school's "Commoditarium." But what's more surprising is Fox's assertion that this scenario
is closer to reality than we might think.*

*What Fox calls "Salespeak" is infiltrating all aspects of our lives, but in
this selection he is most interested with the ways that advertising and merchandising have established themselves in classrooms and schools across the
country, changing the content and purpose of education. Fox is a Professor of
Education at the University of Missouri at Columbia, and the author of
Mediaspeak, from which this selection was excerpted.*

***Before you read,** reflect on your experience as a student in a variety of
schools. Have you been exposed to advertising or merchandising in the classrooms, hallways, or cafeterias of your schools, or at school-sponsored events?
Does this strike you as odd?*

No profit whatsoever can possibly be made but at the expense of another.
—Michel de Montaigne, "Of Liars," 1580

WHAT IS SALESPEAK?

Salespeak is any type of message surrounding a transaction between   1
people. First, Salespeak is persuasive in nature. It can convince us to purchase products and services. It can also persuade us, directly and indi-
rectly, to "buy into" political candidates, beliefs, ideologies, attitudes,
values, and lifestyles. Salespeak persuades by presenting us with facts,
where logic, language, and numbers dominate the message. More often,
though, it persuades by massaging us—entertaining and arousing us,
and changing our emotions with imagery, sound effects, and music.

Second, Salespeak can function as a type of entertainment or   2
escapism—as an end in itself, where we are more focused on the experiences surrounding consumerism (e.g., browsing through an L. L. Bean

catalog) than we are on actually purchasing something. Salespeak occurs when messages are crafted so as to "hit" a specific, "targeted" audience. Therefore, Salespeakers collect and analyze information about their audiences to help them shape their messages.

Third, Salespeak usually employs a systematic approach in target-   3
ing its audience. A theme for Boltz laundry detergent, such as, "It's white as lightning!" might unify different types of messages communicated through different channels. The goal here is to create "overlapping fields of experience" (Ray 1982), hitting us from several sides in different ways, in short, to create an "environment" of persuasion. In this chapter, Sales- peak also includes any type of message about transactions between peo- ple, such as a market report describing a specific group of consumers.

We live in a market-driven economy in which we consume more   4
than we produce. It's little wonder, then, that Salespeak flows constantly—from television, billboards, print ads, and blinking Inter- net messages. Because Salespeak touches nearly every area of life, its infinite tones and painstakingly crafted imagery appear in an endless variety of forms. Salespeak ranges from the hard-sell radio pitch of the local Ford dealer to the vague, soft, amorphous TV commercial that merely wants you to know that the good folks at Exxon care.

Salespeak includes the envelope in your mailbox that states,   5
"God's Holy Spirit said, 'Someone connected with this address needs this help.'" Salespeak ranges from the on-screen commercial loops play- ing on the ATM machine while you wait for your cash, to the plugs for car washes that appear on the screens affixed to the gas pump as you fill up your car. Salespeak even shows up in slot machines designed to entice children (Glionna 1999). These slots for tots now feature themes such as Candyland, Monopoly, the Three Stooges, the Pink Panther, and South Park. This is the gaming industry's attempt to promote a "family-friendly" image, which will help ensure that future genera- tions will support the casino industry (Ruskin 1999). Salespeak also sprouts from the "product information" about a new computer embed- ded within the instructions for installing a software program, from the camera shot in a popular film that lingers on a bag of Frito's corn chips, and from the large sign inside Russia's Mir space station that states, "Even in Space . . . Pepsi is Changing the Script." Salespeak is indeed the script, on earth as it is in heaven.

A DAY IN THE LIFE

At 6:03 A.M., Mrs. Anderson's voice comes over the intercom into her   6
teenaged daughter's bedroom. Mrs. Anderson asks, "Pepsi? It's time to wake up, dear. Pehhhp-si . . . are you up and moving?"

Pepsi answers groggily, "Yeah. . . I'm up. Morning, Mom." As   7
Pepsi sits up in bed, she reaches over and hits the button on her old
pink Barbie alarm clock, which rests on her old American Girl traditional oak jewelry box. As both cherished items catch her eye, she
pauses and wistfully recalls those happy days of girlhood, rubbing her
hand over the *Little Mermaid* bedsheet. If only she hadn't given away
her favorite purple My Little Pony to her best childhood friend,
Microsoft McKenzie, who lives next door.

Just then her mother's voice calls her back to reality, "Good deal,   8
sweetie. Let me know when you finish your shower. I just got your Gap
sweatshirt out of the dryer, but I couldn't get that Gatorade stain out of
your Tommy Hilfiger pants, so I'm washing them again."

Once upstairs, Pepsi sits down for a bowl of Cap'n Crunch cereal.   9
She peels a banana, carefully pulling off a bright yellow sticker, which
states, "ABC. Zero calories." She places the used sticker onto her
McDonald's book cover. Pepsi's younger brother, Nike, dressed in his
Babylon Five T-shirt, places a Star Trek notebook into his Star Wars
book bag as he intently watches the Amoco morning newscast on the
video wall. The network anchor tells about the latest corporate merger
as he reads from his perch within the "N" of the giant MSNBC logo.
Then Mrs. Anderson walks into the nutrition pod.

Mrs. Anderson: Hey, Peps, what's going on at school today?
Pepsi: Nothing much. Just gotta finish that dumb science
    experiment.
Mrs. Anderson: Which one is that?
Pepsi: That one called "Digging for Data." We learned about sci-
    entific inquiry stuff and how to deduce conclusions. We
    learned that American settlers were short because they didn't
    eat enough meat and stuff like that.
Mrs. Anderson: Oh, yes! That was one of my favorites when I was
    in school. Those National Livestock and Meat Board teaching
    kits are wonderful! I liked it even better than Campbell Soup's
    "Prego Thickness Experiment." How 'bout you?
Pepsi: I dunno. Everyone already knows that Prego spaghetti
    sauce is three times thicker and richer than Ragu's sauce.
Mrs. Anderson: Well, yes, of course they do. But that's not the
    only point. There are larger goals here, namely, your becoming
    the best high-volume consumer possible. Isn't that right, dear?
Pepsi: Yeah, I guess so.

Pepsi's school bus, equipped with the latest electronic wraparound   10
billboard, mentions that the price of Chocolate Cheetah Crunch "is being
sliced as you read this—down to $48.95 per ten-pounder!" Pepsi takes

her seat and discusses this price reduction with her locker partner, Reebok Robinson. They engage in a lively conversation about which of them loves Cheetah Crunch more. Next, the screen on the back of the seat in front of them catches their attention: a large dancing lamb sings, "Be there! Tonight only! At the IBM Mall! All remaining Rickon collectibles must go! Pledge bidding only! Be there!" Even Reebok cannot contain a squeal.

At school, Pepsi watches Channel One, the National Truth Channel, during her first three classes. The first news story documents the precise steps in which Zestra, the new star of the Z-5 Lectradisk corporate communication spots, went about purchasing her new video wall unit. Afterward, Pepsi and her peers receive biofeedback printouts of their responses registered during this program via the reaction console on their desks. Next, the students use voice-print technology to describe what they were feeling during the broadcast.   11

Then their teacher, Ms. Qualcomm, tells them to take a twenty-minute recess at the Commoditarium before they return for Tech Lab, where they will begin the unit "Product Scanning: Art or Science?" At the Commoditarium, Pepsi purchases one bag of Kwizzee sticks, one can of Channel One soda, and a One-der Bar, in addition to a pair of Golden Arch earrings she can't live without. The accessories for the earrings, which she also longs for, will have to wait.   12

Back at Tech Lab, Pepsi and her peers receive a half hour of AT&T ("Allotted Time & Testing," sponsored by AT&T, in which students are free to explore their own interests on the GodNet). In the upper-left corner of her computer screen, Pepsi watches what appears to be an enlarged part of human anatomy, alternately shrinking and enlarging, as one of her favorite new songs beats in sync. The olfactory port of her computer emits a musky odor. In the background of this pulsating image, sticks of lightning flare randomly against a deep blue sky. Pepsi looks at them more closely and detects that each one contains three small letters: A, T, and T. She smiles, points, and clicks on the window.   13

Immediately, this message forms on screen in large, puffy blue letters: "A, T, & T Loves You." Then the message begins dissolving and enlarging simultaneously, so that the background is now the same blue as the message. Huge lips fill the screen. Pepsi is unsure whether they are the lips of a man or woman. The lips slowly murmur, "You, Pepsi . . . You're the one . . . Oh, yes . . . Nobody else. Just you."   14

Pepsi, mesmerized, half whispers to herself, "Me?" as the lips fade at the same time that the blue background re-forms into the previous message, "A, T, & T Loves You." Pepsi clicks again. Three golden books appear on screen. One is titled "A, T, & T's Pledge to You, Pepsi Anderson." Another one is titled, "Making Love Rich," and the third is titled, "Us . . . Forever." The lights of the Tech Lab dim, signaling students that it's time   15 to begin their new unit. The lights slowly fade out until the lab is nearly dark. Pepsi hears muffled patriotic music from the opposite side of the room—a flute and drum, playing the tune of "Yankee Doodle Dandy." From the far end of the ceiling, an image of the traditional "fyfe and drum corps"—the three ragged soldiers in Revolutionary Army garb—come marching across the screen; above the U.S. flag flies a larger one, with a golden arch on it.

As the tattered trio exit via a slow dissolve on the opposite end of the ceiling screen, the room goes completely dark. Pepsi twists her head and limbers up, as her classmates do, almost in unison. Then, on instinct, Pepsi and her peers look upward to the neon green and pink Laser Note swirling above them: "To thine own self, be blue. And rakest thou joy into thine own taste sphere! Tru-Blu Vervo Dots: now half price at Commoditarium!" A laser image of Shakespeare forms from the dissolving lights. Next, the bard's face dissolves into blue Vervo Dots. Pepsi, feeling vaguely tired and hungry, saves her place on screen so she can return later to find out what's in the three golden books. Before she exits, she is automatically transferred to another screen so that she can input her biofeedback prints from the past half hour. 16

At home that night, Pepsi and her family gather in the Recipient Well. To activate the video wall, Mrs. Anderson submits a forehead print on the ConsumaScan. Before any audio can be heard, a Nike logo appears on the screen for two minutes. Mrs. Anderson turns to her daughter. 17

Mrs. Anderson: So, Peps, you were awfully quiet at dinner. Are you okay? Everything all right at school?

Pepsi: Fine. I just get tired of learning all the time.

Mrs. Anderson (sighing): Well, sweetie, I know. Things are so much different nowadays than when I was your age. You kids have to work harder in school because there are so many more products and services to keep up with.

Pepsi: Yeah, I guess so. . . .

Mrs. Anderson: But you've also got many luxuries we never had. Why, when I was born, parents were completely ignorant about giving their children beautiful names. My family just called me "Jennifer." Ugh! Can you believe it?

Pepsi: Oh, gag me, Mom! "Jennifer"?! You're kidding! How did you and Dad name me?

Mrs. Anderson: Well, let's see. . . . We first fell in love with your name when Pepsico offered us a lifetime membership at the Nova Health Spa if we'd name you "Pepsi." I thought it was so refreshing—not to mention thirst quenching and tasty. Besides—it's your generation!

Pepsi: And I'll always love you and Dad for bestowing me with
    eternal brandness . . .

Mrs. Anderson: It's just because we love you, that's all. Growing
    up branded is a lot easier these days—especially after the
    Renaissance of 2008, just after you were born.

Pepsi: What was that?

Mrs. Anderson: You know—*life cells!* We got them a few years
    after the Second Great Brand Cleansing War.

Pepsi: But I thought we always had life cells, that we were just
    born with 'em. . . .

Mrs. Anderson: My gosh, no, girl! When I was your age we had to
    stay glued to National Public Radio to keep up with the latest
    fluctuations of the NASDAQ and high tech markets.

Pepsi: Jeez . . . I can't imagine life without life cells.

Mrs. Anderson: Me either—now! Back then, it all started with
    Moletronics and the first conversions of Wall Street datastreams
    into what they used to call "subcutaneous pseudo-neurons."
    But that's ancient history for you!

Pepsi: Mom?

Mrs. Anderson: Yes, dear?

Pepsi: Can we set aside some special family time, so we can talk
    about that relationship portfolio with AT&T?

Mrs. Anderson: Well, of course! Maybe during spring break at the
    cabin? That's not the kind of thing we ever want to slight.

At this moment, the video wall's audio activates. The Nike   18
swoosh logo forms into a running cheetah as a male voice-over states,
"Nike Leopard-Tech Laser Runners. Be the Cheetah you were born free
to be." Mrs. Anderson turns back to her daughter and asks, "Would
you mind running to the Pantry Pod and seeing if there's any more of
that Chocolate Cheetah Crunch left?" "Sure," says Pepsi, turning as she
leaves the room, "*If* we can talk about those new shoes I need." . . .

IS PEPSI'S WORLD ALREADY HERE?

Yes. Most of what happens to Pepsi in this scenario is based on fact. A   19
few other parts are extensions or exaggerations of what already occurs
in everyday life. Let's begin with a girl named Pepsi. In Pepsi's world
of Salespeak, nearly every facet of life is somehow linked to sales.
Pepsi, the girl, lives in a Pepsi world, where person, product, and hype
have merged with everyday life.

Salespeak is all-powerful. As small children, as soon as we become   20
aware that a world exists outside of ourselves, we become a "targeted

audience." From then on, we think in the voices of Salespeak. We hear them, we see them. We smell them, taste them, touch them, dream them, become them. Salespeak is often targeted at young people, the group marketers most prize because first, they spend "disposable" income, as well as influence how their parents spend money (see the following section, "Notes from the World of Salespeak"); second, people tend to establish loyalties to certain brands early in life; and third, young people are more likely to buy items on impulse. For these reasons and more, Salespeak is most prevalent and vivid for children and young adults. Hence, most of this chapter focuses on the layers of Salespeak that surround these groups. The core issue is targeting kids in the first place, regardless of the product being sold.

What's in a Name?

At this writing, I've neither read nor heard of a human being legally 21
named after a product or service (though I feel certain that he or she is out there). I have, though, heard that school administrators in Plymouth, Michigan, are considering auctioning off school names to the highest bidder. It's only a matter of time before kids attend "Taco Bell Middle School" or "Gap Kids Elementary School" (Labi 1999). Appropriating names—and hence identities—is essentially an act of aggression, of control over others' personal identity. Our practice of naming things for commercial purposes is not new. Consider San Diego's Qualcomm Stadium. Unlike St. Louis's Busch Stadium or Denver's Coors Field, the name Qualcomm has no connections to people or things already traditionally linked with baseball. In Pepsi's world, "AT&T" stood for "Allotted Time for Testing." To my knowledge, commercial or corporate names have yet to be used for identifying processes. However, they have been used to identify specific places where educational processes occur.

For example, the Derby, Kansas, school district named its elemen- 22
tary school resource center the GenerationNext Center. The district agreed to use the Pepsi slogan to name their new facility, as well as to serve only Pepsi products, in exchange for one million dollars (Perrin 1997, 1A). Even ice cream is now named so that it can advertise something else: the name of Ben and Jerry's butter almond ice cream is called "Dilbert's World: Totally Nuts" (Solomon 1998a).

Every time we see or read or hear a commercial name, an 23
"impression" registers. Advertising profits depend on the type and number of impressions made by each ad message. Therefore, Pepsi Anderson and her friend, Microsoft McKenzie, are walking, breathing, random ad messages. (Similar important names) are now devised

solely for purposes of advertising. Nothing more. Such names become ads. In earlier times and in other cultures, as well as our own, names were sacred: they communicated the essence of our identity, not just to others but to ourselves as well. To rob someone of her name was to appropriate her identity, to deny her existence. In *I Know Why the Caged Bird Sings*, Maya Angelou speaks of how demoralizing it was for African Americans to be "called out of name" by white people, who would refer to any African American male as "boy," "Tom," or "Uncle."

Similarly, several years ago, the rock musician and composer known as Prince changed his name to a purely graphic symbol. The result, of course, was that nobody could even pronounce it! By default he became known as "The Artist Formerly Known as Prince." In an interview on MTV, this musician-composer explained that the public believed he was crazy because print and electronic media had proclaimed him so, over and over. He therefore changed his name to something unpronounceable to halt this labeling. It worked. In effect, this man regained control of his own life because he found a way to stop others from controlling it for him, as they were doing by writing about him in the media. This man understands the general semantics principle that the word is not the thing symbolized—that the map is not the territory. . . .   24

The long-term effects of replacing real names with commercial labels (of important spaces, processes, and possibly even people) can benefit nobody except those doing the appropriating—those reaping revenue from increased sales. At the very least, this practice demonstrates, in concrete, definitive ways, that we value materialism and the act of selling above all else.   25

Celebrating Coke Day at the Carbonated Beverage Company

At century's end, the question is not "Where and when does Salespeak appear?" Rather, the real question is, "Where and when does Salespeak *not* appear?" Only in churches and other places of worship? (Not counting, of course, the church that advertised itself by proclaiming on its outside message board: "Come in for a faith lift.") Salespeak is more than a voice we hear and see: we also wear it, smell it, touch it, play with it. Ads on book covers, notebooks, backpacks, pencils, and pens are common. So are the girl Pepsi's Gap sweatshirt, Tommy Hilfiger pants, Barbie alarm clock, and *Little Mermaid* bedsheets. The bulletins that Pepsi and her classmates received about current sales are also   26 authentic: PepsiCo has offered free beepers to teens, who are periodically contacted with updated ad messages.

Salespeak is seeping into the smallest crevices of American life.   27
As you fill your car with gas, you can now watch commercials on a small screen on the gas pump. As you wait for your transaction at the ATM machine, you can view commercials. As you wait in the switchback line at an amusement park, you can watch commercials on several screens. As you wait in your doctor's office, you can read about medicines to buy, as well as watch commercials for them. As you stand in line at Wal-Mart's customer service desk, you can watch ads for Wal-Mart on a huge screen before you. As you wait for the phone to ring when making a long-distance call, you'll hear a soft, musical tinkle, followed by a velvety voice that intones, "AT&T."

As your children board their school bus, you'll see ads wrapped   28
around it. When you pick up a bunch of bananas in the grocery store, like our friend Pepsi in the earlier scenario, you may have to peel off yellow stickers that state, "ABC. Zero calories." When you call a certain school in Texas and don't get an answer, you'll hear this recorded message: "Welcome to the Grapevine-Colleyville Independent School District, where we are proudly sponsored by the Dr. Pepper Bottling Company of Texas" (Perrin 1997).

Salespeak also commonly appears under the guise of school   29
"curriculum"—from formal business-education partnerships, to free teacher workshops provided to introduce new textbooks. Corporate-produced "instructional materials" are sometimes thinly veiled sales pitches that can distort the truth. The curriculum unit "Digging for Data," mentioned earlier as part of Pepsi's school day, is actual material used in schools.

For another "learning experience," students were assigned to be   30
"quality control technicians" as they completed "The Carbonated Beverage Company" unit, provided free to schools by PepsiCo. Students taste-tested colas, analyzed cola samples, took video tours of the St. Louis Pepsi plant, and visited a local Pepsi plant (Bingham 1998, 1A). Ads have even appeared in math textbooks. *Mathematics: Applications and Connections*, published by McGraw-Hill, and used in middle schools, includes problems that are just as much about advertising as they are arithmetic—salespeak masquerading as education. Here's a sample decimal division problem: "Will is saving his allowance to buy a pair of Nike shoes that cost $68.25. If Will earns $3.25 per week, how many weeks will Will need to save?" Directly next to this problem is a full-color picture of a pair of Nike shoes (Hays 1999). The 1999 edition of this book contains the following problem: "The best-selling packaged cookie in the world is the Oreo cookie. The diameter of the Oreo cookie is 1.75 inches. Express the diameter of an Oreo cookie as a fraction in simplest form." It seems no

accident that "Oreo" is repeated three times in this brief message; repetition is an ancient device used in propaganda and advertising. More insidious is the fact that such textbooks present the act of saving money for Nike shoes as a *natural* state of affairs, a given in life. Requiring captive audiences of kids to interact with brand names in such mentally active ways helps ensure product-identification and brand-name loyalty during kids' future years as consumers.

Some schools slavishly serve their corporate sponsors. After sealing a deal with Coca-Cola, a school in Georgia implemented an official "Coke Day" devoted to celebrating Coca-Cola products. On that day, Mike Cameron, a senior at the school, chose to exercise his right to think by wearing a T-shirt bearing the Pepsi logo. He was promptly suspended ("This School Is Brought to You By: Cola? Sneakers?" 1998, 11A).

31

This intense focus on selling products to a captive audience of students is illustrated by the following letter sent to District 11's school principals in Colorado Springs, Colorado. The letter was written by the district's executive director of "school leadership." In September 1997, the district had signed an $8 million contract with Coca-Cola (Labi 1999).

32

Dear Principal:

Here we are in year two of the great Coke contract. . . .

First, the good news: This year's installment from Coke is "in the house," and checks will be cut for you to pick up in my office this week. Your share will be the same as last year.

Elementary School	$3,000
Middle School	$15,000
High School	$25,000

Now the not-so-good news: we must sell 70,000 cases of product (including juices, sodas, waters, etc.) at least once during the first three years of the contract. If we reach this goal, your school allotments will be guaranteed for the next seven years.

The math on how to achieve this is really quite simple. Last year we had 32,439 students, 3,000 employees, and 176 days in the school year. If 35,439 staff and students buy one Coke product every other day for a school year, we will double the required quota.

Here is how we can do it:

1. Allow students to purchase and consume vended products throughout the day. If sodas are not allowed in classes, consider allowing juices, teas, and waters.
2. Locate machines where they are accessible to the students all day. Research shows that vender purchases are closely linked to availability. Location,

location, location is the key. You may have as many machines as you can
handle. Pueblo Central High tripled its volume of sales by placing vending
machines on all three levels of the school. The Coke people surveyed the
middle and high schools this summer and have suggestions on where to
place additional machines.
3. A list of Coke products is enclosed to allow you to select from the entire
menu of beverages. Let me know which products you want, and we will get
them in. Please let me know if you need electrical outlets.
4. A calendar of promotional events is enclosed to help you advertise Coke
products.

I know this is "just one more thing from downtown," but the long-term benefits are worth it.
Thanks for your help.

John Bushey
The Coke Dude
(Bushey 1998)

With visionary leaders such as "The Coke Dude" to inspire them,   33
students will be well prepared to perpetuate a world ruled by Salespeak. Of course, Pepsi (the girl), Mike (the actual student expelled for
wearing a Pepsi T-shirt), and their fellow students did not begin
encountering ads in high school. It begins much earlier. . . .

The National Truth Channel

Many other details of Pepsi's day are anchored in fact, not fiction. In   34
Pepsi's not-too-distant world, Channel One television has become the
"National Truth Channel." Today Channel One, owned by a private
corporation, beams daily commercials to more than 8 million American
kids attending middle schools and high schools. It therefore imposes
more uniformity on public school kids and their curriculum than the
federal government ever has. For all practical purposes, it has indeed
been our "national" channel for several years.

Although I made up the "Truth" part of "The National Truth   35
Channel," I want to note that it serves as Doublespeak nested within
Salespeak—a common occurrence in real life. For example, the term
"corporate communication" (used in Pepsi's world, above, to refer to
commercials) is a euphemism that the Benetton company actually used
to refer to its ads. And although laser ads have yet to appear on the ceil-
ings of classrooms, as they do in Pepsi's world, it is true that a few
years ago, a company wanted to launch into geosynchronous orbit a
massive panel that could be emblazoned with a gigantic corporate
logo, visible for periods of time, over certain cities (Doheny-Farina 1999).

Here, the promise of reality far exceeds what happened in Pepsi's fictional classroom.

Also, remember that "news story" about Zestra, a star of "corporate communication" spots that Pepsi watched on Channel One? More truth than fiction here, too. Since 1989, Channel One has sometimes blurred the lines between news, commercials, and public service announcements. In one study (Fox 1996), many students mistook commercials for news programs or public service announcements, such as those that warn viewers about drunk driving. The result was that students knew the product being advertised and regarded it warmly because, as one student told me, "They [the manufacturers and advertisers] are trying to do good. They care about us."   36

In the worst case of such blurring that I observed during the two-year period of this study, the students could hardly be faulted. Instead, the Salespeak was highly deceptive (merging with Doublespeak). That is, PepsiCo's series of ads called "It's Like This" were designed to look very much like documentary news footage and public service announcements. The actors spoke directly into the swinging, handheld camera, as if they were being interviewed; the ads were filmed in black and white, and the product's name was never spoken by any of the people in the commercial, although the rapid-fire editing included brief shots of the Pepsi logo, in color, on signs and on merchandise.   37

Just as in Pepsi's world, described earlier in this chapter, real-life ads are often embedded within programs, as well as other commercials, products, instructions, and even "transitional spaces" between one media message and another. For example, when the girl Pepsi took a break from her "learning," she went to the school's Commoditarium, or mini-mall, to shop for items that had been advertised at school. Again, there is truth here. Although schools do not yet contain mini-malls, they do contain stores and increasing numbers of strategically placed vending machines. A ninth-grade girl told me that after students viewed Channel One in the morning and watched commercials for M&Ms candies, her teacher allowed them to take a break. The student said she'd often walk down the hall and purchase M&Ms from the vending machine. In such schools, operant conditioning is alive and well. This is not the only way in which many schools are emulating shopping malls. My daughter's high school cafeteria is a "food court," complete with McDonald's and Pizza Hut.   38

By establishing itself in public schools, Channel One automatically "delivers" a captive, well-defined audience to its advertisers, more than was ever possible before. "Know thy audience"—as specifically as possible—is the name of the advertising game. Marketers have become increasingly effective at obtaining all kinds of demographic and psychographic information on consumers. Channel One increasingly hones its   39 messages based on the constant flow of demographic information it extracts from viewers, often under the guise of "clubs" and contests, which seek information on individuals, teams, classes, and entire schools ("Be a Channel One School"). Channel One's printed viewing and "curriculum" guides for teachers, as well as its Web site for students, also constantly solicit marketing information.

NOTES FROM THE WORLD OF SALESPEAK

More than anything else, dominant voices may be shaped by their   40
environment. Consider the following facts about the environment that
generates Salespeak:

- *$150 billion:* Amount spent by American advertisers each year, a cost that is passed on to consumers in higher prices. Landay (1998) summarizes our relationship with advertisers: "We pay their ad bills, we provide their profits, and we pay for their total tax write-off on the ads they place."
- *12 billion and 3 million:* The number of display ads and broadcast ads that Americans are collectively exposed to each day (Landay 1998).
- *2:* The number of times that we pay for advertising. First, advertising costs are built into the product. We pay again in terms of the time, money, and attention spent when processing an ad message.
- *1,000:* The number of chocolate chips in each bag of Chips Ahoy! cookies. The cookie company sponsored a "contest" in which students tried to confirm this claim (Labi 1999, 44).
- *$11 billion:* The amount of money dedicated to market research throughout the world (*World Opinion* Web site, November 11, 1998).
- *"Gosh, I don't understand—there are so many brands":* This is what one marketing firm has its researchers say, after they go into stores and place themselves next to real shoppers, in an effort to elicit what consumers are thinking in an authentic context (from the May 30, 1997, issue of the *Wall Street Journal* [McLaren 1998]).
- *$66 billion:* The amount of money spent by kids and young adults (ages 4–19) in 1992 (Bowen 1995).
- *16 million:* Approximate number of American children who use the Internet (*Brill's Content,* December 1998, 140).
- *115.95:* The number of banner ads viewed per week by the average Web user (*World Opinion* Web site, November 11, 1998).
- *"Save water. It's precious":* Message on a Coca-Cola billboard in Zimbabwe, where, according to the August 25, 1997, issue of the

Wall Street Journal, the soft drink has become the drink of choice (necessity?) because of a water shortage (McLaren 1998).

- *$204 billion:* The estimated amount of Web-based transactions in 2001, up from $10.4 billion in 1997 (Zona Research 1999 on the *World Opinion* Web site).
- *89:* Percentage of children's Web sites that collect users' personal information (*Brill's Content,* December 1998, 140).
- *23:* Percentage of children's Web sites that tell kids to ask their parents for permission before sending personal information. (*Brill's Content,* December 1998, 140).
- *$29 million:* Net income for Nielsen Media Research during the first six months of 1998. (*Brill's Content,* December 1998, 140).
- *$36 billion:* The amount of money spent by kids and young adults in 1992 (ages 4–19) that belonged to their parents (Bowen 1995).
- *$3.4 million:* The amount of money received by the Grapevine-Colleyville Texas School District for displaying a huge Dr. Pepper logo atop the school roof. This school is in the flight path of Dallas-Fort Worth International Airport (Perrin 1997).
- *$8 million:* The amount of money received by the Colorado Springs School District in Colorado from Coca-Cola for an exclusive ten-year service agreement (Perrin 1997).
- *"A tight, enduring connection to teens":* What Larry Jabbonsky, a spokesman at Pepsi headquarters, said his company seeks (Perrin 1997).
- *9,000:* The number of items stocked in grocery stores in the 1970s (Will 1997).
- *30,000:* The number of items now stocked in grocery stores (Will 1997).
- *99:* The percentage of teens surveyed (N = 534 in four cities) who correctly identified the croaking frogs from a Budweiser television commercial (Horovitz and Wells 1997, 1A).
- *93:* The percentage of teens who reported that they liked the Budweiser frogs "very much" or "somewhat" (Horovitz and Wells 1997, 1A).
- *95 and 94:* The percentages of teens who know the Marlboro man and Joe Camel (Wells 1997, 1A).
- *Great Britain's white cliffs of Dover:* The backdrop for a laser-projected Adidas ad (Liu 1999).
- *$200 million:* The amount of money Miller Beer spends on advertising each year.
- *Time Warner:* A corporate empire that controls news and information in America. (There are fewer than twelve.) Time Warner owns large book publishers, cable TV franchises, home video firms, CNN and other large cable channels, and magazines such as *Time,*

Life, People, Sports Illustrated, Money, Fortune, and *Entertainment Weekly* (Solomon 1999b).

- *$650 billion:* Annual sales of approximately 1,000 telemarketing companies, which employ 4 million Americans (Shenk 1999, 59).
- *350,000:* The number of classrooms that view two minutes of television commercials every day on Channel One ("Selling to School Kids" 1995).
- *154:* The number of Coca-Cola cans that students must find on a book cover and then color in, to reveal a hidden message ("Selling to School Kids" 1995).
- *50:* The percentage of increase in advertising expenditures during the past fifteen years (Bowen 1995).
- *560:* The daily number of ads targeted at the average American in 1971 (Shenk 1999, 59).
- *3,000:* The daily number of ads targeted at the average American in 1991 (Shenk 1999, 59).
- *Business Update:* An hourly segment broadcast on National Public Radio. Even though NPR is supposed to focus on "public broadcasting," it does not offer a *Labor Update.*
- *3.4 trillion:* The number of e-mail messages that crossed the Internet in the United States in 1998—a number expected to double by 2001 (McCafferty 1999).
- *80 percent:* The percentage of America's e-mail messages in 1998 that were mass-produced e-mailings, "most from corporations with something to sell" (McCafferty 1998).

It's hardly unusual for a free enterprise system to employ Salespeak. Advertising is a necessary ingredient for informing consumers about the goods and services they need. This is true for much of America's history. A sign hung in a trading post at the beginning of the Oregon Trail, 150 years ago, stating, "Sugar, 2 cents per lb.," contains necessary information for specific readers who had definite goals. Today, though, America is quite different.   41

First, unlike even forty years ago, most of today's advertising carries scant information about the product or service. Second, the more affluent America becomes, the fewer true "needs" we have. To make up for it, advertisers now focus not so much on what we truly need, but on what we may desire. Third, very few limits are placed upon advertising: we have little control over where it appears, who can see it (note how many of the previous items focus on young people), how often it appears, how messages are constructed, or how much money is budgeted for them (at the expense of, say, improving the product). The field of advertising itself is now a major industry. The Bureau of Labor   42

Statistics reports that in 1995, more people died on the job in advertising than in car factories, electrical repair companies, and petroleum refining operations (*Advertising Age,* August 19, 1996). Because advertising has such free rein in America, it's become one of our most dominating voices, if not the most dominating voice.

Examining the Text
1. Which parts of Pepsi's story ("A Day in the Life") are based on fact, according to Fox? Which parts of the story are "extensions or exaggerations of what already occurs in everyday life"? Do you find any of these "extensions or exaggerations" unrealistic or difficult to believe?
2. According to Fox, what's wrong with naming a person or a place after a product? Do you think there are qualitative differences between giving a product's name to a person, to a baseball stadium, or to a school?
3. What is a euphemism? List some of the euphemisms that Fox mentions in this reading. What problems does Fox see with these euphemisms?
4. *Thinking rhetorically:* In this article, Fox juxtaposes the fictional, futuristic, and seemingly outrageous story of the girl Pepsi with paragraphs of exposition and argument based on research. Do you find one of these strategies more persuasive than the other? How do they work together to prove his points?

For Group Discussion
In this article, Fox shows that he is particularly concerned with Salespeak in educational settings. In your discussion group, make a list of all the examples Fox gives to show where Salespeak is found in schools. Add examples to this list based on your own experience with Salespeak in your grade school, high school, and college experience. As a group, discuss whether your experiences tend to confirm or contradict Fox's claims that Salespeak exerts an undue influence in education.

Writing Suggestion
The article ends with a list of statistics about advertising. Use some of these statistics as evidence in an essay in which you give your opinion of the influence of advertising on our society. Consider using quotations from the article. You can use these statistics and quotations to support a position in which you agree with Fox's argument, or you can construct your essay by arguing against Fox, reinterpreting the statistics he offers and taking issue with statements that you quote from the article.

Advertising's Fifteen Basic Appeals

Jib Fowles

In the following essay, Jib Fowles looks at how advertisements work by examining the emotional, subrational appeals that they employ. We are confronted daily by hundreds of ads, only a few of which actually attract our attention. These few do so, according to Fowles, through "something primary and primitive, an emotional appeal, that in effect is the thin edge of the wedge, trying to find its way into a mind." Drawing on research done by the psychologist Henry A. Murray, Fowles describes fifteen emotional appeals or wedges that advertisements exploit.

Underlying Fowles's psychological analysis of advertising is the assumption that advertisers try to circumvent the logical, cautious, skeptical powers we develop as consumers, to reach, instead, the "unfulfilled urges and motives swirling in the bottom half of [our] minds." In Fowles's view, consumers are well advised to pay attention to these underlying appeals in order to avoid responding unthinkingly.

***As you read,** note which of Fowles's fifteen appeals seem most familiar to you. Do you recognize these appeals in ads you can recall? How have you responded?*

EMOTIONAL APPEALS

The nature of effective advertisements was recognized full well by the late media philosopher Marshall McLuhan. In his *Understanding Media*, the first sentence of the section on advertising reads, "The continuous pressure is to create ads more and more in the image of audience motives and desires."   1

By giving form to people's deep-lying desires, and picturing states of being that individuals privately yearn for, advertisers have the best chance of arresting attention and affecting communication. And that is the immediate goal of advertising: to tug at our psychological shirt sleeves and slow us down long enough for a word or two about whatever is being sold. We glance at a picture of a solitary rancher at work, and "Marlboro" slips into our minds.   2

Advertisers (I'm using the term as a shorthand for both the products' manufacturers, who bring the ambition and money to the process, and the advertising agencies, who supply the know-how) are ever more compelled to invoke consumers' drives and longings; this is the   3 "continuous pressure" McLuhan refers to. Over the past century, the American marketplace has grown increasingly congested as more and more products have entered into the frenzied competition after the public's dollars. The economies of other nations are quieter than ours since the volume of goods being hawked does not so greatly exceed demand. In some economies, consumer wares are scarce enough that no advertising at all is necessary. But in the United States, we go to the other extreme. In order to stay in business, an advertiser must strive to cut through the considerable commercial hub-bub by any means available—including the emotional appeals that some observers have held to be abhorrent and underhanded.

The use of subconscious appeals is a comment not only on condi-   4
tions among sellers. As time has gone by, buyers have become stoutly resistant to advertisements. We live in a blizzard of these messages and have learned to turn up our collars and ward off most of them. A study done a few years ago at Harvard University's Graduate School of Business Administration ventured that the average American is exposed to some 500 ads daily from television, newspapers, magazines, radio, billboards, direct mail, and so on. If for no other reason than to preserve one's sanity, a filter must be developed in every mind to lower the number of ads a person is actually aware of—a number this particular study estimated at about seventy-five ads per day. (Of these, only twelve typically produced a reaction—nine positive and three negative, on the average.) To be among the few messages that do manage to gain access to minds, advertisers must be strategic, perhaps even a little underhanded at times.

There are assumptions about personality underlying advertisers'   5
efforts to communicate via emotional appeals, and while these assumptions have stood the test of time, they still deserve to be aired. Human beings, it is presumed, walk around with a variety of unfulfilled urges and motives swirling in the bottom half of their minds. Lusts, ambitions, tendernesses, vulnerabilities—they are constantly bubbling up, seeking resolution. These mental forces energize people, but they are too crude and irregular to be given excessive play in the real world. They must be capped with the competent, sensible behavior that permits individuals to get along well in society. However, this upper layer of mental activity, shot through with caution and rationality, is not receptive to advertising's pitches. Advertisers want to circumvent this shell of consciousness if they can, and latch on to one of the lurching, subconscious drives.

In effect, advertisers over the years have blindly felt their way   6
around the underside of the American psyche, and by trial and error have discovered the softest points of entree, the places where their messages have the greatest likelihood of getting by consumers' defenses. As

McLuhan says elsewhere, "Gouging away at the surface of public sales resistance, the ad men are constantly breaking through into the *Alice in Wonderland* territory behind the looking glass, which is the world of subrational impulses and appetites."

An advertisement communicates by making use of a specially 7 selected image (of a supine female, say, or a curly-haired child, or a celebrity) which is designed to stimulate "subrational impulses and desires" even when they are at ebb, even if they are unacknowledged by their possessor. Some few ads have their emotional appeal in the text, but for the greater number by far the appeal is contained in the artwork. This makes sense, since visual communication better suits more primal levels of the brain. If the viewer of an advertisement actually has the importuned motive, and if the appeal is sufficiently well fashioned to call it up, then the person can be hooked. The product in the ad may then appear to take on the semblance of gratification for the summoned motive. Many ads seem to be saying, "If you have this need, then this product will help satisfy it." It is a primitive equation, but not an ineffective one for selling.

Thus, most advertisements appearing in national media can be 8 understood as having two orders of content. The first is the appeal to deeprunning drives in the minds of consumers. The second is information regarding the good[s] or service being sold: its name, its manufacturer, its picture, its packaging, its objective attributes, its functions. For example, the reader of a brassiere advertisement sees a partially undraped but blandly unperturbed woman standing in an otherwise commonplace public setting, and may experience certain sensations; the reader also sees the name "Maidenform," a particular brassiere style, and, in tiny print, words about the material, colors, price. Or, the viewer of a television commercial sees a demonstration with four small boxes labeled 650, 650, 650, and 800; something in the viewer's mind catches hold of this, as trivial as thoughtful consideration might reveal it to be. The viewer is also exposed to the name "Anacin," its bottle, and its purpose.

Sometimes there is an apparently logical link between an ad's 9 emotional appeal and its product information. It does not violate common sense that Cadillac automobiles be photographed at country clubs, or that Japan Air Lines be associated with Orientalia. But there is no real need for the linkage to have a bit of reason behind it. Is there anything inherent to the connection between Salem cigarettes and mountains, Coke and a smile, Miller Beer and comradeship? The link being forged in minds between product and appeal is a pre-logical one.

People involved in the advertising industry do not necessarily talk 10 in the terms being used here. They are stationed at the sending end of this communications channel, and may think they are up to any number of things—Unique Selling Propositions, explosive copywriting, the optimal use of demographics or psychographics, ideal media buys, high recall ratings, or whatever. But when attention shifts to the receiving end of the channel, and focuses on the instant of reception, then commentary becomes much more elemental: an advertising message contains something primary and primitive, an emotional appeal, that in effect is the thin end of the wedge, trying to find its way into a mind. Should this occur, the product information comes along behind.

When enough advertisements are examined in this light, it becomes   11
clear that the emotional appeals fall into several distinguishable categories, and that every ad is a variation on one of a limited number of basic appeals. While there may be several ways of classifying these appeals, one particular list of fifteen has proven to be especially valuable.

Advertisements can appeal to:

1. The need for sex
2. The need for affiliation
3. The need to nurture
4. The need for guidance
5. The need to aggress
6. The need to achieve
7. The need to dominate
8. The need for prominence
9. The need for attention
10. The need for autonomy
11. The need to escape
12. The need to feel safe
13. The need for aesthetic sensations
14. The need to satisfy curiosity
15. Physiological needs: food, drink, sleep, etc.

MURRAY'S LIST

Where does this list of advertising's fifteen basic appeals come from?   12
Several years ago, I was involved in a research project which was to have as one segment an objective analysis of the changing appeals made in post–World War II American advertising. A sample of magazine ads would have their appeals coded into the categories of psychological needs they seemed aimed at. For this content analysis to happen, a complete roster of human motives would have to be found.

The first thing that came to mind was Abraham Maslow's famous   13
four-part hierarchy of needs. But the briefest look at the range of

appeals made in advertising was enough to reveal that they are more varied, and more profane, than Maslow had cared to account for. The search led on to the work of psychologist Henry A. Murray, who together with his colleagues at the Harvard Psychological Clinic has constructed a full taxonomy of needs. As described in *Explorations in Personality,* Murray's team had conducted a lengthy series of in-depth interviews with a number of subjects in order to derive from scratch what they felt to be the essential variables of personality. Forty-four variables were distinguished by the Harvard group, of which twenty were motives. The need for achievement ("to overcome obstacles and obtain a high standard") was one, for instance; the need to defer was another; the need to aggress was a third; and so forth.

Murray's list had served as the groundwork for a number of   14
subsequent projects. Perhaps the best-known of these was David C. McClelland's extensive study of the need for achievement, reported in his *The Achieving Society.* In the process of demonstrating that a people's high need for achievement is predictive of later economic growth, McClelland coded achievement imagery and references out of a nation's folklore, songs, legends, and children's tales.

Following McClelland, I too wanted to cull the motivational   15
appeals from a culture's imaginative product—in this case, advertising. To develop categories expressly for this purpose, I took Murray's twenty motives and added to them others he had mentioned in passing in *Explorations in Personality* but not included on the final list. The extended list was tried out on a sample of advertisements, and motives which never seemed to be invoked were dropped. I ended up with eighteen of Murray's motives, into which 770 print ads were coded. The resulting distribution is included in the 1976 book *Mass Advertising as Social Forecast.*

Since that time, the list of appeals has undergone refinements as a   16
result of using it to analyze television commercials. A few more adjustments stemmed from the efforts of students in my advertising classes to decode appeals; tens of term papers surveying thousands of advertisements have caused some inconsistencies in the list to be hammered out. Fundamentally, though, the list remains the creation of Henry Murray. In developing a comprehensive, parsimonious inventory of human motives, he pinpointed the subsurface mental forces that are the least quiescent and most susceptible to advertising's entreaties.

FIFTEEN APPEALS

1. *Need for sex.* Let's start with sex, because this is the appeal   17
which seems to pop up first whenever the topic of advertising is raised. Whole books have been written about this one alone, to find a large

audience of mildly titillated readers. Lately, due to campaigns to sell blue jeans, concern with sex in ads has redoubled.

The fascinating thing is not how much sex there is in advertising, but how little. Contrary to impressions, unambiguous sex is rare in these messages. Some of this surprising observation may be a matter of definition: the Jordache ads with the lithe, blouse-less female astride a similarly clad male is clearly an appeal to the audience's sexual drives, but the same cannot be said about Brooke Shields in the Calvin Klein commercials. Directed at young women and their credit-card carrying mothers, the image of Miss Shields instead invokes the need to be looked at. Buy Calvins and you'll be the center of much attention, just as Brooke is, the ads imply; they do not primarily inveigle their target audience's need for sexual intercourse. 18

In the content analysis reported in *Mass Advertising as Social Forecast* only two percent of ads were found to pander to this motive. Even *Playboy* ads shy away from sexual appeals: a recent issue contained eighty-three full-page ads, and just four of them (or less than five percent) could be said to have sex on their minds. 19

The reason this appeal is so little used is that it is too blaring and tends to obliterate the product information. Nudity in advertising has the effect of reducing brand recall. The people who do remember the product may do so because they have been made indignant by the ad; this is not the response most advertisers seek. 20

To the extent that sexual imagery is used, it conventionally works better on men than women; typically a female figure is offered up to the male reader. A Black Velvet liquor advertisement displays an attractive woman wearing a tight black outfit, recumbent under the legend, "Feel the Velvet." The figure does not have to be horizontal, however, for the appeal to be present as National Airlines revealed in its "Fly me" campaign. Indeed, there does not even have to be a female in the ad; "Flick my Bic" was sufficient to convey the idea to many. 21

As a rule, though, advertisers have found sex to be a tricky appeal, to be used sparingly. Less controversial and equally fetching are the appeals to our need for affectionate human contact. 22

2. *Need for affiliation.* American mythology upholds autonomous individuals, and social statistics suggest that people are ever more going it alone in their lives, yet the high frequency of affiliative appeals in ads belies this. Or maybe it does not: maybe all the images of companionship are compensation for what Americans privately lack. In any case, the need to associate with others is widely invoked in advertising and is probably the most prevalent appeal. All sorts of goods and services are sold by linking them to our unfulfilled desires to be in good company. 23

According to Henry Murray, the need for affiliation consists of   24
desires "to draw near and enjoyably cooperate or reciprocate with
another; to please and win affection of another; to adhere and remain
loyal to a friend." The manifestations of this motive can be segmented
into several different types of affiliation, beginning with romance.

Courtship may be swifter nowadays, but the desire for pairbond-   25
ing is far from satiated. Ads reaching for this need commonly depict a
youngish male and female engrossed in each other. The head of the
male is usually higher than the female's, even at this late date; she may
be sitting or leaning while he is standing. They are not touching in the
Smirnoff vodka ads, but obviously there is an intimacy, sometimes frol-
icsome, between them. The couple does touch for Martell Cognac when
"The moment was Martell." For Wind Song perfume they have
touched, and "Your Wind Song stays on his mind."

Depending on the audience, the pair does not absolutely have to   26
be young—just together. He gives her a DeBeers diamond, and there is
a tear in her laugh lines. She takes Geritol and preserves herself for
him. And numbers of consumers, wanting affection too, follow suit.

Warm family feelings are fanned in ads when another generation   27
is added to the pair. Hallmark Cards brings grandparents into the picture, and Johnson and Johnson Baby Powder has Dad, Mom, and baby,
all fresh from the bath, encircled in arms and emblazoned with "Share
the Feeling." A talc has been fused to familial love.

Friendship is yet another form of affiliation pursued by advertisers.   28
Two women confide and drink Maxwell House coffee together; two
men walk through the woods smoking Salem cigarettes. Miller Beer
promises that afternoon "Miller Time" will be staffed with three or four
good buddies. Drink Dr. Pepper, as Mickey Rooney is coaxed to do,
and join in with all the other Peppers. Coca-Cola does not even need to
portray the friendliness; it has reduced this appeal to "a Coke and
a smile."

The warmth can be toned down and disguised, but it is the same   29
affiliative need that is being fished for. The blonde has a direct gaze and
her friends are firm businessmen in appearance, but with a glass of Old
Bushmill you can sit down and fit right in. Or, for something more
upbeat, sing along with the Pontiac choirboys.

As well as presenting positive images, advertisers can play to the   30
need for affiliation in negative ways, by invoking the fear of rejection.
If we don't use Scope, we'll have the "Ugh! Morning Breath" that
causes the male and female models to avert their faces. Unless we
apply Ultra Brite or Close-Up to our teeth, it's good-bye romance. Our
family will be cursed with "House-a-tosis" if we don't take care. Without Dr. Scholl's antiperspirant foot spray, the bowling team will keel
over. There go all the guests when the supply of Dorito's nacho cheese

chips is exhausted. Still more rejection if our shirts have ring-around-the-collar, if our car needs to be Midasized. But make a few purchases, and we are back in the bosom of human contact.

As self-directed as Americans pretend to be, in the last analysis 31 we remain social animals, hungering for the positive, endorsing feelings that only those around us can supply. Advertisers respond, urging us to "Reach out and touch someone," in the hopes our monthly bills will rise.

3. *Need to nurture.* Akin to affiliative needs is the need to take care 32 of small, defenseless creatures—children and pets, largely. Reciprocity is of less consequence here, though; it is the giving that counts. Murray uses synonyms like "to feed, help, support, console, protect, comfort, nurse, heal." A strong need it is, woven deep into our genetic fabric, for if it did not exist we could not successfully raise up our replacements. When advertisers put forth the image of something diminutive and furry, something that elicits the word "cute" or "precious," then they are trying to trigger this motive. We listen to the childish voice singing the Oscar Mayer weiner song, and our next hotdog purchase is prescribed. Aren't those darling kittens something, and how did this Meow Mix get into our shopping cart?

This pitch is often directed at women, as Mother Nature's chief 33 nurturers. "Make me some Kraft macaroni and cheese, please," says the elfin preschooler just in from the snowstorm, and mothers' hearts go out, and Kraft's sales go up. "We're cold, wet, and hungry," whine the husband and kids, and the little woman gets the Manwiches ready. A facsimile of this need can be hit without children or pets: the husband is ill and sleepless in the television commercial, and the wife grudgingly fetches the NyQuil.

But it is not women alone who can be touched by this appeal. The 34 father nurses his son Eddie through adolescence while the John Deere lawn tractor survives the years. Another father counts pennies with his young son as the subject of New York Life Insurance comes up. And all over America are businessmen who don't know why they dial Qantas Airlines when they have to take a trans-Pacific trip; the koala bear knows.

4. *Need for guidance.* The opposite of the need to nurture is the 35 need to be nurtured: to be protected, shielded, guided. We may be loath to admit it, but the child lingers on inside every adult—and a good thing it does, or we would not be instructable in our advancing years. Who wants a nation of nothing but flinty personalities?

Parent-like figures can successfully call up this need. Robert 36 Young recommends Sanka coffee, and since we have experienced him for twenty-five years as television father and doctor, we take his word for it. Florence Henderson as the expert mom knows a lot about the advantages of Wesson oil.

The parent-ness of the spokesperson need not be so salient; some-   37
times pure authoritativeness is better. When Orson Welles scowls and
intones, "Paul Masson will sell no wine before its time," we may not
know exactly what he means, but we still take direction from him.
There is little maternal about Brenda Vaccaro when she speaks up for
Tampax, but there is a certainty to her that many accept.

A celebrity is not a necessity in making a pitch to the need for guid-   38
ance, since a fantasy figure can serve just as well. People accede to the
Green Giant, or Betty Crocker, or Mr. Goodwrench. Some advertisers can
get by with no figure at all: "When E.F. Hutton talks, people listen."

Often it is tradition or custom that advertisers point to and con-   39
sumers take guidance from. Bits and pieces of American history are used
to sell whiskeys like Old Crow, Southern Comfort, Jack Daniel's. We conform to traditional male/female roles and age-old social norms when we
purchase Barclay cigarettes, *which informs us "The pleasure is back."*

The product itself, if it has been around for a long time, can con-   40
stitute a tradition. All those old labels in the ad for Morton salt convince us that we should continue to buy it. Kool-Aid says "You loved it
as a kid. You trust it as a mother," hoping to get yet more consumers to
go along.

Even when the product has no history at all, our need to conform   41
to tradition and to be guided are strong enough that they can be
invoked through bogus nostalgia and older actors. Country-Time
lemonade sells because consumers want to believe it has a past they
can defer to.

So far the needs and the ways they can be invoked which have   42
been looked at are largely warm and affiliative; they stand in contrast
to the next set of needs, which are much more egoistic and assertive.

5. *Need to aggress.* The pressures of the real world create strong   43
retaliatory feelings in every functioning human being. Since these
impulses can come forth as bursts of anger and violence, their display
is normally tabooed. Existing as harbored energy, aggressive drives
present a large, tempting target for advertisers. It is not a target to be
aimed at thoughtlessly, though, for few manufacturers want their
products associated with destructive motives. There is always the danger that, as in the case of sex, if the appeal is too blatant, public opinion
will turn against what is being sold.

Jack-in-the-Box sought to abruptly alter its marketing by going   44
after older customers and forgetting the younger ones. Their television
commercials had a seventy-ish lady command, "Waste him," and the
Jack-in-the-Box clown exploded before our eyes. So did public reaction
until the commercials were toned down. Print ads for Club cocktails
carried the faces of octogenarians under the headline, "Hit me with a
Club"; response was contrary enough to bring the campaign to a stop.

Better disguised aggressive appeals are less likely to backfire: 45
Triumph cigarettes has models making a lewd gesture with their uplifted
cigarettes, but the individuals are often laughing and usually in close
company of others. When Exxon said, "There's a Tiger in your tank," the
implausibility of it concealed the invocation of aggressive feelings.

Depicted arguments are a common way for advertisers to tap the   46
audience's needs to aggress. Don Rickles and Lynda Carter trade gibes,
and consumers take sides as the name of Seven-Up is stitched on
minds. The Parkay tub has a difference of opinion with the user; who
can forget it, or who (or what) got the last word in?

6. *Need to achieve.* This is the drive that energizes people, causing   47
them to strive in their lives and careers. According to Murray, the need
for achievement is signalled by the desires "to accomplish something
difficult. To overcome obstacles and attain a high standard. To excel
one's self. To rival and surpass others." A prominent American trait, it
is one that advertisers like to hook on to because it identifies their product with winning and success.

The Cutty Sark ad does not disclose that Ted Turner failed at his   48
latest attempt at yachting's America Cup; here he is represented as a
champion on the water as well as off in his television enterprises. If we
drink this whiskey, we will be victorious alongside Turner. We can also
succeed with O.J. Simpson by renting Hertz cars, or with Reggie Jackson by bringing home some Panasonic equipment. Cathy Rigby and
Stayfree Maxipads will put people out front.

Sports heroes are the most convenient means to snare consumers'   49
needs to achieve, but they are not the only one. Role models can be
established, ones which invite emulation, as with the profiles put forth
by Dewar's scotch. Successful, tweedy individuals relate they have
"graduated to the flavor of Myer's rum." Or the advertiser can establish a prize: two neighbors play one-on-one basketball for a Michelob
beer in a television commercial, while in a print ad a bottle of Johnnie
Walker Black Label has been gilded like a trophy.

Any product that advertises itself in superlatives—the best, the   50
first, the finest—is trying to make contact with our needs to succeed.
For many consumers, sales and bargains belong in this category of
appeals, too; the person who manages to buy something at fifty percent
off is seizing an opportunity and coming out ahead of others.

7. *Need to dominate.* This fundamental need is the craving to be   51
powerful—perhaps omnipotent, as in the Xerox ad where Brother
Dominic exhibits heavenly powers and creates miraculous copies.
Most of us will settle for being just a regular potentate, though. We
drink Budweiser because it is the King of Beers, and here comes the
powerful Clydesdales to prove it. A taste of Wolfschmidt vodka and
"The spirit of the Czar lives on."

The need to dominate and control one's environment is often   52
thought of as being masculine, but as close students of human nature
advertisers know, it is not so circumscribed. Women's aspirations for
control are suggested in the campaign theme, "I like my men in English
Leather, or nothing at all." The females in the Chanel No. 19 ads are
"outspoken" and wrestle their men around.

Male and female, what we long for is clout; what we get in its   53
place is Mastercard.

8. *Need for prominence.* Here comes the need to be admired and   54
respected, to enjoy prestige and high social status. These times, it
appears, are not so egalitarian after all. Many ads picture the trappings
of high position; the Oldsmobile stands before a manorial doorway, the
Volvo is parked beside a steeplechase. A book-lined study is the setting
for Dewar's 12, and Lenox China is displayed in a dining room chock
full of antiques.

Beefeater gin represents itself as "The Crown Jewel of England"   55
and uses no illustrations of jewels or things British, for the words are
sufficient indicators of distinction. Buy that gin and you will rise up the
prestige hierarchy, or achieve the same effect on yourself with Sea-
gram's 7 Crown, which ambiguously describes itself as "classy."

Being respected does not have to entail the usual accoutrements   56
of wealth: "Do you know who I am?" the commercials ask, and we
learn that the prominent person is not so prominent without his American Express card.

9. *Need for attention.* The previous need involved being *looked up*   57
to, while this is the need to be *looked at.* The desire to exhibit ourselves
in such a way as to make others look at us is a primitive, insuppressible
instinct. The clothing and cosmetic industries exist just to serve this
need, and this is the way they pitch their wares. Some of this effort is
aimed at males, as the ads for Hathaway shirts and Jockey under-
clothes. But the greater bulk of such appeals is targeted singlemindedly
at women.

To come back to Brooke Shields: this is where she fits into Ameri-   58
can marketing. If I buy Calvin Klein jeans, consumers infer, I'll be the
object of fascination. The desire for exhibition has been most strikingly
played to in a print campaign of many years' duration, that of Maidenform lingerie. The woman exposes herself, and sales surge. "Gentlemen prefer Hanes" the ads dissemble, and women who want eyes
upon them know what they should do. Peggy Fleming flutters her legs
for L'eggs, encouraging females who want to be the star in their own
lives to purchase this product.

The same appeal works for cosmetics and lotions. For years, the   59
little girl with the exposed backside sold gobs of Coppertone, but now
the company has picked up the pace a little: as a female, you are

supposed to "Flash 'em a Coppertone tan." Food can be sold the same way, especially to the diet-conscious; Angie Dickinson poses for California avocados and says, "Would this body lie to you?" Our eyes are too fixed on her for us to think to ask if she got that way by eating mounds of guacamole.

10. *Need for autonomy.* There are several ways to sell credit card   60
services, as has been noted: Mastercard appeals to the need to dominate, and American Express to the need for prominence. When Visa
claims, "You can have it the way you want it," yet another primary
motive is being beckoned forward—the need to endorse the self. The
focus here is upon the independence and integrity of the individual;
this need is the antithesis of the need for guidance and is unlike any of
the social needs. "If running with the herd isn't your style, try ours,"
says Rotan-Mosle, and many Americans feel they have finally found
the right brokerage firm.

The photo is of a red-coated Mountie on his horse, posed on a   61
snow-covered ledge; the copy reads, "Windsor—One Canadian stands
alone." This epitome of the solitary and proud individual may work
best with male customers, as may Winston's man in the red cap. But
one-figure advertisements also strike the strong need for autonomy
among American women. As Shelly Hack strides for Charlie perfume,
females respond to her obvious pride and flair; she is her own person.
The Virginia Slims tale is of people who have come a long way from
subservience to independence. Cachet perfume feels it does not need a
solo figure to work this appeal, and uses three different faces in its ads;
it insists, though, "It's different on every woman who wears it."

Like many psychological needs, this one can also be appealed to   62
in a negative fashion, by invoking the loss of independence or self-
regard. Guilt and regrets can be stimulated: "Gee, I could have had a
V-8." Next time, get one and be good to yourself.

11. *Need to escape.* An appeal to the need for autonomy often co-   63
occurs with one for the need to escape, since the desire to duck out of
our social obligations, to seek rest or adventure, frequently takes the
form of one-person flight. The dashing image of a pilot, in fact, is a
standard way of quickening this need to get away from it all.

Freedom is the pitch here, the freedom that every individual   64
yearns for whenever life becomes too oppressive. Many advertisers
like appealing to the need for escape because the sensation of pleasure
often accompanies escape, and what nicer emotional nimbus could
there be for a product? "You deserve a break today," says McDonald's,
and Stouffer's frozen foods chime in, "Set yourself free."

For decades men have imaginatively bonded themselves to the   65
Marlboro cowboy who dwells untarnished and unencumbered in
Marlboro Country some distance from modern life; smokers' aching

needs for autonomy and escape are personified by that cowpoke. Many women can identify with the lady ambling through the woods behind the words, "Benson and Hedges and mornings and me."

But escape does not have to be solitary. Other Benson and Hedges 66 ads, part of the same campaign, contain two strolling figures. In Salem cigarette advertisements, it can be several people who escape together into the mountaintops. A commercial for Levi's pictured a cloudbank above a city through which ran a whole chain of young people.

There are varieties of escape, some wistful like the Boeing 67 "Someday" campaign of dream vacations, some kinetic like the play and parties in soft drink ads. But in every instance, the consumer exposed to the advertisement is invited to momentarily depart his everyday life for a more carefree experience, preferably with the product in hand.

12. *Need to feel safe.* Nobody in their right mind wants to be intimi- 68 dated, menaced, battered, poisoned. We naturally want to do whatever it takes to stave off threats to our well-being, and to our families'. It is the instinct of self-preservation that makes us responsive to the ad of the St. Bernard with the keg of Chivas Regal. We pay attention to the stern talk of Karl Malden and the plight of the vacationing couples who have lost all their funds in the American Express travelers cheques commercials. We want the omnipresent stag from Hartford Insurance to watch over us too.

In the interest of keeping failure and calamity from our lives, we 69 like to see the durability of products demonstrated. Can we ever forget that Timex takes a licking and keeps on ticking? When the American Tourister suitcase bounces all over the highway and the egg inside doesn't break, the need to feel safe has been adroitly plucked.

We take precautions to diminish future threats. We buy Volkswa- 70 gen Rabbits for the extraordinary mileage, and MONY insurance policies to avoid the tragedies depicted in their black-and-white ads of widows and orphans.

We are careful about our health. We consume Mazola margarine 71 because it has "corn goodness" backed by the natural food traditions of the American Indians. In the medicine cabinet is Alka-Seltzer, the "home remedy"; having it, we are snug in our little cottage.

We want to be safe and secure; buy these products, advertisers are 72 saying, and you'll be safer than you are without them.

13. *Need for aesthetic sensations.* There is an undeniable aesthetic 73 component to virtually every ad run in the national media: the photography or filming or drawing is near-perfect, the type style is well chosen, the layout could scarcely be improved upon. Advertisers know there is little chance of good communication occurring if an ad is not visually pleasing. Consumers may not be aware of the extent of their own sensitivity to artwork, but it is undeniably large.

Sometimes the aesthetic element is expanded and made into an   74
ad's primary appeal. Charles Jordan shoes may or may not appear in the
accompanying avant-grade photographs; Kohler plumbing fixtures
catch attention through the high style of their desert settings. Beneath the
slightly out of focus photograph, languid and sensuous in tone, General
Electric feels called upon to explain, "This is an ad for the hair dryer."

This appeal is not limited to female consumers: J&B scotch says   75
"It whispers" and shows a bucolic scene of lake and castle.

14. *Need to satisfy curiosity.* It may seem odd to list a need for infor-   76
mation among basic motives, but this need can be as primal and
compelling as any of the others. Human beings are curious by nature,
interested in the world around them, and intrigued by tidbits of knowledge and new developments. Trivia, percentages, observations counter
to conventional wisdom—these items all help sell products. Any advertisement in a question-and-answer format is strumming this need.

A dog groomer has a question about long distance rates, and Bell   77
Telephone has a chart with all the figures. An ad for Porsche 911 is
replete with diagrams and schematics, numbers and arrows. Lo and
behold, Anacin pills have 150 more milligrams than its competitors;
should we wonder if this is better or worse for us?

15. *Physiological needs.* To the extent that sex is solely a biological   78
need, we are now coming around full circle, back toward the start of
the list. In this final category are clustered appeals to sleeping, eating,
drinking. The art of photographing food and drink is so advanced,
sometimes these temptations are wondrously caught in the camera's
lens: the crab meat in the Red Lobster restaurant ads can start us sali-
vating, the Quarterpounder can almost be smelled, the liquor in the
glass glows invitingly. Imbibe, these ads scream.

STYLES

Some common ingredients of advertisements were not singled out for   79
separate mention in the list of fifteen because they are not appeals in
and of themselves. They are stylistic features, influencing the way a
basic appeal is presented. The use of humor is one, and the use of
celebrities is another. A third is time imagery, past and future, which
goes to several purposes.

For all of its employment in advertising, humor can be treacher-   80
ous, because it can get out of hand and smother the product information. Supposedly, this is what Alka-Seltzer discovered with its comic
commercials of the late sixties; "I can't believe I ate the whole thing,"
the sad-faced husband lamented, and the audience cackled so much it
forgot the antacid. Or, did not take it seriously.

But used carefully, humor can punctuate some of the softer   81
appeals and soften some of the harsher ones. When Emma says to the
Fruit-of-the-Loom fruits, "Hi, cuties. Whatcha doing in my laundry
basket?" we smile as our curiosity is assuaged along with hers. Bill
Cosby gets consumers tickled about the children in his Jell-O commercials, and strokes the need to nurture.

An insurance company wants to invoke the need to feel safe, but   82
does not want to leave readers with an unpleasant aftertaste; cartoonist
Rowland Wilson creates an avalanche about to crush a gentleman who
is saying to another, "My insurance company? New England Life, of
course. Why?" The same tactic of humor undercutting threat is used in
the cartoon commercials for Safeco when the Pink Panther wanders
from one disaster to another. Often humor masks aggression: comedian
Bob Hope in the outfit of a boxer promises to knock out the knock-
knocks with Texaco; Rodney Dangerfield, who "can't get no respect,"
invites aggression as the comic relief in Miller Lite commercials.

Roughly fifteen percent of all advertisements incorporate a   83
celebrity, almost always from the fields of entertainment or sports. The
approach can also prove troublesome for advertisers, for celebrities are
human beings too, and fully capable of the most remarkable behavior.
If anything distasteful about them emerges, it is likely to reflect on the
product. The advertisers making use of Anita Bryant and Billy Jean
King suffered several anxious moments. An untimely death can also
react poorly on a product. But advertisers are willing to take risks
because celebrities can be such a good link between producers and
consumers, performing the social role of introducer.

There are several psychological needs these middlemen can play   84
upon. Let's take the product class of cameras and see how different
celebrities can hit different needs. The need for guidance can be
invoked by Michael Landon, who plays such a wonderful dad on "Little House on the Prairie"; when he says to buy Kodak equipment,
many people listen. James Garner for Polaroid cameras is put in a similar authoritative role, so defined by a mocking spouse. The need to
achieve is summoned up by Tracy Austin and other tennis stars for
Canon AE-1; the advertiser first makes sure we see these athletes playing to win. When Cheryl Tiegs speaks up for Olympus cameras, it is the
need for attention that is being targeted.

The past and future, being outside our grasp, are exploited by   85
advertisers as locales for the projection of needs. History can offer up
heroes (and call up the need to achieve) or traditions (need for guidance) as well as art objects (need for aesthetic sensations). Nostalgia is a
kindly version of personal history and is deployed by advertisers to
rouse needs for affiliation and for guidance; the need to escape can
come in here, too. The same need to escape is sometimes the point of

futuristic appeals but picturing the avant-garde can also be a way to get at the need to achieve.

ANALYZING ADVERTISEMENTS

When analyzing ads yourself for their emotional appeals, it takes a bit   86
of practice to learn to ignore the product information (as well as one's own experience and feelings about the product). But that skill comes soon enough, as does the ability to quickly sort out from all the non-product aspects of an ad the chief element which is the most striking, the most likely to snag attention first and penetrate brains farthest. The key to the appeal, this element usually presents itself centrally and for-wardly to the reader or viewer.

Another clue: the viewing angle which the audience has on the   87
ad's subjects is informative. If the subjects are photographed or filmed from below and thus are looking down at you much as the Green Giant does, then the need to be guided is a good candidate for the ad's emo-tional appeal. If, on the other hand, the subjects are shot from above and appear deferential, as is often the case with children or female models, then other needs are being appealed to.

To figure out an ad's emotional appeal, it is wise to know (or have   88
a good hunch about) who the targeted consumers are; this can often be inferred from the magazine or television show it appears in. This piece of information is a great help in determining the appeal and in decid-ing between two different interpretations. For example, if an ad fea-tures a partially undressed female, this would typically signal one appeal for readers of *Penthouse* (need for sex) and another for readers of *Cosmopolitan* (need for attention).

It would be convenient if every ad made just one appeal, were   89
aimed at just one need. Unfortunately, things are often not that simple. A cigarette ad with a couple at the edge of a polo field is trying to hit both the need for affiliation and the need for prominence; depending on the attitude of the male, dominance could also be an ingredient in this. An ad for Chimere perfume incorporates two photos: in the top one the lady is being commanding at a business luncheon (need to dominate), but in the lower one she is being bussed (need for affiliation). Better ads, however, seem to avoid being too diffused; in the study of post–World War II advertising described earlier, appeals grew more focused as the decades passed. As a rule of thumb, about sixty percent have two conspicuous appeals; the last twenty percent have three or more. Rather than looking for the greatest number of appeals, decoding ads is most productive when the loudest one or two appeals are discerned, since those are the appeals with the best chance of grabbing people's attention.

Finally, analyzing ads does not have to be a solo activity and prob-   91
ably should not be. The greater number of people there are involved, the
better chance there is of transcending individual biases and discerning
the essential emotional lure built into an advertisement.

DO THEY OR DON'T THEY?

Do the emotional appeals made in advertisements add up to the sinister manipulation of consumers?

It is clear that these ads work. Attention is caught, communica-   92
tion occurs between producers and consumers, and sales result. It
turns out to be difficult to detail the exact relationship between a
specific ad and a specific purchase, or even between a campaign and
subsequent sales figures, because advertising is only one of a host of
influences upon consumption. Yet no one is fooled by this lack of perfect proof; everyone knows that advertising sells. If this were not the
case, then tight-fisted American businesses would not spend a total of
fifty billion dollars annually on these messages.

But before anyone despairs that advertisers have our number to   93
the extent that they can marshal us at will and march us like automa-
tons to the check-out counters, we should recall the resiliency and
obduracy of the American consumer. Advertisers may have uncovered
the softest spots in minds, but that does not mean they have found
truly gaping apertures. There is no evidence that advertising can get
people to do things contrary to their self-interests. Despite all the
finesse of advertisements, and all the subtle emotional tugs, the public
resists the vast majority of the petitions. According to the marketing
division of the A.C. Nielsen Company, a whopping seventy-five percent of all new products die within a year in the marketplace, the victims of consumer disinterest which no amount of advertising could
overcome. The appeals in advertising may be the most captivating
there are to be had, but they are not enough to entrap the wiley
consumer.

The key to understanding the discrepancy between, on the one   94
hand, the fact that advertising truly works, and, on the other, the fact
that it hardly works, is to take into account the enormous numbers of
people exposed to an ad. Modern-day communications permit an ad to
be displayed to millions upon millions of individuals; if the smallest
fraction of that audience can be moved to buy the product, then the ad
has been successful. When one percent of the people exposed to a television advertising campaign reach for their wallets, that could be one
million sales, which may be enough to keep the product in production
and the advertisements coming.

In arriving at an evenhanded judgment about advertisements   95
and their emotional appeals, it is good to keep in mind that many of the
purchases which might be credited to these ads are experienced as genuinely gratifying to the consumer. We sincerely like the goods or service we have bought, and we may even like some of the emotional
drapery that an ad suggests comes with it. It has sometimes been noted
that the most avid students of advertisements are the people who have
just bought the product; they want to steep themselves in the associated imagery. This may be the reason that Americans, when polled, are
not negative about advertising and do not disclose any sense of being
misused. The volume of advertising may be an irritant, but the product
information as well as the imaginative material in ads are partial
compensation.

A productive understanding is that advertising messages involve   96
costs and benefits at both ends of the communications channel. For
those few ads which do make contact, the consumer surrenders a
moment of time, has the lower brain curried, and receives notice of a
product; the advertiser has given up money and has increased the
chance of sales. In this sort of communications activity, neither party
can be said to be the loser.

Examining the Text

1. Fowles's claim in this essay is that advertisers try to tap into basic
human needs and emotions, rather than consumers' intellect. How
does he go about proving this claim? What examples or other proof
strike you as particularly persuasive? Where do you see weaknesses in
Fowles's argument?

2. What do advertisers assume about the personality of the consumer,
according to Fowles? How do these assumptions contribute to the way
they sell products? Do you think that these assumptions about personality are correct? Why or why not?

3. Fowles's list of advertising's fifteen basic appeals is, as he explains,
derived from Henry Murray's inventory of human motives. Which of
these motives strike you as the most significant or powerful? What
other motives would you add to the list?

4. *Thinking rhetorically*: What do you think is Fowles's ultimate purpose
in writing this article? Who is he targeting as the audience for his arguments, and what do you think he intends this audience to do or to think
after reading the article? What, if any, real world effects do you imagine
Fowles wants to achieve by writing this article?

For Group Discussion

In his discussion of the way advertising uses "the need for sex" and
"the need to aggress," Fowles debunks the persistent complaints about

the use of sex and violence in the mass media. What current examples support Fowles's point? Discuss your responses to his explanations.

Writing Suggestion

Working with Fowles's list of the fifteen appeals of advertising, survey a recent magazine, looking at all the ads and categorizing them based on their predominant appeal. In an essay, describe what your results tell you about the magazine and its readership. Based on your survey, would you amend Fowles's list? What additions or deletions would you make?

How Advertising Informs to Our Benefit

John E. Calfee

This article, adapted from John E. Calfee's book Fear of Persuasion: A New Perspective on Advertising and Regulation, *provides a different view of the effect of advertising on our society. Calfee, a former Federal Trade Commission economist and a resident scholar at the American Enterprise Institute, argues that advertising actually provides many benefits to consumers. Calfee relates several specific cases in which advertisements spread important health information to people who might not have learned about it otherwise. Because advertisers have huge budgets and can reach into virtually every home through television, newspapers, billboards, and radio campaigns, advertisements have the potential to spread information in a way that government-sponsored public service initiatives cannot.*

Calfee also diverges from previous articles in this chapter by suggesting that regulations on advertising are unnecessary and counterproductive. Indeed, Calfee argues that advertising is, to a large extent, self-regulating. Free-market competition compels companies to be truthful, or else competitors will challenge their claims, resulting in negative publicity.

As you read this article, consider your own feelings about advertising: do you think it's a destructive force in our society or a valuable tool for disseminating information? Given the power and reach of advertising, how can it be used as a positive information resource?

A great truth about advertising is that it is a tool for communicating   1
information and shaping markets. It is one of the forces that compel
sellers to cater to the desires of consumers. Almost everyone knows
this because consumers use advertising every day, and they miss
advertising when they cannot get it. This fact does not keep politicians and opinion leaders from routinely dismissing the value of
advertising. But the truth is that people find advertising very useful
indeed.

Of course, advertising primarily seeks to persuade and everyone   2
knows this, too. The typical ad tries to induce a consumer to do one
particular thing—usually, buy a product—instead of a thousand other
things. There is nothing obscure about this purpose or what it means
for buyers. Decades of data and centuries of intuition reveal that all
consumers everywhere are deeply suspicious of what advertisers say
and why they say it. This skepticism is in fact the driving force that
makes advertising so effective. The persuasive purpose of advertising
and the skepticism with which it is met are two sides of a single
process. Persuasion and skepticism work in tandem so advertising can
do its job in competitive markets. Hence, ads represent the seller's
self interest, consumers know this, and sellers know that consumers
know it.

By understanding this process more fully, we can sort out much   3
of the popular confusion surrounding advertising and how it benefits
consumers.

HOW USEFUL IS ADVERTISING?

Just how useful is the connection between advertising and informa-   4
tion? At first blush, the process sounds rather limited. Volvo ads
tell consumers that Volvos have side-impact air bags, people learn
a little about the importance of air bags, and Volvo sells a few
more cars. This seems to help hardly anyone except Volvo and its
customers.

But advertising does much more. It routinely provides immense   5
amounts of information that benefits primarily parties other than the
advertiser. This may sound odd, but it is a logical result of market
forces and the nature of information itself.

The ability to use information to sell products is an incentive to   6
create new information through research. Whether the topic is nutrition, safety, or more mundane matters like how to measure amplifier
power, the necessity of achieving credibility with consumers and critics
requires much of this research to be placed in the public domain, and
that it rest upon some academic credentials. That kind of research

typically produces results that apply to more than just the brands sold by the firm sponsoring the research. The lack of property rights to such "pure" information ensures that this extra information is available at no charge. Both consumers and competitors may borrow the new information for their own purposes.

Advertising also elicits additional information from other 7 sources. Claims that are striking, original, forceful or even merely obnoxious will generate news stories about the claims, the controversies they cause, the reactions of competitors (A price war? A splurge of comparison ads?), the reactions of consumers and the remarks of governments and independent authorities.

Probably the most concrete, pervasive, and persistent example of 8 competitive advertising that works for the public good is price advertising. Its effect is invariably to heighten competition and reduce prices, even the prices of firms that assiduously avoid mentioning prices in their own advertising.

There is another area where the public benefits of advertising are 9 less obvious but equally important. The unremitting nature of consumer interest in health, and the eagerness of sellers to cater to consumer desires, guarantee that advertising related to health will provide a storehouse of telling observations on the ways in which the benefits of advertising extend beyond the interests of advertisers to include the interests of the public at large.

A CASCADE OF INFORMATION

Here is probably the best documented example of why advertising is 10 necessary for consumer welfare. In the 1970s, public health experts described compelling evidence that people who eat more fiber are less likely to get cancer, especially cancer of the colon, which happens to be the second leading cause of deaths from cancer in the United States. By 1979, the U.S. Surgeon General was recommending that people eat more fiber in order to prevent cancer.

Consumers appeared to take little notice of these recommenda- 11 tions, however. The National Cancer Institute decided that more action was needed. NCI's cancer prevention division undertook to communicate the new information about fiber and cancer to the general public. Their goal was to change consumer diets and reduce the risk of cancer, but they had little hope of success given the tiny advertising budgets of federal agencies like NCI.

Their prospects unexpectedly brightened in 1984. NCI received a 12 all from the Kellogg Corporation, whose All-Bran cereal held a commanding market share of the high-fiber segment. Kellogg proposed to use All-Bran advertising as a vehicle for NCI's public service messages. NCI thought that was an excellent idea. Soon, an agreement was reached in which NCI would review Kellogg's ads and labels for accuracy and value before Kellogg began running their fiber–cancer ads.

The new Kellogg All-Bran campaign opened in October 1984. A   13
typical ad began with the headline, "At last some news about cancer you can live with." The ad continued: "The National Cancer Institute believes a high-fiber, low-fat diet may reduce your risk of some kinds of cancer. . . . That's why one of their strongest recommendations is to eat high-fiber foods. If you compare, you'll find Kellogg's All-Bran has nine grams of fiber per serving. No other cereal has more. So start your day with a bowl of Kellogg's All-Bran or mix it with your regular cereal."

The campaign quickly achieved two things. One was to cre-   14
ate a regulatory crisis between two agencies. The Food and Drug Administration thought that if a food was advertised as a way to prevent cancer, it was being marketed as a drug. Then the FDA's regulations for drug labeling would kick in. The food would be reclassified as a drug and would be removed from the market until the seller either stopped making the health claims or put the product through the clinical testing necessary to obtain formal approval as a drug.

But food advertising is regulated by the Federal Trade Com-   15
mission, not the FDA. The FTC thought Kellogg's ads were nondeceptive and were therefore perfectly legal. In fact, it thought the ads should be encouraged. The Director of the FTC's Bureau of Consumer Protection declared that "the [Kellogg] ad has presented important public health recommendations in an accurate, useful, and substantiated way. It informs the members of the public that there is a body of data suggesting certain relationships between cancer and diet that they may find important." The FTC won this political battle, and the ads continued.

The second instant effect of the All-Bran campaign was to unleash   16
a flood of health claims. Vegetable oil manufacturers advertised that cholesterol was associated with coronary heart disease, and that vegetable oil does not contain cholesterol. Margarine ads did the same, and added that vitamin A is essential for good vision. Ads for calcium products (such as certain antacids) provided vivid demonstrations of the effects of osteoporosis (which weakens bones in old age), and recounted the advice of experts to increase dietary calcium as a way to prevent osteoporosis. Kellogg's competitors joined in citing the National Cancer Institute dietary recommendations.

Nor did things stop there. In the face of consumer demand for 17
better and fuller information, health claims quickly evolved from a
blunt tool to a surprisingly refined mechanism. Cereals were advertised as high in fiber and low in sugar or fat or sodium. Ads for an
upscale brand of bread noted: "Well, most high-fiber bran cereals may
be high in fiber, but often only one kind: insoluble. It's this kind of fiber
that helps promote regularity. But there's also a kind of fiber known as
soluble, which most high-fiber bran cereals have in very small
amounts, if at all. Yet diets high in this kind of fiber may actually lower
your serum cholesterol, a risk factor for some heart diseases." Cereal
boxes became convenient sources for a summary of what made for a
good diet.

INCREASED INDEPENDENT INFORMATION

The ads also brought powerful secondary effects. These may have been 18
even more useful than the information that actually appeared in the
ads themselves.

One effect was an increase in media coverage of diet and health. 19
Consumer Reports, a venerable and hugely influential magazine that
carries no advertising, revamped its reports on cereals to emphasize
fiber and other ingredients (rather than testing the foods to see how
well they did at providing a complete diet for laboratory rats). The
health-claims phenomenon generated its own press coverage, with
articles like "What Has All-Bran Wrought?" and "The Fiber Furor."
These stories recounted the ads and the scientific information that
prompted the ads; and articles on food and health proliferated. Anyone
who lived through these years in the United States can probably
remember the unending media attention to health claims and to diet
and health generally.

Much of the information on diet and health was new. This was no 20
coincidence. Firms were sponsoring research on their products in the
hope of finding results that could provide a basis for persuasive advertising claims. Oat bran manufacturers, for example, funded research on
the impact of soluble fiber on blood cholesterol. When the results came
out "wrong," as they did in a 1990 study published with great fanfare
in *The New England Journal of Medicine,* the headline in *Advertising Age*
was "Oat Bran Popularity Hitting the Skids," and it did indeed tumble.
The manufacturers kept at the research, however, and eventually the
best research supported the efficacy of oat bran in reducing cholesterol
(even to the satisfaction of the FDA). Thus did pure advertising claims
spill over to benefit the information environment at large.

The shift to higher fiber cereals encompassed brands that had   21
never undertaken the effort necessary to construct believable ads about
fiber and disease. Two consumer researchers at the FDA reviewed
these data and concluded they were "consistent with the successful
educational impact of the Kellogg diet and health campaign: consumers seemed to be making an apparently thoughtful discrimination
between high- and low-fiber cereals," and that the increased market
shares for high-fiber non-advertised products represented "the clearest
evidence of a successful consumer education campaign."

Perhaps most dramatic were the changes in consumer awareness   22
of diet and health. An FTC analysis of government surveys showed
that when consumers were asked about how they could prevent cancer
through their diet, the percentage who mentioned fiber increased from
4% before the 1979 Surgeon General's report to 8.5% in 1984 (after the
report but before the All-Bran campaign) to 32% in 1986 after a year
and a half or so of health claims (the figure in 1988 was 28%). By far the
greatest increases in awareness were among women (who do most of
the grocery shopping) and the less educated: up from 0% for women
without a high school education in 1984 to 31% for the same group in
1986. For women with incomes of less than $15,000, the increase was
from 6% to 28%.

The health-claims advertising phenomenon achieved what years   23
of effort by government agencies had failed to achieve. With its mastery of the art of brevity, its ability to command attention, and its use of
television, brand advertising touched precisely the people the public
health community was most desperate to reach. The health claims
expanded consumer information along a broad front. The benefits
clearly extended far beyond the interests of the relatively few manufacturers who made vigorous use of health claims in advertising.

A PERVASIVE PHENOMENON

Health claims for foods are only one example, however, of a pervasive   24
phenomenon—the use of advertising to provide essential health information with benefits extending beyond the interests of the advertisers
themselves.

Advertising for soap and detergents, for example, once improved   25
private hygiene and therefore, public health (hygiene being one of the
underappreciated triumphs in twentieth century public health). Toothpaste advertising helped to do the same for teeth. When mass advertising for toothpaste and tooth powder began early in this century, tooth
brushing was rare. It was common by the 1930s, after which toothpaste
sales leveled off even though the advertising, of course, continued.

When fluoride toothpastes became available, advertising generated interest in better teeth and professional dental care. Later, a "plaque reduction war" (which first involved mouthwashes, and later toothpastes) brought a new awareness of gum disease and how to prevent it. The financial gains to the toothpaste industry were surely dwarfed by the benefits to consumers in the form of fewer cavities and fewer lost teeth.

Health claims induced changes in foods, in nonfoods such as   26
toothpaste, in publications ranging from university health letters to mainstream newspapers and magazines, and of course, consumer knowledge of diet and health.

These rippling effects from health claims in ads demonstrated the   27
most basic propositions in the economics of information. Useful information initially failed to reach people who needed it because information producers could not charge a price to cover the costs of creating and disseminating pure information. And this problem was alleviated by advertising, sometimes in a most vivid manner.

Other examples of spillover benefits from advertising are far   28
more common than most people realize. Even the much-maligned promotion of expensive new drugs can bring profound health benefits to patients and families, far exceeding what is actually charged for the products themselves.

The market processes that produce these benefits bear all the clas-   29
sic features of competitive advertising. We are not analyzing public service announcements here, but old-fashioned profit-seeking brand advertising. Sellers focused on the information that favored their own products. They advertised it in ways that provided a close link with their own brand. It was a purely competitive enterprise, and the benefits to consumers arose from the imperatives of the competitive process.

One might see all this as simply an extended example of the eco-   30
nomics of information and greed. And indeed it is, if by greed one means the effort to earn a profit by providing what people are willing to pay for, even if what they want most is information rather than a tangible product. The point is that there is overwhelming evidence that unregulated economic forces dictate that much useful information will be provided by brand advertising, and only by brand advertising.

Of course, there is much more to the story. There is the question of   31
how competition does the good I have described without doing even more harm elsewhere. After all, firms want to tell people only what is good about their brands, and people often want to know what is wrong with the brands. It turns out that competition takes care of this problem, too.

ADVERTISING AND CONTEXT

It is often said that most advertising does not contain very much infor-   32
mation. In a way, this is true. Research on the contents of advertising
typically finds just a few pieces of concrete information per ad. That's
an average, of course. Some ads obviously contain a great deal of information. Still, a lot of ads are mainly images and pleasant talk, with little in the way of what most people would consider hard information.
On the whole, information in advertising comes in tiny bits and pieces.

Cost is only one reason. To be sure, cramming more information
into ads is expensive. But more to the point is the fact that advertising   33
plays off the information available from outside sources. Hardly anything about advertising is more important than the interplay between
what the ad contains and what surrounds it. Sometimes this interplay
is a burden for the advertiser because it is beyond his control. But
the interchange between advertising and environment is also an
invaluable tool for sellers. Ads that work in collaboration with outside information can communicate far more than they ever could on
their own.

The upshot is advertising's astonishing ability to communicate a   34
great deal of information in a few words. Economy and vividness of
expression almost always rely upon what is in the information environment. The famously concise "Think Small" and "Lemon" ads for
the VW "Beetle" in the 1960s and 1970s were highly effective with buyers concerned about fuel economy, repair costs, and extravagant styling
in American cars. This was a case where the less said, the better. The
ads were more powerful when consumers were free to bring their own
ideas about the issues to bear.

The same process is repeated over again for all sorts of products.   35
Ads for computer modems once explained what they could be used for.
Now a simple reference to the Internet is sufficient to conjure an elaborate mix of equipment and applications. These matters are better left
vague so each potential customer can bring to the ad his own idea of
what the Internet is really for.

Leaning on information from other sources is also a way to   36
enhance credibility, without which advertising must fail. Much of the
most important information in advertising—think of cholesterol and
heart disease, antilock brakes and automobile safety—acquires its force
from highly credible sources other than the advertiser. To build up this
kind of credibility through material actually contained in ads would be
cumbersome and inefficient. Far more effective, and far more economi-
cal, is the technique of making challenges, raising questions and otherwise making it perfectly clear to the audience that the seller invites

comparisons and welcomes the tough questions. Hence the classic slogan, "If you can find a better whiskey, buy it."

Finally, there is the most important point of all. Informational sparseness facilitates competition. It is easier to challenge a competitor through pungent slogans—"Where's the beef?", "Where's the big saving?"—than through a step-by-step recapitulation of what has gone on before. The bits-and-pieces approach makes for quick, unerring attacks and equally quick responses, all under the watchful eye of the consumer over whom the battle is being fought. This is an ideal recipe for competition.

37

It also brings the competitive market's fabled self-correcting forces into play. Sellers are less likely to stretch the truth, whether it involves prices or subtleties about safety and performance, when they know they may arouse a merciless response from injured competitors. That is one reason the FTC once worked to get comparative ads on television, and has sought for decades to dismantle government or voluntary bans on comparative ads.

38

"LESS-BAD" ADVERTISING

There is a troubling possibility, however. Is it not possible that in their selective and carefully calculated use of outside information, advertisers have the power to focus consumer attention exclusively on the positive, i.e., on what is good about the brand or even the entire product class? Won't automobile ads talk up style, comfort, and extra safety, while food ads do taste and convenience, cigarette ads do flavor and lifestyle, and airlines do comfort and frequency of departure, all the while leaving consumers to search through other sources to find all the things that are wrong with products?

39

In fact, this is not at all what happens. Here is why: Everything for sale has something wrong with it, if only the fact that you have to pay for it. Some products, of course, are notable for their faults. The most obvious examples involve tobacco and health, but there are also food and heart disease, drugs and side effects, vacations and bad weather, automobiles and accidents, airlines and delay, among others.

40

Products and their problems bring into play one of the most important ways in which the competitive market induces sellers to serve the interests of buyers. No matter what the product, there are usually a few brands that are "less bad" than the others. The natural impulse is to advertise that advantage—"less cholesterol," "less fat," "less dangerous," and so on. Such provocative claims tend to have an immediate impact. The targets often retaliate; maybe their brands are

41

less bad in a different respect (less salt?). The ensuing struggle brings better information, more informed choices, and improved products.

Perhaps the most riveting episode of "less-bad" advertising   42
ever seen occurred, amazingly enough, in the industry that most people assume is the master of avoiding saying anything bad about its
product.

Less-Bad Cigarette Ads

Cigarette advertising was once very different from what it is today.   43
Cigarettes first became popular around the time of World War I, and
they came to dominate the tobacco market in the 1920s. Steady and
often dramatic sales increases continued into the 1950s, always
with vigorous support from advertising. Tobacco advertising was duly
celebrated as an outstanding example of the power and creativity of
advertising. Yet amazingly, much of the advertising focused on what
was wrong with smoking, rather than what people liked about
smoking.

The very first ad for the very first mass-marketed American ciga-   44
rette brand (Camel, the same brand recently under attack for its use of
a cartoon character) said, "Camel Cigarettes will not sting the tongue
and will not parch the throat." When Old Gold broke into the market in
the mid-1920s, it did so with an ad campaign about coughs and throats
and harsh cigarette smoke. It settled on the slogan, "Not a cough in a
carload."

Competitors responded in kind. Soon, advertising left no doubt   45
about what was wrong with smoking. Lucky Strike ads said, "No
Throat Irritation—No Cough . . . we . . . removed . . . harmful corrosive
acids," and later on, "Do you inhale? What's there to be afraid of? . . .
famous purifying process removes certain impurities." Camel's famous
tag line, "more doctors smoke Camels than any other brand," carried a
punch precisely because many authorities thought smoking was
unhealthy (cigarettes were called "coffin nails" back then), and smokers were eager for reassurance in the form of smoking by doctors themselves. This particular ad, which was based on surveys of physicians,
ran in one form or another from 1933 to 1955. It achieved prominence
partly because physicians practically never endorsed non-therapeutic
products.[1]

---

[1]The ad ran in many outlets, including The Journal of the American Medical Association,
which regularly carried cigarette advertisements until the early 1950s. Incidentally,
Camel was by no means the only brand that cited medical authorities in an effort to reassure smokers.

Things really got interesting in the early 1950s, when the first   46
persuasive medical reports on smoking and lung cancer reached the
public. These reports created a phenomenal stir among smokers and
the public generally. People who do not understand how advertising
works would probably assume that cigarette manufacturers used
advertising to divert attention away from the cancer reports. In fact,
they did the opposite.

Small brands could not resist the temptation to use advertising to   47
scare smokers into switching brands. They inaugurated several spectacular years of "fear advertising" that sought to gain competitive
advantage by exploiting smokers' new fear of cancer. Lorillard, the
beleaguered seller of Old Gold, introduced Kent, a new filter brand
supported by ad claims like these: "Sensitive smokers get real health
protection with new Kent," "Do you love a good smoke but not what
the smoke does to you?" and "Takes out more nicotine and tars than
any other leading cigarette—the difference in protection is priceless,"
illustrated by television ads showing the black tar trapped by Kent's
filters.

Other manufacturers came out with their own filter brands, and   48
raised the stakes with claims like, "Nose, throat, and accessory organs
not adversely affected by smoking Chesterfields. First such report ever
published about any cigarette," "Takes the fear out of smoking," and
"Stop worrying . . . Philip Morris and only Philip Morris is entirely free
of irritation used [sic] in all other leading cigarettes."

These ads threatened to demolish the industry. Cigarette sales   49
plummeted by 3% in 1953 and a remarkable 6% in 1954. Never again,
not even in the face of the most impassioned anti-smoking publicity by
the Surgeon General or the FDA, would cigarette consumption decline
as rapidly as it did during these years of entirely market-driven anti-
smoking ad claims by the cigarette industry itself.

Thus advertising traveled full circle. Devised to bolster brands, it   50
denigrated the product so much that overall market demand actually
declined. Everyone understood what was happening, but the fear ads
continued because they helped the brands that used them. The new filter brands (all from smaller manufacturers) gained a foothold even as
their ads amplified the medical reports on the dangers of smoking. It
was only after the FTC stopped the fear ads in 1955 (on the grounds
that the implied health claims had no proof) that sales resumed their
customary annual increases.

Fear advertising has never quite left the tobacco market despite   51
the regulatory straight jacket that governs cigarette advertising. In
1957, when leading cancer experts advised smokers to ingest less tar,
the industry responded by cutting tar and citing tar content figures
compiled by independent sources. A stunning "tar derby" reduced the

tar and nicotine content of cigarettes by 40% in four years, a far more rapid decline than would be achieved by years of government urging in later decades. This episode, too, was halted by the FTC. In February 1960 the FTC engineered a "voluntary" ban on tar and nicotine claims.

Further episodes continue to this day. In 1993, for example, 52 Liggett planned an advertising campaign to emphasize that its Chesterfield brand did not use the stems and other less desirable parts of the tobacco plant. This continuing saga, extending through eight decades, is perhaps the best documented case of how "less-bad" advertising completely offsets any desires by sellers to accentuate the positive while ignoring the negative. *Consumer Reports* magazine's 1955 assessment of the new fear of smoking still rings true:

> . . . companies themselves are largely to blame. Long before the current medical attacks, the companies were building up suspicion in the consumer by the discredited "health claims" in their ads . . . Such medicine-show claims may have given the smoker temporary confidence in one brand, but they also implied that cigarettes in general were distasteful, probably harmful, and certainly a "problem." When the scientists came along with their charges against cigarettes, the smoker was ready to accept them.

And that is how information works in competitive advertising. 53

Less-bad can be found wherever competitive advertising is allowed. 54 I already described the health-claims-for-foods saga, which featured fat and cholesterol and the dangers of cancer and heart disease. Price advertising is another example. Prices are the most stubbornly negative product feature of all, because they represent the simple fact that the buyer must give up something else. There is no riper target for comparative advertising. When sellers advertise lower prices, competitors reduce their prices and advertise that, and soon a price war is in the works. This process so strongly favors consumers over the industry that one of the first things competitors do when they form a trade group is to propose an agreement to restrict or ban price advertising (if not ban all advertising). When that fails, they try to get advertising regulators to stop price ads, an attempt that unfortunately often succeeds.

Someone is always trying to scare customers into switching 55 brands out of fear of the product itself. The usual effect is to impress upon consumers what they do not like about the product. In 1991, when Americans were worried about insurance companies going broke, a few insurance firms advertised that they were more solvent than their competitors. In May 1997, United Airlines began a new ad campaign that started out by reminding fliers of all the inconveniences that seem to crop up during air travel.

Health information is a fixture in "less-bad" advertising. Ads for   56
sleeping aids sometimes focus on the issue of whether they are habit-
forming. In March 1996, a medical journal reported that the pain
reliever acetaminophen, the active ingredient in Tylenol, can cause liver
damage in heavy drinkers. This fact immediately became the focus of
ads for Advil, a competing product. A public debate ensued, conducted
through advertising, talk shows, news reports and pronouncements
from medical authorities. The result: consumers learned a lot more than
they had known before about the fact that all drugs have side effects.
The press noted that this dispute may have helped consumers, but it
hurt the pain reliever industry. Similar examples abound.

We have, then, a general rule: sellers will use comparative adver-   57
tising when permitted to do so, even if it means spreading bad
information about a product instead of favorable information. The
mechanism usually takes the form of less-bad claims. One can hardly
imagine a strategy more likely to give consumers the upper hand in
the give and take of the marketplace. Less-bad claims are a primary
means by which advertising serves markets and consumers rather than
sellers. They completely refute the naive idea that competitive advertising will emphasize only the sellers' virtues while obscuring their
problems.

Examining the Text

1. What points does Calfee make with his example of advertising for
Kellogg's All-Bran cereal? According to Calfee, what are the advantages and disadvantages of using ads to inform consumers about
health issues?
2. According to Calfee, what are the "spillover benefits" of advertising?
3. What are some of the ways that free-market competition in advertising benefits consumers? Does Calfee see any reason for government or
industry regulation of advertising?
4. *Thinking rhetorically*: How would you describe the tone of this article? Considering the fact that Calfee is arguing an unusual position—
that advertising is good for us—how does the tone of the article help
him convey his arguments effectively? What other rhetorical strategies
does Calfee use to make his position persuasive?

For Group Discussion

This activity requires that each member of the group bring four or five
ads to class—either from a magazine, newspaper, or brochure— in
order to test Calfee's proposition that ads provide consumers with useful information. In your group, make a list of the useful information

that each ad presents. That is, what helpful facts do you learn from the ad? Then discuss the other kinds of information or content presented in each ad. (You might reread Jib Fowles's "Advertising's Fifteen Basic Appeals" to get some ideas.) What conclusions can you draw from this comparison? Do your conclusions coincide with Calfee's claims? Are certain kinds of ads—or ads for certain products—more likely to contain helpful information?

Writing Suggestion
Calfee discusses the history of cigarette advertising, noting the predominance of "less-bad" claims and "fear advertising" in mid-twentieth-century cigarette ad campaigns. Find five or six recent cigarette advertisements in magazines or newspapers and analyze the information these ads present and the strategies they use to sell their product. Then write an essay in which you first summarize Calfee's discussion of the history of cigarette advertising; use quotations and paraphrases from the article to develop your summary. In the remainder of your essay, discuss what you see as the current state of cigarette advertising based on your analysis of recent ads.

Images of Women in Advertising

You're Soaking In It

Jennifer L. Pozner

We begin this casebook on images of women and men in advertising with an article, originally published on the Web at Salon.com, *that presents the ideas of a recognized expert in the field, Jean Kilbourne. Kilbourne is the author of several books on advertising, including her most recent* Can't Buy My Love: How Advertising Changes the Way We Think and Feel. *She is also well known as the creator of award-winning documentaries such as* Killing Us Softly, Pack of Lies, *and* Slim Hopes. *She is a popular speaker on college campuses and in communities, where her message is that we should pay attention to the messages that advertising conveys, especially messages that are harmful to girls and women.*

In her publications and lectures, Kilbourne argues that we are inundated with ads telling us that products can meet our deepest needs, that we can be happier, more popular, more successful—more anything, it seems—simply by buying the right products. Kilbourne also draws attention to the damaging stereotypes of women and girls that are often found in advertisements, stereotypes that are all the more damaging because of the accumulated impact of the approximately 3,000 ads that we see daily.

The article that follows begins by showing how Kilbourne's concerns are dealt with in the movie What Women Want, *starring Mel Gibson. Gibson plays the role of a chauvinistic advertising executive who experiences a significant change of heart when, through a bizarre electrocution experience, he gains the ability to hear the inner thoughts of the women around him. According to Pozner and Kilbourne, the movie perpetuates common misconceptions of the advertising business, as well as misrepresentations of men, women, and relationships.*

*As **you read,** note the effect of the interview format in most of this article. How does the question-and-answer structure of the article influence your understanding of Kilbourne's ideas? What's gained (and lost) by including Kilbourne's answers rather than just reporting on them?*

"Advertisers know what womanpower is," explains a self-promotional   1
pitch for the *Ladies' Home Journal*. The ad shows a stylish woman wired
to a mammoth computer that measures her whims with graphs, light
bulbs and ticker tape. The magazine insists that, like the machine, it has

its finger on the pulse of women's desires. Perk and breathlessness permeate its claim to be able to harness the many elements of "womanpower," including "sales power" ("She spots a bright idea in her favorite magazine, and suddenly the whole town's sold on it!"), "will power" ("Can you stick to a nine-day diet for more than four hours at a stretch?") and, of course, "purchasing power" ("Isn't it the power of her purse that's been putting fresh smiles on the faces of America's businessmen?").

That was 1958. Today advertisers are generally more sophisticated in their execution, but their primary message to and about women has remained fundamentally unchanged. To tap into our power, offer us a new shade of lipstick, a fresh-scented floor wax or, in the case of Mel Gibson's patronizing chick flick, What Women Want, L'eggs pantyhose, Wonderbras or Nike Women's Sports gear.   2

The movie—No. 2 at the box office after a month in theaters—stars Gibson as Nick Marshall, a pompous advertising executive dubbed the "T&A King" for his successful reign over Swedish bikini-babe commercials. But Nick's campaigns leave female consumers cold and he loses an expected promotion to women's market whiz Darcy Maguire (Helen Hunt). Nick's boss explains that while he's more comfortable with Nick, men no longer dominate how ad dollars are being spent.   3

Once Nick acquires the ability to read women's minds—after an unfortunate incident with volumizing mousse, a hair dryer and a bathtub—a story unfolds that could only seem romantic to avid Advertising Age readers: Nick and his nemesis Darcy fall in love over Nike storyboards, brainstorming ways to convince consumers that "Nike wants to empower women" and "Nike is state-of-the-art, hardcore womanpower."   4

What Women Want is more than a commercial for Mars vs. Venus gender typing; it's a feature-length product placement, a jarring reminder that the entertainment media is up for grabs by the hawkers of hair spray and Hondas. Which is not to say that the news media is off limits. Take Disney's news giant, ABC. In November, after ABC accepted a hefty fee from Campbell's soup, journalist Barbara Walters and "The View" crew turned eight episodes of their talk show into paid infomercials for canned soup. Hosting a "soup-sipping contest" and singing the "M'm! M'm! Good!" jingle on-air, they made good on ABC's promise that the "hosts would try to weave a soup message into their regular on-air banter."   5

And in March, after Disney bought a stake in Pets.com, the company's snarky sock puppet mascot began appearing as a "guest" on "Good Morning America" and "Nightline." It was a sad day in news when Diane Sawyer addressed her questions to a sock on a stool with a guy's hand up its butt, but that's what passes for "synergy" in today's megamerged media climate.   6

How does advertising's increasing encroachment into every 7
niche of mass media impact our culture in general, and women in particular? Mothers Who Think asked pioneering advertising critic Jean
Kilbourne, author of *Can't Buy My Love: How Advertising Changes the
Way We Think and Feel.*

A favorite on the college lecture circuit, Kilbourne has produced 8
videos that are used as part of media literacy programs worldwide, in
particular *Killing Us Softly,* first produced in 1979 and remade as
Killing Us Softly III in 2000. She shares her thoughts here about advertising's effects on women, children, media and our cultural environment—and explains why salvation can't be found in a Nike sports bra.

In What Women Want, *Mel Gibson and Helen Hunt produce a Nike com-* 9
*mercial in which a woman runs in swooshed-up sportswear while a voice-over
assures her that the road doesn't care if she's wearing makeup, and she doesn't
have to feel uncomfortable if she makes more money than the road—basically
equating freedom and liberation with a pair of $150 running shoes. Is this typ-
ical of advertising to women?*

Absolutely. The commercial in the movie is saying that women who are 10
unhappy with the quality of their relationships can ease their frustration
by literally forming a more satisfying relationship with the road. There's
no hint that her human relationships are going to improve, but the road
will love her anyway.

Advertising is always about moving away from anything that 11
would help us find real change in our lives. In the funniest scene in the
movie, when Mel Gibson finds out how much it hurts to wax his legs,
he wonders, "Why would anyone do this more than once?" That's a
very good question. But, of course, the film doesn't go there. The real
solutions—to stop waxing or to challenge unnatural beauty standards
or to demand that men grow up—are never offered. Instead, the message is that we must continue with these painful and humiliating rituals, but at least we can escape for a while by lacing on our expensive
sneakers and going out for a run.

What Women Want presents a pretty mercenary picture of advertising aimed 12
*at women. You've studied the industry for decades. Does it seem accurate to
you?*

It isn't far off. As in the film, advertisers were kind of slow to really 13
focus on women. Initially they did it by co-opting feminism. Virginia
Slims equated women's liberation and enslavement to tobacco with the
trivializing slogan "You've come a long way, baby" in the '80s; a little
while ago it ran a campaign with the slogan "Find your voice."

Then there were endless ads that turned the women's movement   14
into the quest for a woman's product. Was there ever such a thing as
static cling before there were fabric softeners and sprays? More recently
advertisers have discovered what they call "relationship marketing,"
creating ads that exploit a human need for connection and relationships, which in our culture is often seen as a woman's need.

Advertising and the larger culture often imply that women are failures if we   15
do not have perfect relationships. Of course, "perfect" relationships don't exist
in real life. Why are they so prominent in ads?

This is part of the advertising mentality. Think about *What Women*   16
Want—there's an ad at the heart of this film literally and figuratively.
Everybody lives in spectacular apartments, they're all thin and beautiful, and Mel Gibson makes this incredible instant transformation. He
starts out as a jerk, he's callous, he tells degrading jokes and patronizes
the women he works with, but because of his new mind-reading power
he gains immediate insight into women. He becomes a great lover in
the space of half an hour. At one point his daughter tells him he's never
had a real relationship in his life, but by the end of the film he has
authentic relationships with his daughter and his new love.

The truth is, most men gain insight into women not through   17
quick fixes but by having close relationships with them over time,
sometimes painfully. In the world of advertising, relationships are
instant and the best ones aren't necessarily with people: Zest is a soap,
Happy is a perfume, New Freedom is a maxipad, Wonder is a bread,
Good Sense is a tea bag and Serenity is a diaper. Advertising actually
encourages us to have relationships with our products.

I'm looking at TV Guide right now and there's a Winston ciga-   18
rette ad on the back cover with a woman saying, "Until I find a real
man, I'll take a real smoke." There's another with four different pictures of one man with four different women, and the copy reads, "Who
says guys are afraid of commitment? He's had the same backpack for
years." In another ad, featuring a young woman wearing a pretty
sweater, the copy says, "The ski instructor faded away after one session. Fortunately the sweater didn't."

One automobile spot implied that a Civic coupe would never tell   19
you, "It's not you, it's me. I need more space. I'm not ready for a commitment." Maybe our chances for lasting relationships are greater with
our cars than with our partners, but surely the solution can't be to fall
in love with our cars, or to depend on them rather than on each other.

Basically, men can't be trusted but Häagen-Dazs never disappoints? Love is fleet-   20
ing but a diamond is forever? Sort of a recipe for lowered expectations, isn't it?

A central message of advertising is that relationships with human beings   21
can't be counted on, especially for women. The message is that men will
make commitments only reluctantly and can't be trusted to keep them.
Straight women, and these are pretty much the women in ads, are told
that it's normal not to expect very much or get very much from the men
in their lives. This normalizes really abnormal behavior—with male violence at the extreme and male callousness in general—by reinforcing
men's unwillingness to express their feelings. This harms men, of course,
as well as women.

In What Women Want, *Mel Gibson is literally able to "get into the female*   22
psyche," private thoughts and all, after he waxes his hairy legs and crams
them into a pair of L'eggs pantyhose. Is it unusual for advertisers to imply that
the essence of womanhood can be found in cosmetics and commercialism?

Not at all. The central message of advertising has to be that we are   23
what we buy. And perhaps what's most insidious about this is that it
takes very human, very real feelings and desires such as the need to
love and be loved, the need for authentic connection, the need for
meaningful work, for respect, and it yokes these feeling to products. It
tells us that our ability to attain love depends upon our attractiveness.

By now most of us know that these images are unrealistic and unhealthy, that   24
implants leak, anorexia and bulimia can kill and, in real life, model Heidi
Klum has pores. So why do the images in ads still have such sway over us?

Most people like to think advertising doesn't affect them. But if that   25
were really true, why would companies spend over $200 billion a year
on advertising? Women don't buy into this because we're shallow or
vain or stupid but because the stakes are high. Overweight women do
tend to face biases—they're less likely to get jobs; they're poorer. Men
do leave their wives for younger, more beautiful women as their wives
age. There is manifest contempt and real-life consequences for women
who don't measure up. These images work to keep us in line.

What do these images teach girls about what they can expect from themselves,   26
from boys, from sex, from each other?

Girls get terrible messages about sex from advertising and popular cul-   27
ture. An ad featuring a very young woman in tight jeans reads: "He says
the first thing he noticed about you is your great personality. He lies."
Girls are told that boys are out for sex at all times, and girls should
always look as if they are ready to give it. (But God help them if they
do.) The emphasis for girls and women is always on being desirable, not

being agents of their own desire. Girls are supposed to somehow be innocent and seductive, virginal and experienced, all at the same time.

Girls are particularly targeted by the diet industry. The obsession   28
with thinness is about cutting girls down to size, making sure they're not too powerful in any sense of the word. One fashion ad I use in my presentations shows an extremely thin, very young Asian woman next to the copy "The more you subtract, the more you add."

Adolescent girls constantly get the message that they should   29
diminish themselves, they should be less than what they are. Girls are told not to speak up too much, not to be too loud, not to have a hearty appetite for food or sex or anything else. Girls are literally shown being silenced in ads, often with their hands over their mouth or, as in one ad, with a turtleneck sweater pulled up over their mouth.

One ad sold lipstick with a drawing of a woman's lips sucking on   30
a pacifier. A girl in a particularly violent entertainment ad has her lips sewn shut. Sometimes girls are told to keep quiet in other ways, by slogans like "Let your fingers do the talking" (an ad for nail polish), "Watch your mouth, young lady" (for lipstick), "Make a statement without saying a word" (for perfume), "Score high on non-verbal skills" (for a clothing store).

Let's talk about violence against women in ads. A controversy broke out dur-   31
ing the Olympics when NBC ran a Nike commercial parodying slasher films,
in which Olympic runner Suzy Favor Hamilton is chased by a villain with a
chain saw. Hamilton outruns him, leaving the would-be murderer wheezing in
the woods. The punch line? "Why sport? You'll live longer." The ad shocked
many people, but isn't violence against women, real or implied, common
in ads?

People were outraged that Nike considered this type of thing a joke. A   32
recent Perry Ellis sequence showed a woman apparently dead in a shower with a man standing over her; that one drew protests, too. But ads often feature images of women being threatened, attacked, or killed. Sexual assault and battery are normalized, even eroticized.

In one ad a woman lies dead on a bed with her breasts exposed   33
and her hair sprawled out around her, and the copy reads, "Great hair never dies." A perfume ad that ran in several teen magazines showed a very young woman with her eyes blackened, next to the text "Apply generously to your neck so he can smell the scent as you shake your head 'no.'" In other words, he'll understand that you don't really mean it when you say no, and he can respond like any other animal.

An ad for a bar in Georgetown with a close-up of a cocktail had   34
the headline "If your date won't listen to reason, try a velvet hammer." That's really dangerous when you consider how many sexual assaults

involve alcohol in some way. We believe we are not affected by these images, but most of us experience visceral shock when we pay conscious attention to them.

Are there subtler forms of abuse in ads?   35

There's a lot of emotional violence in ads. For example, in one cologne   36
ad a handsome man ignores two beautiful blonds. The copy reads, "Do
you want to be the one she tells her deep, dark secrets to? Or do you
want to be her deep, dark secret?" followed by a final instruction:
"Don't be such a good boy." What's the deep, dark secret here? That
he's sleeping with both of them? On one level the message is that the
way to get beautiful women is to ignore them, perhaps mistreat them.
The message to men is that emotional intimacy is not a good thing. This
does terrible things to men, and of course to women too.
     There are also many, many ads in which women are pitted   37
against each other for male attention. For example, there's one ad
with a topless woman on a bed and the copy "What the bitch who's
about to steal your man wears." Other ads feature young women
fighting or glaring at each other. This means that when girls hit
adolescence, at a time when they most need support from each other,
they're encouraged to turn on each other in competition for men. It's
tragic, because the truth is that one of the most powerful antidotes
to destructive cultural messages is close and supportive female
friendships.

Over the years we've grown more accustomed to product placements in   38
movies, but What Women Want *takes advertiser-driven content to a new*
level. I tried to keep a running count, but there were so many I lost track:
Sears, L'eggs, Wonderbra, Macintosh, Martha Stewart, CNN, Meredith
Brooks and Alanis Morissette CD covers all get prominent plugs.
     The final commercial Gibson pitches to the Nike reps was similar in   39
style, tone and prime-time-friendly slogan to sports ads we've seen on TV
before. Would you be surprised if Nike's fake ad eventually traveled from the
big screen to the small screen? How did we get to a point where the whole
premise of a film rests on product placements?

I wouldn't be surprised at all. In fact, the ad in the movie was made in   40
connection with Wieden + Kennedy, Nike's real-life ad agency. But
Nike doesn't really need to pay to broadcast the commercial on TV,
since this film was so successful at the box office—there couldn't be a
better launch for a commercial than this movie.
     I think this is the wave of the future. As more and more people   41
use their VCR to skip the commercials when they watch television, the

commercials will begin to become part of the program so they can't be edited out. So while you're watching "Friends," Jennifer Aniston will say to Courteney Cox, "Your hair looks great," and Courteney will say, "Yeah, I'm using this new gel!"

A number of media critics have dubbed the encroachment of advertising in media, education and public spaces "ad creep." You've called it a "toxic cultural environment." Can you explain that?   42

As the mother of a 13-year-old girl, I feel I'm raising my daughter in a toxic cultural environment. I hate that advertisers cynically equate rebellion with smoking, drinking and impulsive and impersonal sex. I want my daughter to be a rebel, to defy stereotypes of "femininity," but I don't want her to put herself in danger. I feel I have to fight the culture every step of the way in terms of messages she gets.   43

Just as it is difficult to raise kids safely in a physically toxic environment, where they're breathing polluted air or drinking toxic water, it's also difficult or even impossible to raise children in a culturally toxic environment, where they're surrounded by unhealthy images about sex and relationships, and where their health is constantly sacrificed for the sake of profit.   44

Even our schools are toxic—when McDonald's has a nutrition curriculum, Exxon has an environmental curriculum and kindergartners are given a program called "Learning to read through recognizing corporate logos." Education is tainted when a student can get suspended for wearing a Pepsi T-shirt on a school-sponsored Coke day, which happened in Georgia in 1998.   45

The United States is one of the few nations in the world that think that children are legitimate targets for advertisers. We allow the tobacco and alcohol industries to use talking frogs and lizards to sell beer and cartoon characters to sell cigarettes. The Budweiser commercials are in fact the most popular commercials with elementary school kids, and Joe Camel is now as recognizable to 6-year-olds as is Mickey Mouse.   46

What advice do you have for parents, for any of us, who want to counteract this toxic cultural environment?   47

Parents can talk to their children, make these messages conscious. We can educate ourselves and become media literate. But primarily we need to realize that this is not something we can fight purely on an individual basis.   48

Corporations are forever telling us that if we don't like what's on TV we should just turn it off, not let our kids watch tobacco ads or violent movies. We constantly hear that if parents would just talk to their   49 kids there would be no problem. But that really is like saying, "If your children are breathing poisoned air, don't let them breathe."

We need to join together to change the toxic cultural environment.   50
That includes things such as lobbying to teach noncorporate media literacy in our schools, fighting to abolish or restrict advertising aimed at children, organizing to get ads out of our schools, banning the promotion of alcohol and tobacco, and other community solutions.

There are great media literacy projects in Los Angeles, New Mexico,   51
Massachusetts and many places throughout the world. There's no quick fix, but I have extensive resources about media criticism groups, social change organizations, educational material, media literacy programs and more available on my Web site. If they want, people could start there.

Examining the Text

1. Why do you think Pozner begins the interview with references to the movie *What Women Want* and to examples of product placement on TV networks? How do these examples set the stage for the interview with Kilbourne?

2. How does Kilbourne define "relationship marketing"? Which of the appeals discussed by Jib Fowles earlier in this chapter are used by "relationship marketing" ads?

3. Focusing on the issues of weight, dieting, and body image, in what ways does Kilbourne believe that advertising is responsible for causing harm to young girls? Why, according to Kilbourne, does advertising contribute to this problem?

4. What kinds of evidence does Kilbourne use to support claims she makes throughout this article? What evidence do you find particularly persuasive? Where in the article do you find yourself disagreeing with or doubting the validity of Kilbourne's claims?

5. The image on page 114, "Your Gaze Hits the Side of My Face," was created by the artist Barbara Kruger. Which of the themes discussed by Pozner and Kilbourne do you see reflected in this image?

6. *Thinking rhetorically*: Following up on the "as you read" question in the introduction to this article, what effect did the interview format of the article have on you as a reader? In general, what are some of the strengths and weaknesses of directly recording the answers of an interviewee rather than paraphrasing and commenting on them? In other words, what's gained and what's lost when we don't have the author—Jennifer Pozner—commenting on Kilbourne's answers?

For Group Discussion

Discuss what you think of the strategies that Kilbourne suggests for fighting the "toxic cultural environment" created by advertising. Which of these strategies do you think are the most likely to have an influence on the current state of advertising? Why would some strategies be more effective than others? Discuss any other strategies you can think of that allow ordinary people ("consumers") to have some impact on the content and techniques of advertising.

Writing Suggestion
As she answers questions in the interview, Kilbourne makes brief references to a number of advertisements that help to prove her points. For this assignment, look through magazines and newspapers for a single advertisement that you think either supports or contradicts one or more of Kilbourne's claims about "relationship marketing." Look for stereotypes, body images, violence, or other forms of advertising where abuses seem to occur. Begin your essay by providing a brief summary of Kilbourne's ideas. Then analyze the advertisement you've

"Your Gaze Hits the Side of My Face," by Barbara Kruger. (*Courtesy of the Mary Boone Gallery, New York*)

chosen. (You may want to review the "Reading Images" section in Chapter 1.) Be sure to connect your analysis of specific features of the ad to specific points that Kilbourne is making, either by providing quotations from Pozner's article or by summarizing Kilbourne's points in your own words.

Getting Dirty

Mark Crispin Miller

Mark Crispin Miller's essay comes from his 1988 book Boxed In, a study of the meaning and influence of television and advertising in contemporary American culture. In "Getting Dirty," Miller analyzes a television ad for Shield soap, paying close attention to seemingly neutral details and finding meanings that may surprise us. For instance, Miller suggests that the ad woos female viewers with a "fantasy of dominance," offering "a subtle and meticulous endorsement of castration," playing on certain "guilts and insecurities" of men and women. The way the commercial reverses stereotypical gender roles makes it an interesting and complex example of the ways images of men and women are used in advertising.

To those who think he is reading too much into the ad, Miller counters that it is through the details, often unnoticed by viewers, that ads convey some of their most powerful—and questionable—messages.

In this essay Miller is analytical but also is trying to persuade readers that his analysis of the advertisement is correct. **As you read,** *note the strategies that Miller uses to construct a persuasive, well-supported analysis, and note as well those moments where Miller does not persuade you of his interpretation.*

We are outside a house, looking in the window, and this is what we see: 1
a young man, apparently nude and half-crazed with anxiety, lunging toward the glass. "Gail!" he screams, as he throws the window open and leans outside, over a flowerbox full of geraniums: "The most important shower of my life, and you switch deodorant soap!" He is, we now see, only half-naked, wearing a towel around his waist; and he shakes a packaged bar of soap—"Shield"—in one accusing hand. Gail, wearing a blue man-tailored shirt, stands outside, below the window, clipping a hedge. She handles this reproach with an ease that suggests years of contempt. "Shield is better," she explains patiently, in a voice somewhat deeper than her husband's. "It's extra strength." (Close-up of the package in the husband's hand. Gail's efficient finger gliding

along beneath the legend. THE EXTRA STRENGTH DEODORANT
SOAP.) "Yeah," whimpers Mr. Gail, "but my first call on J.J. Siss [sic],
the company's *toughest customer,* and *now this!*" Gail nods with broad
mock-sympathy, and stands firm: "Shield fights odor better, so you'll
feel *cleaner,*" she assures her husband, who darts away with a jerk of
panic, as Gail rolls her eyes heavenward and gently shakes her head, as
if to say, "What a half-wit!"

Cut to our hero, as he takes his important shower. No longer fran-   2
tic, he now grins down at himself, apparently delighted to be caked
with Shield, which, in its detergent state, has the consistency of wet
cement. He then goes out of focus, as if glimpsed through a shower
door. "Clinical tests prove," proclaims an eager baritone. "Shield fights
odor better than the *leading* deodorant soap!" A bar of Shield (green)
and a bar of that other soap (yellow) zip up the screen with a festive
toot, forming a sort of graph which demonstrates that Shield does,
indeed, "fight odor better, so you'll feel *cleaner!*"

This particular contest having been settled, we return to the   3
major one, which has yet to be resolved. Our hero reappears, almost
transformed: calmed down, dressed up, his voice at least an octave
lower. "I *do* feel cleaner!" he announces cheerily, leaning into the
doorway of a room where Gail is arranging flowers. She pretends to
be ecstatic at this news, and he comes toward her, setting himself up
for a profound humiliation by putting on a playful air of suave command. Adjusting his tie like a real man of the world, he saunters over
to his wife and her flower bowl, where he plucks a dainty purple
flower and lifts it to his lapel: "And," he boasts throughout all this,
trying to make his voice sound even deeper, "with old J.J.'s business
and my brains—" "—you'll. . . *clean up again?*" Gail asks with suggestive irony, subverting his authoritative pose by leaning against him,
draping one hand over his shoulder to dangle a big yellow daisy
down his chest. Taken aback, he shoots her a distrustful look, and she
titters at him.

Finally, the word SHIELD appears in extreme close-up and the   4
camera pulls back, showing two bars of the soap, one packaged and
one not, on display amidst an array of steely bubbles. "Shield fights
odor better, so you'll feel *cleaner!*" the baritone reminds us, and then
our hero's face appears once more, in a little square over the unpack-
aged bar of soap: "I feel *cleaner* than *ever before!*" he insists, sounding
faintly unconvinced.

Is all this as stupid as it seems at first? Or is there, just beneath the   5
surface of this moronic narrative, some noteworthy design, intended to
appeal to (and to worsen) some of the anxieties of modern life? A serious look at this particular trifle might lead us to some strange
discoveries.

We are struck, first of all, by the commercial's pseudofeminism,   6
an advertising ploy with a long history, and one ubiquitous on television nowadays. Although the whole subject deserves more extended
treatment, this commercial offers us an especially rich example of the
strategy. Typically, it woos its female viewers—i.e., those who choose
the soap in most households—with a fantasy of dominance; and it does
so by inverting the actualities of woman's lot through a number of
imperceptible details. For instance, in this marriage it is the wife, and
not the husband, who gets to keep her name; and Gail's name, moreover, is a potent one, because of its brevity and its homonymic connotation. (If this housewife were more delicately named, called "Lillian"
or "Cecilia," it would lessen her illusory strength.) She is also equipped
in more noticeable ways; she's the one who wears the button-down
shirt in this family, she's the one who's competent both outdoors and in
the house, and it is she, and only she, who wields the tool.

These visual details imply that Gail is quite a powerful house-   7
wife, whereas her nameless mate is a figure of embarrassing impo-
tence. This "man," in fact, is actually Gail's *wife;* he is utterly feminized,
striking a posture and displaying attributes which men have long
deplored in women. In other words, this commercial, which apparently
takes the woman's side, is really the expression (and reflection) of
misogyny. Gail's husband is dependent and hysterical, entirely without that self-possession which we expect from solid, manly types, like
Gail. This is partly the result of his demeanor: in the opening scene, his
voice sometimes cracks ludicrously, and he otherwise betrays the shrill
desperation of a man who can't remember where he left his scrotum.
The comic effect of this frenzy, moreover, is subtly enhanced by the
mise-en-scène, which puts the man in a conventionally feminine position—in dishabille, looking down from a window. Thus we infer that
he is sheltered and housebound, a modern Juliet calling for his/her
Romeo; or—more appropriately—the image suggests a scene in some
suburban red-light district, presenting this husband as an item on display, like the flowers just below his stomach, available for anyone's
enjoyment, at a certain price. Although in one way contradictory, these
implications are actually quite congruous, for they both serve to
emasculate the husband, so that the wife might take his place, or play
his part.

Such details, some might argue, need not have been the conscious   8
work of this commercial's makers. The authors, that is, might have
worked by instinct rather than design, and so would have been no
more aware of their work's psychosocial import than we ourselves:
they just wanted to make the guy look like a wimp, merely for the purposes of domestic comedy. While such an argument certainly does
apply to many ads, in this case it is unlikely. Advertising agencies do

plenty of research, by which we can assume that they don't select their tactics arbitrarily. They take pains to analyze the culture which they help to sicken, and then, with much wit and cynicism, use their insights in devising their small dramas. This commercial is a subtle and meticulous endorsement of castration, meant to play on certain widespread guilts and insecurities; and all we need to do to demonstrate this fact is to subject the two main scenes to the kind of visual analysis which commercials, so brief and broad, tend to resist (understandably). The ad's visual implications are too carefully achieved to have been merely accidental or unconscious.

The crucial object in the opening shot is that flower box with its bright geraniums, which is placed directly in front of the husband's groin. This clever stroke of composition has the immediate effect of equating our hero's manhood with a bunch of flowers. This is an exquisitely perverse suggestion, rather like using a cigar to represent the Eternal Feminine: flowers are frail, sweet, and largely ornamental, hardly an appropriate phallic symbol, but (of course) a venerable symbol of *maidenhood*. The geraniums stand, then, not for the husband's virility, but for its absence.   9

More than a clever instance of inversion, furthermore, these phallic blossoms tell us something odd about this marital relationship. As Gail, clippers in hand, turns from the hedge to calm her agitated man, she appears entirely capable of calming him quite drastically, if she hasn't done so already (which might explain his hairless chest and high-pitched voice). She has the power, that is, to take away whatever slender potency he may possess, and uses the power repeatedly, trimming her husband (we infer) as diligently as she prunes her foliage. And, as she can snip his manhood, so too can she restore it, which is what the second scene implies. Now the flower bowl has replaced the flower box as the visual crux, dominating the bottom center of the frame with a crowd of blooms. As the husband, cleaned and dressed, comes to stand beside his wife, straining to affect a new authority, the flower bowl too appears directly at his lower center; so that Gail, briskly adding flowers to the bouquet, appears to be replenishing his vacant groin with extra stalks. He has a lot to thank her for, it seems: she is his helpmate, confidante, adviser, she keeps his house and grounds in order, and she is clearly the custodian of the family jewels.   10

Of course, her restoration of his potency cannot be complete, or he might shatter her mastery by growing a bit too masterful himself. He could start choosing his own soap, or take her shears away, or—worst of all—walk out for good. Therefore, she punctures his momentary confidence by taunting him with that big limp daisy, countering his lordly gesture with the boutonniere by flaunting that symbol of his   11 floral status. He can put on whatever airs he likes, but she still has his fragile vigor firmly in her hand.

Now what, precisely, motivates this sexless battle of the sexes? That is, what really underlies this tense and hateful marriage, making the man so weak, the woman so contemptuously helpful? The script, seemingly nothing more than a series of inanities, contains the answer to these questions, conveying, as it does, a concern with cleanliness that amounts to an obsession: "Shield fights odor better, so you'll feel cleaner!" "I *do* feel cleaner!" "Shield fights odor better, so you'll feel *cleaner!*" "I feel *cleaner* than *ever before!*" Indeed, the commercial emphasizes the feeling of cleanliness even more pointedly than the name of the product, implying, by its very insistence, a feeling of dirtiness, an apprehension of deep filth. 12

And yet there is not a trace of dirt in the vivid world of this commercial. Unlike many ads for other soaps, this one shows no sloppy children, no sweatsoaked workingmen with blackened hands, not even a bleary housewife in need of her morning shower. We never even glimpse the ground in Gail's world, nor is her husband even faintly smudged. In fact, the filth which Shield supposedly "fights" is not physical but psychological besmirchment: Gail's husband feels soiled because of what he has to do for a living, in order to keep Gail in that nice big house, happily supplied with shirts and shears. 13

"My first call on J.J. Siss, the company's *toughest customer,* and now *this!*" The man's anxiety is yet another feminizing trait, for it is generally women, and not men, who are consumed by doubts about the sweetness of their bodies, which must never be offensive to the guys who run the world. (This real anxiety is itself aggravated by commercials.) Gail's husband must play the female to the mighty J.J. Siss, a name whose oxymoronic character implies perversion: "J.J." is a stereotypic nickname for the potent boss, while "Sis" is a term of endearment, short for "sister" (and perhaps implying "sissy," too, in this case). Gail's husband must do his boyish best to please the voracious J.J. Siss, just as a prostitute must satisfy a demanding trick, or "tough customer." It is therefore perfectly fitting that this employee refer to the encounter, not as a "meeting" or "appointment," but as a "call"; and his demeaning posture in the window—half dressed and bent over—conveys, we now see, a definitive implication. 14

Gail's job as the "understanding wife" is not to rescue her husband from these sordid obligations, but to help him meet them successfully. She may seem coolly self-sufficient, but she actually depends on her husband's attractiveness, just as a pimp relies on the charm of his whore. And, also like a pimp, she has to keep her girl in line with occasional reminders of who's boss. When her husband starts getting uppity 15 *après la douche,* she jars him from the very self-assurance which she had helped him to discover, piercing that "shield" which was her gift.

"And, with old J.J.'s business and my brains—" "—you'll . . . *clean*   16
up again?" He means, of course, that he'll work fiscal wonders with old J.J.'s account, but his fragmentary boast contains a deeper significance, upon which Gail plays with sadistic cleverness. "Old J.J.'s business and my brains" implies a feminine self-description, since it suggests a variation on the old commonplace of "brains vs. brawn": J.J.'s money, in the world of this commercial (as in ours), amounts to brute strength, which the flexible husband intends to complement with his mother wit. Gail's retort broadens this unconscious hint of homosexuality: "—you'll . . . *clean up again?*" Given the monetary nature of her husband's truncated remark, the retort must mean primarily, "You'll make a lot of money." If this were all it meant, however, it would not be a joke, nor would the husband find it so upsetting. Moreover, we have no evidence that Gail's husband ever "cleaned up"—i.e., made a sudden fortune—in the past. Rather, the ad's milieu and *dramatis personae* suggest upward mobility, gradual savings and a yearly raise, rather than one prior killing. What Gail is referring to, in fact, with the "again," is her husband's shower: she implies that what he'll have to do, after his "call" on J.J. Siss, is, quite literally, wash himself off. Like any other tidy hooker, this man will have to clean up after taking on a tough customer, so that he might be ready to take on someone else.

These suggestions of pederasty are intended, not as a literal characteri-   17
zation of the husband's job, but as a metaphor for what it takes to get ahead: Gail's husband, like most white-collar workers, must debase himself to make a good impression, toadying to his superiors, offering himself, body and soul, to the corporation. Maybe, therefore, it isn't really Gail who has neutered him; it may be his way of life that has wrought the ugly change. How, then, are women represented here? The commercial does deliberately appeal to women, offering them a sad fantasy of control; but it also, perhaps inadvertently, illuminates the unhappiness which makes that fantasy attractive.

The husband's status, it would seem, should make Gail happy,   18
since it makes her physically comfortable, and yet Gail can't help loathing her husband for the degradations which she helps him undergo. For her part of the bargain is, ultimately, no less painful than his. She has to do more than put up with him; she has to prepare him for his world of affairs, and then must help him to conceal the shame. Of course, it's all quite hopeless. She clearly despises the man whom she would bolster; and the thing which she provides to help him "feel cleaner than ever before" is precisely what has helped him do the job that's always made him feel so dirty. "A little water clears us of this

deed" is her promise, which is false, for she is just as soiled as her doomed husband, however fresh and well-ironed she may look.

Of course, the ad not only illuminates this mess, but helps perpet-   19
uate it, by obliquely gratifying the guilts, terrors, and resentments that underlie it and arise from it. The strategy is not meant to be noticed, but works through the apparent comedy, which must therefore be studied carefully, not passively received. Thus, thirty seconds of ingenious advertising, which we can barely stand to watch, tell us something more than we might want to know about the souls of men and women under corporate capitalism.

AFTERWORD

Advertising Age came back at this essay with an edifying two-pronged   20
put-down. In the issue for 7 June 1982, Fred Danzig (now the maga-
zine's editor) devoted his weekly column to the Shield analysis: "The professor prunes a television trifle," ran the headline. After a genial paraphrase of my argument, Danzig reported a few of the things I'd told him in a telephone conversation, and then finally got down to the necessary business of dismissive cluckling: "[Miller's] confession that he had watched the Shield spot more than 15 times quickly enabled me to diagnose his problem: Self-inflicted acute soap storyboard sickness. This condition inevitably leads to a mind spasm, to hallucination." The column featured the ad's crucial frames, over a caption quoting an unnamed "Lever executive": "We can hardly wait for Mr. Miller to get his hands on the Old Testament. His comments merit no comment from us; the Shield commercial speaks for itself."

Leaving aside (with difficulty) that naive crack about the Bible,   21
I point here to the exemplary suppressiveness of his seeming "trifle" in *Advertising Age*. Indeed, "the Shield commercial speaks for itself," but the guardians of the spectacle try to talk over it, permitting it no significance beyond the superficial pitch: "—so you'll feel *cleaner!*" Through manager-
ial scorn ("no comment") and journalistic ridicule ("mind spasm. . . hallu-
cination"), they would shut down all discussion. (J. Walter Thompson later refused to send anyone to debate the matter with me on a radio program.) Thus was a divergent reading written off as the perversity of yet another cracked "professor"—when in fact it was the ad itself that was perverse.

Although that campaign did not appeal to its TV audience   22
(J. Walter Thompson ultimately lost the Shield account), such belliger-
ent "common sense" does have a most receptive public. While the admakers—and others—insist that "people today are adwise" in fact most Americans still perceive the media image as transparent, a sign that simply says what it means and means what it says. They therefore

tend to dismiss any intensive explication as a case of "reading too much into it"—an objection that is philosophically dubious, albeit useful to the admakers and their allies. It is now, perhaps, one obligation of the academic humanists, empowered, as they are, by critical theory, to demonstrate at large the faultiness—and the dangers—of that objection.

A historical note on the Shield commercial's pseudofeminism.   23
Since 1982, the contemptuous housewife has all but vanished from the antiseptic scene of advertising; Gail was among the last of an endangered species. By now, the housewife/mother is a despised figure—most despised by actual housewife/mothers, who make up 60% of the primetime audience. Since these viewers now prefer to see themselves represented as executives, or at least as mothers with beepers and attaché cases, the *hausfrau* of the past, whether beaming or sneering, has largely been obliterated by the advertisers. In 1985, Advertising to Women Inc., a New York advertising agency, found that, out of 250 current ads, only nine showed recognizable Moms.

This is a triumph not for women's liberation, but for advertising;   24
for, now that Mom is missing from the ads, presumably off knocking heads together in the boardroom, it is the commodity that seems to warm her home and tuck her children in at night.

In any case, the Shield strategy itself has certainly outlasted the   25
wry and/or perky Mommy-images of yesteryear. Indeed, because the sexes are now at war within the scene of advertising (and elsewhere), the nasty visual metaphors have become ubiquitous.

Examining the Text

1. Briefly define the term "pseudofeminism" (paragraph 6) in your own words. How, according to Miller, does the Shield advertisement display "pseudofeminism"? Is Miller justified in criticizing the ad in these terms?

2. Recalling that the title of this essay is "Getting Dirty," summarize Miller's points about cleanliness and dirt in the Shield advertisement. What do you think of Miller's statement that "the filth which Shield supposedly 'fights' is not physical but psychological besmirchment" (13)?

3. Describe the strategic importance of Miller's eighth paragraph. What is Miller doing in this paragraph, and why does he place it here in the essay rather than earlier or later? Do you agree with Miller's ultimate conclusion that "the ad's visual implications are too carefully achieved to have been merely accidental or unconscious"?

4. What is Miller's main point in the Afterword? To what extent does the Afterword help make the essay itself more persuasive?

5. *Thinking rhetorically*: How would you describe the tone of Miller's essay, particularly in the opening section in which he describes the

Shield commercial? Why do you think Miller adopts this tone? Do you find it helps him convey his points? Why or why not?

For Group Discussion

Miller comments in the Afterword that "In fact most Americans still perceive the media image as transparent, a sign that simply says what it means and means what it says. They therefore tend to dismiss any intensive explication as a case of 'reading too much into it'" (22). How does this quote relate to your own response to Miller's essay? If you think Miller "reads too much into" the Shield ad, where in the essay does this occur? What could he do to make these parts of the essay more persuasive?

Writing Suggestion

Miller's analysis of the Shield advertisement focuses on its hidden misogyny. Reflect on other advertisements that also show some degree of misogyny, and write a description about how misogyny works in one specific ad. How does this ad, like the one for Shield, manage to appeal to female consumers even though its message is essentially derogatory toward women?

Sex, Lies and Advertising

Gloria Steinem

This chapter concludes with an essay by one of the most important and influential figures in the American feminist movement, Gloria Steinem. Steinem's essay, originally published in Ms. *magazine (which she co-founded), addresses some of the broader issues involving advertising and gender. As she demonstrates, we need to be aware not only of the content of advertisements, but also of how advertising agencies and their clients make demands that affect the entire content of magazines, women's magazines in particular.*

Steinem describes the difficulties Ms. *faced when soliciting advertisements for their new magazine in the 1970s. As a magazine with an entirely female readership,* Ms. *had first to convince advertisers that women were intelligent, active consumers. Then, the editors had to placate advertisers who demanded editorials and articles to promote their products. Steinem offers numerous examples of how companies try to influence the magazines they advertise in.*

Before you read, look at a recent issue of a woman's magazine, such as Ms. *or* Working Woman *or* Vogue *to notice what sort of advertisements and articles you find there. To what extent do you think these magazines represent the interests and needs of their female readership?*

About three years ago, as *glasnost* was beginning and *Ms.* seemed to be   1
ending, I was invited to a press lunch for a Soviet official. He entertained us with anecdotes about new problems of democracy in his
country. Local Communist leaders were being criticized in their media
for the first time, he explained, and they were angry.

"So I'll have to ask my American friends," he finished pointedly,   2
"how more *subtly* to control the press." In the silence that followed, I
said, "Advertising."

The reporters laughed, but later, one of them took me aside: How   3
dare I suggest that freedom of the press was limited? How dare I imply
that his newsweekly could be influenced by ads?

I explained that I was thinking of advertising's media-wide   4
influence on most of what we read. Even news magazines use "soft" cover
stories to sell ads, confuse readers with "advertorials,"[1] and occasionally
self-censor on subjects known to be a problem with big advertisers.

But, I also explained, I was thinking especially of women's maga-   5
zines. There, it isn't just a little content that's devoted to attracting ads,
it's almost all of it. That's why advertisers—not readers—have always
been the problem for *Ms.* As the only women's magazine that didn't
supply what the ad world euphemistically describes as "supportive
editorial atmosphere" or "complementary copy" (for instance, articles
that praise food/fashion/beauty subjects to "support" and "complement" food/fashion/beauty ads), *Ms.* could never attract enough
advertising to break even.

"Oh, *women's* magazines," the journalist said with contempt.   6
"Everybody knows they're catalogs—but who cares? They have nothing to do with journalism."

I can't tell you how many times I've had this argument in 25 years   7
of working for many kinds of publications. Except as money-making
machines—"cash cows" as they are so elegantly called in the trade—
women's magazines are rarely taken seriously. Though changes being
made by women have been called more far-reaching than the industrial
revolution—and though many editors try hard to reflect some of them in
the few pages left to them after all the ad-related subjects have been covered—the magazines serving the female half of this country are still far
below the journalistic and ethical standards of news and general interest
publications. Most depressing of all, this doesn't even rate an exposé.

If *Time* and *Newsweek* had to lavish praise on cars in general and   8
credit General Motors in particular to get GM ads, there would be a
scandal—maybe a criminal investigation. When women's magazines
from *Seventeen* to *Lear's* praise beauty products in general and credit
Revlon in particular to get ads, it's just business as usual.

---

[1]**"advertorial"** Advertisement designed to mimic the appearance of a feature article.—EDS.

When *Ms.* began, we didn't consider *not* taking ads. The most impor- 9
tant reason was keeping the price of a feminist magazine low enough
for most women to afford. But the second and almost equal reason was
providing a forum where women and advertisers could talk to each
other and improve advertising itself. After all, it was (and still is) as
potent a source of information in this country as news or TV and movie
dramas.

We decided to proceed in two stages. First, we would convince 10
makers of "people products" used by both men and women but advertised mostly to men—cars, credit cards, insurance, sound equipment,
financial services, and the like—that their ads should be placed in a
women's magazine. Since they were accustomed to the division
between editorial[2] and advertising in news and general interest magazines, this would allow our editorial content to be free and diverse.
Second, we would add the best ads for whatever traditional "women's
products" (clothes, shampoo, fragrance, food, and so on) that surveys
showed *Ms.* readers used. But we would ask them to come in without
the usual quid pro quo of "complementary copy."

We knew the second step might be harder. Food advertisers have 11
always demanded that women's magazines publish recipes and articles on entertaining (preferably ones that name their products) in
return for their ads; clothing advertisers expect to be surrounded by
fashion spreads (especially ones that credit their designers); and shampoo, fragrance, and beauty products in general usually insist on positive editorial coverage of beauty subjects, plus photo credits besides.
That's why women's magazines look the way they do. But if we could
break this link between ads and editorial content, then we wanted
good ads for "women's products," too.

By playing their part in this unprecedented mix of *all* the things 12
our readers need and use, advertisers also would be rewarded: Ads for
products like cars and mutual funds would find a new growth market;
the best ads for women's products would no longer be lost in oceans of
ads for the same category; and both would have access to a laboratory
of smart and caring readers whose response would help create effective
ads for other media as well.

I thought then that our main problem would be the imagery in 13
ads themselves. Car-makers were still draping blondes in evening
gowns over the hoods like ornaments. Authority figures were almost
always male, even in ads for products that only women used. Sadistic,
he-man campaigns even won industry praise. (For instance, *Advertising
Age* had hailed the infamous Silva Thin cigarette theme, "How to Get a

---

[2]**editorial** In the magazine industry, all nonadvertising content in a magazine, including
regular columns and feature articles.—EDS.

Woman's Attention: Ignore Her," as "brilliant.") Even in medical journals, tranquilizer ads showed depressed housewives standing beside
piles of dirty dishes and promised to get them back to work.

Obviously, *Ms.* would have to avoid such ads and seek out the   14
best ones—but this didn't seem impossible. *The New Yorker* had been
selecting ads for aesthetic reasons for years, a practice that only seemed
to make advertisers more eager to be in its pages. *Ebony* and *Essence*
were asking for ads with positive black images, and though their struggle was hard, they weren't being called unreasonable.

Clearly, what *Ms.* needed was a very special publisher and ad   15
sales staff. I could think of only one woman with experience on the
business side of magazines—Patricia Carbine, who recently had become
a vice president of *McCall's* as well as its editor in chief—and the reason
I knew her name was a good omen. She had been managing editor at
Look (really *the* editor, but its owner refused to put a female name at the
top of his masthead) when I was writing a column there. After I did an
early interview with Cesar Chavez, then just emerging as a leader of
migrant labor, and the publisher turned it down because he was worried about ads from Sunkist, Pat was the one who intervened. As
I learned later, she had told the publisher she would resign if the interview wasn't published. Mainly because *Look* couldn't afford to lose Pat,
it *was* published (and the ads from Sunkist never arrived).

Though I barely knew this woman, she had done two things I   16
always remembered; put her job on the line in a way that editors often
talk about but rarely do, and been so loyal to her colleagues that she
never told me or anyone outside *Look* that she had done so.

Fortunately, Pat did agree to leave *McCall's* and take a huge cut   17
in salary to become publisher of *Ms.* She became responsible for training and inspiring generations of young women who joined the *Ms.* ad
sales force, many of whom went on to become "firsts" at the top of
publishing. When *Ms.* first started, however, there were so few
women with experience selling space that Pat and I made the rounds
of ad agencies ourselves. Later, the fact that *Ms.* was asking companies to do business in a different way meant our saleswomen had to
make many times the usual number of calls—first to convince agencies and then client companies besides—and to present endless
amounts of research. I was often asked to do a final ad presentation,
or see some higher decision-maker, or speak to women employees so
executives could see the interest of women they worked with. That's
why I spent more time persuading advertisers than editing or writing
for *Ms.* and why I ended up with an unsentimental education in the
seamy underside of publishing that few writers see (and even fewer
magazines can publish).

Let me take you with us through some experiences, just as they   18
happened:

• Cheered on by early support from Volkswagen and one or two
other car companies, we scrape together time and money to put on a
major reception in Detroit. We know U.S. car-makers firmly believe
that women choose the upholstery, not the car, but we are armed with
statistics and reader mail to prove the contrary: A car is an important
purchase for women, one that symbolizes mobility and freedom.

But almost nobody comes. We are left with many pounds of   19
shrimp on the table, and quite a lot of egg on our face. We blame ourselves for not guessing that there would be a baseball pennant play-off
on the same day, but executives go out of their way to explain they
wouldn't have come anyway. Thus begins ten years of knocking on
hostile doors, presenting endless documentation, and hiring a full-time
saleswoman in Detroit; all necessary before *Ms.* gets any real results.

This long saga has a semihappy ending: foreign and, later, do-   20
mestic car-makers eventually provided *Ms.* with enough advertising
to make cars one of our top sources of ad revenue. Slowly, Detroit
began to take the women's market seriously enough to put car ads in
other women's magazines, too, thus freeing a few pages from the hot-
house of fashion-beauty-food ads.

But long after figures showed a third, even a half, of many car   21
models being bought by women, U.S. makers continued to be uncomfortable addressing women. Unlike foreign car-makers, Detroit never
quite learned the secret of creating intelligent ads that exclude no one,
and then placing them in women's magazines to overcome past exclusion. (*Ms.* readers were so grateful for a routine Honda ad featuring
rack and pinion steering, for instance, that they sent fan mail.) Even
now, Detroit continues to ask, "Should we make special ads for
women?" Perhaps that's why some foreign cars still have a disproportionate share of the U.S. women's market.

• In the *Ms.* Gazette, we do a brief report on a congressional hear-   22
ing into chemicals used in hair dyes that are absorbed through the skin
and may be carcinogenic. Newspapers report this too, but Clairol, a
Bristol-Myers subsidiary that makes dozens of products—a few of
which have just begun to advertise in *Ms.*—is outraged. Not at newspapers or news magazines, just at us. It's bad enough that *Ms.* is the only
women's magazine refusing to provide the usual "complementary"
articles and beauty photos, but to criticize one of their categories—*that*
is going too far.

We offer to publish a letter from Clairol telling its side of the story.   23
In an excess of solicitousness, we even put this letter in the Gazette, not

in Letters to the Editors where it belongs. Nonetheless—and in spite of surveys that show *Ms.* readers are active women who use more of almost everything Clairol makes than do the readers of any other women's magazine—*Ms.* gets almost none of these ads for the rest of its natural life.

Meanwhile, Clairol changes its hair-coloring formula, apparently   24 in response to the hearings we reported.

• Our saleswomen set out early to attract ads for consumer   25 elections: sound equipment, calculators, computers, VCRs, and the like. We know that our readers are determined to be included in the technological revolution. We know from reader surveys that *Ms.* readers are buying this stuff in numbers as high as those of magazines like *Playboy,* or "men 18 to 34," the prime targets of the consumer electronics industry. Moreover, unlike traditional women's products that our readers buy but don't need to read articles about, these are subjects they want covered in our pages. There actually *is* a supportive editorial atmosphere.

"But women don't understand technology," say executives at the   26 end of ad presentations. "Maybe now," we respond, "but neither do men, and we all buy it."

"If women *do* buy it," say the decision-makers, "they're asking   27 their husbands and boyfriends what to buy first." We produce letters from *Ms.* readers saying how turned off they are when salesmen say things like "Let me know when your husband can come in."

After several years of this, we get a few ads for compact sound   28 systems. Some of them come from JVC, whose vice president, Harry Elias, is trying to convince his Japanese bosses that there is something called a women's market. At his invitation, I find myself speaking at huge trade shows in Chicago and Las Vegas, trying to persuade JVC dealers that showrooms don't have to be locker rooms where women are made to feel unwelcome. But as it turns out, the shows themselves are part of the problem. In Las Vegas, the only women around the technology displays are seminude models serving champagne. In Chicago, the big attraction is Marilyn Chambers, who followed Linda Lovelace of *Deep Throat* fame as Chuck Traynor's captive and/or employee. VCRs are being demonstrated with her porn videos.

In the end, we get ads for a car stereo now and then, but no VCRs;   29 some IBM personal computers, but no Apple or Japanese ones. We notice that office magazines like *Working Woman* and *Savvy* don't benefit as much as they should from office equipment ads either. In the electronics world, women and technology seem mutually exclusive. It remains a decade behind even Detroit.

• Because we get letters from little girls who love toy trains, and   30 who ask our help in changing ads and box-top photos that feature little boys only, we try to get toy-train ads from Lionel. It turns out that

Lionel executives have been concerned about little girls. They made a pink train, and were surprised when it didn't sell.

Lionel bows to consumer pressure with a photograph of a boy *and* a girl—but only on some of their boxes. They fear that, if trains are associated with girls, they will be devalued in the minds of boys. Needless to say, *Ms.* gets no train ads, and little girls remain a mostly unexplored market. By 1986, Lionel is put up for sale.

But for different reasons, we haven't had much luck with other kinds of toys either. In spite of many articles on child-rearing; an annual listing of nonsexist, multiracial toys by Letty Cottin Pogrebin; Stories for Free Children, a regular feature also edited by Letty; and other prizewinning features for or about children, we get virtually no toy ads. Generations of *Ms.* saleswomen explain to toy manufacturers that a larger proportion of *Ms.* readers have preschool children than do the readers of other women's magazines, but this industry can't believe feminists have or care about children.

• When *Ms.* begins, the staff decides not to accept ads for feminine hygiene sprays or cigarettes: they are damaging and carry no appropriate health warnings. Though we don't think we should tell our readers what to do, we do think we should provide facts so they can decide for themselves. Since the antismoking lobby has been pressing for health warnings on cigarette ads, we decide to take them only as they comply.

Philip Morris is among the first to do so. One of its brands, Virginia Slims, is also sponsoring women's tennis and the first national polls of women's opinions. On the other hand, the Virginia Slims theme, "You've come a long way, baby," has more than a "baby" problem. It makes smoking a symbol of progress for women.

We explain to Philip Morris that this slogan won't do well in our pages, but they are convinced its success with some women means it will work with *all* women. Finally, we agree to publish an ad for a Virginia Slims calendar as a test. The letters from readers are critical— and smart. For instance: Would you show a black man picking cotton, the same man in a Cardin suit, and symbolize the antislavery and civil rights movements by smoking? Of course not. But instead of honoring the test results, the Philip Morris people seem angry to be proven wrong. They take away ads for *all* their many brands.

This costs *Ms.* about $250,000 the first year. After five years, we can no longer keep track. Occasionally, a new set of executives listens to *Ms.* saleswomen, but because we won't take Virginia Slims, not one Philip Morris product returns to our pages for the next 16 years.

Gradually, we also realize our naiveté in thinking we *could* decide against taking cigarette ads. They became a disproportionate support of magazines the moment they were banned on television, and few magazines could compete and survive without them; certainly not *Ms.*, which lacks so many other categories. By the time statistics in the 1980s showed that women's rate of lung cancer was approaching men's, the necessity of taking cigarette ads has become a kind of prison.

• General Mills, Pillsbury, Carnation, DelMonte, Dole, Kraft,   38
Stouffer, Hormel, Nabisco: You name the food giant, we try it. But no matter how desirable the *Ms.* readership, our lack of recipes is lethal.

We explain to them that placing food ads *only* next to recipes   39
associates food with work. For many women, it is a negative that works *against* the ads. Why not place food ads in diverse media without recipes (thus reaching more men, who are now a third of the shoppers in supermarkets anyway), and leave the recipes to specialty magazines like *Gourmet* (a third of whose readers are also men)?

These arguments elicit interest, but except for an occasional ad for   40
a convenience food, instant coffee, diet drinks, yogurt, or such extras as avocados and almonds, this mainstay of the publishing industry stays closed to us. Period.

• Traditionally, wines and liquors didn't advertise to women: 41
Men were thought to make the brand decisions, even if women did the buying. But after endless presentations, we begin to make a dent in this category. Thanks to the unconventional Michel Roux of Carillon Importers (distributors of Grand Marnier, Absolut Vodka, and others), who assumes that food and drink have no gender, some ads are leaving their men's club.

Beermakers are still selling masculinity. It takes *Ms.* fully eight   42
years to get its first beer ad (Michelob). In general, however, liquor ads are less stereotyped in their imagery—and far less controlling of the editorial around them—than are women's products. But given the underrepresentation of other categories, these very facts tend to create a disproportionate number of alcohol ads in the pages of *Ms.* This in turn dismays readers worried about women and alcoholism.

• We hear in 1980 that women in the Soviet Union have been   43
producing feminist *samizdat* (underground, self-published books) and circulating them throughout the country. As punishment, four of the leaders have been exiled. Though we are operating on our usual shoe-string, we solicit individual contributions to send Robin Morgan to interview these women in Vienna.

The result is an exclusive cover story that includes the first news   44
of a populist peace movement against the Afghanistan occupation, a prediction of *glasnost* to come, and a grassroots, intimate view of Soviet women's lives. From the popular press to women's studies courses, the response is great. The story wins a Front Page award.

Nonetheless, this journalistic coup undoes years of efforts to get   45
an ad schedule from Revlon. Why? Because the Soviet women on our
cover are not wearing make-up.

• Four years of research and presentations go into convincing   46
airlines that women now make travel choices and business trips.
United, the first airline to advertise in *Ms.*, is so impressed with the
response from our readers that one of its executives appears in a film
for our ad presentations. As usual, good ads get great results.

But we have problems unrelated to such results. For instance: 47
Because American Airlines flight attendants include among their labor
demands the stipulation that they could choose to have their last
names preceded by "Ms." on their name tags—in a long-delayed revolt
against the standard. "I am your pilot, Captain Rothgart, and this is
your flight attendant, Cindy Sue"—American officials seem to hold the
magazine responsible. We get no ads.

There is still a different problem at Eastern. A vice president can-   48
cels subscriptions for thousands of copies on Eastern flights. Why?
Because he is offended by ads for lesbian poetry journals in the *Ms.*
Classified. A "family airline," as he explains to me coldly on the phone,
has to "draw the line somewhere."

It's obvious that *Ms.* can't exclude lesbians and serve women.   49
We've been trying to make that point ever since our first issue included
an article by and about lesbians, and both Suzanne Levine, our managing editor, and I were lectured by such heavy hitters as Ed Kosner, then
editor of *Newsweek* (and now of *New York Magazine*), who insisted that
Ms. should "position" itself *against* lesbians. But our advertisers have
paid to reach a guaranteed number of readers, and soliciting new subscriptions to compensate for Eastern would cost $150,000, plus rebating
money in the meantime.

Like almost everything ad-related, this presents an elaborate   50
organizing problem. After days of searching for sympathetic members
of the Eastern board, Frank Thomas, president of the Ford Foundation,
kindly offers to call Roswell Gilpatrick, a director of Eastern. I talk with
Mr. Gilpatrick, who calls Frank Borman, then the president of Eastern.
Frank Borman calls me to say that his airline is not in the business of
censoring magazines: *Ms.* will be returned to Eastern flights.

• Women's access to insurance and credit is vital, but with the   51
exception of Equitable and a few other ad pioneers, such financial services address men. For almost a decade after the Equal Credit Opportunity Act passes in 1974, we try to convince American Express that
women are a growth market—but nothing works.

Finally, a former professor of Russian named Jerry Welsh becomes   52
head of marketing. He assumes that women should be cardholders, and

persuades his colleagues to feature women in a campaign. Thanks to this 1980s series, the growth rate for female cardholders surpass that for men.

For this article, I asked Jerry Welsh if he would explain why American Express waited so long. "Sure," he said, "they were afraid of having a 'pink' card." 53

• Women of color read *Ms.* in disproportionate numbers. This is a source of pride to *Ms.* staffers, who are also more racially representative than the editors of other women's magazines. But this reality is obscured by ads filled with enough white women to make a reader snowblind. 54

Pat Carbine remembers mostly "astonishment" when she requested African American, Hispanic, Asian, and other diverse images. Marcia Ann Gillespie, a *Ms.* editor who was previously the editor in chief of *Essence*, witnesses ad bias a second time: Having tried for *Essence* to get white advertisers to use black images (Revlon did so eventually, but L'Oreal, Lauder, Chanel, and other companies never did), she sees similar problems getting integrated ads for an integrated magazine. Indeed, the ad world often creates black and Hispanic ads only for black and Hispanic media. In an exact parallel of the fear that marketing a product to women will endanger its appeal to men, the response is usually, "But your [white] readers won't identify." 55

In fact, those we are able to get—for instance, a Max Factor ad made for *Essence* that Linda Wachner gives us after she becomes president—are praised by white readers, too. But there are pathetically few such images. 56

• By the end of 1986, production and mailing costs have risen astronomically, ad income is flat, and competition for ads is stiffer than ever. The 60/40 preponderance of edit over ads that we promised to readers becomes 50/50; children's stories, most poetry, and some fiction are casualties of less space; in order to get variety into limited pages, the length (and sometimes the depth) of articles suffers; and, though we do refuse most of the ads that would look like a parody in our pages, we get so worn down that some slip through. Still, readers perform miracles. Though we haven't been able to afford a subscription mailing in two years, they maintain our guaranteed circulation of 450,000. 57

Nonetheless, media reports on *Ms.* often insist that our unprofitability must be due to reader disinterest. The myth that advertisers simply follow readers is very strong. Not one reporter notes that other comparable magazines our size (say, *Vanity Fair* or *The Atlantic*) have been losing more money in one year than *Ms.* has lost in 16 years. No matter how much never-to-be-recovered cash is poured into starting a magazine or keeping one going, appearances seem to be all that matter. 58

(Which is why we haven't been able to explain our fragile state in public. Nothing causes ad flight like the smell of nonsuccess.)

My healthy response is anger. My not-so-healthy response is   59
constant worry. Also an obsession with finding one more rescue. There is hardly a night when I don't wake up with sweaty palms and pounding heart, scared that we won't be able to pay the printer or the post office; scared most of all that closing our doors will hurt the women's movement.

Out of chutzpah and desperation, I arrange a lunch with Leonard   60
Lauder, president of Estée Lauder. With the exception of Clinique (the brainchild of Carol Phillips), none of Lauder's hundreds of products has been advertised in *Ms*. A year's schedule of ads for just three or four of them could save us. Indeed, as the scion of a family-owned company whose ad practices are followed by the beauty industry, he is one of the few men who could liberate many pages in all women's magazines just by changing his mind about "complementary copy."

Over a lunch that costs more than we can pay for some articles, I   61
explain the need for his leadership. I also lay out the record of *Ms.:* more literary and journalistic prizes won, more new issues introduced into the mainstream, new writers discovered, and impact on society than any other magazine; more articles that became books, stories that became movies, ideas that became television series, and newly advertised products that became profitable; and, most important for him, a place for his ads to reach women who aren't reachable through any other women's magazine. Indeed, if there is one constant characteristic of the everchanging *Ms.* readership, it is their impact as leaders. Whether it's waiting until later to have first babies, or pioneering PABA as sun protection in cosmetics, *whatever* they are doing today, a third to a half of American women will be doing three to five years from now. It's never failed.

But, he says, *Ms.* readers are not *our* women. They're not inter-   62
ested in things like fragrance and blush-on. If they were, *Ms.* would write articles about them.

On the contrary, I explain, surveys show they are more likely to   63
buy such things than the readers of, say, *Cosmopolitan* or *Vogue*. They're good customers because they're out in the world enough to need several sets of everything: home, work, purse, travel, gym, and so on. They just don't need to read articles about these things. Would he ask a men's magazine to publish monthly columns on how to shave before he advertised Aramis products (his line for men)?

He concedes that beauty features are often concocted more for   64
advertisers than readers. But *Ms.* isn't appropriate for his ads anyway, he explains. Why? Because Estée Lauder is selling "a kept-woman mentality."

I can't quite believe this. Sixty percent of the users of his products   65
are salaried, and generally resemble *Ms.* readers. Besides, his company
has the appeal of having been started by a creative and hard-working
woman, his mother, Estée Lauder.

That doesn't matter, he says. He knows his customers, and they   66
would *like* to be kept women. That's why he will never advertise in *Ms.*

In November 1987, by vote of the Ms. Foundation for Education and   67
Communication (*Ms.*'s owner and publisher, the media subsidiary of
the Ms. Foundation for Women), *Ms.* was sold to a company whose
officers, Australian feminists Sandra Yates and Anne Summers, raised
the investment money in their country that *Ms.* couldn't find in its
own. They also started *Sassy* for teenage women.

In their two-year tenure, circulation was raised to 550,000 by   68
investment in circulation mailings, and, to the dismay of some readers,
editorial features on clothes and new products made a more traditional
bid for ads. Nonetheless, ad pages fell below previous levels. In addition, *Sassy,* whose fresh voice and sexual frankness were an unprecedented success with young readers, was targeted by two mothers from
Indiana who began, as one of them put it, "calling every Christian
organization I could think of." In response to this controversy, several
crucial advertisers pulled out.

Such links between ads and editorial content was a problem in   69
Australia, too, but to a lesser degree. "Our readers pay two times more
for their magazines," Anne explained, "so advertisers have less power
to threaten a magazine's viability."

"I was shocked," said Sandra Yates with characteristic directness.   70
"In Australia, we think you have freedom of the press—but you don't."

Since Anne and Sandra had not met their budget's projections for   71
ad revenue, their investors forced a sale. In October 1989, *Ms.* and *Sassy*
were bought by Dale Lang, owner of *Working Mother, Working Woman,*
and one of the few independent publishing companies left among the
conglomerates. In response to a request from the original *Ms.* staff—as
well as to reader letters urging that *Ms.* continue, plus his own belief
that *Ms.* would benefit his other magazines by blazing a trail—he
agreed to try the ad-free, reader-supported *Ms.*. . . . and to give us complete editorial control.

In response to the workplace revolution of the 1970s, traditional   72
women's magazines—that is, "trade books" for women working at
home—were joined by *Savvy, Working Woman,* and other trade books
for women working in offices. But by keeping the fashion/beauty/
entertaining articles necessary to get traditional ads and then adding
career articles besides, they inadvertently produced the antifeminist

stereotype of Super Woman. The male-initiative, dress-for-success woman carrying a briefcase became the media image of a woman worker, even though a blue-collar woman's salary was often higher than her glorified secretarial sister's, and though women at a real brief-case level are statistically rare. Needless to say, these dress-for-success women were also thin, white, and beautiful.

In recent years, advertisers' control over the editorial content of women's magazines has become so institutionalized that it is written into "insertion orders" or dictated to ad salespeople as official policy. The following are recent typical orders to women's magazines: 73

- Dow's Cleaning Products stipulates that ads for its Vivid and Spray 'n Wash products should be adjacent to "children or fashion editorial"; ads for Bathroom Cleaner should be next to "home furnishing/family" features; and so on for other brands. "If a magazine fails for the brands or more," the Dow order warns, "it will be omitted from further consideration." 74

- Bristol-Myers, the parent of Clairol, Windex, Drano, Bufferin, and much more, stipulates that ads be placed next to a "full page of compatible editorial." 75

- S.C. Johnson & Son, makers of Johnson Wax, lawn and laundry products, insect sprays, hair sprays, and so on, orders that its ads *"should not be opposite extremely controversial features or material antitheti-cal to the nature/copy of the advertised product."* (Italics theirs.) 76

- Maidenform, manufacturer of bras and other apparel, leaves a blank for the particular product and states: "The creative concept of the _____ campaign, and the very nature of the product itself appeal to the positive emotions of the reader/consumer. Therefore, it is imperative that all editorial adjacencies reflect that same positive tone. The editorial must not be negative in content or lend itself contrary to the _____ product imagery/message (e.g., *editorial relating to illness, disillusionment, large size fashion, etc.*)." (Italics mine.) 77

- The De Beers diamond company, a big seller of engagement rings, prohibits magazines from placing its ads with "adjacencies to hard news or anti-love/romance themed editorial." 78

- Procter & Gamble, one of this country's most powerful and diver-sified advertisers, stands out in the memory of Anne Summers and Sandra Yates (no mean feat in this context): Its products were not to be placed in *any* issue that included *any* material on gun control, abortion, the occult, cults, or the disparagement of religion. Caution was also demanded in any issue covering sex or drugs, even for educational purposes. 79

Those are the most obvious chains around women's magazines. There are also rules so clear they needn't be written down: for instance, an 80 overall "look" compatible with beauty and fashion ads. Even "real" nonmodel women photographed for a woman's magazine are usually made up, dressed in credited clothes, and retouched out of all reality. When editors do include articles on less-than-cheerful subjects (for instance, domestic violence), they tend to keep them short and unillustrated. The point is to be "upbeat." Just as women in the street are asked, "Why don't you smile, honey?" women's magazines acquire an institutional smile.

Within the text itself, praise for advertisers' products has become   81
so ritualized that fields like "beauty writing" have been invented. One of its frequent practitioners explained seriously that "It's a difficult art. How many new adjectives can you find? How much greater can you make a lipstick sound? The FDA restricts what companies can say on labels, but we create illusion. And ad agencies are on the phone all the time pushing you to get their product in. A lot of them keep the business based on how many editorial clippings they produce every month. The worst are products" like Lauder's, as the writer confirmed, "with their own name involved. It's all ego."

Often, editorial becomes one giant ad. Last November, for   82
instance, *Lear's* featured an elegant woman executive on the cover. On the contents page, we learned she was wearing Guerlain makeup and Samsara, a new fragrance by Guerlain. Inside were full-page ads for Samsara and Guerlain antiwrinkle cream. In the cover profile, we learned that this executive was responsible for launching Samsara and is Guerlain's director of public relations. When the *Columbia Journalism Review* did one of the few articles to include women's magazines in coverage of the influence of ads, editor Frances Lear was quoted as defending her magazine because "this kind of thing is done all the time."

Often, advertisers also plunge odd-shaped ads into the text, no   83
matter what the cost to the readers. At *Woman's Day*, a magazine originally founded by a supermarket chain, editor in chief Ellen Levine said, "The day the copy had to rag around a chicken leg was not a happy one."

Advertisers are also adamant about where in a magazine their   84
ads appear. When Revlon was not placed as the first beauty ad in one Hearst magazine, for instance, Revlon pulled its ads from *all* Hearst magazines. Ruth Whitney, editor in chief of *Glamour,* attributes some of these demands to "ad agencies wanting to prove to a client that they've squeezed the last drop of blood out of a magazine." She also is, she says, "sick and tired of hearing that women's magazines are controlled by cigarette ads." Relatively speaking, she's right. To be as censoring as are many advertisers for women's products, tobacco companies would have to demand articles in praise of smoking

and expect glamorous photos of beautiful women smoking their brands.

I don't mean to imply that the editors I quote here share my objec-   85
tions to ads: Most assume that women's magazines have to be the way they are. But it's also true that only former editors can be completely honest. "Most of the pressure came in the form of direct product mentions," explains Sey Chassler, who was editor in chief of *Redbook* from the sixties to the eighties. "We got threats from the big guys, the Revlons, blackmail threats. They wouldn't run ads unless we credited them."

"But it's not fair to single out the beauty advertisers because these   86
pressures came from everybody. Advertisers want to know two things: What are you going to charge me? What else are you going to do for me? It's a holdup. For instance, management felt that fiction took up too much space. They couldn't put any advertising in that. For the last ten years, the number of fiction entries into the National Magazine Awards has declined."

"And pressures are getting worse. More magazines are more bot-   87
tom-line oriented because they have been taken over by companies with no interest in publishing."

"I also think advertisers do this to women's magazines espe-   88
cially," he concluded, "because of the general disrespect they have for women."

Even media experts who don't give a damn about women's   89
magazines are alarmed by the spread of this ad–edit linkage. In a climate *The Wall Street Journal* describes as an unacknowledged Depression for media, women's products are increasingly able to take their low standards wherever they go. For instance: Newsweeklies publish uncritical stories on fashion and fitness. *The New York Times Magazine* recently ran an article on "firming creams," complete with mentions of advertisers. *Vanity Fair* published a profile of one major advertiser, Ralph Lauren, illustrated by the same photographer who does his ads, and turned the lifestyle of another, Calvin Klein, into a cover story. Even the outrageous *Spy* has toned down since it began to go after fashion ads.

And just to make us really worry, films and books, the last media   90
that go directly to the public without having to attract ads first, are in danger, too. Producers are beginning to depend on payments for displaying products in movies, and books are now being commissioned by companies like Federal Express.

But the truth is that women's products—like women's magazines—   91
have never been the subjects of much serious reporting anyway. News and general interest publications, including the "style" or "living" sections of newspapers, write about food and clothing as cooking and fashion, and almost never evaluate such products by brand name.

Though chemical additives, pesticides, and animal fats are major health risks in the United States, and clothes, shoddy or not, absorb more consumer dollars than cars, this lack of information is serious. So is ignoring the contents of beauty products that are absorbed into our bodies through our skins, and that have profit margins so big they would make a loan shark blush.

What could women's magazines be like if they were as free as books? as realistic as newspapers? as creative as films? as diverse as women's lives? We don't know.   92

But we'll only find out if we take women's magazines seriously. If readers were to act in a concerted way to change traditional practices of *all* women's magazines and the marketing of *all* women's products, we could do it. After all, they are operating on our consumer dollars: money that we now control. You and I could: 93

• Write to editors and publishers (with copies to advertisers) that we're willing to pay *more* for magazines with editorial independence, but will *not* continue to pay for those that are just editorial extensions of ads;   94

• Write to advertisers (with copies to editors and publishers) that we want fiction, political reporting, consumer reporting—whatever is, or is not, supported by their ads;   95

• Put as much energy into breaking advertising's control over content as into changing the images in ads, or protesting ads for harmful products like cigarettes;   96

• Support only those women's magazines and products that take *us* seriously as readers and consumers.   97

• Those of us in the magazine world can also use the carrot-and-stick technique. For instance: Pointing out that, if magazines were a regulated medium like television, the demands of advertisers would be against FCC rules. Payola and extortion could be punished. As it is, there are probably illegalities. A magazine's postal rates are determined by the ratio of ad to edit pages, and the former costs more than the latter. So much for the stick.   98

The carrot means appealing to enlightened self-interest. For instance: There are many studies showing that the greatest factor in determining an ad's effectiveness is the credibility of its surroundings. The "higher the rating of editorial believability," concluded a 1987 survey by the *Journal of Advertising Research,* "the higher the rating of the advertising." Thus, an impenetrable wall between edit and ads would also be in the best interest of advertisers.   99

Unfortunately, few agencies or clients hear such arguments. Editors often maintain the false purity of refusing to talk to them at all. Instead, they see ad salespeople who know little about editorial,   100 are trained in business as usual, and are usually paid by commission. Editors might also band together to take on controversy. That happened once when all the major women's magazines did articles in the same month on the Equal Rights Amendment. It could happen again.

It's almost three years away from life between the grindstones of advertising pressures and readers' needs. I'm just beginning to realize how edges got smoothed down—in spite of all our resistance.   101

I remember feeling put upon when I changed "Porsche" to "car" in a piece about Nazi imagery in German pornography by Andrea Dworkin—feeling sure Andrea would understand that Volkswagen, the distributor of Porsche and one of our few supportive advertisers, asked only to be far away from Nazi subjects. It's taken me all this time to realize that Andrea was the one with a right to feel put upon.   102

Even as I write this, I get a call from a writer for *Elle*, who is doing a whole article on where women part their hair. Why, she wants to know, do I part mine in the middle?   103

It's all so familiar. A writer trying to make something of a nothing assignment; an editor laboring to think of new ways to attract ads; readers assuming that other women must want this ridiculous stuff; more women suffering for lack of information, insight, creativity, and laughter that could be on these same pages.   104

I ask you: Can't we do better than this?   105

Examining the Text

1. What do you think of the anecdote at the beginning of the essay, in which Steinem remarks to a Soviet official that advertising is a way to limit freedom of the press? Do you think that her essay supports this assertion? Why or why not?

2. According to Steinem, what is the relationship between advertising and editorial content in magazines? Does your own reading of magazines support the assertion that advertising affects content?

3. In what ways do women's magazines have a different relationship to advertising than other magazines? What are some of the significant problems that *Ms.* encountered in dealing with advertisements and advertisers?

4. *Thinking rhetorically*: How would you describe the structure of this essay? What effect do the numerous specific examples Steinem cites in the first and second parts of the essay have on you as a reader? In general, what are the advantages and disadvantages of using many specific examples, as Steinem does, to help you support a claim or argument that you're making?

For Group Discussion

Steinem asks, "What could women's magazines be like if they were as free as books? as realistic as newspapers? as creative as films? as diverse as women's lives?" (paragraph 92). How would you answer these questions? What would be the content of an "ideal" women's magazine? Would it be different from an "ideal" men's magazine? In what ways? Do any magazines read by group members approach these "ideals"?

Writing Suggestion

Look at recent issues of several women's magazines and test Steinem's assertions about the relationship between advertising and editorial content. Take note of any "complementary copy" in the magazine and any other ways editorial decisions might have been influenced by advertising. In an essay, explore your conclusions about the extent to which advertising affects the content and organization of women's magazines.

ADDITIONAL SUGGESTIONS FOR WRITING ABOUT ADVERTISING

1. Choose a magazine, television, or radio advertisement that you find particularly interesting, appealing, or puzzling, and write a narrative essay describing your response to the ad.

Begin by recording your initial impressions of the ad. What do you notice first, and why are you drawn to that element of the ad? What emotions or thoughts strike you as you first look at the ad? Then describe your step-by-step progress through the ad. Where does your eye go next? How do your thoughts or emotions change as you notice more of the ad? Finally, record your impressions after you've taken in all of the ad. How does this final impression differ from your first impression?

You might conclude your narrative by commenting on whether, based on your response, the ad achieves its objective of selling the product. In other words, do you think you responded as the designers of the ad intended?

2. Devise your own ad campaign for a product with which you're familiar, including several different ads, each appealing to a different audience.

After deciding on the product, briefly describe each audience group. Choose the form in which you want your advertisements to appear (magazine ads, TV commercials, audio presentations, billboards, or other forms and venues) and then decide on the persuasive methods that you want to use. Do you want to appeal to emotion or intellect or both? What motives will you try to reach? You might refer to Fowles's list of advertising's basic appeals.

Finally, design the ads and briefly explain the reasoning behind each design.

3. Choose recent issues of a women's magazine and a men's magazine, and compare and contrast the ads in each.

How many advertisements are there? What products are being advertised? What techniques are used in the ads and how do these techniques differ significantly between men's and women's magazines? What are the differences in the appeals the ads make? What are the differences in the images of men and women?

From your findings, draw conclusions about how advertisers envision and represent differences in gender. What (if any) stereotypes of men and women do the ads present?

4. Imagine that you are a member of a citizens' group working to improve the quality of advertising. What specific recommendations would you make and what standards would you want to see enforced? Illustrate your ideas with ads you can find that either meet or fall below these standards.

Internet Activities

1. On the Web you'll find sites representing the products and services of almost all major U.S. corporations and of many smaller businesses as well. These corporate Web sites can be seen as extensive advertisements. Though they differ in style and strategy from television and magazine advertisements, they share the goal of informing consumers about a product or service and persuading consumers in their purchasing decisions.

At the *Common Culture* Web site, you'll find links to the sites of companies selling a variety of products. Choose one of those product categories and investigate the links. As you browse through the companies' Web sites, make a list of the kind of information that's offered there, the organization of the site, the graphics and other interactive elements that are used, the style and tone of the writing, and the mood created at the site. Then write an essay in which you describe the similarities and differences of two or more sites. What strategies do these sites use to promote the company's products and services? Which strategies do you find effective, and why? You might conclude your essay by commenting on the distinctive features of Web sites as advertisements. How are they different from magazine and television ads?

2. You've probably noticed that many Web sites contain advertisements— called "Web banners"—for other sites or for products and services offered by specific companies. These banners usually appear in the top portion of the Web page and invite viewers to click on an icon to get more information. Also on the Web are sponsor links and extra windows that open up to advertise products when one visits a Web site. At the *Common Culture* Web site, you'll find links to examples and additional information about Web advertising. Visit these links and take some time to browse the Web and familiarize yourself with the advertising strategies there. Then, write an essay in which you first describe the characteristics of advertising on the Web, and then compare and contrast Web advertising to television commercials and to print ads. What common features are shared by ads in these different media? How do the differences in media shape the content and style of advertisements?

Reading Images

The image entitled "Absolute End" on page CI-2 is taken from Adbusters (*http://www.adbusters.org*); it's one of their "Spoof Ads" that draws on familiar themes and motifs in advertising in order to undermine the messages that the ads themselves convey. Adbusters has spoofed such popular ad campaigns as Obsession perfume and the "Joe Camel" cigarette ads. The idea is to turn ads against themselves, to use the very style of the manufacturers' advertisements in exposing the harm that these ads and products can cause.

"Absolute End" is one of several spoofs of the Absolut vodka ads in which the shape of the vodka bottle is superimposed over some geographic location (for instance, New York's Central Park). Here, the familiar bottle shape (made familiar in part by the Absolut vodka ads themselves) is used as a chalk drawing on a pavement, calling to mind the chalk drawings that trace the shape of a murder victim's body.

Clearly, "Absolute End" is not an advertisement for Absolut vodka. However, it's not an ad directly against Absolut vodka, either. It seems, rather, to be an ad against alcohol advertising in general. The text in the image makes the message explicit:

> Nearly 50% of automobile fatalities are linked to alcohol. 10% of North Americans are alcoholics. A teenager sees 100,000 alcohol ads before reaching the legal drinking age.

In an essay, analyze the techniques used in this image to convey its message. For instance, consider how the perspective of the photograph influences your reaction to it: why is the viewer positioned above the scene that the photograph depicts? Consider also what's left out of the photograph: why is there no victim's body in this scene? Who is included in the scene, and why? Consider also the color scheme and other visual components of the image. Finally, be sure to discuss the text that's included: the "title" of the image and the three sentences that state its message.

Conclude your analysis by discussing whether or not you think a "spoof ad" like this one is an effective way to convey a message. What are the advantages and disadvantages of using a visual statement like this rather than a purely textual one (for instance, a newspaper article about alcohol, drunk driving, and advertising)?

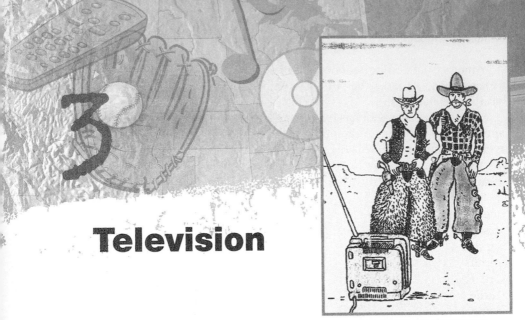

Television

THE BOYS ALWAYS FOUND
SUNSET ON THE PRAIRIE A PAR-
TICULARLY MOVING EXPERIENCE

Drawing by Glen Baxter; © 1991
The New Yorker Magazine, Inc.

We may laugh at these "boys" who stand in the middle of the barren Southwest desert watching a sunset on TV as the real sun sets behind them. Yet the joke is also on us because—like the cowboys—we might often find ourselves more engaged, more entertained, and even more emotionally touched by what we watch on television than by our own experiences in real life.

Some critics even suggest that people regard what they see on television as more real than what goes on around them and thus virtually narrow their world to what comes to them on "the tube." Paradoxically, television's greatest benefit is its potential to broaden our experience, to bring us to places we could never visit, to people we could never meet, and to a range of ideas otherwise unavailable to many people.

This complex relationship between television and people as individuals and as a society leads thoughtful people to examine closely the way television diverts our attention from what could be our own rich, nonmediated experiences; the way it entertains and informs us through otherwise inaccessible experiences; the way it shapes our perceptions of the world around us.

The readings in the first part of this chapter address some of the important questions raised in regard to this ubiquitous medium. Why do Americans spend so much time watching television? What essential needs and desires does television satisfy? How accurately does television represent reality? How strongly do its distortions of reality affect our ideas and behavior? To what extent does television intervene in our everyday lives, influencing families and communities, domestic space, and leisure time? Will new technological developments change how we watch television in the future? Can watching TV actually make us smarter?

The readings in the second part of the chapter expand on these questions by focusing on particular television shows. The first two articles analyze the genre of reality television shows, including reality dating shows, to determine who watches these shows, why they've become popular, and what they have to say about contemporary American culture. Rebecca Gardyn draws on evidence produced from demographic studies and polls of television viewers, along with information gathered from interviews of reality TV fans, in order to answer these questions. Robert Samuels reports on informal surveys of his students and analyzes the reasons they give for their attraction to (or addiction to?) reality dating shows. As both authors show, analyzing specific genres of television shows can yield interesting insights, particularly when that genre is as wildly popular as reality television has been of late.

The last two essays in the chapter have an even narrower focus: *The Simpsons*. Matt Groening's well-known cartoon has been a fixture of television programming since 1989, and Homer, Marge, Bart, and Lisa have become recognizable pop culture icons. But why has *The Simpsons* been so popular for so long? In what ways does this show appeal to us, and what do we learn from watching it? These questions are answered quite differently in the articles by Paul Cantor and Lisa Frank. In fact, it's interesting to read these articles side-by-side to see that a single television show can generate such diverse interpretations.

As you read these essays, remember the television-entranced cowboys at the opening of the chapter. As you hone your own critical abilities, you will go beyond being a passive observer to become an active, critically engaged viewer.

The Cultural Influences of Television

Spudding Out

Barbara Ehrenreich

Do you head straight for the TV when you arrive home after work or school, flicking on the set before you talk to your roommate or feed the cat? If so, you may be exhibiting symptoms of "couch potato" syndrome—a condition cultural critic Barbara Ehrenreich laments in the following essay. Referring to a more active and gregarious America in days past, Ehrenreich observes an onset of a "mass agoraphobia," which she argues has been directly caused by television. This TV-induced phobia—an irrational fear of being away from the tube—has led to a significant loss in human contact and activity, according to Ehrenreich: no longer do people look outside the little box for relaxation or entertainment; instead, Americans have retreated to their living rooms, kitchens, bedrooms, or wherever they lounge comfortably in front of a TV, isolating themselves there before the tube.

Cocooned in chairs, couches, beds, and blankets, and armed with that indispensable accessory of modern life—the remote control—today's Americans are tuned in to the artificial images of TV-land and tuned out from the rest of the world. Moreover, Ehrenreich points to a paradox in our relationship to television: "We love TV because TV brings us a world in which TV does not exist."

As you read *this essay, observe Ehrenreich's tone, which succeeds in being both funny and biting. Notice also how she uses irony and exaggeration to make her critique simultaneously understated and incisive.*

Someone has to speak for them, because they have, to a person, lost the power to speak for themselves. I am referring to that great mass of Americans who were once known as the "salt of the earth," then as "the silent majority," more recently as "the viewing public," and now, alas, as "couch potatoes." What drives them—or rather, leaves them sapped and spineless on their reclining chairs? What are they seeking—beyond such obvious goals as a tastefully colorized version of *The Maltese Falcon*? 1

My husband was the first in the family to "spud out," as the expression now goes. Soon everyone wanted one of those zip-up "Couch Potato Bags," to keep warm in during David Letterman. The youngest and most thoroughly immobilized member of the family 2

relies on a remote that controls his TV, stereo, and VCR, and can also
shut down the neighbor's pacemaker at fifteen yards.

But we never see the neighbors anymore, nor they us. This sad-   3
dens me, because Americans used to be a great and restless people,
fond of the outdoors in all of its manifestations, from Disney World to
miniature golf. Some experts say there are virtues in mass agoraphobia,
that it strengthens the family and reduces highway deaths. But I would
point out that there are still a few things that cannot be done in the den,
especially by someone zipped into a body bag. These include racquet-
ball, voting, and meeting strange people in bars.

Most psychologists interpret the couch potato trend as a negative   4
reaction to the outside world. Indeed, the list of reasons to stay safely
tucked indoors lengthens yearly. First there was crime, then AIDS, then
side-stream smoke. To this list should be added "fear of the infra-
structure," for we all know someone who rashly stepped outside only
to be buried in a pothole, hurled from a collapsing bridge, or struck by
a falling airplane.

But it is not just the outside world that has let us down. Let's face   5
it, despite a decade-long campaign by the "profamily" movement, the
family has been a disappointment. The reason lies in an odd circular
dynamic: we watch television to escape from our families because television shows us how dull our families really are.

Compare your own family to, for example, the Huxtables, the   6
Keatons, or the peppy young people on *Thirtysomething*. In those families, even the three-year-olds are stand-up comics, and the most insipid
remark is hailed with heartening outbursts of canned laughter. When
television families aren't gathered around the kitchen table exchanging
wisecracks, they are experiencing brief but moving dilemmas, which
are handily solved by the youngest child or by some cute extraterres-
trial house-guest. Emerging from *Family Ties* or *My Two Dads*, we are
forced to acknowledge that our own families are made up of slow-
witted, emotionally crippled people who would be lucky to qualify for
seats in the studio audience of *Jeopardy!*

But gradually I have come to see that there is something besides fear   7
of the outside and disgust with our families that drives us to spudhood—
some positive attraction, some deep cathexis to television itself. For a
long time it eluded me. When I watched television, mainly as a way of
getting to know my husband and children, I found that my mind wan-
dered to more interesting things, like whether to get up and make ice
cubes.

Only after many months of viewing did I begin to understand the   8
force that has transformed the American people into root vegetables. If
you watch TV for a very long time, day in, day out, you will begin to
notice something eerie and unnatural about the world portrayed

therein. I don't mean that it is two-dimensional or lacks a well-developed critique of the capitalist consumer culture or something superficial like that. I mean something so deeply obvious that it's almost scary. When you watch television, you will see people doing many things—chasing fast cars, drinking lite beer, shooting each other at close range, etc. But you will never see people *watching television*. Well, maybe for a second before the phone rings or a brand-new, multiracial adopted child walks into the house. But never *really watching*, hour after hour, the way *real* people do.

Way back in the beginning of the television era, this was not so strange, because real people actually did many of the things people do on TV, even if it was only bickering with their mothers-in-law about which toilet paper to buy. But modern people, i.e., couch potatoes, do nothing that is ever shown on television (because it is either dangerous or would involve getting up from the couch). And what they do do— watch television—is far too boring to be televised for more than a fraction of a second, not even by Andy Warhol, bless his boredom-proof little heart.   9

So why do we keep on watching? The answer, by now, should be perfectly obvious: we love television because television brings us a world in which television does not exist. In fact, deep in their hearts, this is what the spuds crave most: a rich, new, participatory life, in which family members look each other in the eye, in which people walk outside and banter with the neighbors, where there is adventure, possibility, danger, feeling, all in natural color, stereophonic sound, and three dimensions, without commercial interruptions, and starring . . . us.   10

"You mean some new kind of computerized interactive medium?" the children asked hopefully, pert as the progeny on a Tuesday night sitcom. But before I could expand on this concept—known to our ancestors as "real life"—they were back at the box, which may be, after all, the only place left to find it.   11

Examining the Text

1. What differences does Ehrenreich note between what we see on television and in "real life"? Could these differences be viewed as criticism of television and/or of how we live our lives? Should television reflect the way most people live?

2. "Couch potato" was widely quoted in the media during the middle and late 1980s when Ehrenreich wrote this essay, but the term is not as common today. Has the "couch potato" phenomenon been a significant aspect of U.S. culture over the last decade or so? How does the way you answer this question color your response to Ehrenreich's essay?

3. *Thinking rhetorically*: Ehrenreich's tone in this essay is basically satirical. Point out several examples of this tone and consider why she adopts it. Does she only intend to be amusing or would you say she is making a serious point? If so, what is it?

For Group Discussion

Working in a group, choose several currently popular programs that focus on family life and list the characteristics of the families they portray—the relationships among family members, the ways they behave, the problems they face and how they solve them. (For balance, choose at least one situation comedy and one hour-long dramatic series.) How well do these characteristics correspond to those that Ehrenreich notes? As a class, consider how accurately these television families reflect the "average" American family and, in fact, whether there is any such thing as an "average" American family.

Writing Suggestion

Based on your own experiences and your observations of your own family and friends, how would you characterize the television viewing habits of most people? In an essay, analyze the different reasons people have for watching television. In doing so, you may wish to expand upon or counter Ehrenreich's observations.

Television Addiction Is No Mere Metaphor

Robert Kubey and Mihaly Csikszentmihalyi

We all know that certain substances are addictive; indeed, we know that cigarettes, alcohol, and drugs are dangerous in large part because we can become addicted to them and end up using them to our own physical and psychological detriment. Certain activities, such as gambling, are also recognized as addictive. But can the activity of watching television be considered addictive? Are heavy television viewers "addicts" in the same way that alcoholics and long-term smokers are?

These questions are addressed by Robert Kubey and Mihaly Csikszentmihalyi in the following article, which was originally published in Scientific American. Kubey and Csikszentmihalyi are both college professors: Kubey is the director of the Center for Media Studies at Rutgers University, and Csikszentmihalyi is the C. S. and D. J. Davidson Professor of Psychology at Claremont Graduate University. In this article, they combine their expertise in media studies and psychology in order to examine the phenomenon of "TV addiction."

*While Barbara Ehrenreich in the previous essay adopts a fairly humorous tone in looking at people "spudding out" in front of the television, Kubey and Csikszentmihalyi bring sociological and biological evidence to bear on their explanation of the addictive power television has over us. **Before you read,** think about what the term "addiction" means to you. Do you know anyone who you think is "addicted" to television? What do you think are the causes and consequences of this addiction?*

Perhaps the most ironic aspect of the struggle for survival is how easily   1
organism can be harmed by that which they desire. The trout is caught by the fisherman's lure, the mouse by cheese. But at least those creatures have the excuse that bait and cheese look like sustenance. Humans seldom have that consolation. The temptations that can disrupt their lives are often pure indulgences. No one has to drink alcohol, for example. Realizing when a diversion has gotten out of control is one of the great challenges of life.

Excessive cravings do not necessarily involve physical substances.   2
Gambling can become compulsive; sex can become obsessive. One activity, however, stands out for its prominence and ubiquity—the world's most popular leisure pastime, television. Most people admit to having a love-hate relationship with it. They complain about the "boob tube" and "couch potatoes," then they settle into their sofas and grab the remote control. Parents commonly fret about their children's viewing (if not their own). Even researchers who study TV for a living marvel at the medium's hold on them personally. Percy Tannenbaum of the University of California at Berkeley has written: "Among life's more embarrassing moments have been countless occasions when I am engaged in conversation in a room while a TV set is on, and I cannot for the life of me stop from periodically glancing over to the screen. This occurs not only during dull conversations but during reasonably interesting ones just as well."

Scientists have been studying the effects of television for decades,   3
generally focusing on whether watching violence on TV correlates with being violent in real life (see "The Effects of Observing Violence," by Leonard Berkowitz; *Scientific American,* February 1964; and "Communication and Social Environment," by George Gerber; September 1972). Less attention has been paid to the basic allure of the small screen—the medium, as opposed to the message.

The term "TV addiction" is imprecise and laden with value   4
judgments, but it captures the essence of a very real phenomenon.

Psychologists and psychiatrists formally define substance dependence as a disorder characterized by criteria that include spending a
great deal of time using the substance; using it more often than one
intends; thinking about reducing use or making repeated unsuccessful efforts to reduce use; giving up important social, family or occupational activities to use it; and reporting withdrawal symptoms
when one stops using it.

All these criteria can apply to people who watch a lot of televi-   5
sion. That does not mean that watching television, per se, is problematic. Television can teach and amuse; it can reach aesthetic
heights; it can provide much needed distraction and escape. The
difficulty arises when people strongly sense that they ought not
to watch as much as they do and yet find themselves strangely
unable to reduce their viewing. Some knowledge of how the
medium exerts its pull may help heavy viewers gain better control
over their lives.

A BODY AT REST TENDS TO STAY AT REST

The amount of time people spend watching television is astonishing.   6
On average, individuals in the industrialized world devote three hours
a day to the pursuit—fully half of their leisure time, and more than on
any single activity save work and sleep. At this rate, someone who
lives to 75 would spend nine years in front of the tube. To some commentators, this devotion means simply that people enjoy TV and make
a conscious decision to watch it. But if that is the whole story, why do
so many people experience misgivings about how much they view? In
Gallup polls in 1992 and 1999, two out of five adult respondents and
seven out of 10 teenagers said they spent too much time watching TV.
Other surveys have consistently shown that roughly 10 percent of
adults call themselves TV addicts.

To study people's reactions to TV, researchers have undertaken   7
laboratory experiments in which they have monitored the brain waves
(using an electroencephalograph, or EEG), skin resistance or heart rate
of people watching television. To track behavior and emotion in the
normal course of life, as opposed to the artificial conditions of the lab,
we have used the Experience Sampling Method (ESM). Participants
carried a beeper, and we signaled them six to eight times a day, at random, over the period of a week; whenever they heard the beep, they
wrote down what they were doing and how they were feeling using a
standardized scorecard.

As one might expect, people who were watching TV when we   8
beeped them reported feeling relaxed and passive. The EEG studies

similarly show less mental stimulation, as measured by alpha brain-wave production, during viewing than during reading.

What is more surprising is that the sense of relaxation ends when   9
the set is turned off, but the feelings of passivity and lowered alertness
continue. Survey participants commonly reflect that television has
somehow absorbed or sucked out their energy, leaving them depleted.
They say they have more difficulty concentrating after viewing than
before. In contrast, they rarely indicate such difficulty after reading. After
playing sports or engaging in hobbies, people report improvements in
mood. After watching TV, people's moods are about the same or worse
than before.

Within moments of sitting or lying down and pushing the   10
"power" button, viewers report feeling more relaxed. Because the
relaxation occurs quickly, people are conditioned to associate viewing
with rest and lack of tension. The association is positively reinforced
because viewers remain relaxed throughout viewing, and it is negatively reinforced via the stress and dysphoric rumination that occurs
once the screen goes blank again.

Habit-forming drugs work in similar ways. A tranquilizer that   11
leaves the body rapidly is much more likely to cause dependence than
one that leaves the body slowly, precisely because the user is more
aware that the drug's effects are wearing off. Similarly, viewers' vague
learned sense that they will feel less relaxed if they stop viewing may
be a significant factor in not turning the set off. Viewing begets more
viewing.

Thus, the irony of TV: people watch a great deal longer than they   12
plan to, even though prolonged viewing is less rewarding. In our ESM
studies the longer people sat in front of the set, the less satisfaction they
said they derived from it. When signaled, heavy viewers (those who
consistently watch more than four hours a day) tended to report on
their ESM sheets that they enjoy TV less than light viewers did (less
than two hours a day). For some, a twinge of unease or guilt that they
aren't doing something more productive may also accompany and
depreciate the enjoyment of prolonged viewing. Researchers in Japan,
the U.K. and the U.S. have found that this guilt occurs much more
among middle-class viewers than among less affluent ones.

GRABBING YOUR ATTENTION

What is it about TV that has such a hold on us? In part, the attraction   13
seems to spring from our biological "orienting response." First described by Ivan Pavlov in 1927, the orienting response is our instinctive
visual or auditory reaction to any sudden or novel stimulus. It is part of

our evolutionary heritage, a built-in sensitivity to movement and potential predatory threats. Typical orienting reactions include dilation of the blood vessels to the brain, slowing of the heart, and constriction of blood vessels to major muscle groups. Alpha waves are blocked for a few seconds before returning to their baseline level, which is determined by the general level of mental arousal. The brain focuses its attention on gathering more information while the rest of the body quiets.

In 1986 Byron Reeves of Stanford University, Esther Thorson of   14
the University of Missouri and their colleagues began to study whether the simple formal features of television—cuts, edits, zooms, pans, sudden noises—activate the orienting response, thereby keeping attention on the screen. By watching how brain waves were affected by formal features, the researchers concluded that these stylistic tricks can indeed trigger involuntary responses and "derive their attentional value through the evolutionary significance of detecting movement. . . . It is the form, not the content, of television that is unique."

The orienting response may partly explain common viewer   15
remarks such as: "If a television is on, I just can't keep my eyes off it," "I don't want to watch as much as I do, but I can't help it," and "I feel hypnotized when I watch television." In the years since Reeves and Thorson published their pioneering work, researchers have delved deeper. Annie Lang's research team at Indiana University has shown that heart rate decreases for four to six seconds after an orienting stimulus. In ads, action sequences and music videos, formal features frequently come at a rate of one per second, thus activating the orienting response continuously.

Lang and her colleagues have also investigated whether formal   16
features affect people's memory of what they have seen. In one of their studies, participants watched a program and then filled out a score sheet. Increasing the frequency of edits—defined here as a change from one camera angle to another in the same visual scene—improved memory recognition, presumably because it focused attention on the screen. Increasing the frequency of cuts—changes to a new visual scene—had a similar effect but only up to a point. If the number of cuts exceeded 10 in two minutes, recognition dropped off sharply.

Producers of educational television for children have found that   17
formal features can help learning. But increasing the rate of cuts and edits eventually overloads the brain. Music videos and commercials that use rapid intercutting of unrelated scenes are designed to hold attention more than they are to convey information. People may remember the name of the product or band, but the details of the ad itself float in one ear and out the other. The orienting response is overworked. Viewers still attend to the screen, but they feel tired and worn

out, with little compensating psychological reward. Our ESM findings show much the same thing.

Sometimes the memory of the product is very subtle. Many ads today are deliberately oblique: they have an engaging story line, but it is hard to tell what they are trying to sell. Afterward you may not remember the product consciously. Yet advertisers believe that if they have gotten your attention, when you later go to the store you will feel better or more comfortable with a given product because you have a vague recollection of having heard of it. 18

The natural attraction to television's sound and light starts very early in life. Dafna Lemish of Tel Aviv University has described babies at six to eight weeks attending to television. We have observed slightly older infants who, when lying on their backs on the floor, crane their necks around 180 degrees to catch what light through yonder window breaks. This inclination suggests how deeply rooted the orienting response is. 19

"TV IS PART OF THEM"

That said, we need to be careful about overreacting. Little evidence suggests that adults or children should stop watching TV altogether. The problems come from heavy or prolonged viewing. 20

The Experience Sampling Method permitted us to look closely at most every domain of everyday life: working, eating, reading, talking to friends, playing a sport, and so on. We wondered whether heavy viewers might experience life differently than light viewers do. Do they dislike being with people more? Are they more alienated from work? What we found nearly leaped off the page at us. Heavy viewers report feeling significantly more anxious and less happy than light viewers do in unstructured situations, such as doing nothing, daydreaming or waiting in line. The difference widens when the viewer is alone. 21

Subsequently, Robert D. McIlwraith of the University of Manitoba extensively studied those who called themselves TV addicts on surveys. On a measure called the Short Imaginal Processes Inventory (SIPI), he found that the self-described addicts are more easily bored and distracted and have poorer attentional control than the nonaddicts. The addicts said they used TV to distract themselves from unpleasant thoughts and to fill time. Other studies over the years have shown that heavy viewers are less likely to participate in community activities and sports and are more likely to be obese than moderate viewers or nonviewers. 22

The question that naturally arises is: In which direction does the correlation go? Do people turn to TV because of boredom and loneliness, 23 or does TV viewing make people more susceptible to boredom and loneliness? We and most other researchers argue that the former is generally the case, but it is not a simple case of either/or. Jerome L. and Dorothy Singer of Yale University, among others, have suggested that more viewing may contribute to a shorter attention span, diminished self-restraint and less patience with the normal delays of daily life. More than 25 years ago psychologist Tannis M. MacBeth Williams of the University of British Columbia studied a mountain community that had no television until cable finally arrived. Over time, both adults and children in the town became less creative in problem solving, less able to persevere at tasks, and less tolerant of unstructured time.

To some researchers, the most convincing parallel between TV   24
and addictive drugs is that people experience withdrawal symptoms when they cut back on viewing. Nearly 40 years ago Gary A. Steiner of the University of Chicago collected fascinating individual accounts of families whose set had broken—this back in the days when households generally had only one set: "The family walked around like a chicken without a head." "It was terrible. We did nothing—my husband and I talked." "Screamed constantly. Children bothered me, and my nerves were on edge. Tried to interest them in games, but impossible. TV is part of them."

In experiments, families have volunteered or been paid to stop   25
viewing, typically for a week or a month. Many could not complete the period of abstinence. Some fought, verbally and physically. Anecdotal reports from some families that have tried the annual "TV turn-off" week in the U.S. tell a similar story.

If a family has been spending the lion's share of its free time   26
watching television, reconfiguring itself around a new set of activities is no easy task. Of course, that does not mean it cannot be done or that all families implode when deprived of their set. In a review of these cold–turkey studies, Charles Winick of the City University of New York concluded: "The first three or four days for most persons were the worst, even in many homes where viewing was minimal and where there were other ongoing activities. In over half of all the households, during these first few days of loss, the regular routines were disrupted, family members had difficulties in dealing with the newly available time, anxiety and aggressions were expressed. . . . People living alone tended to be bored and irritated. . . . By the second week, a move toward adaptation to the situation was common." Unfortunately, researchers have yet to flesh out these anecdotes; no one has systematically gathered statistics on the prevalence of these withdrawal symptoms.

Even though TV does seem to meet the criteria for substance   27
dependence, not all researchers would go so far as to call TV addictive.

McIlwraith said in 1998 that "displacement of other activities by television may be socially significant but still fall short of the clinical requirement of significant impairment." He argued that a new category of "TV addiction" may not be necessary if heavy viewing stems from conditions such as depression and social phobia. Nevertheless, whether or not we formally diagnose someone as TV-dependent, millions of people sense that they cannot readily control the amount of television they watch.

SLAVE TO THE COMPUTER SCREEN

Although much less research has been done on video games and computer use, the same principles often apply. The games offer escape and distraction; players quickly learn that they feel better when playing; and so a kind of reinforcement loop develops. The obvious difference from television, however, is the interactivity. Many video and computer games minutely increase in difficulty along with the increasing ability of the player. One can search for months to find another tennis or chess player of comparable ability, but programmed games can immediately provide a near-perfect match of challenge to skill. They offer the psychic pleasure—what one of us (Csikszentmihalyi) has called "flow"— that accompanies increased mastery of most any human endeavor. On the other hand, prolonged activation of the orienting response can wear players out. Kids report feeling tired, dizzy and nauseated after long sessions.   28

In 1997, in the most extreme medium-effects case on record, 700 Japanese children were rushed to the hospital, many suffering from "optically stimulated epileptic seizures" caused by viewing bright flashing lights in a Pokemon video game broadcast on Japanese TV. Seizures and other untoward effects of video games are significant enough that software companies and platform manufacturers now routinely include warnings in their instruction booklets. Parents have reported to us that rapid movement on the screen has caused motion sickness in their young children after just 15 minutes of play. Many youngsters, lacking self-control and experience (and often supervision), continue to play despite these symptoms.   29

Lang and Shyam Sundar of Pennsylvania State University have been studying how people respond to Web sites. Sundar has shown people multiple versions of the same Web page, identical except for the number of links. Users reported that more links conferred a greater sense of control and engagement. At some point, however, the number of links reached saturation, and adding more of them simply turned   30 people off. As with video games, the ability of Web sites to hold the user's attention seems to depend less on formal features than on interactivity.

For growing numbers of people, the life they lead online may often seem more important, more immediate and more intense than the life they lead face-to-face. Maintaining control over one's media habits is more of a challenge today than it has ever been. TV sets and computers are everywhere. But the small screen and the Internet need not interfere with the quality of the rest of one's life. In its easy provision of relaxation and escape, television can be beneficial in limited doses. Yet when the habit interferes with the ability to grow, to learn new things, to lead an active life, then it does constitute a kind of dependence and should be taken seriously. 31

Examining the Text
1. According to Kubey and Csikszentmihalyi, what factors distinguish TV addiction from simple TV viewing?
2. What biological evidence do Kubey and Csikszentmihalyi summon to support their claims of TV's addictive capabilities? What is the "orienting response" and how does it function in the context of TV viewing?
3. What do Kubey and Csikszentmihalyi mean when they ask "In which direction does the correlation go?" How do they address the problem of correlation and causation in TV addiction?
4. According to Kubey and Csikszentmihalyi, in what ways are video games and computer use similar to and different from TV viewing? How do these similarities and differences affect the question of addiction that Kubey and Csikszentmihalyi discuss?
5. *Thinking rhetorically*: The title of Kubey and Csikszentmihalyi's article draws attention to the fact that many people use the term "addiction" as a metaphor. For instance, you might hear people saying that they're "addicted" to watching "Survivor" or that they're "addicted" to Brown Sugar Cinnamon Frosted PopTarts. What are some of the differences between using "addiction" as a metaphor and using it as a clinical term, as Kubey and Csikszentmihalyi do? Can you think of other terms that function as common metaphors in our culture, like "addiction" does?

For Group Discussion
In a group with several other students, choose an addiction about which you have some knowledge (for instance, gambling, smoking, or drinking alcohol). Make a list of all that you know about this addiction: who suffers from it, what problems it causes, why it occurs, how society

has responded, what laws exist that address the addiction, what economic consequences it has, how it can be "cured," and so on. Then
compare the list you've compiled to the facts about television addiction
that Kubey and Csikszentmihalyi discuss in the reading. Based on this
comparison, do you think that excessive television viewing can genuinely be considered an "addiction"? Why or why not?

Writing Suggestion
For this assignment you'll need access to the Internet in order to research
"TV Turn-Off Week." This annual event, described briefly by Kubey
and Csikszentmihalyi, is organized by Adbusters. At *http://adbusters.
org/campaigns/tvturnoff/* you can read more about this event, including
personal accounts of people who participated and information about
how the television media reported the event. You can also take a look at
posters that people designed to publicize "TV Turn-Off Week," view a
30-second TV "uncommercial" produced for the event, and read
related articles. After reading through all of this information, write an
essay in which you argue either for or against the merits of "TV Turn-
Off Week." Be sure to use quotations and/or statistics from the article
by Kubey and Csikszentmihalyi in your argument. Feel free to include
anecdotes or observations from your own experiences as a TV viewer
to help bolster your position.

Life According to TV

Harry Waters

*The world of television directly influences how people see the "real" world
around them. So says George Gerbner, a noted cultural critic and communications scholar. Gerbner and his staff spent over fifteen years studying the televised programs America watches. Their results paint a damning picture of the
TV industry. In the following essay, Harry Waters summarizes Gerbner's
research about how the televised world matches up to "reality" and to people's
perception of reality. To that end, Gerbner breaks the television-viewing audience into a number of different representative categories—gender, age, race,
and lifestyle, just to name a few—and he observes how people in each category
are portrayed in different television shows.*

    *Frequently, Gerbner's results, as detailed by Waters, are surprising. For
example, contrary to most studies of the relationship between TV and crime,
which suggest that television causes people to become more violent, Gerbner
argues that the prevalence of crime on TV creates a "fear of victimization" in
the viewer. This fear ultimately leads to a "mean-world syndrome" in which*

viewers come to see their social surroundings as hostile and threatening. Waters balances Gerbner's conclusions with comments from network officials who, not surprisingly, often take Gerbner to task.

*As **you read** this selection, pay particular attention to the way Waters maintains his objectivity by attributing most of the opinions and conclusions to Gerbner and his assistants. Notice, too, how Waters's opinions about Gerbner's research can be detected in phrasing such as "the gospel of Gerbner," "tidy explanation," and "comforting."*

Since this is an article originally published in Newsweek, *a magazine which claims to report the news without bias, you might ask just how really objective so-called objective reporting is.*

The late Paddy Chayefsky, who created Howard Beale, would have loved George Gerbner. In "Network," Chayefsky marshaled a scathing, fictional assault on the values and methods of the people who control the world's most potent communications instrument. In real life, Gerbner, perhaps the nation's foremost authority on the social impact of television, is quietly using the disciplines of behavioral research to construct an equally devastating indictment of the medium's images and messages. More than any spokesman for a pressure group, Gerbner has become the man that television watches. From his cramped, book-lined office at the University of Pennsylvania springs a steady flow of studies that are raising executive blood pressures at the networks' sleek Manhattan command posts.

1

George Gerbner's work is uniquely important because it transports the scientific examination of television far beyond familiar children-and-violence arguments. Rather than simply studying the link between violence on the tube and crime in the streets, Gerbner is exploring wider and deeper terrain. He has turned his lens on TV's hidden victims—women, the elderly, blacks, blue-collar workers and other groups—to document the ways in which video-entertainment portrayals subliminally condition how we perceive ourselves and how we view those around us. Gerbner's subjects are not merely the impressionable young; they include all the rest of us. And it is his ominous conclusion that heavy watchers of the prime-time mirror are receiving a grossly distorted picture of the real world that they tend to accept more readily than reality itself.

2

The 63-year-old Gerbner, who is dean of Penn's Annenberg School of Communications, employs a methodology that meshes scholarly observation with mundane legwork. Over the past 15 years, he and a tireless trio of assistants (Larry Gross, Nancy Signorielli and Michael Morgan) videotaped and exhaustively analyzed 1,600 prime-time

3

programs involving more than 15,000 characters. They then drew up multiple-choice questionnaires that offered correct answers about the world at large along with answers that reflected what Gerbner perceived to be the misrepresentations and biases of the world according to TV. Finally, these questions were posed to large samples of citizens from all socioeconomic strata. In every survey, the Annenberg team discovered that heavy viewers of television (those watching more than four hours a day), who account for more than 30 percent of the population, almost invariably chose the TV-influenced answers, while light viewers (less than two hours a day), selected the answers corresponding more closely to actual life. Some of the dimensions of television's reality warp:

SEX

Male prime-time characters outnumber females by 3 to 1 and, with a   4
few star-turn exceptions, women are portrayed as weak, passive satellites to powerful, effective men. TV's male population also plays a vast variety of roles, while females generally get typecast as either lovers or mothers. Less than 20 percent of TV's married women with children work outside the home—as compared with more than 50 percent in real life. The tube's distorted depictions of women, concludes Gerbner, reinforce stereotypical attitudes and increase sexism. In one Annenberg survey, heavy viewers were far more likely than light ones to agree with the proposition: "Women should take care of running their homes and leave running the country to men."

AGE

People over 65, too, are grossly underrepresented on television. Corre-   5
spondingly, heavy-viewing Annenberg respondents believe that the elderly are a vanishing breed, that they make up a smaller proportion of the population today than they did 20 years ago. In fact, they form the nation's most rapidly expanding age group. Heavy viewers also believe that old people are less healthy today than they were two decades ago, when quite the opposite is true. As with women, the portrayals of old people transmit negative impressions. In general, they are cast as silly, stubborn, sexually inactive and eccentric. "They're often shown as feeble grandparents bearing cookies," says Gerbner. "You never see the power that real old people often have. The best and possibly only time to learn about growing old with decency and

grace is in youth. And young people are the most susceptible to TV's messages."

RACE

The problem with the medium's treatment of blacks is more one of image than of visibility. Though a tiny percentage of black characters come across as "unrealistically romanticized," reports Gerbner, the overwhelming majority of them are employed in subservient, supporting roles—such as the white hero's comic sidekick. "When a black child looks at prime time," he says, "most of the people he sees doing interesting and important things are white." That imbalance, he goes on, tends to teach young blacks to accept minority status as naturally inevitable and even deserved. To access the impact of such portrayals on the general audience, the Annenberg survey forms included questions like "Should white people have the right to keep blacks out of their neighborhoods?" and "Should there be laws against marriages between blacks and whites?" The more that viewers watched, the more they answered "yes" to each question.

6

WORK

Heavy viewers greatly overestimated the proportion of Americans employed as physicians, lawyers, athletes and entertainers, all of whom inhabit prime-time in hordes. A mere 6 to 10 percent of television characters hold blue-collar or service jobs vs. about 60 percent in the real work force. Gerbner sees two dangers in TV's skewed division of labor. On the one hand, the tube so overrepresents and glamorizes the elite occupations that it sets up unrealistic expectations among those who must deal with them in actuality. At the same time, TV largely neglects portraying the occupations that most youngsters will have to enter. "You almost never see the farmer, the factory worker or the small businessman," he notes. "Thus not only do lawyers and other professionals find they cannot measure up to the image TV projects of them, but children's occupational aspirations are channeled in unrealistic directions." The Gerbner team feels this emphasis on high-powered jobs poses problems for adolescent girls, who are also presented with views of women as homebodies. The two conflicting views, Gerbner says, add to the frustration over choices they have to make as adults.

7

HEALTH

Although video characters exist almost entirely on junk food and quaff   8
alcohol 15 times more often than water, they manage to remain slim,
healthy and beautiful. Frequent TV watchers, the Annenberg investigators found, eat more, drink more, exercise less and possess an almost
mystical faith in the curative powers of medical science. Concludes
Gerbner: "Television may well be the single most pervasive source of
health information. And its over-idealized images of medical people,
coupled with its complacency about unhealthy life-styles, leaves both
patients and doctors vulnerable to disappointment, frustration and
even litigation."

CRIME

On the small screen, crime rages about 10 times more often than in real   9
life. But while other researchers concentrate on the propensity of TV
mayhem to incite aggression, the Annenberg team has studied the hidden side of its imprint: fear of victimization. On television, 55 percent
of prime-time characters are involved in violent confrontations once a
week; in reality, the figure is less than 1 percent. In all demographic
groups in every class of neighborhood, heavy viewers overestimated
the statistical chance of violence in their own lives and harbored an
exaggerated mistrust of strangers—creating what Gerbner calls "mean-
world syndrome." Forty-six percent of heavy viewers who live in cities
rated their fear of crime "very serious" as opposed to 26 percent for
light viewers. Such paranoia is especially acute among TV entertainment's most common victims: women, the elderly, nonwhites, foreign-
ers and lower-class citizens.

Video violence, proposes Gerbner, is primarily responsible for   10
imparting lessons in social power: it demonstrates who can do what to
whom and get away with it. "Television is saying that those at the bottom of the power scale cannot get away with the same things that a
white, middle-class American male can," he says. "It potentially conditions people to think of themselves as victims."

At a quick glance, Gerbner's findings seem to contain a cause-   11
and-effect, chicken-or-the-egg question. Does television make heavy
viewers view the world the way they do or do heavy viewers come
from the poorer, less experienced segment of the populace that regards
the world that way to begin with? In other words, does the tube create
or simply confirm the unenlightened attitudes of its most loyal audiences? Gerbner, however, was savvy enough to construct a methodology

largely immune to such criticism. His samples of heavy viewers cut across all ages, incomes, education levels and ethnic backgrounds— and every category displayed the same tube-induced misconceptions of the world outside.

Needless to say, the networks accept all this as enthusiastically as 12 they would a list of news-coverage complaints from the Ayatollah Khomeini. Even so, their responses tend to be tinged with a singular respect for Gerbner's personal and professional credentials. The man is no ivory-tower recluse. During World War II, the Budapest-born Gerbner parachuted into the mountains of Yugoslavia to join the partisans fighting the Germans. After the war, he hunted down and personally arrested scores of high Nazi officials. Nor is Gerbner some videophobic vigilante. A Ph.D. in communications, he readily acknowledges TV's beneficial effects, noting that it has abolished parochialism, reduced isolation and loneliness and provided the poorest members of society with cheap, plug-in exposure to experiences they otherwise would not have. Funding for his research is supported by such prestigious bodies as the National Institute of Mental Health, the Surgeon General's office, and the American Medical Association, and he is called to testify before congressional committees nearly as often as David Stockman.

MASS ENTERTAINMENT

When challenging Gerbner, network officials focus less on his findings 13 and methods than on what they regard as his own misconceptions of their industry's function. "He's looking at television from the perspective of a social scientist rather than considering what is mass entertainment," says Alfred Schneider, vice president of standards and practices at ABC. "We strive to balance TV's social effects with what will capture an audience's interests. If you showed strong men being victimized as much as women or the elderly, what would comprise the dramatic conflict? If you did a show truly representative of society's total reality, and nobody watched because it wasn't interesting, what have you achieved?"

CBS senior vice president Gene Mater also believes that Gerbner 14 is implicitly asking for the theoretically impossible. "TV is unique in its problems," says Mater. "Everyone wants a piece of the action. Everyone feels that their racial or ethnic group is underrepresented or should be portrayed as they would like the world to perceive them. No popular entertainment form, including this one, can or should be an accurate reflection of society."

On that point, at least, Gerbner is first to agree; he hardly expects 15 television entertainment to serve as a mirror image of absolute truth.

But what fascinates him about this communications medium is its marked difference from all others. In other media, customers carefully choose what they want to hear or read: a movie, a magazine, a best seller. In television, notes Gerbner, viewers rarely tune in for a particular program. Instead, most just habitually turn on the set—and watch by the clock rather than for a specific show. "Television viewing fulfills the criteria of a ritual," he says. "It is the only medium that can bring to people things they otherwise would not select." With such unique power, believes Gerbner, comes unique responsibility: "No other medium reaches into every home or has a comparable, cradle-to-grave influence over what a society learns about itself."

MATCH

In Gerbner's view, virtually all of TV's distortions of reality can be attrib-   16
uted to its obsession with demographics. The viewers that primetime sponsors most want to reach are white, middle-class, female and between 18 and 49—in short, the audience that purchases most of the consumer products advertised on the tube. Accordingly, notes Gerbner, the demographic portrait of TV's fictional characters largely matches that of its prime commercial targets and largely ignores everyone else. "Television," he concludes, "reproduces a world for its own best customers."

Among TV's more candid executives, that theory draws consider-   17
able support. Yet by pointing a finger at the power of demographics, Gerbner appears to contradict one of his major findings. If female viewers are so dear to the hearts of sponsors, why are female characters cast in such unflattering light? "In a basically male-oriented power structure," replies Gerbner, "you can't alienate the male viewer. But you can get away with offending women because most women are pretty well brainwashed to accept it." The Annenberg dean has an equally tidy explanation for another curious fact. Since the corporate world provides network television with all of its financial support, one would expect businessmen on TV to be portrayed primarily as good guys. Quite the contrary. As any fan of "Dallas," "Dynasty" or "Falcon Crest" well knows, the image of the company man is usually that of a mendacious, dirty-dealing rapscallion. Why would TV snap at the hand that feeds it? "Credibility is the way to ratings," proposes Gerbner. "This country has a populist tradition of bias against anything big, including big business. So to retain credibility, TV entertainment shows businessmen in relatively derogatory ways."

In the medium's Hollywood-based creative community, the   18
gospel of Gerbner finds some passionate adherents. Rarely have TV's

best and brightest talents viewed their industry with so much frustration and anger. The most sweeping indictment emanates from David Rintels, a two-time Emmy-winning writer and former president of the Writers Guild of America, West. "Gerbner is absolutely correct and it is the people who run the networks who are to blame," says Rintels. "The networks get bombarded with thoughtful, reality-oriented scripts. They simply won't do them. They slam the door on them. They believe that the only way to get ratings is to feed viewers what conforms to their biases or what has limited resemblance to reality. From 8 to 11 o'clock each night, television is one long lie."

Innovative thinkers such as Norman Lear, whose work has been 19 practically driven off the tube, don't fault the networks so much as the climate in which they operate. Says Lear: "All of this country's institutions have become totally fixated on short-term bottom-line thinking. Everyone grabs for what might succeed today and the hell with tomorrow. Television just catches more of the heat because it's more visible." Perhaps the most perceptive assessment of Gerbner's conclusions is offered by one who has worked both sides of the industry street. Deanne Barkley, a former NBC vice president who now helps run an independent production house, reports that the negative depictions of women on TV have made it "nerve-racking" to function as a woman within TV. "No one takes responsibility for the social impact of their shows," says Barkley. "But then how do you decide where it all begins? Do the networks give viewers what they want? Or are the networks conditioning them to think that way?"

Gerbner himself has no simple answer to that conundrum. 20 Neither a McLuhanesque shaman nor a Naderesque crusader, he hesitates to suggest solutions until pressed. Then out pops a pair of provocative notions. Commercial television will never democratize its treatments of daily life, he believes, until it finds a way to broaden its financial base. Coincidentally, Federal Communications Commission chairman Mark Fowler seems to have arrived at much the same conclusion. In exchange for lifting such government restrictions on TV as the fairness doctrine and the equal-time rule, Fowler would impose a modest levy on station owners called a spectrum-use fee. Funds from the fees would be set aside to finance programs aimed at specialized tastes rather than the mass appetite. Gerbner enthusiastically endorses that proposal: "Let the ratings system dominate most of prime time but not every hour of every day. Let some programs carry advisories that warn: 'This is not for all of you. This is for nonwhites, or for religious people or for the aged and the handicapped. Turn it off unless you'd like to eavesdrop.' That would be a very refreshing thing."

ROLE
▬▬▬▬

In addition, Gerbner would like to see viewers given an active role in   21
steering the overall direction of television instead of being obliged to
passively accept whatever the networks offer. In Britain, he points out,
political candidates debate the problems of TV as routinely as the issue
of crime. In this country, proposes Gerbner, "every political campaign
should put television on the public agenda. Candidates talk about
schools, they talk about jobs, they talk about social welfare. They're
going to have to start discussing this all-pervasive force."

There are no outright villains in this docudrama. Even Gerbner   22
recognizes that network potentates don't set out to proselytize a point
of view; they are simply businessmen selling a mass-market product.
At the same time, their 90 million nightly customers deserve to know
the side effects of the ingredients. By the time the typical American
child reaches the age of reason, calculates Gerbner, he or she will have
absorbed more than 30,000 electronic "stories." These stories, he suggests, have replaced the socializing role of the preindustrial church:
they create a "cultural mythology" that establishes the norms of
approved behavior and belief. And all Gerbner's research indicates
that this new mythological world, with its warped picture of a sizable
portion of society, may soon become the one most of us think we
live in.

Who else is telling us that? Howard Beale and his eloquent   23
alarms have faded into off network reruns. At the very least, it is comforting to know that a real-life Beale is very much with us . . . and
really watching.

Examining the Text

1. Waters reports extensive studies by George Gerbner and his associates that show that heavy television viewers have a generally "warped"
view of reality, influenced by television's own "reality warp" (paragraph
3). Which viewers do you think would be affected most negatively by
these "warped" viewpoints, and why?

2. Gerbner's studies show that "55 percent of prime-time characters are
involved in violent confrontations once a week; in reality, the figure is
less than 1 percent" (9). While violent crime is known to rank as mid-
dleclass America's primary concern, most violent crime occurs in neighborhoods far removed from most middle-class people. How do you
explain these discrepancies? Why is "violent confrontation" so common
on television? How does the violence you see on television affect you?

3. Waters interviewed a number of different people when he wrote this
article for *Newsweek*. Collectively, they offer a variety of explanations for

and solutions to the limited images television provides. Look closely at these suggested causes and solutions. Which seem most reasonable to you? In general, is Waters's coverage of the issue balanced? Why or why not?

4. *Thinking rhetorically*: Following up on the "as you read" question in the introduction to this article, what is your impression of the objectivity of this article? Where in the article do you see indications that the author is striving to be objective? Where do you see the author's opinions and biases coming through? In general, what is the relationship between objectivity and persuasiveness? That is, do you think it's easier or more difficult to be persuasive when you're also compelled to be objective?

For Group Discussion

This article was first published more than ten years ago. With your group, look again at Gerbner's categories and discuss what significant recent examples suggest about the way current television programming represents reality. Do today's shows seem more accurate than those of ten years ago? As a class, discuss whether or not most viewers want more "reality" on television.

Writing Suggestion

The TV guide is a fine example of nonacademic but very common reading material in our culture. Millions of people read TV schedules every day and think nothing of it. This writing assignment asks you to reflect on *how* you read TV schedules and to interpret what meanings can be found in these common documents.

On page 168 is a reproduction of a page from the TV listings in our local (Santa Barbara, CA) newspaper, listing the televised offerings on Thursday, December 8, 2005. Begin writing about this document by describing it: What are its distinguishing features? How is the information organized? How does its appearance differ from the pages of this textbook? Next, take notes describing the strategies you use in reading this document: Where do you begin? Where does your eye go next? What factors influence your choices? Are there parts of the document that you ignore completely? Why? Finally, write down your thoughts about the content of this schedule: To what extent do the TV programs scheduled for this evening confirm or contradict Waters's claims in "Life According to TV"? As you bring these observations together in an essay, highlight what you see as the two or three most important features of TV schedules in general, based on your observations of this specific example.

TV WEEK

THURSDAY DECEMBER 8, 2005

PRIMETIME		6:00	6:30	7:00	7:30	8:00	8:30	9:00	9:30	10:00	10:30	11:00	11:30
USA	2 43	Law & Order: Criminal Intent: Ex Stasis. (cc) 961156	Law & Order: Special Victims Unit: Resilience. (cc) 562517			Law & Order: Criminal Intent: Shibboleth. (cc) 601137		Movie: "Three Wise Guys" (2006) Tom Arnold. NH finds killers create a tempting miracle. (cc) 604241		Primetime (cc) 5576		Movie: "Three Wise Guys" (2006) 69472	(11:35) Nightline 51427330
KSBY (ABC)	3 3	News 595		Inside Edition (cc) 5098	Seinfeld: The Caddy. 359	Movie: ★★ "Maid of Honor" (2006) Linda Purl. Bride's psychiatrist uncovers family secret. (cc) 8208		The Apprentice: The Final Showdown. (N) 46969				News 7673040	Tonight Show
KSBY (NBC)	6 6	News 5595	News 8175	Jeopardy! (N) (cc) 4750	Wheel of Fortune (N) 5359	Joey Joey's old friend. 8458	Will & Grace (N) (cc) 9205	The Apprentice: The Final Showdown. (N) (cc) 48059		(9:59) ER: All About Christmas Eve. (N) (cc) 5577677		(11:14) "Street" 5454855a	Tonight Show
TBS	7 45	Seinfeld (cc)	Seinfeld (cc)	Raymond	Raymond	Friends 819408	Friends 525243	Movie: ★★★ "Scrooged" (1988) Comedy. (cc) 5045901				(11:10) "Street" 5454855a	South Park (N) 69601
KCAL	9 9	Be a Millionaire	9 on the Town 4021	Dr. Phil 67359		News (cc) 73779		News (cc) 88243		News (cc) 6746345	Sports Central 68373408	South Park (N) 32834	Charlie Rose (N) 124137
KCET (PBS)	10 10	California's Gold 47311	Life and Times (cc) 38663	The NewsHour With Jim Lehrer (N) 90141		Tom Jones: The Legend The singer's hits. (cc) 784885		Bruce Springsteen and the E Street Band: Hammersmith Odeon, London 1975 1975 concert. (N) (cc) 986601			(10:35) Dr. Phil 4130750		Fear Factor
FOX 11 - KKFX	11 11	Malcolm-Mid.	King of the Hill	The Simpsons	'70s Show	The O.C. (N) (cc) 91175		Reunion: 1993. (N) (cc) 71311		Without a Trace: When Darkness Falls. (N) (cc) 72040		News (cc) 5632040	Late Show-Letterman
KCOY (CBS)	12 12	News (cc) 28409		Entertainment Tonight 2934	The Insider (N) (cc) 6243	Survivor: Guatemala – The Maya Empire (N) (cc) 99717		CSI: Crime Scene Investigation: Still Life. (N) 79953		Programa Pagado 48156	Programa Pagado 24576	Programa Pagado 21525	Programa Pagado 94796
KBEH	13	Atrévete 51296				Película: "Suceso en México" (1136, Drama) Magda Montoya. Perro, joven y continúa. Luis Aguilar. NR 96081		Amor en Custodia 14463175		La Chacala	Noticiero	Otra Mitad Sol	Hechos Noche
AZTECA	14	Los Machos 772224	Ventaneando 436985		Casino a la Fama 404130		El Cuerpo del Deseo 74021		Corazón Part	Decisiones	Decisiones 87972	Noticias 30576	Thuiane
KTAS (Tel)	15 16	Noticias 1311	Nol-Telemundo	La Tormenta 68601		Contra Viento y Marea 38175		La Esposa Virgen 13311		Aquí y Ahora 25798		Noticias C. C.	Noticiero Univ.
KPWB (Uni)	16 16	Noticias C. C.	Noticiero Univ	Piel de Otoño 29427		Everybody Hates Chris	Love, Inc. (cc) 7345	Eve: Shelly And... 99243	Cuts: Home Alone. 67779	Seinfeld: The Caddy. 50446	That '70s Show 31866	News 97048	Seinfeld (cc) 82137
KCOP (UPN)	44 13	The Bernie Mac Show	The King of Queens 7137	That '70s Show 5040	The Bernie Mac Show	Joey Joey's old friend. 2750	Will & Grace (N) (cc) 1685	The Apprentice: The Final Showdown. (N) (cc) 5359		(9:59) ER: All About Christmas Eve. (N) 19043427		News (cc) 1568408	Tonight Show
NBC News	4	News (cc) 137	NBC Nightly News (cc) 717	Extra (N) (cc) 6330	Access Hollywood (N) 601	Will & Grace (N) (cc) 23663		Everwood (N) (cc) 42427		Will & Grace	Will & Grace	Sex and-City	Sex and-City
WB	5	Yes, Dear 7563	Yes, Dear 6205	King	King	Smallville: Lexmas. (N) 20663			Paid Program	Community	News 57682	News 60330	Noticias 30576	Music Choice Concert 58865
CO38	6	Education	In Focus	Community	Wellness Hour	Wellness Hour	Paid Program	Celebration 20243		Native 57682	Undercover TV	Permacultura 58865	
COM 17-CMAC	17	Open Hearts Open Doors		SBPU Live		Santa Barbara City Council (cc) 820040						City Calendar 1139663	
City TV	19	The Rediscovery of York 34446		'70s Show	'70s Show	Cops 8251683	Cops 8270798	Cops 3510175		Cops 4945059	Cops 4925779	'70s Show	'70s Show
FX	19 77	King of the Hill	King of the Hill									Classic Arts Showcase	
COUNTY	20 20	(9) Board of Supervisors Meeting 2598882			Mary Anthony: A Life		Phillip Richardson 396934			Creative	Creative	Science Writing Physics	
EDUCATION	21	Innovation-Educ.	MimeWorks 9030966	Anderson Cooper 360 (cc) 209963				Larry King Live 696205		Anderson Cooper 360 699392		Paula Zahn Now 205137	
CNN	22 50	Larry King Live (cc) 976098		Nancy Grace 7828972		Showbiz Tonight 7804392		Prime News Tonight 7924156		Nancy Grace 7627243		Headline News 1305098	Cosby Show
CNN Headln	23 51	Prime News Tonight 3157901		The Big Idea With Deutsch		Apprentice: Martha Stewart		Mad Money 1528514		The Big Idea With Deutsch		Paid Program	Paid Program
CNBC	24 48	Mad Money 9302866		On the Record-Van Susteren		The O'Reilly Factor 5068676		Special Report 5072040		Your World With Neil Cavuto		Hannity & Colmes 8453137	
FOXNEWS	52	Hannity & Colmes 9729399				"Above the Law" (1988) Steven Seagal. A Chicago cop busts a drug cartel. (cc) 472778		"Death Reaction" (1994) Kaya Reyes. A crash-sprinkled drug cartel is groovering big caught in a conspiracy. (cc) 2221137		"Death Reaction" (1994) Kaya Reyes. 219918 A caked and smacking baking ...		Great Tool Gifts 7454446	
AMC	26 46	"Young Guns II" (1990, Western) Emilio Estevez. The Kid and his posse make a mad dash for the border. 22220205				Gifts for Her 752966		Dennis Basso Boutique		Practical Presents 1642717		Law & Order 918755	
QVC	27 7	(5) Craftsman Workshop Holiday Special 6473243				NBA Basketball: Houston Rockets at Sacramento Kings. (Live) 186630				Inside the NBA (cc) 453098		Roseanne (cc)	Roseanne (cc)
TNT	28 44	NBA Basketball: Wizards at Pacers		Odapotolls	SpongeBob	NBA Basketball: Mighty Ducks of Anaheim at Buffalo Sabres. 351682		Full House	Fresh Prince	Roseanne (cc)	Roseanne (cc)	Roseanne (cc)	That's-Raven
NICK	29 70	All Grown Up	Danny Phant.	That's-Raven	That's-Raven	NHL Hockey: Carolina Hurricanes at Los Angeles Kings. (Live) 133966		Full House	Phil of Future	Buzz-Maggie	Sister, Sister	That's-Raven	Best-Sports
DISNEY	30 68	Sister, Sister	Phil of Future	U.S. Marshals: Fugitive	U.S. Marshals: Fugitive	Kim Possible: A Stitch in Time. (cc) 1264359		City Cops 4322959		City Cops (cc) 465446		U.S. Marshals: Fugitive	
Learning	31 69	Martha (N) (cc) 785224		America's Next Top Model		I Shouldn't Be Alive 983791		Living With Tigers (cc) 593995		America's Next Top Model		MythBusters (cc) 901779	
Discovery	32 53	Cash Cab (N)	Cash Cab (N)	I Shouldn't Be Alive 993971		The Planet's Funniest Animals		The Planet's Funniest Animals		Into the Lion's Den 343412		The Most Extreme (cc) 40243	
ANIMAL	33 33	The Planet's Funniest Animals	New Breed Vets (N) 42427		SportsCenter (cc) 427137		NFL Live (N)		New Breed Vets 41798		The Most Extreme (cc) 40243	
ESPN	34 30	College Basketball: Georgetown at Illinois. (Live) (cc) 426408		SportsCenter (cc) 427137			Outside-Lines		SportsCenter (cc) 440088		SportsCenter (cc) 956755	
ESPN 2	35 31	College Basketball: Massachusetts at Connecticut. 8124330		Quite Frankly With Smith		Rodeo: Wrangler National Finals – Seventh Round. From Las Vegas. 3487695			So. Cal. Sports		It's Saw Easy 1590662	
FOXSpNe2	36	NHL Hockey	HS Spotlight	Lexus Gauntlet	Lexus Gauntlet					So. Cal. Sports	HS Spotlight	Lexus Gauntlet	NBA Action (N)
FOXSpNet	37 32	Fant. Football	Chris Myers	Break the Ice	Break the Ice				Best Damn Sports Show	Punk'd 876514		Cosby Show
MTV	38 40	Making Band	Making Band	Making Band	Making Band	Making Band	Making Band	Making Band	Making Band	Making Band		Real World Austin	Top 40 of 2005 (cc)
VH1	39 41	America's Next Top Model	America's Next Top Model		America's Next Top Model		America's Next Top Model		America's Next Top Model		Brokeback Mtn	
LIFETIME	41 62	The Golden Girls 896885	The Golden Girls 894885	Movie: ★★ "The Man Upstairs" (1992) Katharine Hepburn. A jail inmate gives a town a second chance at life. (cc) 930069		Harry & David	Esteban Music	Textiles Year in Review 9269663				Will & Grace 488750	Will & Grace 125427
HomeShop	42	Heidi Daus Fashion Jewelry 9297175										It's Saw Easy 1590662	
Trinity	43 75	Bishop Jakes	This Is Day	Praise the Lord (cc) 688205		Praise		Praise		Dr. Carl Baugh	Hal Lindsey	This Is Day	Praise the Lord (cc) 784476
SPIKE	45 28	World's Wildest Police Videos		CSI: Crime Scene Investigation		CSI: Crime Scene Investigation				TNA IMPACT! (N) (cc) 701137	MXC 795601	MXC 420750	World's Wildest Police Videos

Watching TV Makes You Smarter

Steven Johnson

If your parents have ever complained that you watch too much TV, just tell them, "But Mom, Dad, watching TV is mentally stimulating and can actually make me smarter!" When they look at you in disbelief, refer them to the following article in which Steven Johnson makes precisely that argument: that watching TV—or at least, watching some of the shows currently on TV— gives you a good cognitive workout. The article, adapted from Johnson's recent bestseller, Everything Bad is Good for You: How Today's Popular Culture is Actually Making Us Smarter, *compares past and present TV shows and concludes that viewers today are required to exercise their mental faculties in order to make sense of complex, multilayered plots and characters.*

Although Johnson refers to many past and present shows in this article, his primary examples of intellectually challenging shows are "24," "The West Wing," "The Sopranos," and "ER." He argues that these shows combine the complicated plot threads of soap opera with the realistic characters and important social issues of nighttime drama. As a result, in any given episode of a show, viewers have to follow intersecting narrative threads that include many distinct characters, each with their own continuing story line. These shows often have fast-paced, specialized dialogue that's purposely difficult for viewers to follow. Watching the shows engages viewers in the pleasures of solving puzzles and unlocking mysteries, and so these shows provide a mentally stimulating hour of TV viewing—punctuated, of course, by commercial breaks.

It certainly goes against common perceptions of TV to suggest that watching shows is mentally stimulating; you're far more likely to find arguments like those presented in the previous article by Harry Waters, that TV viewing can give you a skewed perception of reality. Because Johnson makes such an unusual argument, it's interesting to pay attention to the strategies he uses to try to convince readers that he's correct. **As you read,** *notice the different kinds of evidence that Johnson uses to prove his point. What evidence do you find most convincing? What evidence do you find questionable?*

THE SLEEPER CURVE

SCIENTIST A: Has he asked for anything special?

SCIENTIST B: Yes, this morning for breakfast . . . he requested something called "wheat germ, organic honey and tiger's milk."

SCIENTIST A: Oh, yes. Those were the charmed substances that some years ago were felt to contain life-preserving properties.
SCIENTIST B: You mean there was no deep fat? No steak or cream pies or . . . hot fudge?
SCIENTIST A: Those were thought to be unhealthy.

From Woody Allen's "Sleeper"

On Jan. 24, the Fox network showed an episode of its hit drama "24,"   1
the real-time thriller known for its cliffhanger tension and often-gruesome violence. Over the preceding weeks, a number of public controversies had erupted around "24," mostly focused on its portrait of Muslim terrorists and its penchant for torture scenes. The episode that was shown on the 24th only fanned the flames higher: in one scene, a terrorist enlists a hit man to kill his child for not fully supporting the jihadist cause; in another scene, the secretary of defense authorizes the torture of his son to uncover evidence of a terrorist plot.

But the explicit violence and the post-9/11 terrorist anxiety are   2
not the only elements of "24" that would have been unthinkable on prime-time network television 20 years ago. Alongside the notable change in content lies an equally notable change in form. During its 44 minutes—a real-time hour, minus 16 minutes for commercials—the episode connects the lives of 21 distinct characters, each with a clearly defined "story arc," as the Hollywood jargon has it: a defined personality with motivations and obstacles and specific relationships with other characters. Nine primary narrative threads wind their way through those 44 minutes, each drawing extensively upon events and information revealed in earlier episodes. Draw a map of all those intersecting plots and personalities, and you get structure that—where formal complexity is concerned—more closely resembles "Middlemarch" than a hit TV drama of years past like "Bonanza."

For decades, we've worked under the assumption that mass culture   3
follows a path declining steadily toward lowest-common-denominator standards, presumably because the "masses" want dumb, simple pleasures and big media companies try to give the masses what they want. But as that "24" episode suggests, the exact opposite is happening: the culture is getting more cognitively demanding, not less. To make sense of an episode of "24," you have to integrate far more information than you would have a few decades ago watching a comparable show. Beneath the violence and the ethnic stereotypes, another trend appears: to keep up with entertainment like "24," you have to pay attention, make inferences, track shifting social relationships. This is what I call the Sleeper Curve: the most debased forms of mass diversion—video games

and violent television dramas and juvenile sitcoms—turn out to be nutritional after all.

I believe that the Sleeper Curve is the single most important new   4
force altering the mental development of young people today, and I believe it is largely a force for good: enhancing our cognitive faculties, not dumbing them down. And yet you almost never hear this story in popular accounts of today's media. Instead, you hear dire tales of addiction, violence, mindless escapism. It's assumed that shows that promote smoking or gratuitous violence are bad for us, while those that thunder against teen pregnancy or intolerance have a positive role in society. Judged by that morality play standard, the story of popular culture over the past 50 years—if not 500—is a story of decline: the morals of the stories have grown darker and more ambiguous, and the antiheroes have multiplied.

The usual counterargument here is that what media have lost in   5
moral clarity, they have gained in realism. The real world doesn't come in nicely packaged public-service announcements, and we're better off with entertainment like "The Sopranos" that reflects our fallen state with all its ethical ambiguity. I happen to be sympathetic to that argument, but it's not the one I want to make here. I think there is another way to assess the social virtue of pop culture, one that looks at media as a kind of cognitive workout, not as a series of life lessons. There may indeed be more "negative messages" in the mediasphere today. But that's not the only way to evaluate whether our television shows or video games are having a positive impact. Just as important—if not more important—is the kind of thinking you have to do to make sense of a cultural experience. That is where the Sleeper Curve becomes visible.

TELEVISED INTELLIGENCE

Consider the cognitive demands that televised narratives place on   6
their viewers. With many shows that we associate with "quality" entertainment—"The Mary Tyler Moore Show," "Murphy Brown," "Frasier"—the intelligence arrives fully formed in the words and actions of the characters on-screen. They say witty things to one another and avoid lapsing into tired sitcom clichés, and we smile along in our living rooms, enjoying the company of these smart people. But assuming we're bright enough to understand the sentences they're saying, there's no intellectual labor involved in enjoying the show as a viewer. You no more challenge your mind by watching these intelligent shows than you challenge your body watching "Monday Night Football." The intellectual work is happening on-screen, not off.

But another kind of televised intelligence is on the rise. Think of   7
the cognitive benefits conventionally ascribed to reading: attention,
patience, retention, the parsing of narrative threads. Over the last half-
century, programming on TV has increased the demands it places on
precisely these mental faculties. This growing complexity involves
three primary elements: multiple threading, flashing arrows and social
networks.

According to television lore, the age of multiple threads began   8
with the arrival in 1981 of "Hill Street Blues," the Steven Bochco police
drama invariably praised for its "gritty realism." Watch an episode of
"Hill Street Blues" side by side with any major drama from the preceding decades—"Starsky and Hutch," for instance, or "Dragnet"—and
the structural transformation will jump out at you. The earlier shows
follow one or two lead characters, adhere to a single dominant plot and
reach a decisive conclusion at the end of the episode. Draw an outline
of the narrative threads in almost every "Dragnet" episode, and it will
be a single line: from the initial crime scene, through the investigation,
to the eventual cracking of the case. A typical "Starsky and Hutch"
episode offers only the slightest variation on this linear formula: the
introduction of a comic subplot that usually appears only at the tail
ends of the episode, creating a structure that looks like this graph. The
vertical axis represents the number of individual threads, and the horizontal axis is time.

"STARSKY AND HUTCH" (ANY EPISODE)

A "Hill Street Blues" episode complicates the picture in a number   9
of profound ways. The narrative weaves together a collection of distinct strands—sometimes as many as 10, though at least half of the
threads involve only a few quick scenes scattered through the episode.
The number of primary characters—and not just bit parts—swells significantly. And the episode has fuzzy borders: picking up one or two
threads from previous episodes at the outset and leaving one or two
threads open at the end. Charted graphically, an average episode looks
like this:

"HILL STREET BLUES" (EPISODE 85)

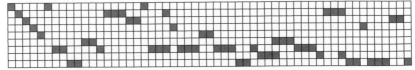

Critics generally cite "Hill Street Blues" as the beginning of "serious drama" native in the television medium—differentiating the series from the single-episode dramatic programs from the 50's, which were Broadway plays performed in front of a camera. But the "Hill Street" innovations weren't all that original; they'd long played a defining role in popular television, just not during the evening hours. The structure of a "Hill Street" episode—and indeed of all the critically acclaimed dramas that followed, from "thirtysomething" to "Six Feet Under"—is the structure of a soap opera. "Hill Street Blues" might have sparked a new golden age of television drama during its seven-year run, but it did so by using a few crucial tricks that "Guiding Light" and "General Hospital" mastered long before.   10

Bochco's genius with "Hill Street" was to marry complex narrative structure with complex subject matter. "Dallas" had already shown that the extended, interwoven threads of the soap-opera genre could survive the weeklong interruptions of a prime-time show, but the actual content of "Dallas" was fluff. (The most probing issue it addressed was the question, now folkloric, of who shot J.R.) "All in the Family" and "Rhoda" showed that you could tackle complex social issues, but they did their tackling in the comfort of the sitcom living room. "Hill Street" had richly drawn characters confronting difficult social issues and a narrative structure to match.   11

Since "Hill Street" appeared, the multi-threaded drama has become the most widespread fictional genre on prime time: "St. Elsewhere," "L.A. Law," "thirtysomething," "Twin Peaks," "N.Y.P.D. Blue," "E.R.," "The West Wing," "Alias," "Lost." (The only prominent holdouts in drama are shows like "Law and Order" that have essentially updated the venerable "Dragnet" format and thus remained anchored to a single narrative line.) Since the early 80's, however, there has been a noticeable increase in narrative complexity in these dramas. The most ambitious show on TV to date, "The Sopranos," routinely follows up to a dozen distinct threads over the course of an episode, with more than 20 recurring characters. An episode from late in the first season looks like this: 12

"THE SOPRANOS" (EPISODE 8)

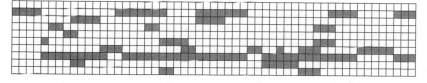

The total number of active threads equals the multiple plots of   13
"Hill Street," but here each thread is more substantial. The show does-
n't offer a clear distinction between dominant and minor plots; each
story line carries its weight in the mix. The episode also displays a
chordal mode of storytelling entirely absent from "Hill Street": a single
scene in "The Sopranos" will often connect to three different threads at
the same time, layering one plot atop another. And every single thread
in this "Sopranos" episode builds on events from previous episodes
and continues on through the rest of the season and beyond.

Put those charts together, and you have a portrait of the Sleeper   14
Curve rising over the past 30 years of popular television. In a sense, this
is as much a map of cognitive changes in the popular mind as it is a map
of on-screen developments, as if the media titans decided to condition
our brains to follow ever-larger numbers of simultaneous threads. Before
"Hill Street," the conventional wisdom among television execs was that
audiences wouldn't be comfortable following more than three plots in a
single episode, and indeed, the "Hill Street" pilot, which was shown in
January 1981, brought complaints from viewers that the show was too
complicated. Fast-forward two decades, and shows like "The Sopranos"
engage their audiences with narratives that make "Hill Street" look like
"Three's Company." Audiences happily embrace that complexity because
they've been trained by two decades of multi-threaded dramas.

Multi-threading is the most celebrated structural feature of the   15
modern television drama, and it certainly deserves some of the honor that
has been doled out to it. And yet multi-threading is only part of the story.

THE CASE FOR CONFUSION

Shortly after the arrival of the first-generation slasher movies—   16
"Halloween," "Friday the 13th"—Paramount released a mock-slasher
flick called "Student Bodies," parodying the genre just as the "Scream"
series would do 15 years later. In one scene, the obligatory nubile
teenage baby sitter hears a noise outside a suburban house; she opens
the door to investigate, finds nothing and then goes back inside. As the
door shuts behind her, the camera swoops in on the doorknob, and we
see that she has left the door unlocked. The camera pulls back and then
swoops down again for emphasis. And then a flashing arrow appears
on the screen, with text that helpfully explains: "Unlocked!"

That flashing arrow is parody, of course, but it's merely an exag-   17
gerated version of a device popular stories use all the time. When a sci-fi
script inserts into some advanced lab a nonscientist who keeps asking
the science geeks to explain what they're doing with that particle accelerator, that's a flashing arrow that gives the audience precisely the

information it needs in order to make sense of the ensuing plot. ("Whatever you do, don't spill water on it, or you'll set off a massive explosion!") These hints serve as a kind of narrative hand-holding. Implicitly, they say to the audience, "We realize you have no idea what a particle accelerator is, but here's the deal: all you need to know is that it's a big fancy thing that explodes when wet." They focus the mind on relevant details: "Don't worry about whether the baby sitter is going to break up with her boyfriend. Worry about that guy lurking in the bushes." They reduce the amount of analytic work you need to do to make sense of a story. All you have to do is follow the arrows.

By this standard, popular television has never been harder to fol- 18
low. If narrative threads have experienced a population explosion over the past 20 years, flashing arrows have grown correspondingly scarce. Watching our pinnacle of early 80's TV drama, "Hill Street Blues," we find there's an informational wholeness to each scene that differs markedly from what you see on shows like "The West Wing" or "The Sopranos" or "Alias" or "E.R."

"Hill Street" has ambiguities about future events: will a convicted 19
killer be executed? Will Furillo marry Joyce Davenport? Will Renko find it in himself to bust a favorite singer for cocaine possession? But the present-tense of each scene explains itself to the viewer with little ambiguity. There's an open question or a mystery driving each of these stories—how will it all turn out?—but there's no mystery about the immediate activity on the screen. A contemporary drama like "The West Wing," on the other hand, constantly embeds mysteries into the present-tense events: you see characters performing actions or discussing events about which crucial information has been deliberately withheld. Anyone who has watched more than a handful of "The West Wing" episodes closely will know the feeling: scene after scene refers to some clearly crucial but unexplained piece of information, and after the sixth reference, you'll find yourself wishing you could rewind the tape to figure out what they're talking about, assuming you've missed something. And then you realize that you're supposed to be confused. The open question posed by these sequences is not "How will this turn out in the end?" The question is "What's happening right now?"

The deliberate lack of hand-holding extends down to the micro- 20
level of dialogue as well. Popular entertainment that addresses technical issues—whether they are the intricacies of passing legislation, or of performing a heart bypass, or of operating a particle accelerator— conventionally switches between two modes of information in dialogue: texture and substance. Texture is all the arcane verbiage provided to convince the viewer that they're watching Actual Doctors at Work; substance is the material planted amid the background texture that the viewer needs make sense of the plot.

Conventionally, narratives demarcate the line between texture   21
and substance by inserting cues that flag or translate the important
data. There's an unintentionally comical moment in the 2004 blockbuster "The Day After Tomorrow" in which the beleaguered climatolo-
gist (played by Dennis Quaid) announces his theory about the imminent
arrival of a new ice age to a gathering of government officials. In his
speech, he warns that "we have hit a critical desalinization point!" At
this moment, the writer-director Roland Emmerich—a master of
brazen arrow-flashing—has an official follow with the obliging remark:
"It would explain what's driving this extreme weather." They might
as well have had a flashing "Unlocked!" arrow on the screen.

The dialogue on shows like "The West Wing" and "E.R.," on the   22
other hand, doesn't talk down to its audiences. It rushes by, the words
accelerating in sync with the high-speed tracking shots that glide
through the corridors and operating rooms. The characters talk faster
in these shows, but the truly remarkable thing about the dialogue is not
purely a matter of speed; it's the willingness to immerse the audience
in information that most viewers won't understand. Here's a typical
scene from "E.R.":

[WEAVER AND WRIGHT push a gurney containing a 16-year-old girl.   23
Her parents, JANNA AND FRANK MIKAMI, follow close behind.
CARTER AND LUCY fall in.]

> WEAVER: 16-year-old, unconscious, history of biliary atresia.
> CARTER: Hepatic coma?
> WEAVER: Looks like it.
> MR. MIKAMI: She was doing fine until six months ago.
> CARTER: What medication is she on?
> MRS. MIKAMI: Ampicillin, tobramycin, vitamins a, d and k.
> LUCY: Skin's jaundiced.
> WEAVER: Same with the sclera. Breath smells sweet.
> CARTER: Fetor hepaticus?
> WEAVER: Yep.
> LUCY: What's that?
> WEAVER: Her liver's shut down. Let's dip a urine. [To CARTER]
>   Guys, it's getting a little crowded in here, why don't you deal
>   with the parents? Start lactulose, 30 cc's per NG.
> CARTER: We're giving medicine to clean her blood.
> WEAVER: Blood in the urine, two-plus.
> CARTER: The liver failure is causing her blood not to clot.
> MRS. MIKAMI: Oh, God. . . .
> CARTER: Is she on the transplant list?
> MR. MIKAMI: She's been Status 2a for six months, but they
>   haven't been able to find her a match.

CARTER: Why? What's her blood type?

MR. MIKAMI: AB.

[This hits CARTER like a lightning bolt. LUCY gets it, too. They share a look.]

There are flashing arrows here, of course—"The liver failure is causing her blood not to clot"—but the ratio of medical jargon to layperson translation is remarkably high. From a purely narrative point of view, the decisive line arrives at the very end: "AB." The 16-year-old's blood type connects her to an earlier plot line, involving a cerebral-hemorrhage victim who—after being dramatically revived in one of the opening scenes—ends up brain-dead. Far earlier, before the liver-failure scene above, Carter briefly discusses harvesting the hemorrhage victim's organs for transplants, and another doctor makes a passing reference to his blood type being the rare AB (thus making him an unlikely donor). The twist here revolves around a statistically unlikely event happening at the E.R.—an otherwise perfect liver donor showing up just in time to donate his liver to a recipient with the same rare blood type. But the show reveals this twist with remarkable subtlety. To make sense of that last "AB" line—and the look of disbelief on Carter's and Lucy's faces—you have to recall a passing remark uttered earlier regarding a character who belongs to a completely different thread. Shows like "E.R." may have more blood and guts than popular TV had a generation ago, but when it comes to storytelling, they possess a quality that can only be described as subtlety and discretion. 24

EVEN BAD TV IS BETTER

Skeptics might argue that I have stacked the deck here by focusing on relatively highbrow titles like "The Sopranos" or "The West Wing," when in fact the most significant change in the last five years of narrative entertainment involves reality TV. Does the contemporary pop cultural landscape look quite as promising if the representative show is "Joe Millionaire" instead of "The West Wing"? 25

I think it does, but to answer that question properly, you have to avoid the tendency to sentimentalize the past. When people talk about the golden age of television in the early 70's—invoking shows like "The Mary Tyler Moore Show" and "All in the Family"—they forget to mention how awful most television programming was during much of that decade. If you're going to look at pop-culture trends, you have to compare apples to apples, or in this case, lemons to lemons. The relevant comparison is not between "Joe Millionaire" and "MASH"; it's between "Joe Millionaire" and "The Newlywed Game," or between "Survivor" and "The Love Boat." 26

What you see when you make these head-to-head comparisons is that a rising tide of complexity has been lifting programming at the bottom of the quality spectrum and at the top. "The Sopranos" is several times more demanding of its audiences than "Hill Street" was, and "Joe Millionaire" has made comparable advances over "Battle of the Network Stars." This is the ultimate test of the Sleeper Curve theory: even the junk has improved.

If early television took its cues from the stage, today's reality programming is reliably structured like a video game: a series of competitive tests, growing more challenging over time. Many reality shows borrow a subtler device from gaming culture as well: the rules aren't fully established at the outset. You learn as you play.   27

On a show like "Survivor" or "The Apprentice," the participants— and the audience—know the general objective of the series, but each episode involves new challenges that haven't been ordained in advance. The final round of the first season of "The Apprentice," for instance, threw a monkey wrench into the strategy that governed the play up to that point, when Trump announced that the two remaining apprentices would have to assemble and manage a team of subordinates who had already been fired in earlier episodes of the show. All of a sudden the overarching objective of the game—do anything to avoid being fired— presented a potential conflict to the remaining two contenders: the structure of the final round favored the survivor who had maintained the best relationships with his comrades. Suddenly, it wasn't enough just to have clawed your way to the top; you had to have made friends while clawing. The original "Joe Millionaire" went so far as to undermine the most fundamental convention of all—that the show's creators don't openly lie to the contestants about the prizes—by inducing a construction worker to pose as man of means while 20 women competed for his attention.   28

Reality programming borrowed another key ingredient from games: the intellectual labor of probing the system's rules for weak spots and opportunities. As each show discloses its conventions, and each participant reveals his or her personality traits and background, the intrigue in watching comes from figuring out how the participants should best navigate the environment that has been created for them. The pleasure in these shows comes not from watching other people being humiliated on national television; it comes from depositing other people in a complex, high-pressure environment where no established strategies exist and watching them find their bearings. That's why the water-cooler conversation about these shows invariably tracks in on the strategy displayed on the previous night's episode: why did Kwame pick Omarosa in that final round? What devious strategy is Richard Hatch concocting now?   29

When we watch these shows, the part of our brain that monitors the emotional lives of the people around us—the part that tracks subtle   30 shifts in intonation and gesture and facial expression—scrutinizes the action on the screen, looking for clues. We trust certain characters implicitly and vote others off the island in a heartbeat. Traditional narrative shows also trigger emotional connections to the characters, but those connections don't have the same participatory effect, because traditional narratives aren't explicitly about strategy. The phrase "Monday-morning quarterbacking" describes the engaged feeling that spectators have in relation to games as opposed to stories. We absorb stories, but we second-guess games. Reality programming has brought that second-guessing to prime time, only the game in question revolves around social dexterity rather than the physical kind.

THE REWARDS OF SMART CULTURE

The quickest way to appreciate the Sleeper Curve's cognitive training is to   31
sit down and watch a few hours of hit programming from the late 70's on Nick at Nite or the SOAPnet channel or on DVD. The modern viewer who watches a show like "Dallas" today will be bored by the content—not just because the show is less salacious than today's soap operas (which it is by a small margin) but also because the show contains far less information in each scene, despite the fact that its soap-opera structure made it one of the most complicated narratives on television in its prime. With "Dallas," the modern viewer doesn't have to think to make sense of what's going on, and not having to think is boring. Many recent hit shows—"24," "Survivor," "The Sopranos," "Alias," "Lost," "The Simpsons," "E.R."—take the opposite approach, layering each scene with a thick network of affiliations. You have to focus to follow the plot, and in focusing you're exercising the parts of your brain that map social networks, that fill in missing information, that connect multiple narrative threads.

Of course, the entertainment industry isn't increasing the cognitive   32
complexity of its products for charitable reasons. The Sleeper Curve exists because there's money to be made by making culture smarter. The economics of television syndication and DVD sales mean that there's a tremendous financial pressure to make programs that can be watched multiple times, revealing new nuances and shadings on the third viewing. Meanwhile, the Web has created a forum for annotation and commentary that allows more complicated shows to prosper, thanks to the fan sites where each episode of shows like "Lost" or "Alias" is dissected with an intensity usually reserved for Talmud scholars. Finally, interactive games have trained a new generation of media consumers to probe complex environments and to think on their feet, and that gamer audience has now come to expect the same challenges from their television shows. In the end, the Sleeper Curve tells us something about the human

mind. It may be drawn toward the sensational where content is concerned—sex does sell, after all. But the mind also likes to be challenged; there's real pleasure to be found in solving puzzles, detecting patterns or unpacking a complex narrative system.

In pointing out some of the ways that popular culture has   33
improved our minds, I am not arguing that parents should stop paying attention to the way their children amuse themselves. What I am arguing for is a change in the criteria we use to determine what really is cognitive junk food and what is genuinely nourishing. Instead of a show's violent or tawdry content, instead of wardrobe malfunctions or the F-word, the true test should be whether a given show engages or sedates the mind. Is it a single thread strung together with predictable punch lines every 30 seconds? Or does it map a complex social network? Is your on-screen character running around shooting everything in sight, or is she trying to solve problems and manage resources? If your kids want to watch reality TV, encourage them to watch "Survivor" over "Fear Factor." If they want to watch a mystery show, encourage "24" over "Law and Order." If they want to play a violent game, encourage Grand Theft Auto over Quake. Indeed, it might be just as helpful to have a rating system that used mental labor and not obscenity and violence as its classification scheme for the world of mass culture.

Kids and grown-ups each can learn from their increasingly shared   34
obsessions. Too often we imagine the blurring of kid and grown-up cultures as a series of violations: the 9-year-olds who have to have nipple broaches explained to them thanks to Janet Jackson; the middle-aged guy who can't wait to get home to his Xbox. But this demographic blur has a commendable side that we don't acknowledge enough. The kids are forced to think like grown-ups: analyzing complex social networks, managing resources, tracking subtle narrative intertwinings, recognizing long-term patterns. The grown-ups, in turn, get to learn from the kids: decoding each new technological wave, parsing the interfaces and discovering the intellectual rewards of play. Parents should see this as an opportunity, not a crisis. Smart culture is no longer something you force your kids to ingest, like green vegetables. It's something you share.

Examining the Text

1. What does Johnson mean by the term "the Sleeper Curve"? How is this term related to the opening quotation from Woody Allen's movie, "Sleeper"?

2. In paragraph 5, Johnson makes a distinction between seeing the media "as a kind of cognitive workout, not as a series of life lessons." Explain this distinction in your own words. What TV shows might fall into the category of "cognitive workout"? What shows would be more likely to offer "life lessons"?

3. What does Johnson mean by "flashing arrows" in TV shows? What function do flashing arrows serve? How have they changed over the years?

4. According to Johnson, what kind of intellectual and social complexity does reality TV provide its viewers? Do you think Johnson's argument about reality TV is persuasive? Why or why not?

5. *Thinking rhetorically*: Following up on the "as you read" suggestion in the introduction to this article, think about the evidence that Johnson uses to support his claim that current TV shows are cognitively stimulating. Select one specific piece of evidence from the article that you find very convincing and one that you find unconvincing. Based on a comparison of these two pieces of evidence, what general conclusions can you draw about the characteristics of good and weak evidence?

For Group Discussion

In a small group, have one of the group members read aloud the last paragraph of the article, in which Johnson discusses how parents and children can benefit from "smart culture" on TV. Make a list of the benefits for kids and the benefits for parents. Then discuss whether you think each of the benefits can be realistically achieved by watching "smart TV." Draw on your own experiences and your own knowledge of TV programs in order to decide whether Johnson's argument is reasonable or whether he's overstating the positives of watching TV.

Writing Suggestion

Johnson provides some visual evidence to support his assertion that TV shows have become increasingly complex. The three graphs included in the article show the number of plot threads in single episodes of "Starsky and Hutch," "Hill Street Blues," and "The Sopranos." A quick visual comparison of these graphs does indeed suggest that "The Sopranos" has more plot threads and more interweaving of these threads than the two earlier shows. Your assignment is to create a similar chart for a current TV show of your choice. Choose a show to watch, and as you're watching keep note of each time a new plot thread occurs or there's a reference to another thread. After the show is over, plot these elements on a simple chart in which the vertical axis represents each plot thread and the horizontal axis represents time. To make the task easier, label each plot thread on the vertical axis (something Johnson doesn't do). After you've finished the chart, write a paragraph in which you draw conclusions about the relative complexity of the show as compared to the three examples Johnson offers.

Interpreting Television

1. REALITY TV

The Tribe Has Spoken

Rebecca Gardyn

At the risk of losing all credibility, I have a confession to make: I, Madeleine Sorapure, am a "Survivor" addict: by day, a relatively normal, fairly well-balanced, reasonably intelligent college teacher; by night (but only Thursday night), a glued-to-the-TV, won't-answer-the-phone, cheering and jeering "Survivor" nut. My co-author, Michael Petracca, has somehow escaped the seductions of this particular reality TV show. Frankly, I think he doesn't know what he's missing, especially when you add the online fantasy "Survivor" games, the cyber-gossip of "Survivor" bulletin board discussions, and, of course, the real-life water-cooler gossip with other "Survivor" nuts.

As long as I'm at it, I might as well also admit that I've been known to watch "Big Brother," "The Real World," "Fear Factor," and "The Apprentice." At one point or another I've probably seen all of the reality dating shows, even including (shudder) that one where the parents give prospective suitors a lie detector test and invariably choose the wrong guy for their daughter. I don't watch very much else on TV, and I understand perfectly well that reality TV is not reality, but for some reason, these shows appeal to me in a big way.

Do I fit the demographic profile of the reality TV fanatic? Yes, but so do you. According to Rebecca Gardyn, 70 percent of 18- to 24-year-olds watch reality television programs, and 44 percent of this group prefer to watch real people over scripted characters on TV. In fact, polls have shown that viewers of reality TV shows come from all demographic groups. While age and gender are important variables in determining why people watch these shows, each group nevertheless seems to have found compelling reasons for watching.

*But, as Gardyn admits, these shows may or may not pass the test of time. The current popularity of reality television may not last, especially as networks struggle to come up with interesting new scenarios to keep viewers hooked. Do any of us really want to see supermodels eat cow intestines? Is it worthwhile and uplifting to watch couples bickering and cheating on each other in exotic locations? Will the reality TV trend be a victim of its own outrageousness? **As you read,** consider your own attitudes toward reality TV shows. Do you enjoy watching them? Why or why not?*

Reality TV may have some staying power after all. This fall season,   1
every major network has at least one reality series on its docket—from
the debut of CBS's *The Amazing Race* to the return of ABC's *The Mole*
and Fox's *Temptation Island*. And for the first time, reality programs will
have the opportunity to jockey alongside sitcoms and dramas for
industry kudos at the Primetime Emmy Awards later this month, since
previously there were no categories that accommodated the genre. This
year, voting procedures and prize categories have been revamped to
make room for reality programs. CBS's *Survivor* has five nominations.
Perhaps a win or two will allow this oft-criticized genre to shed its reputation as a fly-by-night novelty and become a legitimate contender in
the ever-cluttered TV outback.

Or not. While some media experts believe reality television will   2
alter the topography of TV Land, others are sure this season will
mark the beginning of the end for the format, as over-scheduling
tends to lead to overkill. Of course, the ultimate vote will be cast by
the viewing public, and for now, that includes almost half of all
Americans, as well as a full 70 percent of 18- to 24-year-olds and
57 percent of 25- to 34-year-olds—two segments most desired by
advertisers.

What is it about the new crop of reality TV programs that has so   3
many viewers riveted? What personality types are attracted to this
genre? And what advertising messages and tactics are apt to resonate
with these viewers? As the copycats mount, programmers and advertisers who want to connect with consumers through this television
vehicle may benefit from understanding not only the demographic
composition of this vast audience, but its attitudes, character traits and
motivations for tuning in.

Forty-five percent of all Americans watch reality television pro-   4
grams. Of those, 27 percent consider themselves die-hard fans, watching
as many episodes as possible, according to a nationally representative
telephone survey of 1,008 people conducted exclusively for *American
Demographics* by Edison, N.J.-based Bruskin Research. In fact, 37 percent
of all Americans prefer to watch real people on television rather than
scripted characters.

While much has been reported about how reality TV is reeling in   5
teens and young adults for the networks, the programs actually attract
a much wider fan base. Brian Devinny, who writes the online column,
"The Reality Factor," on 3BigShows.com, says he receives e-mail from
"all walks of life," from housewives to lawyers, across all income and
age brackets. "The shows reach out to so many people on so many
levels," Devinny says. "When *Survivor I* was on, I had many retirees
write in to me rooting for 72-year-old Rudy. It's not just young people
tuning in."

The results of the *American Demographics*/Bruskin survey illus-   6
trate that diversity. Of all those who watch reality television, 55 percent
are ages 35 or older. In fact, even though 18- to 24-year-olds are the
most likely age group to tune in, the largest portion of the reality TV
audience (29 percent) is actually the 35- to 49-year-old group. And
when it comes to gender divides, women are the die-hard fans, making
up 64 percent of regular viewers (those who watch as many episodes as
they can), while occasional viewers are slightly more male (55 percent
versus 45 percent). Also noteworthy: reality TV watchers are primarily in
the middle- to low-income brackets—58 percent have annual incomes
under $50,000—and Southerners account for 39 percent of all reality TV
viewers, compared with about 20 percent of residents in each of the
Northeast, North Central and Western regions.

What exactly is it about reality TV that has attracted such a dis-   7
parate group? According to Encino, Calif.-based E-Poll's syndicated
online survey of 2,121 Americans, ages 18 to 54, the No. 1 reason people
watch is the thrill of "guessing who will win or be eliminated from the
show." That thrill is the reason cited by 69 percent of all reality TV
watchers, and 84 percent of regular viewers, who make a point to
watch. The second and third most common reasons viewers tune in are
to "see people face challenging situations" and "imagining how I
would perform in similar situations," stated by 63 percent and 42 percent of all viewers, respectively.

Of course, reasons for watching reality TV differ dramatically   8
across age and gender divides, according to E-Poll's findings. For example, 43 percent of 18- to 34-year-old viewers say they tune in because
they like to see conflict break out among the contestants, compared with
29 percent of 35- to 54-year-olds. The older crowd, on the other hand, is
more intrigued than younger viewers with following the contestants'
strategies (41 percent versus 36 percent). Men are more than three times
as likely as women to tune in to see physically attractive contestants
(31 percent versus 9 percent), while women are more likely than men to
tune in because they like guessing the outcomes (72 percent versus
65 percent).

Before becoming a contestant on *The Mole* and an alternate for *Big* 9
Brother I, Wendi Wendt, 30, from Cedar Rapids, Iowa, was a fan of *Surv-*
ivor, and she continues to be an avid viewer of the reality TV genre.
"It's in my blood now," she says. Her current fave is *Fear Factor*. "I
enjoy seeing real people getting the chance to do extraordinary things,
and how they evolve as people," she says. And while Wendt has heard
the accusations that the producers of *Survivor* and other reality shows
allegedly manipulate outcomes, she's not bothered. Speaking from
experience, she notes: "How the players feel is real. You can see their

true emotions, their frustrations, their joy. That's real enough for me. If some of the smaller details aren't so real, so be it."

But other fans fear that producers of the programs are starting   10
to tread too far off the path of "real" intentions. In so doing, they may start to lose a core group of viewers, says Mary Beam, a 38-year-old reality TV fan from Cleveland, Texas, who founded the Web site, RealityTVFans.com. "Some of the shows have started to cast only beautiful Hollywood types, who are just in it to become actresses, or overly obnoxious people who are obviously playing a role," she says. In fact, of 18- to 54-year-olds who don't watch reality programs, 38 percent say it is because "the contestants are just trying to get famous," according to E-Poll. Says Beam: "The viewers want to see people who look or act like we do. If we wanted fake, we'd be watching sitcoms." In fact, E-Poll also found that 81 percent of viewers who stopped watching a reality program after sampling a show did so because they found the show to be "too scripted or not real enough."

No group is more adamant about keeping reality TV real than the   11
18- to 24-year-old crowd, 44 percent of whom say they prefer to watch real people to scripted characters, according to the *American Demographics/Bruskin* survey. In fact, 27 percent of America's youth says that reality television is better than what's currently offered on the networks during prime time, compared with 15 percent of the total population who say the same.

Reality Bites

Of the 18- to 54-year-olds who avoid reality television shows, 60 percent say they can always find something better to watch.

Reasons for *Not* Watching Reality TV	Total	Men	Women	18–34	35–54
Can always find something better to watch	**60%**	60%	61%	56%	63%
Too trashy or low-class	**55%**	57%	53%	56%	55%
Don't like the human values/traits they present	**49%**	49%	49%	47%	50%
Don't care about the contestants	**44%**	53%	35%	52%	39%
Contestants are just trying to get famous	**38%**	38%	38%	43%	35%
I can't identify with the contestants	**35%**	31%	40%	34%	36%
They are faked or rigged	**35%**	36%	33%	43%	28%
Too voyeuristic/don't like spying on people	**33%**	31%	36%	28%	37%
Contestant strategy is weak or overblown	**24%**	27%	22%	26%	22%
Contestants are not appealing/attractive	**12%**	16%	7%	12%	11%

Note: Multiple answers allowed.

Source: E-Poll

"These kids grew up with cable television, where unscripted,   12
documentary-style shows have always been a staple," says Ed Martin,
programming editor at Myers Reports, which provides research for
and about the media industry. "This is what TV is to them," he adds,
noting that MTV's *The Real World* started making inroads with the
genre 10 years ago. The popularity of this format with youth also has a
lot to do with their growing up in a democratized society, where the
Internet, Web cams and other technologies give the average Joe the
ability to personalize his entertainment, notes Andy Dehnart, a 23-
year-old self-described "reality TV addict." "In today's world, anyone
can create a Web site, like I did," says Dehnart, who founded Reality-
Blurred.com, a site that covers reality show news. "Web logs are huge.
Memoirs have taken off. As a culture, we've become so much more
interested in real people."

Jason Thompson, 20, from League City, Texas, who watches   13
"every reality show I can find," says he likes shows that allow him
to get to know the contestants. After the first *Big Brother* aired last
summer, Thompson felt at ease sending e-mails to contestant
Britney Petros and offered to design a Web page for her fans.
Thompson and Petros ended up talking on the phone for half an
hour, and while he didn't get the job to design her site, the two have
become friends and trade e-mails, he says. Thompson adds that
he, too, would like to be famous someday, and reality shows give
him hope that he could be. "Because the contestants are regular
people just like me, it makes me feel like I could be one of them,"
Thompson says.

This fascination with instant celebrity, focused on everyday peo-   14
ple who find fame overnight, has been fueled by reality TV. But
advertisers, especially those targeting youth, have been slow to catch
on, says Irma Zandl, president of The Zandl Group, a market research
firm in New York that caters to the under-30 segment. She cites a
recent series of Levi's ads as an example of a missed opportunity.
Each ad highlighted a teenager on a karaoke stage, singing horribly.
"If [Levi's executives] had instead [recruited] young people who
could really sing, and used the campaign to find the next 'N Sync,
everyone would have been buzzing about it," says Zandl. She advises
marketers to cash in on the reality TV-driven desire for fame and
attention by creating messages that promise the possibility of overnight success. She suggests that companies incorporate *Star Search*–
like competitions in their campaigns, or offer other contests with
TV-related prizes, such as walk-on parts or backstage passes to a television show.

Why Watch?

Of the 18- to 54-year-old reality TV viewers, only 19 percent cite the physical attractiveness of the contestants as a main reason they watch the programs. But 31 percent of men say that it is, in fact, those beautiful bods that keep them tuned in.

Reasons for Watching Reality TV	Total	Watch Reality TV Regularly	Watch Reality TV Occasionally	Men	Women	18–34	35–54
Guessing who will win or be eliminated	69%	84%	60%	65%	72%	67%	71%
Seeing real people face challenging situations	63%	81%	53%	60%	65%	61%	65%
Imagining how I would act in similar situations	42%	51%	37%	43%	41%	42%	42%
Following contestants' strategies	38%	54%	29%	39%	37%	36%	41%
Fights among contestants	37%	49%	30%	39%	35%	43%	29%
Making fun of contestants	28%	31%	26%	32%	24%	32%	21%
Nothing better to watch	25%	11%	32%	26%	24%	26%	23%
Exotic locations	23%	31%	19%	24%	23%	23%	24%
Physically attractive contestants	19%	25%	16%	31%	9%	23%	14%
Romance/relationships among contestants	18%	23%	15%	16%	21%	22%	13%

Note: Multiple answers allowed.

Source: E-Poll

If You Build It

Those who never watch reality television programs may be enticed with the right plotline: a quarter (26 percent) say they'd be interested in viewing a show that had contestants breaking world records, and 21 percent would like to see a show that challenged contestants to find their way out of a remote location.

Percent Who Would Have Interest in Watching the Following Types of Reality TV Plots:	Total	Watch Reality TV Regularly	Watch Reality TV Occasionally	Never Watch Reality TV	Men	Women	18–34	35–54
Racing across the country	40%	57%	46%	20%	45%	34%	42%	37%
Finding way out of a remote location	56%	86%	69%	21%	58%	54%	62%	50%
Losing weight	19%	28%	19%	12%	13%	24%	20%	17%
Beauty contest	13%	17%	15%	8%	17%	9%	17%	8%
Getting the girl/guy	23%	37%	28%	8%	25%	22%	30%	15%
Breaking a world record	44%	52%	54%	26%	48%	41%	44%	45%
Getting a job	20%	26%	23%	13%	21%	19%	21%	19%
Quitting smoking	16%	18%	19%	10%	13%	19%	16%	16%
Truth or dare	64%	73%	58%	18%	48%	48%	55%	40%

Note: Multiple answers allowed.

Source: E-Poll

Another way to reach reality TV viewers is by tapping in to their   15
adventurous personalities and active lifestyles. According to the
American Demographics/Bruskin survey, 40 percent of reality television
viewers consider themselves adventurous, and 86 percent lead active
lives, compared with 31 percent and 79 percent of nonreality watchers,
respectively. Barbara Hammack, 38, from Houston, has no desire to be
famous, but every desire to add some spice to her life. "People who
watch reality TV, like myself, have some deep desire to go on some
great adventure, but maybe they just never had the opportunity or
resources to do it themselves," she says. Hammack, who works in the
oil and gas industry, describes herself as a "regular job, average-income
kind of gal." She says she always wished she had gone into a more
adventurous field, such as archaeology. Hammack is itching to be a
contestant on a reality show and has already tried out for *The Mole*,
Big Brother 2 and *Survivor 4*. She says she's surprised at how few reality
TV viewers she meets who actually want to participate in the shows.
This observation is supported by our survey, which found that for
many reality TV fans, their adventurous streak is purely a vicarious
one: 57 percent say they are actually cautious by nature.

Reebok, by outfitting the feet of *Survivor* participants, masterfully   16
tapped in to the adventurous spirit of reality fans. And since then,
other advertisers followed, with mixed success. Pontiac, the top advertiser for *Survivor II*, according to Competitive Media Reporting, shelled
out $7.2 million to advertise its outdoorsy Aztek truck/camper during
the program, both in commercial spots and as a coveted prize during
one episode of the show. Jason Thompson, the reality enthusiast from
Texas, says that the car manufacturer made a smart move. "Before seeing it in the program, I didn't really know too much about the car," he
says. However, he adds, some products work better than others.
Regarding the abundance of product placement on *Survivor II* by
Mountain Dew soda and Doritos tortilla chips, Thompson says: "I've
always hated Mountain Dew. I'm not going to run out and buy it now
because it was on Survivor." Dehnart, of RealityBlurred.com, says that
advertisers should also be worried about potential backlash from product placement strategy. "When it starts to interfere with the show, a lot
of fans resent it," he says.

In addition to rethinking commercial messages and appropriate   17
product placements on the programs, advertisers developing new
strategies for this audience may also want to pay attention to what's
happening online. According to E-Poll, a full 70 percent of avid fans,
ages 18 to 54, visit Web sites related to the reality shows they prefer, as
do a third (32 percent) of occasional viewers. Twenty-six percent of all
reality TV viewers read or post messages online regarding the genre;
and 22 percent play Internet games that are based on the shows.

This interactivity is not strictly a phenomenon for the younger   18
viewers: while 34 percent of 18- to 34-year-olds visit Web sites related to reality shows, so do 27 percent of 35- to 54-year-olds. At
RealityTV Fans.com, the average age range of message board visitors
is 35 to 55, and they are primarily women, says webmaster Mary Beam.

Wendy Veazey, a 38-year-old mother of two from Metairie, La., finds   19
plenty of other fans in her age group chatting it up on reality TV message
boards and as her opponents on fantasy *Survivor* games. Talking with
others in real time, guessing strategies and analyzing the possible outcomes brings a whole new component to the shows, says Veazey. "The
Internet completes the whole experience." Last year, during the first
Big Brother series, for example, Veazey, who works from home, kept Internet feeds running all day, so she could eavesdrop on the contestants,
whom she came to think of as "friends." In fact, while the critics panned
Big Brother I, and the TV ratings didn't hold a candle to *Survivor*, the viewers who supplemented their TV watching with online participation overwhelmingly loved the show, says Beam of RealityTVFans.com. "There's a
whole subculture on the Net that a lot of people don't know about."

Ed Martin of the Myers Reports anticipates that real-time interac-   20
tivity will be the next evolution of reality TV, and some networks are
already taking steps toward that end. This fall, the WB network will

Ratings Toppers

Temptation Island tops the Nielsen ratings for teens and young adults.

Nielsen Ratings for Reality Programs Aired During the 2000–2001 Season, by Age Group[*]:	12–17	18–24	18–34	25–54	50+	Women 18+	Men 18+
Temptation Island (FOX)	9.1	10.6	12.0	8.0	3.0	7.0	6.5
Survivor I (CBS)	7.4	9.2	12.1	12.7	12.6	13.3	11.2
Boot Camp (FOX)	7.3	5.9	6.6	5.1	2.1	4.0	4.4
Survivor II (CBS)	7.0	6.6	12.3	13.7	12.5	13.5	11.5
The Mole (ABC)	3.9	4.0	5.7	5.4	5.4	5.9	4.5
Fear Factor (NBC)	3.8	4.4	5.4	5.3	4.5	5.1	4.7
Spy TV (NBC)	2.9	4.4	5.8	5.1	3.4	4.9	4.0
Popstars (WB)	2.7	1.8	1.7	1.2	0.4	1.3	0.7
Chains of Love (UPN)	1.4	0.9	1.2	1.0	0.5	0.9	0.8
Big Brother I (CBS)	N/A	N/A	3.8	4.2	4.7	5.0	3.3

[*]A rating represents the estimated percentage of people in each age group watching the
named show during the 2000–2001 season. For example, Temptation Island received a 9.1
rating among 12- to 17-year-olds, meaning that 9.1 percent of teens tuned in to that program.
Source: Analysis of Nielsen Media Research, 10/2/2000–9/30/2001, by The Media Edge.

Crowd Pleasers

When it comes to reality TV's online community, age doesn't seem to be a factor. Nineteen percent of 18- to 34-year-olds have read or posted messages online about reality TV shows, as have 16 percent of the 35- to 54-year-old crowd.

	Total	Watch Reality TV Regularly	Watch Reality TV Occasionally	Never Watch Reality TV	Men	Women	18-34	35-54
Visit Web sites related to reality TV shows	31%	70%	32%	3%	29%	32%	34%	27%
Play online games based on reality TV shows	16%	35%	16%	2%	16%	16%	17%	14%
Read or post online messages about reality TV shows	18%	41%	18%	2%	18%	17%	19%	16%
Read articles about reality TV shows	47%	84%	53%	13%	43%	50%	49%	44%
Watch interviews with reality TV show contestants	46%	91%	54%	7%	41%	52%	50%	43%

Note: Multiple answers allowed.

Source: E-Poll

191

debut a new program called *Lost in the USA*, that will allow viewers to interact with the contestants, online and by phone, giving them the power to tip off participants to their opponents' strategies. And then there's ABC's much anticipated *The Runner*, which makes its debut in January, and will actually turn viewers into contestants. One man (or woman) will attempt to cross the country without being identified by viewers. If successful, the runner wins $1 million. If unsuccessful, the identifier(s) can claim all or part of the prize. ABC will provide clues online and during the televised show.

To reach the next generation of television viewers, advertisers   21
will have to get more creative about combining efforts across both TV and the Internet, says Ira Matathia, global director of business development for advertising conglomerate Euro RSCG Worldwide. Reality TV has created a whole new range of challenges for advertisers, he says, adding, "We are going to have to work a hell of a lot harder to reach people in the coming years."

But first, let's face the fall.   22

Examining the Text

1. What advice do Gardyn and the television and advertising executives quoted here give about effective advertising on reality TV shows? In what ways is effective advertising on reality shows different from advertising on scripted shows, talk shows, or sports shows?

2. According to Gardyn, what role does the Web (and other interactive forums) play in terms of reality TV programming?

3. From the article, can you discern Gardyn's opinion about whether reality TV programming will gain or decrease in popularity? What clues, if any, are there in the article that let you know what Gardyn thinks about this question? Why might Gardyn want to leave her opinion unstated?

4. *Thinking rhetorically*: Gardyn presents at least two kinds of evidence to support her assertions in this article: statistics from surveys conducted by various organizations, and interviews with individuals who are fans of reality TV programs. How do these two kinds of evidence differ? What are the strengths and weaknesses of each? Why do you think Gardyn begins with mostly statistical evidence and puts most of the interview-based evidence toward the end of the article?

For Group Discussion

In discussing different demographic groups, Gardyn covers such factors as age, gender, and economic class, along with other groupings of people based on their affiliation with reality TV shows and the amount of time they spend watching TV. Working with several other students, choose one group that Gardyn discusses (for instance, 18- to 24-year-old viewers, or men, or "die-hard" reality TV fans). Read through the article, including the tables of data and the interviews with individual viewers, looking for all of the information Gardyn presents on this group. Together, write a brief explanation of what Gardyn reports about this group; compare your results to those of other groups in your class.

Writing Suggestion

Gardyn includes five tables with data from various surveys of television viewers. Take one of the tables and, after carefully studying it, write a four- or five-paragraph explanation of the significant information that this table conveys. You might organize your essay by identifying one key point for each paragraph of your essay; key points can include data from just one answer, or comparisons of data from different answers, or comparisons of data from different demographic groups. Make sure that you don't simply report numbers; rather, provide verbal descriptions that show what the numbers signify. You might also consider including quotations or paraphrases from Gardyn's article to help you explain what the information in the table means.

Keeping It Real: Why We Like to Watch Reality Dating Television Shows

Robert Samuels

In the following article, Robert Samuels, a lecturer in the Writing Programs at the University of California at Los Angeles, reports on what he learned from his students. Specifically, Samuels asked his students what they think about one type of reality television program: the "reality dating show." After all, as Samuels points out, college students are in the demographic group that these shows actively target, so finding out what the target group has to say about the shows that target them should yield interesting conclusions. How do the attitudes and concerns of this audience shape the very programming that they end up watching?

Samuels records the top ten reasons why his students like to watch reality dating shows, but he also takes his investigation a few steps further by analyzing the responses of his students and not accepting them at face value. His analysis ultimately engages questions of privacy and voyeurism, the blurred distinctions between the real and the artificial, and the nature of competition, fame and narcissism, distrust and paranoia. In short, Samuels moves from an analysis of a specific type of television show to a broad social commentary and to speculation on how the media shapes our behavior and guides our actions and beliefs.

Samuels has published extensively on popular culture, psychoanalysis, and philosophy. **As you read,** *keep in mind both the approach and the conclusions of the previous article, "The Tribe has Spoken." In what ways is Samuels's investigative strategy different from Gardyn's? How does the focus on a particular type of reality show influence the kind of conclusions Samuels reaches?*

———————————

Every day from 5 to 7 P.M., millions of Americans tune in to watch other   1
people go on dates. From *Blind Date* to *ElimiDate* to *Rendez-View,* viewers cannot seem to get enough of these new reality TV dating shows. In order to explore why we like to watch these shows and what they say about contemporary American culture, I decided to survey my university students to see what the targeted audience really thinks. The responses I received help us understand the general popularity of reality television shows and the effect these programs are having on contemporary American culture. Like *Big Brother, Survivor,* and countless other reality shows, reality dating programs challenge traditional oppositions between performer and audience, reality and fiction, private and public, and sport and nonsport. By turning everyday experiences—like camping, co-habitating, and dating—into spectator sports, these programs cater to our desire to witness the private lives of our fellow human beings. Moreover, by portraying an edited version of reality as if it is the real thing, these shows are able to combine fiction and reality in new and unexpected ways.

Many critics have traced the roots of reality television to the   2
power of MTV and other cable formats that rely on fast-action, skimpy clothing, and documentary-style fast-cutting to retain an attention-challenged audience. However, my survey of contemporary university students—who, after all, are the main audience of these shows—reveals a more varied and complex explanation for the development of these programs. I found that in order to see why people love to watch reality television, we cannot just focus on how the media has shaped the viewing habits of young adults; rather, we must also discover how the concerns and desires of the target audience have helped to mold the productions of contemporary media culture.

According to my survey, here are the top ten reasons why univer-   3
sity students like to watch reality dating programs:

1. It's fun to watch other people be rejected.
2. The people on these shows are just like us.

3. There are a lot of hot guys and girls on these shows.
4. You can learn a lot by watching other people's mistakes.
5. These shows are more real than other shows.
6. It's like going on a virtual date.
7. It's fun to guess who will be chosen.
8. You can see other people in an uncomfortable situation.
9. Everyone gets their fifteen minutes of fame.
10. These shows celebrate our narcissism and voyeurism.

Many of these responses seem to contradict each other, yet I   4
believe there is a certain logic to the popularity of these shows, and this
logic says a lot about our contemporary culture.

1. *It's fun to watch other people be rejected.* But why do people like to   5
watch other people get rejected? Is it because we have all felt the sting of
rejection in the past, and thus we like to see other people suffer a similar
fate? Or does this response say something about our great human need
to rubberneck and watch other people's difficult moments from a safe
and controlled distance? After all, what is more anxiety-provoking than
going on a nationally broadcasted date where you stand a high chance
of being rejected and ridiculed? To sit in the comfort of our homes,
while other people are out there testing the dating waters, allows us the
chance to relive some of our own worst experiences without any sense
of personal risk. It is like going on an emotional roller coaster, but one
which you know you can get off at anytime.

This question of emotional and personal safety is very important to   6
American daters who have grown up in the age of AIDS and other sexually transmitted diseases. After all, what type of sex could be safer than
the kind you get from watching other people try to have sex? In other
words, even if no one ends up "hooking up" and everyone is eventually
rejected, the audience still receives the gratification of going on a vicarious date without risk and without much effort. And let's not forget that
most of these shows come on right when most Americans are just arriving home from a long day of work. After eight hours at the office, who
has the energy to go on a real date? Isn't it easier to watch someone else
go on the date for you? Moreover, after a long day of surviving the various frustrations and rejections that comprise the work experience for
many Americans, what could be better than watching someone else be
rejected and humiliated? Yet, what is so strange is that not only do we
enjoy watching the suffering of others from the comfort of our own
homes, but we also want those suffering others to be just like us.

2. *The people on these shows are just like us.* Many of my students feel   7
that the real attraction of these reality dating programs is that any

young adult can relate to them because the participants are just ordinary people doing something that everyone else has done before. This need to identify with the "characters" on television shows has motivated many TV programmers to replace paid actors with unpaid ordinary citizens. Not only does this use of real people give many Americans the chance to experience their fifteen minutes of fame, but it also helps to motivate the audience to suspend their disbelief and forget about the mediated nature of these shows.

By using real people and placing them in real situations, reality   8
television programs are thus able to lull the audience into misperceiving controlled situations as being spontaneous events. In these seamlessly mediated productions, we never see the camera, the producer, or the editor. One of the results of this subtle blending between real reality and edited fiction is that our own everyday reality becomes less interesting compared to the controlled television reality. For it is obvious that one of the appeals of these shows is that these people are not really like most of us, since most of us do not spend most of our time trying to look beautiful for the camera. In other words, we watch these shows because the people on them are like us, but in many ways they are superficially more beautiful or extreme versions of our own selves.

In response to a question concerning the attractiveness of the par-   9
ticipants on these programs, one of my students wrote that "it is natural for guys to like girls with fake boobs." Here we see how something that is fake can be considered natural, while something that is natural turns out being fake. The subtle psychological effect of this blending between the natural and the artificial is that constructed aspects of consumer culture become naturalized at the same moment that our natural urges (like sex and eating) become socialized. In many ways, this blending of nature and culture is the key to our capitalist society where sex sells because sex is no longer natural or instinctual; instead of being something real and spontaneous, sex has become a form of advertising and entertainment.

3. *There are a lot of hot guys and girls on these shows.* As my students   10
often remind me, not only are there attractive people on dating shows, but these attractive people are trying to seduce each other, and so they act and dress in a very sexy way. Furthermore, these dating shows are often set up so that viewers feel that they are also on the date, and thus they are able to date people they might not be able to date in their own lives.

Of course, one of the most negative lessons people can learn from   11
watching these beautiful daters is that the only thing that matters when one is considering a potential mate is physical beauty and seductive charm. Furthermore, since none of these dates last longer than a few edited minutes, the whole mating process is sped up into a fast-paced

Darwinian survival of the hottest. The overall drive of these shows is to turn courtship into a superficial competitive sport complete with color commentary and a clear distinction between winners and losers. Like other reality TV shows, dating programs thus turn a seemingly non-competitive aspect of everyday life into a spectator sport.

4. *You can learn a lot by watching other people's mistakes.* Given the contrived nature of these programs, it is strange that many of my students claim they learn a lot of important lessons from these shows. In fact, many of these dating programs do provide a constant commentary on what to do and what not to do on dates. Here, we see another way that sex and courtship have become unnatural processes mediated by expert advice and highly judgmental criticism. As Rochefoucault once said, no one would fall in love if they didn't first read about love. In the same vein, can we say now that no one can date without a thorough knowledge of the popular media's conception of proper dating etiquette? I often wonder if people going on dates today anxiously wait for some pop-up caption to tell them whether they are proceeding in the accepted manner. In any account, it seems apparent from my students' responses that dating has become more performative and self-reflexive than it once was. Yes, it may be odd that TV dating would invade the realm of real dating, yet one of the great powers of reality television shows is that they effectively blur the distinctions between what's real and what's fiction.

5. *These shows are more real than other shows.* Once again, what draws people to reality programs is that they use real people in real situations, and thus they break down the traditional borders between the actor and the spectator and the real and the fictional. As my students often point out, on these programs, one never knows if someone is being real or just acting. On the one hand, this inability to determine the sincerity of the participants allows the viewing audience to identify more easily with the performers on the screen. On the other hand, not knowing who and what is real contributes to a general social atmosphere of distrust and paranoia.

This question of distrust feeds into contemporary culture's fascination with the dark side of public and private personalities. So much of our media is dedicated to showing us people in their worst moments that one must question how we are able to trust anyone with whom we come in contact. Reality dating shows add to this culture of paranoia by bringing together a real situation with a competition or a quest for fame. This combination of reality with competition forces the viewer to question the motives of the performers, and yet this constant confrontation with distrust and paranoia is compensated for by the continual stream of commentary and expert analysis. In other words, at the same time these shows make us distrust other people's real intentions,

12

13

14

they reassure us by telling us what is right and wrong in the dating world.

While it is always a question of how much people actually learn   15
from television shows and how much of this knowledge shapes their behavior, my students often celebrate the way reality TV shows allow the viewers to participate as if they were actually part of the shows themselves. For when students discuss reality dating shows, they stress how the realness of these productions gives them the sense that they are actually along for the ride or are active participants in the date.

6. *It's like going on a virtual date.* This idea that watching reality TV   16
dating shows can make you feel like you are on a virtual date may point to the general sense of virtual reality circulating in contemporary culture. Many of my students who watch reality TV shows also spend a great deal of time on the Internet, and some have experimented with virtual dating and various forms of cyber relationships. Their experiences in a cyber world may help these same students slip more easily into vicarious relationships with the people on reality dating shows.

This connection between the Internet and reality dating shows   17
also points to the ways new communication technologies give people unprecedented access into the private thoughts and experiences of a diverse range of fellow human beings. Like personal home pages and Web diaries, reality dating shows break down many of the traditional boundaries separating the private and public realms. By allowing us to go on other people's dates and hear personal reflections about these dates, reality dating programs open up a previously private realm of personal experience for the pleasure of a public audience. A side-effect of this vicarious dating structure is that it gives the viewer a false sense of activity, while he or she is passively watching other people. Instead of feeling guilty for being lazy and watching meaningless junk, we can convince ourselves that we are actively participating in a learning experience.

7. *It's fun to guess who will be chosen.* One way that these shows   18
help the audience forget about their own passivity is by creating opportunities for them to participate in the process. On many of these programs, this level of participation is limited to the viewer's vicarious experience of picking who will be chosen and who will be rejected in the dating competition.

Not only do people get to predict the future winners and losers,   19
but like many other reality TV shows, the dating programs train people into accepting a Darwinian world view where someone is always being downsized and eliminated. Like a giant corporate training program, these shows help to rationalize an economy where there are constant winners and losers. For the audience members not only enjoy picking

who will be the winner of the dating sweepstakes, but they also love to see who will be rejected and humiliated.

8. *You can see other people in an uncomfortable situation.* Perhaps this 20
great desire to see other people be rejected and humiliated can be derived from the fact that the more we see others in bad situations, the better our own situations look. According to this constant-sum logic, there can only be a certain number of happy people in the world at any given time, and thus the more we view other people failing, the more we can be assured that we are doing okay. Furthermore, we only know how we rate in the great game of life by comparing ourselves to others; thus, the worse off others are, the better off we feel.

Another psychological explanation for our desire to see other peo- 21
ple in uncomfortable situations is that if we can watch a scene of humiliation in a safe and comfortable environment, we gain a sense of control over our own anxieties. In this context, the television frame works to contain or "box in" our own feelings of humiliation and discomfort. From the viewer's perspective, one person's rejection is another person's triumph.

Of course, these shows don't just display people being rejected 22
and placed in humiliating situations, but they also depict a democratic world where everyone gets a chance to be on TV and thus stake a claim to instant celebrity. In many ways, fame is seen as its own prize, and therefore any humiliation one has to endure is worth the chance of being on the other side of the screen.

9. *Everyone gets their fifteen minutes of fame.* This democratization of 23
celebrity on reality television is often proclaimed as a great appeal for both viewers and contestants. When we watch the average Joe and Jane on TV, we are reminded that we could be the next person watched by millions. Instead of just sitting at home and staring at the screen, we can cross the border and have people watch us. And with so many new technologies allowing us to film and be filmed, the desire to be on the other side of the camera is constantly being cultivated.

10. *These shows celebrate our narcissism and voyeurism.* I learned 24
from the responses of my students that not only do people want their fifteen minutes of fame, but they also want to be shown that it is okay to be narcissistic and voyeuristic. After all, we are a culture that loves to celebrate the possibility of anyone making it—whether through talent, good looks, confidence, or sheer luck. Without our national obsession with superficial appearances, there would be no beauty industry, no dieting industry, no work-out industry: in fact, we would have no economy if we did not believe in our inherent need to be more beautiful and instantly powerful.

Reality dating programs may celebrate our most superficial 25
desires for fame, sex, beauty, and quick hook-ups, but isn't that what

twenty-first–century America is all about? Perhaps we should see these shows as public service announcements helping to train us to be effective participants in our consumer economy. Or perhaps we should read these shows as funhouse mirrors reflecting back to us in a distorted form our own social and psychological selves? One thing is clear: reality television programs offer us new insights into previously hidden aspects of American life.

Examining the Text

1. According to Samuels, what are some of the specifically *psychological* appeals of reality dating shows? That is, what psychological gratifications do these shows give their viewers?

2. In what ways, according to Samuels, are the dates on reality dating shows different from dates in real life?

3. *Thinking rhetorically*: What do you think is Samuels's opinion of reality dating shows? Where in the article can you discern his opinion? Do you see this article as being more or less objective than the previous article by Gardyn?

For Group Discussion

In the last paragraph, Samuels proposes two analogies for thinking about reality dating shows: they are "public service announcements helping to train us to be effective participants in our consumer economy"; or, they are "funhouse mirrors reflecting back to us in a distorted form our own social and psychological selves." In a group, discuss the implications of these options. What does it mean to say that these shows are "funhouse mirrors," for instance? How should we watch them and what should we learn from them if we see these shows as distorted reflections of ourselves? After discussing both options, decide which one you think more accurately describes reality dating shows.

Writing Suggestion

Write an essay in which you compare and contrast the article by Samuels and the previous article by Gardyn. Be sure to consider not only the content but also the method of each article. What is the approach of each author to the subject matter? What kinds of evidence does each author include in his or her analysis? How is each article organized, and how do the differences in organization affect the message of the article? You might conclude your comparison by stating from which article you think you learned more about reality television, and why.

2. THE SIMPSONS

The Simpsons: Atomistic Politics and the Nuclear Family

Paul A. Cantor

Paul A. Cantor is a Professor of English at the University of Virginia, member of the National Council on the Humanities, and a noted scholar of Elizabethan and Romantic English literature. In the article that follows, however, Professor Cantor wears the hat of popular culture specialist, as an expert on and devotee of The Simpsons. *The article is part of Cantor's book-length work,* Gilligan Unbound, *which studies the ways in which popular television shows reflect and shape American political and social principles. Clearly, Cantor is an example of a "serious" scholar who takes television seriously.*

While The Simpsons *has often been criticized for presenting horrible role models, particularly in the characters of Bart and Homer, Cantor argues that the show ultimately celebrates the nuclear family and small-town life in American communities. Cantor also argues that the show deals with key social issues, politics, religion, the media, and other important American institutions, so that even though it's "just a cartoon," the show actually provides valuable social commentary and presents "more human, more fully-rounded" characters than those on TV sitcoms and dramas.*

Cantor points out that the basic strategy of The Simpsons *is to simultaneously mock and celebrate; in other words, by satirizing something (education, politics, the police, etc.), the show acknowledges its importance. As you read, think about episodes of* The Simpsons *that you've seen (if you've never seen an episode, take this opportunity to watch one!). Do Cantor's arguments ring true, based on your own experience of watching the show?*

When Senator Charles Schumer (D-N.Y.) visited a high school in upstate   1
New York in May 1999, he received an unexpected civics lesson from an unexpected source. Speaking on the timely subject of school violence, Senator Schumer praised the Brady Bill, which he helped sponsor, for its role in preventing crime. Rising to question the effectiveness of this effort at gun control, a student named Kevin Davis cited an example no doubt familiar to his classmates but unknown to the senator from New York:

> It reminds me of a *Simpsons* episode. Homer wanted to get a gun but
> he had been in jail twice and in a mental institution. They label him as

"potentially dangerous." So Homer asks what that means and the gun dealer says: "It just means you need an extra week before you can get the gun."[1]

Without going into the pros and cons of gun control legislation,   2
one can recognize in this incident how the Fox Network's cartoon series *The Simpsons* shapes the way Americans think, particularly the younger generation. It may therefore be worthwhile taking a look at the television program to see what sort of political lessons it is teaching. *The Simpsons* may seem like mindless entertainment to many, but in fact, it offers some of the most sophisticated comedy and satire ever to appear on American television. Over the years, the show has taken on many serious issues: nuclear power safety, environmentalism, immigration, gay rights, women in the military, and so on. Paradoxically, it is the farcical nature of the show that allows it to be serious in ways that many other television shows are not.[2]

I will not, however, dwell on the question of the show's politics in   3
the narrowly partisan sense. *The Simpsons* satirizes both Republicans and Democrats. The local politician who appears most frequently in the show, Mayor Quimby, speaks with a heavy Kennedy accent[3] and generally acts like a Democratic urban-machine politician. By the same token, the most sinister political force in the series, the cabal that seems to run the town of Springfield from behind the scenes, is invariably portrayed as Republican. On balance, it is fair to say that *The Simpsons*, like most of what comes out of Hollywood, is pro-Democrat and anti-Republican. One whole episode was a gratuitously vicious portrait of ex-President Bush,[4] whereas the show has been surprisingly slow to satirize President Clinton.[5] Nevertheless, perhaps the single funniest political line in the history of *The Simpsons* came at the expense of the Democrats. When Grandpa Abraham Simpson receives money in the mail really meant for his grandchildren, Bart asks him, "Didn't you wonder why you were getting checks for absolutely nothing?" Abe replies, "I figured 'cause the Democrats were in power again."[6] Unwilling to forego any opportunity for humor, the show's creators have been generally evenhanded over the years in making fun of both parties, and of both the Right and the Left.[7]

Setting aside the surface issue of political partisanship, I am inter-   4
ested in the deep politics of *The Simpsons*, what the show most fundamentally suggests about political life in the United States. The show broaches the question of politics through the question of the family, and this in itself is a political statement. By dealing centrally with the family, *The Simpsons* takes up real human issues everybody can recognize and thus ends up in many respects less "cartoonish" than other television programs. Its cartoon characters are more human, more fully

rounded, than the supposedly real human beings in many situation comedies. Above all, the show has created a believable human community: Springfield, USA. *The Simpsons* shows the family as part of a larger community and in effect affirms the kind of community that can sustain the family. That is at one and the same time the secret of the show's popularity with the American public and the most interesting political statement it has to make.

The Simpsons indeed offers one of the most important images of   5
the family in contemporary American culture and, in particular, an image of the nuclear family. With the names taken from creator Matt Groening's own childhood home, *The Simpsons* portrays the average American family: father (Homer), mother (Marge), and 2.2 children (Bart, Lisa, and little Maggie). Many commentators have lamented the fact that *The Simpsons* now serves as one of the representative images of American family life, claiming that the show provides horrible role models for parents and children. The popularity of the show is often cited as evidence of the decline of family values in the United States. But critics of *The Simpsons* need to take a closer look at the show and view it in the context of television history. For all its slapstick nature and its mocking of certain aspects of family life, *The Simpsons* has an affirmative side and ends up celebrating the nuclear family as an institution. For television, this is no minor achievement. For decades, American television has tended to downplay the importance of the nuclear family and offer various one-parent families or other nontraditional arrangements as alternatives to it. The one-parent situation comedy actually dates back almost to the beginning of network television, at least as early as *My Little Margie* (1952–1955). But the classic one-parent situation comedies, like *The Andy Griffith Show* (1960–1968) or *My Three Sons* (1960–1972), generally found ways to reconstitute the nuclear family in one form or another (often through the presence of an aunt or uncle) and thus still presented it as the norm (sometimes the story line actually moved in the direction of the widower getting remarried, as happened to Steve Douglas, the Fred MacMurray character, in *My Three Sons*).

But starting with shows in the 1970s like *Alice* (1976–1985),   6
American television genuinely began to move away from the nuclear family as the norm and suggest that other patterns of child rearing might be equally valid or perhaps even superior. Television in the 1980s and 1990s experimented with all sorts of permutations on the theme of the nonnuclear family, in shows such as *Love, Sidney* (1981–1983), *Punky Brewster* (1984–1986), and *My Two Dads* (1987–1990). This development partly resulted from the standard Hollywood procedure of generating new series by simply varying successful formulas.[8] But the trend toward nonnuclear families also expressed the

ideological bent of Hollywood and its impulse to call traditional family values into question. Above all, though television shows usually traced the absence of one or more parents to deaths in the family, the trend away from the nuclear family obviously reflected the reality of divorce in American life (and especially in Hollywood). Wanting to be progressive, television producers set out to endorse contemporary social trends away from the stable, traditional, nuclear family. With the typical momentum of the entertainment industry, Hollywood eventually took this development to its logical conclusion: the no-parent family. Another popular Fox program, *Party of Five*, now shows a family of children gallantly raising themselves after both their parents were killed in an automobile accident.

Party of Five cleverly conveys a message some television produc-   7
ers evidently think their contemporary audience wants to hear—that children can do quite well without one parent and preferably without both. The children in the audience want to hear this message because it flatters their sense of independence. The parents want to hear this message because it soothes their sense of guilt, either about abandoning their children completely (as sometimes happens in cases of divorce) or just not devoting enough "quality time" to them. Absent or negligent parents can console themselves with the thought that their children really are better off without them, "just like those cool—and incredibly good-looking—kids on *Party of Five*." In short, for roughly the past two decades, much of American television has been suggesting that the breakdown of the American family does not constitute a social crisis or even a serious problem. In fact, it should be regarded as a form of liberation from an image of the family that may have been good enough for the 1950s but is no longer valid in the 1990s. It is against this historical background that the statement *The Simpsons* has to make about the nuclear family has to be appreciated.

Of course television never completely abandoned the nuclear   8
family, even in the 1980s, as shown by the success of such shows as *All in the Family* (1971–1983), *Family Ties* (1982–1989), and *The Cosby Show* (1984–1992). And when *The Simpsons* debuted as a regular series in 1989, it was by no means unique in its reaffirmation of the value of the nuclear family. Several other shows took the same path in the past decade, reflecting larger social and political trends in society, in particular the reassertion of family values that has by now been adopted as a program by both political parties in the United States. Fox's own *Married with Children* (1987–1998) preceded *The Simpsons* in portraying an amusingly dysfunctional nuclear family. Another interesting portrayal of the nuclear family can be found in ABC's *Home Improvement* (1991–1999), which tries to recuperate traditional family values and even gender roles within a postmodern television context. But

The Simpsons is in many respects the most interesting example of this return to the nuclear family. Though it strikes many people as trying to subvert the American family or to undermine its authority, in fact, it reminds us that antiauthoritarianism is itself an American tradition and that family authority has always been problematic in democratic America. What makes *The Simpsons* so interesting is the way it combines traditionalism with antitraditionalism. It continually makes fun of the traditional American family. But it continually offers an enduring image of the nuclear family in the very act of satirizing it. Many of the traditional values of the American family survive this satire, above all the value of the nuclear family itself.

As I have suggested, one can understand this point partly in   9
terms of television history. *The Simpsons* is a hip, postmodern, self-aware show.[9] But its self-awareness focuses on the traditional representation of the American family on television. It therefore presents the paradox of an untraditional show that is deeply rooted in television tradition. *The Simpsons* can be traced back to earlier television cartoons that dealt with families, such as *The Flintstones* or *The Jetsons*. But these cartoons must themselves be traced back to the famous nuclear-family sitcoms of the 1950s: *I Love Lucy, The Adventures of Ozzie and Harriet, Father Knows Best,* and *Leave It to Beaver. The Simpsons* is a postmodern re-creation of the first generation of family sitcoms on television. Looking back on those shows, we easily see the transformations and discontinuities *The Simpsons* has brought about. In *The Simpsons,* father emphatically does not know best. And it clearly is more dangerous to leave it to Bart than to Beaver. Obviously, *The Simpsons* does not offer a simple return to the family shows of the 1950s. But even in the act of re-creation and transformation, the show provides elements of continuity that make *The Simpsons* more traditional than may at first appear.

The Simpsons has indeed found its own odd way to defend the   10
nuclear family. In effect, the show says, "Take the worst-case scenario—the Simpsons—and even that family is better than no family." In fact, the Simpson family is not all that bad. Some people are appalled at the idea of young boys imitating Bart, in particular his disrespect for authority and especially for his teachers. These critics of *The Simpsons* forget that Bart's rebelliousness conforms to a venerable American archetype and that this country was founded on disrespect for authority and an act of rebellion. Bart is an American icon, an updated version of Tom Sawyer and Huck Finn rolled into one. For all his troublemaking—precisely because of his troublemaking—Bart behaves just the way a young boy is supposed to in American mythology, from *Dennis the Menace* comics to the *Our Gang* comedies.[10]

As for the mother and daughter in *The Simpsons,* Marge and Lisa   11
are not bad role models at all. Marge Simpson is very much the

devoted mother and housekeeper; she also often displays a feminist streak, particularly in the episode in which she goes off on a jaunt à la *Thelma and Louise*.[11] Indeed, she is very modern in her attempts to combine certain feminist impulses with the traditional role of a mother. Lisa is in many ways the ideal child in contemporary terms. She is an overachiever in school, and as a feminist, a vegetarian, and an environmentalist, she is politically correct across the spectrum.

The real issue, then, is Homer. Many people have criticized *The Simpsons* for its portrayal of the father as dumb, uneducated, weak in character, and morally unprincipled. Homer is all those things, but at least he is there. He fulfills the bare minimum of a father: he is present for his wife and above all his children. To be sure, he lacks many of the qualities we would like to see in the ideal father. He is selfish, often putting his own interest above that of his family. As we learn in one of the Halloween episodes, Homer would sell his soul to the devil for a donut (though fortunately it turns out that Marge already owned his soul and therefore it was not Homer's to sell).[12] Homer is undeniably crass, vulgar, and incapable of appreciating the finer things in life. He has a hard time sharing interests with Lisa, except when she develops a remarkable knack for predicting the outcome of pro football games and allows her father to become a big winner in the betting pool at Moe's Tavern.[13] Moreover, Homer gets angry easily and takes his anger out on his children, as his many attempts to strangle Bart attest.   12

In all these respects, Homer fails as a father. But upon reflection, it is surprising to realize how many decent qualities he has. First and foremost, he is attached to his own—he loves his family because it is his. His motto basically is, "My family, right or wrong." This is hardly a philosophic position, but it may well provide the bedrock of the family as an institution, which is why Plato's *Republic* must subvert the power of the family. Homer Simpson is the opposite of a philosopher-king; he is devoted not to what is best but to what is his own. That position has its problems, but it does help explain how the seemingly dysfunctional Simpson family manages to function.   13

For example, Homer is willing to work to support his family, even in the dangerous job of nuclear power plant safety supervisor, a job made all the more dangerous by the fact that he is the one doing it. In the episode in which Lisa comes to want a pony desperately, Homer even takes a second job working for Apu Nahasapeemapetilon at the Kwik-E-Mart to earn the money for the pony's upkeep and nearly kills himself in the process.[14] In such actions, Homer manifests his genuine concern for his family, and as he repeatedly proves, he will defend them if necessary, sometimes at great personal risk. Often, Homer is not effective in such actions, but that makes his devotion to his family   14 in some ways all the more touching. Homer is the distillation of pure fatherhood. Take away all the qualities that make for a genuinely good father—wisdom, compassion, even temper, selflessness—and what you have left is Homer Simpson with his pure, mindless, dogged devotion to his family. That is why for all his stupidity, bigotry, and self-centered quality, we cannot hate Homer. He continually fails at being a good father, but he never gives up trying, and in some basic and important sense that makes him a good father.

The most effective defense of the family in the series comes in the episode in which the Simpsons are actually broken up as a unit.[15] This episode pointedly begins with an image of Marge as a good mother, preparing breakfast and school lunches simultaneously for her children. She even gives Bart and Lisa careful instructions about their sandwiches: "Keep the lettuce separate until 11:30." But after this promising parental beginning, a series of mishaps occurs. Homer and Marge go off to the Mingled Waters Health Spa for a well-deserved afternoon of relaxation. In their haste, they leave their house dirty, especially a pile of unwashed dishes in the kitchen sink. Meanwhile, things are unfortunately not going well for the children at school. Bart has accidentally picked up lice from the monkey of his best friend Milhouse, prompting Principal Skinner to ask, "What kind of parents would permit such a lapse in scalpal hygiene?" The evidence against the Simpson parents mounts when Skinner sends for Bart's sister. With her prescription shoes stolen by her classmates and her feet accordingly covered with mud, Lisa looks like some street urchin straight out of Dickens.

Faced with all this evidence of parental neglect, the horrified principal alerts the Child Welfare Board, who are themselves shocked when they take Bart and Lisa home and explore the premises. The officials completely misinterpret the situation. Confronted by a pile of old newspapers, they assume that Marge is a bad housekeeper, when in fact she had assembled the documents to help Lisa with a history project. Jumping to conclusions, the bureaucrats decide that Marge and Homer are unfit parents and lodge specific charges that the Simpson household is a "squalid hellhole and the toilet paper is hung in improper overhand fashion." The authorities determine that the Simpson children must be given to foster parents. Bart, Lisa, and Maggie are accordingly handed over to the family next door, presided over by the patriarchal Ned Flanders. Throughout the series, the Flanders family serves as the doppelgänger of the Simpsons. Flanders and his brood are in fact the perfect family according to old-style morality and religion. In marked contrast to Bart, the Flanders boys, Rod and Todd, are well behaved and obedient. Above all, the Flanders family is pious, devoted to activities

15

16

like Bible reading, and more zealous than even the local Reverend Lovejoy. When Ned offers to play "bombardment" with Bart and Lisa, what he has in mind is bombardment with questions about the Bible. The Flanders family is shocked to learn that their neighbors do not know of the serpent of Rehoboam, not to mention the Well of Zahassadar or the bridal feast of Beth Chadruharazzeb.

Exploring the question of whether the Simpson family really is dysfunctional, the foster parent episode offers two alternatives to it: on one hand, the old-style moral/religious family; on the other, the therapeutic state, what is often now called the nanny state. Who is best able to raise the Simpson children? The civil authorities intervene, claiming that Homer and Marge are unfit as parents. They must be reeducated and are sent off to a "family skills class" based on the premise that experts know better how to raise children. Child rearing is a matter of a certain kind of expertise, which can be taught. This is the modern answer: the family is inadequate as an institution and hence the state must intervene to make it function. At the same time, the episode offers the old-style moral/religious answer: what children need is God-fearing parents in order to make them God-fearing themselves. Indeed, Ned Flanders does everything he can to get Bart and Lisa to reform and behave with the piety of his own children. 17

But the answer the show offers is that the Simpson children are better off with their real parents—not because they are more intelligent or learned in child rearing, and not because they are superior in morality or piety, but simply because Homer and Marge are the people most genuinely attached to Bart, Lisa, and Maggie, since the children are their own offspring. The episode works particularly well to show the horror of the supposedly omniscient and omnicompetent state intruding in every aspect of family life. When Homer desperately tries to call up Bart and Lisa, he hears the official message: "The number you have dialed can no longer be reached from this phone, you negligent monster." 18

At the same time, we see the defects of the old-style religion. The Flanders may be righteous as parents but they are also self-righteous. Mrs. Flanders says, "I don't judge Homer and Marge; that's for a vengeful God to do." Ned's piety is so extreme that he eventually exasperates even Reverend Lovejoy, who at one point asks him, "Have you thought of one of the other major religions? They're all pretty much the same." 19

In the end, Bart, Lisa, and Maggie are joyously reunited with Homer and Marge. Despite charges of being dysfunctional, the Simpson family functions quite well because the children are attached to their parents and the parents are attached to their children. The premise of those who tried to take the Simpson children away is that there is a 20 principle external to the family by which it can be judged dysfunctional, whether the principle of contemporary child-rearing theories or that of the old-style religion. The foster parent episode suggests the contrary—that the family contains its own principle of legitimacy. The family knows best. This episode thus illustrates the strange combination of traditionalism and antitraditionalism in *The Simpsons*. Even as the show rejects the idea of a simple return to the traditional moral/ religious idea of the family, it refuses to accept contemporary statist attempts to subvert the family completely and reasserts the enduring value of the family as an institution.

As the importance of Ned Flanders in this episode reminds us,   21
another way in which the show is unusual is that religion plays a significant role in *The Simpsons*. Religion is a regular part of the life of the Simpson family. We often see them going to church, and several episodes revolve around churchgoing, including one in which God even speaks directly to Homer.[16] Moreover, religion is a regular part of life in general in Springfield. In addition to Ned Flanders, the Reverend Lovejoy is featured in several episodes, including one in which no less than Meryl Streep provides the voice for his daughter.[17]

This attention to religion is atypical of American television in the   22
1990s. Indeed, judging by most television programs today, one would never guess that Americans are by and large a religious and even a churchgoing people. Television generally acts as if religion played little or no role in the daily lives of Americans, even though the evidence points to exactly the opposite conclusion. Many reasons have been offered to explain why television generally avoids the subject of religion. Producers are afraid that if they raise religious issues, they will offend orthodox viewers and soon be embroiled in controversy; television executives are particularly worried about having the sponsors of their shows boycotted by powerful religious groups. Moreover, the television community itself is largely secular in its outlook and thus generally uninterested in religious questions. Indeed, much of Hollywood is often outright antireligious, and especially opposed to anything labeled religious fundamentalism (and it tends to label anything to the right of Unitarianism as "religious fundamentalism").

Religion has, however, been making a comeback on television in   23
the past decade, in part because producers have discovered that an audience niche exists for shows like *Touched by an Angel* (1994–).[18] Still, the entertainment community has a hard time understanding what religion really means to the American public, and it especially cannot deal with the idea that religion could be an everyday, normal part of American life. Religious figures in both movies and television tend to be miraculously good and pure or monstrously evil and hypocritical. While there are exceptions to this rule,[19] generally Hollywood religious

figures must be either saints or sinners, either laboring against all odds and all reason for good or religious fanatics, full of bigotry, warped by sexual repression, laboring to destroy innocent lives in one way or another.[20]

But *The Simpsons* accepts religion as a normal part of life in   24
Springfield, USA. If the show makes fun of piety in the person of Ned Flanders, in Homer Simpson it also suggests that one can go to church and not be either a religious fanatic or a saint. One episode devoted to Reverend Lovejoy deals realistically and rather sympathetically with the problem of pastoral burnout.[21] The overburdened minister has just listened to too many problems from his parishioners and has to turn the job over to Marge Simpson as the "listen lady." The treatment of religion in *The Simpsons* is parallel to and connected with its treatment of the family. *The Simpsons* is not proreligion—it is too hip, cynical, and iconoclastic for that. Indeed, on the surface, the show appears to be antireligious, with a good deal of its satire directed against Ned Flanders and other pious characters. But once again, we see the principle at work that when *The Simpsons* satirizes something, it acknowledges its importance. Even when it seems to be ridiculing religion, it recognizes, as few other television shows do, the genuine role that religion plays in American life.

It is here that the treatment of the family in *The Simpsons* links up   25
with its treatment of politics. Although the show focuses on the nuclear family, it relates the family to larger institutions in American life, like the church, the school, and even political institutions themselves, like city government. In all these cases, *The Simpsons* satirizes these institutions, making them look laughable and often even hollow. But at the same time, the show acknowledges their importance and especially their importance for the family. Over the past few decades, television has increasingly tended to isolate the family—to show it largely removed from any larger institutional framework or context. This is another trend to which *The Simpsons* runs counter, partly as a result of its being a postmodern re-creation of 1950s sitcoms. Shows like *Father Knows Best* or *Leave It to Beaver* tended to be set in small-town America, with all the intricate web of institutions into which family life was woven. In re-creating this world, even while mocking it, *The Simpsons* cannot help re-creating its ambience and even at times its ethos.

Springfield is decidedly an American small town. In several   26
episodes, it is contrasted with Capitol City, a metropolis the Simpsons approach with fear and trepidation. Obviously, the show makes fun of small-town life—it makes fun of everything—but it simultaneously celebrates the virtues of the traditional American small town. One of the principal reasons why the dysfunctional Simpsons family functions as well as it does is that they live in a traditional American small town.

The institutions that govern their lives are not remote from them or alien to them. The Simpson children go to a neighborhood school (though they are bussed to it by the ex-hippie driver Otto). Their friends in school are largely the same as their friends in their neighborhood. The Simpsons are not confronted by an elaborate, unapproachable, and uncaring educational bureaucracy. Principal Skinner and Mrs. Krabappel may not be perfect educators, but when Homer and Marge need to talk to them, they are readily accessible. The same is true of the Springfield police force. Chief Wiggum is not a great crime fighter, but he is well known to the citizens of Springfield, as they are to him. The police in Springfield still have neighborhood beats and have even been known to share a donut or two with Homer.

Similarly, politics in Springfield is largely a local matter, including town meetings in which the citizens of Springfield get to influence decisions on important matters of local concern, such as whether gambling should be legalized or a monorail built. As his Kennedy accent suggests, Mayor Quimby is a demagogue, but at least he is Springfield's own demagogue. When he buys votes, he buys them directly from the citizens of Springfield. If Quimby wants Grandpa Simpson to support a freeway he wishes to build through town, he must name the road after Abe's favorite television character, Matlock. Everywhere one looks in Springfield, one sees a surprising degree of local control and autonomy. The nuclear power plant is a source of pollution and constant danger, but at least it is locally owned by Springfield's own slave-driving industrial tyrant and tycoon, Montgomery Burns, and not by some remote multinational corporation (indeed, in an exception that proves the rule, when the plant is sold to German investors, Burns soon buys it back to restore his ego).[22]   27

In sum, for all its postmodern hipness, The Simpsons is profoundly anachronistic in the way it harks back to an earlier age when Americans felt more in contact with their governing institutions and family life was solidly anchored in a larger but still local community. The federal government rarely makes its presence felt in The Simpsons, and when it does it generally takes a quirky form like former President Bush moving next door to Homer, an arrangement that does not work out. The long tentacles of the IRS have occasionally crept their way into Springfield, but its stranglehold on America is of course all-pervasive and inescapable.[23] Generally speaking, government is much more likely to take local forms in the show. When sinister forces from the Republican Party conspire to unseat Mayor Quimby by running ex-convict Sideshow Bob against him, it is local sinister forces who do the conspiring, led by Mr. Burns and including Rainer Wolfcastle (the Arnold Schwarzenegger lookalike who plays McBain in the movies) and a Rush Limbaugh lookalike named Burch Barlow.[24]   28

Here is one respect in which the portrayal of the local community   29
in *The Simpsons* is unrealistic. In Springfield, even the media forces are
local. There is of course nothing strange about having a local television
station in Springfield. It is perfectly plausible that the Simpsons get
their news from a man, Kent Brockman, who actually lives in their
midst. It is also quite believable that the kiddie show on Springfield
television is local, and that its host, Krusty the Klown, not only lives in
town but also is available for local functions like supermarket openings
and birthday parties. But what are authentic movie stars like Rainer
Wolfcastle doing living in Springfield? And what about the fact that the
world-famous *Itchy & Scratchy* cartoons are produced in Springfield?
Indeed, the entire *Itchy & Scratchy* empire is apparently headquartered
in Springfield. This is not a trivial fact. It means that when Marge campaigns against cartoon violence, she can picket *Itchy & Scratchy* headquarters without leaving her hometown.[25] The citizens of Springfield
are fortunate to be able to have a direct impact on the forces that shape
their lives and especially their family lives. In short, *The Simpsons*
takes the phenomenon that has in fact done more than anything else
to subvert the power of the local in American politics and American
life in general—namely, the media—and in effect brings it within the
orbit of Springfield, thereby placing the force at least partially under
local control.[26]

The unrealistic portrayal of the media as local helps highlight the   30
overall tendency of *The Simpsons* to present Springfield as a kind of
classical polis; it is just about as self-contained and autonomous as a
community can be in the modern world. This once again reflects the
postmodern nostalgia of *The Simpsons;* with its self-conscious re-creation
of the 1950s sitcom, it ends up weirdly celebrating the old ideal of small-
town America.[27] Again, I do not mean to deny that the first impulse of
The Simpsons is to make fun of small-town life. But in that very process,
it reminds us of what the old ideal was and what was so attractive
about it, above all the fact that average Americans somehow felt in
touch with the forces that influenced their lives and maybe even in control of them. In a presentation before the American Society of Newspaper
Editors on April 12, 1991 (broadcast on C-SPAN), Matt Groening said
that the subtext of *The Simpsons* is "the people in power don't always
have your best interests in mind."[28] This is a view of politics that cuts
across the normal distinctions between Left and Right and explains
why the show can be relatively evenhanded in its treatment of both
political parties and has something to offer to both liberals and conservatives. *The Simpsons* is based on distrust of power and especially of
power remote from ordinary people. The show celebrates genuine
community, a community in which everybody more or less knows

everybody else (even if they do not necessarily like each other). By re-creating this older sense of community, the show manages to generate a kind of warmth out of its postmodern coolness, a warmth that is largely responsible for its success with the American public. This view of community may be the most profound comment *The Simpsons* has to make on family life in particular and politics in general in America today. No matter how dysfunctional it may seem, the nuclear family is an institution worth preserving. And the way to preserve it is not by the offices of a distant, supposedly expert, therapeutic state but by restoring its links to a series of local institutions that reflect and foster the same principle that makes the Simpson family itself work—the attachment to one's own, the principle that we best care for something when it belongs to us.

The celebration of the local in *The Simpsons* was confirmed in an   31 episode that aired May 9, 1999, which for once explored in detail the possibility of a utopian alternative to politics as usual in Springfield. The episode begins with Lisa disgusted by a gross-out contest sponsored by a local radio station, which, among other things, results in the burning of a travelling van Gogh exhibition. With the indignation typical of youth, Lisa fires off an angry letter to the Springfield newspaper, charging, "Today our town lost what remained of its fragile civility." Outraged by the cultural limitations of Springfield, Lisa complains, "We have eight malls, but no symphony; thirty-two bars but no alternative theater." Lisa's spirited outburst catches the attention of the local chapter of Mensa, and the few high-IQ citizens of Springfield (including Dr. Hibbert, Principal Skinner, the Comic Book Guy, and Professor Frink) invite her to join the organization (once they have determined that she has brought a pie and not a quiche to their meeting). Inspired by Lisa's courageous speaking out against the cultural parochialism of Springfield, Dr. Hibbert challenges the city's way of life: "Why do we live in a town where the smartest have no power and the stupidest run everything?" Forming "a council of learned citizens," or what reporter Kent Brockman later refers to as an "intellectual junta," the Mensa members set out to create the cartoon equivalent of Plato's *Republic* in Springfield. Naturally, they begin by ousting Mayor Quimby, who in fact leaves town rather abruptly once the little matter of some missing lottery funds comes up.

Taking advantage of an obscure provision in the Springfield char-   32 ter, the Mensa members step into the power vacuum created by Quimby's sudden abdication. Lisa sees no limit to what the Platonic rule of the wise might accomplish: "With our superior intellects, we could rebuild this city on a foundation of reason and enlightenment; we could turn Springfield into a utopia." Principal Skinner holds out hope for "a new Athens," while another Mensa member thinks in terms of B. F. Skinner's "Walden II." The new rulers immediately set out to bring their utopia into existence, redesigning traffic patterns and abolishing all sports that involve violence. But in a variant of the dialectic of enlightenment, the abstract rationality and benevolent universalism of the intellectual junta soon prove to be a fraud. The Mensa members begin to disagree among themselves, and it becomes evident that their claim to represent the public interest masks a number of private agendas. At the climax of the episode, the Comic Book Guy comes forward to proclaim, "Inspired by the most logical race in the galaxy, the Vulcans, breeding will be permitted once every seven years; for many of you this will mean much less breeding; for me, much much more." This reference to *Star Trek* appropriately elicits from Groundskeeper Willie a response in his native accent that calls to mind the *Enterprise's* Chief Engineer Scotty: "You cannot do that, sir, you don't have the power." The Mensa regime's self-interested attempt to imitate the *Republic* by regulating breeding in the city is just too much for the ordinary citizens of Springfield to bear.

With the Platonic revolution in Springfield degenerating into petty squabbling and violence, a *deus ex machina* arrives in the form of physicist Stephen Hawking, proclaimed as "the world's smartest man." When Hawking voices his disappointment with the Mensa regime, he ends up in a fight with Principal Skinner. Seizing the opportunity created by the division among the intelligentsia, Homer leads a counterrevolution of the stupid with the rallying cry: "C'mon you idiots, we're taking back this town." Thus, the attempt to bring about a rule of philosopher-kings in Springfield ends ignominiously, leaving Hawking to pronounce its epitaph: "Sometimes the smartest of us can be the most childish." Theory fails when translated into practice in this episode of *The Simpsons* and must be relegated once more to the confines of the contemplative life. The episode ends with Hawking and Homer drinking beer together in Moe's Tavern and discussing Homer's theory of a donut-shaped universe. 33

The utopia episode offers an epitome of what *The Simpsons* does so well. It can be enjoyed on two levels—as both broad farce and intellectual satire. The episode contains some of the grossest humor in the long history of *The Simpsons* (I have not even mentioned the subplot concerning Homer's encounter with a pornographic photographer). But at the same time, it is filled with subtle cultural allusions; for example, the Mensa members convene in what is obviously a Frank Lloyd Wright prairie house. In the end, then, the utopia episode embodies the strange mixture of intellectualism and anti-intellectualism characteristic of *The Simpsons*. In Lisa's challenge to Springfield, the show calls attention to the cultural limitations of small-town America, but it also 34 reminds us that intellectual disdain for the common man can be carried too far and that theory can all too easily lose touch with common sense. Ultimately, *The Simpsons* seems to offer a kind of intellectual defense of the common man against intellectuals, which helps explain its popularity and broad appeal. Very few people have found *The Critique of Pure Reason* funny, but in *The Gay Science,* Nietzsche felt that he had put his finger on Kant's joke:

> Kant wanted to prove in a way that would puzzle all the world that all the world was right—that was the private joke of this soul. He wrote against the learned on behalf of the prejudice of the common people, but for the learned and not for the common people.[29]

In Nietzsche's terms, *The Simpsons* goes *The Critique of Pure Reason* one better: it defends the common man against the intellectual but in a way that both the common man and the intellectual can understand and enjoy.   35

NOTES

[1]As reported in Ed Henry's "Heard on the Hill" column in *Roll Call,* 44, no. 81 (May 13, 1999). His source was the *Albany Times-Union.*

[2]This essay is a substantial revision of a paper originally delivered at the Annual Meeting of the American Political Science Association in Boston, September 1998. All *Simpsons* episodes are cited by title, number, and original broadcast date, using the information supplied in the invaluable reference work *The Simpsons: A Complete Guide to Our Favorite Family,* ed. Ray Richmond and Antonia Coffman (New York: HarperCollins, 1997). I cite episodes that aired subsequent to the publication of this book simply by broadcast date.

[3]The identification is made complete when Quimby says, "Ich bin ein Springfielder" in "Burns Verkaufen der Kraftwerk," #8F09, 12/5/91.

[4]"Two Bad Neighbors," #3F09, 1/4/96.

[5]For the reluctance to go after Clinton, see the rather tame satire of the 1996 presidential campaign in the "Citizen Kang" segment of the Halloween episode, "Treehouse of Horror VII," #4F02, 10/27/96. Finally in the 1998–1999 season, faced with the mounting scandals in the Clinton administration, the creators of *The Simpsons* decided to take off the kid gloves in their treatment of the president, especially in the February 7, 1999, episode (in which Homer legally changes his name to Max Power). Hustled by Clinton at a party, Marge Simpson is forced to ask, "Are you sure it's a federal law that I have to dance with you?" Reassuring Marge that she is good enough for a man of his stature, Clinton tells her, "Hell, I've done it with pigs—real no foolin' pigs."

[6]"The Front," #9616, 4/15/93.

[7]An amusing debate developed in the *Wall Street Journal* over the politics of *The Simpsons.* It began with an Op-Ed piece by Benjamin Stein titled "TV

Land: From Mao to Dow" (February 5, 1997), in which he argued that the show has no politics. This piece was answered by a letter from John McGrew given the title "The Simpsons Bash Familiar Values" (March 19, 1997), in which he argued that the show is political and consistently left-wing. On March 12, 1997, letters by Deroy Murdock and H. B. Johnson Jr. argued that the show attacks left-wing targets as well and often supports traditional values. Johnson's conclusion that the show is "politically ambiguous" and thus appeals "to conservatives as well as to liberals" is supported by the evidence of this debate itself.

[8]Perhaps the most famous example is the creation of *Green Acres* (1965–1971) by inverting *The Beverly Hillbillies* (1962–1971)—if a family of hicks moving from the country to the city was funny, television executives concluded that a couple of sophisticates moving from the city to the country should be a hit as well. And it was.

[9]On the self-reflexive character of *The Simpsons,* see my essay "The Greatest TV Show Ever," *American Enterprise,* 8, no. 5 (September/October 1997), 34–37.

[10]Oddly enough, Bart's creator, Matt Groening, has now joined the chorus condemning the Simpson boy. Earlier this year, a wire-service report quoted Groening as saying to those who call Bart a bad role model, "I now have a 7-year-old boy and a 9-year-old boy so all I can say is I apologize. Now I know what you were talking about."

[11]"Marge on the Lam," #1F12, 11/4/93.

[12]"The Devil and Homer Simpson" in "Treehouse of Horror IV," #1F04, 10/30/93.

[13]"Lisa the Greek," #8F12, 1/23/92.

[14]"Lisa's Pony," #8F06, 11/7/91.

[15]"Home Sweet Homediddly-Dum-Doodily," #3F01, 10/1/95.

[16]"Homer the Heretic," #9F01, 10/8/92.

[17]"Bart's Girlfriend," #2F04, 11/6/94.

[18]I would like to comment on this show, but it is scheduled at the same time as *The Simpsons,* and I have never seen it.

[19]Consider, for example, the minister played by Tom Skerritt in Robert Redford's film of Norman Maclean's *A River Runs Through It.*

[20]A good example of this stereotyping can be found in the film *Contact,* with its contrasting religious figures played by Matthew McConaughey (good) and Jake Busey (evil).

[21]"In Marge We Trust," #4F18, 4/27/97.

[22]"Burns Verkaufen der Kraftwerk," #8F09, 12/5/91.

[23]See, for example, "Bart the Fink," #3F12, 2/11/96.

[24]"Sideshow Bob Roberts," #2F02, 10/9/94.

[25]"Itchy & Scratchy & Marge," #7F09, 12/20/90.

[26]The episode called "Radioactive Man" (#2517, 9/24/95) provides an amusing reversal of the usual relationship between the big-time media and small-town life. A Hollywood film company comes to Springfield to make a movie featuring the comic book hero, Radioactive Man. The Springfield locals take advantage of the naive moviemakers, raising prices all over town and imposing all sorts of new taxes on the film crew. Forced to return to California

penniless, the moviemakers are greeted like small-town heroes by their caring neighbors in the Hollywood community.

[27]In his review of *The Simpsons: A Complete Guide to Our Favorite Family*, Michael Dirda aptly characterizes the show as "a wickedly funny yet oddly affectionate satire of American life at the end of the 20th century. Imagine the unholy offspring of *Mad* magazine, Mel Brooks's movies, and 'Our Town.'" See the *Washington Post*, Book World, January 11, 1998, p. 5.

[28]Oddly enough, this theme is also at the heart of Fox's other great television series, *The X-Files*.

[29]See *Die fröhliche Wissenschaft*, sec. 193 (my translation) in Friedrich Nietzsche, *Sämtliche Werke: Kritische Studienausgabe*, ed. Giorgio Colli and Mazzino Montinari, vol. 3 (Berlin: de Gruyter, 1967–1977), 504.

Examining the Text

1. What points does Cantor make in his discussion about how the nuclear family has been represented in television shows of the past? According to Cantor, how does the portrayal of the nuclear family in *The Simpsons* comment on previous television families? For instance, how is the Simpson family similar to and different from the family as portrayed in *The Cosby Show, Married with Children, I Love Lucy,* and *The Flintstones*?

2. In your own words, explain how *The Simpsons* can both mock and celebrate a group or institution. Why does Cantor see this as an important strategy in *The Simpsons*?

3. Based on his discussion of *The Simpsons*, how do you think Cantor defines the term "politics"? What does "politics" include for Cantor? How is his notion of politics different from what we usually think of as politics?

4. *Thinking rhetorically*: One of the distinguishing features of Cantor's article is his extensive use of specific examples drawn from episodes of *The Simpsons*. What is the effect of these numerous examples? Do you think the examples are included primarily to entertain or to persuade the reader? Do they help establish Cantor's credibility?

For Group Discussion

Choose any one of the institutions discussed by Cantor in this article, for instance political parties, the family, religion, community groups, or the media. In a group with two or three other students, go over Cantor's points about how *The Simpsons* portrays this institution: for instance, with mockery, praise, nostalgia, rejection, criticism, acceptance, some combination of these approaches, none of the above, or another approach entirely. Then choose another popular television show that comments on the same institution, and compare how the message of this show is similar to and different from that of *The Simpsons*.

Writing Suggestion

This assignment puts on you the onerous burden of watching an episode of *The Simpsons* in order to compare what you see in this episode with Cantor's arguments about the "deep politics" of the show. Before you watch the episode, you should make a list of the categories that Cantor discusses, including partisan politics, the nuclear family (and the roles played by each character in the family), religion, the community and local political institutions, the media, and the high culture and pop culture references in the show. Then, with a pen and notebook ready, watch the episode. Try your best to take extensive notes as you watch, writing down bits of dialogue or plot summary in the categories you've listed. When you've finished watching the episode and while it's still fresh in your memory, write down your impressions of how the show dealt with each of the categories that Cantor discusses; depending on the episode, some of the categories may be dealt with extensively and others not at all. Finally, based on your notes, write an essay in which you either support or take issue with Cantor's analysis of *The Simpsons* in one or more of the categories. Be sure to use

MATT GROENING

quotations from Cantor's article as well as descriptions of the episode you watched in order to develop your argument.

The Evolution of the Seven Deadly Sins: From God to the Simpsons

Lisa Frank

Lisa Frank, a writer who lives in Los Angeles, is also a fan of The Simpsons. *However, her approach to the show is quite different from Cantor's discussion in the previous article. Frank's article, originally published in the* Journal of Popular Culture, *uses examples from* The Simpsons *to help prove her point that our attitude towards sinning and sinfulness has changed drastically since the "invention" of the "seven deadly sins." Frank draws on the writings of early Christian theologians, along with Dante, Chaucer, Milton, and Shakespeare, as she describes the characteristics of each of the seven deadly sins: pride, envy, wrath, sloth, greed, lust, and gluttony. She contrasts these quotations with examples drawn from* The Simpsons *and with anecdotes from everyday life in contemporary culture to show how radically our ideas about sin have changed.*

Frank may not be entirely serious—that's up to you to decide—but one of the central claims she makes in her article is that in contemporary society we "accept and embrace" sinfulness, and even find ways to use sinning to our advantage. Thus, rather than shunning and avoiding the seven deadly sins, as Christian doctrine teaches us, we learn from The Simpsons *and from popular culture in general the value and usefulness of sinning.*

As you read, recall the arguments made by Cantor that The Simpsons *celebrates the nuclear family, religious belief, and community. How is Frank able to use examples from the very same show to prove a dramatically different point? Is it a question of each author's interpretation of the show, where one author is right and the other wrong? Or does* The Simpsons *invite and support these significantly different interpretations?*

———————

I can personally attest that the seven deadly sins are still very much   1
with us. Today, I have committed each of them, several more than once, before my lunch hour even began. Here is my schedule of sin (judge me if you will):

7:00 - I pressed the snooze button three times before dragging myself out of   2
    bed. *Sloth.*

7:11 - I took an obscenely long, hot shower with no consideration for my sister,   3
    with whom I live. (Don't even bother mentioning the ecological implica-
    tions.) *Greed.*
7:52 - I noticed a pool of cat vomit on the floor and chose to ignore it, knowing   4
    that my sister would dutifully clean it up. *Sloth.*
8:22 - I gave someone the finger after they cut me off in traffic. *Wrath.*   5
8:33 - I helped myself to two complementary pastries at the office meeting   6
    (although I had breakfast only an hour before). *Gluttony.*
8:42 - I flirted with the guy next to me, ignoring the speaker to whom I was sup-   7
    posed to be listening. *Lust.*
10:04 - I ignored someone's incessant knocking on the door of the only restroom   8
    in the building where I work in order to spend more time putting on makeup
    in front of the mirror. *Pride.*
10:42 - I lied and told a homeless person that I didn't have any change.   9
    Sloth.
11:02 - I purposely got to class early so that I could take another student's usual   10
    seat, which was much better than mine. *Envy.*
11:27 - I lied and told someone that I got an A on a paper, when in actuality, I   11
    only got a B. *Pride.*
11:49 - I took three free movie passes, although the sign said to only take one.   12
    Covetousness.

Relatively speaking, I am an average person who commits an   13
average number of the deadly sins each day, give or take a sin. I am not
particularly malicious in my sinning, but it would be untrue to say that
they are committed for righteous purposes, either. I am human; therefore, I sin. A lot. As early Christian doctrine repeatedly points out, the
seven deadly sins are so deeply rooted in our fallen human nature, that
not only are they almost completely unavoidable, but like a proverbial
bag of potato chips, we can never seem to limit ourselves to just one.
With this ideology, modern society agrees. However, with regard to
the individual and social effects of the consequences of these sins, we
do not.

The deadly sins of seven were identified, revised, and revised   14
again in the heads and classrooms of reportedly celibate monks as
moral and philosophical lessons taught in an effort to arm men and
women against the temptations of sin and vice in the battle for their
souls. These teachings were quickly reflected in the literature, theater,
art, and music of that time and throughout the centuries to follow.
Today, they remain popular motifs in those media, as well as having
made the natural progression into film and television. Every day and
every hour, acts of gluttony, lust, covetousness, envy, pride, wrath, and
sloth are portrayed on television. Social ethics have shifted dramatically since those early days, as has our regard for the seven deadly sins.
With the possible exception of our presidents, we no longer struggle to

fight our natural tendency to commit these sins. Instead, we have chosen not only to accept them, but also to embrace them and even to use them to our advantage.

THE HISTORY

The seven deadly sins were first discussed as separate entities   15
throughout the scriptures of the Bible. Later, the sins were developed into self-help guides by the early theologians and moralists, as a means to save the souls of their local rubes from the decay of immorality and to teach them some basic manners. They believed that those who were morally and ethically superior (i.e., monks) were happier human beings and, generally, better company. The goal was to teach men and women how to control their behavior, so that their inner virtue would dominate their wrongful tendencies toward sex, wine, and song, therefore guiding them toward the path of magnetic Stepford-like happiness.

Although the seven deadly sins were originally classified as "cap-   16
ital" in the fourth century by some lesser known monastics, it was the final alterations made in the early sixth century by Gregory the Great (who was so great that he was later made a saint), that led society to regard him as the final and true compiler. Gregory was also noted for making two important points: 1) that pride is the root of all sin; and 2) that there is a distinction between the sins of the spirit (pride, envy, wrath, sloth, and greed) and the sins of the flesh (lust and gluttony). However, much to the dismay of his fellow Christians, St. Greg failed to include a top ten list of examples for each or any of the seven deadly sins.

In the thirteenth century, the well known, anally obsessive   17
St. Thomas Aquinas devised the most methodical and concise analysis of sin, virtue, and vice written (that did not, however, include the name Monica Lewinsky) in his three volume series, *Summa Theologiae*. His teachings were then translated from the abstractness of theology into a more accommodating language suited to the common man (much the same service that *Reader's Digest* performs today). By applying his teachings to everyday life situations, Christians were taught practical methods for overcoming temptation. To further the cause, these teachings were then enumerated into classic literature, so they could be casually name dropped at all the VIP, socially-elite cocktail parties of the day (and for centuries to follow). These titles included Dante Alighieri's *The Divine Comedy,* Geoffrey Chaucer's *Canterbury Tales,* and John Milton's *Paradise Lost.*

In modern society, we have accepted our fate as sinning machines.   18
We have taken what the Christians regarded as vices that harmed
humanity and turned them into virtues that aid mankind. We have
come to understand the power that each of these vices holds and how
it can make us happier and stronger people. Advertising agencies and
marketing firms know this and have taken full advantage of it, selling
each of the seven deadly sins in record numbers and encouraging us to
work with what we've got (while still holding focus groups on the
development of sins eight, nine, and ten).

THE SIMPSONS

Since it was created in the late 1980s, *The Simpsons* has continued to   19
parody all facets of American culture with honesty and with humor.
From our daily mundane activities to key events in world news, it mirrors our society in a dark and distorted light, usually with great insight,
and always in jest. Perhaps the most brilliant aspect of the show is its
uncompromising boldness in addressing the various hypocrisies of our
culture in a way that no other show has ever dared to do before, including those of the seven deadly sins. And so without further delay, I
present. . .

THE SEVEN DEADLY SINS

Pride

> [T]hat first archetype
> Of pride, and paragon of all creation
> Who, of the light impatient, fell unripe.
> —*The Divine Comedy*

According to the cloistered Christian monks of long ago, pride is   20
the mother of all capital sin. Not only that, but it is said to prompt each
of the other sins, as well as being present in them. Robert Broderick's
The Catholic Encyclopedia defines pride as the "inordinate desire for
honor, recognition, and distinction" (490–91). It is the result of a lack of
humility and inevitably develops into a self-love, which becomes sinful
when it causes insubordination, especially to God, who like Santa
Claus, watches our every move. In the second part of Dante's *The
Divine Comedy*, Dante and his guide, Virgil, enter Mount Purgatory and
talk with the souls they meet about the sins the souls have committed

during their lives. They learn that in order to get to heaven, the souls must first cleanse themselves of their past sins by performing a corresponding penance. The first souls Dante and Virgil meet are those who have committed the sin of pride. In bewilderment, they watch as the souls are taught the evil of their ways by carrying heavy stones on their backs as a means to lessen their spirits.

In modern society, pride is not just considered a positive trait, but one of absolute necessity. In each aspect of our lives, from our careers to our romantic relationships, we are made to sell ourselves. Pride in our appearance has become increasingly important in modern times. We spend thousands of dollars on clothing, hair products, makeup, plastic surgery, and gym memberships in an effort to improve our image and the probability of being selected as a contestant in the next installment of *Survivor*. In an episode of *The Simpsons* entitled "Simpson and Delilah," our growing fixation with outer appearance is delineated when Homer commits insurance fraud in order to buy a one thousand dollar bottle of miracle hair growth formula. Instead of being punished for his sin of pride, Homer grows a full head of hair, his love life soars, and he lands a promotion.   21

We are also taught to take pride in our endeavors, especially in our regard for sports. In an episode entitled "Lisa On Ice," Bart and Lisa are on opposing teams in a hockey tournament. The spirited Homer tells Marge: "It's your child versus mine! The winner will be showered with praise, the loser will be taunted and booed until my throat is sore." Such pride in mere athletic achievement would surely not have been understood by St. Thomas Aquinas.   22

Envy

> The infernal serpent; he it was, whose guile
> Stirred up with envy and revenge, deceived
> The mother of mankind.
> > —*Paradise Lost*, Book I, 34–36

In his book, *The Seven Deadly Sins*, Solomon Schimmel defines envy as "the pain we feel when we perceive another individual possessing some object, quality, or status we do not possess" (57). This pain may cause feelings of inadequacy in us, which, in turn, may lead us to wish or even to cause the loss of what is envied. As with wrath, envy not only has the power to fully consume our consciousness, but worse yet, it makes us buy sport utility vehicles when we live in well-paved cities.   23

In Milton's *Paradise Lost,* Satan is a character afflicted with the sin   24
of pride, who refuses to pay homage to God. After leading a rebellion of
the angels, he is cast out of heaven by God and is sent down to hell,
where he plots his revenge—the temptation of Adam and Eve. In Books
I and II, the seven deadly sins are presented individually by seven delegate speakers, each representing the embodiment of their vice. Envy is
represented by Satan's Ed McMahon, Beelzebub, who only feels joy in
another's tragedy and feels pain when others are happy. The reader is
shown the immorality of Beelzebub's envious nature that motivates him
to advise the council to seek revenge against God.

In modern society, we view envy not only as a natural emotion,   25
but also as a tool that helps further us toward self-improvement. Without envy, there would be no competition, and without competition we
might lose the motivation to spend our life savings on the Jenny Craig
program in an effort to ensure that we always look better than our
friends and neighbors. In an episode of *The Simpsons* entitled "Lisa's
Rival," Lisa, the token overachiever, becomes envious of a new student, Allison Taylor, who begins to outshine Lisa. At the end of the
episode, the guiltridden Lisa apologizes for resorting to unscrupulous,
Bart-like tactics in an effort to discredit Allison in a science project competition. However, Allison tells Lisa that if it weren't for their mutual
envy and competitiveness, neither of them would have cause to work
toward their maximum capacity. Thus, envy is shown to be a device
that brings us closer toward achievement and success.

Wrath

> I was angry with my friend;
> I told my wrath, my wrath did end.
> I was angry with my foe:
> I told it not, my wrath did grow.
>
> And I water'd it in fears,
> Night & Morning with my tears;
> And I sunned it with smiles,
> And with soft deceitful wiles.
> —William Blake, "A Poison Tree,"
> *Selected Poetry and Prose of William Blake* (1–8)

Wrath, also referred to as anger, also referred to as my personal   26
favorite emotion, is a milieu of pain and pleasure that arises in our human
existence when a person believes he or she has been unjustly wronged.
Pain is received in reaction to the wrongful injury and pleasure is taken in

the sweet taste of vengeance. Picture this: I go outside to have a much needed meditational moment and a cigarette. First, pain is experienced when my moment is interrupted by the endless, high-pitched screams of the monster children next door, jumping up and down on their inflatable trampoline. Then, pleasure is received when I imagine what might result when I toss my still-burning cigarette over the fence in their direction.

Moloch, the embodiment of wrath (much like his modern coun-   27
terpart, Dirty Harry), is the third delegate speaker in *Paradise Lost*. He is persistent in his argument for a large scale war against God's angels in the War in Heaven in Book VI. Later, though, we see the perils of his nature as his wrath diminishes to fear and cowardice as he is stricken by Gabriel's sword.

Today, from *Sesame Street* to the *Jerry Springer Show*, we are taught   28
the importance of expressing our anger and are urged to not let it be bottled up inside ourselves, but rather to vent and to express to others exactly what we're feeling. The effects of bottling up one's anger are presented in an episode of *The Simpsons* entitled "Hurricane Neddy," featuring Homer Simpson's neighbor and friendly Christian, Ned Flanders. When Ned's house is demolished in a hurricane and his specialty store for the left-handed is looted, he becomes unable to control his emotions and checks himself into the same mental hospital that he was committed to as a child. After observing Ned, a doctor renders his opinion that Ned's anger stems from the inferior therapy he received as a child, when he was urged to suppress his anger, rather than to express it constructively. Unlike Moloch, Ned could have averted his downfall, had he been taught to vent properly in the first place.

Lust

> But virtue, as it never will be moved,
> Though lewdness court it in a shape of heaven,
> So lust, though to a radiant angel link'd,
> Will sate itself in a celestial bed,
> And prey on garbage.
>   —*Hamlet*, Act I, Scene V, 54–58

Lust was referred to by the uptight celibates of early Christianity   29
as an unnecessary, excessive, and irrational feeling that ultimately leads to the committing of various unmentionable acts (all of which, of course, the monks were forbidden to participate). The Early Christians tried desperately to tame the hideous beasts that they believed their bodies to be, yet these efforts inevitably proved unsuccessful. For ultimately, the beast was always unleashed. Quite simply, they believed

mankind is made to honor God with the body and to exercise self control. Should man fail and be spotted in a raincoat at a special showing of *Deep Throat,* he will develop an excessive attachment to the material sexual world and will, eventually, fall down the path of madness.

In the second book of *The Divine Comedy,* the reader is shown the   30
consequences of the sin of lust. In Canto XXV, these sinners are punished by being purged in flames (at a time when being flaming did not involve pink feather boas or an excessive love of musicals).

In modern society, we embrace feelings of lust and revel in the   31
energy and excitement it brings to our lives (hopefully over and over again). We all want to feel sexy and we have accepted our nature as condom-carrying, desire machines, who have long since lost control of the lust we feel. In *The Simpsons,* the notion of socially acceptable lust is conveyed in the nonchalant depictions of an affair between the elementary school principal, Seymour Skinner and teacher, Edna Krabapple; the contemplation of extramarital affairs by both Homer and his wife, Marge; and the casual confession of one-night stands that led to bastard children by both town villain, Mr. Burns, and Homer's senior citizen father, Abe. Even though the Christian Right will never confer, lust has come to be regarded as a desirable attribute for people of all ages and social positions.

Gluttony

> And by his side rode loathsome Gluttony,
> Deformed creature, on a filthie swyne.
> His belly was up-blowne with luxury,
> And eke with fatness swollen were his eyne;
> —*The Faerie Queene,* Book 1, Canto IV, Stanza 21

According to *The Catholic Encyclopedia,* gluttony is "the inordinate   32
longing for or the indulgence in food or drink" (241). So, you see, the pleasure that we seek from scarfing down an entire carton of Ben and Jerry's ice cream or getting wasted at family weddings reflects a weakness of our reason and will and defies God's intention for us. Therefore, it is considered a sin. Allowing our bodies to become unhealthy by the excess of fried chicken and Ding-Dongs is also sinful, since according to Christianity, we are meant to preserve ourselves in order to better serve God (who, by their own account, is ultimately responsible for the creation of fried chicken and Ding-Dongs in the first place). Worse yet, early Christians believed that the pursuit of these pleasures can lead to the committing of other sins, such as lying or stealing in order to fulfill our craving.

These notions are conveyed by the pardoner in one of Chaucer's   33
twenty-four short dramatic stories included in the *Canterbury Tales*.
These stories, written as separate tales told by separate narrators on a
pilgrimage to the Canterbury Cathedral, were meant to entertain and
to provide moral lessons, including those of the seven deadly sins, for
the fictional men and women en route to Canterbury. It is thus that the
Pardoner discourages sins of gluttony by creatively linking food and
drink with decay. He says:

> O thou belly! Stinking pod
> Of dung and foul corruption, that canst send
> Thy filthy music forth at either end. (264)

Gluttony may not make us better people (though it may certainly   34
make us bigger people), but nothing makes us happier than food or
drink, with the possible exception of sex. In a segment of *The Simpsons*
entitled "The Devil and Homer Simpson," Homer demonstrates our
inordinate love for food when he sells his soul to the devil for a donut.
Our love for drink is equally well presented in the tales of the family
Simpson. One of the popular tourist attractions in Springfield, the fictional town where the Simpsons live, is Duff Gardens, which features
rides and attractions that "either promote alcohol consumption or simulate inebriation" (Groening 23).

Covetousness

the nature of man, which coveth divination, thinks it no peril to foretell that
which indeed they do but collect.
                                                           —Bacon 780, XXXV

Covetousness, a.k.a. avarice or greed (which makes it sound bad),   35
is referred to in *The Catholic Encyclopedia* as "the inordinate love of temporal or earthly things" (59). It is a perversion of right values of when
we fail to recognize that we really don't need yet another Ginsu knife in
our collection, but, nonetheless, we still find ourselves maxing out our
credit cards in order to buy it.

In Chaucer's *The Pardoner's Tale*, the sin of covetousness is   36
depicted in the portrayal of three greedy gamblers who swear eternal
friendship to one another in God's name. We are shown the evil that
greed leads to after they lie, cheat, and kill one another for a measly pot
of tattered gold.

It may well be argued that coveting is the one thing all of   37
mankind does well. Let's face it, we're a culture of coveting whores. We

are all so proud of our vast CD collections, our matching shoes and sweaters, our tattoos, and our wide-screen TVs. In *The Simpsons*, our tendency to covet is parodied in their elaborate array of specialty stores in Springfield, including All Creatures Great and Cheap (specializing in freeze-dried pets that come to life when watered), and Corpulent Cowboy (for the plus-sized cowboy enthusiast).

In an episode appropriately entitled "Bart Gets Hit By a Car," the   38
current societal trend of filing frivolous lawsuits is depicted perfectly. After Bart is hit by Mr. Burns' car, Homer takes advantage of the situation and sues Mr. Burns for a million dollars, although Bart remains virtually unscathed. Such ludicrous greed can only surely be laughed at . . . or so, we can only hope.

Sloth

If something's hard to do, then it's not worth doing.
—Homer Simpson, *The Simpsons*, "The Otto Show"

The Maryknoll Catholic Dictionary refers to sloth as "the disinclina-   39
tion to spiritual action" that "leads to tepidity in keeping God's law, the desire for that which is forbidden, faint-heartedness and despair of salvation" (538). Translation—sloth equals laziness. St. Thomas Aquinas, who apparently never had a lover to spend Sunday mornings in bed with, argued that because it is our duty to serve God, a refusal to do so is a sinful denial of the purpose of our existence. In canto XVIII of Dante's *Purgatory*, the reader is presented with the ultimate fate of those who commit sins of sloth. The sinners on Mount Purgatory are absolved of their sins by running swiftly up the mountain and proclaiming expressions of zeal (much like high school cheerleaders do today).

In modern society, mankind's tendency to move toward the realm   40
of sloth is most notably present in the creation of the almighty remote control. Without our natural inclination toward sloth, we would actually have to get ourselves up from the couch or risk watching the fifteenth episode of *The Brady Bunch* marathon. If we weren't slothful, cars, fax machines, and Prozac might never have been invented. Then, where would we be? We would actually be forced to walk the two blocks to our local McDonald's, to talk with one another face to face (oh my God, the anxiety that brings us), and to deal with our emotions on our own.

In *The Simpsons*, our social indifference for the ill effects of sloth is   41
most strongly parodied in Homer, who holds the record as the

employee who has worked the most years in an entry-level position at the plant where he works. In an episode entitled "The PTA Disbands," he says to Lisa: "If you don't like your job you don't strike. You just go in every day and do it really half-assed. That's the American way." Perhaps the best example of Homer's weakness toward sloth is in an episode entitled "King-Sized Homer," where, in order to avoid working, he decides to boost his weight up to 300 pounds so that he will be eligible for disability. Who knows? If disability were around when St. Thomas Aquinas was alive, maybe he would have been tempted, too.

Human nature hasn't changed much since the first century and   42
thankfully, the seven deadly sins are still very much alive and well today, providing endless material for contemporary writers and artists. The only difference is that now we work with our vices instead of against them, not only accepting them as the core of who we are and what is natural within us, but also as a measure of what we're capable of. It's a way of coming full circle, if you will, in mankind's understanding of sin. In time, as social ethics continue to evolve, the notion of the seven deadly sins may ultimately surrender to being a mere relic of the past. Consequently, it will be interesting to see how the artistic and fictional depictions of pride, envy, wrath, lust, covetousness, gluttony, and sloth will, then, further evolve. Stay tuned.

NOTE

With kind thanks to Sharon DeLyser, Tracy Dillon, Ph.D., and Aliza Earnshaw.

WORKS CITED

Alighieri, Dante. *The Divine Comedy.* Trans. Jefferson Butler Fletcher. New York: Columbia UP, 1931.

Bacon, Francis. *The Philosophical Works of Francis Bacon.* Trans. Ellis and Spedding. Ed. John M. Robertson. London: George Rutledge and Sons, LTD, 1905.

"Bart Gets Hit By a Car." *The Simpsons.* Fox TV. 10 Jan. 1991.

Blake, William. *Selected Poetry and Prose of William Blake.* Ed. Northrop Frye. New York: Random House, 1953.

Broderick, Robert. *The Catholic Encyclopedia.* Nashville: Thomas Nelson Inc., 1976.

Chaucer, Geoffrey. "The Pardoner's Tale." *The Canterbury Tales.* Ed.
    Edwin Johnston Howard and Gordon Donley Wilson. New York:
    Prentice-Hall, Inc., 1947.
"The Devil and Homer Simpson: Treehouse of Horror IV." *The Simpsons.*
    Fox TV. 30 Oct. 1995.
Groening, Matt. *Are We There Yet: The Simpson's Guide to Springfield.*
    New York: HarperCollins, 1998.
"Hurricane Neddy." *The Simpsons.* Fox TV. 29 Dec. 1996.
"King-Sized Homer." *The Simpsons.* Fox TV. 5 Nov. 1995.
"Lisa On Ice." *The Simpsons.* Fox TV. 13 Nov. 1994.
"Lisa's Rival." *The Simpsons.* Fox TV. 11 Sept. 1994.
Milton, John. *Paradise Lost.* Ed. Scott Elledge. New York: W.W. Norton &
    Company, 1975.
"The Otto Show." *The Simpsons.* Fox TV. 23 Apr. 1992.
"The PTA Disbands." *The Simpsons.* Fox TV. 16 Apr. 1995.
Schimmel, Solomon. *The Seven Deadly Sins.* New York: Free Press, 1992.
Shakespeare, William. *The Complete Works of William Shakespeare.* Ed.
    David Bevington. 3rd ed. Glenview: Scott, Foresman and Company,
    1980.
"Simpson and Delilah." *The Simpsons.* Fox TV. 18 Oct. 1990.
"Sloth." *The Maryknoll Catholic Dictionary.* Ed. Albert J. Nevins. New
    York: Grosset and Dunlap, 1965
Spenser, Edmund. *The Faerie Queene.* Ed. J. C. Smith. Oxford: Clarendon
    Press, 1909.

Examining the Text
1. Why do you think the article begins as it does, with a list of the sins
that Frank has ostensibly committed on a given morning? What effect
does this opening have on you as a reader? In what ways does it signal
the tone and approach of the rest of the article?
2. In what ways does *The Simpsons* serve as evidence for Frank's argument? What function does the description of episodes from this show
serve in her article?
3. Why do you think Frank includes quotations from *Paradise Lost,
The Divine Comedy, Hamlet,* and other classic works of literature?
4. How would you describe the tone of Frank's article? What specific
words, phrases, and sentences convey that tone? In what ways does
Frank's tone contribute to (or detract from) the argument she presents?
5. *Thinking rhetorically*: Following up on the "as you read" question in
the introduction to this article, what general conclusions can you draw
about the differences between the arguments offered by Frank and
those offered by Cantor? Since both authors use evidence from
episodes of *The Simpsons*, does that mean that they're both correct? Is

one author using evidence more effectively than another? If so, in what ways? Or does *The Simpsons* somehow invite contradictory interpretations?

For Group Discussion

Frank argues that nowadays "we have chosen not only to accept [the seven deadly sins], but also to embrace them and even to use them to our advantage." In your groups, discuss whether you think Frank is serious about this statement and other similar statements she makes in the article. Do you think that she truly thinks we now "work with our vices instead of against them, not only accepting them as the core of who we are and what is natural within us, but also as a measure of what we're capable of"? What evidence can you point to in the article that might indicate Frank is being sincere in making these statements? What evidence is there in the article that might cause you to question her sincerity? If you decide that you think Frank is being sarcastic or ironic and doesn't really believe that nowadays we accept and embrace sin, why do you think she would focus her article on this argument?

Writing Suggestion

Write an essay in which you compare and contrast the article by Frank and the previous article by Cantor. As you develop your comparison, consider the following questions: How does each author deal with the issue of religion in the context of "The Simpsons" and popular culture in general? How does each author use evidence to support his or her assertions? What kind of evidence is used? How is evidence from "The Simpsons" used differently in each article? How does the tone of the author differ in each article? In what ways are the articles organized differently? You might conclude your comparison with an explanation of which article you found more persuasive.

ADDITIONAL SUGGESTIONS FOR WRITING ABOUT TELEVISION

1. This chapter includes two essays about reality television shows. Choose another genre (such as game shows, situation comedies, detective shows, cartoons, talk shows, soap operas, or live police dramas) and analyze the underlying presuppositions of this genre. What specific beliefs, actions, and relationships do these shows encourage? How and why do these shows appeal to the audience? If everything that you knew were based on your exposure to this genre of show, what kind of world would you expect to encounter, how would you expect people to behave toward each other, and what sort of values would you expect them to have? To support your analysis of the genre, use examples from specific shows, but keep in mind that your essay should address the genre or category of shows in general.

2. According to sociologists and psychologists, human beings are driven by certain basic needs and desires. Most of the essays in this chapter attempt to account for the powerful appeal of television in our culture, and several suggest that we rely on television to fulfill needs that aren't met elsewhere. Consider some of the following basic needs and desires that television might satisfy for you or for the broader viewing public:

> to be amused
>
> to gain information about the world
>
> to have shared experiences
>
> to find models to imitate
>
> to see authority figures exalted or deflated
>
> to experience, in a controlled and guilt-free situation, extreme emotions
>
> to see order imposed on the world
>
> to reinforce our belief in justice
>
> to experience thrilling or frightening situations
>
> to believe in romantic love
>
> to believe in magic, the marvelous and the miraculous
>
> to avoid the harsh realities of life
>
> to see others make mistakes

Referring to items on this list, or formulating your own list of needs and desires, compose an essay in which you argue that television succeeds or fails in meeting our basic needs and desires. Use specific television programs that you're familiar with as concrete evidence for your assertions.

3. As the two articles on *The Simpsons* indicate, it's possible for people to interpret the messages of a television show in radically different ways. Choose a show that you're familiar with and about which you think there can be multiple interpretations. You might think about older shows, such as *The X-Files* or *Star Trek,* or more recent shows, such as *South Park* or *The Sopranos.* You might want to watch a few episodes of the show (all of the ones mentioned above have past episodes available on video and DVD) just to remind yourself of the characters, setting, typical plot structure, and other details. Then write an essay in which your thesis states two (or more) possible interpretations of the show. In the body of the essay, explain what details of the show support each of these interpretations. You might conclude the essay by stating which interpretation you find most persuasive.

Internet Activities

1. Game shows have long been a popular television genre, and their popularity of late seems to be on the rise. One reason may be found in their similarity to reality TV shows, in that they allow for a degree of audience interactivity that scripted shows like dramas and comedies lack; after all, viewers can become participants on game shows and gain instant celebrity if they do well. Game shows also seem to appeal to our greed (or our desire to get rich quickly and without too much work) as well as to our competitive nature. In preparation for writing an essay on game shows, recall some of the ones that you've seen on TV, and check the *Common Culture* Web site for links to sites related to game shows. Then, write an essay in which you analyze the reasons why this television genre is appealing to viewers. As part of your essay, you might decide to compare and contrast game shows to reality television shows to determine the relative appeal of these two genres.

2. Although it's difficult to predict developments having to do with the Internet, a possibility discussed by experts is that television and the World Wide Web will, in some way, merge. Perhaps your TV screen will become your computer monitor, or you'll be able to order movies and view television shows through your computer and Internet connection. Already we see some early connections between the two media, for instance in the live Web casts that some TV shows are doing, or in exclusive Web casts (that is, programs or videos that are shown only on the Web and not on TV). In addition, most news and sports shows have companion Web sites that offer viewers additional information, pictures, interviews, etc. Consider some of these developments, discussed in further detail at the links provided at the *Common Culture* Web site. Then, write an essay in which you discuss the ways in which the Web competes with or complements television. Do the two media provide the same kind of information and entertainment, or do they offer fundamentally different viewing experiences?

Reading Images

The image at the bottom of page CI-2 is a still photograph of Nam June Paik's video installation art work, entitled "TV Buddha Reincarnated." Paik is a well-known Korean-American artist whose works incorporate television, video, and other technologies in thought-provoking and aesthetically interesting ways. (If you're intrigued by "TV Buddha

Reincarnated," you can find out more information about Paik and view some of his other work at the Artcyclopedia Web site [*http://www. artcyclopedia.com/artists/paik_nam_june.html*].)

The title of this piece—"TV Buddha Reincarnated"—refers to an earlier and simpler work by Paik, entitled "TV Buddha." In "TV Buddha," Paik positioned a statue of the Buddha looking at a television set; on top of the television set was a video camera, trained on the statue of the Buddha. In essence, the Buddha statue was "watching" himself (or itself) on television.

As you can see, "TV Buddha Reincarnated" incorporates more technologies than the earlier piece: there's a video camera, but also a telephone and a computer. The statue of the Buddha has been refashioned as well, with what appears to be an interior of wires, circuit boards, and batteries.

Begin an analytical essay about this image by first describing it as clearly and in as much detail as possible. Consider issues of perspective, color, positioning, shapes, sizes, and focal point. Next, identify what you see as the three or four most significant components of the work, whether it's the use of the Buddha statue as part of this piece (with the meditational and religious overtones that the statue conveys), the Buddha's high-tech (but seemingly antique) interior, the telephone, the video camera, the computer (replacing the television from the earlier "TV Buddha" piece), or some other component. In separate paragraphs, offer an interpretation of each of these components, attempting to explain what meaning they add to the work. Keep in mind that although what you see in this textbook is a photograph, "TV Buddha Reincarnated" was an installation piece (with the video camera turned on and recording). People viewing the work could walk around it and see it from different angles. You might want to comment on how this interactive viewing experience could change the meaning of different components of the work.

Finally, draw your analysis together in a statement that articulates what you see as the message of "TV Buddha Reincarnated." What story does this art work tell? What point do you think Paik is trying to convey through this piece? In your conclusion, draw on any of the readings in the "Television" chapter that are relevant to your analysis.

Popular Music

A naked man, arms outstretched suggestive of Christ on the cross or an Olympian swimmer about to take the plunge, stands atop a cassette deck. Electric pulses from the tape player reach his brain through head-phones as he gazes heavenward as if in a trance. The phrase "Be the music" scrolls about his midsection, concealing—perhaps replacing—his maleness, as the music fills his every cell. Such is the power music has over us, this TDK ad suggests, that it can take us over completely—mentally, physically, emotionally.

By virtue of its sheer volume, rhythm, and encompassing presentation, music has the capacity to take us to "completely different" psychic spaces. It can lift us from our ordinary sense of reality and profoundly affect our moods, emotions, energy level, and even our level of sexual arousal. Furthermore, the lyrics, when combined with these powerful aural appeals, become all the more potent and suggestive, influencing our feelings of isolation or belonging, our relation to parents and friends, our attitudes toward authority figures, our notions about romance, and our views about gender and race.

The articles in this chapter discuss the ways in which people are "constructed" by what they hear—that is, how their beliefs, values, attitudes, and morals are shaped by the music they listen to. Some observers see this phenomenon as potentially dangerous, since it encourages people—especially young people—to transgress the boundaries imposed by civilized society. However, other critics contend that popular music plays a very positive role in contemporary society, since it allows people to voice feelings and ideas that would otherwise not be widely heard. This is especially the case with rap and hip-hop music, as several writers in the second section of this chapter observe. Originally created by and intended for young, African American inner-city audiences, this music has gained more widespread acceptance, to the point that it appears regularly on MTV and has been adopted by major recording labels, thus giving previously disenfranchised urban youth a more pervasive presence in the popular culture.

As you read these essays, perhaps hooked up to your Walkman and blasting the latest Black Eyed Peas, Coldplay, Gwen Stefani, Papa Roach, or Tupac posthumous release, you might consider the implications of music in your life: the reasons why you listen to certain kinds of music, the messages embodied in their lyrics and rhythm, and the pleasures and possible dangers inherent in letting popular music move you to a "completely different" frame of mind.

The Hip-Hop Generation

Rap and Race: It's Got a Nice Beat, But What About the Message?

Rachel E. Sullivan

Over roughly three decades, hip-hop music has traveled from the Bronx, across the country and around the world. Rap's roots are in New York's African-American neighborhoods, but its audience is just as likely to be Caucasian suburbanites. In the following article, published in the Journal of Black Studies, *author Rachel Sullivan attempts to discern differences in attitude towards rap based on race. She wants to know, for example, whether Black adolescents are more committed to, and more knowledgeable about hip-hop and its practitioners than White youths.*

As Sullivan develops her article, she closely scrutinizes earlier research on rap, which primarily explored rap's role as a form of resistance among Black listeners. In reviewing and analyzing previous research, Sullivan focuses on a key question: Does rap retain a role in racial identification even as its audience grows in size and racial diversity? The article details the result of a poll she conducted among young people—both Black and White—in a Midwestern city.

*As **you read**, notice how the author develops her background information and her hypotheses first before delving into the actual research she conducted. Why do you think it's important for her to acknowledge both the previous research and critique its shortcomings? How did her findings differ from her expectations, as stated at the beginning of the piece?*

RACE AND RAP'S ROOTS

Rap music emerged in the mid-1970s in New York City. Since that period, it has grown from a New York phenomenon to a mainstay of popular music in the United States and around the world (McGregor, 1998). Most of the research on rap music explores its history and development as a social movement (Rose, 1991, 1994) and analyzes the content of lyrics (Henderson, 1996; Martinez, 1993, 1997; Pinn, 1999). Although these studies have contributed to our understanding of

1

hip-hop, they are more focused on music artists and less on rap fans.[1]
Thus, this article marks a departure from much of the research because
it focuses mostly on rap's listeners and their interpretations of rap,
specifically racial differences in adolescents' opinions of rap.

In its early years, rap's fans were primarily Black and Latino;   2
however, the 1980s saw the popularity of rap music expand dramatically. Artists such as Run DMC, LL Cool J, Salt N' Pepa, and the Beastie
Boys all gained popularity not only with urban African Americans and
Latinos but also with White adolescents outside the inner city (Rose,
1994). By the late 1980s, rap was no longer viewed as a fad but as a distinctive musical form. In spite of the increasing numbers of White rap
fans, many people still viewed rap consumers as African American.[2]

How these fans interpret and reinterpret rap music and how   3
important rap music is in their lives have not been thoroughly explored.
Furthermore, studies on the potential differences that racial/ethnic
groups may have are often limited in much of the literature. Given the
racialized political themes in rap (Martinez, 1997), it is possible that
rap's White fans may see rap in a different light. They may also try to
avoid listening to rap that involves a more explicit critique of racism.

During the 1980s, genres of rap became more noticeable, and many   4
rappers turned to more overtly political themes.[3] They addressed gang
violence, police brutality, and other politically charged issues, such as
poverty and racism (Martinez, 1997). The more politically oriented rap
became very popular in the late 1980s and early 1990s (Rose, 1991), a
period that some refer to as the golden era of rap (Powell, 2000). The
group Public Enemy was at the forefront of this movement with songs
like "Fight the Power," "By the Time I Get to Arizona," and "911 is a
Joke" (Drayton, Shocklee, & Sadler, 1990; Ridenhour, Shocklee, & Sadler,
1991; Shocklee, Sadler, & Ridenhour, 1989), all of which addressed the
effects of White racism in the United States (Rose, 1991, 1994). Even
"gansta rappers" injected political views into their music; for example,
Ice Cube's (1991) "How to Survive in South Central" criticizes the Los
Angeles Police Department's treatment of African Americans.[4]

Although more overtly political rap lost popularity in the mid-   5
1990s, some critical discourse is still embedded in the lyrics of many
recent rap songs. Nevertheless, rap's more critical voices have been
marginalized in recent years. Some say that corporate control and marketing have deadened hip-hop's political edge (Powell, 2000). Rather
than offering a critique of the postindustrial United States, which was
more evident in early rap (Rose, 1994), rap's critical voice has faded into
the background. Even though this may not be directly connected to rap's
widening and "Whitening" audience, it is probably not coincidental.

From the start, the public viewed hip-hop culture and rap music   6
through a racist lens. Rappers and rap fans were often portrayed as

menacing Black adolescents, and rap music was vilified as violent and misogynistic (Feagin, Vera, & Batur, 2001; Rose, 1994). As Rose (1994) noted, rap music has both overt and covert political dimensions: "Rap's poetic voice is deeply political in content and spirit, but its hidden struggle—that of access to public space and community resources and the interpretation of Black expression—constitutes rap's hidden politics" (p. 145). She also pointed out the "struggle between rappers' counter-dominant speech and the exercise of institutional and discursive power against them." Rose (1994) highlighted the role of institutional racism leveled against rappers, who were given poor record contracts and forced into recording divisions that had smaller budgets. Moreover, these same acts found it nearly impossible to put together concert tours because insurance companies refused to insure their concerts. These companies argued that rap acts were a great risk because of their allegedly violent fans (Rose, 1994). Thus, the struggle for rap artists and fans to gain respect has taken place in the context of pervasive, institutionalized White racism.

Of particular interest are the criticisms leveled by White politi-   7
cians, almost all of whom viewed rap as producing potential victimizers. Vice President Dan Quayle attacked rapper Tupac Shakur for promoting violence. President George H. W. Bush also voiced his antirap (anti-Black) sentiments when he criticized Ice-T and Body Count's song "Cop Killer" (Rose, 1994). (Ironically, neither politician had heard these albums; in fact, Dan Quayle did not even pronounce Tupac's name correctly, and Bush failed to realize that Body Count was in fact a heavy metal group.) President Bill Clinton also leveled similar charges at rapper Sista Souljah, arguing that she advocated killing Whites (Feagin et al., 2001). Other well-known political figures, such as Bob Dole and Supreme Court nominee Robert Bork, have also added their own critiques of rap music (Ogbar, 1999). All these criticisms of rappers were made by politicians in a highly racialized (racist) context. Even though many of their criticisms may have relayed legitimate concerns about violence, their discussions also appealed to fears that these rappers would somehow incite violence among Black youth; moreover, they appealed to Whites' fears of Black youth.

Rap music has long been the target of criticism from the popular   8
media, White politicians, and even some older African Americans. Often, antirap sentiments are thinly veiled anti-Black comments. Moreover, these antirap comments are often framed differently from those attacking White musicians, as Binder's (1993) analysis of media accounts indicates. Her study indicated that White heavy metal fans were viewed as potential victims of the music, whereas predominantly Black rap fans were viewed by media outlets as potential victimizers.

A small number of African American leaders have also criticized   9
rap on similar grounds. C. Deloris Tucker and Reverend Calvin Butts
have both argued that rap music promotes violence and misogyny and
have publicly criticized rap music on these grounds (Ogbar, 1999; Rose,
1994). White media outlets, possibly in search of African Americans to
make criticisms, have quickly picked up Black leaders' criticisms.

In the new millennium, critics from within the hip-hop commu-   10
nity have argued that many contemporary artists have abandoned
antiracism messages and focused instead on money and sexual exploits
(Powell, 2000). They go on to say that corporate control and the desire to
reach a "wider and Whiter" audience has led rap away from overtly
antiracist sentiments. Although hip-hop artists have always been
diverse and self-critical (Ogbar, 1999), criticism from within hip-hop
seems to have increased in recent years.

Although many leaders have argued about the effects of rap on   11
its fans, studies exploring effects of rap are few. This is partly because
the small body of research on hip-hop focuses more on artists, lyrical
content, and the history of hip-hop. Moreover, any social differences
(gender, age, race, social class, etc.) in fans that could be correlated with
influence are generally overlooked.

RACE AND RAP'S AUDIENCE

Debates regarding the effects of rap music are missing one very critical   12
voice—that of fans. While politicians and other community leaders
argue over "how corrupting" rap can be and researchers look at the
themes and history of the music, few people speak directly to rap
fans asking them what they feel about rap and how important it is in
their lives.

In spite of the criticism, the popularity of rap continues to grow.   13
Billboard's top 100 albums of April 11, 1998, included 13 rap albums,
whereas *Billboard*'s top 100 albums of January 20, 2001, included 21 rap
acts.[5] Given the tremendous increase in rap's popularity, it is evident
that rap's White audience has grown dramatically. In the early 1990s,
Public Enemy's Chuck D estimated that 60% of his audience was White
(Rose, 1994). However, it is very difficult to make any precise estimates
of the racial makeup of the rap audience because no specific information has been collected.

Even though many people have made claims about rap music   14
and its effect on its listeners, research on music effects generally focuses
on young Whites and their attitudes about rock and roll, punk, or heavy
metal (Arnett, 1992, 1993, 1995; Fox, 1987; Gold, 1987; Rosenbaum &
Prinsky, 1991; Roe, 1995; Snow, 1987; Stack, Gundlach, & Reeves, 1994).

Jonathon Epstein's (1994) collection of essays, *Adolescents and Their Music: If It's Too Loud, You're Too Old*, does include 1 essay on rap music, but this is surrounded by 13 other essays all dealing with rock and heavy metal.

Many of the studies analyzing rap have been more qualitative   15
and theoretical, focusing on the role of rap music in popular culture (Fenster, 1995; Martinez, 1997) and its use as a form of resistance (Berry, 1994; Martinez, 1993; Pinn, 1996; Rose, 1991). However, these studies did not examine multiracial samples and did not ask specific questions focusing on the attitudes of rap's audience.

One study by Epstein, Pratto, and Skipper (1990) analyzed the   16
relationship between behavior problems and preference for rap and heavy metal music. This study indicates that preference for heavy metal and rap was highly correlated with race: 96% of those who preferred heavy metal were White, and 98% of those who preferred rap were Black. In addition, they found that preference for both forms of music was not associated with behavior problems.

Three studies have focused on young people's opinions of rap.   17
One study written by Berry (1994) concluded that rap helps low income African American youth develop empowering beliefs that help them connect with their culture and develop positive identities. However, the weakness of this study is that it does not give a detailed analysis of students' responses or the questions students were asked, so it is difficult to gain a thorough understanding of the students' attitudes. Moreover, the sample only included low income African Americans in an Upward Bound program.

The second study from *American Demographics* magazine reported   18
on a survey conducted by Teenage Research Unlimited (Spiegler, 1996). This study revealed that 58% of those younger than 18 years and 59% of those 18 to 20 years *liked* or *strongly liked* rap. This study also found that several fashions associated with hip-hop were considered "in" by 12- to 19-year-olds. Seventy-eight percent of adolescents said that baggy clothes were in, 76% said pro sports apparel was in, and 69% said hooded sweatshirts were in. The author argued that rap has expanded the market for White designers such as Tommy Hilfiger and DKNY; moreover, style of dress has become a way for Whites to connect with Blacks without actually having any face-to-face contact. Although this indicates that there are racial differences, those differences were not the focus of the survey.

Finally, the most detailed study of rap's effect on adolescents was   19
conducted by Kuwahara (1992). This study found that 13.3% of Black college students listened to rap all the time, and 29.7% listened to rap often. Kuwahara also found that Black men had a stronger preference for rap than Black women. The analysis of White college students

revealed that 51.6% of White men and 68.9% of White women *seldom* or *never* listened to rap. When the two groups were compared, White students demonstrated less knowledge of rap acts regardless of their preference for rap music. However, Whites and Blacks did not differ much in their reasons for listening to rap. Both groups preferred the beat most and the message second. Drawing on qualitative responses from Black students, Kuwahara argued that rap music and the styles of dance associated with it serve as forms of resistance to the dominant culture. However, findings from this study may be dated. Rap's popularity has increased significantly since 1992, and the White audience for rap has increased (*The Source*, 1998).

Because of the rapid change in rap's popularity, it is necessary to   20
reevaluate youth's attitudes toward rap. More literature on rap is also needed because the current writings are few and many theoretical claims have not been substantiated through empirical work.

METHOD AND HYPOTHESES

To explore the relationship between racial identity and preference   21
for rap music, I conducted surveys in a small Midwestern city. I approached teenagers on a Saturday afternoon in a local mall and asked them to fill out a brief survey about the music they listened to. In creating this survey, I developed four major hypotheses related to racial differences in adolescents' reactions to and interpretations of rap music.

First, I predicted that Black adolescents would have stronger   22
preferences for rap music than White adolescents. Given the high percentage of African American rappers and rap's history of articulating concerns of Black youth, I expected that young African Americans would like rap music more than Whites. Moreover, at least two prior studies found this (Epstein et al., 1990; Kuwahara, 1992).

For the second hypothesis, I expected that Black respondents   23
would be more likely to agree with the statements, "Rap is a truthful reflection of society," "I find myself wearing clothes similar to rappers," and "I find myself using words or phrases similar to rappers." If Kuwahara's 1992 study is still accurate and Black students like rap music more than their White counterparts, then I expect that Black adolescents will incorporate rap music and rap acts into their everyday life to a greater extent than White adolescents.

Next, I hypothesized that Black adolescents would listen to a   24
wider variety of rap acts. In spite of rap's increasing popularity with Whites, I expected that Black adolescents will still be more knowledgeable about rap acts (Kuwahara, 1992).

Finally, I expected that Whites (who are rap fans) would be most   25
likely to say that rap has affected their opinions about racism. If rap
does act as an interracial socializer, then it may very well be that White
fans learn about the effects of racism and discrimination through rap
music. White adolescents may also be more affected because African
American adolescents are more likely to have many more sources, such
as parents, religious leaders, or peers, through whom they learn about
racism. On the other hand, White adolescents are probably less likely to
hear about racism through peers and family members; therefore, they
may be most affected by rap. Although the study was generally guided
by hypotheses, I also put an open-ended question at the end of the survey, asking rap fans why they listened to rap, which was designed to
give the respondents an opportunity to express their feelings outside of
the narrow categories that I previously provided.

FINDINGS

The response rate was very high: Only 3 adolescents refused to partici-   26
pate in the study. There were a total of 51 respondents—21 Blacks,
17 Whites, 7 Latinos, and 6 who marked other categories. Nineteen of
the respondents were girls and 32 were boys, and the mean age of
respondents was 16 years old. The questionnaire included 13 questions. Participants were asked their age, gender, and race as basic
demographic questions. Then they were asked how much they liked
rap on a scale ranging from 10 (*It's my favorite music*) to 1 (*I don't like it at
all*). Participants were also asked how many hours they listened to rap
and which three rap artists they listen to most. The next 4 questions
asked how rap had influenced them, and the final, open-ended question asked those who listened to rap why they listened.

Rap music appeared to be very popular within the sample. Over-   27
all, students rated rap 7.98 on the 10-point scale. The mean rating was
8.57 for Blacks, 7.18 for Whites, and 8.29 for Latinos.[6] However, the difference between racial groups was not statistically significant.[7] What
was most surprising was that 22 of the respondents gave rap a 10, saying that it was their favorite music. Within this group, racial differences
were more evident: 13 of these respondents were Black, 3 were Latino,
4 were White, and 2 marked multiple racial categories or no category.[8]
This does provide some evidence that rap is more popular with African
Americans; however, the difference did not appear to be significant in
this sample.

Overall, respondents registered slight agreement with the state-   28
ment, "Rap is a truthful reflection of society." Moreover, there were not
strong racial differences. African Americans had a mean of 3.3, and

Whites had a mean 3.1 (on a 5-point scale where 5 represented *strongly agree*). So the hypothesis that Blacks would be more likely to agree with this statement was not confirmed. However, another finding did come out of this particular question. Those who were rap fans were much more likely to agree that rap is a truthful reflection of society.[9]

The hypotheses that African Americans were more likely to agree   29
with the statements, "I find myself wearing clothes similar to rappers" and "I find myself using words or phrases similar to rappers" were supported. Black adolescents were much more likely to report wearing clothes similar to rappers, and they were somewhat more likely to say that they used words similar to rappers. Only 1 White respondent agreed that he wore clothes similar to rappers; however, 8 Whites reported that they used words or phrases similar to rappers.

White fans were more likely to say that rap had affected their   30
opinion about racism than Black fans. However, what was even more interesting was that the overall agreement for Whites, regardless of whether they were fans, was higher than that of African Americans. Even though there were racial differences in agreement with this statement, overall the respondents moderately disagreed; they did not believe rap has had much of an effect on their opinions about racism.

The two open-ended questions in the survey provided the most   31
interesting answers. They were used to address the third hypothesis that Black adolescents would be more knowledgeable about rap. I asked the respondents to name their three favorite rap acts, and provided them with three blanks. African Americans did name a wider variety of rap acts; they named a total of 27 different acts, and only 3 answers were left blank. In contrast, White adolescents named only 15 different acts, and left 14 blanks. Racial differences in whom adolescents named as their favorite rap acts were small.[10]

Although I formulated no hypotheses about racial differences in   32
reasons for listening to rap music, some differences were evident. Whites, particularly young women, were much more likely to say that they listened to rap because it had a "nice beat." Black adolescents gave more diverse responses, and the most common response was variations of "I like it." However, a significant number of African American adolescents gave responses that indicated that rap was an affirmation of their experiences. The following five responses were indicative of these responses:

> Teach me things or tell me things about life. (Black male, 17)
>
> Because it hits home, when I listen to it it's something I can relate to. (Black male, 18)
>
> Because it tells the truth about how us Black people live being raised in the ghetto. (Black female, 15)

> Because I like the way it sounds and some rapper just tell the truth
> and the way things really are. (Black female, 17)
>
> Mostly because of the way they talk and state about people's real
> life. (Black female, 13)

Only one White respondent had a similar response: 33

> Because some of the things the rappers rap about is the same type of shit
> that happens in everyday life to sombody [sic] from the hood. (White
> male, 18)

Even the response by this 18-year-old White male is written in   34
third person, indicating some distance between this young man and
"sombody [sic] from the hood."

These statements indicate that there are some racial differences in   35
why African Americans and Whites listen to rap and how knowledgeable they are about rap. Unfortunately, the methodology limited the
ability to probe on many of these questions, which could have provided
more detailed answers and revealed more specific racial differences.

Overall, this survey indicates that the racial gap in adolescents'   36
desirability ratings for rap is closing. Nevertheless, racial differences in
adolescents' perceptions of rap still exist. However, this survey is primarily exploratory. It does not include a random sample and does not
allow us to further explore how Whites and Blacks are affected by and
committed to rap.[11]

RAP'S RACIAL IMPLICATIONS

The most striking finding from this study is that the racial gap in pref-   37
erence for rap music is closing. Unlike the previous research (Epstein
et al., 1990), this study shows that preference for rap was not significantly different for Blacks and Whites; however, this may be misleading. Black adolescents named more rap artists and were more likely
to say that they wore clothes like rappers and used words or phrases
similar to rappers. Moreover, African Americans were more likely to
say that they listened to rap because it was truthful and taught them
about life. Although White adolescents say they like rap, many of the
White respondents in this survey had difficulty naming three rap
artists, which indicated that they did not have a high level of commitment to the music. Rap may only be a fad and a phase, as indicated
by this statement given when a respondent was asked why he listened to rap:

> I used to but now I don't anymore. (White male, 16)

The responses to the open-ended questions on the survey support   38
the idea that African Americans have higher commitment to rap. The
wider variety of rap acts Black adolescents listed provides evidence
that they have a broader knowledge of rap. Some of the White respondents' answers to the question, "Why do you listen to rap?" indicated
that Whites were listening to rap because it has a "good beat," so the
message of the music was not as important as the sound. This leads me
to believe that although Black and White adolescents are saying that
they like rap, they may be getting two different messages from the
same music. Many young African Americans appear to be looking at
rap for its messages about life and its aesthetically pleasing sound, yet
Whites seem to be listening almost exclusively because of the aesthetically pleasing sound. In many ways, these findings support Berry's
(1994) and Martinez's (1997) arguments that rap is a form of resistance.
Although young African American rap fans are not arguing that rap
leads them into social protest, they seem to be indicating that it offers
a counterdominant message that they use as an affirmation of their
experiences.

Not only are rap music and hip-hop culture a potential form of   39
resistance, they may also have broad-reaching implications for identity
development and maintenance. Although many may see music as a
passing phase, it is often a source of information about one's group (or
other groups), and it can also be a (re)affirmation of one's identity. This
could be particularly true for young African Americans, who are less
likely to have their experiences reflected in the dominant culture.

Therefore, future research needs to examine not just how much   40
adolescents report they like to rap but their knowledge and commitment to the music. Furthermore, the extent to which Black and White
adolescents are getting different messages from the same rap songs
must be clarified.

Because so many young Whites listen to rap, future research   41
should also focus on rap as an interracial socializer. Whites in this study
(who were fans) indicated that rap had affected their opinions about
racism. The survey did not measure how rap had affected their opinions
of racism or how it has affected their opinions of African Americans
more generally. However, rap as an interracial socializer may be detrimental for many reasons. First, many Whites who listen to rap may be
motivated by curiosity. Rap may allow White adolescents to satisfy
their curiosities without ever having face-to-face contact or interper-
sonal relationships with any African Americans, so rap can be a way
for Whites to vicariously learn about African Americans. They may be
able to satisfy curiosities about African Americans and even mimic
what they may see as African American life without having
an understanding or appreciation of African American experiences.

Second, rap music does not reflect the diversity of African Americans. Rap often operates from the perspectives of young, urban, Black men. White adolescents may get a picture of African American life that is not inclusive of those who are older, from rural areas, or female (or other important social characteristics). The third reason this could be detrimental is because it may perpetuate prejudices, particularly the view that African Americans are materialistic and hedonistic, which could inadvertently promote stereotypes more than it dismantles them. Although rappers themselves are not fully accountable for how their music is interpreted, many fans may not be accessing alternative sources of information about African Americans. In addition, many rap songs are fictional and do not even represent the artists' true beliefs or those beliefs of African Americans in general. Rap, like any other cultural product, is also subjected to corporate control, which could potentially limit antiracist messages because those messages may not be as economically profitable.

I am not making the case that rap sends only negative messages   42
to White adolescents. Many artists do have images that are less stereotypical (Ogbar, 1999); however, those voices are often less commercially successful. Rap would probably be best when combined with other forms of interracial socialization, particularly in a society that has been built on racism, sexism, and capitalism. Daily interactions or interactions that are not from media could be beneficial.

One of the more interesting findings in this study is the overall   43
agreement with the statement that rap is a truthful reflection of society.[12] Future research has many questions to answer in this respect. If adolescents agree that rap is a truthful reflection of society, do they value rappers' opinions about political and social issues? Moreover, it is important to understand what aspects of rap adolescents think are truthful. Do young people believe what rappers say about topics such as gender, sexuality, racism, police brutality, wealth, and poverty? This may be very difficult to ascertain, given the ambivalence and the great diversity found within rap. This also has practical applications for political organizers who want to mobilize the hip-hop generation.

Rap music research has a very promising future. There is little   44
work in this field, so virtually any aspect of rap music is open to research. Moreover, rap music and hip-hop culture are the products of the first generation to be raised in the postindustrial era (Rose, 1994). Research on racial formations and their effects on the post–baby-boomer generations need to be pursued further given the unique technological and social changes experienced by the hip-hop generation.[13]

Although this article focuses primarily on racial differences,   45
future studies can focus on several other areas. Factors such as gender,

class, age, and urbanicity affect the production and consumption of rap
and preferences for rap. The area of racial differences also needs to be
explored further. Many of the responses to this survey need elabora-
tion. Precisely why and how there are racial differences in consumption of rap can be identified through in-depth interviews. In addition,
rap's effects on Latinos also need to be analyzed. Latino rappers, such
as Mellow Man Ace, Kid Frost, Fat Joe, Cuban Link, and Cypress Hill
(who have Black and Hispanic members), have made strong contributions to hip-hop, and much research, including this, does not explore
Latino opinions. The role of rap as a form of interracial socialization
should also be analyzed because such a large number of White adolescents are listening to rap, even those who are not fans cannot help
being exposed to at least some rap. Adolescents' interpretations of
rap songs must also be examined so researchers can better understand
what they are listening to and why they think it is important or unimportant. Finally, more research must be done because rap is constantly
changing.

Even though rap music is a relatively new phenomenon, it con-   46
tinues to expand. The current market for rap and hip-hop products is a
lucrative business. What started out in the Bronx has spread nationwide. Although rap music is reaching a multiracial audience, this
research indicates that Black and White adolescents are influenced by
rap in different ways. These differences need to be further examined
and interpreted.

NOTES

[1]It is important here to explain the difference between the term *rap* and
hip-hop. In the movie *Rhyme and Reason* (Block, Spirer, & Sollinger, 1997), rapper
KRS-One defines hip-hop as the cultural phenomenon that appeared in the
mid- to late 1970s. Hip-hop culture is primarily organized around the experiences of urban, minority youth, and the primary expressions of hip-hop culture
include rapping, break dancing, and graffiti art (Rose, 1994). Some also include
DJing as the fourth pillar of hip-hop. So, rap music is a form of expression used
by people within the hip-hop community or culture.

[2]It is interesting to note that the Puerto Rican members of the early hip-
hop culture were ignored and forgotten by the popular media and many later
rap fans.

[3]It is very difficult to make clear distinctions between the genres of rap.
Some divide rap into East Coast and West Coast. East Coast rap generally comes
from New York, and West Coast rap comes from Los Angeles and its surrounding cities. Dividing rap by coast has some merit because most rappers come from
these cities, but it fails to address differences in rap beyond geographic subcultures. Moreover, the division also ignores the recent ascendance of rappers from

the South. Others have used the terms *old school* and *new school*—old school rap would be anything before the late 1980s, and new school anything after that point. Rap has also been classified as gansta rap, political rap, dance rap, fast rap (*The Source*, 1998), and gospel rap.We would also argue that materialistic rap and bravado rap should also be added to the list of rap genres.

[4]Ice Cube and other rappers have long been critical of the Los Angeles Police Department, which seems quite appropriate given the recent revelations about police brutality and misconduct in that department.

[5]Artists such as Snoop Doggy Dogg, Tupac, Notorious B.I.G., Eminem, and others have produced multiplatinum records.

[6]Because there were only 7 Latinos in the study, it is difficult to make any accurate generalizations.

[7]All tests of statistical significance were conducted using chi-square. Results are significant if they have a p value of .05 or less.

[8]Only 2 of the Black respondents giving rap a 10 were Black young women. In fact, only 3 of the 22 were females.

[9]Those who rated rap 6 or higher were considered to be fans.

[10]Black adolescents chose Master P as their favorite rap act followed by Tupac, Puff Daddy, Notorious B.I.G., and Ice Cube. The most popular rap artists, according to White adolescents, were Master P followed by Mase, Tupac, Puff Daddy, and Bone Thugs-n-Harmony.

[11]Commitment in this study is operationalized as: the ability to name rap artists, wearing clothes similar to rappers, using words or phrases similar to rappers, belief that rap is a truthful reflection of society, and listening to rap because it is truthful or teaches about life.

[12]This question was included in the survey because it is one main argument used to justify explicit and violent lyrics in rap.

[13]I intentionally avoid using the term *Generation X*; we find this term to be racially loaded. I argue that this term has been used almost exclusively to refer to young, middle-class, White men and their experiences. Personally, I prefer the *hip-hop generation*. Although many may think this is also racially loaded, hip-hop has always been a multiracial movement, which makes the term more inclusive.

REFERENCES

Arnett, J. (1992). The soundtrack of recklessness: Musical preferences and reckless behavior among adolescents. *Journal of Adolescent Research, 7,* 313–331.

Arnett, J. (1993). Three profiles of heavy metal fans: A taste for sensation and a subculture of alienation. *Qualitative Sociology, 16,* 423–443.

Arnett, J. (1995). Adolescents' uses of media for self socialization. *Journal of Youth and Adolescence, 24,* 519–533.

Berry, V. (1994). Redeeming the rap music experience. In J. Epstein (Ed.), *Adolescents and their music: If it's too loud you're too old.* New York: Garland.

Binder, A. (1993). Constructing racial rhetoric: Media depictions of harm in heavy metal and rap music. *American Sociological Review, 58,* 753–767.

Block, C. X., Spirer, P., & Sollinger, D. (1997). *Rhyme and reason* [Video recording]. Produced by City Block and Asian Pictures. West Hollywood, CA: Miramax Films.

Drayton, W., Shocklee, K., & Sadler, E. (1990). 911 is a joke. On *Fear of a Black Planet.* New York: Def Jam Records.

Epstein, J. S. (Ed.). (1994). *Adolescents and their music: If it's too loud you're too old.* New York: Garland.

Epstein, J. S., Pratto, D., & Skipper, J., Jr. (1990). Teenagers, behavioral problems, and preferences for heavy metal and rap music: A case study of a southern middle school. *Deviant Behavior, 11,* 381–394.

Feagin, J. R., Vera, H., & Batur, P. (2001). *White racism: The basics* (2nd ed.). New York: Routledge.

Fenster, M. (1995). Understanding and incorporating rap: The articulation of alternative popular musical practices within dominant cultural practices and institutions. *Howard Journal of Communications, 5,* 223–244.

Fox, K. J. (1987). Real punks and pretenders: The social organization of a counterculture. *Journal of Contemporary Ethnography, 16,* 344–370.

Gold, B. D. (1987). Self-image of punk rock and nonpunk rock juvenile delinquents. *Adolescence, 22,* 535–544.

Henderson, E. A. (1996). Black nationalism and rap music. *Journal of Black Studies, 26,* 308–339.

Ice Cube. (1991). How to survive in South Central. On *Boyz N the Hood* [Cassette]. Burbank, CA: Qwest Records.

Kuwahara, Y. (1992). Power to the people y'all: Rap music, resistance, and Black college students. *Humanity and Society, 16,* 54–73.

Martinez, T. (1993). Recognizing the enemy: Rap music in the wake of the Los Angeles riots. *Explorations in Ethnic Studies, 16,* 115–127.

Martinez, T. (1997). Popular culture: Rap as resistance. *Sociological Perspectives, 40,* 265–286.

McGregor, T. (1998). Worldwide worldwide. *The Source: The Magazine of Hip-Hop Culture & Politics, 100,* 109.

Ogbar, J. (1999). Slouching toward Bork: The culture wars and self-criticism in hip hop music. *Journal of Black Studies, 30*(2), 164–183.

Pinn, A. (1996). Gettin' grown': Note on gansta rap music and notions of manhood. *Journal of African American Men, 2,* 61–73.

Pinn, A. (1999). How ya livin'? Notes on rap music and social transformation. *Western Journal of Black Studies, 23*(1), 10–21.

Powell, K. (2000, October 9). My culture at the crossroads: A rap devotee watches corporate control and apolitical times encroach on the music he has loved all his life. *Newsweek,* p. 66.

Ridenhour, C., Shocklee, H., & Sadler, E. (1991). By the time I get to Arizona. On *Apocolypse 91 . . . The Enemy Strikes Back*. New York: Def Jam Records.

Roe, K. (1995). Adolescents' use of socially devalued media: Towards a theory of media delinquency. *Journal of Youth and Adolescence, 24,* 617–630.

Rose, T. (1991). "Fear of a Black planet": Rap music and Black cultural politics in the 1990s. *Journal of Negro Education, 60,* 276–290.

Rose, T. (1994). *Black noise: Rap music and Black culture in contemporary America.* Hanover, NH: Wesleyan University Press.

Rosenbaum, J. L., & Prinsky, L. (1991). The presumption of influence: Recent responses to popular music subcultures. *Crime & Delinquency, 37,* 528–535.

Shocklee, H., Sadler, E., & Ridenhour, C. (1989). *Fight the Power*. New York: Def Jam Records.

Snow, R. P. (1987). Youth, rock' n roll, and electronic media. *Youth and Society, 18,* 326–343. *The Source: The Magazine of Hip Hop Music, Culture & Politics.* (1998, January). Special 100th Issue.

Spiegler, M. (1996, November). Marketing street culture: Bringing hip-hop style to the mainstream. *American Demographics,* pp. 28–34.

Stack, S., Gundlach, J., & Reeves, J. (1994). The heavy metal subculture and suicide. *Suicide and Life Threatening Behavior, 24,* 15–23.

Examining the Text

1. The author states that debates regarding the effects of rap have tended to exclude the voice of fans. Other studies have been more "qualitative and theoretical." In trying to figure out the role of rap in society, why is it important to speak to fans of the music? Why is it important to examine rap on the basis of race? What insights can fans provide that might not be available by simply looking at music sales, concert attendance, fashion adoption, and so on?

2. Author Sullivan calls rap an "interracial socializer" (Line 25). What do you understand by this term? What are the positive and negative consequences of using rap in this role? In your opinion, does music have the power to bring people of differing backgrounds together?

3. What specific racial differences did the author find in her study? How do these differ from the results she predicted in her hypotheses? Does anything about her study surprise you or challenge previously held beliefs or opinions?

4. If you had been asked the same questions as those surveyed for the article, what would your answers have been? Would your responses align with those surveyed, based on your cultural background?

5. *Thinking rhetorically:* Based upon the tone and the format of this piece, who would you say its intended audience is? Provide textual evidence to support your contention that this article was written to enable hip-hop fans to understand better why they listen to the music. Do you think the author is trying to persuade readers to adopt a particular position; if so, what do you think that position is? Find samples in the text that illustrate the article's thematic core belief. By the end of the text, do you feel that the article provided satisfactory answers or raised more questions?

For Group Discussion
Historically, music has played an important role as a force for social change: in the Civil Rights, Anti-Vietnam War, and Labor Movements, for example. Rap has also a social justice element to it. Discuss whether you think that role is diminished as rap becomes more mainstream or that the power of the lyrics will be lost when audiences cannot identify with its Black-oriented message.

Writing Suggestion
Imagine you are conducting research attempting to measure the influence of rap music on students at your school. Design fifteen to twenty questions that you think would be key to ask, and then administer your survey to as many students as is feasible. In an essay, explain the reasoning behind your choice of questions, making sure to explain your hypotheses and intended methodology, and then discuss the results of your study. Consider this question as a possible thematic center for your paper: Is your sample student population representative of the youthful American population at large, or is it significantly different?

The Miseducation of Hip-Hop

Evelyn Jamilah

In this article, the author points to criticisms currently being leveled at rap music and hip-hop culture from within the community of African American educators. No one would deny that rap culture has unprecedented popularity among young people. Nevertheless, many of these observers believe that while the themes embodied in rap music may reflect real-life situations within America's inner cities, rap's influence may be ultimately counterproductive, causing Black students to perform worse in school—which, in turn, will perpetuate the negative economic and social conditions which rappers dramatize in their lyrics. Some observers go so far as to insist that young African American students turn away from this popular artform, while others suggest that some university courses focus their attention on rap, to make some connections between this popular form and the work of Black historians, sociologists, urban psychologists, and so forth.

As you read this article, attempt to determine the author's own stance toward this topic. Does she play the role of dispassionate observer, merely recording journalistically the arguments swirling around this hotly debated topic, or can you detect a certain agenda, a rhetorical stance underlying her reportage? Note also your own reactions to points raised during this piece. The commentators presented in this article will probably cause you to have some emotional reaction; try to set your emotions aside momentarily, make note of specific points of agreement or disagreement as they arise.

When Jason Hinmon transferred to the University of Delaware two years ago from Morehouse College in Atlanta, the 22-year-old senior says he almost dropped out his first semester.   1

He says that for financial reasons, he came back here to his home-town. But in many ways, he had never felt so abandoned.   2

"I came to class and my professors didn't know how to deal with me," he says, between bites of his a-la-carte lunch. "I could barely get them to meet with me during their office hours."   3

Dark-hued, dreadlocked and, well, young, he says many of his mostly White professors figured they had him pegged.   4

"They took one look at me and thought that I was some hip-hop hoodlum who wasn't interested in being a good student," he says.   5

But if Hinmon represents the "good" students with grounds to resent the stereotype, there are faculty who profess there's no shortage of young people willing to live up—or down—to it.   6

"You see students walking on campus reciting rap lyrics when they should be reciting something they'll need to know on their next test. Some of these same students you won't see back on campus next semester," says Dr. Thomas Earl Midgette, 50, director of the Institute for the Study of Minority Issues at historically Black North Carolina Central University.   7

"These rap artists influence the way they dress," he continues. "They look like hoochie mamas, not like they're coming to class. Young men with pants fashioned below their navel. Now, I used to wear bell-bottoms, but I learned to dress a certain way if I was negotiating the higher education maze. I had to trim my afro."   8

The difference between today's students and their parents, faculty and administrators is marked, no doubt. Technology's omnipresence—apparent in kids with little patience for anything less than instant meals, faster Internet information and cellular ubiquity—is certainly at play when it comes to explaining the divide.   9

But what causes more consternation among many college and   10
university officials is a music form, a culture and a lifestyle they say is
eating away at the morals, and ultimately the classroom experience, of
today's college students.

Hip-hop—brash, vulgar, in-your-face hip-hop—is indisputably   11
the dominant youth culture today. Its most controversial front men
floss mad ice (wear lots of diamonds and other expensive jewelry),
book bad bitches (usually scantily clad, less than the take home kind of
girl), and in general, party it up. Its most visible females brag about
their sexual dexterity, physical attributes, and cunning tactics when it
comes to getting their rent paid.

With college completion statistics at an embarrassing low and the   12
Black–White achievement gap getting wider by the semester, perhaps
it's time to be concerned whether the culture's malevolent message is
at play.

But can atrocious retention rates really be linked to reckless   13
music? Or do university officials underestimate their students? Is it
that young folk today have no sense of history, responsibility and plain
good manners? Or are college faculty a bunch of old fogies simply
more comfortable with Marvin Gaye's "Sexual Healing" than Little
Kim's sexual prowess?

Is this no different than the divide we've always seen between   14
young people and their college and university elders? Or do the dis-
parities between this wave of students and those charged with educating them portend something more disparaging?

THE GAP

At the heart of the rift between the two groups is a debate that has both   15
sides passionately disturbed.

Young people say they feel pigeonholed by an image many of   16
them don't support. They say the real rub is that their teachers—Black
and White—believe the hype as much as the old lady who crosses the
street when she sees them coming.

And they'd like their professors to consider this: They can listen   17
to the music, even party to it, but still have a response just as critical, if
not more so, than their faculty and administrators.

Others point out that the pervasiveness of hip-hop's immoral   18
philosophies is at least partly rooted in the fact that the civil rights
movement—the older generation's defining moment—surely did not
live up to all its promises for Black America.

And further, they say it's important to note that not all hip-hop is   19
irresponsible. In fact, some argue that it's ultimately empowering,

uplifting and refreshing. After all, when was the last time a biology professor sat down with a Mos Def CD? How many can even pronounce his name?

Older faculty, administrators and parents alike respond that the   20
music is downright filth. And anyone associated with it ought to have their mouths and their morals cleansed.

There's a real problem when a marijuana-smoking ex-con named   21
Snoop Doggy Dog can pack a campus auditorium quicker than Black historian John Hope Franklin; when more students deify the late Tupac Shakur and his abrasive lyrics than those who ever read the great Martin Luther King Jr.'s "I Have a Dream" speech; when kids decked out in sweats more pricey than their tuition complain that they can't afford a semester's books; when the gains they fought so hard for are, in some ways, slowly slipping away.

"I think what causes us the most grief is that hip-hop comes   22
across as heartless, valueless, nihilistic and certainly anachronistic if not atheistic," says Dr. Nat Irvin, president of Future Focus 2020, an urban futures think tank at Wake Forest University in North Carolina. "Anyone who would argue with that needs to take a look for themselves and see what images are prevalent on BET and MTV."

"But I don't think there's any question that the disconnect comes   23
from the fact that old folks don't have a clue. They don't understand technology. The world has changed. And there's an enormous age gap between most faculty on college campuses and the rest of America," he says.

More than 60 percent of college and university faculty are over   24
the age of 45. Meanwhile, nearly 53 percent of African Americans are under 30 and some 40 percent are under 20.

That means more than half of all Blacks were born after the civil   25
rights movement and the landmark *Brown vs. Board of Education* case.

"There's no big puzzle why these kids are coming with a different   26
ideology," Irvin, 49, says.

THIS IS WHAT BLACKNESS IS

It is universally acknowledged that rap began in New York City's   27
Bronx borough nearly 30 years ago, a mix of Jamaican reggae's dancehall, America's funk music, the inner city's pent-up frustrations and Black folks' general propensity to love a good party.

Pioneering artists like the The Last Poets, The Sugar Hill Gang,   28
Kurtis Blow and Run-DMC combined creative genius and street savvy to put hip-hop on the map.

Its initial associations were with graffiti and party music, according   29
to Dr. Robin D. G. Kelley, professor of history and Africana studies at
New York University.

"Then in the late '80s, you begin to see more politicized manifesta-   30
tions of that. BDP, Public Enemy . . . In essays that students wrote that
were not about rap music, but about the urban condition itself, they
would adopt the language. They would quote Public Enemy lyrics,
they would quote Ghetto Boys," says Kelley, 38.

"This whole generation of Blacks in particular were trying to   31
carve out for themselves an alternative culture," he continues. "I saw a
whole generation for the first time say, 'I don't want to go to corporate
America. I don't want to be an attorney. I don't want to be a doctor.
I don't want to get paid. I want to make a revolution.'"

"The wave that we're in now is all over the place," he explains.   32

But even hip-hop's fans stop short at endorsing some of the
themes prevailing in today's music and mindset.

Kevin Powell, noted cultural critic and former hip-hop journalist,   33
says the biggest difference between the music today and the music at
its onset is that "we don't own it."

"Corporate America completely commodified hip-hop," he says.   34
"We create the culture and corporate America takes it and sells it back
to us and tells us, 'This is what Blackness is.'"

And while Powell, 34, says he is disappointed in some of the   35
artists, especially the older ones who "should know better," many students are their staunchest defenders.

Caryn Wheeler, 18, a freshman at Bowie State University, explains   36
simply that "every day isn't about love." Her favorite artists? Jay-Z,
OutKast, Biggie Smalls, Tupac and Little Kim, many of whom are
linked to hip-hop's controversial side. "We can relate because we see
what they are talking about every day," she says.

Mazi Mutafa, 23, is a senior at the University of Maryland College   37
Park and president of the Black Student Union there. He says he listens
to jazz and hip-hop, positive artists and those who capture a party
spirit. "There's a time to party and have fun, and Jay-Z speaks to that,"
he says. "But there needs to be a happy medium."

Interrupting, senior Christine Gonzalez, 28, says a lot of artists   38
like Jay-Z tend to be revered by younger students. "As you get older,
you tend to tone down your style and find that happy medium," she
says. "It's all a state of mind."

"People have to understand that Jay-Z is kind of like a 100-level   39
class—an intro to hip-hop. He brings a lot of people into its fan base,"
Mutafa chimes in. "But then you have groups like The Roots, which are
more like a 400-level class. They keep you engaged in the music. But
one is necessary for the other."

Erick Rivas, 17, a freshman also at the University of Maryland, says   40
he listens to Mos Def, Black Star, Mobb Deep, Wu-Tang Clan and sometimes other, more mainstream acts like Jay-Z. "Hip-hop has been a driving force in our lives. It is the soundtrack to our lives," he explains.

KEEPIN' IT REAL

But if hip-hop is the soundtrack to their lives, it may also mark the fail-   41
ure of it.

De Reef Jamison, a doctoral candidate who teaches African   42
American history at Temple University in Philadelphia, surveyed 72 Black
male college students last summer for his thesis. Then a graduate student
at Florida, A&M State University, Jamison was interested in discovering if there are links between students' music tastes and their cultural
identity, their grades and other key indicators.

"While the lines weren't always so clear and distinct, I found that   43
many of the students who had a low African self-consciousness, who
overidentified with a European worldview and who were highly materialistic were often the students who listened to the most 'gangster'
rap, or what I prefer to call reality rap," he explains.

As for grades, he says the gangster rap devotees' tended to be   44
lower than those students who listened mostly to what he calls more
conscious rap. Still, he's reluctant to draw any hard and fast lines
between musical preference and student performance.

"I'd recommend that scholars take a much closer look at this," he   45
says.

Floyd Beachum, a graduate student at Bowling Green State   46
University in Ohio, surveyed secondary [school] students to try to
ascertain if there was a correlation between their behavior and the
music they listened to.

"The more hyper-aggressive students tended to listen to more   47
hardcore, gangster rap," he says. "Those who could identify with the
violence, the drive-by shootings, the stereotypes about women—many
times that would play out in their lives."

But Beachum, who teamed up with fellow Bowling Green gradu-   48
ate student Carlos McCray to conduct his research, says he isn't ready
to draw any sweeping conclusions either.

"Those findings weren't across the board," he says, adding that   49
he believes school systems can play a role in reversing any possible
negative trends.

"If hip-hop and rap influence behavior and you bring all that to   50
school, then the schools should create a very different environment and
maybe we'll see more individuals go against the grain," he says.

Even undergraduates say they must admit that they see hip-hop's   51
squalid influence on some of their peers.

"It upsets me when some young people complain that they can't   52
get a job but when they go into that interview, they refuse to take off
their do-rags, their big gold medallion and their baggy pants," says
Kholiswa Laird, 18, a freshman at the University of Delaware. "But for
some stupid reason, a lot of them feel like they're selling out if they
wear proper clothes."

"That's just keepin it real," explains Davren Noble, 20, a junior at   53
the University of Delaware. "Why should I have to change myself to
get a job? If somebody wants to hire me but they don't like my braids,
then either of two things will happen: They'll just have to get over it or
I just won't get the job."

It's this kind of attitude that many in higher education see as the   54
crux of the problem.

"We're not gonna serve them well in the university if we don't   55
shake their thinking about how dress is going to influence job opportunities," says Central's Midgette.

Noble, from Maplewood, N.J., is a rapper. And he says that while   56
he grew up in a posh suburb, he often raps about violence.

"I rap about positive stuff too, but as a Black person in America,   57
it's hard to escape violence," he explains. "Mad Black people grew up
in the ghetto and the music and our actions reflect that."

For sure, art has been known to imitate life. Hip-hop icon Sean   58
"Puffy" Combs—who two years ago gave $750,000 to his alma mater,
Howard University—is currently facing charges on his involvement in a
Manhattan nightclub shooting last December. Grammy-winning rapper
Jay-Z, also was connected with a night club dispute that ended with a
record company executive being stabbed last year.

A BAD RAP?

A simple explanation for the boldness of much of rap's lyrics is that   59
"artists have always pushed the limits," Kelley says.

But what's more, there is a politically conscious, stirring, enrich-   60
ing side of hip-hop that many of its fans say is often overlooked.

"Urban radio stations play the same songs every day," says   61
Powell, a former reporter for *Vibe* magazine. "The media is ghettoizing
hip-hop. They make it look passe."

Those often included in hip-hop's positive list are Lauryn Hill,   62
Common, Mos Def, Dead Prez, Erykah Badu, Talib Kweli and other
underground acts. Indeed, many of them have been active in encouraging

young people to vote. Mos Def and other artists recently recorded a song in memory of Amadou Diallo, "Hip-Hop for Respect."

This is the side of hip-hop many young people say they'd like 63 their faculty to recognize. This is also the side that some people say faculty must recognize.

"There are scholars—I've seen them do this before—who will 64 make a disparaging remark about a whole genre of music, not knowing a doggone thing," NYU's Kelley says. "That's the same thing as saying, 'I've read one article on rational choice theory and it was so stupid, I dismissed the whole genre.' . . . People who are trained in their own fields would never do that with their own scholarship and yet they are willing to make these really sweeping statements."

"And they don't know. They don't have a critical understanding of 65 the way the music industry operates or the way in which people engage music," he says. "But they are willing to draw a one-to-one correlation between the students' failure and music."

Some professors argue that another correlation should be made: 66 "My most serious students are the die-hard hip-hop fans," says Dr. Ingrid Banks, assistant professor of Black Studies at Virginia Tech. "They are able to understand politics because they understand hip-hop."

Banks says that more of her colleagues would be wise to better 67 understand the music and its culture. "You can't talk about Reagan's policies in the '80s without talking about hip-hop," says the 30-something scholar. "If you start where students are, they make these wonderful connections."

CURRICULAR CONNECTIONS

If the augmentation of hip-hop scholarship is any indication, academe 68 just may be coming around to at least tolerating this formidable medium.

Courses on hip-hop, books, essays and other studied accounts of 69 the genre are being generated by a pioneering cadre of scholars. And while many people see that as notable, there's not yet widespread belief that academe has completely warmed to the idea of hip-hop as scholarship.

Banks, who has taught "Race, Politics and Rap Music in Late 70 Twentieth Century America" at the Blacksburg, Va., school, says she's experiencing less than a speedy response to getting her course included into the department's curriculum.

"I understand that it usually takes a while to get a course 71 approved, but there have been courses in bio-history that were signed off on rather quickly," she says.

But if academe fails to find ways to connect with hip-hop and its   72
culture, then it essentially will have failed an entire generation, many
critics say.

"What's happening is that administrators and teachers are faced   73
with a real crisis. And that crisis they can easily attach to the music,"
Kelley says. "It's the way they dress, the way they talk. The real crisis is
their failure to educate; their failure to treat these students like human
beings; their failure to come up with a new message to engage students."

"Part of the reason why there is such a generational gap is   74
because so few educators make an effort to understand the times in
which they live. You can't apply '60s and '70s methods to teaching in
the new millennium. You can't apply a jazz aesthetic to hip-hop
heads," says Powell, who lectures at 70 to 80 colleges and universities a
year. "You have to meet the students where they are. That's the nature
of education. That's pedagogy."

And while Wake Forest's Irvin says he would agree with that   75
sentiment, he also sees a role that students must play.

"What I see as being the major challenge that these kids will deal   76
with is the image of young, urban America," Irvin says. "Young people
need to ask themselves, 'Who will control their identity?'"

"If they leave it up to the media to define who they are, they'll be   77
devastated by these images," he says. "That's where hip-hop is killing us."

Examining the Text

1. What judgment does Dr. Thomas Earl Midgette of North Carolina
Central University make about students he sees on campus? What
judgment do you make about Dr. Midgette—that is, do you agree with
his belief that hip-hop attitude and fashion might somehow contribute
to academic and/or social failure?

2. The article alludes to "technology's omnipresence." Describe this
concept and cite some concrete examples to support its validity. What
effect does technology have on young people, according to this article,
and how does Jamilah associate technology with the generation gap
that exists within school systems?

3. Where did rap music originate, according to the author? How did it
come about, and how did it evolve through subsequent decades? What
form(s) does rap take today?

For Group Discussion

Jamilah asks the question concerning hip-hop styles and attitude, "Is
this no different than the divide we've always seen between young
people and their college and university elders?" Based upon your own
experience as a member of the hip-hop generation (even if you're not a

rabid fan of hip-hop), attempt to answer this question: Are the styles
and behaviors of today the same as the bell-bottoms and Afros to
which Dr. Midgette refers near the beginning of this article, or is there
something more insidious in hip-hop culture and its effect on students?

Writing Suggestion

Write an essay in which you comment on Jamilah's statement, "There's
a real problem when a marijuana-smoking ex-con named Snoop Doggy
Dogg can pack a campus auditorium quicker than Black historian John
Hope Franklin; when more students deify the late Tupac Shakur and
his abrasive lyrics than those who ever read the great Martin Luther
King Jr.'s 'I have a dream' speech." As you formulate a thesis, decide
first whether or not you agree with this statement by the author. Next,
spend some time freewriting on the topic, letting your mind range over
a wide range of points of contention or agreement. Having accomplished this activity, begin to cut and paste those supporting points into
an order that has a coherent logical development, and then fill in that
framework with supporting paragraphs that contain concrete evidence
and examples from your experience, reading, and music listening.

Pop Goes the Rapper: A Close Reading of Eminem's Genderphobia

Vincent Stephens

*In this article, author Vincent Stephens uses the term genderphobe to critique
the lyrics of hip-hop artist Eminem. Stephens defines genderphobe as someone
who uses language more typically invoked by homophobes but applies it irre-
spective of the recipient's sexual orientation. In other words, in his songs
Eminem uses anti-gay terms broadly and does not confine the derogatory
remarks to those who are homosexual.*

Originally published in the journal Popular Music, *Stephens's article
examines closely the semantics of Eminem's songs, attempting to link language to perceptions of behavior and image. The article also analyzes responses
to the rapper's lyrics, including those by the Pet Shop Boys and Mariah
Carey—both of whom are critical of Eminem—along with Eminem's chastising responses to his critics' accusations.*

*Underlying the article's dissection of the rapper's lyrics is an attempt to
understand the connection between the songs and issues of masculinity as well
as the role of gender.* **As you read**, *attempt to gain a clear understanding of
how the author uses very specific definitions for certain sociological and/or*

*social-scientific terms. These may be somewhat different from your current
understanding and are central to the pivotal argument the author makes in the
article.*

INTRODUCTION

Hip-hop musician Eminem (real name Marshall Mathers; alter ego   1
'Slim Shady') is the most provocative and controversial musical performer at the end of the twentieth century and the beginning of the
twenty-first century. Catchy songs and a shrewdly crafted public
image define the popular 'white trash' rapper's 'appeal'. Underlying
his pop packaging is a menacing ability to artfully capture latent and
explicit levels of cultural misogyny and homophobia in his songs. It is
unclear if he is a sophisticated satirist and/or a shameless exploiter
revelling in misogyny and homophobia for commercial gain. Both
arguments continue to inspire discourse questioning his moral responsibility as a performer and influence on his largely teenage audience.

In this article I argue that Eminem is more properly termed a gen-   2
derphobe than a homophobe because he explicitly uses homophobic
language to critique gender behavior, not sexual orientation. To begin,
I define Eminem's relation to genderphobia and the term's social implications. Next, I discuss the centrality of genderphobia in establishing
Eminem as an 'authentic' rapper. Then, I examine the Gay and Lesbian
Association Against Defamation's (GLAAD) accusations that Eminem's
lyrics on the 2000 album *The Marshall Mathers LP* are homophobic, and
his response. Finally, I analyse the Pet Shop Boys and Mariah Carey's
answer songs, which directly address Eminem's genderphobia and
authenticity. The tension between celebrities critiquing other celebrities
for having contrived images and *all* celebrities' need to construct a
marketable image haunts the Pet Shop Boys and Carey, as well as
Eminem. Thus a consideration of persona informs my reading of pop
and hip-hop personas.

EMINEM: GENDERPHOBE OR HOMOPHOBE?

Numerous critics and organisations brand Eminem as a homophobe   3
because of his explicit use of epithets such as 'faggot' and 'lez' in his lyrics
(from 2001's 'Criminal'). Such accusations are credible because they highlight Eminem's blithe exploitation of homophobia (and misogyny) in his

music. However, Eminem's critics fail to expose the complexity of his lyrics. Through a close reading of Eminem's lyrics and persona, I identify the distinctions between sexual object-choice and gender behaviour that the rapper makes in his lyrics and rhetoric. Too many critics unjustifiably collapse genderphobic aspects of hip-hop rhetoric under the rubric of homophobia. Conflating gender behaviour and sexual object-choice distorts the arguably dominant role of gender as an impetus for discrimination.

DEFINING GENDERPHOBIA

Genderphobia must be understood in relation to homophobia and   4
transphobia because they are easy to conflate but quite distinct. The distinctions between homophobia, transphobia and genderphobia are less about semantics than recognising the specific tensions defining subcultural experiences. Flattening out differences among gays, lesbians and transpeople obscures palpable tensions between these groups. Conflation also ignores the way gender discrimination affects the gender behaviour of heterosexually oriented people. The tyranny of gender is that no one is safe from rigid, hegemonic notions of appearance and behaviour.

   Homophobia is a common term in the cultural lexicon that essen-   5
tially refers to discrimination against gay and lesbian people. Transphobia (sometimes defined interchangeably with genderphobia) is a more recent term academics, activists and journalists employ that refers to transgender and transsexual discrimination. Genderphobia is a more obscure term, related to the terms effeminaphobia and sissyphobia (Bergling 2001), that refers to a more covert form of gender discrimination based primarily on behaviour rather than sexual object-choice or appearance.

   Many US advocacy organisations, such as the Sexual Minority   6
Youth Assistance League (SMYAL), utilise T. Aaron Hans' 'Gender Terminology List'. The List formally defines homophobia as 'The irrational fear of love, affection, and erotic behaviour between people of the same gender'. This definition's emphasis on sexual object-choice overlooks the conflation of gender and sexual object choice that informs homophobic language and violence in practice (Hans 1998). As Canada's Trans Accessibility Project notes, '. . . much homophobia name-calling is related to gender roles. Calling a man a 'pansy' or a 'fairy' is to call him effeminate; in other words, he is not doing his part in upholding the masculine gender standard' (Trans Accessibility Project). Clearly, the appearance of non-conformist *gender behaviour*, rather than knowledge about *sexual behaviour*, fuels homophobic incidents.

SMYAL defines transphobia/genderphobia as 'The irrational fear   7
of those who are perceived to break and/or blur cultural/stereotypical
gender roles, often assumed to be queer' (Hans 1998). Though this definition conflates the terms, they are not exactly interchangeable. Transphobia, particularly the marginalisation of transpeople in lesbian and
feminist communities, is an oft-debated topic among feminist, women's
studies and gender studies scholars. Transphobia literature focuses on the
tensions between those who believe that 'woman' is a biological category
and those who believe 'woman' should be based in self-definition.[1]
These tensions surface in numerous arenas, most infamously the US
Michigan Womyn's Music Festival's 'womyn born womyn' admission
policy (Cvetkovich and Wahng 2001, pp. 131–51).

Genderphobia is a more surreptitious form of dicrimination than   8
transphobia because it quietly adheres to hegemonic notions of gender
behaviour. For example, heterosexual people, wearing gender normative clothing, are sometimes victims of what is termed homophobia.
However, because these victims are not homosexual and are not
marked as transpeople, they are more *properly* termed victims of genderphobia. Eminem, along with other hip-hop musicians, often
espouses homophobic rhetoric, but his most inflammatory attacks are
usually directed at male rivals who deviate from gender roles. Thus he
is as much a *genderphobe* as he is a homophobe.

Gender conformity is often more central of hip-hop's aesthetic   9
than sexual behaviour. My emphasis on gender does not discount
homophobia. Rather, I argue that the gender aspect of sex/gender discrimination is particular to hip-hop and relevant among all sexual
orientations. For example, the answer songs I discuss later challenge
cultural perceptions of Eminem, and, hip-hop culture as singularly
homophobic. The Pet Shop Boys and Carey address Eminem's masculinist gender notions alongside the homophobic subtext. The popular media's more recent exposure of 'homo thug' culture and academic
attention to transphobia, illustrate the growing need for scholarship on
cultures which discriminate primarily on the basis of gender role
behaviour.

The increased integration of 'out' gay, lesbian, bisexual and trans-   10
expression, characterises the 1990s (Walters 2001). Increased visibility
does not inherently erase discrimination, but heightens cultural awareness of what constitutes homophobia and opens up spaces for addressing
it. The presence of queer studies in academe, 'out' personnel in popular
media, and prominent national queer political organisations indicate
growing public interest in queer cultural and political concerns. The
anti-homophobic politics such cultural shifts represent do not, however, directly address or challenge the role of *gender* in shaping cultural

attitudes about behavioural propriety. Genderphobic violence is largely aimed toward persons who violate hegemonic codes of masculine and feminine behaviour. From the mid-1980s through the present, hip-hop culture continues to shape and reflect the values of its audience, particularly teenagers and young adults. Hip-hop is masculinist genre with explicit notions of gender appropriate behaviour which several scholars explore in the context or its own self-defined authenticity of 'realness'.

AUTHENTICITY DISCOURSE AND EMINEM

Gender and sexuality are central to the study of music's cultural and emotional resonance, often referred to as authenticity, in popular music studies. Authenticity is particularly common in studies of rock and pop music genres (Frith 1981, 1983; Gracyk 1996; Dolan and Coyle 1999; Weinstein 1999; Leach 2001; McLeod 2001; Shuker 2001) and country (Lewis 1997; Peterson 1997; Jensen 1998). Several hip-hop scholars (Rose 1992, 1994; Williams 1992; White 1996; Boyd 1997; Watkins 1998) trace authenticity's relevance to the genre and culture. One of the most eloquent, detailed and systematic account of hip-hop authenticity is Kembrew McLeod's 'Authenticity within hip-hop and other cultures threatened with assimilation'. McLeod's article is particularly notable for outlining the centrality of gender conformity to hip-hop culture. 11

Table. Semantic dimensions (McLeod 1999, pp. 138–9).

Semantic dimensions	Real	Fake
Social-psychological	Staying true to yourself	Following mass trends
Racial	Black	White
Political-economic	The underground	Commercial
Gender-sexual	Hard	Soft
Social locational	The street	The suburbs
Cultural	The old school	The mainstream

McLeod notes that as hip-hop's commercial profile increases, the culture becomes more self-conscious about preserving its identity from becoming too mainstream (McLeod 1999, p. 136). Through an analysis of hip-hop magazine articles, letters to the editor, Internet postings and interviews with hip-hop fans, artists and related personnel, she constructs six semantic dimensions of meaning hip-hop community members invoke in discussions of authenticity (McLeod 1999, pp. 138–9). 12

The six areas include social-psychological, racial, political-economic, gender-sexual, social-locational and cultural. Within these six dimensions are several binaries, which speak to specific genre efforts to preserve hip-hop's distinct identity from pop. I reproduce McLeod's chart to illustrate the binaries invoked in each dimension (see Table).

My analysis focuses on McLeod's analysis of the gender-sexual   13 dimension because gender explicitly informs Eminem's rhetoric, including his disavowal of teen pop, and attempts to mimic black hypermasculinity. McLeod notes, 'Selling out is also associated with being soft, as opposed to hard. Within the context of hip-hop, these oppositional terms are very clearly gender-specific, with soft representing feminine attributes and hard representing masculine attributes' (McLeod 1999, p. 142).

Krims further localises authenticity by addressing conventions   14 characterising various rap genres (party rap, mack rap, jazz/bohemian, reality rap). Eminem best fits the 'reality rap' category, which describes 'any rap that undertakes the project of realism, in the classical sense, which in this context would amount to an epistemological/ontological project to map the realities of (usually black) inner-city life' (Krims 2000, p. 70). One of the central characteristics of the genre are musical elements (pitch, bass) connoting a 'hardness' connected to a mythical 'ghettocentricity and masculinity' with an implied disdain or even hostility toward elements perceived as soft or weak (Krims 2000, p. 72–3). Eminem sometimes diverts from the 'reality rap' genre, incorporating skits and songs lighter in tone, exemplifying Krims' notion that rappers' often incorporate multiple genres on albums even if they have a predominant style (Krims 2000, p. 87).

Eminem's biographical narrative aims to validate the 'reality' of   15 his raps. His roots as a white rapper, with a *working-class* background raised in *the streets* of Detroit (he was actually born in Missouri) is central to critics' and audiences' perceptions of him as an 'authentic' white rapper performing in an African-American performance tradition. Further, his often-explicit depictions of genderphobia, violence, misogyny, homophobia and hostility toward pop singers (particularly teen pop singers N'Sync and Christina Aguilera) rhetorically position him as an *enfant terrible*, resistant to mainstream culture.

Though Eminem is white, his poor economic background, affilia-   16 tion with and acceptance by black producers and performers and hypermasculine behaviour validate his social-locational and racial 'realness.' Indeed Richard Goldstein locates Eminem's acceptance by many liberals and black rappers as the result of his avowed populism. Eminem's status as a working-class hero (elevated by the pseudo-autobiographical 2002 film, *8 Mile*) obscures what Goldstein views as the true bond among rappers, sexism toward women (Goldstein 2002, p. 53).

STRANGE BEDFELLOWS: EMINEM AND GLAAD

Hip-hop performer/producer/mogul Dr. Dre discovered Eminem in   17
1998, and he made his commercial debut in 1999 with the single 'My
Name Is' and album *The Slim Shady LP*. The album chronicles
Eminem's sometimes macabre, juvenile and violent imagination and
tongue-in-cheek 'humour'. The track ' '97 Bonnie & Clyde', a murder
fantasy toward his girlfriend, particularly generated controversy for its
violent and misogynist imagery. The album also chronicles his 'white
trash' childhood and contempt toward his mother. By the winter of
2000, the album had gone multi-platinum, won two Grammys and
earned the ire of critics and women's groups.

His 2000 follow-up, *The Marshall Mathers LP*, topped the album   18
charts and catapulted him into the public consciousness as one of the
most notorious performers in contemporary music. Critics often praise
Eminem's fluid delivery, fresh beats and deft rhyming. However,
his violent images and epithet-filled lyrics divide critics who appreciate
his form over his attitudes (George-Warren and Romanowski 2001, p. 304).

GLAAD promptly criticised Eminem's lyrics from the outset of its   19
May 2000 release. According to a GLAAD press release, 'Eminem's
lyrics are soaked with violence and full of negative comments about
many groups, including lesbians and gay men' (Dansby 2000). The
release critiques Eminem and his record label UNI/Interscope that it
deems irresponsible for producing and promoting 'such defamatory
material that encourages violence and hatred'. The release grounds its
concerns in the presumption that 'the market for this music has been
shown to be adolescent males, the very group that statistically commits
the most hate crimes'. GLAAD's release passionately argues 'such disregard for others can lead to discrimination, physical abuse and even
death' (Dansby 2000).

The GLAAD press release clearly defines Eminem's lyrics as   20
homophobic. Tellingly the release does not explicitly reference transpeople discrimination. Nor does it mention the way people of *all* sexu-
alities are potentially vulnerable to discrimination based on their
failure to exhibit socially acceptable *gender behaviour*. GLAAD's over-
sights opened rhetorical space for Eminem to address homophobia
without addressing gender, which is precisely what he did to vindicate
himself. In a July 2000 interview in response to GLAAD's accusations,
Eminem said, 'The term "faggot" doesn't necessarily mean a gay person. To me, it don't' (DeCurtis 2000, p. 18). Eminem uses the term 'faggot' the way hip-hop performers typically employ the term, as a sign of
weakness. In an MTV interview he elaborated: 'Faggot is like taking
away your manhood—you're a sissy, you're coward . . . It doesn't necessarily mean you're being a gay person' (Douglas-Brown 2002, p. 83).

For example, in 'Remember Me?' he rants 'Two faggots can van-   21
ish to volcanic ash and re-appear in hell with a can of gas, AND a
match'. In the more sombre 'Marshall Mathers', he lashes out at teen
pop: 'Boy/girl groups make me sick/And I can't wait 'til I catch all you
faggots in public'. He also addresses his rivalry with rap group the
Insane Clown Posse in the same song, rapping, 'Plus I was here to put
fear in faggots who spray Faygo Root Beer/And call themselves
"Clowns" 'cause they look queer/Faggot2Dope and Silent Gay/Claimin'
Detroit, when y'all live twenty mile away (fuckin' punks)/And I don't
wrestle, I'll knock you fuckin' faggots the fuck out', and the lyrics, 'I
don't get fucked in mine you two little flaming faggots!'.

In these excerpts from *The Marshall Mathers LP*, Eminem specifi-   22
cally uses the term 'faggot' or 'fag' as a battle cry to taunt his rivals by
mocking their masculinity and strength. Eminem's rhetoric is actually
two-fold. First, by using a historically loaded term used as an epithet
for homosexual men, he exploits the term's omnipresent stigma,
regardless of his stated intentions. As Bruce Vilanch notes in a commentary on Eminem and the term 'faggot', 'Lots of younger straight
guys do call each other "fag" when they're not calling each other
"wuss", "pussy", or "dweeb". But most of them know that "fag" has a
harsher connotation. They must because they use it when they really
want to score, when they really want to get under somebody's skin—
which is exactly the way Eminem uses it' (Vilanch 2000, p. 39). Second,
in the context of hip-hop, Eminem's usage of 'faggot' to embarrass or
shame his enemies conforms to hip-hop's genderphobic, masculinist
rhetoric. According to McLeod, 'Within hip-hop, being a real man
does't merely entail having the proper sex organ; it means acting in a
masculine manner' (McLeod 1999, p. 142). Eminem's lyrics and public
persona present him as a jokester and provocateur, but he is aware of
the typical masculinist behaviour in the cultural domain of hip-hop.

In one of the first national stories on underground homosexual   23
hip-hop culture or 'homo thug' culture, journalist Guy Trebay notes
that 'In the hip-hop hierarchy, the faggot is the un-man: passive, dis-
empowered, he's down in the gutter with the bitches and 'hos. By faggot is meant, of course, the girlie man–who vogues in his spare time,
worships the anthemic divas, and takes it up the keister when he isn't
giving head in the local park' (Trebay 2000, p. 46). Indeed, most articles
on 'homo thug' culture consist mostly of African-American men who
do not identify as gay because it signifies effeminate culture (Edwards
2001; Venable 2001, p. 101).

Though Eminem references anal sex in 'Marshall Mathers', his lyrics   24
aim for gender through referencing sex acts. Eminem tends to attack the
feminine 'softness' of boy bands and male rivals like the Insane Clown
Posse more than he attacks their actual sexuality. My aim is not to discredit

or ignore the latent homophobia of the term faggot or his repugnant use of the term. Rather I hope to place it in the cultural context of hip-hop and note the relationship between homophobia and genderphobia, which the single term homophobia does not adequately capture. Eminem blithely dismisses the homophobic charge because he uses the term the way hip-hoppers often do rendering it benign in his mind. Further, he and his interviewers neglect the unquestioned genderphobia of his lyrics. The latent nature of genderphobia slips past the musician and his critics.

GLAAD followed up its initial anti-Eminem release in January 2001   25
when The National Academy of Recording Arts & Sciences (N.A.R.A.S) nominated *The Marshall Mathers LP* for four 2001 Grammy awards, including Album of the Year. In response GLAAD again issued a press release noting the threat of violence lyrics could pose to 'lesbians and gay men', but overlooking the specific threats to gender outsiders his lyrics actually embody (Dansby 2001). GLAAD also organised a protest against his nominations and televised performance outside the ceremony. In a shocking and ironic move, 'out' gay musician Elton John performed 'Stan', a tale of an obsessed fan where Eminem rejects the fan's obsessive fandom and a homosexual advance, with Eminem at the ceremony.

In 2002 Eminem released the chart-topping album, *The Eminem*   26
Show, and his film debut, the semi-autobiographical film, *8 Mile*. *The Eminem Show* (released 29 May) received generally positive reviews and critics noted a slightly milder, more introspective tone to his songs. Critics positively reviewed *8 Mile* (released 8 November) and the film and soundtrack are commercial hits. Interestingly, in *8 Mile*, during a confrontation, Eminem actually defends a gay co-worker when he raps that 'Paul's gay/But you're a faggot'. In response to this, Scott Seomin, entertainment media director for GLAAD, responds 'I believe that scene was strategically put in there to get media attention as well as reveal in an artificial way the many layers of this man. But I don't think he's all that complicated' (Fierman 2002, p. 28). Once again, contempt for Eminem's suspected homophobia obscures his genderphobic rhetoric.

ANSWER SONGS MOCK EMINEM'S AUTHENTICITY

The Pet Shop Boys (PSB) (singer/instrumentalist/writer Neil Tennant   27
and instrumentalist/writer Chris Lowe) are a British dance-pop band formed in 1981 who garnered international commercial success from the mid 1980s to the early 1990s. Since the mid 1990s, they have fallen out of the commercial mainstream, though they have a large US cult following and maintain their commercial success in the United Kingdom. In 1994 both members officially came out and solidified their

status as prominent gay icons by performing at gay political and cultural events.

Critics often praise (and condemn) The Boys for their sly, witty, arch and ironic sensibilities (George-Warren and Romanowski 2001, p. 753). Their pointed, observational style emerges on 2002's *Release*'s boldest track, the cheeky 'The Night I Fell In Love', a song clearly targeted at an Eminem-like rapper. In an MTV.com interview, Tennant discusses the song's genesis. According to Tennant,   28

> Eminem's defence of the homophobic lyrics on his albums has always been that he's not speaking as himself, he's speaking as a character, and he's representing homophobia in America, Tennant explained. I thought it would be interesting to take that method and just to imagine a scene where a boy meets a famous rap star backstage at his concert and is surprised to discover he's gay and ends up sleeping with him. Just to present rap in this homosexual content. I mean there are obviously gay rap stars. (Neil Tennant, cited in Moss 2002)

Tennant elaborates, noting, 'I'm not suggesting he [Eminem] is gay, but he's really fascinated by homoeroticism' (Seymour 2002, p. 1D). Given Tennant's reputation for sly lyrics and statements, it's likely that these statements are somewhat tongue-in-cheek. 'The Night I Fell In Love' does not merely describe a scenario. Intentionally or not, the song questions many elements fundamental to the hip-hop discourse's self-construction, not just Eminem. The fact that Tennant casually declares that there are 'obviously' gay rap stars strongly suggests he exposes hip-hop's often unwelcoming masculinist facade to a wider range of relations. The Pet Shop Boys deconstruct Eminem and hip-hop by shrewdly critiquing the artificiality of hip-hop's hypermasculine rhetoric.   29

Singer/songwriter/producer Mariah Carey is the most popular female recording artist of the 1990s. Carey's songs have grown increasingly personal and shifted from pop toward a more hip-hop soul sound (George-Warren and Romanowski 2001, p. 149). In the fall of 2001, Carey had a physical and emotional breakdown preceding the release of her oft-delayed film and soundtrack project, *Glitter*. During her breakdown, tabloids and magazines published numerous rumours about her, including one about an alleged affair and break-up with Eminem (Keeps 2001, p. 28).   30

In December 2002 during promotion for her comeback album *Charmbracelet*, she tersely asserted in TV interviews that she and Eminem met on several occasions but have no romantic involvement.[2] On the track 'Clown', Carey answers Eminem who 'dissed' Carey on *The Eminem Show* track 'Superman'. In the song, Eminem suggests that   31 he rejects Carey because she is demanding and refuses to have sex with him.[3] In 'Clown', Carey bitterly vents frustration with Eminem's conjecture by mocking his macho image and hip-hop authenticity using specifically gendered language.

In the heated musical battle between Eminem, PSB and Mariah   32
Carey, it is important to consider how their personas inform their lyrical approaches. Dyer's *Stars* focuses on film stars but his discussion of image-making media texts and cinematic 'types' relates to popular musicians. Management-generated promotion, press publicity, film images (in the case of musicians, music videos and TV appearances) and criticism and commentary are the chief texts comprising public star images (Dyer 1979, pp. 68–72). One can loosely define pop singers, who rely on media texts for their images and personas, as discernible types. Based on a broad survey of their public images, PSB are postmodern pop stars on the periphery of pop culture with a self-awareness and sense of detachment. Their type is contemporary and unique among pop singers and notably distinct from film actors. Mariah Carey is a more conventional 'ordinary' girl-next-door who achieves the American Dream but struggles to preserve 'ordinary' self from a corrupting industry (*ibid.*, pp. 49–50). Finally, Eminem is the proverbial 'tough guy' and 'rebel' types Dyer adapts from O.E. Klapp. Similar to a heroic 'tough guy', Eminem is embroiled in a battle against something evil (pop) and uses numerous visual and linguistic tools of ambiguous morality in his quest for 'justice', making him an ambivalent but intangibly charismatic hero (*ibid.*, pp. 55–6). Simultaneously he is a 'rebel' with angst rooted in anomie, self-defining as a misfit but with no clear structural target beyond a generalised conformity (*ibid.*, pp. 59–61). Eminem's need to rebel against pop music is rooted in a reactionary masculine impulse to object to the feminised nature of it. The PSB and Carey challenge his faux rebellion by musically critiquing his constructed masculinity.

INTRODUCING ANSWER SONGS

The PSB's and Carey's songs are answer songs that use a fictional sce-   33
nario and a personal reflection to question the 'realness' of Eminem, which has implications for the performance of 'realness' in hip-hop. 'The Night I Fell In Love' and 'Clown's' lyrics are not notable because they reveal contradictions between Eminem's public image and private self, which, according to Dyer are to be expected. However, they highlight an unusual *depth* of contradiction between Eminem's public masculinist rhetoric and his demure private self. Suggestions that one of

the most notoriously aggressive 'reality' male rappers so drastically differs in image and self negates the fundamentals of a genre premised on credibility and truth. These suggestions are especially significant coming from a gay pop duo and a female pop singer, both from the 'soft' pop music spectrum and representing social identities that hypermasculinity, genderphobia and sexism typically affect.

The PSB use a fictional teen character to mock Eminem's hyper-   34 masculine 'hardness'. The character illustrates Eminem's safe appeal to the 'soft' suburban teen audience and portrays Eminem as an exaggeratedly docile man in a way that teasingly feminises him. Carey posits Eminem as an emotionally underdeveloped boy, rather than a fully grown man, unable to transcend childhood demons. She continually asserts that Eminem is a purely artificial act, an accusation critics usually level at 'pop', whose true self is deeply buried beneath a controlled 'authenticity' facade. 'The Night I Fell In Love' and 'Clown' ultimately reveal a masculinist performance of gender as the key to Eminem's public persona, a performative dimension which extends to hip-hop culture in general. Eminem espouses and exploits homophobic language in his lyrics, but his chief tactic is a celebration of hypermasculinity rooted in the anxieties informing genderphobia and sexism.

'The Night I Fell In Love'

Unlike most rock stars, PSB are overt about their attempts to control   35 their image and dismiss rock culture's investment in authenticity. In *Pet Shop Boys, Literally*, PSB are very conscious of their public images and open about constructing an aura of mystery and emotional affect that is 'anti-nice' and resistant to the 'jolly fun' ethos characterising 1980s and 1990s pop singers (Heath 1992, pp. 35–6, 51–2, 93–6, 195–6, 284–5). The PSB criticise rock stars' and rock critics' self-conscious claims of rock's spontaneity and authenticity (*ibid.*, pp. 31–3, 133, 218). Further, they question the critical coronation of rock as a 'serious', 'political' genre based on rock singers publicly adopting trendy political causes (*ibid.*, pp. 93, 176–8). The PSB's self-awareness and critique of rock's signifiers for authenticity does not exempt them from being stars. But PSB generally avoid conflating their public image with their personal identity and make very few claims to being 'authentic' or 'real'. They are ideal critics of the antics of self-consciously 'authentic' performers.

The PSB use a narrator as a stand-in for Eminem's teen audience   36 and as commentary on the tension between Eminem the performer and person. A male teenager narrates 'The Night I Fell In Love' in the first person voice. The narrator, an eager fan, begins describing his wait after an Eminem-like rapper's concert to meet him. 'I was backstage/Couldn't believe my luck was in/I saw him approach wearing a most approachable grin'. This establishes the fan as a teenager anxious to meet the pop idol. These lyrics resemble a commonly imagined scenario of teenage girls and groupies waiting to meet their idols. However, the narrator is clearly a male. The rapper asks the fan, 'Hey man!/Your name isn't Stan is it?' a clever ode to Eminem's song title of the same name and clearly indicating the fan as a male.

Further clues indicating the young fan's young, suburban sensibility are the narrator's awkward and diffident language and simple rhymes. For example, the narrator expresses surprise that '. . . he spoke so politely/I said I liked his show/Well he just smiled/I guess it happens nightly/And so/I fell in love'. After the narrator and the rapper go to the rapper's dressing room, the rapper takes out a video camera and the fan notes how 'I was so nervous/I had to try hard not to stammer'. The teen's halting tone suggests someone young, frightened and inexperienced. Tennant also carefully modulates his tenor voice to indicate a character younger and more naïve than himself.

The narrator is elated when the rapper breaks the tension and says, 'I'm glad you like the show/That crowd was dope out there tonight, alright'. These comforting words grow into an invitation when he says 'You wanna see some more?/Well be my guest/You can have a private performance'. The teenage narrator naively exclaims, 'I'd fallen in love'. As the song ends, the narrator wakes up post-coitus and joins the rapper at breakfast. The fan jovially notes how 'he couldn't have been a nicer bloke' and that 'I was already late for school by then/I'd fallen in love'.

These excerpts illustrate the young, upbeat suburban sensibility characteristic of rap's primary audience, suburban white teenagers. In the 'Social-Locational (the Street vs the Suburbs)' dimension, McLeod notes that 'Hip-hop artists are often considered sellouts when they distance themselves from their community and sell records primarily to suburban kids . . . ' (McLeod 1999, p. 143). The PSB deftly hint at the immense presence of suburban adolescents among Eminem's fan base through skilfully using language and tone. The fact that the narrator has a homosexual experience with the rapper is less surprising to the narrator than Eminem's docility. The song acknowledges Eminem's alleged homophobia but primarily mocks his genderphobia. 'The Night I Fell In Love' unmasks Eminem and by association, hip-hop's hypermasculine masquerade, and reveals its importance for the genre's authenticity.

To fend off such associations, Eminem is relentlessly critical of teen pop singers in his lyrics. All of his anti-teen pop lyrics rhetorically function to distance him from pop singers with large white, teenage suburban audiences. For example, in the somewhat light-hearted radio and video single, 'The Real Slim Shady', he declares, 'I'm sick of you little girl and

37

38

39

40

boy groups/All you do is annoy me/So I have been sent here to destroy you'. The popular and more sombre follow-up single, 'The Way I Am', elaborates these sentiments when he says, 'I'm not Mr. N'SYNC/I'm not what your friends think'. In 'Marshall Mathers', the rapper vacillates between rapping as Marshall and as Eminem. To differentiate himself from teen pop, Eminem professes, 'I'm anti-Backstreet and Ricky Martin/ With instincts to kill N'SYNC, don't get me started/These fuckin' brats can't sing and Britney's garbage/What's this bitch retarded'. In the same song he notes how 'Boy/girl groups make me sick'.

Eminem doth protest too much however, because his career *is*   41
largely the result of the teenage fans that request his videos on MTV's Total Request Live (TRL) and relish his rebellious persona. The kids populating TRL's soundstage are predominantly white teenagers, not 'hard', urban street kids whose consumption would confer authenticity on the rapper. Eminem attempts to distance himself from the type of gawking suburban fans 'The Night I Fell In Love' hints at, to maintain his credibility as a rapper with street appeal. Though his records appeal to various audiences, his success is largely attributable to white, suburban teenage audiences.

Eminem avoids alienating these fans by simultaneously chastising   42
teens' taste in pop *and* glorifying their intelligence. In an interview in which he addresses *The Slim Shady LP* controversy, he says, 'I think kids are smarter than we give them credit for' (DeCurtis 2000). His acknowledgement demonstrates that teens can distinguish between fantasy and fiction in lyrics and protects his interests. The teenage audience is comprised of fragmented taste cultures which seem contradictory but coexist. The notion that suburban teens exclusively buy pop and urban teens buy edgier forms of music is a fallacy feeding hip-hop's self-mythology. The constructed dichotomy between suburban and urban teen taste cultures is a discursive strategy that maintains hip-hop's authenticity and sells records. Eminem has no investment in what teens purchase, but to ensure that rebellious and wannabe rebellious teens purchase his records, he validates the intelligence of both while slyly skewering teen pop. 'The Night I Fell In Love' captures the contradictions characteristic of Eminem, and hip-hop mythology.

'Clown'

Carey's persona is more precarious than PSB because she tends to pro-   43
ject a literal-minded notion of music as autobiography, thus the liner notes of *Charmbracelet* read, 'This album is like a charmbracelet I'm passing down to you. Here's my story . . .'. Carey's mockery of Eminem does not absolve her of the image issues defining celebrityhood. Carey,

like Eminem, is a celebrity with a constructed persona to project to her audience. Her recent shift toward 'personal' song lyrics presumably aims to present her 'authentic self', much like Eminem defines Marshall Mathers as the 'real' him and Slim Shady as a persona. The obviousness of Carey's self-consciously 'personal' lyrics actually highlights her attempt to restore the ordinary, girl-next-door image she temporarily abandoned for a highly sexualised makeover. In light of her 2001 breakdown, 'Clown' can be understood chiefly as a critique of Eminem *and* an attempt to separate her from Eminem by amplifying her comparative ordinariness and realness.

Ordinariness is a trope of celebrity image-making that can be understood as a construct. As Richard Dyer notes in his discussion of Judy Garland's unique appeal to gay men, 'It is not, in any case, Garland's direct embodiment of ordinariness that is important ... What is important is rather a special relationship with ordinariness, particularly in the disparity between the image and the imputed real person ...'. (Dyer 1986, p. 156). Burdette notes explicit parallels between Dyer's Garland argument and film-maker Todd Haynes' characterisation of singer Karen Carpenter in *Superstar: The Karen Carpenter Story*. Carey, Carpenter and Garland project ordinary images that mask reservoirs of emotional issues (Burdette 1998, pp. 71–2).   44

In 'Clown' Mariah Carey focuses on the constructed nature of Eminem's persona and the gaps between his public and private personas. Carey's account may be tainted by their supposed relationship, indeed much of 'Clown's' tone is petty and vindictive, but her lyrics are worth describing because they complement some of PSB's assertions. Because Ms Carey does not grant lyric reprint permissions, I will discuss the content of 'Clown' and refer to specific verses and choruses when possible.[4] Carey questions Eminem's masculinity employing *his own terms* rather than espousing a broad notion that men cannot be masculine and emotive. Thus when she applies markers of femininity to Eminem's private behaviour and asserts that his image is acutely artificial, she challenges his masculinity and legitimacy using his definitions.   45

Carey tends to write in non-sequiturs rather than narrative form. Still, within the song her gendered accusations are clear. In Verse One her language posits the rapper as a child, rather than a man, and reiterates this with the 'accusation' that he is an extremely emotional, sad person who expresses himself via the feminine mode of tears. Both statements are direct blows to Eminem's professed investment in 'manhood'. Instead of playfully suggesting the rapper is docile, she attempts to expose him as self-pitying.   46

During the Bridge she directly asserts to him that he is in emotional pain and ponders the long-term toll on his life. However, the   47 initial lyrics build from empathy to an assertion that the rapper is deeply wounded and vulnerable in a manner belying his tough image. Carey ends the song in Chorus Four with a lyric capitalising on Eminem's well-publicised legal disputes and emotional resentment toward his mother infantilising the rapper and rhetorically trapping him in a childhood characterised by a domineering mother. Carey's portrait of Eminem as emotionally frail, cuckolded and child-like is interesting because it comes from a female who rejects his narrow definition of masculinity and is one of the few explicit critiques of rap from a pop singer who perceives frailty and insecurity behind the 'hard' façade.

'Clown' mirrors 'The Night I Fell In Love' in noting and mocking   48
the performativity of 'realness'. Structurally, Carey begins each verse expressing regret that she ever shared herself with Eminem and speaks in code about the details of their association. What is key is the chorus, which questions who will care for Eminem once the controversies surrounding him diminish and the audience moves on to the next pop phenomenon. There are two notable elements in the chorus. First, like most hip-hoppers, Eminem surrounds himself with an entourage of rappers. For example, in 2001 he launched the career of protégé rap group D12. Carey implies that much of his industry support will disappear as his popularity and prosperity fade. Second, Carey asserts that Eminem is an ephemeral cultural phenomenon, the proverbial one-hit wonder lacking any enduring appeal beyond his provocative persona. This hints at a deeper implication, that a 'hard' and 'real' genre like rap is as constructed and vulnerable to exploitation as pop. She ends the chorus reiterating that Eminem is a public performer with an unusually wide distance between his image and self, suggested by the imagery of a crying clown. She later continues the puppet show theme likening him to a marionette and coyly asking who is pulling the strings?

Finally, throughout the song, Carey asserts that she had access to   49
a 'real' Eminem obscured from the public. Though all pop celebrities have personas, Carey's references to his 'woeful stories', the 'little boy' inside and 'hidden pain' assert that the rapper's public realness dramatically differs from his private self. In Chorus Four the vague yet boastful lyrics strongly *suggest* Carey possesses insider knowledge regarding the rapper that gives her some licence to critique the dichotomy. However tainted Carey's 'insider's view' may be, 'Clown' is provocative precisely because it suggests that Eminem is inauthentic. The song also breaches one of hip-hop's realness tenets by illustrating how one of its chief icons extensively fails to sustain hip-hop hardness/ realness in everyday life.

HYPERMASCULINITY, GENDERPHOBIA AND GENRE REALNESS

The construction of gender is predicated on patriarchal, heterosexual   50
biases, which subordinate women and persons who resist gender conformity, such as the transgendered. Judith Butler's discussion of gender as performance challenges unquestioned assumptions about the
naturalness of gender behaviour in everyday life (Butler 1990, p.
270–82). Butler argues that gender governs language, clothing, movement, etc., in seemingly invisible ways that disguise the constructed
nature of gender. Butler's argument that gender is performative illuminates the hostile tone of Eminem's lyrics toward women, particularly
his mother and ex-wife, and sex and gender outsiders. Jody Norton
points out that 'The successful performance of masculinity crucially
involves the repression or masking of cultural signs of feminity and, like
all repression, it generates anxiety that expresses itself in various kinds
of acting out: especially misogynistic and homophobic violence'
(Norton 1997, p. 24). Eminem's masculinist performance blends misogyny
and homophobia together in ways linked ultimately to genderphobia.

As a white rapper, Eminem must constantly reify his 'realness',   51
and performing 'hardness' is central to this gesture. According to *Vibe*,
'part of the success in marketing the black man involves selling an
image of him–forbidding, full of untamed rage. He must look tough
and dark and mysterious and sensual. Presentations of black men continue to perpetuate this image, this standard of manliness' (Venable
2001, p. 104). Physically, Eminem will never embody the constructed
hardness of black masculinity, but overcompensates through perpetually espousing his masculinity. He may be White, but he is adamant
about being the toughest and most vitriolic White rapper. The PSB and
Carey's song lyrics mock hip-hop's gender imperative through their
acute characterisations of Eminem.

As 'The Night I Fell In Love' progresses, the narrator relays that   52
'though he seemed like a regular guy/He said we could be secret
lovers/Just him and me'. In these passages the narrator reveals the
tension between the rapper's constructed 'regular guy' masculine performance and homosexual orientation. The mutually exclusive relationship between gender 'hardness' and homosexuality are at odds
with hip-hop's gendered realness. Thus, the narrator recognises the
rapper's gendered masquerade. Toward the end of their encounter the
narrator notes how 'When I asked why have I heard so much about
him being charged with homophobia and stuff/He just shrugged'.
Here the rapper passively acknowledges his gender performance as an
integral part of participating in the hip-hop community.

The narrator's shocked response to the disparity between the   53
rapper's persona and personal demeanour is a veiled critique of gender realness in hip-hop. Hip-hop 'realness' hinges on public perceptions of rappers as storytellers who convey unfiltered truth about their
life experiences. The investment in 'realness' is precisely how hip-hop
artists define themselves against pop, which they characterise as contrived. Eminem is adamant that his songs, notably those performed in
his 'real' Marshall Mathers persona, are genuine chronicles of his life. If
his albums express the real him, even in veiled form, PSB and Carey, to
a lesser extent, suggest that such a sizeable disparity exists between the
'realness' of the performer and the real person that he is transparent.
These distinctions are important because they suggest that Eminem
performs for his audience and for the hip-hop community and only
becomes himself privately. McLeod's construction of hip-hop realness,
based on a broad survey of texts, leaves little room for gaps between
the hip-hop performer and the person. These pop answer records suggest that Eminem violates whatever space for fantasy exists between
rappers and their lives, by continually burying himself in a self-conscious
performance. If the performer and person are supposed to be one in
hip-hop, particularly in the arena of realness, 'The Night I Fell In Love'
and 'Clown' posit Eminem as the ultimate fake.

Hypermasculinity, signified via machismo and compulsory het-   54
erosexuality, are usually central markers distinguishing hip-hop from
pop and other 'softer' genres. However, gender realness is ultimately
more essential to the way in which record companies and artists construct and market hip-hop than sexual orientation. Thus 'The Night I
Fell In Love''s boldest assertion that a rapper could be gay, but would
mask his orientation beneath a masculinist façade, is more believable
than outrageous.[5]

Both 'The Night I Fell In Love' and 'Clown' emerge at a time   55
when the centrality of hypermasculinist behaviour to hip-hop is
increasingly being separated from sexuality. If 'The Night I Fell In
Love' is a fictional depiction of a scenario and 'Clown' is rooted in a
personal vendetta, their critiques are perhaps less isolated than they
seem. It is unclear if the notion of a popular and accepted gay rapper
contradicts hip-hop's deeply masculinist rhetoric. However, if hip-hop
demands hypermasculine performance at all costs, regardless of sexual
orientation, then perhaps the genre has opened up a space where a
masculine homosexual can pass for real, just as the 'fake' Marshall
Mathers passes for the 'Real Slim Shady'. This possible shift does not
necessarily represent progress. Hip-hop's genderphobia is a perverse
demonstration of how the increased salience of gender shifts the
emphasis from homophobia, but does not eliminate the centrality of
gender and sexual conformity in defining our cultural consciousness.

Neither 'The Night I Fell In Love' nor 'Clown' proves that Eminem   56
is gay, a homophobe or even a hypocrite, *per se*. The songs deconstruct
the multi-layered performativity he enacts and suggests a broader pattern of performed authenticity in hip-hop. The answer songs also
reveal the centrality of gendered myths in defining musical genres and
their performers. Hip-hop tolerates sexual deviancy as long as gender
remains intact and tolerates racial outsiders as long as they perform
'realness'. When pop musicians resist the contrived nature of so-called
'outside' genres, it should inspire scholars and critics to reconsider
whom and what such genres symbolically and materially rebel against.
Some may applaud the way hip-hop continues for providing many
ethnic minorities and financially underprivileged urban youth access
to the music industry. However, such seeming race and class gains
have yet to be equalled by progressive challenges toward gender and
sexual hegemony.

END NOTES

[1]Janice G. Raymond's 1979 book, *Transsexual Empire: The Making of the She-
Male* (Boston, Beacon Press) posits male-to-female transsexuals (M-t-F) as infil-
trators to feminism. Riki Anne Wichins speaks as a genderqueer frustrated
with the transphobia of the gay rights movement in 1997's *Read My Lips: Sexual
Subversion and the End of Gender* (Ithaca, Firebrand Books). Other examples of
discussions of transphobia include the following: Wyss, Shannon, 'True Spirit
Conference: facing lesbian and feminist transphobia', in *GW Feminist Review*,
available at *http://www.gwu.edu/~wstu/newsletter/spring99/page10.htm* and
'Genderphobia . . . Do you have it, asks Katrina Fox', first published in *Lesbians
on the Loose*, April 2002, available at *www.katrinafox.com/genderltl.htm*
[2]Carey appeared on 3 December 2002 broadcasts on MTV, NBC's *Dateline
NBC* and 19 December 2002's *Larry King Live* on CNN.
[3]The excerpt of 'Superman''s lyrics mentioning Carey says, 'Play no games,
say no names, ever since I broke up with what's her face/I'm a different man,
kiss my ass, kiss my lips, bitch why ask?/Kiss my dick, hit my cash, I'd rather
have you whip my ass/Don't put out? I'll put you out/Won't get out, I'll push
you out?/Puss blew out, copin' shit/Wouldn't piss on fire to put you out/Am
I too nice? buy you ice/Bitch if you died, wouldn't buy you life/What you
tryin' to be, my new wife?/What you Mariah? fly through twice'.
[4]Full lyrics to 'Clown' can be viewed on *http://www.monarc.com/
mariahcarey/music/M_1.las?click=charmbracelet*
[5]As the rapper and the starstruck narrator in PSB's song move from backstage to the rapper's room (most likely a hotel room), they have a sexual
encounter. The rapper offers the fan 'a private performance', alluding to genital
sex. The narrator says 'he [the rapper] said we could be secret lovers', indicating the rapper's awareness that his homosexuality would have to remain private for the sake of his career. The rapper further discredits realness when he

mocks his own homophobic anxiety from the song 'Stan'. According to the narrator, 'Then he joked/Hey, man!/Your name isn't Stan, is it?/We should be
together!/And he was passionate'. The rapper emerges less as a 'closet case'
than self-conscious purveyor of homophobic rhetoric in service of his career.

REFERENCES

Bergling, T. 2001. *Sissyphobia: Gay Men and Effeminate Behavior* (New York)

Boyd, T. 1997. *Am I Black Enough For You?: Popular Culture From the
'Hood and Beyond* (Bloomington)

Burdette, K. 1998. 'Queer readings/queer cinema: an examination of
the early work of Todd Haynes', *The Velvet Light Trap*, 41, pp. 68–80

Butler, J. 1990. 'Performative Acts and Gender Constitution: an essay
in phenomenology and feminist theory', in *Performing Feminisms:
Feminist Critical Theory and Theatre*, ed. S.-E. Case (Baltimore),
pp. 270–82

Cvetkovich, A., and Wahng, S. 2001. 'Don't stop the music: roundtable
discussion with workers from the Michigan Womyn's Music Festival',
GLQ: A Journal of Lesbian and Gay Studies, 7/1, pp. 131–51

Dansby, A. 2000. 'GLAAD Takes Aim at "Marshall Mathers"', *http://
www.rollingstone.com/news*, 31 May
    2001 'GLAAD Urges Responsible Coverage of Eminem Noms',
    http://www.rollingstone.com/news, 5 January

DeCurtis, A. 2000. 'Eminem responds: the rapper addresses his critics',
Rolling Stone, 3 August, p. 18

Dolan, J., and Coyle, M. 1999. 'Modeling authenticity, authenticating commercial models', in *Reading Rock and Roll: Authenticity, Appropriation,
Aesthetics*, ed. K.J.H. Dettmar and W. Richey (New York), pp. 17–35

Douglas-Brown, L. 2002. 'Another chance for Eminem and gays?', *The
Washington Blade*, 22 November, p. 83

Dyer, R. 1979. *Stars* (London)
    1986. *Heavenly Bodies* (New York)

Edwards, T. 2001. 'Men who sleep with men: brothers on the down
low pose a serious AIDS risk to black women', *Essence*, October,
pp. 76. 187–8

Fierman, D. 2002. 'Acting his rage', *Entertainment Weekly*, 8 November,
p. 28

Frith, S. 1981. *The Sociology of Rock* (London)
    1983. *Sound Effects: Youth, Leisure and the Politics of Rock 'N' Roll*
    (London)

George-Warren, H., and Romanowski, P. (eds.) 2001. *The Rolling Stone
Encyclopedia of Rock & Roll* (New York)

Goldstein, R. 2002. 'The Eminem Consensus', *The Village Voice*,
19 November, p. 53

Gracyk, T. 1996. *Rhythm and Noise: An Aesthetics of Rock* (Durham)

Hans, T. A. 1998. 'Gender Terminology List', *www.smyal.org*

Heath, C. 1992. *Pet Shop Boys, Literally* (New York)

Jensen, J. 1998. *The Nashville Sound: Authenticity, Commercialization, and Country Music* (Nashville)

Keeps, D.A. 2001. 'Mariah's Meltdown', *US Weekly*, 13 August, p. 28

Krims, A. 2000. *Rap Music and the Poetics of Identity* (Cambridge)

Leach, E.E. 2001. 'Vicars of "Wannabe": authenticity and the Spice Girls', *Popular Music*, 20, pp. 143–67

Lewis, G.H. 1997. 'Lap dancer or hillbilly deluxe? The cultural constructions of modern country music', *Journal of Popular Culture*, 31/3, pp. 163–73

McLeod, K. 1999. 'Authenticity within hip-hop and other cultures threatened with assimilation', *Journal of Communication*, 49/4, pp. 134–50 2001.'"*1/2": a critique of rock criticism in North America'. *Popular Music*, 20, pp. 47–60

Moss, C. 2002. 'Pet Shop Boys "In Love" With Gay Eminem Character', *www.mtv.com/news/articles/1453441/20020416/pet_shop_boys.jhtml*, 16 April

Norton, J. 1997. 'Bodies that don't matter: The discursive effacement of sexual difference', *Women and Language*, 20/1, p. 24

Peterson, R.A. 1997. *Creating Country Music: Fabricating Authenticity* (Chicago)

Rose, T. 1992. 'Black Texts/Black Contexts', in *Black Popular Culture: A Project by Michele Wallace*, ed. G. Dent (Seattle), pp. 223–7 1994. *Black Noise: Rap Music and Black Culture in Contemporary America* (Hanover)

Seymour, C. 2002. 'On "Release", Pet Shop Boys show their grown-up side; but track about Eminem may become most noticed', *Atlanta Journal-Constitution*, 16 May, p. 1D

Shuker, R. 2001. *Understanding Popular Music*, 2nd edn (New York)

Trans Accessibility Project: Transphobia and Discrimination, *www.queensu.ca/humanrights/tap/3discrimination.htm*

Trebay, G. 2000. 'Homo thugz blow up the spot', *Village Voice*, 2–8 February, p. 46

Venable, M. 2001. 'A question of identity', *Vibe*, July, pp. 98–106

Vilanch, B. 2000. 'Eminem's fag jag', *The Advocate*, 12 September, p. 39

Walters, S.D. 2001. *All The Rage: The Story of Gay Visibility in America* (Chicago)

Watkins, S.C. 1998. *Representing: Hip Hop Culture and the Production of Black Cinema* (Chicago)

Weinstein, D. 1999. 'Art versus commerce: deconstructing a (useful) romantic illusion', in *Stars Don't Stand Still in the Sky: Music and Myth*, ed., K., K., and E. McDonnell (New York), pp. 56–69

White, A. 1996. 'Who wants to see ten niggers play basketball?', in *Droppin' Science: Critical Essays on Rap Music and Hip-Hop Culture*, ed. W.E. Perkins (Philadelphia), pp. 192–202

Williams, S.A. 1992. 'Two Words on Music: Black Community', in *Black Popular Culture: A Project by Michele Wallace*, ed. G. Dent (Seattle), pp. 164–72

DISCOGRAPHY

Mariah Carey, 'Clown', *Charmbracelet*. Island Def Jam, 440 063 467–2. 2002

Eminem, 'Criminal', 'Marshall Mathers', 'Remember Me', 'The Real Slim Shady', *The Marshall Mathers LP*. Interscope Records, B00004T9UF. 2000

Eminem, 'Superman', *The Eminem Show*. Interscope Records, B00006690G. 2002

The Pet Shop Boys, 'The Night I Fell In Love', *Release*. EMI Records. 7243 5381502 8. 2002

Examining the Text

1. "Gender conformity is often more central to hip-hop's aesthetic than sexual behavior," states Vincent Stephens. What do you think the author means by this statement? Likewise, what do you think he means by "sexual object-choice?" Does this imply that homophobia is *not* part of Eminem's repertoire, or does it have some other meaning as regards the rapper's lyrics?

2. The author states that gender and sexuality are central to the study of music's cultural and emotional resonance. What do you understand by that assertion? In your opinion, is the ability to comprehend the broader context of popular music dependent on the two elements of gender and sexuality? As he develops his argument, whose gender and sexuality does the author seem to be talking about: the listener's or the performers'. . . or both?

3. Stephens quotes another researcher named McLeod, who broke down the semantic dimensions of hip-hop. As evidenced in the discussion and accompanying table, what are the specific findings and conclusions of this piece of scholarship? Do you agree with the assertions made there? Whether you agree or disagree, what does the table provide you in understanding the gender dimension of Eminem's lyrics?

4. *Thinking rhetorically*: What kind of readership was this article written for: a body of Eminem fans or a group of literary/pop culture critics concerned with social meanings encoded in texts . . . or both? Explain the specific means by which the author attempted to convince this audience that Eminem's lyrics have more to do with gender role/behavior than homophobia?

For Group Discussion

Informed by your reading of the text, discuss whether the lyrics of rap songs like those by Eminem have any influence on how people think and behave. Are these songs mere entertainment or do they set a standard for how to treat women, gay people and how to behave based on one's gender? Do you think they are harmful in any way? Can something be offensive to some people and not be harmful in society?

Do you agree with the article's position that the true bond between rappers of all races is sexism? Why do you think sexism seems to have such a dominant place in rap song lyrics? Or is sexism and gender stereotyping commonplace in all popular music?

Writing Suggestion

Using the Internet, research the lyrics of four hit songs; two must be rap numbers from the past five years and the other two should be pop songs from the seventies or eighties. A hit would be any song that reached the top 10 on the *Billboard* magazine charts. Examine the words carefully in all four songs. What inferences can you make from the lyrics about gender roles, sexism, homophobia and other stereotyping? Write a three-page essay in which you compare and contrast the use of lyrics from your old hit song to a more contemporary rap song. Be sure to develop a thesis for your essay and provide evidence (from the songs you select) in support of your position.

Music and Contemporary Culture

Marilyn Manson and the Apt Pupils of Littleton

Gary Burns

In this relatively brief but well-documented popular culture research essay, the author examines a variety of textual responses to youth violence, in order to determine whether or not pop stars such as Marilyn Manson actually cause adolescents to commit murder and other heinous acts. What he uncovers is a species of hypocrisy. According to Burns, the news media tend to "scapegoat" high-profile celebrities such as Marilyn Manson, while ignoring other factors that the author finds much more insidious and dangerous. The author takes great pains to speculate on what these specific factors might be.

As you read this essay, pay attention to any political biases the author may bring to the table. How does he view the mainstream media, and how do his views of the media perhaps color his interpretation of the Marilyn Manson/youth violence issue? If possible, observe at the same time your own preconceptions: do you share the author's views toward the news media and therefore find yourself favorably disposed toward his arguments, or do you find his underlying premises flawed—therefore leading you to question his conclusions about the connections between pop stars and violence?

"America: Love it or leave it mother fuckers. All you racist (and if you think im [sic] a hypocrite, come here so I can kill you) mother fucking assholes in America who burn our flag and disgrace my land, GET OUT! And to you assholes in Iraq and Iran and all those other little piece of shit desert lands who hate us, shut up and die! We will kick your ass if you try and fuck with us, or at least I will!"

—Eric Harris's web site (Wilkinson 53)

A reporter from a Detroit radio station called and wanted to know what I thought about the killings in Colorado. He seemed to have an agenda—as is often the case with journalists. Specifically, he wanted to know whether I thought Marilyn Manson was to blame for the massacre and that parents should police what their children listen to.

I thought this was a most peculiar question, since it was only a   2
day or two after the killings and, to my knowledge, it had not been
definitively established that Eric Harris and Dylan Klebold even listened to or liked Marilyn Manson. As I write now in September 1999, I
still don't think it has been established. *Time* says yes (Cloud 37);
Rolling Stone says "[t]hey thought Marilyn Manson kind of sucked"
(Wilkinson 54).

What seemed more obvious to me, as I talked to the reporter, was   3
the significance of the date of the killings—April 20, which is Hitler's
birthday and one day after the anniversaries of both Waco (1993) and
Oklahoma City (1995). I talk to reporters fairly often, and I must say
that I find no evidence in those quarters of the so-called "liberal
media." The reporter in this particular case had picked up, somewhere,
the conservative scapegoating of Marilyn Manson.

I did what I always do, which was to try to redirect and broaden   4
the reporter's narrowly focused attention. Often, reporters don't want
to hear a contrary view, even though they are trained to seek out "the
other side." The blindness and deafness of the media in the Columbine
case are especially pronounced and troubling. It seems that we have a
new rite of spring in the form of rightwing violence every couple of
years around the time of Hitler's birthday. That is the story—not
Marilyn Manson.

The mainstream media have done practically nothing to expose,   5
let alone defuse, the rightwing culture of guns, militarism, and government and antigovernment violence in the United States. One war follows another with scarcely a peep from reporters, anchors, or pundits.
Practically nobody in the media elite even has the gumption to say:
"Golly, for a peace-loving nation, the United States sure invades and
bombs a lot of countries." Nor do the media "connect the dots"
between military and civilian violence. When the decorated soldier
Timothy McVeigh returned home from the Gulf War and bombed
Oklahoma City, the militia movement received momentary scrutiny,
but that's not where McVeigh learned how to make bombs. His teachers in the military remain unstigmatized and even unnamed in media
coverage of the slaughter.

Similarly, McVeigh's motive remains mysterious, but curiously   6
absent from most discussions of it was any serious consideration of
possible "cultural" influences. In McVeigh's case, this would have
meant rightwing radio host William Cooper (see Alterman), not a musician. In the wake of Oklahoma City, there was a minor and temporary
stir about rightwing radio nuts such as convicted Watergate felon
G. Gordon Liddy, who somehow "landed on his feet" with a nationally
syndicated daily talk radio show. The fact that he provided on-air
instruction in how to kill government agents was only momentarily

scandalous ("Head shots, head shots . . . Kill the sons of bitches").[1]
Indeed, parents should police what their children listen to.

Indirect evidence suggests at least some military influence in the   7
Columbine murders. According to the *New York Times*:

> [a]n essay in which Eric Harris portrayed himself as a shotgun shell
> prompted [a] teacher to have a . . . talk with his father, Wayne Harris.
> Once the teacher learned that Mr. Harris was a retired Air Force officer
> and that his son hoped to enlist in the military, she concluded that the
> essay was consistent with his future career aspirations, [school district
> spokeswoman Marilyn] Saltzman said. (Brooke A14)[2]

The hapless figure of Marilyn Manson is positively benign when   8
compared with Hitler, McVeigh, and the likes of Liddy, but even
Manson's weirdness has a military explanation, at least partially. Manson
reports in his autobiography that one of his few "source[s] of friends"

> was a study and play group for the children of parents who had come in
> contact with Agent Orange during Vietnam. My father, Hugh, was a . . .
> member of the . . . covert group responsible for dumping the hazardous
> herbicide all over Vietnam. . . . Because I wasn't deformed, I didn't fit in
> with the other children in the group or at the regular retreats for kids
> whose parents were suing the government for exposure to the chemical.
> The other children had prosthetic limbs, physical irregularities and de-
> generative diseases, and not only was I comparatively normal but my
> father was the one who had actually sprayed the stuff on their fathers,
> most of whom were American infantry soldiers. (Manson, Long 28–29)

Manson is clearly some combination of jester and shaman, draw-   9
ing his fabricated identity equally from the tragic glitter (Marilyn
Monroe) and detritus (Charles Manson) of popular culture. If he did
somehow inspire Harris and Klebold, that would be interesting and
disturbing, but it still has not been proven. Manson's influence, if any,
must also be considered in the light of at least three questions: What
other popular culture did these teenagers consume?[3] Why haven't
Marilyn Manson's thousands or millions of other fans shot up the local
high school? Is "shoot up your school" really a plausible message to
draw from Manson's songs? Obviously, the second question partially
answers the third.

Manson himself, in a post-massacre *Rolling Stone* column   10
("Columbine"), says that his message is positive and the opposite of
what his detractors claim. This, of course, is what one would expect
him to say under the circumstances. However, critic James Blandford,
several months before Columbine, made basically the same point in a
defense of Manson: "He does not . . . promote the illnesses of society,

Marilyn Manson

but forces us to confront them" (86). This type of confrontation, practiced to varying degrees by many contemporary musicians, is presumably what prompts fans to write to the newsletter *Rock & Rap Confidential* with testimonials to the effect that music saved their lives.

Be that as it may, we should not let Manson—Charles or Marilyn—   11
off the hook entirely. It was Charles Manson who perverted the cultural connotation of the Beatles in particular and rock culture in general.[4] Marilyn's choice of that last name is deliberately dangerous and provocative. He had to know that something like Columbine could eventually happen and drag him into a present-day criminal case.

What's in a name? While "Manson" is certainly bad, "Marilyn" is   12
potentially good. Even so, "Marilyn" was probably not chosen admiringly, and in any case the bad name semiotically overwhelms the good. The murderer has come home to roost, along with the ghosts of Vietnam.

Another act of naming deserves mention here. Why did Klebold's   13
parents name him Dylan? One can only speculate, but I would guess that his parents, who must be baby boomers, had some Sixties sense of idealism at least in the back of their minds. One of the lessons of Columbine should be that Bob Dylan and Hitler do not mix. You can model yourself after one or the other, but not both. As we used to say in the Sixties, if you are not part of the solution, you are part of the problem.

Eric Harris's Web site, quoted above, proves the point. In one   14
breath he condemns racism—a noble gesture he might easily have learned from a Bob Dylan song. In the next breath he delivers a racist

diatribe against Iraq, Iran, and "those other little piece of shit desert lands." What "cultural influences" might lead an aspiring antiracist to such a contradictory position? Not Bob Dylan or even Marilyn Manson. But quite possibly the promilitary, prowar, anti-Iraq, anti-Iran propaganda that has freely circulated, practically without challenge, in the increasingly rightwing cultural climate that has prevailed in the United States for the past two decades.

Rolling Stone's coverage of Columbine captured the contradiction   15
that must have troubled Harris and Klebold:

> It's been said that Eric and Dylan were fascists or Hitlerites. Eric spoke German, having studied the language since eighth grade. He spoke German at work and wore shirts with German sayings on them that, he'd say when asked, meant things like "go away." But so far, there is little direct evidence of supremacist thought on the part of Eric or Dylan, or a racial motive in the killings. "The only swastika I've seen at Columbine was the one that was etched in my desk," says one student. (Wilkinson 54)

On the other hand: "Guns change hands easily in the wild king-   16
dom known as gun shows, where David Koresh, Tim McVeigh, and serial killer Thomas Lee Dillon all have felt at home, where swastika flags may not raise an eyebrow and where all the guns used in the Littleton massacre were purchased" (Fortgang 51).[5]

Michael Shoels, father of the only black student killed at   17
Columbine, "has accused a Columbine dean of ignoring a complaint he made in early April [1999] that his son had received racist death threats from the trench coat mafia, a school clique that included Eric Harris and Dylan Klebold" (Brooke A14).[6] ABC radio news reported on 11 September 1999 that Shoels complained about three swastikas discovered at Columbine High School at the start of the 1999–2000 school year (i.e., four months after the killings).

Contradictory accounts are to be expected in a case like Columbine,   18
where perceptions differ and conflicting interests compete for dominance in the historical record of events. Despite the contradictions (or to account for them), a picture emerges of Harris and Klebold as reluctant racists, nice kids who turned into apt pupils. As in the film *Apt Pupil* (1998), fascination with Nazi evil led to experimentation, seduction, and catastrophe.

The dominant rightwing media culture in the United States   19
unfortunately facilitates such calamities by failing to provide sufficient reminders that Nazism, fascism, racism, and militarism, despite their attractions, are pathological and disastrous. Instead, a child or teenager can easily get the impression that these things are normal and respectable, just as gun shows, a war every six months, and violent,

reactionary "political commentary" such as Liddy's are normal and respectable.

We are asleep and having a nightmare. Set the alarm for April   20
2000, April 2001, and April 2002. If those months pass without another Waco, Oklahoma City, or Littleton, the nightmare may be over. If our springtime ritual of rightwing violence continues, it will be a sign of deepening sickness, from which we may never recover—and it won't have a thing to do with Marilyn Manson.

NOTES

[1]26 Aug. 1994, quoted in Federal Communications Commission complaint quoted by *Indianapolis News*, Jorgenson 22. For additional examples of Liddy's inflammatory on-air comments, see Bottoms. For a post-Oklahoma City critique of rightwing talk radio, see Naureckas.

[2]My attention was drawn to this *New York Times* article by Pollitt.

[3]*Time*'s summary of Harris and Klebold's "cultural influences" reads as follows: "Music: Marilyn Manson; hero: Hitler; video games: *Doom* and *Quake*" (Cloud 36–37). As I already pointed out, the reference to Manson may be inaccurate. Wilkinson reported that Harris and Klebold "listened to KMFDM, Rammstein, and Nine Inch Nails, as well as Dr. Octagon and DJ Spooky" (54). *Time* mentioned in a different article that Harris was a devotee of the rightwing novelist and essayist Ayn Rand (Pooley 30).

[4]For a recent, insightful discussion of Charles Manson, see Dalton.

[5]Colorado, perhaps not coincidentally, is a relative hotbed of militia activity and rightwing talk radio (see Jorgenson).

[6]However, Wilkinson reports that "Eric and Dylan weren't charter members or even full-fledged members of any clique, not even the Trench Coat Mafia. They bounced around" (49).

WORKS CITED

Alterman, Eric. "Little Limbaughs and the Fire Next Time." *The Nation* 27 Sept. 1999: 10.

Blandford, James R. "Antichrist Reborn." *Record Collector* Nov. 1998: 86–88.

Bottoms, Richard. "Liddy's Lethal Advice: Red Meat for Republican Voters." *Extra*! July/Aug. 1995:18.

Brooke, James. "Teacher of Colorado Gunmen Alerted Parents." *New York Times* 11 May 1999: A14.

Cloud, John. "Just a Routine School Shooting." *Time* 31 May 1999: 34–43.

Dalton, David. "Pleased to Meet You . . . ". *Mojo* Sept. 1999: 68–76.

Fortgang, Erika. "How They Got the Guns." *Rolling Stone* 10 June 1999:51–53.

Jorgenson, Leslie. "AM Armies." *Extra!* Mar./Apr. 1995: 20–22.

Manson, Marilyn. "Columbine: Whose Fault Is It?" *Rolling Stone* 24 June 1999: 23–24+.

Manson, Marilyn, with Neil Strauss. *The Long Hard Road Out of Hell.* New York: HarperCollins, 1998.

Naureckas, Jim. "Talk Radio on Oklahoma City: Don't Look at Us." *Extra!* July/Aug. 1995: 17–18.

Pollitt, Katha. "Humanitarian, All Too Humanitarian." *The Nation* 31 May 1999: 10.

Pooley, Eric. "Portrait of a Deadly Bond." *Time* 10 May 1999: 26–32.

Wilkinson, Peter, with Matt Hendrickson. "Humiliation and Revenge: The Story of Reb and VoDkA [sic]." *Rolling Stone* 10 June 1999: 49–54+.

Examining the Text

1. Explain what Burns means when he refers to "conservative scapegoating" in this piece. What evidence, if any, does he bring to bear on such a charge of scapegoating? Do you agree or disagree with this charge, and why?

2. The author contends that the news media have done nothing "to expose, let alone defuse, the rightwing culture of guns, militarism, and government and antigovernment violence in the United States." How does he support this assertion, and how does this claim factor into a discussion of Marilyn Manson's impact on youth violence?

3. While focusing on other factors that may play more of a role in inciting teen violence, author Burns also allows that "we should not let Manson . . . off the hook entirely." In what ways do Marilyn Manson and other media figures contribute to the culture of youth violence, according to the author?

For Group Discussion

The author, writing at the turn of the millennium, says, "Set the alarm for April 2000, April 2001, and April 2002. If those months pass without another Waco, Oklahoma City, or Littleton, the nightmare may be over." Of course, on September 11, 2001, the nightmare escalated to a level unimagined by the author. As a class, discuss what factors discussed in this essay—as well as other factors not discussed by the author—may have contributed to the culture of terror and antiterror which pervades the United States today.

Writing Suggestion

In an essay, respond to the author's thematic position: that the media use pop music artists as easy scapegoats for many of society's ills, while ignoring more pervasive and dangerous influences. Based upon your own reading of newspapers and magazines, and your watching of television and movies, do you find evidence to support Burns' assertions? Be specific in incorporating textual material from all forms of media as you develop your argument. Also, feel free to adopt a contrarian position: either that pop stars *are* to blame for youth violence, or that media scapegoating of music stars is a myth perpetuated by certain observers such as Burns . . . or both.

The Money Note: Can the Record Business Be Saved?

John Seabrook

The music business has always embraced the latest recording technology. Over the decades, music has changed with the tide of technical innovation: from sheet music to mechanical cylinders to 78 rpm records to 8-track and cassette tapes and, most recently, to CDs and MP3s. In the following article originally published in the New Yorker *magazine, author John Seabrook explains how the recorded music business moved from pressing long-playing records to issuing music on compact discs, the latter representing a technology that held promise of more resilience than easily scratched vinyl records and reduced production costs.*

However, while the medium on which music is recorded has changed over the years, the process of selecting and marketing talent altered little since World War II. According to Seabrook, "a few guys still determine the fate of many." By "the few," he means the artist and repertoire (A&R) men celebrated as heroes by recording-industry insiders for recognizing and promoting the performers who go on to become stars. Yet, the success rate of the A&R specialists is no greater than ten percent: for every one success, there are nine failures, a rate that is less successful than a computer program developed to determine pop music successes by scientists in Barcelona.

Although A&R men like the one profiled in Seabrook's article still retain a high importance in the music industry, their ability to help propel future stars to huge record sales has been dented by the ability of consumers to copy CDs for sharing via the Internet. Seabrook says that young people in particular no longer think of purchasing music when it can be copied for free from the Internet.

As you read, pay special attention to ways in which the author's descriptive language conveys the visceral experiences involved in listening to music, while at the same time informing the reader about popular music history and economic trends.

When he was a teen-ager, growing up in New York City in the nineteen-   1
seventies, Jason Flom wrote songs, sang, and played guitar for two
rock bands, which he named Relative Pleasure and Selective Service.
But Flom's dreams of rock stardom ended around the time he started
working at Atlantic Records, in 1979, when he was nineteen, and began
redirecting his energies into making other people stars. Now forty-two,
he is one of the most successful record men of the past twenty years,
scoring hits in genres as varied as heavy metal (Twisted Sister), Celtic
pop (the Corrs), and rock (Matchbox 20, Sugar Ray). Altogether, his
artists have sold more than a hundred million CDs.

In an era when many of the top-selling acts have "flava"—the edgy   2
sound of hip-hop artists and R. & B. singers and rap-metal groups, who
emerge from niches and achieve broad recognition—Flom has continued to have success with pop music, that sweet, beguiling, never-too-
challenging sound which has been a record industry staple from Bing
Crosby to Doris Day to Britney Spears. Flom's specialty is delivering
"monsters"—records that sell millions of copies and become rainmak-
ers for everyone else in the record business, because they bring fans
into the music stores. Successful record men are commonly said to have
"ears," but prospecting for monsters requires eyes for star quality as
well as a nose for the next trend. You have to be able to go to thousands
of sweaty night clubs, and sit through a dozen office auditions each
week, and somehow not become so jaded that you fail to recognize a
superstar when you encounter one. Like the night in 1981 when Clive
Davis, then the head of Arista Records, happened to go to a New York
supper club and hear a nineteen-year-old gospel singer who was
Dionne Warwick's cousin—Whitney Houston. Or the day when Bruce
Lundvall, the head of Blue Note Records, had a routine office audition from
a singer recommended by an employee in the accounting department—
Norah Jones. Or the time in 1997 when Flom met Kid Rock, then an
obscure m.c. who had made a couple of records that "stiffed" (sold
poorly), in the basement of a Detroit disco at two-thirty in the morning.
It is necessary to recognize that ineffable quality a great pop star communicates (Flom calls it "the thing"), but it isn't always necessary to
love the way the music sounds. Chris Blackwell, who founded Island
Records, told me that he didn't especially like listening to U2 when he
first heard them play, in the early nineteen-eighties, but "I could see
that they had something," and so he signed them to his label.

Why should the latent capacity for superstardom in pop, which is   3
perhaps the most egalitarian of art forms, be obvious to only a gifted
few like Jason Flom—those great A. & R. (artist-and-repertoire) men
whom the record industry celebrates as its heroes? (And they are
invariably male.) After all, even the great record men are wrong much
more often than they are right about the acts they sign (nine misses for

each hit is said to be the industry standard). One wonders how much of the art of hit-making is just dumb luck. Scientists in Barcelona say they have created a computer-based "Hit Song Science" that picks hits much more efficiently than a human can. There's even a Web site, hitsongscience.com, where aspiring pop stars can test themselves on a hit-o-meter.

"American Idol," the popular "Star Search"-style Fox TV show, in which the viewers pick their own stars by voting over the telephone, is considered a "reality show," but the democratic process is not the way stars are actually discovered. In the record business, a few guys still determine the fare of many. 4

One day last October, I was sitting with Flom in his office at Atlantic, which is part of the Warner Music Group, at Sixth Avenue and Fifty-first Street, when he played me a song by a new artist he had recently signed to his label, Lava Records. (Flom began the label as a joint venture with Atlantic, and then sold his share to the company two years ago, for a reported fifty million dollars.) Lava has a roster of twenty-three artists, and Flom can afford to take "a big bet," as he puts it, on two or three new artists a year. The artist's name was Cherie, he explained, and she was a young French singer whose specialty was the sweeping pop ballad. She was a "belter," as they say in the business— one of those singers who don't hold back. 5

Flom often has a startled expression in his eyes, as if he were wait- ing for something to go wrong—a look of disappointed optimism, the feeling that anyone who makes a career out of betting on talent must routinely suffer. But today he looked positively grim as he talked about the record business. Sales of recorded music in the United States have dropped by more than a hundred million units in the past two years, falling well below seven hundred million. The eighteen-year-old Canadian singer Avril Lavigne is the idol of ten-year-old girls across the country, but her debut album, "Let's Go," sold far fewer records in its first six months (four million) than did Alanis Morissette's debut album, "Jagged Little Pill" (seven million), which was released in 1995. Around the globe, the record business is sixteen per cent smaller than it was in 2000. Record labels blame the fans, for lacking the long-term loyalty to pop acts which record buyers used to have, and for engaging in wholesale "piracy" of music, either by copying CDs or by down- loading music illegally from the Internet. "There is no precedent for what's happening now in the music business," Flom said. "What would happen if groceries suddenly became free, or hotels—do you think those businesses would survive?" 6

However, Flom brightened at the prospect of playing Cherie's demo CD. "I guess you'd call her a diva," he said. "She's seventeen, and she's classically trained, but she sings these pop ballads—and she 7 is phenomenal." He was excitedly hunting for the demo amid the stacks of disks that cover every surface in his office. "I honestly believe she is one of the most important artists I've ever signed." Seeing the skeptical look on my face—a French pop star?—Flom quickly said, "She's also Jewish, and there aren't too many of them left in France, if you know what I mean, so it's a little different from being just French. And," he added, "she doesn't sound French when she sings."

Flom lacks the star quality that he divines in other people. He is   8
neither tall nor physically imposing, and he seems more like a laid-back lawyer than like a record man (his father is Joseph Flom, a patriarch of the New York law firm Skadden, Arps, Slate, Meagher & Flom). He is a friend of Bill Clinton's, and a generous supporter of the American Civil Liberties Union. He is not wild and crazy, although his office, like the offices of most record executives, is full of photographs of him posing with wild and crazy guys such as Kid Rock, who usually has his middle finger extended in the picture. During the nineteen-eighties, Flom tried living like a rock star, but when he was twenty-eight he checked into the Hazelden clinic, in Minnesota, for thirty days of rehab, and he hasn't had a drink or a line since. Now he lives with his wife and their two kids on the Upper West Side.

He had never heard Cherie sing before she and her manager, Jeff   9
Haddad, turned up in his office the previous February, on Valentine's Day, for an audition. Haddad had given Flom his pitch, which, Haddad told me later, included this question: "There are maybe twenty people in the world who can deliver a song the way Faith Hill sings the Diane Warren song that is the theme in the movie 'Pearl Harbor,' and out of those people how many can do it in four different languages?" Then Cherie performed two songs, one in French and the other in English; her only accompaniment was the noisy heating system in Flom's office. On the basis of that half-hour meeting, and Flom's gut feeling that the girl, whose real name is Cindy Almouzni, had that special quality which can move a massive amount of product, Flom signed her to a million-dollar, five-album contract, and was prepared to do everything that a major label like Warner can do to make an artist a big star— "Whatever it takes to put her over," Flom told me. He declined to say how much that would cost, but David Foster, another top hitmaker with Warner Music, told me, "It's basically a five-million-dollar bet. It might cost only five hundred thousand dollars to make the record, but it's so expensive to promote it. If you get on the 'Today' show, you've got to get a band together, fly everyone in and put them up, and by the time you're done it has cost you fifty thousand dollars."

Last year, the Wall Street Journal ran a story about an unknown   10
eighteen-year-old Irish singer named Carly Hennessy, whose debut

CD, from Universal, was the subject of a $2.2-million marketing campaign yet wound up selling only three hundred and seventy-eight copies in its first three months. "If that happens to me," Flom said, "a lot of people are going to look at me funny." For the artist, the stakes were higher. "This is her shot. It's very rare for an artist to get a buildup like this and then, if things don't go well, come back from it and reinvent herself."

The song Flom played for me that day in his office, "My Way Back   11
Home," is a love ballad written for Cherie by the Canadian singer-songwriter Corey Hart, who has also composed songs for Celine Dion. The lyrics are solidly within the convention of self-help, which is one of the main tropes of the popular love ballad. The singer is finding her way through the darkness, and, in spite of winter storms, bitter cold, and loneliness, manages to reach high and touch the sky, and to find . . . My Way Back Home. It was a surprising choice from the man who gave the world Twisted Sister's "We're Not Gonna Take It," although perhaps this is Flom's genius—understanding how a conventional love ballad and a heavy-metal anthem stimulate the same adult-contemporary emotions. As Doug Morris, the head of Universal Music Group, who was Flom's mentor when Morris ran Atlantic, said to me, "The basic thing is you've got a singer, and you've got a song, and you put them together and it makes people feel good. And if they feel good enough they buy it! That's what it's all about! And it's a beautiful thing when you see it happen—the singer up there singing his song and all the fans are screaming for him. It makes me wanna cry, when I see it."

And Cherie's voice was remarkably appealing. She had the vocal   12
power of Whitney Houston and the feel-good-around-the-edges shimmer of Shania Twain. But she wasn't a screamer; she could sustain the note at the end of a phrase without resorting to vibrato. She hit the high notes effortlessly, could soar from tragedy to triumph in a single breath, and seemed to inhabit the lyrics with complete sincerity. As the chorus rolled around for the second time, I sensed that the song was building toward an emotional climax that people in the record business sometimes refer to as "the money note"—that moment on the record which seems to have an almost involuntary effect on your insides. (According to researchers at Dartmouth who recently studied the brains of people listening to music, the brain responds physiologically to dramatic swoops in range and pitch.) The money note is the moment in Whitney Houston's version of the Dolly Parton song "I Will Always Love You" at the beginning of the third rendition of the chorus: pause, drum beat, and then "Iiiiiieeeeeeiiieeii will always love you." It is the moment in the Celine Dion song from "Titanic," "My Heart Will Go On": the key change that begins the third verse, a note you can hear a

hundred times and it still brings you up short in the supermarket and transports you from the price of milk to a world of grand romantic gesture—"You're here/There's nuthing I fear."

David Foster, the producer of "I Will Always Love You," who is 13 among the contemporary masters of the pop ballad (he has written and produced songs for Natalie Cole and Toni Braxton, among others), says that he came up with the expression during a session with Barbra Streisand. "Barbra had hit this high note, and she wanted to know how it sounded, because although you'd think Barbra was real confident she's not," he told me. "And I said, 'That sounds like money!'" He added, "And I don't mean money in the crass sense of that will make a lot of money, although that's certainly part of it. I mean expensive. It sounds expensive."

Cherie hit the money note with full force—"When I cry I'm weak/ 14 I'm learning to fly." As her voice went up on "fly," an electric guitar came floating up with it, and the tone was so pure that a chill spread over my shoulders, prickling the skin. Flom pumped his fist when the moment hit, lifted his leg a little, and grimaced.

When the song ended, he asked me what I thought, and I admit- 15 ted that I had found the money note shattering. But would it produce the reaction Flom was looking for—the effect he had mimed for me earlier, by taking an imaginary wallet from his back pocket, fingering an imaginary bill, and slapping it down on an imaginary counter? What was to stop people from taking the money notes for free?

Flom pointed out that Cherie's music, like that of Norah Jones, 16 should appeal to older people, who are less likely to download music from the Internet. "But who knows?" he said. "It's difficult to compete with free. All I know is what I know—if the star is big enough, people will buy the album, because it's like a piece of the artist. But if the star doesn't have that kind of irresistible appeal then people just say, 'What the heck, I'll download the good songs.' So we just have to figure out how to make her a big star."

Five global music companies control more than eighty-five per cent 17 of the record business. (The remaining fifteen per cent is divided among some ten thousand independent labels.) Universal Music Group, which is owned by Vivendi Universal, is the dominant player among the majors; then comes the Warner Music Group, a division of AOL Time Warner; Sony Music Entertainment; the Bertelsmann Music Group (BMG); and the EMI Group. From the early seventies to the mid-nineties, Warner was the leading company in the record industry, but by the end of 2002, with a sixteen-per-cent share of the domestic market, the company had fallen behind Universal, which had a twenty-nine-per-cent share.

The story of Warner Music is a parable for the music industry—a   18
tale of corporate dyssynergy. Over the course of the rock era, which
began almost fifty years ago, virtually all the original record companies
have been bought by larger media corporations. The industry has
changed from an art-house business run by the founders of the labels—
men with ears, like Ahmet Ertegun, a founder of Atlantic; Chris
Blackwell, of Island Records; and Jerry Moss, the co-founder, with
Herb Alpert, of A&M Records—into a corporate enterprise run by
managers, who in addition to making records have to worry about
quarterly earnings and timely results.

Atlantic Records was co-founded in 1947 by the Turkish-born   19
Ertegun, with money borrowed from the family dentist. He began by
recording artists like Ray Charles and the New Orleans juke-joint
bluesman Professor Longhair. In the nineteen-fifties, Ertegun, working
with his partners—his brother Nesuhi and Jerry Wexler, a writer for
Billboard—had a string of hit records with singers like Ruth Brown and
Big Joe Turner, before the dominant power in the music business, CBS
Records (now owned by Sony), discovered the commercial possibility
of black R. & B. music. In the mid-sixties, Atlantic expanded into pop
(Bobby Darin, Sonny and Cher) and, later, into rock (Buffalo Springfield).
In 1968, Ertegun sold the label to Warner-Seven Arts, and the following
year Steve Ross's Kinney National bought that company, creating
Warner Communications. During the nineteen-seventies, the collection
of Warner labels assembled by Ross, and run by the legendary record
man Mo Ostin (including Atlantic, Warner Bros., Reprise, Elektra, and
Asylum), eclipsed those of CBS, and Warner became the leader of the
record industry. Its acts included the Grateful Dead; Crosby, Stills,
Nash & Young; the Eagles; Fleetwood Mac; and the Doobie Brothers.
"Steve Ross's never got involved in anything we did," Ertegun, who
continued to run Atlantic after its sale, told me. "He was just happy to
see the results." But as Warner Communications grew—it merged with
Time, in 1990, and AOL, in 2001—the music business faltered. Ross,
who might have been able to run the labels effectively, died in 1992,
and Gerald Levin took over.

The business rationale behind the record companies' role in   20
these huge conglomorations was that their corporate owners would
use the cash generated by monster hits to pay for other parts of their
operations, and the companies would be able to survive the stiffs,
thanks to their corporate backing. Corporate ownership also gave
record men like Ertegun the financial resources to compete for
expensive established acts, like the Rolling Stones, whom he signed
in the nineteen-seventies. However, it gradually became apparent
that the corporate culture might not provide the best environment

for nurturing new talent. Chris Blackwell, who sold Island to PolyGram in 1989 (he now has another independent label, Palm Pictures), told me, "I don't think the music business lends itself very well to being a Wall Street business. You're always working with individuals, with creative people, and the people you are trying to reach, by and large, don't view music as a commodity but as a relationship with a band. It takes time to expand that relationship, but most people who work for the corporations have three-year contracts, some five, and most of them are expected to produce. What an artist really needs is a champion, not a numbers guy who in another year is going to leave."

Moreover, the kind of controversy that often helps sell records is   21
not good for the corporate image. In the mid-nineties, Warner was well positioned to control the exploding rap market, through its half ownership of Interscope, a label that had been developed by the producer Jimmy Iovine and had recently signed Tupac Shakur. Interscope was allied with Death Row Records, the label run by Dr. Dre and Marion (Suge) Knight, which recorded seminal gangsta-rap acts like Snoop Doggy Dogg. But bad publicity from these acts was hurting Time Warner's other businesses and straining the political connections that the corporation needed in Washington. In 1995, Levin made the decision to sell the company's half share of Interscope, and it eventually became part of Universal. Iovine went on to amass a remarkable streak of hits, including records by Eminem and the rapper 50 Cent. Warner missed out on the rap boom almost entirely.

In the past three years, under the leadership of Roger Ames, a   22
suave, cigarette-smoking, fifty-two-year-old Trinidadian, who took over the Warner Music Group in 1999, the company has had major hits with Linkin Park, Enya, and Faith Hill. Ames has also cut costs to improve profits. However, Warner is fourth among the majors in sales of new music and did not have a record on the list of Top Ten-selling albums in 2002:

1. "The Eminem Show"/Eminem, 7.6 million (Interscope).
2. "Nellyville"/Nelly, 4.9 million (Universal).
3. "Let's Go"/Avril Lavigne, 4.1 million (Arista, a BMG label).
4. "Home"/Dixie Chicks, 3.7 million (Sony).
5. "8 Mile"/Soundtrack, 3.5 million (Interscope).
6. "Missundaztood"/Pink, 3.1 million (Arista).
7. "Ashanti"/Ashanti, 3.09 million (Murder Inc., Universal).
8. "Drive"/Alan Jackson, 3.05 million (Arista Nashville).
9. "Up"/Shania Twain, 2.9 million (Universal).
10. "O Brother, Where Art Thou?"/Soundtrack, 2.7 million (Universal).

But is a winner-take-all strategy the best way to run a record   23
company—for any of the majors? Hit-making is an imprecise method
of doing business. Of thirty thousand CDs that the industry released
last year in the United States, only four hundred and four sold more
than a hundred thousand copies, while twenty-five thousand releases
sold fewer than a thousand copies apiece. No one seems to be able to
predict which those four hundred and four big sellers will be. The
chairman of BMG, Rolf Schmidt-Holtz, told *Billboard* in December, "We
need reliable calculations of returns that are not based solely on hits
because the way people get music doesn't go with hits anymore." He
added, "We have to get rid of the lottery mentality."

I asked Flom whether he thought hits might become less impor-   24
tant to the record business. "That ain't gonna happen," he said. "If anything, hits can be more important than ever, because you can make
stars on a global scale now. If the star is big enough, people will want to
buy the CD." When I repeated what Schmidt-Holtz had said, Flom
looked momentarily stunned. Then he said, "Something must be getting lost in the translation there, because the day we stop seeing hits is
the day people stop buying records."

When Cindy Almouzni was eight, in 1992, the video of the Whitney   25
Houston song "I Will Always Love You" came out, accompanied by
shots of the singer playing opposite Kevin Costner in the film "The
Bodyguard." Cindy was the youngest of three children in a religious
household in Marseilles. Her parents are Sephardic Jews from North
Africa. As a child, her father fled during the Algerian war, and met his
wife years later in France. When Cindy's mother was too busy to watch
her, she would put her in front of music videos on TV. Cindy learned "I
Will Always Love You," exactly the way Whitney sings it—the breathing, the key change in the third chorus—and she sang it over and over
again. At first, she sang the song to herself, then to her family, and then
in school. The summer that she was nine, she sang "I Will Always Love
You" for several hundred people at a campground where the Almouznis
went during August.

Her parents sent her to singing school, and after that she received   26
private lessons. She learned the songs of Jacques Brel and Edith Piaf,
but she also continued to sing "I Will Always Love You." At fourteen,
she won a local karaoke contest, and went to Paris for a national competition. There, she met a record producer, who invited her to his studio to record a song he had written called "I Don't Want Nobody
(Telling Me What to Do)." The vocals were remixed, and the song
became a dance track, which wound up in the hands of Jeff Haddad, a
languid, affable Californian. "I heard her sing, and she blew me away,
and I thought, Let's do what we can to make this happen," Haddad

told me. He flew to France to meet her parents, and they agreed to let him try to make their daughter a star.

Haddad is a manager, but, like many other people in the music   27
industry—producers, songwriters, engineers, lawyers—he functions as a filter between undiscovered talent and a major-label deal. He and Dave Moss, the owner of a small record label, put out a single of Cindy's dance song, and it became an international hit for Cherie Amore, as they decided to call her, back in 2000, when there was a vogue for French house music. On the strength of that success, Haddad commissioned a British songwriter and producer named Paul Moessl to create a pop ballad for Cherie. Moessl wrote a song called "Older" ("My love is older than my years/It's wiser than your fears"). There was considerable interest in the demo, and Haddad scheduled a week of office auditions in L.A. and a week in New York, with people like Tommy Mottola, who was then the head of Sony Music. It was cold in New York, and people were coughing and sneezing while Cindy sang. Jason Flom was the last record guy they saw. "Within thirty seconds of hearing her sing," he said, "I just knew." In Cherie, Flom encountered a singer whose artistic sensibility was derived from the kind of commer-cial music that record men like Flom produce—her flava was pop. He signed her within a week.

The traditional course in star-making is to begin with a local fan   28
base and gradually grow to global renown. Flom was proposing to mar-ket Cherie the other way around—she would appear on the scene as a "worldwide artist," with campaigns in France, Italy, England, and Spain, as well as in the United States. Although the music industry more or less invented the hit, it has struggled to make songs and artists into the kind of global properties that movies have become. (The recent film "X2" opened simultaneously in ninety-five countries.) Music is sup-posed to be the universal language, but pop depends on regional associ-ations, and on language, which is why the charts in France and Spain and Germany are so different from the pop charts in the United States.

Last summer, Flom presented his future star at the Warner Music   29
Group summit meeting, held in Barcelona and attended by affiliates from more than a hundred and thirty countries. ("There were some affiliates from countries I didn't even know they had records in," Flom said.) Cherie was a hit, and Flom and Haddad decided that she should sing several of the tracks on her debut album in Spanish and French, as well as in English. They solicited songs from successful pop songwrit-ers, like Kara Dioguardi and Paul Barry, and they hired producers who had scored hits in European and South American countries to work on possible singles for those countries.

Flom told me that in some ways Cherie's youth and obscurity   30
were advantages in making her into a worldwide sensation. Stars often

balk at travelling to other countries to perform, and don't want to keep up the relentless schedule of public appearances which is necessary to sustain a hit record. "The nice thing about Cherie is she's portable," Flom said. "She'll go places and do stuff if we think she should do it."

But, if Cherie truly is an extraordinary artist, why not build her   31
career more slowly? "In an era like this," Flom said, "when the audience has more distractions than ever, you have to reach critical mass to put an artist over. And the outlets you need to do that, the Teen Peoples and whatever, are not going to take you seriously unless they know you are putting a major push behind it."

Of course, it was possible that Flom was wrong about Cherie's   32
talent. Perhaps she wasn't a great artist; maybe she was merely a great karaoke singer, and the audience would be able to tell the difference. On the other hand, maybe the current pop scene is a "karaoke world"—the phrase that the pop impresario Malcolm McLaren uses to describe contemporary pop culture—in which all the great artistic statements have already been made, and the newer artists are merely doing karaoke versions of their predecessors.

In November, I attended a marketing meeting in Flom's spacious   33
corner office to draw up an outline for launching Cherie's career, or, as they say in the business, "blowing her up." Seven Lava staff members were in attendance: Richard Bates, creative; Nikki Hirsch and Lee Trink, marketing; Aaron Simon, product management; Doug Cohen, video promotion; Janet Stampler, new media; and Lisbeth Cassaday, publicity. Before the meeting started, Aaron Simon told the others about the experience of having Cherie sing for him, in the office. "I was, like, 'Do you want me to close the door?'" he reported. "And she was, like, 'No, it's cool.' And she just did it right there. And it was, like—chills."

Flom began by saying that they hoped to take the first single, prob-   34
ably a mid- to up-tempo dance number, to American radio in June, 2003. When record guys hear fans complaining that pop music has become too commercial, they are often quick to blame radio. Radio doesn't play as much new music as it used to, they argue, and the music that is played has to fit into a certain format, which is based on research about what people like to listen to—or, at least, will tolerate. Many stations also carry between fifteen and twenty minutes of commercials an hour. ("If anyone said we were in the radio business, it wouldn't be someone from our company," Lowry Mays, the founder and C.E.O. of Clear Channel, which is the country's largest radio-station operator, with some hundred million listeners nationwide, told Fortune in March. "We're not in the business of providing well-researched music. We're simply in the business of selling our customers products.")

Cherie's music fits almost perfectly into the adult-contemporary   35
format, radio's largest; Flom thought that Cherie was tailor-made for

New York's WLTW 106.7 Lite-FM, the city's most popular music radio station, which is owned by Clear Channel. Jim Ryan, a programming executive there, told me that when Flom played "My Way Back Home" for him, along with two other songs, during a car ride home from an industry event, he said, "Jason, I want to quit my job at Clear Channel and sign up on the Cherie bandwagon."

With luck, Flom went on, Cherie's first single would be a hit, and would cross over from the light-FM stations to the Top Forty stations. At that point, Lava would release the second single, a ballad. Flom was also looking at other ways to promote Cherie. One was a Time Warner DVD, a Batman movie called "Batman: Mystery of the Batwoman"; Cherie was being animated in the film as a sexy singer whom Batman encounters in a late-night *boite*, and who sings a song called "Betcha Neva" (a song that would be on Cherie's album). He added that there had been tremendous interest in Cherie from "the soundtrack community," especially from makers of animated films, and reminded everyone that Celine Dion's big break came with the theme song from the Disney movie "Beauty and the Beast." "I'm not saying she's another Celine, but there's a road map there."   36

The group then discussed the possibility of getting Cherie a product-endorsement deal with a company like Revlon. As the expense of blowing up an artist increases, and the prospective payoff in record sales becomes ever more in doubt, the industry is shifting the cost of promoting artists onto advertisers. Sting's 1999 album, "Brand New Day," an Interscope release, sold sluggishly until the artist was featured in a Jaguar commercial singing music from the album—and then sales took off.   37

The staff addressed the subject of "imaging" Cherie—what kind of look the artist should affect. Cherie's personal style was a work in progress. She was not a dressy kind of girl: she was partial to jeans. Richard Bates, the art director, said that in examining the images of current pop stars he had noticed that there was a middle ground between Britney Spears and Shania Twain, which no one was trying to fill. "The older singers are very polished and classy, and then it jumps down to young and trashy—which we don't want her to be," he said. The danger was that in trying to strike a balance between these extremes you might wind up with nothing at all. In photos from Cherie's first shoot, the artist, dressed in a sleeveless jersey and neat jeans, well scrubbed, her long hair pushed back from her face, looked as if she were ready for a college interview.   38

Lee Trink talked about making Cherie a keyword on AOL Time Warner's Internet service, and launching a "Who Is Cherie?" instant-messaging campaign.   39

The staff was undecided on the use of what Lisbeth Cassaday referred as "the 'd' word." Cassaday thought it was best not to call   40

Cherie a diva; Flom wasn't so sure. "I mean, she is a diva, right?" he said. It was a conundrum. Operatic divas inhabit classic dramatic roles like Tosca and Madame Butterfly, but pop divas, one way or another, have to play themselves, which may be why pop divas wear out faster than operatic divas. The constant blowing up they require eventually causes them to explode.

Once the album went platinum—hit a million in sales—Flom   41
said, they would go to the media with the story of Cherie's life. Flom reminded everyone that the artist was Jewish. He had heard that her synagogue in Marseilles was burned recently, and, "while this should obviously be treated as a very sensitive subject, we could go to Oprah and pitch her as an artist who has suffered violence in her life as a result of her religion."

Everyone nodded.   42

"You know. It's a story line."   43

In 1983, the president of PolyGram, Jan Timmer, introduced what   44
he hoped would become the new platform for the sale of recorded music—the compact disk—at a recording-industry convention in Miami. Technically, CDs were a big advance over vinyl and tape. On a CD, music takes the form of digital strings of ones and zeros, which are encoded on specially treated plastic disks. If the disk is properly cared for, there is no "fidelity degradation"—none of those hisses and pops that vinyl develops over time. The high-tech allure of the CD would allow the industry to raise the cost of an album from $8.98 to $15.98 (even though CDs were soon cheaper to manufacture than vinyl records), and the record companies would get a larger share of money, because the industry would persuade artists not to raise royalty rates, arguing that the extra money was needed to market the new format to customers.

Timmer's group was booed by record men in the audience that   45
day. This may have been because the co-inventors of the CD—Philips, which was a corporate partner of PolyGram, and Sony—wanted a patent royalty on the disks. The booing, however, also reflected the music industry's long history of technophobia. A hundred years ago, music publishers were trying to sue player-piano makers out of existence, fearing that no one would ever buy sheet music again. In the nineteen-twenties, the music industry sued radio broadcasters for copyright infringement. Although history has repeatedly shown that new technologies inevitably bring opportunities and create new markets, the industry's attitude toward new technology remains hostile. (Technophobia is also rampant in the film industry: in 1992, when movie studios were suing Sony over the Betamax, claiming that it was a threat to the film business, Jack Valenti, the president of the Motion Picture Association of America, said, "The VCR is to the American film producer and the American public as the Boston Strangler is to a

woman alone." Fortunately for the movie industry, it lost the Betamax case: today, videos and DVDs account for more than fifty per cent of a studio's revenues.)

The CD, of course, turned out to be extremely popular with   46 record buyers. Many fans who already owned music on vinyl dutifully replaced their records with CDs. By 1986, CD sales had climbed to a hundred million worldwide, and by the early nineties hit albums on CD were selling in greater numbers than hit albums on vinyl had sold. In 1999, in what now looks like hubris, the industry's trade organization, the Recording Industry Association of America (R.I.A.A.), created a super-platinum prize with which to honor the new megahits—the Diamond Award, bestowed on records that sell more than ten million copies. (Flom has two Diamond Awards, for Matchbox 20's "Yourself or Someone Like You" and for Kid Rock's "Devil Without a Cause.") CDs also turned out to be a brilliant way of repackaging a label's "catalogue"—all the recordings that were no longer in production on vinyl. CDs spawned a generation of record executives whose skill was in putting together compilations of existing music, rather than in discovering new artists. Through the stock market crash of 1987 and the recession of the early nineties, the CD market grew steadily, until sales abruptly declined in 2001, by six per cent, and then dropped nine per cent in 2002.

Lyor Cohen, the head of Island Def Jam, which is owned by   47 Universal, thinks that the record industry would have been better off without the CD. "The CD kept the whole business on artificial life support," he told me. Without it, the old record industry would have died in the early eighties, and a new, more modern industry would have replaced it. But the CD preserved the status quo. "The record business became a commodity business, not a content-and-creation business," Cohen said. He rubbed his fingertips together. "What was lost was secchie—it means 'touch.' "

Unlike Jason Flom, who has always worked at a record label,   48 Cohen got his start as an artist's representative; he co-managed the Beastie Boys and Public Enemy. Now forty-three, he is tall and speaks with a slight Israeli accent. On the morning I visited Cohen in his office, in Manhattan, he was dressed in jeans and an expensive-looking dress shirt and was puffing on a cigar. He propped his size-13 New Balance sneakers up on his desk as he spoke.

"The A. & R. guys at the record companies had gotten a little   49 older and didn't feel like standing in the back of some filthy hole to listen to a new band," he said. "So, instead, they started repackaging stuff from when they were younger. We got the theme album—'Summer of Love,' 'Splendor in the Grass,' whatever—and by the end of the eighties most of the industry's profits were in catalogue."

Finally, CDs made piracy possible, by making music much easier   50
to copy. Had the platform never shifted from vinyl, the piracy problem
wouldn't be nearly so bad. The zeal with which the labels flogged their
catalogues on CD insured that a large amount of previously recorded
music was rendered into digital form—almost none of it protected
from copying. "None of us wondered what the digitizing of sound
waves would mean to our business," Stan Cornyn, a longtime Warner
marketing man, wrote in "Exploding," a recent history of Warner
Music. "How fidelity degradation, which had held back some from
making free tape copies, would no longer be a factor once sound waves
got turned into digits. . . . Digital sound, being so casually accepted
into our world, was free to cause an epidemic. It would make data
copying easy, clean, free, and something that felt about as immoral as
killing an ant."

During the past decade, virtually every piece of popular music   51
ever recorded on CD has been "ripped," converted into a compressed
digital file known as an MP3 (short for Moving Picture Experts Group
Layer Three), and made available online, where anyone with a computer can get it. Once a song is converted into an MP3, it can be copied
millions of times without any fidelity degradation. New music is
ripped from CDs and uploaded as soon as the records come out (often
before they come out, by studio technicians or by music journalists
who receive advance copies). Music fans, who used to hear a song they
liked on the radio, go to the record store, and buy the album, now hear
a song they like on the radio, go to the Internet, and help themselves to
it for free. Teen-agers who were once the labels' best customers are now
their worst enemies. "Younger fans, at whom pop music is aimed, tend
to be comfortable with computers, which is why downloading hurts
the best-selling hits more than other kinds of music," I was told by
Hilary Rosen, the departing C.E.O. of the R.I.A.A. "As a result, records
that might have sold eight million copies now sell five. Unfortunately,
these blockbuster sales pay for the development of new artists—Kid
Rock pays for all the others." In 2002, the industry shipped 33.5 million
copies of the year's ten best-selling albums, barely half the number it
shipped in 2000.

Whether or not the record business figures out how to make   52
money from MP3s, the format is here to stay. Just as CDs replaced
vinyl, so will MP3s replace CDs. But, whereas CDs made the record
business extraordinarily lucrative, MP3s are making it extraordinarily
painful—a gigantic karmic correction that may lead to a bigger music
business one day, although not before things get worse. Daniel Strickland,
a twenty-three-year-old student at the University of Virginia, told me
recently, "Maybe it's because I'm in college and I have an eighteen-
year-old sister and a ten-year-old brother, but, let me tell you, nobody

I know buys CDs anymore. My sister—she just gets on her computer, and she knows only two things, file sharing and instant messaging. She and friends go online, and one instant-messages the other, and says, 'Oh, there's this cool song I just found,' and they go and download it, play it, and instant-message back about it. My brother has never even seen a CD—except for the ones my sister burns."

Napster, the first widely used music-sharing software, appeared   53
in 1999. It was based on a program developed by a nineteen-year-old college student named Shawn Fanning. Later that year, the R.I.A.A. charged Napster with copyright infringement, and, after a hearing in San Francisco, a California federal judge ruled against Napster and eventually closed the service down. But that action did almost nothing to diminish the availability of free music online; people simply began to use other file-sharing programs, like KaZaA, Morpheus, Grokster, and LimeWire. Unlike Napster, these programs, which operate on what are known as P2P (peer-to-peer) computer networks, have no central computer that keeps an index of all the files on the system. Instead, any computer using one of these programs can search and share files with any other computer using the same software. The number of people downloading music files over P2P networks today is thought to be many times greater than the number of people who used Napster at its height; by some estimates, fifty million Americans have downloaded music illegally.

The music industry has launched alternatives to the P2P net-   54
works—legal, online music services like Emusic, Pressplay, and Rhapsody. But so far these have failed to attract many fans, partly because they require users to pay monthly subscription fees, rather than selling individual songs and albums. Sony and Universal recently sold Pressplay to Roxio, a software company, which is expected to give its service a new, sexier-sounding name—Napster. Apple's iTunes Music Store, which was launched in April, selling downloadable songs for ninety-nine cents and albums for ten dollars, is the best-designed and best-stocked of the legal services, and the company sold three million songs in the first month of operation. Although sales have fallen sharply, other companies, including Microsoft, are reportedly planning similar services. Meanwhile, the labels are quietly beginning to harvest the marketing data on songs and artists that the illegal networks offer. Warner Music Group worked with Big Champagne, a company that mines data from the P2P networks, but Big Champagne's C.E.O., Eric Garland, isn't allowed to talk about it. "We are still very much the mistress," he told me.

In 2001, the R.I.A.A. joined the film industry in bringing a copy-   55
right-infringement suit against some of the larger P2P networks, including Morpheus and Grokster. But suing peer-to-peer networks

Barbie and Ken
Branding
Photographer: Aaron
Goodman

"Conversion Barbie," by
Kimmy McCann

"Absolute End," by Adbusters

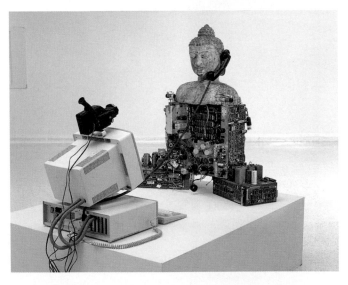

"TV Buddha Reincarnated," by Nam June Paik
Carl Solway Gallery, Cincinnati, Ohio. Photographers: Tom Allison
and Chris Gomien

Gwen Stefani
© Frank Trapper/CORBIS SYGMA

Tupac Shakur
Getty Images/Time Life Pictures

Still photo from the film, *Johnny Mnemonic*
The Kobal Collection/Limited Partnership/Alliance/Seida, Takashi

Still photo from the film, *The Matrix*
The Kobal Collection/Warner Bros.

Brandi Chastain in her sports bra

Jesus and Mel

isn't as easy as suing Napster; for one thing, there's no one to sue. (KaZaA is based on software that was commissioned by two Scandinavian businessmen. The programmers are Estonian. The right to license the program was acquired by Sharman Networks, an Australian company that has no direct employees and is incorporated in the Pacific island nation of Vanuatu.) Also, P2P networks offer a wide range of legitimate applications for research and businesses. In April, a federal judge in Los Angeles ruled that, because Morpheus and Grokster can be used for both legal and illegal purposes, the companies that distribute the software can't be sued for copyright infringement.

Last fall, several Microsoft programmers released a study of some   56
of the social implications of P2P. They foresaw the networks converging into what the authors called "the Darknet"—a vast, illegal, anarchic economy of shared music, TV programs, movies, software, games, and pornography which would come to rival the legitimate entertainment industry. Unless the government does something about P2P, our entertainment industry could one day resemble China's, where piracy is endemic. With no means of support, many artists would be forced to stop working, and a cultural dark age would ensue. The movie industry, which is a bigger and more politically powerful force than the record business, has yet to see its profits eroded by illegal downloading, but it may be only a matter of waiting until DVD burners become the standard item in PCs that CD burners are now. Unlike the music industry, the film industry is incorporating copy protection into its digital recordings, but the Darknet is full of bright hackers determined to prove their mettle by breaking through the most robust encryption.

In the face of the recent legal setbacks in the R.I.A.A.'s campaign   57
against the P2P networks, the organization's war on piracy has shifted toward the people who steal music. In April, the R.I.A.A. named four university undergraduates in a multimillion-dollar claim for copyright infringement, forcing them to pay between twelve thousand and seventeen thousand dollars each in fines. The day before the R.I.A.A. lost in the Grokster case, it won an important victory in a legal action against Verizon, when a federal judge in New York upheld a ruling that Verizon was required, under the 1998 Digital Millennium Copyright Act, to turn over to the R.I.A.A. the names of customers whom the record industry suspected of illegally sharing music files. (Verizon, which is in the business of selling broadband Internet connectivity, does not want to discourage potential customers, even if downloading music illegally is what they want broadband for.) Last week, the R.I.A.A. announced that it would begin preparing hundreds of lawsuits against individuals, charging the defendants up to a hundred and fifty thousand dollars per song. "It's easy to figure out whose computer is doing it," Hilary Rosen told me.

The record industry has also engaged in less conventional ways   58
of harassing people who use P2P networks, including posting music
files that are corrupt or empty, and has explored the legality of using
software that temporarily "locks up" any computer that downloads it.
Orrin Hatch, the chairman of the Senate Judiciary Committee, when
asked a couple of weeks ago whether he favored passing legislation
that would override federal anti-hacking laws, said that if other means
of stopping illegal downloaders failed, "I'm all for destroying their
machines. If you have a few hundred thousand of those, I think people
would realize the seriousness of their actions."

Sir Howard Stringer, the chairman of the Sony Corporation of   59
America, calls downloaders "thieves." "That's a reasonably polite way
of saying it," he observed recently. "A shoplifter is a thief. That actress
wandering around Hollywood helping herself, she was a thief. She
should have adopted the Internet defense—'I was downloading music
in the morning, downloading movies in the afternoon, and then I
thought I'd rustle a few dresses out of the local department store. And
it's been a good day, and all of a sudden I'm arrested. How is that
fair?'" Many people I met within the record industry seem to regard
today's music fans with disapproval. Tom Whalley, the head of Warner
Bros. Records, said, "I think the audience is less loyal today than it used
to be. The artist has to prove him- or herself with every new album; it
feels like you're starting over each time." Fans I spoke to had, for their
part, almost nothing good to say about the record industry. "I think the
record companies are greedy pigs," said Oliver Ignatius, a fourteen-
year-old music fan who lives in Brooklyn, and who knows as much
about pop music as anyone I know. Ignatius is the type of fan a record
guy would kill for: he downloads, but he also uses file-sharing services
to discover new music and to research previously recorded material,
and if he likes what he hears he buys the CD. He keeps his CDs in
scrapbook-size folders, like a collection of stamps or baseball cards.
Oliver thinks that the price of a CD should be six dollars. The industry
is currently drawing the line at ten dollars—the price of downloading
an album from Apple's iTunes Music Store.

One could argue that the record industry has helped to create   60
these thieving, lazy, and disloyal fans. By marketing superficial, disposable pop stars, labels persuade fans to treat music as superficial
and disposable. By placing so much emphasis on hit singles that
fit into the radio formats, the record industry has created a fan who
has no interest in albums. And the values of the people who share
music illegally over P2P networks are, after all, rock-and-roll values:
freedom, lack of respect for authority, and a desire for instant
gratification—the same values that made so many people in the
record business rich.

Still, one of the most galling things about the piracy problem, if   61
you happen to be in the record business, is that not only are the fans
gleefully and remorselessly taking the hits you make; they are doing so
because they think you deserve it—it's your payback for ripping off
artists with years of "plantation accounting." "I hope it all goes down
the crapper," Joni Mitchell said of the record industry in Rolling Stone
last year. "I would never take another deal in the record business. . . .
I'll be damned if I'll line their pockets." The following month, in W, she
called the record industry a "corrupt cesspool," saying that she was
leaving the major-label system because "record companies are not
looking for talent. They're looking for a look and a willingness to cooperate." (Mitchell's most recent album came out on Nonesuch, a Warner
label.) As Malcolm McLaren observed to me, "The amazing thing
about the death of the record industry is that no one cares. If the movie
industry died, you'd probably have a few people saying, 'Oh, this is
too bad—after all, they gave us Garbo and Marilyn Monroe.' But now
the record industry is dying, and no one gives a damn."

In December, I went to Los Angeles to visit the recording studio   62
where work on Cherie's album was under way, and to meet the artist.
Cherie had moved there in June, shortly after finishing school in
France. The label had found her a house in Beverly Hills, and she was
living there by herself, although Haddad was keeping a close watch
over her. Her mother had come to help her settle in, but she had
returned home to Marseilles.

Haddad briefed me on Cherie's schedule in L.A. "Her routine is   63
very intense, and it's all about her," he said. "She gets up early, and she
works out at home, sometimes with her trainer, then she does her voice
lessons, and she does her English lessons, and if she's recording she
spends afternoons and evenings at the studio, and if she isn't she meets
with agents and movie producers and a bunch of other people who are
interested in her."

Westlake Studios is in Hollywood, in a one-story building with   64
blackout windows, at the corner of Santa Monica and Poinsettia. It's an
expensive, state-of-the-art studio. These days, almost all the effects that
were once only possible to create in a professional studio like this can
now be achieved on a home computer with a software program. (A
program called Pro Tools will even correct your voice when you sing
off key.) Flom's reason for spending the money anyway, as I understood it, was: Anyone can make a record these days, but only a major
label can make a really expensive record. This is what economists call
"retreating upmarket," which is the classic response of an entrenched
industry threatened with a disruptive technology.

Inside, Cherie, who had recently turned eighteen, was behind a   65
glass wall that separated the recording area from the control room. She

was singing "pickups"—the bits of the song in which the vocal needed work. Most of the pickups were the "U" sounds, where Cherie sounded most French.

At the controls of an immense mixing board was Humberto   66
Gatica, a producer of hits by, among others, Celine Dion and Michael Jackson. Gatica had silver hair, a slight Spanish accent (he was born in Chile), and a voluble manner. Beside him, co-producing, was the song-writer Paul Moessl, who had written Cherie's original demo, "Older," and was the co-writer of the song they were working on now, "Fool." The musicians had already recorded their parts—the label had bought the services of the best studio musicians, including the rock star Beck's father, David Campbell, who specializes in arrangements for strings. Moessl estimated that there were fifty thousand dollars' worth of strings on the record. Now Gatica was mixing everything together on the hundred-and-twenty-track system.

Moessl, who was in his early thirties and had lank blond hair,   67
said, "Did you pull down the crunchy loop?" referring to part of the complicated percussion mix.

"No," said Gatica, not taking his eyes off the flashing lights on the   68
console. "I just took a little pressure off the snare."

Moessl turned his attention to a volume on his lap, which was   69
entitled "The Book of Positive Quotations." He was looking for ideas for lyrics for a new song he was writing with Cherie.

"If you are writing an artistic song, you write from inside your-   70
self," he said. "You say, oh, I don't know, 'My dog died today,' or some-thing like that. But if it's a commercial song you look for uplifting things."

The recording of the album had not been going as smoothly as   71
Flom had hoped. For one thing, the songwriters were having trouble creating the right up-tempo number for Cherie—the song that would become the all-important first single. "Ballads are about love," Flom explained to me, "but, at least for the last twenty years, most dance songs are about sex. But Cherie doesn't sing about sex. She sings about love. So we need a dance song about love. 'Push Push in the Bush' is not the right song for Cherie."

Gatica, his back stiff from bending over the mixing board,   72
seemed to have become temporarily confused by all the sonic possi-bilities at his fingertips. He paused from his work, sat down with his head in his hands, and remained that way in silence for a minute or so. Cherie waited patiently for him to recover. Finally, he sat up and said, "I was riding in the car the other day, and an Annie Lennox song came on, from ten years ago or so—and, man, it was brilliant. Brilliant production. But now the kids don't want that sound anymore." He threw his hands in the air. "They want simple! Like it's made in a

garage! So you do an expensive production like this one, made in a facility like this that costs many thousands of dollars a day, and then you end up grunging it up so that it sounds like it was made in a garage."

Cherie finished her pickups and emerged from the recording 73 room. She wore a navy turtleneck, Levi's, black boots with pointed toes and stiletto heels, and silver bracelets on each wrist, which she twisted with her long, thin fingers. She wasn't as sultry as the animated Cherie in the Batman movie, but she was much more beautiful than she appeared in the label's first photo shoot, with dramatic cheekbones and striking dark eyes. When she smiled, her mouth went up in the middle but turned down at the corners, in a way that looked French. Her English was passable, and when she was stuck for a word Haddad supplied it. She seemed like a nice, modest girl who was trying hard to please.

We went to a room at the back which was used as a place to hang 74 out between sessions. There were candles burning, and plants, and low, comfortable furniture. Cherie said that she had never been interviewed before, but if she was nervous it added to her charm. I asked her about the feeling she is able to put into a song, adding that Flom had described it as "the thing." Cherie, her eyes bright, responded, "Yes! This is eet! It is the thing. That is exactly what it is—it's just this thing." She gestured toward her chest. "I don't know where it comes from, just comes from inside you—the thing."

As we were talking, I could hear Gatica shouting in Spanish as he 75 worked on the word "learn," which sounded particularly Gallic, playing it over and over again, adding what were to me inaudible effects, and shouting some more.

"So now I will sing for you, it's O.K.?" Cherie asked. She stood up 76 and launched into her lucky song—a Jacques Brel belter called "Quand on n'a que l'amour." The money note is the last note in the piece, and Cherie hit it perfectly, arms reaching to embrace her amour. Chills.

Flom arrived, wearing a suit, and hugged his star. They walked 77 back into the control room, where Gatica was at work. The producer played the song. Flom listened with his head inclined downward, rocking with the beat back and forth, his fist cocked, ready to punch the air when he heard the money note.

But the note never came. When the song ended, Flom looked 78 crestfallen. He said he missed some of the simplicity of the earlier demo.

"Right," Gatica said. "I am combing it now. The idea is to keep it 79 fresh—transparent. Today, records are simpler. People will say this sounds like Whitney Houston. Well, it is a ballad. But we have to make it for a new generation."

They played the song again. "We have been very, very careful not   80
to let the accent get in the way," Gatica said.

"Though you can still tell she's French," Flom said.   81

"You can tell?" the producer said, sounding alarmed.   82

"It's not that that's bad," Flom said. "She's French. Hey—it is a   83
Romance language, after all."

Flom departed and Gatica went back to work. Hours later, when I   84
left, he was still at it.

On the subject of whether the record industry will survive, there   85
are optimists and pessimists. The optimists think record companies
will eventually figure out how to sell music over the Internet, and
when that happens the market for music will be three times bigger than
it is now. The pessimists say that the industry has missed a crucial
opportunity to control the new distribution platform and that unless
the government intervenes the recording industry will disappear, and
the music business will return to what it was in the nineteenth century,
when publishing and performing were the main sources of revenue.
Chris Blackwell thinks the online music business will be a boon to
independent labels because manufacturing and distribution costs will
be much cheaper; Ahmet Ertegun says, "Yes, but independents still
have to get people to buy their records." And, with so much music out
there, artists will need more blowing up than ever.

Historically, popular music has been heavily influenced by its for-   86
mat. In the nineteenth century, before Edison invented the phono-
graph, the music business was a publishing enterprise in which sheet
music was the primary commodity. People performed the music themselves, at home, usually on the piano. Songs were made into hits by the
popular performers who travelled around the country putting on concerts and musicals. The length of the songs varied. It was a singles business. When recorded music became popular, early in the twentieth
century, and the format changed to the shellac 78-r.p.m. disk, popular
songs became about three minutes long, which was as much time as a
disk could hold. The invention of the LP—the 33-r.p.m. long-playing
record—in the late nineteen-forties, created the market for albums. For
the record companies, albums cost about the same as singles to produce, but they could be sold for much more. In the CD era, the record
industry all but killed off the singles business.

MP3s might revive that business. For artists, this will mean that,   87
instead of making grand artistic statements with an album released
once every three or four years, they will focus their talent on individual
songs, which they will release every month or so. Moby, the popular
recording artist, told me he thought this would be a terrible development for artists, "because an album is so much more interesting artistically than a song." Fans will buy this music in part because it will

include goods and services like concert tickets and merchandise. Traditionally, record labels have earned money only from the sale of recorded music, but increasingly record companies may make deals like the one EMI made last year with the British pop star Robbie Williams, in which the label paid the artist some eighty million dollars to become a full partner in all of Williams's earnings—from publishing, touring, and merchandise, as well as from record sales.

As with CDs, MP3s will probably cause a boom in catalogue   88
sales. At the moment, because of traditional retailing constraints, only a small fraction of a label's catalogue is for sale. In an online music store, everything can be offered. Niche markets could become much more important, and artists with small but loyal followings, who are not economically viable in a winner-take-all market, might hold more appeal. Danny Goldberg, a former president of Warner Bros. Records, who is a founder of the independent Artemis Records, told me, "The Internet will be good for Latin music, jazz, world, and anything that sells five to ten thousand." The singer-songwriter Jimmy Buffett, who decided to leave the major-label system and put out music on his own label, Mailboat Records, told me that he thinks that more artists will go into the music business for themselves. "At Mailboat, we have three people, and we take care of our customers, and we handle the shows, and everyone has a good time—it's just like the old record business," he said.

Arguably, the most important function that record-industry pro-   89
fessionals perform—the task that people like Jason Flom, Jeff Haddad, David Foster, Lyor Cohen, Humberto Gatica, and Paul Moessl are all engaged in, one way or another—is filtering through the millions of aspiring artists who think they can sing or play and finding the one or two who really can. Record men of the future might not need to do A. & R.; they might not even make records. They may prepare monthly playlists of new songs or artists that will be beamed wirelessly to your portable MP3 player. But their essential task—filtering—will remain the same.

Everything depends on getting people to pay for recorded music   90
that they now get for free. When radio threatened the music business in the nineteen-twenties and thirties, the broadcasters agreed to pay a fee to the various rights holders for the music they played, based on an actuarial accounting system. Rights holders' societies like Ascap administered those payments. Some have argued that a similar system should be adapted to the Internet, but many users would refuse to pay their share, and would go on taking music for free. It may make more sense to address the P2P problem with a government-imposed, statutory license, such as many countries in Europe impose on TV owners. Anyone with an Internet connection would be charged a few dollars a

month, regardless of whether he downloaded music or not. That money would be distributed to the rights holders, based on an online sampling system. As Jim Griffin, a former executive at Geffen Records and a digital-rights visionary, explained the concept to me, "You monetize anarchy. Charge them five dollars a month to be thieves."

As the music business shifts online, the hitmakers may give way   91
to people who understand the financial restructuring that's needed. In January, Sir Howard Stringer replaced Tommy Mottola, the head of Sony Music, with Andrew Lack, an executive from NBC with no previous experience in the record industry. The uber bosses of the record labels aren't even necessarily from the entertainment industry. Universal Vivendi is now run by Jean-René Fourtou, an ex-pharmaceuticals executive; and the head of Bertelsmann is Gunter Thielen, who formerly ran the company's printing and industrial operations. In some ways, the record business of the future sounds more like a public utility than like a music company. It also doesn't sound like as much fun.

In April, Flom decided to postpone Cherie's record. Instead of   92
coming out this summer, it will be released sometime during the first quarter of next year. "It's just taking them a lot longer in the studio than we had anticipated," he told me, and I had a vision of Gatica, the producer, driving himself to distraction with the crunchy loops.

I said that it seemed as though worldwide politics had given the   93
lie to the idea of a "worldwide artist," especially if the artist is French. "They're not going to boycott the fucking album because she's French," Flom replied. Still, it was perhaps not the ideal time to break a worldwide artist named Cherie.

The last time I saw Flom, the numbers for the first quarter of 2003   94
had just come in, showing that the record industry's downward spiral was continuing. Sales were even lower than those of the first quarter of the disastrous previous year. The top-selling album in the country was a collection of songs sung by Kelly Clarkson, Fox's first "American Idol" winner, who has been discovered and blown up without much help from a record label—television made her a star. (Before too long, the United States' pop charts could begin to resemble Spain's, where seven of the spots on the Top Ten charts were recently occupied by reality-show contestants, causing real recording artists to complain that they aren't getting a fair shake.) And there was talk of a merger between BMG and Warner Music, which could mean that the man who called for the end of Flom's type of "lottery mentality," Rolf Schmidt-Holtz, could be Flom's boss.

Still, on this warm, springlike day, Flom seemed to be in a sunnier   95
mood about the future than he had been when we first met, six months earlier. He had recently signed a new, all-girl country-rock group called Antigone Rising, whom he expected to be huge. And he was happily

immersed in looking for the right song that would be the first single for Cherie, confident that sooner or later the perfect up-tempo love song would present itself. Jerry Wexler, one of Ertegun's partners at Atlantic, once said that artist-and-repertoire was just a fancy expression for putting a singer together with a song, and in this respect the record business does not seem to have changed at all.

Flom said he had even thought about trying to write a song for Cherie himself. But this idea hadn't got very far.   96

"I can't imagine writing a song today," he said. "I don't know where I'd start."   97

Can the record business survive?   98

Examining the Text

1. Beyond the implications of new technology and the recording industry's response to it, what other issues does the author address in this article? On reflection, do you believe that illegal downloading is the main issue confronting the recording industry? Why, or why not?

2. Author Seabrook quotes Jason Flom making the above statement: "If the star is big enough, people will buy the album, because it's like a piece of the artist. But if the star doesn't have that kind of irresistible appeal then people just say, 'what the heck, I'll download the good songs.' So we just have to figure out how to make her a big star." Looking back on recently successful bands and singers, how much of their popularity do you think is owed to this kind of "blowing up" by recording-industry executives like Flom? Using some of your own favorite musicians as examples, examine whether you think Flom's statement is accurate: can record sales be driven by record companies' marketing efforts?

3. Examine the quote from Clear Channel CEO Lowry Mays, who says: "We're simply in the business of selling products." What does this imply about the role of commercial radio and other media in the development and dissemination of your favorite music? When you listen to a radio station that plays current songs (as opposed to hits from the past), do you notice how many get frequent plays? Do you ever consider that record companies might be influencing what gets played on the radio; if so, do you object to such "manipulation"?

4. *Thinking rhetorically*: Based on the title, what sorts of information and themes did you expect from the article? After reading it, did the article meet your expectations? What specific persuasive techniques does the writer employ with this article? By the end of the article, did these techniques alter your views on whether or not the record business can be saved? If so, how; if not, why not? Might the author have approached the subject using different rhetorical strategies and still attained the same result for you?

For Group Discussion

By now, everyone knows that downloading copyrighted music from the Internet is illegal, yet still it persists. Knowing that it is legally wrong has not dissuaded the majority of Americans who still download music, seemingly unconcerned about the ethical issues involved. In light of what you've read in the article, discuss what would have to change in order for people to stop downloading music. Are there steps that the recording industry should take? Should universities and other providers of high-speed Internet connections be held responsible when users download music illegally? Alternatively, take a pro-downloading position and defend the rights of MP3-sharers to access music freely and without legal consequence.

Writing Suggestion

Imagine you are a record label executive faced with declining sales of CDs as a result of downloading from the Internet. Write a letter to the *New Yorker* magazine in which you defend recent efforts to sue networks like Napster as well as individual heavy users of file-swapping networks. Address how you're trying to win the battle in the court of public opinion as well as legally.

I Hate Classical Music

Alex Ross

Dying music written by long-dead composers enjoyed by aging, fussy elitists: is that a fair image of classical music, as detailed by author Alex Ross in the following article published in the New Yorker *magazine? Ross laments the ways in which classical music has been relegated to the margins of popular culture, laden with upper-class rituals and, ultimately, misunderstood. Followers of classical music have burdened it with invented traditions, such as dressing up to hear it and not applauding during performances, that have further distanced it from other music forms. While other music remains dynamic and changing, the author argues that classical music is largely stuck in the past, favoring dead over living composers.*

    Yet sonatas, symphonies, and other classical forms have the power to move you, to rekindle a "child-like energy, a happy ferocity about the world," says the author. Classical music continues to attract talented youngsters from all over the world, and there are pioneers who are taking the form into a new, post-classical phase that blends in electronic instruments. There are also practitioners who have abandoned the starched suits of old and take a more theatrical approach to playing. **As you read**, *notice how the author juxtaposes his own musical evolution with the history of classical music. What do you think the author's personal story lends to the article?*

I hate "classical music": not the thing but the name. It traps a tena- 1
ciously living art in a theme park of the past. It cancels out the possibility that music in the spirit of Beethoven could still be created today. It
banishes into limbo the work of thousands of active composers who
have to explain to otherwise well-informed people what it is they do
for a living. The phrase is a masterpiece of negative publicity, a tour de
force of anti-hype. I wish there were another name. I envy jazz people
who speak simply of "the music." Some jazz aficionados also call their
art "America's classical music," and I propose a trade: they can have
"classical," I'll take "the music."

For at least a century, the music has been captive to a cult of 2
mediocre elitism that tries to manufacture self-esteem by clutching at
empty formulas of intellectual superiority. Consider some of the rival
names in circulation: "art" music, "serious" music, "great" music,
"good" music. Yes, the music can be great and serious; but greatness
and seriousness are not its defining characteristics. It can also be stupid, vulgar, and insane. Music is too personal a medium to support an
absolute hierarchy of values. The best music is music that persuades
us that there is no other music in the world. This morning, for me, it
was Sibelius's Fifth; late last night, Dylan's "Sad-Eyed Lady of the
Lowlands"; tomorrow, it may be something entirely new. I can't rank
my favorite music any more than I can rank my memories. Yet some
discerning souls believe that the music should be marketed as a luxury
good, one that supplants an inferior popular product. They say, in
effect, "The music you love is trash. Listen instead to our great, arty
music." They gesture toward the heavens, but they speak the language
of high-end real estate. They are making little headway with the
unconverted because they have forgotten to define the music as something worth loving. If it is worth loving, it must be great; no more need
be said.

When people hear "classical," they think "dead." The music is 3
described in terms of its distance from the present, its resistance to the
mass—what it is not. You see magazines with listings for Popular
Music in one section and for Classical Music in another, so that the

latter becomes, by implication, Unpopular Music. No wonder that stories of its imminent demise are so commonplace. The Web site Art-
sJournal features a media file with the deliberately ridiculous name
Death of Classical Music Archive, whose articles recycle a familiar
litany of problems: record companies are curtailing their classical divisions; orchestras are facing deficits; the music is barely taught in public
schools, almost invisible on television, ignored or mocked by Hollywood. But the same story could have been written ten years ago or
twenty. If this be death, the record is skipping. A complete version of
the Death of Classical Music Archive would go back to the fourteenth
century, when the sensuous melodies of ars nova were thought to signal the end of civilization.

The classical audience is assumed to be a moribund crowd of the   4
old, the white, the rich, and the bored. Statistics provided by the
National Endowment for the Arts suggest that the situation is not quite
so dire. Yes, the audience is older than that for any other art—the
median age is forty-nine—but it is not the wealthiest. Musicals, plays,
ballet, and museums all get larger slices of the $50,000-or-more income
pie (as does the ESPN channel, for that matter). If you want to see an
in-your-face, Swiss-bank-account display of wealth, go look at the
millionaires sitting in the skyboxes at a Billy Joel show, if security lets
you. Nor is the classical audience aging any faster than the rest of
America. The music may not be a juggernaut, but it is a major world.
American orchestras sell around thirty million tickets each year. Brilliant new talents are thronging the scene; the musicians of the august
Berlin Philharmonic are, on average, a generation younger than the
Rolling Stones.

The music is always dying, ever-ending. It is an ageless diva on a   5
non-stop farewell tour, coming around for one absolutely final appearance. It is hard to name because it never really existed to begin with—
not in the sense that it stemmed from a single time or place. It has no
genealogy, no ethnicity: leading composers of today hail from China,
Estonia, Argentina, Queens. The music is simply whatever composers
create—a long string of written-down works to which various performing traditions have become attached. It encompasses the high, the
low, empire, underground, dance, prayer, silence, noise. Composers
are genius parasites; they feed voraciously on the song matter of their
time in order to engender something new. They have gone through a
rough stretch in the past hundred years, facing external obstacles
(Hitler and Stalin were amateur music critics) as well as problems of
their own invention ("Why doesn't anyone like our beautiful twelve-
tone music?"). But they may be on the verge of an improbable renaissance, and the music may take a form that no one today would recognize.

For now, it is like the "sunken cathedral" that Debussy depicts in one of his Preludes—a city that chants beneath the waves.

The critic Greg Sandow recently wrote in his online journal that 6 we partisans of the classical need to speak more from the heart about what the music means. He admits that it's easier to analyze his ardor than to express it. The music does not lend itself to the same generational storytelling as, say, "Sgt. Pepper." There may be kids out there who lost their virginity during Brahms's D-Minor Piano Concerto, but they don't want to tell the story and you don't want to hear it. The music attracts the reticent fraction of the population. It is an art of grand gestures and vast dimensions that plays to mobs of the quiet and the shy. It is a paradise for passive-aggressives, sublimation addicts, and other relics of the Freudian world. Which may explain why it has a hard time expressing itself in the time of Dr. Phil.

I am a thirty-six-year-old white American male who first started 7 listening to popular music at the age of twenty. In retrospect, this seems strange; perhaps "freakish" is not too strong a word. Yet it seemed natural at the time. I feel as though I grew up not during the seventies and eighties but during the thirties and forties, the decades of my parents' youth. They came of age in the great American middlebrow era, when the music had a much different place in the culture than it does today. In those years, in what now seems like a surreal dream world, millions listened as Toscanini conducted the NBC Symphony on national radio. Walter Damrosch explained the classics to schoolchildren, singing ditties to help them remember the themes. (My mother remembers one of them: "This is/The sympho-nee/That Schubert wrote but never fi-nished . . .") NBC would broadcast Ohio State vs. Indiana one afternoon, a recital by Lotte Lehmann the next. In my house, it was the Boston Symphony broadcast followed by the Redskins game. I was unaware of a yawning gap between the two.

Early on, I reached for my parents' record collection, which was 8 well stocked with artifacts of the Golden Age. I listened to Toscanini's Brahms, Koussevitzky's Sibelius, the Budapest Quartet. The look and feel of the records were inseparable from the sound they made. They said so much to me that for a long time I had no curiosity about other music. There was Otto Klemperer's Zeppelin-like, slow-motion account of "The St. Matthew Passion," with nightmare-spawning art by the Master of Delft. Toscanini's fierce recordings were decorated with Robert Hupka's snapshots of the Maestro in motion, his face registering every emotion between ecstasy and disgust. Mozart's Divertimento in E-Flat featured the famous portrait in which the composer looks down at the world in sorrow, like a general surveying a hopeless battle. While listening, I read along in the liner notes, which were

generally written in the over-the-top everymanorator style that Orson
Welles parodied brilliantly in "Citizen Kane." Tchaikovsky's Violin
Concerto, for example, was said to be "melancholy, sometimes progressing to abysmal depths." None of this made sense at the time; I had
no acquaintance with melancholy, alone abysmal depths. What mat-
tered was the exaggerated swoop of the thought, which roughly
matched the pattern of the sound.

The first music that I loved to the point of distraction was   9
Beethoven's "Eroica" Symphony. My parents had a disk of Leonard
Bernstein conducting the New York Philharmonic—one of a series of
Music-Appreciation Records put out by the Book-of-the-Month Club.
A companion record provided Bernstein's analysis of the symphony, a
road map to its forty-five-minute sprawl. I now had names for the
shapes that I perceived. (The conductor's "Joy of Music" and "Infinite
Variety of Music" remain the best introductory books of their kind.)
Bernstein drew attention to something that happens about ten seconds
in—a C-sharp that unexpectedly sounds against the plain E-flat-major
harmony. "There has been a stab of intrusive otherness," he said, cryp-
tically but seductively, in his nicotine baritone. Over and over, I listened to this note of otherness. I bought a score and deciphered the
notation. I learned some time-beating gestures from Max Rudolf's conducting manual. I held my family hostage in the living room as I led
the record player in a searingly intense performance of the "Eroica."

Did Lenny get a little carried away when he called that soft   10
C-sharp in the cellos a "shock," a "wrench," a "stab"? If you were to play
the "Eroica" for a fourteen-year-old hip-hop scholar versed in the works
of Eminem and 50 Cent, he might find it shockingly boring at best.
No one is slicing up his wife or getting shot nine times. But I would submit to my young gangsta interlocutor that those artists are relatively
shocking—relative to the social norms of their day. Although the
"Eroica" ceased to be controversial in the these-crazy-kids-today sense
around 1830, within the "classical" frame it has continued to deliver its
surprises right on cue. Seven bars of E-flat major, then the C-sharp that
hovers for a moment before disappearing: it is like a speaker stepping
up to a microphone, launching into the first words of a grand oration,
and then faltering, as if he had just remembered something from childhood or seen a sinister face in the crowd.

I don't identify with the listener who responds to the "Eroica" by   11
saying, "Ah, civilization." That wasn't what Beethoven wanted: his
intention was to shake the European mind. I don't listen to music to be
civilized; sometimes, I listen precisely to escape the ordered world.
What I love about the "Eroica" is the way it manages to have it all, unit-
ing Romanticism and Enlightenment, civilization and revolution, brain
and body, order and chaos. It knows which way you think the music is

going and veers triumphantly in the wrong direction. The Danish composer Carl Nielsen once wrote a monologue for the spirit of Music, in which he or she or it says, "I love the vast surface of silence; and it is my chief delight to break it."

Around the time I got stabbed by Beethoven's C-sharp, I began 12 trying to write music myself. My career as a composer lasted from the age of eight to the age of twenty. I lacked both genius and talent. My spiral-bound manuscript book includes an ambitious program of future compositions: thirty piano sonatas, twelve violin sonatas, various symphonies, concertos, fantasias, and funeral marches, most of them in the key of D minor. Scattered ideas for these works appear in the following pages, but they don't go anywhere, which was the story of my life as a composer. Still, I treasure the observation of one of my college teachers, who wrote on the final page of my end-of-term submission that I had created a "most interesting and slightly peculiar sonatina." I put down my pen and withdrew into silence, like Sibelius in Jarvenpa.

My inability to finish anything, much less anything good, left me 13 with a profound respect for this impossible mode of making a living. Composition at its most intense is a rebellion against reality. No one except the very young demands new music, and even when we are young the gates of inattention crash down quickly. Composers manufacture a product that is universally deemed superfluous—at least until their music enters public consciousness, at which point people begin to say that they could not live without it. For more than a century, the repertory has consisted largely of music by dead composers. Yet half of those on the American Symphony Orchestra League's top-ten most-performed list—Mahler, Strauss, Ravel, Shostakovich, Prokofiev—hadn't been born when the first draft of the repertory got written.

Throughout my teens, I took piano lessons from a man named 14 Denning Barnes. He also taught me composition, music history, and the art of listening. He was a wiry man with tangled hair, whose tweed jackets emitted an odd smell that was neither pleasant nor unpleasant, just odd. He was intimate with Beethoven, Schubert, and Chopin, and he also loved twentieth-century music. Scriabin, Bartok, and Berg were three favorites. He opened another door for me, in a wall that I never knew existed. His own music, as far as I can remember, was rambunctious, jazzy, a little nuts. One day he pounded out one of the variations in Beethoven's final piano sonata and said that it was an anticipation of boogie-woogie. I had no idea what boogie-woogie was, but I was excited by the idea that Beethoven had anticipated it. The marble-bust Beethoven of my childhood suddenly became an eagle-eyed sentinel on the ramparts of sound, spying nameless entities on the horizon. "Boogie-woogie" was a creature out of Bernstein's serious-fun world, and Mr. Barnes was my private Bernstein. There was not a snobbish bone in his body; he was a skeleton of enthusiasm, a fifteen-dollar-an-hour guerrilla fighter for the music he loved. He died of a brain tumor in 1989. The last time I saw him, we played a hair-raising version of Schubert's Fantasia in F Minor for four hands. It was full of wrong notes, most of them at my end of the keyboard, but it felt great and made a mighty noise, and to this day I have never been able to tolerate any other performance of the work, not even Britten and Richter's.

By high school, a terrible truth had dawned: I was the only person   15
my age who liked this stuff. Actually, there were other classical nerds at my school, but we were too diffident to form a posse. Several "normal" friends dragged me to a showing of "Pink Floyd—The Wall," after which I conceded that one passage sounded Mahlerian. Only in college did my musical fortress finally crumble. I spent most of my days and nights at the campus radio station, where I had a show and helped organize the classical contingent. I fanatically patrolled the boundaries of the classical broadcasting day, refusing to surrender even fifteen minutes of "Chamber Music Masterworks" and the like. At 10 p.m., the schedule switched from classical to punk, and only punk of the most recondite kind. Once a record sold more than a few hundred copies, it was kicked off the playlist. The d.j.s liked to start their sets with the shrillest, crudest songs in order to scandalize the classical crowd. I tried to one-up them by ending my show with squalls of Xenakis. They hit back with Sinatra singing "Only the Lonely." Once, they followed up my heartfelt tribute to Herbert von Karajan with Skrewdriver's rousing neo-Nazi anthem "Prisoner of Peace": "Free Rudolf Hess/How long can they keep him there? We can only guess." Touche.

The thing about these cerebral punk rockers is that they were   16
easily the most interesting people I'd ever met. Between painstakingly researched tributes to Mission of Burma and the Butthole Surfers, they composed undergraduate theses on fourth-century Roman fortifications and the liberal thought of Lionel Trilling. I began hanging around in the studio after my show was over, suppressing an instinctive fear of their sticker-covered leather jackets and multicolored hair. I informed them, as Mr. Barnes would have done, that Schoenberg had anticipated all of this. And I began listening to new things. The first two rock records I bought were Pere Ubu's "Terminal Tower" compilation and Sonic Youth's "Daydream Nation." I crept from underground rock to alternative rock and finally to the full-out commercial kind. Soon I was astounding my friends with pronouncements like "'Highway 61 Revisited' is a pretty good album," or "The White Album is a masterpiece." I abandoned the notion of classical superiority, which led to a crisis of faith: if the music wasn't great and serious and high and mighty, what was it?

For a little while, living in Northern California after college, 17 I thought of giving up on the music altogether. I sold off a lot of my CDs, including all my copies of the symphonies of Arnold Bax, in order to pay for more Pere Ubu and Sonic Youth. I cut my hair short, wore angry T-shirts, and started hanging out at the Berkeley punk club 924 Gilman Street. I became a fan of a band called Blatz, which was about as far from Bax as I could get. (Their big hit was "Fuk Shit Up.") Fortunately, no one needed to point out to my face that I was in the wrong place. It is a strange American dream, this notion that music can give you a new personality, a new class, even a new race. The out-of-body experience is thrilling as long as it lasts, but most people are eventually deposited back at the point where they started, and they may begin to hate the music for lying to them. When I went back to the classical ghetto, I chose to accept its limitations. I realized that, despite the outward decrepitude of the culture, there was still a bright flame within. It occurred to me that if I could somehow get from Brahms to Blatz, others could go the same route in the opposite direction. I have always wanted to talk about classical music as if it were popular music and popular music as if it were classical.

For many, popular music is the soundtrack of raging adolescence, 18 while the other kind chimes in during the long twilight of maturity. For me, it's the reverse. Listening to the "Eroica" reconnects me with a kind of childlike energy, a happy ferocity about the world. Since I came to pop music late, I invest it with more adult feeling. To me, it's penetrating, knowing, full of microscopic shades of truth about the way things really are. Dylan's "Blood on the Tracks" anatomizes a doomed relationship with a saturnine clarity that a canonical work such as "Die Schöne Müllerin" can't match. (Listening recently to Ian Bostridge sing the Schubert cycle, I had the thought that the protagonist might never have spoken to the miller girl for whose sake he drowns himself. How classical of him.) If I were in a perverse mood, I'd say that the "Eroica" is the raw, thuggish thing—a blast of ego and id—whereas a song like Radiohead's "Everything in Its Right Place" is all cool adult irony. The idea that life is flowing along with unsettling smoothness, the dark C-sharpness of the world sensed but not confirmed, is a resigned sort of sentiment that Beethoven probably never even felt, much less communicated. What I refuse to accept is that one kind of music soothes the mind and another kind soothes the soul. Depends on whose mind, whose soul.

On my iPod I've been listening to the new Missy Elliott song 19 "Wake Up." It's an austere hip-hop track with a political edge. Something about the music sets off my classical radar. There are, effectively, only three notes, free-floating and ambiguous. The song begins with a clip of a voice shouting "Wake up!" The voice rises up a tritone, and that interval determines the notes. The idea of generating music from the singsong of speech is ancient, but "Wake Up" reminds me in particular of two minimalist pieces by Steve Reich, "It's Gonna Rain" and "Come Out." Both use tapes of impassioned black voices to create seething electronic soundscapes. Whether Elliott and her producer, Timbaland, have listened to Reich is beside the point. (If you say, "Of course they haven't," ask yourself what makes you so certain.) The song works much like Reich's compositions, building a world from a sliver of sound. It's almost manic and obsessive enough to be classical music.

The fatal phrase came into circulation late in the game. From 20 Monteverdi to Beethoven, modern music was the only music, bartered about in a marketplace that resembled modern pop culture. Concerts were eclectic hootenannies in which opera arias collided with chunks of sonatas. Barrel-organ grinders carried the best-known arias out into the streets, where they were blended with folk tunes. Concerts in pre-classical America were a stylistic free-for-all, a mirror of the country's mixed-up nature. Walt Whitman mobilized grand opera as a metaphor for democracy; the voices of his favorite singers were integral to the swelling sound of his "barbaric yawp."

In Europe, the past began to overwhelm the present just after 21 1800. Johann Nikolaus Forkel's 1802 biography of Bach, one of the first major books devoted to a dead composer, may be the founding document of the classical mentality. All the earmarks are there: the longing for lost worlds, the adulation of a single godlike entity, the horror of the present. Bach was "the first classic that ever was, or perhaps ever will be," Forkel proclaimed. "If the art is to remain an art and not to be degraded into a mere idle amusement, more use must be made of classical works than has been done for some time." By "idle amusement" Forkel had in mind the prattling of Italian opera; his biography is addressed to "patriotic admirers of true musical art," namely the German. The notion that the music of Forkel's time was teetering toward extinction is, of course, amusing in retrospect; in the summer of 1802, Beethoven began work on the "Eroica." Scholars eventually defined the Classical Era as Viennese music of the late eighteenth century, especially Mozart and Haydn, who, in their day, had been racy, modern figures. The word was nonsense from the outset.

The rise of "classical music" mirrored the rise of the commercial 22 middle class, which employed Beethoven as an escalator to the social heights. Concert halls grew quiet and reserved, habits and attire formal. Improvisation was phased out; the score became sacred. Audiences were discouraged from applauding while the music was going on—it had been the custom to clap after a good tune or a dazzling solo—or between movements. Patrons of the Wagner festival in Bayreuth proved notoriously militant in the suppression of applause. At an early performance of "Parsifal," listeners hissed an unmusical vulgarian who yelled out "Bravo!" after the Flower Maidens scene. The troublemaker had reason to feel embarrassed; he had written the opera. The Wagnerians were taking Wagner more seriously than he took himself—an alarming development.

Composers liked the fact that listeners were quieting down; the   23
subtle shock of a C-sharp wouldn't register if the crowd were chattering away. Even so, the emergence of a self-styled elite audience had limited appeal for the likes of Beethoven and Verdi, who did not come from that world. The nineteenth-century masters were, most of them, monstrous egomaniacs, but they were not snobs. Verdi wrote for the masses, and he scandalously proclaimed the box office the only barometer of success. Wagner, surrounded by luxury, royalty, and extreme pretension, nonetheless railed against the emergence of a "classical" repertory, for which he blamed the Jews. His nauseating anti-Semitism went hand in hand with a sometimes deeply charming populism. In a letter to Liszt, he raged against the "monumental character" of the music of his time, the "clinging and sticking to the past." Another letter demanded, "Kinder! macht Neues! Neues!, und abermals Neues!" Ezra Pound condensed this thought as "Make it new."

Unfortunately, the European bourgeoisie, having made a   24
demigod of Beethoven, began losing interest in even the most vital living composers. In 1859, a critic wrote, "New works do not succeed in Leipzig. Again at the fourteenth Gewandhaus concert a composition was borne to its grave." The crazy modern music in question was Brahms's First Piano Concerto. By 1870, seventy-five per cent of works in the Gewandhaus repertory were by dead composers. The fetishizing of the past had a degrading effect on composers' morale. They began to doubt their ability to please this implacable audience, which seemed prepared to reject their wares no matter what style they wrote in. If no one cares, composers reasoned, we might as well write for connoisseurs—or for each other. This was the mentality that gave birth to the phenomenon of Arnold Schoenberg. The relationship between composer and public became a vicious circle; the more the composer asserted independence, the more the public clung to the past. A critic who attended the premiere of the "Eroica" saw the impasse coming: "Music could quickly come to such a point, that everyone who is not precisely familiar with the rules and difficulties of the art would find absolutely no enjoyment in it."

The American middle class carried the worship of the classics to a   25
necrophiliac extreme. Lawrence Levine, in his book "Highbrow/Lowbrow,"

gives a devastating portrait of the country's musical culture at the turn of the twentieth century. It was a world that abhorred virtuosity, extravagance, anything that smacked of entertainment. Orchestras dedicated themselves to "the great works of the great composers greatly performed, the best and profoundest art, these and these alone," in the redundant words of the conductor Theodore Thomas, who was the founder of the modern American orchestra. Early in his career, Thomas tried to attract the masses, conducting in parks and beer gardens. Later, he decided that the working classes could never appreciate greatly great great music like Beethoven's. He was a marvellous conductor, by all accounts, but his infatuation with "cultivated persons" set a bad precedent.

Within a decade or two, American symphonic culture was so ossi-   26
fied that progressive spirits were calling for change. "America is saddled, hag-ridden, with culture," the critic-composer Arthur Farwell wrote in 1911. "There is a conventionalism, a cynicism, a self-consciousness, in symphony concert, recital, and opera." Daniel Gregory Mason, a maverick Columbia professor, similarly attacked the "prestige-hypnotized" plutocrats who ran the New York Philharmonic. He found more excitement at open-air concerts at Lewisohn Stadium, in Harlem, where the audience freely expressed its enthusiasm. Mason delightedly quoted a notice that read, "We would respectfully request that the audience refrain from throwing mats." His sentiment still rings true—concerts would be better if there were more throwing of mats.

In the nineteen-thirties, Farwell's populist philosophy took root.   27
A generation of composers, conductors, and broadcasters embraced the idea of "music for all." The storied middlebrow age began. David Sarnoff, the head of NBC, had a vision of Toscanini conducting for a vast public, and the public duly materialized. The first broadcast day of CBS featured an American opera: "The King's Henchman," by Deems Taylor. Hollywood studios hired composers such as Korngold, Copland, and Herrmann and pursued the modernist giants Schoenberg and Stravinsky (both of whom asked for too much money). F.D.R. funded a Federal Music Project that in two and a half years entertained ninety-five million people; there were concerts in delinquent-boys' homes and rural Oklahoma towns. A Boston reporter pictured one Federal opera performance as a storming of the Bastille: "Drivers, chauffeurs, and footmen were occupying the seats of the master and the madame at 83 cents a chair."

Perhaps the boldest forward leap was the invention of a hybrid   28
music combining European tradition and new popular forms. Duke Ellington wrote symphonic jazz for Carnegie Hall; his "Black, Brown, and Beige" was heard there in 1943. Morton Gould and Leonard Bernstein wrote for orchestra, jazz ensemble, and Broadway without worrying about the ranking of each. The ultimate phenomenon was George

Gershwin, who rose through Tin Pan Alley and then through the orchestral world, transforming America's idea of what a composer was. For all his Jazz Age glamour, some part of Gershwin remained a lonely classical kid—the hard-practicing pianist who had filled scrapbooks with concert programs from Cooper Union and Wanamaker's Auditorium. In Vienna, in 1928, Gershwin met his idol, Alban Berg, who had the Kolisch Quartet play him the "Lyric Suite." Gershwin then sat down at the piano, but hesitated, wondering aloud whether he was worthy of the occasion. "Mr. Gershwin," Berg said sternly, "music is music."

The middlebrow utopia sputtered out quickly, and for a variety of   29
reasons. Federally funded arts projects fell victim to a classic American culture war—the Republicans versus the New Deal—for which fanatics on both the left and the right were to blame. Orchestras that had flourished on radio foundered on television. (No one wants to get that close to oboists.) But the real problem was with the competition. Jazz was satisfying a hunger for popular art that in previous eras only classical composers had been able to satisfy. Ellington and Mingus were pulling off the same synthetic feat that Mozart and Verdi had accomplished before them; they were picking up pieces of every form of available music—African-American, Latin, Gypsy, Debussy, operetta—and transforming them through the force of their personalities.

Lately, I have been reading the young intellectuals who embraced   30
jazz in the twenties, and I recognize their urge to join the party. Carl Van Vechten, the notorious author of "Nigger Heaven," started out as a music critic for the Times; he witnessed "The Rite of Spring" and embraced Stravinsky as a savior. Then his attention began to wander. He found more life and truth in ragtime, Tin Pan Alley, and, eventually, blues and jazz. In a 1917 article for Vanity Fair, he predicted that Tin Pan Alley songwriters were likely to be considered "the true grandfathers of the Great American Composer of the year 2001." For young African-American music mavens, the disenchantment was more bitter and more personal. Some were children of a middle class that had taken to heart Dvorak's 1893 prophecy of a great age of Negro music. The likes of James Weldon Johnson awaited the black Beethoven who would write the music of God's trombones. Soon enough, these aspiring violinists, pianists, and composers came up against a wall of racism. Only in popular music could they make a living. Many—Fletcher Henderson, for example—turned to jazz.

The twenties saw a huge change in music's social function. Classical   31
music had given the middle class aristocratic airs; now popular music helped the middle class to feel down and dirty. There is American musical history in one brutally simplistic sentence. I recently watched a silly 1934 movie entitled "Murder at the Vanities," which seemed to sum up the genre wars of the era. It is set behind the scenes of a

Ziegfeld-style variety show, one of whose numbers features a performer, dressed vaguely as Franz Liszt, who plays the Second Hungarian Rhapsody. Duke Ellington and his band keep popping up behind the scenes, throwing in insolent riffs. Eventually, they drive away the effete classical musicians and play a takeoff called "Ebony Rhapsody": "It's got those licks, it's got those tricks / That Mr. Liszt would never recognize." Liszt comes back with a submachine gun and mows down the band. The metaphor wasn't so far off the mark. Although many in the classical world were fulsome in their praise of jazz—Ernest Ansermet lobbed the word "genius" at Sidney Bechet—others fired verbal machine guns in an effort to slay the upstart. Daniel Gregory Mason, the man who wanted more throwing of mats, was one of the worst offenders, calling jazz a "sick moment in the progress of the human soul."

The contempt flowed both ways. The culture of jazz, at least in its white precincts, was much affected by that inverse snobbery which endlessly congratulates itself on escaping the elite. (The singer in "Murder at the Vanities" brags of finding a rhythm that Liszt, of all people, could never comprehend: what a snob.) Classical music became a foil against which popular musicians could assert their earthy cool. Composers, in turn, were irritated by the suggestion that they constituted some sort of moneyed behemoth. They were the ones who were feeling bulldozed by the power of cash. Such was the complaint made by Lawrence Gilman, of the Tribune, after Paul Whiteman and his Palais Royal Orchestra played "Rhapsody in Blue" at Aeolian Hall. Gilman didn't like the "Rhapsody," but what really incensed him was Whiteman's suggestion that jazz was an underdog fighting against symphony snobs. "It is the Palais Royalists who represent the conservative, reactionary, respectable elements in the music of today," Gilman wrote. "They are the aristocrats, the Top Dogs, of contemporary music. They are the Shining Ones, the commanders of huge salaries, the friends of Royalty." The facts back Gilman up. By the late twenties, Gershwin was making at least a hundred thousand dollars a year. In 1938, Copland, the best-regarded composer of American concert music, had $6.93 in his checking account.

All music becomes classical music in the end. Reading the histories of other genres, I often get a warm sense of deja vu. The story of jazz, for example, seems to recapitulate classical history at high speed. First, the youth-rebellion period: Satchmo and the Duke and Bix and Jelly Roll teach a generation to lose itself in the music. Second, the era of bourgeois grandeur: the high-class swing band parallels the Romantic orchestra. Stage 3: artists rebel against the bourgeois image, echoing the classical modernist revolution, sometimes by direct citation (Charlie Parker works the opening notes of "The Rite of Spring" into "Salt

Peanuts"). Stage 4: free jazz marks the point at which the vanguard loses touch with the mass and becomes a self-contained avant-garde. Stage 5: a period of retrenchment. Wynton Marsalis's attempt to launch a traditionalist jazz revival parallels the neo-Romantic music of many late-twentieth-century composers. But this effort comes too late to restore the art to the popular mainstream. Jazz recordings sell about the same as classical recordings, three per cent of the market.

The same progression worms its way through rock and roll. What were my hyper-educated punk-rock friends but Stage 3 high modernists, rebelling against the bloated Romanticism of Stage 2 stadium rock? Right now, there seems to be a lot of Stage 5 classicism going on in what remains of rock and roll. The Strokes, the Hives, the Vines, the Stills, the Thrills, and so on hark back to some lost pure moment of the sixties or seventies. Their names are all variations on the Kinks. Many of them use old instruments, old amplifiers, old soundboards. One rocker was recently quoted as saying, "I intentionally won't use something I haven't heard before." Macht Neues, kids! So far, hip-hop has proved resistant to this kind of classicizing cycle, but you never know. It is just a short step from old school to the Second Viennese School.   34

The original classical is left in an interesting limbo. It has a chance to be liberated from the social cliches that currently pin it down. It is no longer the one form carrying the burden of the past. Moreover, it has the advantage of being able to sustain constant reinterpretation, to renew itself with each repetition. The best kind of classical performance is never a retreat into the past but rather an intensification of the present. When you hear a great orchestra perform Beethoven's "Eroica," it isn't like a rock band trying to mimic the Beatles—it is like the Beatles re-incarnated. The mistake that apostles of the classical have always made is to have joined their love of the past to a dislike of the present. The music has other ideas: it hates the past and wants to escape.   35

I have seen the future, and it is called Shuffle—the setting on the iPod that skips randomly from one track to another. I've transferred about a thousand songs, works, and sonic events from my CD collection to my computer and on to the MP3 player. There is something thrilling about setting the player on Shuffle and letting it decide what to play next. Sometimes its choices are a touch delirious—I had to veto an attempt to forge a link between Gyorgy Kurtag and Oasis—but the little machine often goes crashing through barriers of style in ways that change how I listen. For example, it recently made a segue from the furious crescendo of "The Dance of the Earth," ending Part I of "The Rite of Spring," right into the hot jam of Louis Armstrong's "West End Blues." The first became a gigantic upbeat to the other. For a second, I felt that I was at some madly fashionable party at Carl Van Vechten's.   36

On the iPod, music is freed from all fatuous self-definitions and delusions of significance. There are no record jackets depicting bombastic Alpine scenes or celebrity conductors with a family resemblance to Rudolf Hess. Instead, music is music.

It seems to me that a lot of younger listeners think the way the   37
iPod thinks. They are no longer so invested in a single genre, one that promises to mold their being or save the world. This gives the life-style disaster called "classical music" more of a chance. Although the music is far from attaining any sort of countercultural cachet, it is no longer a plausible target for teen rebellion, given that all the parents listen to the Eagles. (A colleague pointed out to me that the movie "School of Rock" pictures a private school where classical music is forced down students' throats. The closing credits don't specify which alternate universe this is set in.) Committed rock fans are likely to know a fair amount about twentieth-century composition, especially the avant-garde. Mavens of electronic dance music list among their heroes Stockhausen, Terry Riley, and, especially, Steve Reich, who avoids the temptation to sue his less inventive admirers. Mark Prendergast's book "The Ambient Century," a history of the new electronic genres, begins, startlingly enough, with Gustav Mahler.

The new buzzword in progressive circles is "post-classical." The   38
phrase was coined by the writer Joseph Horowitz, and it neatly expresses exasperation with the C word without jettisoning it. It also hints that life will go on even if monuments of the old classical empire falter. The scholar Robert Fink is even predicting a Richard Strauss-style "death and transfiguration." Post-classical composers are writing music heavily influenced by minimalism and its electronic spawn, but they are still immersed in the complexity of composition. They just don't need to advertise an entire course of study on the surface of a work. Likewise, new generations of musicians are dropping the mask of Olympian detachment (silent, stone-faced musician walks onstage and begins to play). They've started mothballing the tuxedo, explaining the music from the stage, using lighting and backdrops to produce a mildly theatrical experience. They are finding allies in the "popular" world, some of whom care less about record sales than the average star violinist. The London Sinfonietta, for example, will be playing a program next month of Aphex Twin, Jamie Lidell, and other sonic scientists from the Warp Records label, pairing their work with the constructions of Reich and Cage. The borders between "popular" and "classical" are becoming creatively blurred, and only the Johann Forkels in each camp see a problem.

The strange thing about the music in America today is that large   39
numbers of people seem aware of it, curious about it, even mildly knowledgeable about it, but they do not go to concerts. The people

who try to market orchestras have a name for these annoying phantoms: they are "culturally aware non-attenders," to quote a recent article in the magazine Symphony. I know the type; most of my friends are case studies. They know the principal names and periods of musical history: they know what Nietzsche said about Wagner, they can pick Schoenberg and Stravinsky out of a lineup, they own Glenn Gould's "Goldberg Variations" and some Mahler and perhaps a CD of Arvo Part. They follow all the other arts—they go to gallery shows, read new novels, see art films. Yet they have never paid money for a classical concert. They almost make a point of their ignorance. "I don't know a thing about Beethoven," they say, which is not what they would say if the subject were Henry James or Stanley Kubrick. This is one area where even sophisticates wrap themselves in the all-American anti-intellectual flag. It's not all their fault: centuries of classical intolerance have gone into the creation of the culturally aware non-attender. When I tell people what I do for a living, I see the same look again and again—a flinching sideways glance, as if they were about to be reprimanded for not knowing about C-sharps. After this comes the serene declaration of ignorance. The old culture war is fought and lost before I say a word.

I'm imagining myself on the other side—as a thirty-six-year-old pop fan who wants to try something different. On a lark, I buy a record of Otto Klemperer conducting the "Eroica," picking this one because Klemperer is the father of Colonel Klink, on "Hogan's Heroes." I hear two impressive loud chords, then something that the liner notes allege is a "truly heroic" theme. It sounds kind of feeble, lopsided, waltz-like. My mind drifts. A few days later, I try again. This time, I hear some attractive adolescent grandeur, barbaric yawps here and there. The rest is mechanical, remote. But each time I go back I map out a little more of the imaginary world. I invent stories for each thing as it happens. Big chords, hero standing backstage, a troubling thought, hero orating over loudspeakers, some ideas for songs that don't catch on, a man or woman pleading, hero shouts back, tension, anger, conspiracies—assassination attempt? The nervous splendor of it all gets under my skin. I go to a bookstore and look at the classical shelf, which seems to have more books for Idiots and Dummies than any other section. I read Bernstein's essay in "The Infinite Variety of Music," coordinate some of the examples with the music, read fun stories of the composer screaming about Napoleon, and go back and listen again. Sometime after the tenth listen, the music becomes my own; I know what's around almost every corner and I exult in knowing. It's as if I could predict the news.

I am now enough of a fan that I buy a twenty-five-dollar ticket to hear a famous orchestra play the "Eroica" live. It is not a very heroic experience. I feel dispirited from the moment I walk in the hall. My

40

41

black jeans draw disapproving glances from men who seem to be mod-
elling the Johnny Carson collection. I look around dubiously at the
twenty shades of beige in which the hall is decorated. The music starts,
but I find it hard to think of Beethoven's detestation of all tyranny over
the human mind when the man next to me is a dead ringer for my dentist. The assassination sequence in the first movement is less exciting
when the musicians have no emotion on their faces. I cough; a thin
man, reading a dog-eared score, glares at me. When the movement is
about a minute from ending, an ancient woman creeps slowly up the
aisle, a look of enormous dissatisfaction on her face, followed at a few
paces by a blank-faced husband. Finally, three grand chords to finish,
which the composer obviously intended to set off a roar of applause. I
start to clap, but the man with the score glares again. One does not
applaud in the midst of greatly great great music, even if the composer
wants one to! Coughing, squirming, whispering, the crowd visibly
suppresses its urge to express pleasure. It's like mass anal retention.
The slow tread of the Funeral March, or Marcia funebre, as everyone
insists on calling it, begins. I start to feel that my newfound respect for
the music is dragging along behind the hearse.

But I stay with it. For the duration of the Marcia, I try to disregard   42
the audience and concentrate on the music. It strikes me that what I'm
hearing is an entirely natural phenomenon, nothing more than the
vibrations of creaky old instruments reverberating around a boxlike
hall. Each scrape of a bow translates into a strand of sound; what I see
is what I hear. So when the cellos and basses make the floor tremble
with their big deep note in the middle of the march (what Bernstein
calls the "wham!") the force of the moment is purely physical. Amplifiers are for sissies, I'm starting to think. The orchestra isn't playing
with the same cowed intensity as Klemperer's heroes, but the tone is
warmer and deeper and rounder than on the CD. I make my peace
with the stiffness of the scene by thinking of it as a cool frame for a hot
event. Perhaps this is how it has to be: Beethoven needs a passive audience as a foil. To my left, a sleeping dentist; to my right, an angry aes-
thete; and, in front of me, the funeral march that rises to a fugal fury,
and breaks down into softly sobbing memories of themes, and then
gives way to an entirely new mood—hard-driving, laughing, lurching,
a little drunk.

Two centuries ago, Beethoven bent over the manuscript of the   43
"Eroica" and struck out Napoleon's name. It is often said that he made
himself the protagonist of the work instead. Indeed, he engendered an
archetype—the rebel artist hero—that modern artists are still recycling.
I wonder, though, if Beethoven's gesture meant what people think it
did. Perhaps he was freeing his music from a too specific interpretation, from his own preoccupations. He was setting his symphony

adrift, as a message in a bottle. He could hardly have imagined it travelling two hundred years, through the dark heart of the twentieth century and into the pulverizing electronic age. But he knew it would go
far, and he did not weigh it down. There was now a torn, blank space
on the title page. The symphony became a fragmentary, unfinished
thing, and unfinished it remains. It becomes whole again only in the
mind and soul of someone listening for the first time, and listening
again. The hero is you.

A classical kid learns to love pop—and wonders why he has to   44
make a choice.

Examining the Text

1. According to the author, "Music is always dying, ever-ending. It is
an ageless diva on a non-stop farewell tour, coming around for one
absolutely final appearance." What does this mean in the context of
this article, and do you agree with the statement? How does this statement support or contrast with the author's specific pronouncements
about classical music?

2. What does the writer mean when he says that the "best music is the
music that persuades you that there is no other music in the world"?
Based upon your own experience with music, both popular and classical, do you agree or disagree with this assertion?

3. What kinds of imagery does the writer invoke when describing classical and popular music? Do those images draw positive or negative
associations with their respective musical genres?

4. The author comments, "I have seen the future and it is called 'shuffle,' the setting on the iPod that skips randomly from one track to
another . . . on the iPod, music is freed from all fatuous self-definitions
and delusions of significance." What broad point is the author making
about the categorization of music in contemporary culture?

5. *Thinking rhetorically*: What do you think was the rhetorical intention
of the author in writing this article? Is it clear that he has a persuasive
purpose here? What role does his own personal history play in your
overall understanding of the topic? Do the details about his musical
evolution help you gain a clearer impression of classical music's
plight? By the end of the article, were you inclined to agree or disagree
with the author? What caused you to reach that position?

For Group Discussion

Conduct an informal survey of your class to discover how many people (if any) listen to classical music at least once a month or attend concerts. For those that don't ever listen to classical music, discuss what you

know about it and why you don't listen to it. Did any of the complaints raised by the author—about the music being elitist, for example—resonate with you? For those that do listen to classical music, do you agree with the author's contention about the problems related to classical music?

Writing Suggestion

Write an autobiographical essay in which you explore your own musical interests and tastes. Have they changed over the years? Do you imagine that, like those of the author, your tastes will continue to evolve as you get older? Do you listen to a variety of musical genres or restrict yourself to one or two? What factors most heavily influence your musical taste? If you typically listen to only one or two types of music, what has stopped you from exploring other music genres? Do you still like the music you enjoyed when you were twelve or fourteen years old? If not, what do you think has changed? If you still like the same music, has your repertoire of musical pleasure expanded in other ways?

ADDITIONAL SUGGESTIONS FOR WRITING ABOUT POPULAR MUSIC

1. Americans receive a great deal of information about important issues—for example, presidential elections, gender-role attitudes, the legalization of drugs—from popular music and the media that purvey it. Write an essay in which you examine the representation of one important social issue or problem through music. For instance, you might focus on how AIDS is represented in recent song lyrics, on AM and FM radio stations, and in videos and advertisements on channels such as MTV and VH1.

2. Write an essay in which you first construct a detailed description of a band whose music you know very well, and then analyze the themes embodied in that band's songs. Discuss the effects the band's music has on its listeners and some possible reasons for the band's popularity or lack thereof with mainstream listeners.

3. Imagine that you've recently arrived in the United States; you turn on the television and find yourself watching an hour of programming on MTV. Based on this one hour of viewing, write a description of the interests, attitudes, lifestyles, and customs of young Americans. Try to include information that you gather from everything you've seen during that hour—the videos, game shows, advertisements, promos for upcoming shows, and so on—and make sure that you render your descriptions in vivid detail, so that somebody from another country might visualize all the elements you describe.

4. Write an essay in which you discuss the relative advantages and disadvantages of the three primary sources of popular music: television, radio, and record albums or compact discs. Which one of the three do you think most effectively conveys the messages intended by contemporary recording artists, and why? Which source do you think trivializes the music, turning it into a popular product without redeeming social relevance? What are the advantages and disadvantages of each pop-music source?

Internet Activities

1. Visit the Web sites of some diverse musicians (possible options are available on the *Common Culture* Web site). Write an essay describing these sites. What features do these Web sites offer? What differences similarities can you note in the presentations of the different musical genres? How would you account for these differences/similarities? For instance, is there anything offered on a Web site devoted to a rock group that isn't available on a jazz Web site? Are the Web site's features indicative of the genre in any way; that is, do the form/appearance/layout of the site mirror the musical genre it presents?

2. With the advent of various forms of media on the Web, such as radio broadcasts and videos, music has a new forum to reach an immediate, worldwide audience. Explore some sites that offer music from across the country and the world (options are available at the *Common Culture* Web site). Once you have sampled a diverse selection of music, write an essay categorizing and/or describing your findings. How is the availability of music on the Web changing how listeners access music and what they listen to? What type of music is available? Are any musical types represented more heavily than others? Are any music genres woefully lacking, in your opinion? How would you account for this representation (or lack thereof)?

Reading Images

Write an essay in which you compare and contrast the images of the two popular musicians, Gwen Stefani and Tupac Shakur, as illustrated on pages CI3 and CI4 in the color section of this book.

In this type of essay, you want to spend some time describing each image, so that the reader has a sense of the key visual features of each. Next, you might explore the ways in which the superficial appearances of both illustrations are similar or different (depending on your "reading" of the pictures, following the directions toward the end of Chapter 1). Finally, you will want to show how the images' other elements (coloration, composition, text, and so forth, also as described in Chapter 1 of this book) work in similar or different ways to put forth the images' messages, which may be subtly implied or blatantly "in-your-face."

The problem with this kind of essay is one of organization. Since a comparison/contrast essay by its nature involves looking at both similarities and differences, make sure that you structure your paper so that you don't have to jump back and forth too much from issue to issue, point to point. While many writers, when writing comparison/contrast-type pieces, sometimes favor this approach, you might want to experiment with discussing *all* the elements of the Tupac image and *then* going on to the Stefani, pointing out all its areas of likeness and dissimilarity. Ideally, your paper will flow smoothly and progress logically, while still covering all elements of likeness and dissimilarity.

5

Technology

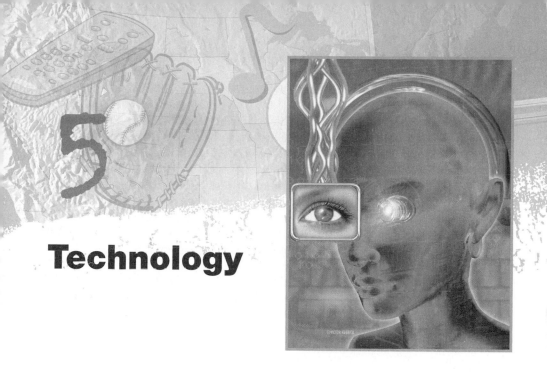

The image above seems to be clearly drawn from the realm of cyborgs and science fiction. After all, our eyeballs are not and could never be attached to a set of wires, or our eye sockets replaced with cybernetic implants. Or could they be? Although this computer-generated image is still a fiction, at least one real-life experiment comes pretty close to it. Steve Mann, a Professor of Electrical Engineering at the University of Toronto, has designed a device called the Eye-Tap, a very high-tech set of computerized eyeglasses that cause the eye to function as if it were a digital camera. This eye/camera feeds images back into a computer, which can then process the images and can actually alter what the user sees (*http://www.eyetap.org*). Mann has also designed other kinds of wearable computers, devices that allow humans to change how they interact with their environments and to live in a computer-mediated reality.

The cyborg image—and even the EyeTap system—may both seem extreme, but how far are they really from other technologies that we use every day to enhance our lives and mediate our interactions with the world? Just thinking of our sense of sight, the technologies we commonly use range from simple eyeglasses and sunglasses to contact lenses and Lasik surgery. A wearable computer like the EyeTap is perhaps just the next logical step, one that harnesses the power of the computer in order to augment and alter the capabilities of the human eye. And why wouldn't a cybernetic implant be the next step after that?

But even if you never wear an EyeTap or have a computer implanted in your eye, you probably have a lot of experience with technologies that shape your everyday activities and augment your capabilities. For example, communications technologies like the Internet, instant messaging, and cell phones enable you to interact in an inexpensive and immediate way with people who are physically distant from you; video games let you experience unusual sorts of situations, challenges, and puzzles; and, of course, computers affect almost every aspect of our lives. Technologies like these are extremely influential because they're so common. Indeed, like the other subjects in *Common Culture*, technology exerts a profound and mostly unexamined impact on our lives.

Technology, Individuals, and Communities

Breaking Down Borders: How Technology Transforms the Private and Public Realms

Robert Samuels

One important premise of Common Culture *is that the culture all around us is worthy of investigation. Indeed, we believe that paying attention to the activities we are involved in every day is particularly important because these activities are highly likely to influence who we are, what we do, and what we value. Robert Samuels, a Lecturer in the Writing Programs at UCLA, takes precisely this approach in the article that follows. Samuels reports on a mundane, everyday sort of event: a trip to his local Borders Café. But in describing and analyzing what he sees at the Café, he is able to draw conclusions about larger changes and challenges in our culture. Specifically, Samuels focuses his attention on the different technologies used by people at the Café, and he analyzes how the use of technologies blurs the borders between public and private and between work and play.*

Samuels' article begins our chapter on technology, and the ideas he introduces here are taken up by the next two readings as well. So, before you read, make a list of the technologies you use on a regular basis, particularly those associated with media, communication, and culture: cell phone, computer, MP3 player, TV, VCR, DVD player, remote control, and other technologies like these. How do you think the technologies you regularly use have influenced the way you live your life? What would your everyday life be like without these technologies?

It's a Tuesday morning and I'm walking through the Borders Café just   1
south of the UCLA campus in Westwood, CA. My plan is to find a table, drink my coffee, and read some of the novel that I just bought in the bookstore section. As I head for one of the few empty chairs, I pass by a man sitting at a table, the sports section of the *L.A. Times* spread out in front of him, a cup of coffee and a blueberry muffin to one side, his cell phone close at hand on the other side. He's wearing a t-shirt and shorts, but he might as well be in pajamas and slippers; it's as if

he's in his own kitchen, reading his paper and having his breakfast, just following his morning routine.

I move past breakfast-man and notice a twenty-something 2 woman sitting in one of the five or six comfy upholstered chairs that Borders provides its customers. She's curled up cozily in the chair with one foot stretched out and resting on a matching upholstered footstool. Actually, the foot isn't resting; it's wagging back and forth in time, I assume, to the music that's coming through the headphones attached to her ears and her iPod. Keeping time to the music, she taps her yellow highlighter pen against the textbook that she's ostensibly reading. As I watch, she begins to hum out loud—it sounds like a wildly out-of-tune version of "Dancing Queen"—and then she abruptly looks up and stops humming, a bit startled, remembering that she's in Borders and not in her living room.

I sit at my own table with my coffee and novel, but I don't get past 3 the first page before I'm distracted by a woman at the table to my left who's talking on her cell phone. I see that she's also got her laptop computer open on the table and a magazine on her lap, but it's her phone conversation that's getting all of her attention—and, of course, the attention of everyone around her. We learn that she's terribly sorry but she has to cancel her job interview that Friday because of a doctor's appointment; our dismay is quickly alleviated when, in her next call, she tells a friend that, yes, the trip to Las Vegas that weekend is back on. The café, it seems, is her personal office.

Each of these people seems to have carved a little semi-private, 4 personalized space out of the larger public, commercial space of Borders Café. As people come and go, these spaces change, so that a time-lapse video of Borders Café would have to show it as not just one space but rather as an aggregate of small, shifting living rooms, kitchens, and offices (no bedrooms—yet!). And of course it's not just Borders; this kind of activity goes on at bookstores and coffee shops across the country. These new commercial public squares have become shared spaces that are neither private nor public. In fact, they compel us to redefine what private and public mean. The cell phone woman, for example, seems to have no problem sharing her Las Vegas plans with everyone sitting around her. But then I look around again and notice that I'm one of the few people who can actually hear her. Most of the other people here have headphones on and they're listening to their own iPods or MP3 players, perhaps precisely in order to avoid having to listen to conversations that should be private in the first place.

What I see at Borders convinces me that there are new rules for 5 how to act in public places and for how to socialize with and around one another. It's clear, as well, that none of these changes would have occurred without new technologies helping to break down borders. For instance, the telephone used to be firmly located in the private realm, physically attached to the kitchen wall or set on a desk in an office. Now, however, cell phones allow for a high level of mobility and access, and thus they help us transform any public place into a setting for a private conversation. The laptop, too, has not only transformed the desktop computer but has also reinvented the desktop itself as any table or flat surface. Indeed, your very own lap becomes a desktop of sorts when you put your laptop computer on it.

With wireless technology, laptops and cell phones not only help   6
us cross back and forth between the public and the private, but they also function to undermine the distinction between work and play. For instance, people often jump quickly from doing work on their computers to emailing their friends and playing video games. Likewise, cell phones can combine work functions and play functions, incorporating games as well as digital cameras, video, and, of course, sound clips for ring tones. Some critics of new communication technologies argue that cell phones, laptops, iPods, and the other devices we take with us throughout our day encourage a high level of multitasking and prevent us from concentrating on any single activity. Thus, they argue, people not only become more superficial, but the constant switching between work and leisure activities creates a fragmented sense of self and gives everyone a bad case of attention deficit disorder.

However, another way of looking at these new technologies is to   7
see how they allow people to re-center their sense of self by creating what can be called "personal culture." In other words, instead of seeing culture as a social and public activity, like going to a concert hall, devices like iPods and laptops allow people to take culture with them wherever they go. More importantly, instead of having to let the radio station tell them what to listen to or the newspaper limit their choice of news sources, people are able to personalize their own media and decide on their own what culture they want to consume.

Personal culture derives much of its power from the fact that many   8
of the new media devices are highly immersive: people on cell phones and laptops can become so involved in their own mediated worlds that they forget where they actually are and what they are supposed to be doing. Some states have laws now against driving while talking on a cell phone, but in addition to the physical danger there also may be a social cost. After all, we are social beings who live in public worlds, and therefore we cannot simply forget that other people exist. As I look around me at the people who have temporarily transformed Borders Café into a set of small personal spaces, I realize that although we're all together here there's very little chance that we'll interact with one another. Most of us are plugged in to technologies that, while allowing us to personalize our environment, also effectively isolate us from our neighbors.

But is there really anything wrong with that? We adapt to our   9
new technologies and to the new spaces these technologies create; we
adapt, in fact, by using more technologies. To tune out the cell phones,
we put on our headphones. There seems to be no way of escaping
from a technologically mediated environment, even in a place devoted
to selling those old-fashioned, low-tech items called books. But, in
Borders, at least, on this sunny Tuesday morning, we seem to be cop-
ing well enough even as the borders all around us are shifting and
transforming.

Examining the Text
1. Why do you think Samuels begins his article with the detailed
descriptions of three people he sees at Borders Café? What do you learn
from these descriptions? How does this opening strategy help Samuels
introduce his argument?
2. What does Samuels mean by "personal culture"? According to
Samuels, how do technologies help us create "personal culture"?
3. Reread the last two paragraphs of the article. What do you think is
Samuels' opinion of technology's influence on our culture?
4. *Thinking rhetorically*: Who do you think are the target readers of
Samuels' article? And what do you see as its overall purpose? Point to
specific features of the article that help you determine its audience and
purpose.

For Group Discussion
Samuels discusses two different borders in this article: the border
between public and private, and the border between work and play. In
your group, choose one of these borders, and make a list of all the technologies that contribute to breaking down this border. You can begin
with the technologies that Samuels himself describes; for instance, he
discusses how the cell phone helps to break down the border between
public and private as well as the border between work and play. Be
sure to continue your list with examples of other technologies. Then list
any technologies that you think help to maintain or increase the border.
As a group, try to come to some general conclusions about the role of
technology in the particular border area you're discussing.

Writing Suggestion
Samuels acts as an amateur anthropologist in this essay in the sense
that he goes to a particular place, observes how people act there, and
records and analyzes his observations in an article. Your assignment is
to do something similar. Choose a place where people congregate: a
coffee shop, a dorm lounge, an outdoor park or playground, a living

room. Ideally the place you choose will be somewhere where you can sit and observe and take notes without being too distracted and without distracting others. Spend an hour or two at the place, watching to see what technologies people use and how the people interact with each other. Then write an essay modeled after Samuels' article. Begin the essay with a couple of detailed descriptions of specific people or activities you observed. In the body of the essay, discuss and analyze the ways that you saw technologies influence people's interactions. You might want to cite Samuels' article in your essay, perhaps in order to argue for or against the conclusions he draws.

Cyberhood vs. Neighborhood

John Perry Barlow

This essay on "virtual communities" is written by an unlikely expert. John Perry Barlow grew up in the small town of Pinedale, Wyoming, and ran the family cattle ranch there until he was forced to sell it in 1988. Seeing the decline of the community all around him and searching, as he explains here, for evidence "that community in America would not perish altogether," Barlow started exploring the possibilities of virtual communities—that is, communities that don't exist in a particular place but rather are formed by participants in Internet mailing lists, conferences, discussion groups, and virtual "chat rooms." In this essay, Barlow describes his initial enthusiasm for these virtual communities, as well as his subsequent disillusionment.

Barlow's strategy here is to evaluate virtual communities in terms of how closely they can reproduce the qualities of real communities, in terms of human interaction and connection as well as in terms of shared interests, diversity, and meaningfulness. In comparing real and virtual communities, Barlow defines what is essential to the concept of "community"—what makes a community thrive? Why do we form and maintain communities in the first place?

As you read, make a list of the elements that Barlow believes are essential to a community. Which of those elements do you find in the communities you currently participate in?

"There is no there there."

—Gertrude Stein (speaking of Oakland)

"It ain't no Amish barn-raising in there . . . "

—Bruce Sterling (speaking of cyberspace)

I am often asked how I went from pushing cows around a remote   1
Wyoming ranch to my present occupation (which *Wall Street Journal*
recently described as "cyberspace cadet"). I haven't got a short answer,
but I suppose I came to the virtual world looking for community.

Unlike most modern Americans, I grew up in an actual place, an   2
entire nonintentional community called Pinedale, Wyoming. As I
struggled for nearly a generation to keep my ranch in the family, I was
motivated by the belief that such places were the spiritual home of
humanity. But I knew their future was not promising.

At the dawn of the 20th century, over 40 percent of the American   3
workforce lived off the land. The majority of us lived in towns like
Pinedale. Now fewer than 1 percent of us extract a living from the soil.
We just became too productive for our own good.

Of course, the population followed the jobs. Farming and ranch-   4
ing communities are now home to a demographically insignificant percentage of Americans, the vast majority of whom live not in ranch
houses but in more or less identical split level "ranch homes" in more
or less identical suburban "communities." Generica.

In my view, these are neither communities nor homes. I believe   5
the combination of television and suburban population patterns is simply toxic to the soul. I see much evidence in contemporary America to
support this view.

Meanwhile, back at the ranch, doom impended. And, as I   6
watched the community in Pinedale growing ill from the same economic forces that were killing my family's ranch, the Bar Cross, satel-
lite dishes brought the cultural infection of television. I started looking
around for evidence that community in America would not perish
altogether.

I took some heart in the mysterious nomadic City of the Deadheads, 7
the virtually physical town that follows the Grateful Dead around the
country. The Deadheads lacked place, touching down briefly wherever
the band happened to be playing, and they lacked continuity in time,
since they had to suffer a new diaspora every time the band moved on
or went home. But they had many of the other necessary elements
of community, including a culture, a religion of sorts (which, though
it lacked dogma, had most of the other, more nurturing aspects of
spiritual practice), a sense of necessity, and most importantly, shared
adversity.

I wanted to know more about the flavor of their interaction, what 8
they thought and felt, but since I wrote Dead songs (including "Estimated

Prophet" and "Cassidy"), I was a minor icon to the Deadheads, and was thus inhibited, in some socially Heisenbergian way, from getting a clear view of what really went on among them.

Then, in 1987, I heard about a "place" where Deadheads gathered   9
where I could move among them without distorting too much the field of observation. Better, this was a place I could visit without leaving Wyoming. It was a shared computer in Sausalito, California, called the Whole Earth 'Lectronic Link, or WELL. After a lot of struggling with modems, serial cables, init strings, and other Computer arcana that seemed utterly out of phase with such notions as Deadheads and small towns, I found myself looking at the glowing yellow word "Login:" beyond which lay my future.

"Inside" the WELL were Deadheads in community. There were   10
thousands of them there, gossiping, complaining (mostly about the Grateful Dead), comforting and harassing each other, bartering, engaging in religion (or at least exchanging their totemic set lists), beginning and ending love affairs, praying for one another's sick kids. There was, it seemed, everything one might find going on in a small town, save dragging Main Street and making out on the back roads.

I was delighted. I felt I had found the new locale of human   11
community—never mind that the whole thing was being conducted in mere words by minds from whom the bodies had been amputated. Never mind that all these people were deaf, dumb, and blind as paramecia or that their town had neither seasons nor sunsets nor smells.

Surely all these deficiencies would be remedied by richer, faster   12
communications media. The featureless log-in handles would gradually acquire video faces (and thus expressions), shaded 3-D body puppets (and thus body language). This "space" which I recognized at once to be a primitive form of the cyberspace William Gibson predicted in his sci-fi novel *Neuromancer*, was still without apparent dimensions of vistas. But virtual reality would change all that in time.

Meanwhile, the commons, or something like it, had been redis-   13
covered. Once again, people from the 'burbs had a place where they could encounter their friends as my fellow Pinedalians did at the post office and the Wrangler Cafe. They had a place where their hearts could remain as the companies they worked for shuffled their bodies around America. They could put down roots that could not be ripped out by forces of economic history. They had a collective stake. They had a community.

It is seven years now since I discovered the WELL. In that time, I co-   14
founded an organization, the Electronic Frontier Foundation, dedicated to protecting its interests and those of other virtual communities like it from raids by physical government. I've spent countless hours

typing away at its residents, and I've watched the larger context that contains it, the Internet, grow at such an explosive rate that, by 2004, every human on the planet will have an e-mail address unless the growth curve flattens (which it will).

My enthusiasm for virtuality has cooled. In fact, unless one   15
counts interaction with the rather too large society of those with whom I exchange electronic mail, I don't spend much time engaging in virtual community, at all. Many of the near-term benefits I anticipated from it seem to remain as far in the future as they did when I first logged in. Perhaps they always will.

Pinedale works, more or less, as it is, but a lot is still missing from   16
the communities of cyberspace, whether they be places like the WELL, the fractious newsgroups of USENET, the silent "auditoriums" of America Online, or even enclaves on the promising World Wide Web.

What is missing? Well, to quote Ranjit Makkuni of Xerox Corpo-   17
ration's Palo Alto Research Center, "the *prāna* is missing," *prāna* being the Hindu term for both breath and spirit. I think he is right about this and that perhaps the central question of the virtual age is whether or not *prāna* can somehow be made to fit through any disembodied medium.

Prāna is, to my mind, the literally vital element in the holy and   18
unseen ecology of relationship, the dense mesh of invisible life, on whose surface carbon-based life floats like a thin film. It is at the heart of the fundamental and profound difference between information and experience. Jaron Lanier has said that "information is alienated experience," and, that being true, *prāna* is part of what is removed when you create such easily transmissible replicas of experience as, say, the evening news.

Obviously a great many other, less spiritual, things are also miss-   19
ing entirely, like body language, sex, death, tone of voice, clothing, beauty (or homeliness), weather, violence, vegetation, wildlife, pets, architecture, music, smells, sunlight, and that ol' harvest moon. In short, most of the things that make my life real to me.

Present, but in far less abundance than in the physical world,   20
which I call "meat space," are women, children, old people, poor people, and the genuinely blind. Also mostly missing are the illiterate and the continent of Africa. There is not much human diversity in cyberspace, which is populated, as near as I can tell, by white males under 50 with plenty of computer terminal time, great typing skills, high math SATs, strongly held opinions on just about everything, and an excruciating face-to-face shyness, especially with the opposite sex.

But diversity is as essential to healthy community as it is to   21
healthy ecosystems (which are, in my view, different from communities only in unimportant aspects).

I believe that the principal reason for the almost universal failure   22
of the intentional communities of the '60s and '70s was a lack of diversity in their members. It was a rare commune with any old people in it,
or people who were fundamentally out of philosophical agreement
with the majority.

Indeed, it is the usual problem when we try to build something   23
that can only be grown. Natural systems, such as human communities,
are simply too complex to design by the engineering principles we
insist on applying to them. Like Dr. Frankenstein, western civilization
is now finding its rational skills inadequate to the task of creating and
caring for life. We would do better to return to a kind of agricultural
mind-set in which we humbly try to re-create the conditions from
which life has sprung before. And leave the rest to God.

Given that it has been built so far almost entirely by people with   24
engineering degrees, it is not so surprising that cyberspace has the kind
of overdesigned quality that leaves out all kinds of elements nature
would have provided invisibly.

Also missing from both the communes of the '60s and from cyber-   25
space are a couple of elements that I believe are very important, if not
essential, to the formation and preservation of a real community: an
absence of alternatives and a sense of genuine adversity, generally
shared. What about these?

It is hard to argue that anyone would find losing a modem liter-   26
ally hard to survive, while many have remained in small towns, have
tolerated their intolerances and created entertainment to enliven their
culturally arid lives simply because it seemed there was no choice but to
stay. There are many investments—spiritual, material, and temporal—
one is willing to put into a home one cannot leave. Communities are
often the beneficiaries of these involuntary investments.

But when the going gets rough in cyberspace, it is even easier   27
to move than it is in the burbs, where, given the fact that the average
American moves some 12 times in his or her life, moving appears to be
pretty easy. You cannot only find another bulletin board service (BBS) or
newsgroup to hang out in; you can, with very little effort, start your own.

And then there is the bond of joint suffering. Most community is   28
a cultural stockade erected against a common enemy that can take
many forms. In Pinedale, we bore together, with an understanding
needing little expression, the fact that Upper Green River Valley is the
coldest spot, as measured by annual mean temperature, in the lower
48 states. We knew that if somebody was stopped on the road most
winter nights, he would probably die there, so the fact that we might
loathe him was not sufficient reason to drive on past his broken pickup.

By the same token, the Deadheads have the Drug Enforcement   29
Administration, which strives to give them 20-year prison terms

without parole for distributing the fairly harmless sacrament of their faith. They have an additional bond in the fact that when their Microbuses die, as they often do, no one but another Deadhead is likely to stop to help them.

But what are the shared adversities of cyberspace? Lousy user   30 interfaces? The flames of harsh invective? Dumb jokes? Surely these can all be survived without the sanctuary provided by fellow sufferers.

One is always free to yank the jack, as I have mostly done. For me,   31 the physical world offers far more opportunity for *prāna* rich connections with my fellow creatures. Even for someone whose body is in a state of perpetual motion, I feel I can generally find more community among the still-embodied.

Finally, there is that shyness factor. Not only are we trying to   32 build community here among people who have never experienced any in my sense of the term, we are trying to build community among people who, in their lives, have rarely used the word we in a heartfelt way. It is a vast club, and many of the members—following Groucho Marx—wouldn't want to join a club that would have them.

And yet . . .   33

How quickly physical community continues to deteriorate. Even   34 Pinedale, which seems to have survived the plague of ranch failures, feels increasingly cut off from itself. Many of the ranches are now owned by corporate types who fly their Gulfstreams in to fish and are rarely around during the many months when the creeks are frozen over and neighbors are needed. They have kept the ranches alive financially, but they actively discourage their managers from the interdependence my former colleagues and I require. They keep agriculture on life support, still alive but lacking a functional heart.

And the town has been inundated with suburbanites who flee   35 here, bringing all their terrors and suspicions with them. They spend their evenings as they did in Orange County, watching television or socializing in hermetic little enclaves of fundamentalist Christianity that seem to separate them from us and even, given their sectarian animosities, from one another. The town remains. The community is largely a wraith of nostalgia.

So where else can we look for the connection we need to prevent   36 our plunging further into the condition of separateness Nietzsche called sin? What is there to do but to dive further into the bramble bush of information that, in its broadest forms, has done so much to tear us apart?

Cyberspace, for all its current deficiencies and failed promises, is   37 not without some very real solace already.

Some months ago, the great love of my life, a vivid young woman   38 with whom I intended to spend the rest of it, dropped dead of undiagnosed viral cardiomyopathy two days short of her 30th birthday. I felt as if my own heart had been as shredded as hers.

We had lived together in New York City. Except for my daugh-   39
ters, no one from Pinedale had met her. I needed a community to wrap around myself against colder winds than fortune had ever blown at me before. And without looking, I found I had one in the virtual world.

On the WELL, there was a topic announcing her death in one of   40
the conferences to which I posted the eulogy I had read over her before burying her in her own small town of Nanaimo, British Columbia. It seemed to strike a chord among the disembodied living on the Net. People copied it and sent it to one another. Over the next several months I received almost a megabyte of electronic mail from all over the planet, mostly from folks whose faces I have never seen and probably never will.

They told me of their own tragedies and what they had done to   41
survive them. As humans have since words were first uttered, we shared the second most common human experience, death, with an openheartedness that would have caused grave uneasiness in physical America, where the whole topic is so cloaked in denial as to be considered obscene. Those strangers, who had no arms to put around my shoulders, no eyes to weep with mine, nevertheless saw me through. As neighbors do.

I have no idea how far we will plunge into this strange place.   42
Unlike previous frontiers, this one has no end. It is so dissatisfying in so many ways that I suspect we will be more restless in our search for home here than in all our previous explorations. And that is one reason why I think we may find it after all. If home is where the heart is, then there is already some part of home to be found in cyberspace.

So . . . does virtual community work or not? Should we all go off   43
to cyberspace or should we resist it as a demonic form of symbolic abstraction? Does it supplant the real or is there, in it, reality itself?

Like so many true things, this one doesn't resolve itself to a black   44
or a white. Nor is it gray. It is, along with the rest of life, black/white. Both/neither. I'm not being equivocal or whishy-washy here. We have to get over our Manichean sense that everything is either good or bad, and the border of cyberspace seems to me a good place to leave that old set of filters.

But really it doesn't matter. We are going there whether we want   45
to or not. In five years, everyone who is reading these words will have an e-mail address, other than the determined Luddites who also eschew the telephone and electricity.

When we are all together in cyberspace we will see what the   46
human spirit, and the basic desire to connect, can create there. I am convinced that the result will be more benign if we go there open-minded,

open-hearted, and excited with the adventure than if we are dragged into exile.

And we must remember that going to cyberspace, unlike previ-   47
ous great emigrations to the frontier, hardly requires us to leave where we have been. Many will find, as I have, a much richer appreciation of physical reality for having spent so much time in virtuality.

Despite its current (and perhaps in some areas permanent) insuf-   48
ficiencies, we should go to cyberspace with hope. Groundless hope, like unconditional love, may be the only kind that counts.

In Memoriam, Dr. Cynthia Horner (1964–1994).

Examining the Text
1. What does Barlow see as the essential elements of community? How do the various physical and virtual communities Barlow discusses embody or fail to embody these elements?
2. What does Barlow mean when he suggests that the *"prāna"* is missing from cyberspace communities? Why does he nevertheless find virtual communities worthwhile?
3. *Thinking rhetorically*: Examine the organization of Barlow's essay. How does he structure his argument? Do you think that the conclusions he comes to at the end (particularly in paragraph 44) are supported by what he says in the body of the essay?

For Group Discussion
Barlow observes that when he first entered the virtual community of Deadheads and others on the WELL, he saw a place where people "could put down roots that could not be ripped out by forces of economic history." To what forces is Barlow referring? Can you think of other forces—economic, social, cultural, political, historical, religious—that have affected the sense of community in America? As a group and then as a class, make a list of these factors. Which have helped strengthen a sense of community in America and which have brought about the decline of community?

Writing Suggestion
Define the characteristics of an ideal community, using ideas from Barlow's essay as well as ideas from your own experiences and observations. Then choose one community that you inhabit or know about: for example, the college or university community to which you belong; your high school community; the community in which you grew up; communities that you've visited; or perhaps a virtual community on the Internet that you're familiar with. Describe this community and compare it with your ideal definition. How well does this particular community meet your definition of the ideal? In what ways does it fall

short? What are the reasons, in your opinion, that the community you're discussing is less than ideal?

Our Cell Phones, Ourselves

Christine Rosen

If you had to choose between going to the dentist and sitting next to someone who's talking on a cell phone, which would you find more painful? If you're like most Americans, it's the latter. According to a USA Today poll, fifty-nine percent of Americans would rather get their teeth scraped and drilled than deal with the aggravation and annoyance of sitting next to someone using a cell phone. And yet, as the cartoon on page 352 illustrates, we find ourselves more and more often in situations where cell phones intrude: in restaurants, busses, movie theaters, libraries—even (gasp!) in classrooms.

The author of this article, Christine Rosen, is a senior editor of The New Atlantis *(where the article first appeared) and a fellow of the Ethics and Public Policy Center. In "Our Cell Phones, Ourselves," Rosen assesses the impact of cell phones on individuals and communities and she tries to understand our particular attachment to this technology. For despite the aggravation they cause, cell phones today are more frequently used and more highly valued by Americans than ever before.*

This is a long article and one in which Rosen brings up quite a few different but related points about how cell phones function in our culture and in other cultures. In order to have a good understanding of the article, it would be wise to take notes as you read, either in the margins or on a separate piece of paper. So **as you read***, each time Rosen makes a new point about cell phones, make a note of it; then when you're finished reading you'll have an outline of her key points to guide you as you discuss and write about the article.*

"Hell is other people," Sartre observed, but you need not be a misan-   1
thrope or a diminutive French existentialist to have experienced similar feelings during the course of a day. No matter where you live or what you do, in all likelihood you will eventually find yourself participating in that most familiar and exasperating of modern rituals: unwillingly listening to someone else's cell phone conversation. Like the switchboard operators of times past, we are now all privy to calls being put through, to the details of loved ones contacted, appointments made, arguments aired, and gossip exchanged.

Today, more people have cell phones than fixed telephone lines, both in the United States and internationally. There are more than one billion cell phone users worldwide, and as one wireless industry analyst recently told *Slate*, "some time between 2010 and 2020, everyone who wants and can afford a cell phone will have one." Americans spend, on average, about seven hours a month talking on their cell phones. Wireless phones have become such an important part of our everyday lives that in July, the country's major wireless industry organization featured the following "quick poll" on its website: "If you were stranded on a desert island and could have one thing with you, what would it be?" The choices: "Matches/Lighter," "Food/Water," "Another Person," "Wireless Phone." The World Health Organization has even launched an "International EMF Project" to study the possible health effects of the electromagnetic fields created by wireless technologies.

FARRIS
USA

CARTOONISTS & WRITERS SYNDICATE http://CartoonWeb.com

"Cell phone or non-cell phone section?"

But if this ubiquitous technology is now a normal part of life, our   3
adjustment to it has not been without consequences. Especially in the
United States, where cell phone use still remains low compared to
other countries, we are rapidly approaching a tipping point with this
technology. How has it changed our behavior, and how might it continue to do so? What new rules ought we to impose on its use? Most
importantly, how has the wireless telephone encouraged us to connect
individually but disconnect socially, ceding, in the process, much that
was civil and civilized about the use of public space?

UNTETHERED

Connection has long served as a potent sign of power. In the era before   4
cell phones, popular culture served up presidents, tin-pot dictators,
and crime bosses who were never far from a prominently placed row of
phones, demonstrating their importance at the hub of a vast nexus.
Similarly, superheroes always owned special communications devices:
Batman had the Batphone, Dick Tracy his wrist-phone, Maxwell Smart
his shoe spy phone. (In the Flash comics of the 1940s, the hero simply
outraces phone calls as they are made, avoiding altogether the need for
special communication devices.) To be able to talk to anyone, at any
time, without the mediator of the human messenger and without the
messenger's attendant delays, is a thoroughly modern triumph of
human engineering.

In 1983, Motorola introduced DynaTAC, now considered the first   5
truly mobile telephone, and by the end of that year, the first commercial cellular phone systems were being used in Chicago and in the
Baltimore/Washington, D.C. area. Nokia launched its own mobile
phone, the cumbersome Cityman, in 1987. Americans were introduced
to the glamour of mobile telephone communication that same year in a
scene from the movie *Wall Street*. In it, the ruthless Gordon Gekko
(played by Michael Douglas) self-importantly conducts his business on
the beach using a large portable phone. These first-generation cell
phones were hardly elegant—many people called them "luggables"
rather than "portables," and as one reporter noted in *The Guardian*,
"mobiles of that era are often compared to bricks, but this is unfair.
Bricks are quite attractive and relatively light." But they made up in
symbolic importance what they lacked in style; only the most powerful
and wealthiest people owned them. Indeed, in the 1980s, the only other
people besides the elite and medical professionals who had mobile
technologies at all (such as pagers) were presumed to be using them for
nefarious reasons. Who else but a roving drug dealer or prostitute
would need to be accessible at all times?

This changed in the 1990s, when cell phones became cheaper,   6
smaller, and more readily available. The technology spread rapidly, as
did the various names given to it: in Japan it is *keitai*, in China it's *sho ji*,
Germans call their cell phones *handy*, in France it is *le portable* or *le G*,
and in Arabic, *el mobile, telephone makhmul*, or *telephone gowal*. In countries where cell phone use is still limited to the elite—such as Bulgaria,
where only 2.5 percent of the population can afford a cell phone—its
power as a symbol of wealth and prestige remains high. But in the
rest of the world, it has become a technology for the masses. There
were approximately 340,000 wireless subscribers in the United States
in 1985, according to the Cellular Telecommunications and Internet
Associate (CTIA); by 1995, that number had increased to more than
33 million, and by 2003, more than 158 million people in the country
had gone wireless.

Why do people use cell phones? The most frequently cited reason   7
is convenience, which can cover a rather wide range of behaviors. Writing in the *Wall Street Journal* this spring, an executive for a wireless
company noted that "in Slovakia, people are using mobile phones to
remotely switch on the heat before they return home," and in Norway,
"1.5 million people can confirm their tax returns" using cell phone
short text messaging services. Paramedics use camera phones to send
ahead to hospitals pictures of the incoming injuries; "in Britain, it is
now commonplace for wireless technology to allow companies to
remotely access meters or gather diagnostic information." Construction workers on-site can use cell phones to send pictures to contractors
off-site. Combined with the individual use of cell phones—to make
appointments, locate a friend, check voicemail messages, or simply to
check in at work—cell phones offer people a heretofore unknown level
of convenience.

More than ninety percent of cell phone users also report that own-   8
ing a cell phone makes them feel safer. The CTIA noted that in 2001,
nearly 156,000 wireless emergency service calls were made every
day—about 108 calls per minute. Technological Good Samaritans place
calls to emergency personnel when they see traffic accidents or crimes-
in-progress; individuals use their cell phones to call for assistance
when a car breaks down or plans go awry. The safety rationale carries a
particular poignancy after the terrorist attacks of September 11, 2001.
On that day, many men and women used cell phones to speak their final
words to family and loved ones. Passengers on hijacked airplanes called
wives and husbands; rescue workers on the ground phoned in to report
their whereabouts. As land lines in New York and Washington, D.C.,
became clogged, many of us made or received frantic phone calls
on cell phones—to reassure others that we were safe or to make sure

that our friends and family were accounted for. Many people who had never considered owning a cell phone bought one after September 11th. If the cultural image we had of the earliest cell phones was of a technology glamorously deployed by the elite, then the image of cell phones today has to include people using them for this final act of communication, as well as terrorists who used cell phones as detonators in the bombing of trains in Madrid.

Of course, the perceived need for a technological safety device   9 can encourage distinctly irrational behavior and create new anxieties. Recently, when a professor at Rutgers University asked his students to experiment with turning off their cell phones for 48 hours, one young woman told *University Wire*, "I felt like I was going to get raped if I didn't have my cell phone in my hand. I carry it in case I need to call someone for help." Popular culture endorses this image of cell-phone-as-lifeline. The trailer for a new suspense movie, *Cellular*, is currently making the rounds in theaters nationwide. In it, an attractive young man is shown doing what young men apparently do with their camera-enabled cell phones: taking pictures of women in bikinis and e-mailing the images to himself. When he receives a random but desperate phone call from a woman who claims to be the victim of a kidnapping, he finds himself drawn into a race to find and save her, all the while trying to maintain that tenuous cell phone connection. It is indicative of our near-fetishistic attachment to our cell phones that we can relate (and treat as a serious moment of suspense) a scene in the movie where the protagonist, desperately trying to locate a cell phone charger before his battery runs out, holds the patrons of an electronics store at gunpoint until the battery is rejuvenated. After scenes of high-speed car chases and large explosions, the trailer closes with a disembodied voice asking the hero, "How did you get involved?" His response? "I just answered my phone."

Many parents have responded to this perceived need for personal   10 security by purchasing cell phones for their children, but this, too, has had some unintended consequences. One sociologist has noted that parents who do this are implicitly commenting on their own sense of security or insecurity in society. "Claiming to care about their children's safety," Chantal de Gournay writes, "parents develop a 'paranoiac' vision of the community, reflecting a lack of trust in social institutions and in any environment other than the family." As a result, they choose surveillance technologies, such as cell phones, to monitor their children, rather than teaching them (and trusting them) to behave appropriately. James E. Katz, a communications professor at Rutgers who has written extensively about wireless communication, argues that parents who give children cell phones are actually weakening the traditional bonds of authority; "parents think they can reach kids any time they want, and thus are more indulgent of their children's wanderings," Katz notes. Not surprisingly, "my cell phone battery died" has become a popular excuse among teenagers for failure to check in with their parents. And I suspect nearly everyone, at some point, has suffered hours of panic when a loved one who was supposed to be "reachable" failed to answer the cell phone.

Although cell phones are a technology with broad appeal, we do   11
not all use our cell phones in the same way. In June 2004, Cingular announced that "for the fourth year in a row, men prove to be the more talkative sex in the wireless world," talking 16 percent more on their phones than women. Women, however, are more likely to use a cell phone "to talk to friends and family" while men use theirs for business— including, evidently, the business of mating. Researchers found that "men are using their mobile phones as peacocks use their immobilizing feathers and male bullfrogs use their immoderate croaks: To advertise to females their worth, status, and desirability," reported the *New York Times*. The researchers also discovered that many of the men they observed in pubs and nightclubs carried fake cell phones, likely one of the reasons they titled their paper "Mobile Phones as Lekking Devices Among Human Males," a lek being a "communal mating area where males gather to engage in flamboyant courtship displays." Or, as another observer of cell phone behavior succinctly put it: "the mobile is widely used for psychosexual purposes of performance and display."

The increasingly sophisticated accessories available on cell phones   12
encourage such displays. One new phone hitting the market boasts video capture and playback, a 1.2 megapixel camera, a 256 color screen, speakerphone, removable memory, mp3 player, Internet access, and a global positioning system. The *Wall Street Journal* recently reported on cell phones that will feature radios, calculators, alarm clocks, flash- lights, and mirrored compacts. Phones are "becoming your Swiss army knife," one product developer enthused. Hyperactive peacocking will also be abetted by the new walkie-talkie function available on many phones, which draws further attention to the user by broadcasting to anyone within hearing distance the conversation of the person on the other end of the phone.

With all these accoutrements, it is not surprising that one contrib-   13
utor to a discussion list about wireless technology recently compared cell phones and BlackBerrys to "electronic pets." Speaking to a group of business people, he reported, "you constantly see people taking their little pets out and stroking the scroll wheel, coddling them, basically 'petting' them." When confined to a basement conference room, he found that participants "were compelled to 'walk' their electronic pets on breaks" to check their messages. In parts of Asia, young women

carry their phones in decorated pouches, worn like necklaces, or in pants with specially designed pockets that keep the phone within easy reach. We have become thigmophilic with our technology—touch-loving— a trait we share with rats, as it happens. We are constantly taking them out, fiddling with them, putting them away, taking them out again, reprogramming their directories, text messaging. And cell phone makers are always searching for new ways to exploit our attachments. Nokia offers "expression" phones that allow customization of faceplates and ring tones. Many companies, such as Modtones, sell song samples for cell phone ringers. In Asia, where cell phone use among the young is especially high, companies offer popular anime and manga cartoons as downloadable "wallpaper" for cell phones.

Cell phone technology is also creating new forms of social and 14 political networking. "Moblogging," or mobile web logging, allows cell phone users to publish and update content to the World Wide Web. An increasing number of companies are offering cell phones with WiFi capability, and as Sadie Plant noted recently in a report she prepared for Motorola, "On the Mobile," "today, the smallest Motorola phone has as much computing power in it as the largest, most expensive computer did less than a generation ago." In his *Forbes* "Wireless Outlook" newsletter, Andrew Seybold predicted, "in twenty five years there aren't going to be any wired phones left and I think it might happen even much sooner than that—ten to fifteen years." As well, "the phone will be tied much more closely to the person. Since the phone is the person, the person will be the number." It isn't surprising that one of Seybold's favorite movies is the James Coburn paranoid comedy, *The President's Analyst* (1967), whose premise "centered on attempts by the phone company to capture the president's psychoanalyst in order to further a plot to have phone devices implanted in people's brains at birth." Ma Bell meets *The Manchurian Candidate*.

Dodgeball.com, a new social-networking service, applies the princi- 15 ples of websites such as Friendster to cell phones. "Tell us where you are and we'll tell you who and what is around you," Dodgeball promises. "We'll ping your friends with your whereabouts, let you know when friends-of-friends are within ten blocks, allow you to broadcast content to anyone within ten blocks of you or blast messages to your groups of friends." The service is now available in fifteen cities in the U.S., enabling a form of friendly pseudo-stalking. "I was at Welcome to the Johnson's and a girl came up behind me and gave a tap on the shoulder," one recent testimonial noted. "'Are you this guy?' she inquired while holding up her cell phone to show my Dodgeball photo. I was indeed."

Political organizers have also found cell phone technology to be a 16 valuable tool. Throughout 2000 in the Philippines, the country's many cell phone users were text-messaging derogatory slogans and commentary about then-President Joseph Estrada. With pressure on the Estrada administration mounting, activists organized large demonstrations against the president by activating cell phone "trees" to summon protesters to particular locations and to outmaneuver riot police. Estrada was forced from office in January 2001. Anti-globalization protesters in Seattle and elsewhere (using only non-corporate cell phones, surely) have employed the technology to stage and control movements during demonstrations.

COMMUNICATION DELINQUENTS

The ease of mobile communication does not guarantee positive results   17
for all those who use it, of course, and the list of unintended negative consequences from cell phone use continues to grow. The BBC world service reported in 2001, "senior Islamic figures in Singapore have ruled that Muslim men cannot divorce their wives by sending text messages over their mobile phones." (Muslims can divorce their wives by saying the word "talaq," which means "I divorce you," three times).

Concerns about the dangers of cell phone use while driving have   18
dominated public discussion of cell phone risks. A 2001 study by the National Highway Traffic Safety Administration estimated that "54 percent of drivers 'usually' have some type of wireless phone in their vehicle with them" and that this translates into approximately 600,000 drivers "actively using cell phones at any one time" on the road. Women and drivers in the suburbs were found to talk and drive more often, and "the highest national use rates were observed for drivers of vans and sport utility vehicles." New York, New Jersey, and Washington, D.C. all require drivers to use hands-free technology (headsets or speakerphones) when talking on the cell.

Cell phones can also play host to viruses, real and virtual. A 2003   19
study presented at the American Society for Microbiology's conference on infectious disease found that twelve percent of the cell phones used by medical personnel in an Israeli hospital were contaminated with bacteria. (Another recent cell phone-related health research result, purporting a link between cell phone use and decreased sperm counts, has been deemed inconclusive.) The first computer virus specifically targeting cell phones was found in late June. As *The Guardian* reported recently, anti-virus manufacturers believe that "the mobile phone now mirrors how the Net has developed over the past two or three years—blighted with viruses as people got faster connections and downloaded more information."

With technology comes addiction, and applicable neologisms   20
have entered the lexicon—such as "crackberry," which describes the dependence exhibited by some BlackBerry wireless users. In a 2001

article in *New York* magazine about feuding couples, one dueling duo, Dave and Brooke, traded barbs about her wireless addictions. "I use it when I'm walking down the street," Brooke said proudly. "She was checking her voice mail in the middle of a Seder!" was Dave's exasperated response. "Under the table!" Brooke clarified. A recent survey conducted by the Hospital of Seoul National University found that "3 out of 10 Korean high school students who carry mobile phones are reported to be addicted" to them. Many reported feeling anxious without their phones and many displayed symptoms of repetitive stress injury from obsessive text messaging.

The cell phone has also proven effective as a facilitator and alibi   21
for adulterous behavior. "I heard someone (honest) talking about their 'shag phone' the other day," a visitor to a wireless technology blog recently noted. "He was a married man having an affair with a lady who was also married. It seems that one of the first heady rituals of the affair was to purchase a 'his and her' pair of pre-pay shag phones." A recent story in the *New York Times* documented the use of cell phone "alibi and excuse clubs" that function as an ethically challenged form of networking—Dodgeball for the delinquent. "Cell phone-based alibi clubs, which have sprung up in the United States, Europe, and Asia, allow people to send out mass text messages to thousands of potential collaborators asking for help. When a willing helper responds, the sender and the helper devise a lie, and the helper then calls the victim with the excuse," the report noted. One woman who started her own alibi club, which has helped spouses cheat on each other and workers mislead their bosses, "said she was not terribly concerned about lying," although she did concede: "You wouldn't really want your friends to know you're sparing people's feelings with these white lies." Websites such as Kargo offer features like "Soundster," which allows users to "insert sounds into your call and control your environment." Car horns, sirens, the coughs and sniffles of the sick room—all can be simulated in order to fool the listener on the other end of the call. Technology, it seems, is allowing people to make instrumental use of anonymous strangers while maintaining the appearance of trustworthiness within their own social group.

Technology has also led to further incursions on personal privacy.   22
Several websites now offer "candid pornography," peeping-Tom pictures taken in locker rooms, bathrooms, and dressing rooms by unscrupulous owners of cell phone cameras. Camera phones pose a potentially daunting challenge to privacy and security; unlike old-fashioned cameras, which could be confiscated and the film destroyed, digital cameras, including those on cell phones, allow users to send images instantaneously to any e-mail address. The images can be stored indefinitely, and the evidence that a picture was ever taken can be destroyed.

WILL YOU PLEASE BE QUIET, PLEASE?

Certain public interactions carry with them certain unspoken rules   23
of behavior. When approaching a grocery store checkout line, you
queue behind the last person in line and wait your turn. On the sub-
way, you make way for passengers entering and exiting the cars.
Riding on the train, you expect the interruptions of the ticket taker
and the periodic crackling blare of station announcements. What
you never used to expect, but must now endure, is the auditory
abrasion of a stranger arguing about how much he does, indeed,
owe to his landlord. I've heard business deals, lovers' quarrels, and
the most unsavory gossip. I've listened to strangers discuss in
excruciating detail their own and others' embarrassing medical conditions; I've heard the details of recent real estate purchases, job triumphs, and awful dates. (The only thing I haven't heard is phone sex,
but perhaps it is only a matter of time.) We are no longer *overhearing*,
which implies accidentally stumbling upon a situation where two
people are talking in presumed privacy. Now we are all simply
hearing. The result is a world where social space is overtaken by
anonymous, unavoidable background noise—a quotidian narration
that even in its more interesting moments rarely rises above the tone
of a penny dreadful. It seems almost cruel, in this context, that
Motorola's trademarked slogan for its wireless products is "Intelligence Everywhere."

Why do these cell phone conversations bother us more than lis-   24
tening to two strangers chatter in person about their evening plans or
listening to a parent scold a recalcitrant child? Those conversations are
quantitatively greater, since we hear both sides of the discussion—so why
are they nevertheless experienced as qualitatively different? Perhaps it is
because cell phone users harbor illusions about being alone or assume a
degree of privacy that the circumstances don't actually allow. Because
cell phone talkers are not interacting with the world around them, they
come to believe that the world around them isn't really there and
surely shouldn't intrude. And when the cell phone user commandeers
the space by talking, he or she sends a very clear message to others that
they are powerless to insist on their own use of the space. It is a pas-
sive-aggressive but extremely effective tactic.

Such encounters can sometimes escalate into rude intransigence   25
or even violence. In the past few years alone, men and women have
been stabbed, escorted off of airplanes by federal marshals, pepper-
sprayed in movie theaters, ejected from concert halls, and deliberately
rammed with cars as a result of their bad behavior on their cell phones.
The *Zagat* restaurant guide reports that cell phone rudeness is now the
number one complaint of diners, and *USA Today* notes that "fifty-nine

percent of people would rather visit the dentist than sit next to someone using a cell phone."

The etiquette challenges posed by cell phones are universal,   26
although different countries have responded in slightly different ways.
Writing about the impact of cell phone technology in *The Guardian* in
2002, James Meek noted, with moderate horror, that cell phones now
encourage British people to do what "British people aren't supposed to
do: invite strangers, spontaneously, into our personal worlds. We let
everyone know what our accent is, what we do for a living, what kind
of stuff we do in our non-working hours." In France, cell phone companies were pressured by the public to censor the last four digits of
phone numbers appearing on monthly statements, because so many
French men and women were using them to confirm that their significant other was having an affair.

In Israel, where the average person is on a cell phone four times   27
as much as the average American, and where cell phone technology
boasts an impressive 76 percent penetration rate (the United States isn't
projected to reach that level until 2009), the incursion of cell phones
into daily life is even more dramatic. As sociologists Amit Schejter and
Akiba Cohen found, there were no less than ten cell phone interruptions
during a recent staging of *One Flew Over the Cuckoo's Nest* at Israel's
National Theater, and "there has even been an anecdote reported of an
undertaker's phone ringing inside a grave as the deceased was being
put to rest." The authors explain this state of affairs with reference to the
Israeli personality, which they judge to be more enthusiastic about technology and more forceful in exerting itself in public; the subtitle of their
article is "chutzpah and chatter in the Holy Land."

In the U.S., mild regional differences in the use of cell phones are   28
evident. Reporting on a survey by Cingular wireless, CNN noted that
cell phone users in the South "are more likely to silence their phones in
church," while Westerners "are most likely to turn a phone off in
libraries, theaters, restaurants, and schools." But nationwide, cell
phones still frequently interrupt movie screenings, theater performances, and concerts. Audience members are not the sole offenders,
either. My sister, a professional musician, told me that during one performance, in the midst of a slow and quiet passage of Verdi's *Requiem*,
the cell phone of one of the string players in the orchestra began ringing, much to the horror of his fellow musicians.

We cannot simply banish to Tartarus—the section of Hades   29
reserved for punishment of the worst offenders—all those who violate
the rules of social space. And the noise pollution generated by rude cell
phone users is hardly the worst violation of social order; it is not the
same as defacing a statue, for example. Other countries offer some reason for optimism: In societies that maintain more formality, such as

Japan, loud public conversation is considered rude, and Japanese people will often cover their mouths and hide their phones from view when speaking into them.

Not surprisingly, Americans have turned to that most hallowed but least effective solution to social problems: public education. Cingular Wireless, for example, has launched a public awareness campaign whose slogan is "Be Sensible." The program includes an advertisement shown in movie theaters about "Inconsiderate Cell Phone Guy," a parody of bad behavior that shows a man talking loudly into his cell phone at inappropriate times: during a date, in a movie, at a wedding, in the middle of a group therapy session. It is a miniature manners nickelodeon for the wireless age. July is now officially National Cell Phone Courtesy Month, and etiquette experts such as Jacqueline Whitmore of the Protocol School of Palm Beach advise companies such as Sprint about how to encourage better behavior in their subscribers. Whitmore is relentlessly positive: "Wireless technology is booming so quickly and wireless phones have become so popular, the rules on wireless etiquette are still evolving," she notes on her website. She cites hopeful statistics culled from public opinion surveys that say "98 percent of Americans say they move away from others when talking on a wireless phone in public" and "the vast majority (86 percent) say they 'never' or 'rarely' speak on wireless phones while conducting an entire public transaction with someone else such as a sales clerk or bank teller." If you are wondering where these examples of wireless rectitude reside, you might find them in the land of wishful thinking. There appears to be a rather large disconnect between people's actual behavior and their reports of their behavior.

Whitmore is correct to suggest that we are in the midst of a period of adjustment. We still have the memory of the old social rules, which remind us to be courteous towards others, especially in confined environments such as trains and elevators. But it is becoming increasingly clear that cell phone technology itself has disrupted our ability to insist on the enforcement of social rules. Etiquette experts urge us to adjust—be polite, don't return boorish behavior with boorish behavior, set a standard of probity in your own use of cell phones. But in doing so these experts tacitly concede that every conversation is important, and that we need only learn how and when to have them. This elides an older rule: when a conversation takes place in public, its merit must be judged in part by the standards of the other participants in the social situation. By relying solely on self-discipline and public education (or that ubiquitous modern state of "awareness"), the etiquette experts have given us a doomed manual. Human nature being what it is, individuals will spend more time rationalizing their own need to make cell phone calls than thinking about how that need might affect others.

Worse, the etiquette experts offer diversions rather than standards, encouraging alternatives to calling that nevertheless still succeed in removing people from the social space. "Use text messaging," is number 7 on Whitmore's Ten Tips for the Cell Phone Savvy.

These attempts at etiquette training also evade another reality: the decline of accepted standards for social behavior. In each of us lurks the possibility of a Jekyll-and-Hyde-like transformation, its trigger the imposition of some arbitrary rule. The problem is that, in the twenty-first century, with the breakdown of hierarchies and manners, all social rules are arbitrary. "I don't think we have to worry about people being rude intentionally," Whitmore told *Wireless Week*. "Most of us simply haven't come to grips with the new responsibilities wireless technologies demand." But this seems foolishly optimistic. A psychologist quoted in a story by UPI recently noted the "baffling sense of entitlement" demonstrated by citizens in the wireless world. "They don't get sheepish when shushed," he marveled. "You're the rude one." And *contra* Ms. Whitmore, there is intention at work in this behavior, even if it is not intentional rudeness. It is the intentional removal of oneself from the social situation in public space. This removal, as sociologists have long shown, is something more serious than a mere manners lapse. It amounts to a radical disengagement from the public sphere. 32

SPECTATOR SPORT

We know that the reasons people give for owning cell phones are largely practical—convenience and safety. But the reason we answer them whenever they ring is a question better left to sociology and psychology. In works such as *Behavior in Public Spaces*, *Relations in Public*, and *Interaction Ritual*, the great sociologist Erving Goffman mapped the myriad possibilities of human interaction in social space, and his observations take on a new relevance in our cell phone world. Crucial to Goffman's analysis was the notion that in social situations where strangers must interact, "the individual is obliged to 'come into play' upon entering the situation and to stay 'in play' while in the situation." Failure to demonstrate this presence sends a clear message to others of one's hostility or disrespect for the social gathering. It effectively turns them into "non-persons." Like the piqued lover who rebuffs her partner's attempt to caress her, the person who removes himself from the social situation is sending a clear message to those around him: I don't need you. 33

Although Goffman wrote in the era before cell phones, he might have judged their use as a "subordinate activity," a way to pass the time such as reading or doodling that could and should be set aside 34 when the dominant activity resumes. Within social space, we are allowed to perform a range of these secondary activities, but they must not impose upon the social group as a whole or require so much attention that they remove us from the social situation altogether. The opposite appears to be true today. The group is expected never to impinge upon—indeed, it is expected to tacitly endorse by enduring—the individual's right to withdraw from social space by whatever means he or she chooses: cell phones, BlackBerrys, iPods, DVDs screened on laptop computers. These devices are all used as a means to refuse to be "in" the social space; they are technological cold shoulders that are worse than older forms of subordinate activity in that they impose visually and auditorily on others. Cell phones are not the only culprits here. A member of my family, traveling recently on the Amtrak train from New York, was shocked to realize that the man sitting in front of her was watching a pornographic movie on his laptop computer—a movie whose raunchy scenes were reflected in the train window and thus clearly visible to her. We have allowed what should be subordinate activities in social space to become dominant.

One of the groups Goffman studied keenly were mental patients, 35 many of them residents at St. Elizabeth's Hospital in Washington, D.C., and his comparisons often draw on the remarkable disconnect between the behavior of people in normal society and those who had been institutionalized for mental illness. It is striking in revisiting Goffman's work how often people who use cell phones seem to be acting more like the people in the asylum than the ones in respectable society. Goffman describes "occult involvements," for example, as any activity that undermines others' ability to feel engaged in social space. "When an individual is perceived in an occult involvement, observers may not only sense that they are not able to claim him at the moment," Goffman notes, "but also feel that the offender's complete activity up till then has been falsely taken as a sign of participation with them, that all along he has been alienated from their world." Who hasn't observed someone sitting quietly, apparently observing the rules of social space, only to launch into loud conversation as soon as the cell phone rings? This is the pretense of social participation Goffman observed in patients at St. Elizabeth's.

Goffman called those who declined to respond to social overtures 36 as being "out of contact," and said "this state is often felt to be full evidence that he is very sick indeed, that he is, in fact, cut off from all contact with the world around him." To be accessible meant to be available in the particular social setting and to act appropriately. Today, of course, being accessible means answering your cell phone, which brings you in contact with your caller, but "out of contact" in the physical social situation, be it a crosstown bus, a train, an airplane, or simply walking down the street.

In terms of the rules of social space, cell phone use is a form of 37
communications panhandling—forcing our conversations on others
without first gaining their tacit approval. "The force that keeps people
in their communication place in our middle-class society," Goffman
observed, "seems to be the fear of being thought forward and pushy, or
odd, the fear of forcing a relationship where none is desired." But middle class society itself has decided to upend such conventions in the
service of greater accessibility and convenience. This is a dramatic shift
that took place in a very short span of time, and it is worth at least considering the long-term implications of this subversion of norms. The
behavioral rules Goffman so effectively mapped exist to protect everyone, even if we don't, individually, always need them. They are the
social equivalent of fire extinguishers placed throughout public buildings. You hope not to have to use them too often, but they can ensure
that a mere spark does not become an embarrassing conflagration. In a
world that eschews such norms, we find ourselves plagued by the
behavior that Goffman used to witness only among the denizens of the
asylum: disembodied talk that renders all of us unwilling listeners.

We also use our cell phones to exert our status in social space, like 38
the remnants of the entourage or train, which "led a worthy to demonstrate his status by the cluster of dependent supporters that accompanied
him through a town or a house of parliament." Modern celebrities still
have such escorts (a new cable television series, *Entourage*, tracks a fictional celebrity posse). But cell phones give all of us the unusual ability to
simulate an entourage. My mother-in-law recently found herself sharing
an elevator (in the apartment building she's lived in for forty years) with
a man who was speaking very loudly into his cell phone. When she asked
him to keep his voice down, he became enraged and began yelling at her;
he was, he said, in the midst of an "important" conversation with his secretary. He acted, in other words, as if she'd trounced on the hem of his
royal train. She might have had a secretary too, of course—for all he knew
she might have a fleet of assistants at her disposal—but because she
wasn't communicating with someone *at that moment* and he, thanks to his
cell phone, was, her status in the social space was, in effect, demoted.

The language of wireless technology itself suggests its selfishness 39
as a medium. One of the latest advances is the "Personal Area Network,"
a Bluetooth technology used in Palm Pilots and other personal digital
assistants. The network is individualized, closed to unwelcome intrud-
ers, and totally dependent on the choices of the user. We now have our
own technological assistants and networks, quite an impressive kingdom for ordinary mortals. In this kingdom, our cell phones reassure us
by providing constant contact, and we become much like a child with a
security blanket or Dumbo with his feather. Like a security blanket, which
is also visible to observers, cell phones provide the "'publicization' of

emotional fulfillment," as French sociologist Chantal de Gournay has argued. "At work, in town, while traveling—every call on the mobile phone secretly expresses a message to the public: 'Look how much I'm in demand, how full my life is.'" Unlike those transitional objects of childhood, however, few of us are eager to shed our cell phones.

ABSENT WITHOUT LEAVE

Our daily interactions with cell phone users often prompt heated   40
exchanges and promises of furious retribution. When *New York Times* columnist Joe Sharkey asked readers to send in their cell phone horror stories, he was deluged with responses: "There is not enough time in the day to relay the daily torment I must endure from these cell-yellers," one woman said. "There's always some self-important jerk who must holler his business all the way into Manhattan," another commuter wearily noted. Rarely does one find a positive story about cell phone users who behaved politely, observing the common social space.

Then again, we all apparently have a cell phone *alter idem*, a second   41
self that we endlessly excuse for making just such annoying cell phone calls. As a society, we are endlessly forgiving of our own personal "emergencies" that require cell phone conversation and easily apoplectic about having to listen to others'. At my local grocery store around 6:30 in the evening, it is not an uncommon sight to see a man in business attire, wandering the frozen food aisle, phone in hand, shouting, "Bird's Eye or Jolly Green Giant? What? Yes, I got the coffee filters already!" How rude, you think, until you remember that you left your own grocery list on the kitchen counter; in a split second you are fishing for your phone so that you can call home and get its particulars. This is the quintessential actor-observer paradox: as actors, we are always politely exercising our right to be connected, but as observers we are perpetually victimized by the boorish bad manners of other cell phone users.

A new generation of sociologists has begun to apply Goffman's   42
insights to our use of cell phones in public. Kenneth J. Gergen, for example, has argued that one reason cell phones allow a peculiar form of diversion in public spaces is that they encourage "absent presence," a state where "one is physically present but is absorbed by a technolog-ically mediated world of elsewhere." You can witness examples of absent presence everywhere: people in line at the bank or a retail store, phones to ear and deep into their own conversations—so unavailable they do not offer the most basic pleasantries to the salesperson or cashier. At my local playground, women deep in cell phone conversa-tions are scattered on benches or distractedly pushing a child on a

swing—physically present, to be sure, but "away" in their conversations, not fully engaged with those around them.

The first time you saw a person walking down the street having a   43
conversation using a hands-free cell phone device you intuitively
grasped this state. Wildly gesticulating, laughing, mumbling—to the
person on the other end of the telephone, their street-walking conversation partner is engaged in normal conversation. To the outside
observer, however, he looks like a deranged or slightly addled escapee
from a psychiatric ward. Engaged with the ether, hooked up to an ear-
piece and dangling microphone, his animated voice and gestures are
an anomaly in the social space. They violate our everyday sense of
normal behavior.

The difficulty of harmonizing real and virtual presence isn't new.   44
As Mark Caldwell noted in *A Short History of Rudeness* about the first
telephones, "many early phone stories involved a bumpkin who nods
silently in reply to a caller's increasingly agitated, 'Are you there?'"
Even young children know Goffman's rules. When a parent is in front
of a child but on the telephone (physically present but mentally
"away"), a child will frequently protest—grabbing for the phone or
vocalizing loudly to retrieve the parent's attention. They are expressing a
need for recognition that, in a less direct and individualized way, we all
require from strangers in public space. But the challenge is greater given
the sheer number of wireless users, a reality that is prompting a new
form of social criticism. As a "commentary on the potential of the mobile
phone for disrupting and disturbing social interactions," the Interaction
Design Institute Ivrea recently sponsored a project called "Mass
Distraction." The project featured jackets and cell phones that only
allowed participants to talk on their phones if the large hood of the jacket
was closed completely over their head or if they continued to insert coins
into the pocket of the jacket like an old fashioned pay phone. "In order to
remain connected," the project notes, "the mobile phone user multitasks
between the two communication channels. Whether disguised or not,
this practice degrades the quality of the interaction with the people in
his immediate presence."

Cocooned within our "Personal Area Networks" and wirelessly   45
transported to other spaces, we are becoming increasingly immune to
the boundaries and realities of physical space. As one reporter for the
Los Angeles Times said, in exasperation, "Go ahead, floss in the elevator.
You're busy; you can't be expected to wait until you can find a bathroom. . . . [T]he world out there? It's just a backdrop, as movable and
transient as a fake skyline on a studio lot." No one is an outsider with a
cell phone—that is why foreign cab drivers in places like New York and
Washington are openly willing to ignore laws against driving-and-talking.
Beyond the psychic benefits cell phone calls provide (cab driving is a

lonely occupation), their use signals the cab driver's membership in a community apart from the ever-changing society that frequents his taxi. Our cell phones become our talismans against being perceived as (or feeling ourselves to be) outsiders.

TALK AND CONVERSATION

Recently, on a trip to China, I found myself standing on the Great Wall. 46 One of the members of our small group had hiked ahead, and since the rest of us had decided it was time to get back down the mountain, we realized we would need to find him. Despite being in a remote location at high altitude, and having completely lost sight of him in the hazy late morning air, this proved to be the easiest of logistical tasks. One man pulled out his cell phone, called his wife back in the United States, and had her send an e-mail to the man who had walked ahead. Knowing that our lost companion religiously checked his BlackBerry wireless, we reasoned that he would surely notice an incoming message. Soon enough he reappeared, our wireless plea for his return having successfully traveled from China to Washington and back again to the Wall in mere minutes.

At the time, we were all caught up in the James Bond-like excite- 47 ment of our mission. Would the cell phone work? (It did.) Would the wife's e-mail get through to our companion's BlackBerry? (No problem.) Only later, as we drove back to Beijing, did I experience a pang of doubt about our small communications triumph. There, at one of the Great Wonders of the World, a centuries-old example of human triumph over nature, we didn't hesitate to do something as mundane as make a cell phone call. It is surely true that wireless communication is its own wondrous triumph over nature. But cell phone conversation somehow inspires less awe than standing atop the Great Wall, perhaps because atop the Great Wall we are still rooted in the natural world that we have conquered. Or perhaps it is simply because cell phones have become everyday wonders—as unremarkable to us as the Great Wall is to those who see it everyday.

Christian Licoppe and Jean-Philippe Heurtin have argued that 48 cell phone use must be understood in a broader context; they note that the central feature of the modern experience is the "deinstitutionalization of personal bonds." Deinstitutionalization spawns anxiety, and as a result we find ourselves working harder to build trust relationships. Cell phone calls "create a web of short, content-poor interactions through which bonds can be built and strengthened in an ongoing process."

But as trust is being built and bolstered moment by moment   49
between individuals, public trust among strangers in social settings is
eroding. We are strengthening and increasing our interactions with the
people we already know at the expense of those who we do not. The
result, according to Kenneth Gergen, is "the erosion of face-to-face community, a coherent and centered sense of self, moral bearings, depth of
relationship, and the uprooting of meaning from material context: such
are the dangers of absent presence."

No term captures this paradoxical state more ably than the word   50
"roam," which appears on your phone when you leave an area
bristling with wireless towers and go into the wilds of the less well connected. The word appears when your cell phone is looking for a way to
connect you, but the real definition of roam is "to go from place to place
without purpose or direction," which has more suggestive implications. It suggests that we have allowed our phones to become the link
to our purpose and the symbol of our status—without its signal we
lack direction. Roaming was a word whose previous use was largely
confined to describing the activities of herds of cattle. In her report on
the use of mobile phones throughout the world, Sadie Plant noted,
"according to the *Oxford English Dictionary*, one of the earliest uses of the
word 'mobile' was in association with the Latin phrase *mobile vulgus*,
the excitable crowd," whence comes our word "mob."

Convenience and safety—the two reasons people give for why   51
they have (or "need") cell phones—are legitimate reasons for using
wireless technology; but they are not neutral. Convenience is the major
justification for fast food, but its overzealous consumption has something to do with our national obesity "epidemic." Safety spawned a
bewildering range of anti-bacterial products and the overzealous prescription of antibiotics—which in turn led to disease-resistant bacteria.

One possible solution would be to treat cell phone use the way we   52
now treat tobacco use. Public spaces in America were once littered with
spittoons and the residue of the chewing tobacco that filled them,
despite the disgust the practice fostered. Social norms eventually rendered public spitting déclassé. Similarly, it was not so long ago that cigarette smoking was something people did everywhere—in movie theaters,
restaurants, trains, and airplanes. Non-smokers often had a hard time
finding refuge from the clouds of nicotine. Today, we ban smoking in all
but designated areas. Currently, cell phone users enjoy the same privi-
leges smokers once enjoyed, but there is no reason we cannot reverse the
trend. Yale University bans cell phones in some of its libraries, and
Amtrak's introduction of "quiet cars" on some of its routes has been
eagerly embraced by commuters. Perhaps one day we will exchange
quiet cars for wireless cars, and the majority of public space will revert

to the quietly disconnected. In doing so, we might partially reclaim something higher even than healthy lungs: civility.

This reclaiming of social space could have considerable conse-   53
quences. As sociologist de Gournay has noted, "the telephone is a device ill suited to listening . . . it is more appropriate for exchanging information." Considering Americans' obsession with information— we are, after all, the "information society"—it is useful to draw the distinction. Just as there is a distinction between information and knowledge, there is a vast difference between conversation and talk.

Conversation (as opposed to "talk") is to genuine sociability what   54
courtship (as opposed to "hooking up") is to romance. And the technologies that mediate these distinctions are important: the cell phone exchange of information is a distant relative of formal conversation, just as the Internet chat room is a far less compelling place to become intimate with another person than a formal date. In both cases, however, we have convinced ourselves as a culture that these alternatives are just as good as the formalities—that they are, in fact, improvements upon them.

"A conversation has a life of its own and makes demands on its   55
own behalf," Goffman wrote. "It is a little social system with its own boundary-making tendencies; it is a little patch of commitment and loyalty with its own heroes and its own villains." According to census data, the percentage of Americans who live alone is the highest it has ever been in our country's history, making a return to genuine sociability and conversation more important than ever. Cell phones provide us with a new, but not necessarily superior means of communicating with each other. They encourage talk, not conversation. They link us to those we know, but remove us from the strangers who surround us in public space. Our constant accessibility and frequent exchange of information is undeniably useful. But it would be a terrible irony if "being connected" required or encouraged a disconnection from community life—an erosion of the spontaneous encounters and everyday decencies that make society both civilized and tolerable.

Examining the Text
1. According to Rosen, what are the primary reasons why people use cell phones? What are the primary dangers of cell phone use?
2. Rosen notes that the etiquette of cell phone use is still evolving. What examples does she give to show that people are breaking expected rules of behavior with their cell phone use?
3. In paragraph 33, Rosen refers to the theories of Erving Goffman to explain how people determine how to behave in public places. In your own words, summarize the key ideas of Goffman that Rosen incorporates in this section.

4. Overall, what would you say is Rosen's opinion of cell phones? Do you find her opinion stated directly anywhere in the article?

5. *Thinking rhetorically*: In paragraph 46, Rosen tells the story of how a cell phone was used to help locate a person at the Great Wall of China. What point is Rosen trying to prove with this anecdote? How is the anecdote related to the larger point of the article? In general, what function is served by some of the other specific anecdotes in Rosen's article? How do they help Rosen advance her arguments?

For Group Discussion

Following up on our "as you read" suggestion at the beginning of the article, discuss with others in your group what you saw as the key points Rosen makes about cell phones. Then categorize these points. For instance, one category might focus on why people use cell phones, while another category focuses on the negative impact of cell phones on social behavior. As a group, decide on what categories make sense, and then go through the entire article to make sure you've dealt with all of the points Rosen makes about cell phones.

Writing Suggestion

Rosen's article should give you many ideas as to how cell phones affect the culture as a whole as well as individual cell phone users. Your assignment now is to test some of Rosen's ideas by interviewing three or four people you know who use cell phones frequently. First, decide on which of Rosen's claims you want to test, and write these claims down. Next, develop one or two questions for each claim. For instance, if you want to test the claim that people feel safer with cell phones, ask your interviewees questions about this: Would they feel less safe if they didn't have their cell phones? If so, why? Have they ever used their cell phones in a dangerous situation? After you've developed your list of questions and interviewed your cell phone users, write up the results of your research. Consider beginning the paper by referring to Rosen to explain the claim that you're testing. Then present information gathered from your interviews, including quotations and paraphrases. Finally, conclude the paper by commenting on whether your findings corroborate or contradict Rosen's argument.

Applications

1. Video Games

Let the Games Begin: Gaming Technology and Entertainment Among College Students

Steve Jones

As you read the following report, it will be interesting to see if you think it offers a good representation of the way you and your fellow students use video games and computer games. The purpose of the report is to present an accurate picture of how gaming—on computers, on the Internet, and on video devices like Nintendo and Playstation—fits into the lives of college students. Researchers surveyed students at twenty-seven colleges and universities across the country in order to find out the following: when, where, and how often do you play computer, online, and video games? What kinds of games do you play? Why do you play these games? And what effect does gaming have on your education?

One of the most interesting results of the study is that gaming is woven into the fabric of everyday life for most college students. Gaming is integrated into daily activities like socializing and studying; students play games as a break from their coursework, to occupy free time and stave off boredom, and as a means of interacting with others. It's also interesting that all of the 1,162 students surveyed said that they had played a video, computer, or online game at one time or another, and sixty-five percent of respondents described themselves as regular or occasional game players. These results show that gaming technology is a significant presence in the lives of college students.

The report was written by Steve Jones, who is a Professor of Communication at the University of Illinois at Chicago. Jones is also a Senior Research Fellow with the Pew Internet Research group, which commissioned the study as part of the Pew Internet & American Life Project. This Project aims to be an authoritative source of information on the civic and social impact of the Internet, and it releases 15 to 20 reports a year that present research on various aspects of the Internet. **Before you read***, take a look at the information that's available at the website for the Pew Internet & American Life Project: http://www.pewinternet.org. It's a wonderful resource for finding out about how computer technology and networks are impacting American culture.*

GAMING COMES OF AGE

College students are often considered a bellwether of Internet use, but   1
the Internet is not the only technology they have incorporated into
everyday life. Thanks to a plethora of technologies (video game consoles, computers, handheld devices, Internet) a range of entertainment
options is at their disposal, a range that is much wider than was available to their predecessors. Furthermore, today's college students are
using technologies like cell phones, mp3 players and other devices to
entertain themselves wherever they may be.

The goal of this study was to learn about college students' use of   2
video, computer and online games, and to determine the impact of that
use on their everyday life. To meet those goals the researchers used
three approaches. First, surveys were randomly distributed to college
students at a wide range of two-year and four-year public and private
colleges and universities in the continental United States. Students
from 27 colleges and universities participated and the surveys were
collected between March 2002 and June 2002, and September 2002 and
October 2002. This sample was intended to produce results that would
correspond to the demographics for all U.S. college students as
reported in *The Chronicle of Higher Education*'s annual almanac issue.[1]
The sample was tested against known population parameters (gender,
race, age) and found to be reflective of the national population of college students. In all, 1,162 surveys were returned. For results based on
the total sample, one can say with 95% confidence that the error attributable to sampling and other random effects is plus or minus 3 percentage points. This study focused on traditional college students, ones
who are seeking a college degree and who devote much or all of their
time to their studies.

Second, a team of graduate student researchers at the University   3
of Illinois at Chicago was recruited to observe the behaviors of college
students at 10 Chicago area institutions of higher education. The
researchers were trained in ethnographic methods of observation and
data collecting, and rotated the times of the day and days of the week
they spent in various public settings where college students could be
found using computers and the Internet. Third, additional material was
based on a previous study of college students' Internet use conducted
by this research team for the Pew Internet & American Life Project[2] and
on the findings of surveys of Americans about their use of the Internet

---

[1] *The Chronicle of Higher Education*, Almanac Issue 2001–2, 158(1), August 31, 2001 and
Almanac Issue 2002–3, 159(1), August 30, 2002.

[2] http://www.pewinternet.org/reports/toc.asp?Report=73.

conducted by Princeton Survey Research Associates in 2001 and 2002
for the Pew Internet & American Life Project.

The Context for Games

The 1980s were a boom time for video games. Beginning with *Pong*,   4
progressing to *Space Invaders*, and following on to the PC boom with
computer-based games, the gaming industry evolved its grip on entertainment slowly but surely. By the late 1990s the Internet's growth and
popularity seemed a logical match for video games, but bandwidth,
computer processor speed, and the gaming industry's investment in its
own devices (Nintendo, PlayStation, etc.) postponed the inevitable
merger of interactive games and Internet.

The last few years have been another boom time for the gaming   5
industry. Internet-ready game consoles from Nintendo, Sony and Microsoft
(among others), increasing bandwidth, and computers primed for multi-
media, have made gaming an increasingly popular form of entertainment. Research conducted in 2002 showed that 60% of U.S. residents
age six and older play computer games, and that over 221 million computer and video games were sold in the U.S.[3] Earlier research found
that 35% of U.S. residents surveyed said that video games were the
most entertaining media activity, while television came in second with
18% saying it was most entertaining. The gaming industry reported
sales of over $6.5 billion that same year.[4] Datamonitor estimates online
gaming revenues will reach $2.9 billion by 2005.[5] Additional research
has claimed that 90% of U.S. households with children rented or owned
a video or computer game[6] and that U.S. children spend an average of
20 minutes a day playing video games.[7]

Research conducted by the Pew Internet and American Life   6
Project showed that 66 percent of U.S. teenagers play or download games

[3]Interactive Digital Software Association (2003). Available: http://www.idsa.com/
pressroom.html.

[4]Sherry, J., Lucas, K., Rechtsteiner, S., Brooks, C., Wilson, B. (2001, May 26). *Video game
uses and gratifications as predictors of use and game preference.* Paper presented at the International Communication Association convention. Available: http://icdweb.cc.purdue.
edu/~sherryj/videogames/VGUG.pdf; and Anderson, C. A (2001, August 14). *Violent
video games and aggressive thoughts, feelings and behaviors* [On-line]. Available: http://
psychserver.iastate.edu/faculty/caa/abstracts/2000–2004/02A.jcc.pdf.

[5]Datamonitor (August 30, 2002). *Online gamers console themselves.* Available at http://
www.datamonitor.com/.

[6]Quittner, J. (1999, May 10). *Are video games really so bad?* Time.

[7]Jensen, E. (1999, Nov. 18). *Study finds TV tops kids' big diet of media.* Los Angeles Times,
pp. A1, A29.

online.[8] While 57 percent of girls play online, 75 percent of boys reported that they play Internet-games. Although teenagers are reported to play video and computer games for nearly 4 hours a week, some researchers have found that college aged men report playing these games over 15 hours per week.

General Findings

Responses to questions about college students' use of video games   7
(*e.g.*, those requiring consoles and television sets, like Nintendo, Sega, Xbox, etc.), computer games (*e.g.*, those that require a PC only) and online games (those that require an Internet connection, typically for multiplayer interaction) lead to the undeniable conclusion that college students comprise an active video, computer, and online gaming community. Indeed, gaming is a regular part of college students' lives. Seventy percent (70%) of college students reported playing video, computer or online games at least once in a while. Some 65% of college students reported being regular or occasional game players. All of those surveyed reported to have played a video, computer or online game at one time or another. Of the 27% of college students who said they do not occasionally or regularly play video, computer, or Internet games at all, "lack of interest" (20%) and "waste of time" (13%) were their primary reasons for not playing. Only a handful of students cited a lack of electronic gaming resources (2%) or unfamiliarity (.5%) as their reasons for not gaming. The universe of entertainment options for them clearly includes gaming as an important category of activity.

Surprisingly, slightly more women than men reported playing   8
computer and online games (approximately 60% women compared to 40% men) while about the same number of men and women reported playing video games. Part of the reason more women than men play computer games may be that video games are generally focused on action and adventure (often violent in nature), while computer games are typically traditional games (*e.g.* solitaire, board games). Video games are also often rigid in their game options and narrative structure. In most video games the types of characters one can choose are pre-set by the game designers, and gender roles are stereotyped and exaggerated. Computer games generally do not require the player to choose a character. Online games may be more popular for women than men partly because gender can be disguised and manipulated in

---

[8]Lenhart, A., Rainie, L., Levis, O. (2001). *Teenage life online*. Available: http://www.pewinternet.org/reports/pdfs/PIP_Teens_Report.pdf.

an online game, and because online gaming sites specifically designed for women can provide a comfortable gaming environment. The racial profile of college student gamers is roughly similar to the overall college student population, with a slight skew toward non-white students playing games in comparison to the overall population (Table 1).

Computer games held a slight edge in popularity (Table 2) compared to computer and online games. When asked which they play the most, 30% said video games, 27% said computer games, and 14% said online games. But when asked which they played at least once a week, 37% said computer games, 31% said online games, and 27% said video games. The differing responses likely have to do with the technologies involved and college students' whereabouts. While computer games may be played anywhere there is a computer (*e.g.*, most computer operating systems include some games as part of their standard installation), online games require Internet access, and video games are generally played in the home on gaming consoles like the ones made by Nintendo, Sega and others. This assertion is further supported by students' own reports that they play video games most at their parents' or friend's houses and play online games at a school computer lab.

Computer games have an edge over video games and online games when time-use is considered. Just over one fourth (27%) reported playing video games once a week or more often, and slightly more (31%) reported playing online games once a week or more often. But

Table 1.   Racial characteristics:

	Overall	Video Gamer	Computer Gamer	Online Gamer
White	72%	63%	63%	61%
African-American	11%	9%	11%	12%
Asian	6%	14%	14%	13%
Hispanic	9%	9%	8%	10%

Source: Pew Internet & American Life Project College Students Gaming Survey, n = 1162. Margin of error is ± 3.5%.

Table 2.   Do you ever:

Play computer games	71%
Play video games	59%
Play online games	56%

Source: Pew Internet & American Life Project College Students Gaming Survey, n = 1162. Margin of error is ±3.5%.

over a third (37%) reported playing computer games once a week or more often. Daily, twice as many college students play an online (14%) or a computer (13%) game as play a video game (6%). The computer's prominence as a tool related to gaming is illustrated by the finding that nearly half (45%) of college students reported going online simply to play or download games.

Students' commitment to gaming comes as little surprise consid- 11 ering their long history of interaction with video and computer games. By high school 77% of our respondents had played computer games, and just over two-thirds (69%) of them had been playing video games since elementary school. Table 3 illustrates the trend over time—college students first encountered video games as children in elementary school, and are just beginning to discover the relatively recent phenomenon of online games in high school and college. The fundamental point, however, is that gaming is a part of growing up in the U.S., and by the time the current cohort of college students graduates virtually all of them will have had some kind of experience with gaming. And although only 14% of college students reported that online gaming is the game format they played most, the continuing saturation of wireless technology (particularly in cell phones, and personal digital assistants) with gaming capabilities, along with the availability of broadband connections, will likely affect these numbers significantly in the future and allow college students to maintain and even increase their online gaming activities once they leave the college environment.

Gaming and College Life

College students have readily accepted online gaming into their lives 12 and have adapted gaming activities to the unique environment of college life. College students are notorious "night owls" due in part to all night study sessions and regular (if not continual) socializing, and their gaming activity reflects this. Close to half (41%) of college gamers

Table 3. First started playing this type of game during:

	College	Jr. High/High School	Elementary School
Video games	2%	15%	69%
Computer games	9%	49%	28%
Online games	22%	43%	6%

Source: Pew Internet & American Life Project College Students Gaming Survey, n = 1162. Margin of error is ±3.5%.

reported playing after 9 p.m. Only 8% reported gaming before noon, while another 37% play between 5 p.m. and 9 p.m.

In our observation of college students in campus computer labs it was common to see students who appeared to be stopping by their dormitory computer lab for a postclass/pre-dinner gaming session. The atmosphere in the labs was usually very relaxed during these hours, and the types of computer use by students, including gaming, seemed to provide relaxation. In observations of computer use in public computer labs on college campuses it was found that male students more frequently than female ones often had online games open on their computer's screen alongside their schoolwork (typically written papers). 13

However, the games most commonly seen were billiards, solitaire, crossword puzzles, poker and other arcade and card games, rather than multiple player games. These are readily available via the web, and many students had browser windows open with such games, to which they would turn to take a break while writing a paper. Among the reasons those games are most common is that they are not intended to be a lengthy distraction from work, they are easily accessible on the Internet and do not require fast processors, bandwidth or sound, and they do not require installation of specific programs on the computer.[9] A number of students were seen quickly entering a lab, playing some games in an apparent effort to kill time, and then leaving. The manner of some such students suggested a routine, perhaps an after-class relaxation ritual. We sometimes observed students sitting next to one another and playing an online game together on different, but adjacent machines. In most all cases gaming was one of several simultaneous activities and rarely the sole thing to which a student paid attention. 14

Further observation showed a distinct difference between types of campus computer labs. In residence hall, or dormitory, computer labs, students were directly observed playing various online and offline games on public computers. These students typically had no class materials around them and seemed to be visiting the lab purely for entertainment reasons. Gaming in labs located in academic buildings was much less frequently observed. Public settings, such as school computer labs, the library and Internet cafes lack appeal for student gamers, with only small numbers (5%, 2% and 2% respectively) citing these locations as their favorites for gaming. Reasons for this may include restrictions on the types of computer use allowed on public 15

---

[9] During one observation a student was seen trying to load a multiple player online game onto a computer. After several unsuccessful attempts, likely due to security software on the computer, he gave up and left.

Table 4.   Where do you play games the most?

Parent's home	31%
Friend's home	27%
Dorm room	23%

Source: Pew Internet & American Life Project College Students
Gaming Survey, $n = 1162$. Margin of error is 3.5%.

machines. Although most college students (66%) were unaware of restrictions on playing games in campus or dormitory computer labs, the 16% who were aware of use restrictions reported that campus computer labs had more rules regarding gaming, downloading programs, or looking at pornography than computer labs located in dormitories.

Although college students have access to many settings that can   16
accommodate gaming, including campus computer labs and dormitories, they tend to make their home the primary gaming environment (Table 4). Comfortable surroundings and accessibility to gaming equipment (i.e. TV set, gaming consoles and accessories, computers, and the Internet) appear to be important features in for college students when choosing a place to play games. This suggests that gaming is placed alongside other entertainment forms in their residence, and that it likely forms part of a larger multitasking setting in which college students play games, listen to music and interact with others in the room.

Gaming vs. Studying

According to students, gaming has little impact, either positive or neg-   17
ative, on their academic lives. About two-thirds (66%) felt that gaming had no influence on their academic performance. However, in response to another question close to half (48%) of college student gamers agreed that gaming keeps them from studying "some" or "a lot." In addition, about one in ten (9%) admitted that their main motivation for playing games was to avoid studying. Nevertheless college student gamers' reported hours studying per week match up closely with those reported by college students in general, with about two-thirds (62%) reporting that they study for classes no more than 7 hours per week, and 15% reported studying 12 or more hours per week.

While some educators have noted the possible benefits of gaming   18
as a learning tool, most gamers (69%) reported having no exposure to video, computer, or Internet gaming in the classroom for educational purposes. However, one third (32%) of students surveyed admitted

playing games that were not part of the instructional activities during classes.

Impact of Gaming on College Students' Social Lives

Students felt that gaming had mostly positive, and few negative, effects   19
on their social lives. Most college student gamers seem to associate positive feelings with gaming, such as "pleasant" (36%), "exciting"(34%), and "challenging" (45%). Fewer students reported feeling frustrated (12%), bored (11%), or stressed (6%) by gaming. Specifically, students cited gaming as a way to spend more time with friends. One out of every five (20%) gaming students felt moderately or strongly that gaming helped them make new friends as well as improve their existing friendships. When asked if gaming has taken away time they might spend with friends and family, two-thirds of respondents (65%) said gaming has had little to no influence in this regard. Gaming also appears to play a surrogate role for some gamers when friends are unavailable. Nearly two-thirds (60%) of students surveyed agreed that gaming, either moderately or strongly, helped them spend time when friends were not available.

Based on college student responses, video and online gaming   20
seem especially well suited to their social nature, while computer gaming appears a more solitary activity. Nearly half (46%) of video gamers reported playing multi-player games, while only 1 in 5 (20%) of them reported playing online games. During our observations of computer use in public settings, some students were seen sitting at neighboring computers directing each other to interesting games and entertainment on their terminals, and sharing "war stories" about victories and defeats in particular games. Some were also seen typing into instant message-like dialogue boxes featured on interactive, multi-player games such as Yahoo! Towers.

College students are indeed aware of possible negative conse-   21
quences from gaming, although they seem to perceive these risks as minimum. Despite some agreement among them that gaming can have a positive impact on friendships, more than half (57%) felt moderately or strongly that time spent gaming with friends was not "quality time." Still, almost one in three (28%) reported that gaming took them away from other leisure activities either "some" or "a lot." A majority of college students (62%) said that only "some" or "vulnerable" players[10] are negatively influenced by video, computer, or

---

[10]"Vulnerable" players are those who respondents believed might be more at risk of social isolation due to gaming, while "some" players include all types of gamers.

online games. And an even greater majority (76%) felt that only some or few college students exposed to gaming become "gaming addicts."

Specific Game Preferences

College students' specific gaming preferences varied more within   22
video gaming than in computer and video formats, but all contained elements of excitement and engagement. College students ranked realistic graphics (23%) as the most important feature of a good game, with excitement a very close second (22%), and interactivity (15%) third in importance. Racing (26%), role-playing/adventure (17%), and arcade (16%) games were the most popular among college video gamers, while card games were the predominant interest of both computer (70%) and Internet (15%) student gamers. All other game types were played in marginal numbers among Internet gamers.

Students reported little interest in "socially undesirable" games.   23
Less than 4% reported playing sex games of any kind (video .5%, computer .5%, Internet 1% or other 1%) and only a small number (4%) have gambled online. Self-reporting on such behaviors is notoriously inaccurate, especially in regard to pornography use. While it is possible that the number of users of such games may be higher the confidential and anonymous nature of this survey ought to have promoted accurate responses.

IMPLICATIONS OF COLLEGE STUDENTS' GAMING FOR THE FUTURE

Despite the fact that online gaming is one of the fastest growing enter-   24
tainment industry branches, there is remarkably little data on the development and acceptance of this new medium and even less about its impact on adults. Market research tends to focus on game adoption and revenue and is largely predictive. Research by social scientists tends to focus on potential social problem areas, such as gaming addiction, social isolation, or emerging violence and aggression primarily in children 18 years and younger. So far, studies dealing with everyday use and the integration of gaming in children's social lives are still neglected. Based on the studies available, one does not even know who is playing electronic games based on categories of race, gender, age, religion, and income, all of which are important in understanding who does or does not have access to online gaming technology and whether it is used at home, at school, at work, or at some other publicly accessible gaming operation.

Table 5.   Which one of the following do you play the most?

	Video games	Computer games	Internet games
Male	53%	19%	12%
Female	17%	32%	15%

Source: Pew Internet & American Life Project College Students Gaming Survey, n=1162. Margin of error is ±3.5%.

This study attempted to remedy some of those shortcomings. In   25
our research, for example, significant gender differences were found.
While men mainly reported their main reason for playing games as
being for fun (45%), most women reported playing them mainly when
bored (33%) and half (22%) as many women as men said their main
reason for playing games is for fun. Women were much less likely to
believe that gaming improved their relationship with friends than men
believed (51% of women compared with 34% of men). Women reported
playing computer games the most, while men reported playing video
games the most (Table 5).

Young people in academic settings have been found to be heavy   26
users of the Internet, and early adopters of new technology.[11] This
makes them an ideal group for studying trends in Internet and technology use and therefore and ideal population on which to focus the
research of gaming use. While the study of new technology use can
only claim to capture a snapshot of a continually metamorphosing
geography, it is our hope that this early attempt to more clearly define
the path of electronic and online gaming will provide a strong foundation for future research in the field.

Perhaps the most important trend spotted is the integration of   27
gaming into other activities. Students would take time between classes
to play a game, play a game while visiting with friends or instant messaging, or they would play games as a brief distraction from writing
papers or doing other work. The compartmentalization of leisure activities that their parents have internalized is largely unknown to the current group of college students. That is not to say that they are unable to
relax—quite the contrary. But their leisure is taken in sips rather than
gulps, as a breather between other activities.

Gaming is also leading today's college students toward consider-   28
ing interaction as a routine component of entertainment. The number
that were observed either playing multiplayer online games, instant
messaging while gaming or chatting with friends in the same room

---

[11]See Jones, Steve, et al, "College Students and the Web" (available at: http://www.
pewinternet.org/reports/toc.asp?Report=73)

while gaming, along with the number that reported playing games frequently at a friend's house, leads to the conclusion that gaming is less a solitary activity and more one that is shared with friends and others. Increasing adoption of "always on" broadband technologies and Internet enabled cell phones will likely further contribute to the interactive uses of gaming and entertainment today's college student will pursue.

METHODOLOGY

This report is based on the findings of a survey given to college students at two-year and four-year public and private colleges and universities in the continental United States. Paper surveys were randomly distributed at a wide range of higher education institutions by researchers at the University of Illinois at Chicago between March 2002 and June 2002 and between August 2002 and October 2002. Conducting a survey in this manner allowed researchers to guarantee that participants would remain anonymous as the surveys asked questions regarding students' feelings and attitudes about certain aspects of Internet usage as well as other information that might be considered personal or sensitive. Paper surveys also made it possible for researchers to reach college students in a manner that telephone surveying would not have allowed.

29

Surveys were distributed to undergraduate and graduate students enrolled in degree-seeking programs at 27 institutions of higher education across the United States. The sample was intended to produce results that would correspond to the demographics for college students reported in *The Chronicle of Higher Education*'s annual almanac issue.[12] The sample was tested against known population parameters (gender, race, age) and found to be reflective of the national population of college students as reported by *The Chronicle*. Each student was asked to fill out either a survey about his/her academic uses of the Internet or his/her social uses of the Internet. In all, 1162 surveys were returned between March 2002 and June 2002, and September 2002 and October 2002. For results based on the total sample, one can say with 95% confidence that the error attributable to sampling and other random effects is plus or minus 3.5 percentage points. In addition to sampling error, question wording and practical difficulties in conducting surveys may introduce some error or bias into the findings.

30

Ethnographic data was collected by a team of graduate student researchers at the University of Illinois at Chicago. The researchers

31

---

[12]*The Chronicle of Higher Education*, Almanac Issue 2001–2, 158(1), August 31, 2001 and Almanac Issue 2002–3, 159(1), August 30, 2002.

were recruited to observe the behaviors of college students at numerous Chicago area institutions of higher education. The researchers were trained in ethnographic methods of observation and data collecting, and rotated the times of the day and days of the week they spent in various public settings where college students could be found using the Internet. Observations took place between March 2002 and June 2002.

Additional material is based on the findings of a survey of   32
Americans about their use of the Internet. These results are based on data from telephone interviews conducted by Princeton Survey Research Associates in 2001, among a sample of 16,125 Internet users, 18 and older, who have broadband Internet access. For results based on the total sample, one can say with 95% confidence that the error attributable to sampling and other random effects is plus or minus 2 percentage points. In addition to sampling error, question wording and practical difficulties in conducting telephone surveys may introduce some error or bias into the findings of opinion polls. At least 10 attempts were made to complete an interview at every household in the sample. The calls were staggered over times of day and days of the week to maximize the chances of making contact with a potential respondent. Interview refusals were re-contacted at least once in order to try again to complete an interview.

Examining the Text

1. What distinctions does the author make between video games, computer games, and Internet games? Do you think these are accurate distinctions or do you see any overlap among these categories?

2. According to Jones, what gender differences are there in the playing of video games, computer games, and Internet games? Do you see these gender differences in the game playing of your friends as well?

3. Comparing the leisure activities of students today to the "compartmentalization" of their parents, Jones writes that students today take their leisure "in sips rather than gulps" (paragraph 27). What does he mean by this mean analogy? What do you think of his comparison of the leisure patterns of students and parents?

4. Briefly explain the methodology of this study. What do you see as the strengths and weaknesses of this method of research?

5. *Thinking rhetorically*: Imagine that administrators at your college are considering building a video arcade on campus. They've scheduled a public debate on the project in order to hear the views of the campus community. Which facts and findings could supporters of the video arcade project take from the article to help them advance their argument? Conversely, which facts and findings could opponents of the project take from the article in order to advance their argument? What

overall conclusions can you draw from the fact that this article can be
used to support arguments that are diametrically opposed?

For Group Discussion
Jones presents the results of many questions asked by researchers at various universities and colleges. Before meeting with others in your discussion group, go back through the article and choose two or three results of
the study that you found surprising. Be prepared to say what you thought
was surprising about each result. Then in your group, have each person
explain what they selected as surprising results and why. As a group, discuss where your own experiences and expectations about video, computer, and Internet game use differ from what was reported in the study.

Writing Suggestion
The report includes five small charts that visually represent results of
the study—that is, charts that give percentages and categories for specific questions asked by the researchers. Choose a result that isn't
already visually represented, and create a chart or graph to show the
percentages and categories for the question. You can either draw the
chart or use a word processing program (such as Microsoft Word) or a
charting program (such as Microsoft Excel) to create the chart. After
you've created the chart, write a paragraph to describe and analyze the
results that are represented in the chart.

Playing War: The Emerging Trend of Real Virtual Combat in Current Video Games

Brian Cowlishaw

*While the previous article gives a broad overview of the gaming habits of col-
lege students, the following article focuses in on a particular genre of video
game—the realistic war game—and attempts to discover why this genre is
popular and what influence it might have on people who play it. According to
Brian Cowlishaw, an Assistant Professor of English at Northeastern State
University, the realistic war game video is a type of first-person shooter that
purports to recreate an actual war battle. As Cowlishaw discusses, certain elements in realistic war games are much more realistic than what is found in the
usual first-person shooter video games. But there are important ways in which
these "real virtual combat" games are unrealistic and present a misleading*

view of what war is like. Cowlishaw also traces connections between realistic war video games and training and recruitment in the U.S. military. Here he demonstrates a very specific influence that video games have on individuals, particularly on young people who are thinking of joining the military.

*It isn't until the last paragraph of the article that Cowlishaw explicitly states his opinion of realistic war video games—and he states it very forcefully. **As you read**, try to anticipate what Cowlishaw's ultimate opinion will be. What clues do you see as you read the article that indicate Cowlishaw's opinion on what he's writing about?*

While video games have been around for some time now, they have   1
emerged, in recent years, as a major player on the profit scene. Indeed, for the past two years, the video game market has made more money than the motion picture business. Perhaps that's why filmmakers often release video game versions of their films months before theatrical release—in order to heat up the marketplace for their film.

The latest trend in video games, such as the *Medal of Honor* series,   2
the *Battlefield* series, and *America's Army*, is to be especially "realistic." Such games proudly transport the gamer into immersive, gut wrenching virtual battlefields. They persuade the gamer that, in an echo of WWII-era journalism, "You Are There"—on the beaches of Normandy, in the jungles of Vietnam, in modern military hotspots.

Upon examination, this now-common claim raises other key   3
questions. First, and perhaps most obviously: To what degree is this claim to realism justified? In other words, are the games truly as historically accurate as their makers and players claim? Answering that question raises a series of more significant and telling questions: What do these games signify? Being war games, why are they so popular now? Who benefits from this popularity, and how?

The games that most stridently and persuasively claim to be realistic,   4
and therefore those games on which I will focus, are first-person shooters (FPSs) which purport to recreate full-scale real-world battles. For the uninitiated, the phrase "first-person" in "first-person shooters" refers to the player's point of view: onscreen appears a pair of forearms and hands aiming a weapon forward "into" the screen. The hands are "you." That gun is "your" gun. Players use controls (keyboard, mouse, and/or game controller) to virtually look up, down, and around onscreen, and the result looks and feels like brandishing a weapon. The word "shooter" in "first-person shooter" refers to what the player does: move around a "map" (virtual battlefield) and deploy an arsenal of weapons against virtual enemies.

Unreal Tournament provides clear examples of standard FPS con- 5
ventions. One key convention is that weapons, ammunition, armor,
and first-aid kits regularly and frequently "spawn," that is, suddenly
appear out of nowhere. Simply running over them onscreen confers
their benefits immediately; there is almost no time wasted simulating
using the first-aid kits, or reloading the weapons. Second, all FPS players die a lot, even when they're winning. The goal is to rack up the
most "frags," or kills, so how often they die is really irrelevant. Dead
players immediately respawn at a semi-random spot on the map, then
get right back to killing. Finally, FPSs revel in offering ungenteel, gore-
intensive gameplay. Players can be slimed, shot, sniped, razored,
exploded, or chainsawed to death onscreen. Bodies hit just right, with
the right weapon, fly apart into bloody chunks of flesh.

Realistic war games are recent specialized offshoots of the 6
broader FPS genre. The first FPS was *Wolfenstein*; *Medal of Honor*,
published a decade later, is probably the first realistic war game. This
genealogical relationship—realistic war games' direct descent from
FPSs—becomes apparent with close scrutiny. This genealogical relationship also means that while realistic war games are generally
more realistic than other FPSs, they still retain significant unrealistic
qualities.

One key unrealistic quality of putatively realistic war games 7
might be called "self-assessment." Players have onscreen at all times
thorough, accessible-at-a-glance information regarding their condition. They can see the status of their armor, their physical health
expressed as a precise percentage, and their ammunition stores for
every single weapon. Obviously, this level of self-knowledge is
unavailable in real life. We may have a fairly keen sense of how healthy
or unhealthy we feel, and if we have just had a blood or other test we
may even be able to express this feeling with some precision. But this
precision never approaches that in a FPS: we could never say, "I'm
81% healthy, and my clothes are providing 34% protection." Thus, for
a simulation of war truly to be realistic, such information would have
to remain vague or difficult to obtain. Yet there it is, right onscreen
constantly in all of the new war games—just as in unashamedly unrealistic other FPSs.

Surprisingly, another FPS convention preserved by the realistic 8
war games is respawning. For example, in the *Medal of Honor* games,
when players die they are magically transported back to the beginning
of the scenario, with all their original weapons and health restored, to
try again. This makes sense not only from a games-history perspective,
but also from an entertainment perspective: it's no fun if dying
onscreen means the game is over. Players want to get right back up and

fight some more. Obviously, though, real life does not work this way. Death tends to be final—but not in war video games.

Not only is death in this way banished from the games, but sig-   9
nificantly, so is bodily dismemberment. Game makers systematically exclude it, much in the way Paul Fussell shows it was excluded from images and accounts of World War II. He observes that in such accounts, with very few exceptions, "the bodies of the dead, if inert, are intact. Bloody, sometimes, and sprawled in awkward positions, but except for the absence of life, plausible and acceptable simulacra of the people they once were. . . . American bodies (decently clothed) are occasionally in evidence, but they are notably intact." The famous photographic collection *Life Goes to War*, for example, shows only three dismembered bodies—specifically, heads. It is significant that they are not American but Asian heads. They are displayed as trophies of our soldiers' prowess. Always showing American bodies intact directly counters real-world facts and probabilities: as Fussell points out, it was "as likely for the man next to you to be shot through the eye, ear, testicles, or brain as (the way the cinema does it) through the shoulder. A shell is as likely to blow his whole face off as to lodge a fragment in some mentionable and unvital tissue." In fact, it was also quite common for a soldier to be wounded or killed not by a bullet or shell but by a flying body part—a foot, a skull, a ribcage.

Obviously, game makers could include such graphic details if   10
they wanted to: *Unreal Tournament*, five years old at this writing, which is a dinosaur in computer time, displays gore galore. The technology for depicting dismemberment convincingly onscreen is quite capable nowadays, so clearly war game makers choose not to do it. They do in war video games what wartime journalists such as Ernie Pyle did in writing: purposely, systematically remove gory details so as to make the war more palatable—as opposed to more truly realistic. One of Pyle's best-known stories involves the return of the body of one Captain Henry T. Waskow "of Belton, Texas," to his grieving company. One of the men reportedly sat by the body for a long time, holding the captain's hand and looking into his face; then he "reached over and gently straightened the points of the captain's shirt collar, and then he sort of arranged the tattered edges of the uniform around the wound." As Fussell points out, Pyle's geographical and behavioral precision calls attention to the essential information that he glosses over:

1. What killed Captain Waskow? Bullet, shell fragments, a mine, or what?
2. Where was his wound? How large was it? He implies that it was in the traditional noble place, the chest. Was it? Was it a little hole, or was it a great red missing place? Was it perhaps in the crotch,

or in the testicles, or in the belly? Were his entrails extruded, or in any way visible?

3. How much blood was there? Was the captain's uniform bloody? Did the faithful soldier wash off his hands after toying with those "tattered edges"? Were the captain's eyes open? Did his face look happy? Surprised? Satisfied? Angry?

Like wartime press reports, war video games carefully elide this most basic fact of wartime: bodily damage.   11

The most plainly unrealistic element of the war games is the existence of the games themselves. That is, players always remain inescapably aware of two very important facts. First, the war is never finally real. Players are not, in fact, dashing around a battlefield but rather sitting in a comfortable chair. They grip a controller, or keyboard and mouse, not a Garand rifle. There is no actual danger of being killed, or physically harmed beyond getting stiff and fat from playing video games too long. No matter how immersive or even realistic the game, one can never forget that it is "just a game." Second, players may play the game, but in an important sense the game plays them. There is always a "proper" outcome, a pre-scripted story one must complete correctly, especially when the game pits the player against the computer rather than against other flesh-and-blood players. There is always a specific task to carry out, such as to storm Normandy Beach and rout the Germans from their bunkers; the ideal for game programmers is to make such tasks challenging but possible. Players' job, then, is to find the correct solution to a puzzle someone else constructed; they are in a significant sense acted upon rather than acting. In life, of course, we can choose badly or well, but we can choose. This rat-in-a-maze aspect, together with the game's inescapable "game-ness," reminds players every moment that games fundamentally differ from real life; playing a game is inherently unrealistic.   12

Nevertheless, talk abounds regarding how realistic the current war video games are. *Official Xbox Magazine*'s comments on *Full Spectrum Warrior* are typical of the glee with which players and critics greet the newly "realistic" war games. The magazine effuses, "Now when you send your troops into a slaughter in *Full Spectrum Warrior*, you'll have to look in their eyes and hear their screams." Apparently this is a good thing. *OXM* also raves, "with [its] 5:1 [sound] it really feels like you are in the middle of a combat zone (turn it up loud enough and your neighbors might think so as well)." One fan anticipating *Battlefield: Vietnam*'s release on EBGames.com writes, "this will alow a more real taste of the war [sic]." Another, purporting to   13 speak for all of us, claims, "U know how u always wanted to know what the Vietnam War was like [sic]. I think this game will show you."

There is some justification for these claims to realism. Sound is one   14
area in which the new war games truly do reproduce wartime accurately. Sound effects are as accurate and inclusive as visual representations are sanitized and edited. The realistic war games—for example, *America's Army*, the *Battlefield* series, and the *Medal of Honor* series—reproduce all of the rumbling machinery, gunfire, artillery, explosions, footsteps, splats, ricochets, shouted orders, swearing, and wounded cries one would hear in a real war. And current computer/television sound technology—now standardized at seven points in the room—reproduces all these sounds with perfect clarity at 100+ decibels.

In addition to sound, the war games also reproduce historical cir-   15
cumstances with comparative accuracy. The games do allow players to virtually fight in battles that really did occur—famous ones such as the Normandy invasion, Pearl Harbor, and the Tet Offensive. In-game soldiers use weapons that look and perform more or less like real weapons that real soldiers used. In-game soldiers dress, look, and speak like real soldiers did. The games may not be completely historically faithful in these elements, but they certainly are more so than other, older FPSs. The genealogical relationship makes the newer war games seem more realistic than they are.

Compare any current realistic war game, for example, with   16
Unreal Tournament. In *UT*, the voices and character models ("skins") are a self-consciously over-the-top assortment of idealized macho warriors and ridiculous comic figures. In addition to the macho grunts, my copy features the downloaded voices of Fat Bastard (from the Austin Powers movies), Eric Cartman (from *South Park*), and Homer Simpson (from *The Simpsons*). Players can choose *UT* deathmatchers' appearances: onscreen fighters can be assigned any skin from a giant, scary lizardman, to a stereotypical macho male (or female), to Captain America, to Dr. Frankenfurter (from *The Rocky Horror Picture Show*). Any voice can be assigned to any skin: one might arrange a Dr. Frankenfurter with Cartman's voice, or a skull-faced badass who talks like Homer Simpson. These zany characters' weapons similarly aim for entertaining gameplay rather than factual accuracy. *UT* features rocket launchers, handheld frag cannons, plasma rifles, and sludge guns. The battles in which these crazy weapons are used take place on obviously artificial, nonreferential staging grounds. That is, the in-game battle sites are not intended to reproduce historical locations. They clearly exist solely so that players can virtually blast the hell out of each other in visually interesting, strategically challenging settings—and the more fantastic, the better. References to real-world locales tend to be ironic, humorous: "Hey look, here's a map like a football field!" "Here's one set on a

cruise ship!" I certainly hope real deathmatches never take place in such locales. Classic FPSs, as opposed to realistic war games, are judged by how intense a deathmatch they can produce, not by how accurately they reproduce "the real Normandy."

Overall "presentation," too, proves comparatively realistic in the new war games. "Presentation" refers to the way a game is laid out for the player in terms of menu choices, art, and sound; we might call it "atmosphere." In *Medal of Honor: Frontline*, for example, menu choices take the form of file folders stamped with the (now-defunct) Office of Strategic Services logo. All in-game fonts look typewritten by period typewriters. "Your" portrait in the menu file appears attached by low-tech paper clip. Selecting a menu option produces a gunshot or file-rustling sound. In the *America's Army* game, menu headings use terminology lifted from the real-world America's Army: "Personnel Jacket," "Training Missions," "Deployment," and so on. This kind of attention to making the presentation realistic enhances the overall impression that the game accurately recreates history. Compared to the three-ring FPS circus that is their origin, the new realistic war games appear positively photographic in their historical fidelity. Even gamers, disposed by nature to find all flaws, perceive them as faithful to what the games purport to recreate.

So far, I have discussed two fairly black-and-white categories, "realistic" and "unrealistic," so that I can make descriptions clearly. But the truth is, the issue is much more complicated than that binary choice. It's more accurate to say that the games blur the boundaries between real and virtual, or mix elements of the one in among the other, so thoroughly that players finally cannot tell where reality ends and virtual reality begins.

One telling example appears in the required marksman-training mission that begins *America's Army*. The player must hit a specified number of targets within a time limit. After passing the test, the player receives hearty applause from the drill sergeant: "Congratulations, soldier! You have just qualified as a marksman in the United States Army!" I must admit: the first time I passed this test, I became moderately alarmed—he did mean I virtually qualified, right? So many other kinds of transactions take place online nowadays; why not real-life recruitment and qualification?

The idea that by playing a realistic war game for a few minutes I may have inadvertently enlisted is not as outlandish as it may seem out of context. Consider: the real-world *America's Army* created, programmed, and distributed, for free online, the game called *America's Army*, specifically for the purpose of recruitment. Anyone can download it for free, right now, at americasarmy.com. The real army counts on people, mostly young men ripe for recruitment, to download the game, enjoy it, think to themselves, "Hey, you know, I should do this for real," and then go enlist. Apparently the strategy is working very effectively. In late March 2004, the *CBS Evening News* reported on a huge *America's Army* gaming tournament. Hundreds of thousands of dollars in prize money and computer equipment were at stake. Several recruiters sat in the competition room. Hundreds of players walked directly from their round of competition over to sign up with recruiters. CBS reported that since the game was released in 2002, recruitment has spiked; the video game is the most effective recruitment tool since the Uncle Sam "I Want You" posters during World War II.

This video game recruitment strategy meshes very neatly with   21
the Army's recent advertising campaign. The Army shows images of underage kids essentially playing games—flying a remote-controlled plane in one, and actually playing a video game in another. Then the same people (presumably) are shown as young adults doing pretty much the same activities in the Army: the model plane flyer pilots a decoy drone plane, and the video gamer efficiently directs real tanks and troops around a battlefield. The clear message is: "You should join the real Army because we will pay you to play pretty much the same games you play for fun right now. You were born for this."

Full Spectrum Warrior blurs reality and gaming perhaps even more   22
thoroughly. Like *America's Army*, this game was produced by the real U.S. Army. In fact, it's not entirely clear that the end result was the choice of the game's original developer, William Stahl. In an interview with *Official Xbox Magazine*, Stahl describes how the game got made: "Three years ago, I was pitching a... game for the PC. Representatives of the Army were looking for a developer to create a training simulation on a videogame console. They got ahold of those early documents and thought the concept was right in line with what they wanted to achieve. . . . This game was developed in conjunction with the Army. They were essentially our publisher, and as such, they had the final say on what they wanted in the game, how it looked, etc." This statement raises worrisome questions:

1. How did the Army get "ahold" of those early documents?
2. How much choice of publisher did Stahl and company actually have?

In any case, the Army ultimately made two versions, one of   23
which is being used right now by real American soldiers for training, and a very similar version being sold in stores. Real soldiers and couch bound warriors alike learn battle tactics by playing a video game. Thus, the real and the virtual become indistinguishable. The U.S. Army

recruits real soldiers by appealing to them through video games and suggests that video gamers' virtual prowess and enjoyment translate directly into real-world Army suitability and success.

In one important sense, the first-person-shooter genre itself 24 contributes to this fusion of the real and the virtual. In recent years, in-game instructions have become standard parts of all FPSs and most video games in general; James Paul Gee explains in detail, in his book *What Video Games Have to Teach Us about Learning and Literacy*, how they help the player learn to "read" and understand the game, to figure out what to do in the game world. So, for example, in *America's Army*, the sergeant character gives the player basic directions to get started. He gives commands like, "Press <G> to fix jammed weapon," "Press <T> to bring up sights," and "Press <B> to reload." In doing so, he merges the player's onscreen and real-life identities. The sergeant is onscreen, talking to the player's onscreen representation; but he's giving directions that only the real-world person can carry out. The onscreen representation doesn't have a G, T, or B button to push—it's the real-world person doing that. Similarly, in *Medal of Honor: Frontline* the player is to "press Select to get hints from HQ," and "press Start to review mission objectives." In-game, players are spoken to as their real-world self and their onscreen self simultaneously and without differentiation, which means those identities merge.

With the real and the virtual mingling so thoroughly in war 25 video games, perhaps it's only natural that both players and game makers reproduce and perpetuate this fusion in the way they talk. It's not some kind of schizophrenia or delusion, it's the ordinary, proper response to the postmodern facts. For example, imagining someone playing *Full Spectrum Warrior* with guns blazing rather than cautiously and strategically, William Stahl predicts, "His men will die. Mothers will lose their son, wives will lose their husbands, and children will lose their fathers." *OXM* also warns, "Don't press [the Action] button [in this game] until you've assessed the situation and made the right plan or it'll be the last button you press." Er, they do mean in-game. . . right? Thus, it's not so outlandish for the magazine to call *Full Spectrum Warrior* "The Game That Captured Saddam." *OXM* explains, "This game was made to train the US Army infantry. . . they're the ones who dug Saddam out of his hole. So technically this game caught Saddam." Nor is it as insane as it might first appear when one gamer writes in anticipation of playing *Battlefield: Vietnam*, "The Vietnam War was said to be a draw, but when this game comes out everyone will see that the U.S.A. is the best army in the world." His comment suggests that an alleged misperception of history—namely, that the U.S. did not decisively win that war—will be corrected by people's playing the game. He's epistemologically assuming, and rhetorically suggesting, that not only do video games refer to and simulate real-world battles, but because this is so, they also provide players an accurate recreative picture of history. In this understanding, war games not only borrow from history, they also teach it.   26

Many veterans' and historical organizations have bestowed awards on games such as the *Medal of Honor* series for their educational value. *Medal of Honor: Frontline*'s official sales copy at EBGames.com boasts, "Authentic WWII content with the assistance of the Smithsonian's . . . expert Russ Lee and renowned technical consultant Capt. Dale Dye," and, "The MOH team continues to work closely with the Congressional Medal of Honor Society to ensure the ideals and integrity of this prestigious commendation." Not incidentally, that game awards the Congressional Medal of Honor for especially meritorious military action—in-game. If players complete a given mission quickly enough and safely enough, they win a virtual medal. *MOH: Frontline* also unlocks documentary movie clips and historical speech excerpts as rewards for good performance in the game, and it mixes game elements, such as the game's logo and menus, and historical elements, such as documentary film clips and an exhortative speech by Dwight D. Eisenhower, without any differentiation of importance or validity. They all "feel real." Current war video games have blended and blurred the real and the virtual.   27

Because that is so, the games' romanticizing of war becomes all the more seductive and powerful. Any truly realistic recreation of war would cast some doubt on the idea that war is cool and enjoyable, and that, as in sports, all one has to do is "step up" and become an instant hero. But the titles alone hint at how current war video games support this old myth: *Call of Duty, Full Spectrum Warrior, Medal of Honor*. Players can almost taste the medals, just reading the game box. In-game, it immediately becomes clear that the war effort would never get off the ground without the player's personal, constant heroics. What the U. S. Army claims in its current advertising slogan is absolutely true: the player really is "An Army of One." Never mind the Army's famous unwieldy, illogical bureaucracy made famous in works such as *Catch-22* and *M*A*S*H*. Never mind the fact that boot camp is famously designed to tear down the individual to replace that entity with a small cog in a giant machine. Contrary to common-sense facts, the war game player is always "An Army of One." *Medal of Honor: Frontline*'s first mission provides a brilliant example of this. During this mission, "you" are ordered onscreen to storm the beach at Normandy under heavy machine-gun and rifle fire, provide covering fire for three soldiers widely separated along the beach, run lengthwise down the beach to an engineer then cover his run all the way back, cross a minefield, storm a machine-gun nest and take it over, mow down a wave of advancing German soldiers with that machine-gun, and finally snipe two far-off machine-gunners while still under fire. And that's just the first mission! What must the odds be that any individual would a) be present at D-Day; b) be asked to personally complete every single necessary task at that battle; and c) survive to complete them all successfully, thus winning that battle singlehandedly? The whole game continues like that: the player is assigned all the work at all the key European battles, eventually bringing about V-E Day completely solo.   28

This begins to answer the important question, "Why would someone want to realistically recreate the experience of war? Isn't it just common sense to avoid being there?" One game magazine editor raises exactly this question when he writes, "With the new wave of games pushing the envelope of realism it begs the question: how real do we want it? Do we want games that'll simulate war to such a degree that it's possible to suffer from post-game-atic syndrome?" Judging by the state of the games now, the answer for both gamers and game makers is a resounding "No." For all their attention to accurately recreating sounds, weapons, locales, and uniforms, and for all their visual drama and flair, the new "realistic" war video games do not, in fact, reproduce the real conditions of war. They still play too much like other FPSs, and significantly, like goreless FPSs. Although players see soldiers being blown into the air by mines, riddled with machine-gun fire, and sniped from all directions, they never see blood or a flying body part, ever.   29

Thus, I would argue, what the new war games are is not realistic, but cinematic. They don't reproduce the real world experience of war; they do reproduce the theatrical experience of war. Games use all of the same techniques as movies for framing shots, editing, pacing, and narration. Playing one of the new war video games is very much like starring in a war movie. For example, the *MOH: Frontline* opening mission is a rather accurate, if condensed, version of the first thirty minutes of *Saving Private Ryan*, even down to individual camera shots: bullets whizzing along underwater past slowly sinking soldiers, and the company's seeking cover under a low hill while the engineer blows away the barbed wire barrier. *Medal of Honor: Rising Sun* similarly steals heavily from the much less well-made movie Pearl Harbor. H. L. Mencken once described art as "life with all the boring parts taken out." War has been described as 99 percent boredom punctuated by short bursts of abject terror. No one in their right mind would want to reproduce that, and, in recent war video games, no one does. Instead, the games are, in essence, interactive movies about war with all the boring parts taken out. But the boring parts were already pretty much taken out by the movies, so in the games, all that's left is action, action, action—the player winning a war single handedly. The war games make players heroes, in a bloodless, risk-free environment where they can show off their "mad skillz."

As it turns out, then, logical answers do exist for the question, "Why in the world would anyone want to recreate the experience of war?" First, the games don't do quite that; rather, they recreate movies about the experience of war. The additional remove is key. Playing the games provides an entertaining, cinematic experience, rather than the horrible one a true recreation would give. Even if the imagery is not pleasing, it certainly is immersive. And as Miroslaw Filiciak points out, we value the experience of immersion in itself. We intentionally over-look unconvincing elements of the experience so as to become more fully immersed: "We desire the experience of immersion, so we use our intelligence to reinforce rather than to question the reality of the experi-ence." In short, it doesn't really matter that the war games aren't fully realistic; gamers enjoy them for what they are, interactive movies that temporarily immerse us in the games' battles. The second answer to the question, "Why would anyone want to recreate the experience of war?" is to play the hero, in a cinematically intense experience in which we can play an active part rather than just settling passively down into our couches and watching as movies force us to do. And third, we get to see ourselves onscreen playing the hero. Filiciak observes: "Contemporary people have a fascination with electronic media, something we cannot define, something that escapes our rationalizations. . . . We make the screen a fetish; we desire it, not only do we want to watch the screen but also to 'be seen' on it . . . being on the screen ennobles. All the time we have the feeling (more or less true) that others are watching us. The existence of an audience is an absolute necessity." We can see "our-selves" onscreen in any video game, but in online war games such as *America's Army* and *Battlefield: Vietnam*, we can also be seen by other players. We can show off our skills, and brag about our victories, to others who have just witnessed them. We can enact the electronic equivalent of dancing in the end zone.

The reasons for making the new war video games are even more obvious than those for playing them. Foremost, there's the money. As I mentioned at the beginning of this article, Americans now spend more money on video games than on movies. Games are huge business, and they're steadily getting huger. One key game maker, the real-world U.S. Army—and by extension, the other service branches and the federal government as a whole—reaps huge benefits from the games' popularity. Not only does the current hawkish regime gain flesh-and-blood recruits for the armed services, it also gains general credibility and support as the games work their propagandist magic. By hiding ugly realities and

30

31

producing cinematic cotton candy, the games make real war seem exciting, heroic, even fun. And so hawkish political candidates seem not bellicose, but reasonable. Rapidly escalating defense costs look not wasteful, but common-sensical. Thus our two-front war rolls on and on and on.

Examining the Text

1. According to Cowlishaw, what is the relationship between realistic war games and first-person shooter (FPS) games? What are the similarities and differences between these two types of video games?

2. What are some of the differences between playing a realistic war video game and being involved in an actual, real-world war battle? Why do you think Cowlishaw spends the first part of his article focusing on the differences between video games depicting wars and real life war experiences?

3. In what ways, according to Cowlishaw, do war video games blur the distinctions between real and virtual fighting? What examples does Cowlishaw provide to show the results of this blurring?

4. What does Cowlishaw mean when he says that realistic war games reproduce the cinematic experience of war? What problems result from this, according to Cowlishaw?

5. *Thinking rhetorically*: Following up on the "as you read" suggestion in the introduction to this article, what features of the article did you identify as giving clues about Cowlishaw's opinion of video war games? What are the advantages in Cowlishaw's strategy of waiting until the end of the article to state his opinion explicitly? What are the disadvantages?

For Group Discussion

Cowlishaw draws a number of connections between video war games and the U.S. military. For instance, he notes that the U.S. Army uses a video game for the training of actual soldiers. As a group, make a list of all the connections that are mentioned by Cowlishaw. Then discuss which of these connections you think are appropriate and which ones you think are questionable or misleading. Keep in mind that people in the group might have strong opinions that differ from your own. Try to present evidence to support your opinion and to argue for it reasonably.

Writing Suggestion

Cowlishaw focuses on a particular genre of video game in order to find out why it's appealing to users and what effect it might have on our culture. Your assignment is to choose another genre of video game and do a similar analysis. Choose a genre that you're familiar with, or interview someone you know who is familiar with this genre of video game. Begin your analysis of the game by first describing it: What is the purpose of the game? Who are the characters and what activities do they engage in? How does one win the game? Once you've described the game, speculate on what its influence might be on people who play it regularly. What skills do they develop and what lessons do they learn from the game? How do these lessons translate in real life? You might conclude your analysis by suggesting whether you think the game exerts a mostly positive or negative influence on its players.

2. Blogging

Weblogs: A History and Perspective

Rebecca Blood

You might find it a bit odd to be reading the "history" of something that's less than a decade old. Even odder is the fact that the first weblog (or blog) was published in 1998, and the first "history" of weblogs, which you're about to read, was published just two years later in 2000. But as Rebecca Blood points out, in those two years many changes took place, most notably in the number of blogs that existed on the Web. From a handful in November of 1998 to thousands in September of 2000, blogs grew exponentially. Blood notes that software like Blogger (http://www.blogger.com) made it easy and cheap (that is, free!) for people to publish their words on the Web, and people did.

Blood discusses two different types of weblogs that you can find on the Web: filter-style and journal-style. Filter-style bloggers essentially "pre-surf" the web for their readers. These bloggers usually focus on a particular topic— like baseball, or typography, or the Oklahoma wine industry—and the blogs present commentary and links to sites on this topic. If the topic and the blogger are interesting enough, the blog will gain a wide readership. The second type of blog—the journal-style blog—is a lot like an online diary; bloggers write about events and people in their lives as well as about issues that they think are important. Both types of blogs allow people to publish and be read by others— potentially by hundreds or thousands of others.

As you read, *think about whether you'd ever consider keeping a blog (if you don't already!). Would you want to create a filter-style blog, with commentary and links to sites on topics that you care about? Or would you want to share with the world your thoughts, feelings, and everyday experiences? What do you think motivates other bloggers to create their sites?*

In 1998 there were just a handful of sites of the type that are now identified as weblogs (so named by Jorn Barger in December 1997). Jesse James Garrett, editor of Infosift, began compiling a list of "other sites like his" as he found them in his travels around the web. In November of that year, he sent that list to Cameron Barrett. Cameron published the list on Camworld, and others maintaining similar sites began sending their URLs to him for inclusion on the list. Jesse's 'page of only weblogs' lists the 23 known to be in existence at the beginning of 1999.

Suddenly a community sprang up. It was easy to read all of the   2
weblogs on Cameron's list, and most interested people did. Peter
Merholz announced in early 1999 that he was going to pronounce it
'wee-blog' and inevitably this was shortened to 'blog' with the weblog
editor referred to as a 'blogger.'

At this point, the bandwagon jumping began. More and more   3
people began publishing their own weblogs. I began mine in April of
1999. Suddenly it became difficult to read every weblog every day, or
even to keep track of all the new ones that were appearing. Cameron's
list grew so large that he began including only weblogs he actually followed himself. Other webloggers did the same. In early 1999 Brigitte
Eaton compiled a list of every weblog she knew about and created the
Eatonweb Portal. Brig evaluated all submissions by a simple criterion:
that the site consist of dated entries. Webloggers debated what was
and what was not a weblog, but since the Eatonweb Portal was the
most complete listing of weblogs available, Brig's inclusive definition
prevailed.

This rapid growth continued steadily until July 1999 when Pitas,   4
the first free build-your-own-weblog tool launched, and suddenly
there were hundreds. In August, Pyra released Blogger, and Groksoup
launched, and with the ease that these web-based tools provided, the
bandwagon-jumping turned into an explosion. Late in 1999 software
developer Dave Winer introduced Edit This Page, and Jeff A. Campbell
launched Velocinews. All of these services are free, and all of them are
designed to enable individuals to publish their own weblogs quickly
and easily.

The original weblogs were link-driven sites. Each was a mixture   5
in unique proportions of links, commentary, and personal thoughts
and essays. Weblogs could only be created by people who already
knew how to make a website. A weblog editor had either taught herself
to code HTML for fun, or, after working all day creating commercial
websites, spent several off-work hours every day surfing the web and
posting to her site. These were web enthusiasts.

Many current weblogs follow this original style. Their editors   6
present links both to little-known corners of the web and to current
news articles they feel are worthy of note. Such links are nearly always
accompanied by the editor's commentary. An editor with some expertise in a field might demonstrate the accuracy or inaccuracy of a highlighted article or certain facts therein; provide additional facts he feels
are pertinent to the issue at hand; or simply add an opinion or differing viewpoint from the one in the piece he has linked. Typically this
commentary is characterized by an irreverent, sometimes sarcastic
tone. More skillful editors manage to convey all of these things in the

sentence or two with which they introduce the link (making them, as Halcyon pointed out to me, pioneers in the art and craft of microcontent). Indeed, the format of the typical weblog, providing only a very short space in which to write an entry, encourages pithiness on the part of the writer; longer commentary is often given its own space as a separate essay.

These weblogs provide a valuable filtering function for their readers. The web has been, in effect, pre-surfed for them. Out of the myriad web pages slung through cyberspace, weblog editors pick out the most mind-boggling, the most stupid, the most compelling.   7

But this type of weblog is important for another reason, I think. In Douglas Rushkoff's *Media Virus*, Greg Ruggerio of the Immediast Underground is quoted as saying, "Media is a corporate possession . . . You cannot participate in the media. Bringing that into the foreground is the first step. The second step is to define the difference between public and audience. An audience is passive; a public is participatory. We need a definition of media that is public in its orientation."   8

By highlighting articles that may easily be passed over by the typical web user too busy to do more than scan corporate news sites, by searching out articles from lesser-known sources, and by providing additional facts, alternative views, and thoughtful commentary, weblog editors participate in the dissemination and interpretation of the news that is fed to us every day. Their sarcasm and fearless commentary reminds us to question the vested interests of our sources of information and the expertise of individual reporters as they file news stories about subjects they may not fully understand.   9

Weblog editors sometimes contextualize an article by juxtaposing it with an article on a related subject; each article, considered in the light of the other, may take on additional meaning, or even draw the reader to conclusions contrary to the implicit aim of each. It would be too much to call this type of weblog "independent media," but clearly their editors, engaged in seeking out and evaluating the "facts" that are presented to us each day, resemble the public that Ruggerio speaks of. By writing a few lines each day, weblog editors begin to redefine media as a public, participatory endeavor.   10

Now, during 1999 something else happened, and I believe it has to do with the introduction of Blogger itself.   11

While weblogs had always included a mix of links, commentary, and personal notes, in the post-Blogger explosion increasing numbers of weblogs eschewed this focus on the web-at-large in favor of a sort of short-form journal. These blogs, often updated several times a day, were instead a record of the blogger's thoughts: something noticed on the way to work, notes about the weekend, a quick reflection on some   12 subject or another. Links took the reader to the site of another blogger with whom the first was having a public conversation or had met the previous evening, or to the site of a band he had seen the night before. Full-blown conversations were carried on between three or five blogs, each referencing the other in their agreement or rebuttal of the other's positions. Cults of personality sprung up as new blogs appeared, certain names appearing over and over in daily entries or listed in the obligatory sidebar of "other weblogs" (a holdover from Cam's original list). It was, and is, fascinating to see new bloggers position themselves in this community, referencing and reacting to those blogs they read most, their sidebar an affirmation of the tribe to which they wish to belong.

Why the change? Why so many? I have always suspected that   13
some of the popularity of this form may be a simple desire to emulate the sites of head Pyra kids Ev and Meg. As the creators of Blogger, their charming, witty blogs are their company's foremost advertisement for its most popular product.

More than that, Blogger itself places no restrictions on the form of   14
content being posted. Its web interface, accessible from any browser, consists of an empty form box into which the blogger can type . . . anything: a passing thought, an extended essay, or a childhood recollection. With a click, Blogger will post the . . . whatever . . . on the writer's website, archive it in the proper place, and present the writer with another empty box, just waiting to be filled.

Contrast this with the web interface of Metafilter, a popular   15
community weblog. Here, the writer is presented with three form boxes: the first for the URL of the referenced site, the second for the title of the entry, and the third for whatever commentary the writer would like to add. The Metafilter interface instructs the writer to contribute a link and add commentary; Blogger makes no such demands. Blogger makes it so easy to type in a thought or reaction that many people are disinclined to hunt up a link and compose some text around it.

It is this free-form interface combined with absolute ease of use   16
which has, in my opinion, done more to impel the shift from the filter-style weblog to journal-style blog than any other factor. And there has been a shift. Searching for a filter-style weblog by clicking through the thousands of weblogs listed at weblogs.com, the Eatonweb Portal, or Blogger Directory can be a Sisyphean task. Newcomers would appear to be most drawn to the blog rather than filter style of weblogging.

Certainly, both styles still exist; certainly the particular mixture of   17
links, commentary, and personal observation unique to each individual site has always given each weblog its distinctive voice and personality;

and certainly the weblog has always been an infinitely malleable format. But the influx of blogs has changed the definition of weblog from "a list of links with commentary and personal asides" to "a website that is updated frequently, with new material posted at the top of the page." I really wish there were another term to describe the filter-style weblog, one that would easily distinguish it from the blog. On the principle of truth in advertising, this would make it much easier for the adventuresome reader to find the type of weblog he most enjoys.

So, what of the weblog? Is it of interest or importance to anyone who does not produce one? Well, I think it should be.   18

A filter-style weblog provides many advantages to its readers. It reveals glimpses of an unimagined web to those who have no time to surf. An intelligent human being filters through the mass of information packaged daily for our consumption and picks out the interesting, the important, the overlooked, and the unexpected. This human being may provide additional information to that which corporate media provides, expose the fallacy of an argument, perhaps reveal an inaccurate detail. Because the weblog editor can comment freely on what she finds, one week of reading will reveal to you her personal biases, making her a predictable source. This further enables us to turn a critical eye to both the information and comments she provides. Her irreverent attitude challenges the veracity of the "facts" presented each day by authorities.   19

Shortly after I began producing Rebecca's Pocket I noticed two side effects I had not expected. First, I discovered my own interests. I thought I knew what I was interested in, but after linking stories for a few months I could see that I was much more interested in science, archaeology, and issues of injustice than I had realized. More importantly, I began to value more highly my own point of view. In composing my link text every day I carefully considered my own opinions and ideas, and I began to feel that my perspective was unique and important.   20

This profound experience may be most purely realized in the blog-style weblog. Lacking a focus on the outside world, the blogger is compelled to share his world with whomever is reading. He may engage other bloggers in conversation about the interests they share. He may reflect on a book he is reading, or the behavior of someone on the bus. He might describe a flower that he saw growing between the cracks of a sidewalk on his way to work. Or he may simply jot notes about his life: what work is like, what he had for dinner, what he thought of a recent movie. These fragments, pieced together over months, can provide an unexpectedly intimate view of what it is to be a particular individual in a particular place at a particular time.   21

The blogger, by virtue of simply writing down whatever is on his mind, will be confronted with his own thoughts and opinions. Blogging   22 every day, he will become a more confident writer. A community of 100 or 20 or 3 people may spring up around the public record of his thoughts. Being met with friendly voices, he may gain more confidence in his view of the world; he may begin to experiment with longer forms of writing, to play with haiku, or to begin a creative project—one that he would have dismissed as being inconsequential or doubted he could complete only a few months before.

As he enunciates his opinions daily, this new awareness of his inner   23
life may develop into a trust in his own perspective. His own reactions—to a poem, to other people, and, yes, to the media—will carry more weight with him. Accustomed to expressing his thoughts on his website, he will be able to more fully articulate his opinions to himself and others. He will become impatient with waiting to see what others think before he decides, and will begin to act in accordance with his inner voice instead. Ideally, he will become less reflexive and more reflective, and find his own opinions and ideas worthy of serious consideration.

His readers will remember an incident from their own childhood   24
when the blogger relates a memory. They might look more closely at the other riders on the train after the blogger describes his impressions of a fellow commuter. They will click back and forth between blogs and analyze each blogger's point of view in a multi-blog conversation, and form their own conclusions on the matter at hand. Reading the views of other ordinary people, they will readily question and evaluate what is being said. Doing this, they may begin a similar journey of self-discovery and intellectual self-reliance.

The promise of the web was that everyone could publish, that a   25
thousand voices could flourish, communicate, connect. The truth was that only those people who knew how to code a web page could make their voices heard. Blogger, Pitas, and all the rest have given people with little or no knowledge of HTML the ability to publish on the web: to pontificate, remember, dream, and argue in public, as easily as they send an instant message. We can't seriously compare the creation of the World Wide Web itself with the availability of free technology that allows anyone with a web browser to express their unique, irrepro-ducible vision to the rest of the world . . . can we?

In September of 2000 there are thousands of weblogs: topic-   26
oriented weblogs, alternative viewpoints, astute examinations of the human condition as reflected by mainstream media, short-form jour-nals, links to the weird, and free-form notebooks of ideas. Traditional weblogs perform a valuable filtering service and provide tools for more critical evaluation of the information available on the web. Free-style blogs are nothing less than an outbreak of self-expression. Each is evi-dence of a staggering shift from an age of carefully controlled information provided by sanctioned authorities (and artists), to an unprecedented

opportunity for individual expression on a worldwide scale. Each kind of weblog empowers individuals on many levels.

So why doesn't every bookmark list contain five weblogs? In the beginning of 1999 it really seemed that by now every bookmark list would. There was a bit of media attention and new weblogs were being created every day. It was a small, quick-growing community and it seemed to be on the edge of a wider awareness. Perhaps the tsunami of new weblogs created in the wake of Pitas and Blogger crushed the movement before it could reach critical mass; the sudden exponential growth of the community rendered it unnavigable. Weblogs, once filters of the web, suddenly became so numerous they were as confusing as the web itself. A few more articles appeared touting weblogs as the next big thing. But the average reader, hopefully clicking through to the Eatonweb portal, found herself faced with an alphabetical list of a thousand weblogs. Not knowing where to begin, she quickly retreated back to ABCnews.com.   27

I don't have an answer. In our age the single page website of an obscure Turk named Mahir can sweep the web in days. But the unassailable truth is that corporate media and commercial and governmental entities own most of the real estate. Dell manages more webpages than all of the weblogs put together. Sprite's PR machine can point more man-hours to the promotion of one message—"Obey Your Thirst"—than the combined man-hours of every weblogger alive. Our strength—that each of us speaks in an individual voice of an individual vision—is, in the high-stakes world of carefully orchestrated messages designed to distract and manipulate, a liability. We are, very simply, outnumbered.   28

And what, really, will change if we get weblogs into every bookmark list? As we are increasingly bombarded with information from our computers, handhelds, in-store kiosks, and now our clothes, the need for reliable filters will become more pressing. As corporate interests exert tighter and tighter control over information and even art, critical evaluation is more essential than ever. As advertisements creep onto banana peels, attach themselves to paper cup sleeves, and interrupt our ATM transactions, we urgently need to cultivate forms of self-expression in order to counteract our self-defensive numbness and remember what it is to be human.   29

We are being pummeled by a deluge of data and unless we create time and spaces in which to reflect, we will be left with only our reactions. I strongly believe in the power of weblogs to transform both writers and readers from "audience" to "public" and from "consumer" to "creator." Weblogs are no panacea for the crippling effects of a media-saturated culture, but I believe they are one antidote.   30

Examining the Text
1. According to Blood, what are the key features of filter-style blogs and journal-style blogs? How did Blogger help facilitate the development of journal-style blogs?
2. What benefits come to readers and writers of each type of blog?
3. What does Blood see as the relationship between blogs and mainstream media? What important role does Blood think blogs can serve in our culture?
4. *Thinking rhetorically*: At the beginnings of several paragraphs in the article, Blood uses a familiar rhetorical strategy of asking a question or questions, which she subsequently answers in the rest of the paragraph. Choose one of these paragraphs and reread it. Do you think that the strategy of beginning with a question is effective in this particular instance?

For Group Discussion
Before you read Rebecca Blood's article, you might have had some exposure to blogs; perhaps you or someone you know has kept a blog, or perhaps you've read some blogs on the Web. As a group, discuss what experience each of you has had with blogs. You might also discuss your exposure to blog-related sites like LiveJournal, Friendster, MySpace, and The Facebook—journal-style sites in which people write about themselves and make contact with others who have similar interests. How does Blood's article affect your understanding of blogs and of blog-related sites? What did you learn from the article that might cause you to see these sites differently?

Writing Suggestion
A site called "Technorati" (*http://www.technorati.com*) tracks the world of blogs on the Web. At this site there is a page that lists the 100 most popular blogs: *http://www.technorati.com/pop/blogs/*. For Technorati's ratings, the popularity of a blog is measured by the number of other sites that link to it. Visit the Technorati page and choose one of the 100 most popular blogs listed there. Spend a few hours reading through the blog to get an idea of its content, organization, and writing style. Then write an analysis of the blog in which you offer an explanation of why it's popular. What kind of people would be likely to visit and link to this blog? What does the blog offer that would make it popular? If it's a filter-style blog or a journal-style blog, does Blood's article help explain why it's popular?

Borg Journalism
John Hiler

In 2000, when Rebecca Blood wrote the previous article, blogs had not yet taken on the function that they're best known for today: Web-based, amateur journalism. Neither purely filter-style nor journal-style (though perhaps with a bit of both), journalistic blogs focus on current events, investigating and discussing stories, and sometimes breaking new stories of their own. Though there may not be as many journalistic blogs as the other two types, the journalistic blogs have had a lot of impact, particularly in the political arena and particularly during elections.

John Hiler helped build Xanga.com, one of the largest weblog community sites. He also maintains a blog called MicrocontentNews.com, which is devoted to covering weblogs and other forms of personal publishing on the Web. As Hiler explains, there's sometimes a competition between bloggers and journalists to see who can break a story or uncover hidden evidence. Hiler uses the Borg metaphor, taken from Star Trek, to explain how resistance to the collective power of thousands of bloggers seems to be futile for journalists. But Hiler also notes that bloggers and journalists can work well together when they each do what they're good at. In this synergy, readers benefit by getting more complex, rich, and informative news stories.

Before you read, *think about what forms of journalism you rely on and where you find out about what's going on in the world. Television, newspapers, radio, and news-based websites are probably the primary sources. But do you—or would you consider—getting some of your news from a blog or two? What do you think are the strengths and weaknesses of this source of information?*

As a journalist covering the weblog beat, I officially love weblogs. But sometimes that love can be sorely tested.   1

Weblogs scoop you at every turn, breaking "your" stories before you have a chance to rush your article to press. And even if you do manage to break a story, weblogs take it over, dissecting every point you made and pushing your logic to every inevitable conclusion. Forget that follow-up you had planned—blogs have already anticipated and published every point you might have made.   2

Welcome to the world of Borg Journalism. Resistance is futile: journalism is being assimilated.   3

BLOGS: THE NEW BORG

Star Trek's Federation of Planets faced its greatest challenge in the   4
Borg, a race of cyborgs (half human/half-machine) who assimilate alien
life forms into their collective. Like an army of ants, the Borg Collective
possesses a shared consciousness infused with a ferocious determination
to crush their enemy, at any cost.

Weblogs aren't nearly so malevolent, and most bloggers get the   5
warm fuzzies when they think about online content. But allow me to
share the flip side of the story: if you're a journalist trying to break
news, Blogs are the new Borg.

Blogs relentlessly track down every scrap of news, assimilating it   6
into the Blog Collective hive-mind with stunning efficiency. It doesn't
stop there: individual blogs each add a small insight to the story, drawing on their personal experience and contributing to the conversation.
Then the conversation takes over, exploring every possible implication
and insight with a ferocity that astounds.

When all is said and done, what is the role of journalists in break-   7
ing news? Are journalists relics of a golden era, now useful only as a
conduit to pass along the whispers of the hive-mind to the unplugged
masses? Or have we been reduced to Stamps of Approval, as we validate blog-based trends with the imprimatur of the New York Times or
the Washington Post?

A PERSONAL STORY

My first article on *Microcontent News* mapped out the incredible impact   8
that weblogs were having on Google searches.

Here was my angle: traditional journalists have often been quick   9
to dismiss weblogs by citing a single poorly written online diary as
"proof" of the failure of the weblog format. But it's not the *individual*
weblog that fascinates me. It's when you tap the *collective power* of
thousands of weblogs that you start to see all sort of interesting behavior emerge. It's a property of what scientists call complex adaptive systems and it's enabling weblogs as a collective to become more than the
sum of its parts.

One example of this is a phenomenon called "Google Bombing",   10
in which weblogs can work together to have a quick and dramatic
impact on Google's search engine results. I had lots to say about
Google Bombs, but I was already over 1,500 words. A separate Google
Bomb follow-up just two days later sounded like the perfect solution.

FIRST CONTACT

That was my first contact with the Blog Collective. In just two days, I   11
got thousands of hits, with hundreds of weblogs linking and discussing the implications of Google's blog-friendly algorithms. At first, I
was thrilled by the impact of the article.

　　But then, a reader blogged one of the key insights from my follow-   12
up. And then another blogger did the same. Wait a minute . . . what was
going on here?

　　Point by point, the Blog Collective was scooping all of the ideas for   13
my follow-up article! Rather than fight for intellectual priority, I rebuilt my
story around quotes from the various weblogs and rushed it into print.

AT WAR WITH THE BLOG COLLECTIVE

Something about the whole experience bothered me. My ego was too   14
wrapped up in the process. In my mind, I was at war with the Blog Collective. Getting scooped had really bothered me. This was MY story!
Who were these bloggers who were stealing my story?!

　　But wait . . . blogs are my friend! What was happening to me?!   15
I was getting sucked into the ego-driven world of exclusive scoops
and breaking news. That's not what I'm all about. Besides, I WANT
people to be reading my articles. I don't want to think about blogs as
my competition.

　　But if the Blog Collective isn't my competition, then what are they?   16

PREPARE TO BE ASSIMILATED

Naturally, I came to terms with this troubling question by watching a   17
lot of Star Trek. As the most popular Star Trek villain, the Borg are often
featured in a lot of the new episodes from Voyager, the recent Star Trek
series. Somewhere in the seventh season of reruns, I found my answer.

　　In the episode "Shattered", Captain Janeway and her first officer   18
Chakotay are talking to Seven of Nine, a borg drone who has become a
member of the Star Trek crew. As usual, there's a crisis involved and
the crew is scrambling to come up with a solution.

　　Seven (the Borg drone) identifies a flaw in the proposed solution: 19

Seven:　"Your plan is inefficient."
Janeway:　"Why?"

> Seven: "There are only two of you. If I were to assimilate you
> into a small Borg collective, you could then assimilate others.
> The work would proceed more rapidly."
> Janeway: "Sorry, but I like my plan better. We'll be back."

Seven's point got me thinking: what's wrong with being part of a   20
collective? Whether it's a Borg Collective or a Blog Collective, Seven
might have the right idea: maybe being assimilated *is* more efficient.

RESISTANCE IS FUTILE

In America, individuality is a core part of our culture. Competition and   21
individuality is woven into the very fabric of our value systems. In that
worldview, the Blog Collective is the competition, and a good journalist will do their best to scoop them.

But not all journalists subscribe to that worldview. One brave   22
journalist who doesn't is Dan Gillmor over at the San Jose Mercury
News. Dan does more than maintain a weblog — he's fully assimilated
with the Blog Collective. Lately, he's even been speculating on the relationship between weblogs and journalism.

Four of his key principles (from a recent blog post on his site):   23

1. My readers know more than I do;
2. That is not a threat, but rather an opportunity;
3. We can use this together to create something between a seminar
   and a conversation, educating all of us;
4. Interactivity and communications technology—in the form of e-mail,
   weblogs, discussion boards, websites and more—make it happen.

Clearly, Dan Gillmor has found value in assimilating with the   24
Blog Collective. Dan's first principle resonated deeply with me: it's
clear to me that my readers know more than I do.

BREAKING NEWS

A few days later, they proved it. One day around two in the morning,   25
I started hearing my readers telling me about a new story: Google
seemed to be "censoring" an anti-Scientology site from its database!
This was ten hours before Wired News came out with the first mainstream article on the subject, so it was breaking news indeed.

As I explained in the first article I wrote on the subject,   26

> Late Tuesday night, we noticed an increasing number of hits from a
> Google Group on Scientology™. When I clicked on the link, I came
> across this alarming development:
>   Operation Clambake, that is *http://xenu.net*, appears to have entirely
> disappeared from the Google search engine.
>   A few exploratory searches confirmed this claim. Xenu.net had
> been completely eliminated from the Google database.

The results came from a Usenet group rather than a weblog, but   27
the central idea is clear: listen to your readers, and you will break many
more stories. And if your readers are online and writing weblogs, you
will break more stories than you could possibly imagine.

AN UNSTOPPABLE BLOG COLLECTIVE?

I started thinking of the Blog Collective as an unstoppable force. And   28
whether you call it P2P Journalism, Personal Journalism, or Emergent
Journalism, most bloggers concur: Weblogs represent a new model of
journalism that threatens to render many journalists obsolete.

Watching the Google/Scientology piece play out across various   29
weblogs forced me to rethink that idea. Writing this complicated story
took me 16 hours and over 4,000 words. I found that I needed to
research and write-up at least four major sets of ideas to get my arms
around the subject:

1. The DMCA (Digital Millennium Copyright Act) legislation
   • with a special focus on the "Safe Harbor" provision
2. Intellectual Property Law (Trademark and Copyrights)
3. Jurisdiction of international law
4. History on how the Church of Scientology:
   • has used copyright and trademark law in the past
   • has gamed Google's search engine in the past

With my absolute faith in the power of the Blog Collective, I was   30
really looking forward to seeing the Collective's reaction to the
Google/Scientology story — not just to my piece, but also to the dozens of
similar articles published on the subject. I had been really impressed by the
Collective's response to my previous Googlebombing story, and was looking forward to dozens of fresh new perspectives on the Scientology story.

LIMITATIONS OF THE BLOG COLLECTIVE

The Google/Scientology story got a lot of play in the blogging commu-   31
nity over the next few days. It had all the ingredients of a hot story cus-
tom-built for bloggers: a sexy brand (Google), a controversial subject
(Scientology), and that perennial online rallying cry: a challenge to free
speech and the First Amendment.

This time around, though, the Blog Collective disappointed me.   32
To be honest, a lot of weblog posts over-simplified the story or just got
the facts plain wrong, especially as the complicated story evolved.

For example, Google restored the frontpage of the anti-Scientology   33
site (xenu.net) shortly afterwards, claiming that it had made a mistake.
Much of the weblog world posted responses talking about how "Google
finally backed down" and "stood up to Scientology".

But the central issue hadn't changed at all: Google was still elimi-   34
nating much of Xenu's content because of a DMCA *copyright* complaint
by the Church of Scientology, a complaint that was part of an aggressive usage of copyright and trademark law by Scientologists. That
Google could restore Xenu's frontpage was just a technicality in
trademark law. Unless it's willing to incur significant legal liability,
Google can't and won't index the rest of Xenu's pages.

Ok, the details *are* tough to grok, but still . . . The Blog Collective   35
is the same powerful entity that has scooped just about every thought I
ever had on GoogleBombing. And the Blog Collective had truly amazed
me with its coverage of the KayCee blog hoax, when members of the
community weblog Metafilter swiftly discovered the truth behind the
fictitious weblog of a fake cancer patient. But this time, the Blog Collective wasn't as efficient as I had thought it'd be.

The truth must lie somewhere in the middle. If the Blog Collective   36
isn't all-powerful, then what are its limitations? More important, if I
can better understand the limitations of the Blog Collective, does that
allow me to find a sustainable role for myself as a journalist?

THE TRUTH ABOUT BLOGS

I started by looking more closely at stories where I knew the Blog   37
Collective had really contributed to the coverage. Once I combined
those data points with my own experiences at *Microcontent News*, I
started to notice some places where weblogs shine.

As the KayCee blog hoax showed, Weblogs are ideally suited for   38
what I call *conspiracy journalism*: the act of debunking conspiracies

using journalistic techniques. Another good example from a year ago: psychoexgirlfriend.com, a website where a man uploaded voicemails left on his answering machine by his seemingly psychotic ex-girlfriend. Newstrolls.com, a community weblog "dedicated to the expression of free speech through our links, articles and postings", debunked the psychoexgirlfriend website, digging into the html source code and researching the domain name registration to discover that a traffic-starved company had made the whole thing up.

The Blog Collective is also extremely skilful at what I call   39
speculative blogging: exploring the implications of a new idea or piece of data. Within thirty-six hours of my first piece mentioning Google Bombs, no less than ten separate weblogs had separately scooped parts of my planned follow-up.

PUTTING THE PUZZLE TOGETHER

To use a crude metaphor, if you think about covering a story as putting   40
together puzzle pieces, then the Blog Collective tends to shine when it's finding new puzzle pieces, and putting together simpler puzzles.

Journalists, on the other hand, tend to do their best work with   41
really tough puzzles, or in finding puzzle pieces that demand primary research: phone calls, interviews, and the like.

In a way, Weblogs and Journalism combine to create a powerful   42
new synergy, a theme we'll be exploring over the next two weeks as we complete a three-part series on Weblogs and Journalism.

WEBLOGS AND WATERGATE

As a journalist covering weblogs, this sense of synergy rang true. The   43
Blog Collective represents a powerful new way to cover stories. But Journalists will continue have an important role in this post-Blog world, through primary research and synthesizing complex stories.

To put it another way, Weblogs would never have broken Water-   44
gate. But you can bet they would have blogged the heck out of the story, hashing out its implications on **metafilter** and kuro5hin. And weblogs with dedicated writers can and will break important stories. Just ask Matt Drudge about the Monica Lewinsky scandal if you have any doubts left on that front.

BLOGGING AND ME

As a journalist, I've learned firsthand to respect the power of the Blog   45
Collective.

Cutting-edge journalists are already tapping into the Blog hive-   46
mind, floating potential story ideas past their readers, and getting new
story ideas from reader email. Rather than fight the blogs, journalists
are learning how to work with them. Slowly but surely, journalists are
being assimilated into the Blog Collective.

It's not as easy as it sounds. Truly assimilating with weblogs   47
requires a real attitude adjustment as a journalist. It's more than just
surfing Blogdex for hot trends, and ripping them off in stories you sell
to mass-media outlets. True assimilation requires a journalist to learn
about blogrolling, to follow referer links, to read dozens of blogs, to
learn how to follow distributed conversations across scores of blogs.
It's an intense level of involvement and commitment, which is why
many of the first wave of journalists assimilated have been early
adopters and blog evangelists who happen to cover technology.

But make no doubt: Borg Journalism is a powerful new force   48
that's helping to redefine what it means to be a journalist. If you write
articles for a living, then you ignore weblogs at your own peril.

Or to put it in more familiar terms, *Resistance is futile. Journalism*   49
will be assimilated.

Examining the Text

1. The Borg metaphor used in this article reveals a lot about what Hiler
thinks of blogs. In what sense, according to Hiler, do blogs assimilate
journalism? In what sense is resistance futile?
2. What is "google bombing"? How does it prove Hiler's point about
the collective power of blogs?
3. Explain in your own words the Google/Scientology story that Hiler
relates. What conclusions does Hiler draw from this story?
4. *Thinking rhetorically*: Not all writers include personal anecdotes, but
in this article Hiler relies on them to help him advance his argument.
He uses quite a few examples and stories of his own experiences as a
journalist who works with bloggers. What function do these personal
anecdotes serve? To what extent do you think they help Hiler establish
his credibility and expertise?

For Group Discussion

Hiler discusses the ways in which bloggers and journalists compete with
each other, as well as the ways in which they can work together. In your
group, make a list of the ways in which journalists and bloggers compete

with each other. Make a second list of the ways in which journalists and bloggers can work together. In both lists, draw from Hiler's argument as well as from your own observations and insights. Discuss as a group whether you think bloggers ultimately improve journalism or detract from it, based on Hiler's article as well as on your own opinion.

Writing Suggestion

John Hiler maintains his own blog, Microcontent News (*http://www. microcontentnews.com*), in which he writes about news and events related to blogging. Visit his site and read some of the articles he has published there. Then choose one of these articles and write a summary of it. Be prepared to make a presentation of your summary to others in your class.

ADDITIONAL SUGGESTIONS FOR WRITING ABOUT TECHNOLOGY

1. Though the authors in the first section of this chapter—Samuels, Barlow, and Rosen—deal with different topics and write in different styles, all three of them are concerned with the ways that technologies are redefining the borders between public spaces and private spaces. Write an essay in which state your own opinion about technology's impact in these areas, and try to draw information from all four authors as well as from your own experiences and observations. What are the key technologies that have helped to shape your understanding of the differences between public and private spaces? What technologies change the way you behave in public and in private?

Drawing from the articles, you can use quotations that you agree with to support claims that you make, and you can also use quotations that you disagree with in order to provide you with material to argue against.

2. Several of the articles in this chapter provide a brief historical look at a technology; for instance, Rosen gives some background on the history of the cell phone, and Blood discusses the early development of blogs. Write a research-based report in which you describe the history of another technology, emphasizing the impact that this technology has had on popular culture or on a specific subculture.

To choose a technology for your research topic, think in terms of categories; there are, for instance, technologies associated with music, movies, entertainment, health and medicine, science, communication, sports, cooking, cleaning, and so on. Once you've chosen a category that interests you, it should be easier to choose a specific technology. Do research both in the library and on the Web in order to find out when the technology was invented, how it evolved through the years, when its popularity grew and declined, and, most importantly, what impact it has had on the people who have used it. You might end your research report with speculations about the future of this technology: what new developments are in store for it, and in what new ways do you imagine will people use it in the future?

3. This is a tough assignment: go and play a video game. Actually, the tough part comes next: write an essay in which you analyze the video game you played. To prepare for this assignment, before you play the game you should review your notes from the two articles on video games in this chapter: Steve Jones' "Let the Games Begin" and Brian Cowlishaw's "Playing War." In particular, with Jones' article, give some thought to the different motivations and effects of game playing that he discusses; with Cowlishaw's article, pay attention to the way he describes details of specific games and connects those details to larger interpretations of the games and their genre.

Next, give some thought to the video game you choose to play. You might want to choose a game with which you're very familiar, so that you have a complete understanding of its characters, rules, scenarios, and strategies. On the other hand, you might want to choose a game that's entirely new to you so that you come to it from a fresh perspective.

After you've chosen a video game to play, go ahead and play— but as you're playing, pay attention to both the game and your reactions to it. This may require that you play the game more than once! Ultimately you want to walk away from the experience with something to say about the underlying premises of the game as well as about how playing the game affected you. After playing, be sure to jot down some notes about the most salient and interesting features of the game; you can use these notes as you develop your essay.

In writing your analysis of the video game you played, begin with a specific claim about the game, and use evidence from the game and from your experience of playing it to support the claim you make.

Internet Activities
1. Perhaps in response to the changing ideas of individuality and community that the writers in this chapter (especially John Perry Barlow) have commented on, a number of sites on the World Wide Web have been created to foster a sense of community among groups that may feel marginalized or excluded by the new information technologies. Visit one of these sites; you'll find some listed as links from this chapter at the *Common Culture* Web site. After exploring all that the site has to offer, write an analysis of the strategies it uses to welcome members into its community. How does the content of the site cater to the needs

and interests of its audience? How does the design of the site—its colors and images, its organization—help the audience feel welcome and "at home" at this place on the Internet? Are there any interactive components of the site that allow visitors to communicate with each other? If so, what is the content and tone of these discussions? What other features of the site are employed to respond to its target audience? Finally, assess the overall effectiveness of the Web site in creating a responsive virtual community for a particular group of people.

2. Following up on the two articles about blogging in this chapter, this assignment asks you to give blogging a try yourself. Visit Blogger (*http://www.blogger.com*) or one of the other free blogging sites on the Web and follow the directions there to get started with your own blog. If you have questions or run into problems setting up your blog, services like Blogger have excellent Help functions to guide you along.

Once you've got your blog set up, what should you write? Your teacher might have some specific suggestions for you, but we'd suggest that you start with the filter-style blog that Rebecca Blood describes. That is, write an entry that has a link to a site on the Web that you find interesting or important or surprising or otherwise worthy of note. Along with the link, write a paragraph or two with your commentary on this link: why have you chosen it? Why should people visit the site you're linking to? After you've written one filter-style entry, try writing another one; perhaps you could write one filter-style entry each day for a week or two. You might conclude your blog-writing adventure by writing an entry analyzing your experience: what do you find worthwhile or problematic about writing in a blog? How is it different from writing for print? Do you think you might continue blogging in the future?

Reading Images

The color image on page CI-5 is a still photo from the 1995 film *Johnny Mnemonic*; the color image on page CI-6 comes from the 1999 film *The Matrix*. In both, we see depictions of "the human" and of "the technological." Your task in this analytical essay is to compare the ways that each image represents people, technology, and their relationship. If you've seen one or both of the movies, try to refrain from discussing them in your analysis; stick to the images and to the meanings they convey.

Look first at how "the human" is represented in each image: what are the similarities and differences in the human figures that the images include? Next, write about how "the technological" is represented: how do we know that these movies are about computer technology? How does each image represent technology? As you discuss each of these components, remember to consider color, dimension, contrast, perspective, focal point, and other issues discussed in the "Reading Images" section of Chapter 1.

Move next to a discussion of the relationship that each image creates between human and technology. What words would characterize this relationship: harmonious? antagonistic? intimate? distant? Be sure to provide evidence from each image to support the assertions you make about it.

Finally, select one of the key ideas discussed by Samuels, Gergen, Barlow, or Rosen as they portray the effects of computer technology on individuals and communities. After explaining this idea with the help of quotes from the essay, discuss whether this idea is confirmed or contradicted by the images taken from these two popular sci-fi movies.

Sports

The United States seems to be a nation obsessed with sports, an obsession nowhere more evident than in some fans' virtual addiction to sports statistics. Somewhere there's probably a statistics maven who knows the number of foot faults in the final 1956 Davis Cup match or the most triples by a left-handed batter during Tuesday afternoon World Series games. Fans crave statistics, no matter how minute, as a way of measuring the achievements of their favorite athletes and teams—and perhaps also as a way of holding the memory of never-to-be-repeated athletic performances.

It's not difficult to find further evidence of America's preoccupation with sports. Most daily newspapers allocate an entire section to sports reports and statistics; a number of national weekly and monthly publications concentrate exclusively on sports. Special sporting events such as the Super Bowl are consistently among the most highly rated TV broadcasts, and several cable networks are devoted solely to sports twenty-four hours a day. Americans play sports trivia games, call sports telephone hotlines, and participate in a multibillion dollar sports gaming industry; they display team logos on t-shirts, sweatshirts, baseball caps, and countless other articles of clothing. Many colleges and universities capitalize on the prominence of their sports programs to increase enrollments and donations.

Sports can affect fans in surprisingly intense ways. We all probably know people whose moods fluctuate with the fortunes of their favorite team, who might "bleed Dodger blue," as they say. Indeed, entire cities rejoice when their team brings home a championship, and our national mood lifts when an American underdog takes a medal at the Olympics or when the "Dream Team" squashes an opponent. Given this obsession, it's no wonder that professional athletes are among our most revered—and highly paid—citizens.

How can we explain the popularity of professional sports? The essays in the first part of this chapter offer views about the role of sports in American life in general, including a timely discussion of a wildly popular new "sport"—no-limit hold'em tournament poker— and an insightful discussion of the ways in which American sports are affecting (or *in*fecting, in the opinion of some critics) cultures world-wide. The essays in the second part focus on boxing, golf, and the newer "extreme" sports, and, by implication, the factors—physical ability, the influence of family and friends, climate and environment, even race and gender—that govern an individual's choice to partici-pate in or follow a particular sport.

Obviously, sports can influence the way we speak and the way we feel, our notions of teamwork and individuality, success and failure, and male and female roles. From sports we learn how to deal with pres-sure, adversity, and physical pain and we discover models of grace, skill, and style. As you read the essays in this chapter, think of the sports you play and watch, of the athletes you admire, of the role sports play (or have played) in your life.

Sport in America, American Sports Across the Globe

Fixing Kids' Sports

Peter Cary, Randy Dotinga, and Avery Comarow

The following article was originally published in the journal Science & Society. *In it, the authors explore the changing face of children's team sports in the United States. The authors document the increasing seriousness applied to youth sports such as baseball, soccer, basketball, and softball, and contrast this with a corresponding decline in family activities like dinners together and vacations.*

In addition to the emergence of "select" and "elite" programs designed to tap the most talented youngsters in a particular sport, the authors also note that children are specializing in just one sport, playing more frequently and spending large amounts of time (as well as money) traveling to distant tournaments and competitions. As a result, the article states, children are becoming injured, disillusioned and, ultimately, abandoning sports they formerly enjoyed. Experts, including a pediatrician, a parks administrator, a sports director, and others lend support to the authors' position on what's happening to kids' sports. They also use former professional player Cal Ripken, Jr., who has expertise both as a player and a sports parent, in support of the article's central theme.

As you read, *notice the writers' technique of using statistics to establish the legitimacy of claims they make in the article. Also, note how the quotes used at the beginning of the article signal clearly to the reader the direction the article will take. Quotes used throughout the story underscore the particular slant of the article, which urges readers to agree with the premise that youth sports in the U.S. need a new approach. Consider your own response to these techniques: did you appreciate the wealth of hard evidence, or did you feel as though you were being positioned or manipulated by the authors to agree with their position?*

Fred Engh has seen it all. A wiry former college wrestler and father of 1
seven, Engh has been a baseball dad, a coach, an athletic director, and,
for nearly 30 years, an evangelist out to fix youth sports. Mention any
ugliness at a kids' sporting event, and Engh, the founder of the
National Alliance for Youth Sports, can counter with tales even worse.

There's the father telling the kid, "You little bastard, you could never get anything right." Or the beefy guy, captured on video, telling his young baseball player, "I'm gonna get you tonight because you let me down, buddy." Or the one that started Engh on his crusade, the kid pitching in a local recreation league, who, after every pitch, grabbed his elbow and winced. When the umpire stopped the game, the boy's father and coach came out to the mound. "What's wrong?" he asked the boy. "It's my arm; it hurts," said the child, crying. "Son," said the coach, "this is a man's game. Now stay in there and pitch."

Cal Ripken Jr., the former Baltimore Orioles star shortstop and a   2
father of two, has his own catalog of youth sports at their worst. He has seen coaches use what he calls the "loopholes" just to get wins. They will, in the younger leagues, tell players not to swing the bat because of the likelihood that the pitcher will throw more balls than strikes. Soon the bases are loaded. "So," Ripken continues, "you exploit the base-running, and you create an environment that is frustrating to the defensive team, especially the pitcher. He starts crying. He's thinking, 'How terrible that all these kids are crossing the plate on passed balls and wild pitches and they are stealing on me. It's not fair; it's not fair.' And they break the kids down emotionally, and that's how you win."

On a plane not long ago, Ripken read Engh's *Why Johnny Hates Sports*   3
and found himself highlighting passage after passage. "I was struck by how the things he wrote about were things I cared about," Ripken recalls. He arranged to meet with Engh, and last week they got together again to talk. The topic: How to give kids' sports back to the kids.

That Ripken, a perennial all-star, would find common ground with   4
Engh, a 68-year-old grandfather of 13, isn't quite as surprising as it may sound. Just about anyone who has spent time around youth sports these days has had a bad experience or has heard of plenty more. A survey of 3,300 parents published in the January/February issue of *SportingKid* magazine last year found that 84 percent had witnessed "violent parental behavior" toward children, coaches, or officials at kids' sports events; 80 percent said they had been victims of such behavior. A survey in South Florida in 1999 of 500 adults found 82 percent saying parents were too aggressive in youth sports, and 56 percent said they had personally witnessed overly aggressive behavior. An informal survey of youngsters by the Minnesota Amateur Sports Commission found 45 percent saying they had been called names, yelled at, or insulted while playing. Twenty-two percent said they had been pressured to play while injured, and an additional 18 percent said they had been hit, kicked, or slapped while participating. Not surprisingly, the dropout rate of all children from organized sports is said to be 70 percent.

Suffer the family. In the past decade, some disturbing new trends   5
have emerged. Children are starting in sports younger, specializing in one

sport earlier, and may play the same sport year-round. The consequences of such activity are not yet fully understood, but sports physicians say stress injuries among kids are way up, and coaches say some of the most talented athletes drop out by their teens. And for many parents the demands of toting kids to practice, travel games, and tournaments are taking a big toll on what used to be called family life. In the past 20 years, says Alvin Rosenfeld, a New York psychiatrist who specializes in adolescents, structured sports time has doubled while family dinners have been cut by a third and family vacations have decreased 28 percent. "There's been a huge growth in youth sports," says Paul Roellig, a Virginia coach and parent. "The question nobody's asking is, is this a good thing?"

Perhaps it all began way back in 1929, when the owner of a   6
Philadelphia factory set out to stop neighborhood youths from breaking his windows. He got a friend to organize a youth football league to keep the kids busy. Five years later, they named their club after the legendary Temple University football coach, Glenn Scobie "Pop" Warner. About the same time, in Williamsport, Pa., a sandpaper plant worker named Carl Stotz decided to organize a league for the little kids left out of sandlot play. It came to be called "Little League." The first pitch was thrown on June 6, 1939.

From those humble beginnings, kids' sports exploded. Pop   7
Warner Football came to enroll more than 225,000 children in 36 states. Little League has 2.5 million kids playing in 50 states. Babe Ruth League baseball, whose younger divisions now bear Cal Ripken's name, has 945,000 players and, like Little League, a World Series of its own.

The real boom in youth sports, however, was driven by soccer.   8
Here was a sport—unlike batting a pitched ball or shooting a basketball through a high hoop—that any tot could play. In 1964, the American Youth Soccer Organization was formed in Torrance, Calif. Its founding principles included the ideas that every kid had to play at least half of every game and that teams had to be balanced in talent to ensure fairness. Soccer leagues grew like kudzu. In 2003, the Sporting Goods Manufacturers Association reported that 6.1 million kids from ages 6 to 17 played soccer more than 25 days a year. All told, more than 26 million, or two thirds of America's youth, play a team sport in America.

The boom in youth sports coincided with the suburbanization of   9
America, but it was stoked by the maturing of the baby boom generation and its unprecedented focus on its children. Parenting became "the most competitive sport in America," says Rosenfeld, the psychiatrist. "Soccer mom," meanwhile, came to conjure up more than just the image of a mother shuttling her kids to and from practice. "It's the culture," says Andrew Holzinger, athletic programs coordinator for Palm Beach County, Fla. "Maybe all I wanted to do was have my daughter kick the soccer ball around because she's driving me crazy. But Soccer Mom

gets out to the field, and she has a new personality. She gets to bond with the other parents about the lousy call, or 'Why is this an 11 o'clock game; I told them to schedule it earlier.' Soccer Mom, she gets to have her own sport."

"Child abuse." As parents got more involved, some got *too*   10
involved, and things turned ugly. By the mid-'70s, Engh had seen enough. His daughter played on a softball team whose coach was caught urging his girls to shoplift for him, Engh says. And then, coaching his own son's baseball team, he ran into the father who told his boy with the sore elbow to stay in there and pitch. This was nothing more, Engh says, than "legalized child abuse."

He decided to do something about it. By 1980, he began working   11
out of a tiny second-floor office in West Palm Beach, creating a training manual for coaches. The idea: to make team sports less pressurized, safer, and more child friendly. Engh still remembers the day when the bank called and told his wife, Michaele, they were $440 overdrawn. With seven kids to feed, Engh thought it was the end. Then he opened his mail, and in it was his first order for the new manual, a check for $732. He never looked back.

Today, Engh's National Alliance for Youth Sports has certified   12
2.1 million volunteer coaches. But that, he says, isn't enough; everyone in youth sports—administrators, coaches, officials, parents—should be trained and sensitized. Indeed, one evening in February 2000, the Jupiter-Tequesta Athletic Association in Florida packed more than 1,500 parents into a stadium to watch a video on how to be a good sports parent, pick up a handbook, and sign a sportsmanship pledge—or their children could not play. Engh's National Alliance has even created a program to teach basic skills to kids as young as 3, so they can enjoy sports from the start. Near Buffalo, N.Y., the town of Hamburg adopted all of the alliance programs. "The coaches used to show up like, 'We're going to war here,'" says Tim Jerome, president of the junior football league. "It was pretty bad." Verbal abuse, shoving matches, parents misbehaving, it's all "changed dramatically," he says.

"The one thing people need to understand," Engh emphasizes,   13
"is that they don't need to put up with this anymore." Mike Murray agrees. "Here in Northern Virginia," says Murray, a high school coach, teacher, and a director of youth baseball training programs, "you've seen a real cultural shift. All the things you'd want, people policing themselves. I think in large part people have bought into this." Murray is a trainer for another organization, the Positive Coaching Alliance. The alliance shares many of the same goals as Engh's organization—and even some of the same tips—but their approaches are different. Engh's organization wants all volunteers trained and certified; the Positive Coaching Alliance is focused more on the zen of coaching.

The PCA is the brainchild of a soft-spoken former college basket-   14
ball player named Jim Thompson. While studying at Stanford University
Business School in the mid-1980s, he found himself coaching his son's
baseball and basketball teams. Seeing too many "negative interactions"
between coaches and players, he recalled his earlier experiences working at the Behavioral Learning Center in St. Paul, Minn. There he had
learned the power that positive reinforcement had on severely disturbed children. He wrote a book called *Positive Coaching*, which
stressed some basic principles: Athletes perform best when they feel
good about themselves. The way to keep them confident is with positive comments. Athletes so motivated will be confident, try hardest,
take chances, and play "over their heads." And when that happens, the
team wins.

Thompson's manuscript made its way to Phil Jackson, then the   15
head coach of the Chicago Bulls. Jackson, recalling his own trying years
in youth sports, was struck: "It fused a lot of my thinking," he said. He
decided to test Thompson's theory at the pro level. At the time, Jackson
was riding one of his players, Horace Grant, pretty hard, and their relationship had fallen apart. Jackson tried the positive approach, and
things turned around. Jackson, now with the Los Angeles Lakers,
became the PCA's national spokesman.

Its influence has been sizable. The PCA's 65 trainers have run   16
workshops for 400 youth sports organizations, training an estimated
60,000 coaches and parents. "I can tell you the first year we ran PCA
programs the number of coaches being ejected from games was cut
drastically," says Tim Casey, former vice president of Chicagoland Pop
Warner football conference. The Dallas Parochial League, with 3,500
fifth to eighth graders enrolled in 11 sports, began offering PCA workshops to all coaches. In basketball, "our most volatile sport," says athletic director B. J. Antes, technical fouls dropped from over 100 to 26 in
three years. This year, PCA workshops will no longer be optional,
Antes says. "It's too darned important not to make it mandatory."
Coaches say they like the PCA's "dual goal" approach: striving to win,
but using sports to teach life lessons. PCA workshops stress "honoring
the game," mastering sports skills, and shrugging off mistakes. "The
way I see the world of youth sports," Thompson says, "is that the win-
at-all-costs mentality is the root of all evil."

Studies confirm this. A survey last summer at the National PTA   17
Convention in Charlotte, N.C., found 44 percent of parents saying that
their child had dropped out of a sport because it made him or her
unhappy. These parents were not wimps. In fact, 92 percent of the respondents said sports were either important or very important to the overall
development of their children. But 56 percent said that youth sports
were too competitive, nearly half said that organized youth sports need

to be completely revamped, and half said if they could change one thing, they would want their coach to be less focused on winning. Many surveys support this conclusion: Most kids would prefer to play a lot on a team that loses than sit on the bench of a team that wins.

For all the progress that the Fred Enghs and Jim Thompsons have made, however, they have yet to address a development of the '80s and '90s that has swept up many families. Known as travel teams, they are formed of the best players in a league or a community, may be coached by a volunteer parent or a well-paid coach, and travel to other towns—and sometimes even other states—to play teams of their own caliber. Also known as elite, select, or club teams, they're found in virtually every town in the nation.   18

At their best, travel teams provide young players with professional-level coaching, better competition, and even family bonding. "The clubs get very tight. They like each other; they travel with each other; they go on trips. It becomes much more of a long-term social thing as well as a competitive thing," says Craig Ciandella, California director of United States Specialty Sports Association baseball, which has 1,300 teams. Many young athletes believe their clubs give them the accelerated development they need to make the high school varsity or go beyond. "It's no longer a myth: If your kid wants to make a high school team, he has to play club ball," says Jim Tuyay, a tournament director with the California Beach Volleyball Association. "They're getting the training and the attention that the normal rec leagues are not providing."   19

Pressure. Travel teams can be nothing if not intense. They may practice twice a week and play twice more. They can travel one, two, three hours each way for games, chewing up entire Saturdays or weekends. "It becomes a way of life. It winds up being what you do on weekends. You don't go away; you don't go on vacation; you do baseball. I wouldn't have had it any other way," says Ciandella. And most kids playing on elite teams are encouraged to play the same sport again in one, two, or three more seasons—even if they are playing other sports. Some are told—and believe—that if they don't play, say, soccer year-round, they will fall behind their peers.   20

One effect is even more pressure in the early years. Children now play travel hockey at the age of 7, and baseball tournaments are organized featuring pitchers as young as 8. "Where we live, travel soccer starts at the U-9 [8-year-old] level," says Virginia father Roellig. If you resist, he says, "you will be told, 'Your kids will quickly fall behind and not make the team when they are 10.' If you want your kid to play in high school, you have to start [travel] at 10, and if you want to travel at 10, you have to play travel at 8." Roellig says his community recently   21 started a U-5 soccer program. Called the "Little Kickers," children can play at age 3 1/2. In 2003 it enrolled 50 kids, he says; now it has more than 150. "It's an arms race," complained one soccer mom in Washington, D.C.

Some wonder whether things have not gotten out of hand. Roellig,   22
who coaches soccer, has three children, ages 10, 15, and 16—all involved in sports. His 15-year-old daughter, a high school freshman, plays year-round soccer and two other sports to boot. In the spring, she plays high school and travel soccer. In the summer she attends camps, does a basketball league, and has August soccer practice. In the fall, she has travel soccer and field hockey. And in the winter, she plays indoor travel soccer and basketball. Most nights she gets home at 7:00 or 7:30 from practice, has to eat and do her homework. She may make it to bed by 10 p.m., but she has to get up at 5:40 for school. "What gives is the homework and the sleep," Roellig says, adding that his daughter often looks exhausted. "If I had to do it again as a parent, I'd definitely scale back sports," he says. "I think I'm doing more harm than good."

He's not alone. Holzinger, the parks administrator in Palm Beach   23
County, oversees 120 athletic fields and issues permits for their use by 65 different youth organizations. Only 2 to 5 percent of children under the age of 13, he believes, qualify as "elite" athletes. But in his region, the proportion of kids being placed on "elite" teams has grown to 25 to 30 percent of the athletic pool in the area. It's not that more kids have become better athletes; more parents are simply insisting that their kids be enrolled on select teams. "As we see these children as elite players, we stop thinking of them as children," Holzinger says. "You're not a child; you're my defensive line that nobody ever gets through. So if someone gets through, you let me down." The 25 percent of kids who shouldn't be on the select teams, in other words, frustrate the team and the coach. Parents get down on the coach because the team isn't winning, and coaches sometimes take it out on the kids. Or some kids simply ride the bench. "You, the kid," Holzinger explains, "are now becoming frustrated with a sport, and it's a sport you loved. Past tense."

Much of the problem, Holzinger and others say, stems from   24
coaches. "You'd be surprised," Holzinger says, "by how many parents are really impressed when a coach tells them, 'I'll have your child in a scholarship; stick with this program.'" What parents don't understand, and what the coaches don't tell them, are the real numbers. Dan Doyle, a former collegiate basketball player and head coach, is the executive director of the Institute for International Sport at the University of Rhode Island. For his forthcoming book, *The Encyclopedia of Sports Parenting* (to be published in September 2005), Doyle's research team surveyed young basketball players. Using data from nationally affiliated

basketball leagues, they estimated that the total number of fourth-grade boys playing organized basketball was about 475,000. At the same time, the team found, only 87,000 teens were playing basketball as seniors in high school. Of the 87,000, they say, 1,560 will win Division I college scholarships, 1,350 will get Division II scholarships, and 1,400 more will play at Division III schools. And of those 4,310, about 30 will make it to the National Basketball Association. An additional 130 will play pro ball in Europe.

In soccer, the odds are even longer, because so many colleges recruit foreign players. "It's not a worthy objective at the fourth- or fifth- or sixth-grade level," Doyle says, "which is what some of these coaches are telling them. You know, 'If you don't play for me you're not going to get to college.'" And tennis? Doyle found that there are approximately 3 million males between 10 and 18 worldwide aspiring to be top tennis players. How many make money on the pro circuit? 175. "The professional aspiration," he says, "it's just crazy."   25

Equally crazy, experts say, is the idea that child stars can be created by starting early. "It doesn't matter when you start a sport. If you start at 3, it doesn't necessarily help," says Paul Stricker, a pediatric sports medicine specialist in San Diego. "Kids develop sports skills in a very sequential manner, just like they do sitting up and walking and talking. Parents and coaches just don't understand that sequence. They feel that after they're potty trained, if they practice something enough they'll get it." Parents, some coaches say, are often fooled by "early maturers," kids who are big and well-coordinated at a young age. But often it's the late bloomers, who had to work longer and harder at sports, who turn into the stars.   26

Breakdown. Pushing kids to play sports too early and too often can result in pain and worse. Since he began his specialty practice in 1991, Stricker says, "I've had at least a 30 to 40 percent increase in overuse injuries like stress fractures and tendinitis. Those are things we just didn't see much in kids previously." Stress fractures, which occur when kids overtax their bones, are common. "These only come from forces that are repetitive," Stricker explains. "The bone breaks down faster than it can build up." Tendinitis is also common, especially in pitchers and swimmers, because young muscles aren't strong enough yet to keep up with adult training regimens. In young pitchers, Stricker says, "the growth plate gets pulled apart like an Oreo cookie."   27

The American Academy of Pediatrics has taken note. "Those who participate in a variety of sports and specialize only after reaching the age of puberty," the academy said in a statement four years ago, "tend to be more consistent performers, have fewer injuries, and adhere to sports play longer than those who specialize early."   28

What overeager parents should really worry about, some experts   29
say, is burnout. Jim Perry is director of athletics at La Quinta High
School in Westminster, Calif., a public school where club sports are
hugely popular. He says he recently read an article about a national
powerlifting championship for kids as young as 9. "What 9-year-old
gets up in the morning and says, 'I want to be powerlifting'?" he asks.
"That came about because of a coach or a parent." Perry says many
kids, so pushed, tire of sports by the time they reach high school. "It's
not a matter of [club sports] sucking talent away [from high school].
They're driving high-end kids away from athletics in general," he says.
"They're sick and tired of playing 135 travel baseball games a year by
the time they're 12 years old. They're sick of playing 100 soccer games
a year before they ever set foot in high school. They don't need it
anymore."

Besides, it's not yet proven that year-round play, travel teams,   30
and specialization make better athletes. "Most of today's top professional athletes didn't even think to specialize in just one sport until
they were in high school, around the age of 15," says Rick Wolff, chairman of the Center for Sports Parenting at the University of Rhode
Island. Cal Ripken, for one, attributes his success on the diamond
partly to playing three sports into high school. Soccer taught him foot-
work and balance, he says. Basketball gave him explosiveness and
quick movements. "I think athleticism is developed," he says, "by
everything you do." For that reason, he tells his 10-year-old son, Ryan,
"put down your glove" when spring baseball is over.

All the emphasis on winning, perversely, can make for inferior   31
skills. The Virginia Youth Soccer Association, with 138,000 registered
players, recently posted a long note on its website from Technical
Director Gordon Miller assailing "overly competitive travel soccer." In
their zeal to win games, Miller warned, some Virginia travel teams
emphasize the wrong things. Big kids are recruited and taught to kick
the ball long down the field instead of being taught to make tight, short
passes and ball-handling skills. "You don't encourage flair, creativity,
and passion for the game," he says, emphasizing that it is in practice,
not games, that young athletes develop their skills. Studies show,
Miller says, that in a typical game a player on average has the ball in his
or her control for only two to three minutes. "The question is, 'Is playing all of these matches the best way to develop players?'" he asks.
"And the answer is, 'No.'"

If we could only start over—that's one of Fred Engh's dreams.   32
Engh has been traveling and speaking abroad, hoping to learn from
others and to find countries where it's not too late to fix things. In the
course of his travels, he came across the tiny Caribbean nation of

Dominica, a place where organized youth sports do not yet exist. The Dominicans agreed to let Engh and his Alliance for Youth Sports start a complete roster of kids' sports there, from scratch. Engh told Ripken of the venture. Ripken says he was intrigued by the idea of starting a youth sports program with the slate entirely clean. "I never thought there was a place on this planet that hadn't played baseball as an organized sport," he says. "Maybe I could help participate in something like that—rebuilding the joy of baseball."

DROPPING OUT

Although the number of kids ages 6 to 17 rose by more than 7 million between 1990 and 2002, the most popular team sports lost significant numbers of players.

(Millions of players)

Basketball	
1990	20
1998	22
2002	18

Soccer	
1990	12
1998	14
2002	13

Softball	
1990	12
1998	9
2002	6

Baseball	
1990	10
1998	8
2002	7

Source: American Sports Data Inc.,
Sporting Goods Manufacturers Association

Examining the Text
1. In what ways do the authors appear to support the contention of Fred Engh that youth sports need fixing? Do you think this article is about the mission of Engh to reform kids' sports, or does it represent a broader criticism of youth sports? What role does Engh play in the article; could it have been written without any mention of him?

2. Look carefully at the statistics the authors quote. What information do they convey? Do you think those statistics provide a complete picture? What other perspectives might benefit by the inclusion of some statistics or other hard data?

3. The technical director of the Virginia Youth Soccer Association is quoted as saying that "overly competitive travel soccer" doesn't encourage "flair, creativity and passion for the game." In your opinion, is it reasonable to draw conclusions about travel soccer based on the comments of one particular technical director? How might the inclusion of several other sports program directors' opinions have altered the tone and/or argumentative position and credibility of this article?

4. Parents seem to come in for much criticism in this article, yet the authors appear to have not spoken to anyone representing parents. Do you think this was a deliberate omission on their part? If so, why? If not, do you think hearing from parents would have altered your perception of the article? Based on the way the authors wrote the story and the emphasis given in the article, do you believe they have succeeded in addressing the source of the problem? Does the article offer a viable solution to the problems it highlights?

For Group Discussion

How many people in your group played sports regularly as kids? How many do so now? If, as the authors of this article predict, a significant number of your group members have stopped playing organized sports, discuss whether the reasons cited by the author match the reasons put forward by members of your group. In the opinion of your group members, are there other reasons why youngsters stop playing baseball, soccer, and other team sports?

Writing Suggestions

As an exercise in critical thinking and writing, develop an essay that counters the arguments put forth in this article. You might begin by making a list of all the statistics the authors use in their story about kids' sports, noting what categories they fall into. You might proceed to conduct some research via the library and the Internet, trying to find statistics that contradicts the statistics used in the article. For example, one survey by the Minnesota Amateur Sports Commission reportedly found that forty-five percent of participants had been called names, yelled at or insulted while playing for a youth team. The explicit goal of this assignment will be to conduct research and write a persuasive essay in which you defend the role of competitive team sports. Explain why you think there are benefits for children from specializing at a young age, practicing frequently, and taking part in tournaments. Use the statistics you find to support your arguments.

Baby, You're The Greatest

Tom Farrey

The greatest athletes have drive, determination, dedication, talent and physical prowess appropriate to their chosen sports. But does every winning sprinter have specific physical traits in common with other great sprinters? What about Olympian rowers, cyclists, and marathon runners? Can science, using DNA techniques, determine if certain groups of champion athletes share genetic characteristics? The following article, originally published in ESPN Magazine, examines whether science can come up with a common DNA thread to link medal-winning athletes in a particular sport. Further, it explores whether a young person's DNA profile can predict in advance what sport that individual might be best suited to.

Scientists in Australia are leading efforts to determine whether sports performance can be predicted using DNA samples. The Australians have developed a test using one of the approximately 30,000 genes present in human DNA. For example, The ACTN3 gene, Australian researchers discovered, is tied to a protein required in fast-twitch muscle fiber. Two copies of the gene were found present more frequently in sprinters and power-event participants sampled from a pool of Australia's top athletes than among average members of the Australian public. By comparison, endurance athletes from the same pool were more likely to have no copies of the gene. The ability to make connections between the human genome and sports performance is only just developing, the article acknowledges, but as the database of tested athletes that scientists can draw from grows, so to will the ability to come up with more definitive answers.

The testing of athletes is occurring in a handful of countries around the world. It's therefore not such a leap, the article suggests, to imagine DNA analysis conducted on juvenile athletes to see if their genomic structure matches their chosen sport. To that end, the author offers his one-year-old as a test subject. Does the baby have the ACTN3 gene that is linked to fast-twitch muscles, and thereby suited to such pursuits as baseball, tennis, basketball, and other sports that require highly responsive skills coupled with good eye-hand coordination? If so, should he be directed to a particular sport or perhaps steered away from a sport that science suggests he won't excel at?

As you read, study the style and tone of the article carefully. Look for ways in which the author appears to be playful—using his own child as a study subject—and examine how that seems to contrast with an underlying subject matter. What do you think is the author's intention here?

It's noontime in small-town Connecticut as Kellen, my 1-year-old, awakens from his nap. The shades are drawn, the room dark, the air purifier on a low hum, as I slowly push open the door. He's sitting up in his crib, one hand holding his favorite blue blanket, the other rubbing blue eyes that blink back the hall light. Next to him is the music-box pillow that had sung him to sleep to the ting-ting-ting of "Here Comes Peter Cottontail." 1

"Hi, kicker boy," I say, using his nickname du jour, so given because of his diaper-time obsession with whacking his heels on the changing table as rapidly as possible, like a Benihana chef with new knives. Kellen, of course, does not get my reference, as he does not yet talk, or walk. 2

But he does drool. And it's a sample of that saliva that I'm looking to harvest right now—because his wipe-away spit, clear as a crystal ball, offers genetic insight into his future as an athlete. As Kellen squints back up at me, I slide the end of a Q-tip into the side of his mouth, rub it around the gum area for 20 seconds and drop it into a "Sample Transportation Bag" with his name scrawled in pen on the outside. 3

In two hours, my flight leaves for Australia. "All right, kicker boy," I say, sealing the baggie. "Let's go find your destiny." 4

The Founding Fathers declared that all men are created equal, a bedrock principle that has been extended to define the ethics of American sports. Despite evidence to the contrary—notably all the kids of retired pros who are now pros themselves—we still pledge allegiance to the notion that hard work separates the great from the ordinary. That Tom Brady just wanted it more. That Serena simply fought her way to glory. That Ichiro hustled up the single-season hits chart. 5

The Aussies, blunt about everything, are more willing to explore the role that inherited traits play in athletic achievement. "I think anyone who opens their eyes will realize that certain people have talent for activity A, whereas others have talent for activity B," says Deon Venter, chief pathologist at Genetic Technologies in Melbourne. The doctor, a former Ironman champion, is sitting on a raised swivel chair inside the company's quiet lab, where DNA samples are being processed. A robotic machine on the counter behind him extracts samples, including Kellen's, and drops them into rows of vials. 6

In December, at Venter's urging, Genetic Technologies began selling what it calls the world's first DNA test for sports performance. 7

Available over the Internet to anyone with a mouth swab and 110 Australian dollars ($100 U.S.), the test evaluates just one gene, ACTN3, whose relevance was discovered more than a year ago by a University of Sydney researcher. When there is no mutation, the gene creates the protein alpha-actinin-3, which fuels the explosive machinery in fast-twitch muscle fiber.

Every human being gets two copies of every gene (one from 8 Mom, one from Dad). So for ACTN3, the genetic lottery determines whether a child gets two, one or zero copies of the form linked to fast-twitch fibers. Not surprisingly, when testing the genotypes of 429 of Australia's top athletes in 14 sports, including 50 Olympians, researchers found that participants in sprint and power events were far more likely than average Australians to have two copies. In effect, they were getting a double shot of fast-twitch espresso. By contrast, athletes in endurance sports were more likely to have no copies, suggesting that an advantage in those events is gained when the muscles must rely on slow-twitch fiber.

"Sports performance is a jigsaw puzzle, and this is just piece 9 No. 1," Venter warns. But as we stare at a monitor that gradually displays Kellen's results, which are being decoded in a gene machine about the size of a microwave oven, I am filled with anticipation and queasiness. How bizarre will it be to know if he's cut out for sprinting while he still can only crawl? As a parent, even one whose instinct is to expose my kids to the diversity of life and let them find their own way, can I be trusted with such information?

A lab tech copies the results onto a CD, converts them to a graph- 10 ically pleasing format and hands the disc to Venter, who pulls up a series of bar charts on his laptop. "Well, Tom, here are the results," he says in a gentle voice. The vertical bars on Kellen's graph are absent. In ACTN3 terms, he's a zero (like 20 percent of the population).

"This is more likely to fit with an endurance athlete," Venter 11 confirms.

"So we'll skip the 100-meter dash," I say. 12

"He can do it if he wants to do it," the doctor replies, "but statisti- 13 cally speaking, based on what we know now, he's less likely to do well because he will not apparently make sufficient power."

Venter is a geneticist, not a sports physiologist, so I'll save the 14 question of which activities would be best tailored to Kellen for tomorrow. That's when I meet with the experts at the Australian Institute of Sport, which made its elite athletes available for DNA analysis in the landmark ACTN3 study. But I'm curious to know if Venter, an accomplished endurance athlete himself who happens to have the same ACTN3 architecture as Kellen, thinks my baby boy has the stuff of an Ironman.

"He might, if he can stand the pain," Venter says. "That's some-   15
thing we don't know how to measure yet."

Yet. It's the geneticist's favorite word.   16

The ancient Greeks attributed many human acts to the whims of   17
mythical gods and goddesses. Dionysus made folks get drunk. Aphrodite
made the furniture move. Nike made victory (and still does, at least
some of the time). Modern science has unlocked many secrets. But even
now that we know the instructions for life can be found in the 30,000 or
so genes that make up the human genome, we're still a bit like those
old Greeks, guessing at the source of powerful forces.

For years, people simply assumed that Eero Maentyranta, the   18
great Finnish cross-country skier, was doping when he won two golds
at the 1964 Olympics. After all, others trained much harder. Only later
was he discovered to be a genetic freak, the beneficiary of a mutation
that allowed his body to produce 50 percent more red blood cells than
normal. Those cells carried extra oxygen to his muscles. It's the same
advantage drug-cheats try to get by taking EPO.

So far, researchers around the world have associated 124 genes   19
with physical activity. But the emphasis of many studies has been on
fitness, not performance. Scientists expect to find that a lot of athletic
traits, such as hand-eye coordination, involve a cluster of genes.
Even the ACTN3 test, which included only white subjects and
focused on muscle type, has its detractors. "If you want to find out
which kids have fast-twitch fiber, just line them up and fire a gun
in the air," says Steve Fleck, a former U.S. Olympic Committee scientist who now works with Sports Potential, a Bay Area startup that
helps kids and adults find their ideal sport. "You'll see which ones
run fast."

Still, as more elite athletes get tested, the genetic database will   20
grow, revealing patterns and allowing for predictions with greater
accuracy, based on statistics. Ultimately, it's possible that when a boy
like Kellen is born, the vial of blood taken to genetically screen for diseases could also be used to spot athletic traits. Plug the results into
the Theo Epstein All-Athlete Database, and before leaving the hospital,
the baby's parents could get a report on which stars best match his
DNA—quite the head start if they hope to create the next Freddy Adu
or Matt Leinart.

Some of the most cutting-edge research is being done at the   21
Australian Institute of Sport, a three-hour drive north of Melbourne, in
the capital city of Canberra. The AIS gets $40 million a year from the
government to identify and develop potential stars, many of whom
live and train at the 160-acre facility. It's as much a sports factory as
anything East Germany ever sponsored, minus the institutional doping
and coercion.

Inside his office, the director of the sports science unit taps his   22
fingers nervously on a table. With his thin face, modest eyewear and
measured demeanor, Peter Fricker looks nothing like a mad scientist.
"Is this for the AIS to do?" he wonders. "Open the lid on Pandora's
box?" He knows that by making his athletes available for DNA
analysis, he's helping move sports in a new and uncertain direction.
Concerned that such knowledge could lead to gene doping, the
Australian government temporarily suspended genetic testing by the
AIS in 2003.

But the country can't afford to stand idly by: athletes in England,   23
Mexico, China and elsewhere are being tested, and the Aussies' role
as the leader in sports science is at stake. With the AIS feeding its pipeline,
the nation won more medals per capita in Athens than any other except
the Bahamas (the U.S. was 39th by that measure). So Fricker expects to
receive the green light on gene work from the minister for sport in the
coming months, provided the AIS adheres to an ethical code he hopes
the rest of the world's athletic bodies will adopt. There can be no AIS
testing of kids under the age of 12, for instance. And its researchers
must work hard to understand the value of each genetic marker, so
coaches don't just cut a player for atypical DNA. (After all, Lleyton
Hewitt was supposedly too short for tennis.)

Some cold decisions are inevitable, though. I can hear the echo of   24
Charles Darwin in the chipper voice of AIS exercise physiologist David
Martin, an American who left the U.S. Olympic training center a
decade ago because of the Aussies' embrace of sports science. We meet
on campus at the biomechanics dome. In the background, on a red rub-
ber track, a doctoral student obediently holds a stick upright for a
bearded, slightly obsessive-looking technician tapping furiously on a
laptop, calibrating a camera that analyzes a runner's stride. Clearly, the
geeks run the show here.

"There's only so much taxpayer money," Martin says. "If three or   25
four athletes are performing at similar levels, the coach could use the
genetic test to persuade himself to go with one athlete instead of
another, to increase the likelihood of success."

My mind drifts to Kellen and what we know of his evolutionary   26
stew. His maternal grandmother, who played college tennis, marvels at
how well he whacks a rolling ball with either hand. Starts low. Finishes
high. Topspin deep into the corners?

"With tennis," Martin says, "you want to have fast-twitch fibers   27
to move dynamically."

"What about basketball?" I ask.   28
"Same thing."   29
"Baseball?"   30
"I'd be going for fast-twitch."   31

"Football?" At least Kellen has the right name. But I anticipate the   32
doctor's answer.

"The most explosive guys on the planet."   33

Martin is now chuckling sympathetically. "Good hand-eye coor-   34
dination and endurance," he says, mulling the optimal sport for Kellen.
"How about biathlon? They ski for long distances and shoot a rifle."

And so it shall be. Meet the next Ole Einar Bjoerndalen.   35

All kidding aside, I have something of a dilemma now, right? It's   36
not as if we in the United States have the smartest sports system in the
world. Most kids get funneled into the same four or five mainstream
games, not because their bodies and minds are tailored for success but
because those are what Mom and Dad played. More than 70 percent of
them quit sports by age 13, usually because they can no longer make
the team or they're not having fun. Now, Couch Potato Nation has an
obesity epidemic. Maybe biathlon isn't the answer for Kellen, but a
more thoughtful approach to sports selection has its benefits.

I can see those rewards in the blue eyes of Emma Lincoln-Smith.   37
In December, I found the blond, sturdy 19-year-old near the top of a
snowy mountain in Park City, Utah, half a world away from the golden
beaches of Narrabeen, Australia, where she practically grew up on a
surfboard. Until the previous month, she'd never heard of the sport of
skeleton, in which competitors sled headfirst down a twisting chute at
speeds reaching 80 mph, their chins mere inches above the ice. The AIS,
which gives physical tests to teenagers all over Australia, liked her 30-
meter sprint power on dry land, so the institute invited her to join a
new national skeleton team. Now she was representing Australia at an
America's Cup race as her nation's top sledder.

As we talked after the race (she finished eighth), Emma winced   38
while holding ice packs on her left hip and knee, deeply bruised from a
crash on Turn 12. Her coach figures she's good enough to win an
Olympic medal someday if she can learn how to steer. "I feel like this
has been coming all my life, that fate brought me here," she says. "I
love going fast. I love dangerous sports. So when the opportunity came
up, I just had to take it. It's the best thing that's ever happened in
my life."

Genetic screening is the logical extension of Talent Identification   39
or TI, as the Australians call it. Venter, for one, says his ACTN3 test,
which hits the U.S. market this spring, is intended to help kids and
adults find lifelong avenues of exercise, not to further professionalize
youth sports. "We don't see how a genetic test is going to put any more
pressure on children than has already been applied by parents for generations," he says. "In fact, it might help stop a father from pushing his
child to do well in a sport he wishes he had done well in but for which
the child is not genetically suited."

Venter advises me not to act on what little we know about   40
Kellen's genes until after he's had time to climb trees, experiment with
a few sports and define his interests on his own. I agree. It's his life, not
mine. But I'm glad I have the information. That's all it is, data, not
Dolly the sheep. I trust that I will know when the time is right, if ever,
to use it as a resource. If Kellen picks a power-based sport, we can
always tailor his training. Destinies are surely as much made as found.

Still, after returning from Australia, I couldn't resist one last   41
experiment in ridiculously early TI. I had learned that elite soccer players have unusually long ring fingers (compared to their index fingers)
on their left hands. It's apparently a marker of prenatal testosterone,
which helps form a strong cardiovascular system. So, in the interest of
science, I sent a photocopy of my kid's paw to John Manning, the English
pioneer of this quirky research. On the morning of Kellen's first birthday,
I reach Manning in his office at the University of Central Lancashire. He
greets me with an amused laugh. "I've not looked at many hands of
people so young," he says.

But digit length is fixed for life, so I want to know: Can Kellen's   42
fingers point us in a direction? Manning sets the phone down to measure with his calipers. There is silence for half a minute, as he does the
math, then does the math again. Kellen's left index finger is 30.75 millimeters long; his ring finger is 34 millimeters. "So if you divide those
two, his ratio is .90," Manning says. "That is very low, the kind of ratio
that one sees in international-level soccer players."

Now that's more like it. Kicker boy wakes from his nap in about   43
20 minutes.

Examining the Text

1. Since scientific evaluation of an individual's potential sporting prowess
is still in its infancy—barely a year old when the article was written—how
does the author overcome a lack of firm information? What do you think
the DNA testing of his own baby son contributes to the story? Without the
personal aspect of the story the writer provides, do you think the article
would have been compelling? Would the article been more convincing to
you if it had been written in a more traditional, third-person format?

2. "It's as much a sports factory as anything East Germany ever
sponsored. . . " states the author about the Australian Institute of Sport
(AIS). What do you think he means by this? What, in your opinion, is
the intention of the author in using this reference? What assumptions
does he make about the audience who is writing the article? Is that a
reasonable assumption that does not require additional explanation
for the reader? What might the author add to help those readers who
might not get the reference?

3. On reflection, do you believe the goal of the article was to influence you against the use of DNA science in sports or in favor of it? What aspects of the article swayed you one way or the other? Does the title of the article hint at the angle or perspective of the article, and did that influence your perception of it?

4. *Rhetorical question*: Look over the article again and decide which category of writing it best belongs in: journalism, academic essay, humorous feature, scientific report, or some combination of these. Are there any areas of the article that you feel could be improved, either in terms of its persuasiveness or the degree to which you found it interesting and engaging? Explain your choices. Why do you think that the author chose to use humor and personal example to develop his persuasive points? What other methods might have been used to address this same topic, and what do you think another method might achieve that this method lacked? Since the article is addressing a topic that is still evolving, the writer had few statistical sources to quote. How else might he have addressed this apparent lack of factual information?

For Group Discussion

Using what you've learned from the article, consider the following premise: just as technological developments have led to better shoes, superior running tracks and more improved training regimens, it's only natural that science will reach further and further into athletes' lives. DNA is just one step on that long road of innovation. It's inevitable and worth it. In groups of three of four, assemble a list of points that support or contradict the statement. With group work finished, reassemble as a class and debate the pros and cons of this assertion.

Writing Suggestion

Imagine you're living in 2015 and the use of DNA has become standard in school and college athletic programs in your community. You personally love cross-country running and tennis but testing reveals that your genetic traits make you better suited to basketball and the 100-meter dash. Your coaches have made it clear that they'll only support those athletes with the traits that best match the scientific testing: you're a mediocre tennis player and a moderately successful runner, but with good coaching and your commitment, you could be a great basketball player and maybe a champion sprinter. Write an essay in which you explore how you would deal with this issue. Would you accept your fate as a second-string tennis player or jump at the chance to possibly excel at basketball and sprinting? Explain your decision.

Discipline and Push-Up: Female Bodies, Femininity, and Sexuality in Popular Representations of Sports Bras

Jaime Schultz

On a warm summer day it's common to see women runners, cyclists, or those simply out strolling or socializing wearing sports bras. The garment has become nearly as ubiquitous and socially acceptable as shorts and is worn equally for athletic and sedentary activities. But it hasn't always been that way, as Jaime Schultz explains in this comprehensive article tracing the evolution and public perception of the sports bra. Schultz describes the 1999 World Cup final in which a player removes her shirt, and then the author launches into an analysis of media—and by implication, public—reaction to this act. Schultz uses the public reaction as a way of examining broader societal attitudes towards women in sports, including issues of sexism, power, breast infatuation, eroticism, and the objectification of the female body. Through this broader lens, Schultz attempts to determine whether the public display of Brandi Chastain's sports bra was simply a continuation of a tradition of (men) soccer players removing (and sometimes swapping) jerseys at the end of an important game or an erotic act . . . or was it a symbol of the progression of women's sports? Interpreting Chastain's act is, like understanding art, open to numerous theories, which Schultz seeks to explore in this article, recently published in the Sociology of Sports *journal.*

As you read, notice how Schultz uses soccer player Chastain as an anchor for the article, continuing to review the broader issues with a reference to the World Cup final. Although this is an academic work, the author seeks to inform and take the reader on an exploration of those wider, societal issues through a single event—Chastain's jersey removal—that was (and continues to be) relatively well known. Most people can identify with a major sporting event televised to a mass audience, in this case one with forty million viewers. This makes the bra-removal event an ideal, easily identifiable central point around which to examine the various thematic points that Schultz raises.

It is true that a clue to a woman's view of her femininity might be found in her choice of underwear?

(Benson & Esten, 1996, p. 26)

The author is with the University of Iowa, Dept. of Health & Sport Studies, Iowa City, IA.

On July 10, 1999, over 90,000 people gathered in the Pasadena, California,   1
Rose Bowl to watch the U.S. women's soccer team play China in the final
game of the World Cup. It was the largest crowd that ever gathered to
watch a women's sporting event. An estimated 40 million television
viewers tuned in as well, making it the most watched soccer game, men's
or women's, in U.S. history (Longman, 1999, p. D1). The peak 18.8
Nielsen rating of the Women's World Cup final more than doubled the
previous high for a televised soccer match in the US, the 1994 men's
World Cup match between the United States and Brazil, which registered
a 9.3 rating (Kimball, 1999).

What spectators observed, either from their bleacher seats or on   2
their television sets, was 120 minutes of spectacular, tense, and ultimately scoreless play between the two teams. As a result, a penalty kick
shoot out determined the 1999 World Cup champion. Five players from
each team took their turns shooting against the opposing goalkeeper.
With the score tied at 4–4, Brandi Chastain was the tenth and final
player to take her penalty kick. A goal by Chastain would mean victory
for the U.S. Chastain placed the ball on the designated penalty spot,
12 yards away from the goal line. Not daring to look at Chinese goalkeeper Gao Hong, Chastain approached the ball and struck it with her
left foot. Hong dove in futility. Chastain's shot hammered against
the side paneling of the net, just inside the right goal post, and secured
the win for the U.S. women's soccer team.[1]

Spectators and viewers next witnessed an image that would per-   3
vade the media and cultural memories for months, even years to come.
As one writer put it, "the ball had barely settled into the net when
[Chastain] whipped off her jersey and stood there clad—from the waist
up, anyway—only in her black sports bra" (Kimball, 1999). As Chastain
celebrated with teammates in her black Nike Inner Actives sports bra,
she was immediately and simultaneously lauded, ogled, scrutinized,
and criticized for her actions. Debates over whether the bra exposure
was acceptable or unacceptable, spontaneous or calculated, celebratory
or opportunistic were played out in the media and at proverbial water
coolers at the national and the international levels.

Just over two weeks after the World Cup final, Githens (1999)   4
wrote that the image of Chastain in her sports bra was, "so startling . . .
that it graced the front pages of numerous newspapers the next day, the
cover of *Newsweek* and *Sports Illustrated* and, as of last week, racked up
more than 70 Web site mentions on the Internet." Chastain was named
one of *People* magazine's 20 most intriguing people of 1999 and one of
Street & Smith's 100 most powerful sports figures (Penner, 2000, p. D1).
In the interview round of the 1999 Junior Miss America pageant, contestants were asked whether Chastain's bra display had set a negative
example for young girls. So much attention to Chastain's actions after
her final goal raises the question: why all the fuss about a sports bra?

That seemingly simple question serves as the foundation on which I construct this article.

The sports bra seems to be a relatively uncomplicated though,   5
nonetheless, important garment. The invention of the commercial sports bra in 1977 was a significant advancement for physically active women. Design innovations led to the creation of a garment that allowed women greater support and comfort in their various types of movement. Despite its humble origins as an enabling technology, the sports bra has since been invested with new and varied cultural meanings and currencies. These meanings reflect shifts in ideals of femininity, the increasing acceptance of athletic female bodies, and the subsequent sexualization of those bodies. In addition, the bodily display of sports apparel in nonathletic settings has allowed the sports bra to become an item of fashion, as well as function.

In this article I examine popular mediated representations of   6
sports bras, specifically advertisements and what I call "iconic sports-bra moments." These moments pertain to Brandi Chastain's celebration of the U.S. women's soccer team's victory in the 1999 World Cup, as well as to reactions her celebration inspired. My analysis of these representations relies on the methodology that McDonald and Birrell (1999) refer to as "reading sport critically," a critical cultural studies approach that "focuses analytical attention on specific sporting incidents and personalities and uses them to reveal a nexus of power that helps produce their meaning" (pp. 283–284). In their anthology *Reading Sport*, Birrell and McDonald (2000) argue that incidents such as the Tonya Harding–Nancy Kerrigan figure skating spectacle (Braughman, 1995), the sexual harassment of Lisa Olson (Disch & Kane, 2000), and the Billie Jean King–Bobby Riggs "Battle of the Sexes" (Spencer, 2000) can be read as texts, offering unique points of access for interrogating the ideological production of power.

In particular, Birrell and McDonald (2000) recommend that schol-   7
ars attend to the mediated accounts produced around specific incidents because the "easiest way to get to ideology is through the media" (p. 11). In addition, the narratives that circulate around sporting personalities provide material for reading sport critically. Indeed, as Vande Berg (1998) argues, the mass media is primarily responsible for the construction of modern sporting celebrities. Andrews and Jackson's (2001) *Sports Star* attests to the role of the media complex in manufacturing and promoting the celebrity status of sports figures in an increasingly global cultural economy. The essays in *Sport Stars* constitute critical studies of sporting personalities, such as Wayne Gretzky (Jackson, 2001) and Cathy Freeman (Bruce & Hallinan, 2001), interrogated largely through attention to mediated representations of these individuals (see

also Whannel, 2002). My intent in the first part of this article is to critically read the narrated reports of Brandi Chastain, her World Cup celebration, and the associated iconic sports-bra moments, paying particular attention to patriarchal power relations embedded in these cultural texts.

These power relations are also located in advertising discourse. In   8
the second part of this article, I draw from advertisements for sports bras that I found in women's health and fitness magazines, particularly *Women's Sport and Fitness*. Several scholars have argued that such magazines often promote oppressive, patriarchal notions of femininity using the rhetoric of wellbeing and empowerment (Duncan, 1994; Duquin, 1989; Eskes, Duncan, & Miller, 1998; Hargreaves, 1994; Leath & Lumpkin, 1992; Markula, 1995, 2001). White and Gillett (1994) similarly argue that bodybuilding magazines marketed to men (re)construct dominant masculine ideologies. Based on their critical decoding of advertisements in *Flex* magazine, White and Gillett (1994) propose that the "visual and narrative texts represent the male muscular body as a 'naturalized' embodiment of power, authority, and natural superiority" (p. 33). That this masculine ideal is "taken for granted as desirable affirms the insecurity of the reader who does not measure up to the envied image on the page" and pursuit of this standard is frequently inimical to men's health (p. 26). Likewise, the visual and narrative content of sports-bra advertisements convince female readers that the consumption of their products will assist in obtaining the particular ideal of femininity—one that is active, slender, and toned, and often difficult or impossible to achieve.

The representations I examine construct the sports bra as much   9
more than a piece of athletic apparel for women. Although I do not call the utility of the garment into question, I suggest that the way it is considered, discussed, and framed in popular media results in the construction of the sports bra as an eroticized item. By extension, the breasts the bras cover, and the female bodies of which those breasts are a part, are similarly held up for scrutiny. The bra is constructed as an object of sexual desire, a means of disciplining the breast (both for the purposes of exercise and an objectifying gaze[2]) and disciplining the body. I further argue that these popular representations homogenize and normalize ideals of femininity that are considered achievable through technologies of disciplined body management.

After briefly discussing the evolution of the sports bra, I organize   10
this article under the guise of a rhetorical disrobing. I begin with the act of removing one's shirt so that the sports bra is publicly exposed. The next layer I examine is the sports bra itself, specifically as it is constructed and understood as both functional and fashionable. Then, I analyze the implications that popular representations of sports bras have

on women's breasts. Finally, I discuss the ways that these representations work to discipline women's bodies—bodies that are at once externally bound and internally managed by the sports bra. I refer to this organizational structure as a guise, for it implies that one might peel back the layers of discursive dress and reveal some naked truth about what the sports bra really means. I do not suggest that the sports bra has a singular or unitary meaning that can be uncovered through careful analysis; various contextualizations of the garment inspire a multiplicity of meanings (Birrell & McDonald, 2000, p. 11). Meaning is also dependent on the individuals who interpret the texts, and I do not presume to know how historical subjects will decode the moments or advertisements (Duncan, 1990; Fiske, 1989; Hail, 1980). Instead, I argue that there is one meaningful strand I find in popular representations of the sports bra that suggests the garment can be considered an eroticized object. More important, when the sports bra is infused with sexual connotations, those connotations are in turn associated with the bodies of women who wear the garment.

A HISTORICAL FOUNDATION

The history of women's undergarments has inspired a considerable amount of research (see, for example, Benson & Esten, 1996; Carter, 1992; Ewing, 1972; Ewing, 1978; Ferrell-Beck & Gau, 2002; Reyburn, 1971; Saint-Laurent, 1966). More often than not, however, the role that undergarments have played in the lives of active women has gone unexamined. In particular, it seems that what to do with one's breasts is a dilemma that has plagued the physically active female throughout time. For example, the Amazons, a legendary tribe of women in ancient Greece, were believed to have cut off their right breasts to facilitate archery (Yalom, 1997, p. 23). In less extreme cases, women worked merely to stabilize their breasts during activity. Women in ancient Rome supported their breasts by wearing bands around their chests or binding their breasts with a length of cloth or leather (Phillips & Phillips, 1993, p. 137). A vase from the fifth century BCE depicts Atalanta, a female athlete from Greek mythology, wearing an outfit akin to the modem bikini. Likewise, Lee (1984) argues that a fourth-century mosaic found in Sicily depicts ten bikini-clad women participating in athletic competition. Part of the bikini costume is a "fairly wide band which is worn high under the arms, and appeared designed to strap down the breasts for vigorous activity" (Lee, 1984, p. 62).

Women also used corsets as a means of stabilizing their breasts, though the primary purpose of the garment was to constrict waistlines. In Minoan Crete women wore laced corsets that supported their breasts but left them bare (Benson & Esten, 1996, p. 49). Corsets reached the pinnacle of their popularity in the Victorian Era, when they served to discipline the entirety of women's torsos, including the hips, abdomen, and breasts. Even with the restricting technology of corsetry, some women did manage to participate in sports; the traditional use of rigid stays in corsets, however, made movement difficult and even dangerous. Delaney (1998) writes that women competing in the 1887 Wimbledon tennis tournament had to retire to the dressing rooms between matches to "unhitch their bloody corsets. As they endeavored to twist, turn and lunge on the courts, the women were repeatedly stabbed by the metal and whale bone stays of the cumbersome garments." Though as early as 1837, Madam George had introduced a "Callisthenic Corset" that was "totally devoid of bone," to avoid such injuries during exercise (in Carter, 1992, p. 36).

The advent of elastic was a boon for the athletic, yet still-corseted woman. In 1911 a significantly named "sports corset" was one of the first such undergarments to incorporate the flexible material (Phillips & Phillips, 1993, p. 138). Ewing (1972) argues that the 1914 tango craze inspired a "dancing corset." Constructed with elastic insets, the dancing corset facilitated movement, not just for the tango but also for other energetic dances, including the Charleston, Turkey Trot, and Bunny Hop (Carter, 1992, p. 90). Additional items were designed for other specific physical activities, such as an elastic skating girdle, which was introduced by the Treo Company in 1915.

Farrell-Beck and Gau (2002) note that, although the first patent for a brassiere was filed in 1863, it was not until the 1920s that brassieres began to replace corsets as the favored undergarment of women in the U.S. With the introduction of the brassiere, support for breasts came from above (via shoulder straps) rather than from below, as corsets previously provided. Like corsets, brassieres were adapted to suit active women's lifestyles. For example, bras were incorporated into swimwear. Farrell-Beck and Gau (2002) found that brassieres for athletic women were patented as early as 1906 for acrobatic dancing and other theatrical use, yet the style did not seem to catch on (p. 31). It was not until the late 1970s that a bra specially designed for athletic women would achieve popular acceptance and commercial success. The advancements of women in sport, coupled with the fitness boom of the 1970s, undoubtedly contributed to the need for equipment specifically designed for female athletes.

In 1977, runners Hinda Miller and Lisa Lindahl created a prototype for the modern sports bra. Inspiration for the garment came when the two women considered the utility of jockstraps for male athletes. "We said," recalled Miller, "what we really need to do is what men have been doing: pull everything close to the body" (Sharp, 1994, p. 25). Originally dubbed the "Jockbra," Miller and Lindahl created the sports bra by sewing two jockstraps together. The front panels of the bra were made from the two oval jockstrap pouches and compressed the breasts to the ribcage. The women used the waistband of the jockstrap to construct the bra's wide elastic band that encircled the torso. The over-the-shoulder straps were reconfigured from the leg straps and crossed in the back to further stabilize the breasts and keep the straps from slipping down (Barr, 1997). The original appellation of the garment was changed to JogBra when storeowners in South Carolina found Jockbra offensive (Purdie, 1988, p. 63).[3] In the first year of production, 25,000 sports bras were sold (Nyad & Hogan, 1998, p. 49). In 1998, the sports bra industry rang up $412 million in retail sales (Peck, 1999), and statistics for sports bra sales in 2002 showed that the garment comprised 6.1% of the $4.5 billion bra market (Dolbow, 2002, p. 9). Based on these figures, it seems safe to claim that the sports bra has become a popular garment.

It is difficult to dispute the benefits of the sports bra in the lives of   16
physically active women; it constitutes something of a technological revolution. The sports bra has taken on symbolic importance as well, becoming emblematic of the progress of women's sports. Hinda Miller, one of the inventors of the sports bra, said that the garment has been "as important to the growth of women's sports as the passage of Title IX" (Peck, 1999), and others agree, calling it the "cloth symbol of Title IX" (Gerhart, 1999, p. C01).

Despite the undeniably positive utility and symbolic significance   17
of this piece of apparel, popular representations of sports bras give rise to competing meanings. One frequent mediated construction of the sports bra is that it can be construed as a sexualized article that contributes to the objectification of female bodies.

Brandi Chastain's celebration of the U.S. women's 1999 World   18
Cup victory provides a salient example of the ways in which the popular media sexualizes sports bras and athletic female bodies. When Brandi Chastain immediately ripped off her jersey after scoring the game-winning goal, she provided the world with both a topic for public debate and the most enduring image of the 1999 World Cup. Who can forget the image of Brandi Chastain, her muscular body clenched and her emotion undeniably euphoric, clad from the waist up in only her black Nike Inner Actives sports bra?

TEMPEST IN A B-CUP

"Where were you when Brandi Chastain ripped off her shirt?". . . For a certain generation of teenage girls, the Brandi question will someday resonate with the same timbre as does the Kennedy question for the Boomer parents.

(McKee, 2000, p. W4)

It appears that Brandi Chastain's celebration will persist in our cultural memory for some time to come, though our interpretations of the incident vary. For some, the moment was empowering—the spectacle of a strong woman excelling at her sport—and representative of how far women's sports have come. For others, the moment seemed to signify public acceptance of a new version of femininity. The repeated publication of Chastain in her sports bra legitimized an athletic, strong, active, and autonomous female form. Still others read the gesture with a more skeptical eye, suggesting that the moment was calculated to increase either the marketability of the Nike bra or of Chastain herself. Thus, Brandi Chastain was concomitantly framed as a triumphant athlete, a poster girl for the success of Title IX, a paragon of changing feminine ideals, and a calculating opportunist. Despite competing readings of Chastain's celebration, discourse consistently turned to what it meant for Chastain to take off her shirt, and how the public did or should understand the display of a woman in her bra.   19

Though it is impossible to objectively read the moment, Chastain's gesture seemed instantaneous after the goal; it appeared spontaneous rather than designed. Chastain had already begun to take off her jersey in the minuscule amount of time it took for the announcer to declare "goal!" In less than two full seconds after her shot sailed past the Chinese goalkeeper, Chastain had yanked her jersey over her head and fallen to her knees with fists raised in triumph. Chastain has claimed the moment was nothing more than "temporary insanity" (see for example, Ackerman, 1999, p. 42; Brown, 1999; Davies, 1999, p. 10; Saporito & Willwerth, 1999, p. 58), and after analyzing the moment, I suggest that her gesture bears little resemblance to a seductive act.   20

Popular discourse, however, frequently constructed an eroticized account of the incident. A significant number of writers used the term "striptease" in stories relating Chastain's gesture (see, for example, Bartolomeo, 2000; Harvey, 1999; Hickey 1999; Hummer, 2000; Jones, 2000; Kent, 2000; Kimball, 1999; Kimball, 2000; Middleton, 2000; Smoron, 1999). Similarly, the maneuver has been referred to as a "peel-down" (Peck, 1999), a "strip-down" (Brodeur, 1999), a "provocative gesture" (Ackerman, 1999, p. 42), a "half Monty" (Penner, 1999, p. D1), and designated as "the most brazen bra display this side of Madonna" (Tresniowski, 1999, p. 56). Such terms suggest that Chastain acted with the deliberate intention of titillating onlookers. Supporting this contention, some authors were also quick to include mention that several weeks before the 1999 World Cup, Chastain had appeared in *Gear*, a   21 men's magazine. In her *Gear* pictorial, Chastain posed naked, save her cleats and strategically placed soccer balls. Chastain's decision to appear as she did in *Gear* was juxtaposed with her World Cup celebration and used to undermine both her athletic accomplishment and the sincerity of her revelry.

That male athletes seem to have set the precedent for this type of divestiture further complicates the "Brandi bra moment" (Gerhart, 1999, p. C01; Riley, 2000). Andre Agassi and Pete Sampras have flung their sweat-drenched shirts into the stands after tennis matches. Dennis Rodman did the same after several professional basketball games. It is in soccer, however, that the action most frequently occurs. The practice is so widespread in men's soccer that Federation Internationale de Football Association (FIFA), soccer's international governing body, deemed it illegal to take off one's shirt in celebration (Payne, 1999). "Men do it all the time," said Roger Rogers, editor of *Women's Soccer World Magazine*. "It wasn't as though [Chastain] didn't have a bra on. It certainly would be discriminating to suggest a woman can't do it if a man does" (Welts & Oldenburg, 1999, p. 1A).   22

The resultant discrimination, however, is not based on whether female athletes should have the same public disrobing rights as male athletes, but, rather, what is made of those athletes once their tops come off. Male athletes who doff their shirts do not come under the same media scrutiny that Brandi Chastain inspired.[4] There seems to be a dimension of sexuality connected with a woman who removes her jersey that is not found with male athletes who do the same. Addressing tennis player Goran Ivanisevic's ritual of "yanking off" his shirt en route to winning the 2001 Wimbledon tournament, Givhan (2001) wrote that he was reminded of Chastain's "impromptu striptease." Givhan continued,   23

> Her personal unveiling was one of those cultural touchstones, a moment when talk of female athleticism, body image and the objectification of women all converged. With Ivanisevic, the only talk is pretty much "Nice biceps." One wishes that Chastain had been greeted with simply "Nice six-pack."
>
> (Givhan, 2001, p. C02)

Other public responses to the mediated aftermath of Chastain's celebration attended to this double standard. For example, Mead (1999) astutely noted that, "Girl Takes Top Off . . . is freighted with an entirely different symbolic weight" than "Sports Figure Takes Top Off" (p. 25). Ann Hollander (1978), an art and dress historian, proposes that, for women, the removal of the shirt or blouse has always signified an erotic invitation. So whether or not Chastain's gesture was calculated   24 becomes somewhat irrelevant. Despite the many ways her celebration is read, the act of removing her shirt is largely understood as a public disrobing equivalent to a striptease. It seems the public views Chastain's gesture as an erotic invitation that begs repeating.

Shortly after the 1999 Women's World Cup, a commercial appeared on ESPN. The commercial showed Chastain playing football with three men, including professional basketball player Kevin Garnett. When Chastain scored, all three men turned to her and waited. Finally Garnett broke the silence, asking Chastain, "What's with the shirt?" The men expected that Chastain would celebrate the football goal as she did the soccer goal in the World Cup—by taking off her shirt. It was not Chastain's sporting abilities that the men seemed to admire, but her body. Such anticipation suggests that sport offers another venue in which men can look forward to a woman undressing. These expectations are not limited to carefully orchestrated television commercials. Chastain wrote of a similar incident in which "this guy yells down from a railing three floors up in a hotel: 'Hey Brandi, what's up with the shirt?'" (Chastain, 1999, p. 76). Likewise, in a parking lot before a San Francisco 49er's game, a man asked Chastain, "Are you going to take off your shirt?" Chastain obliged by lifting up her sweatshirt to reveal a 49er's jersey (Harvey, J999, p. D2). [25]

An incident in the 2001 US Major League Soccer (MLS) All-Star game attested to the persistent association of Chastain, the removal of one's top, and the sports bra. In this game, two male players performed what they called "tributes" to Brandi Chastain (Mahoney, 2001, p. D10). First, Jim Rooney and then, later, Landon Donovan took off their jerseys when they scored in the MLS All-Star game. As previously mentioned, this celebratory reaction is somewhat common among male soccer players. This time, however, both men took off their jerseys to reveal black Nike sports bras. When Rooney stripped, teammate Mamadou Diallo caressed his sports bra. When Donovan revealed the bra, he was shown "prancing" about the field (Wagman, 2001). [26]

Like other popular mediated representations of sports bras, a complicated network of power relations lie below the surface of the seemingly uncomplicated actions of Donovan and Rooney. Chastain's celebratory actions in the 1999 World Cup emulated those of male soccer players. Because she is a woman, however, her actions came under scrutiny not usually associated with men taking off their jerseys. The effect of Chastain's emulation is sexualized. When men mimicked Chastain's actions, however, in a complex case of male soccer players imitating a female soccer player imitating the ritual behavior of male soccer players, the effect was comical. Jack Edwards, one of ABC's commentators for the game, remarked of Rooney, "Not the most beautiful sight we've ever seen, but certainly one of the more humorous" [27]

(Jones, 2001, p. D9). To dismiss Rooney and Donovan's actions as simply humorous, however, is to ignore more important implications. Though Rooney commented that it was "just a good laugh for us" (Gardner, 2001), the men's actions also involve misogyny. By mocking a significant moment in women's sports, the male athletes detracted from the moment's importance, reducing it to an incident of frivolity. In addition, the use of humor is one way of diffusing potential threats. Consider the following elements: soccer (a traditionally male sport), the Rose Bowl (a traditionally male venue), and taking off one's jersey upon scoring (a traditionally male style of celebration). Now substitute women in all these male-centered traditions and there is apt to be a sense of threat. Perhaps a humorous tribute to Chastain is one way that male athletes feel they can reassert their dominance when that power is contested.

Though Chastain was recalled in this incident, the media did not reinvoke the same type of rhetoric in reporting it. Donovan and Rooney were described as "taking off" (Eisenberg, 2001), "whipping off" (Leonard, 2001), "ripping off" (Mahoney, 2001, p. D10), and "removing" (Gardner, 2001) their jerseys to reveal black Hike sports bras. The actions of the male players are not described as "stripteases" or "peeldowns." The language, significantly, is not overtly sexualized as in the case of Chastain, though the men's antics certainly pointed to a sexual dimension of removing one's shirt. Furthermore, the acts of Donovan and Rooney removing their shirts are not enough to invoke memories of Chastain. It is only when the bodies are coded with the sports bras that particular meanings are generated, making the gestures comical and, consequently, able to detract from the seriousness of women's sport. Masculine markers, such as referring to Rooney as "balding" (Jones, 2001, p. D9), pronounce the incongruity between the men and the bras. The conventional masculinity of Donovan and Rooney is important. Ian Bishop, also a member of the MLS All-Star game, said he never considered wearing a sports bra like his teammates. Bishop said, "Me with long hair, people would have thought other things" (Eisenberg, 2001). The combined feminine codings of long hair and a sports bra on a man might negate the humor of the gesture and call his gender and sexuality into question.

28

WHAT LIES BENEATH

In the case of Donovan and Rooney, the media give the sports bras primacy after the removal of their jerseys. In the case of Brandi Chastain, however, it is somewhat more difficult to discern whether her 1999

29

World Cup celebration is better understood as the act of a woman taking off her shirt or about the exposure of her bra. The act of displaying the bra and the bra itself are two separate, yet closely conjoined, aspects of Chastain's celebration. After the World Cup, photos of Chastain in her sports bra appeared in magazines throughout the world. The image of the sports-bra-clad Chastain made the covers of *Time, Newsweek,* and *Sports Illustrated*—all in the same week. When Chastain's picture graced the cover of *Sports Illustrated*, the magazine's managing editor, William Colson, deemed it, "the greatest picture of a sports bra in the history of publishing" (Hyman, 1999). To Colson, it was neither a picture of a great athlete nor a memorable moment in sports history. Instead, his reading of the cover photograph concentrated on the bra. Chastain and her team's accomplishment became secondary to the undergarment, so much so that the public still attends to her, not as an athlete, not as the woman who scored the winning goal in the 1999 World Cup, but simply as "that girl in the sports bra" (see for example, Crothers, 2000, p. 64). The reduction of Chastain to "that girl in the sports bra" was reinforced at the 2000 Olympics in Sydney, Australia. As the U.S. women's soccer team played Norway in the Sydney Football Stadium, several spectators held up signs that read, "Show us your sports bra" (More Brandi, Please, 2000).

Like Brandi Chastain, many women do not seem to mind   30
whether their sports bras are visible to the general public, perhaps because, in recent history, the sports bra has marked a categorical elision of function and fashion. As function, the sports bra falls under the heading of "sports equipment." Like shoes or bicycles specifically designed for women, the sports bra has allowed women to more fully enjoy physically active lives. As fashion, however, the sports bra takes on different meanings. The sports bra might be seen as simply another item of lingerie, as in several mediated cases of Brandi Chastain. Nevertheless, Chastain has also increased the public acceptance of the bra as a piece of outerwear. Mike May, of the Sporting Goods Manufacturers Association, said that Chastain "made it OK for women to wear sports bras without anything else on top" (Hiestand, 1999, p. 3C). As a piece of lingerie, the sports bra can be seen as a fashionable dressing down of the female body. Conversely, when worn without a covering top, the sports bra can also be construed as fashionable dressing up of the female body as well.

The act of dressing, of wearing clothes and adopting one fashion   31
or another, is both a cultural practice and a semiotic system. As cultural practice, it has become increasingly popular and acceptable for a woman to wear a sports bra as she would any other shirt. Payne (1999) wrote that although "such bras are designed for sports, they have

become big business fashion items on and off the field with more and more women using them uncovered as casual wear." Similar articles attest to the use of sports bras as stand-alone wear. For example, a 2000 article in *Women's Sport and Fitness* asked, "When is a sports bra really an athletic top?" The answer: "Whenever the hell *you* want it to be" (Bartolomeo 2000, p. 42).[5]

In the semiotic system of fashion, the sports bra has become a   32
way for female athletes and nonathletes alike to present a particular type of image. Susan Willis (1990) writes that women who wear work-out clothes outside of an athletic setting "unabashedly define them-selves as workout women. In making a public body statement, a woman affirms herself as someone who has seized control over the making and shaping of her body" (p. 7). Therefore, a woman might appear publicly in her sports bra to assert her identity as a workout woman. Wearing workout apparel outside of a physically active context allows women to convey the ways that they have disciplined and managed their bodies, and by extension, their lives.

SHAPING UP (AND OUT)

The sexualization of sports bras, and women who wear them, did not   33
begin and end with these iconic sports-bra moments. Sports-bra adver-tisements offer another site for investigating how particular meanings of the garment are generated. One such meaning emphasizes the ways in which bras inevitably draw attention to women's breasts. As a result, advertisements for sports bras often play on the importance of present-ing female breasts in ways that are considered attractive, particularly to an objectifying gaze.

Bras are essentially for and about breasts in some way or another.   34
The first bra a girl owns is a "training bra"—whether it is the girl or her breasts that are being trained is open to interpretation. Throughout her lifespan, a woman's breasts might be supported, separated, squeezed together, shoved forward, rounded out, flattened down, or pushed up by the bra she chooses to wear. Bras can create the illusion of breasts where very little or none exist. Bras can also give the impression of an absence of breasts if that effect is desired. Bras construct bodily silhou-ettes to suit ephemeral fashions—from the minimized bustline of the 1920s to the projectile profile of the 1950s. Iris Marion Young (1990) writes that bras objectify and normalize breasts, molding them to suit an ideal (p. 195). The sports bra is not exempt from the normalizing and disciplining nature of other bras. On the surface, it might seem that the sports bra is unconcerned with creating a socially desirable shape for women's breasts, as the general principle of the garment is to

compress the breasts for protection and comfort during physical activity. Based on my analysis of sports-bra advertisements, however, I propose that the sports bra is implicated in the creation and maintenance of dominant cultural ideals of women's breasts.

There are several ways in which advertising discourse constructs women's breasts as objects for scrutiny. It is interesting that this objectification often comes packaged in the rhetoric of empowerment. Myra Macdonald (1995) writes that in the 1980s and 1990s advertisers "happily made use of concepts that had acquired new status thanks to the feminist and other civil liberties movements." In addition to empowerment, Macdonald also noted that values such as "'freedom,' 'independence,' and 'pleasure' . . . were reduced to matters of lifestyle and consumption" (p. 92). Advertisements for sports bras are no exception. For instance, early sports-bra advertising advocated empowerment through physical activity. Bras with names such as "You Can Do It Running Bra" and "Bound to Win" suggest as much. Themes of empowerment were stressed in the first sports-bra ad (Jogbra, 1979), which articulated a woman-centered approach to the garment by asserting, "no man-made sporting bra can touch it." For the purpose of this article, however, I am interested in examining the ways in which women are encouraged to use their breasts as symbols of agency, control over their sexuality, and as indicative of overall body management. This encouragement is conveyed as another way in which women might be empowered by a sports bra. Writing specifically about Nike, Cole and Hribar (1995) argue that in the postfeminist imaginary, "a popular knowledge of empowerment" is embedded in the intersection of bodily maintenance and the consumption of athletic-lifestyle products (p. 362).

Bodily maintenance, particularly conveyed as concern for the appearance of women's breasts, tends to pervade sports-bra advertisements. For example, several present-day ads discuss the importance of combating the "uniboob." The term *uniboob* refers to the simultaneous flattening and seeming lack of division between the two separate breasts. An ad for Lucy.com (2000), titled "The Uniboob Epiphany," provided a vignette of a woman in a gym who learns that the company has a sports bra to liberate her from the insidious uniboob. The ad concluded with a heroic Lucy declaring, "I will not rest until all the boobs in the world stand as strong and as proud as the women who bear them."[6] Liberation is thus connected not only to the right bra but also to the best possible presentation of women's breasts, making both active lifestyles and women's bodies objects of consumption.

Likewise, an ad for the Champion Jogbra (2000) invoked memories of Brandi Chastain by depicting a female soccer player in a black bra. The text of the ad stated, "Our latest innovation has a unique cup design that eliminates 'uniboob.' " The woman in the ad attests to this

35

36

37

claim, as her gravity-defying breasts remain round, firm, and separate from one another as she performs a "bicycle-kick" maneuver that places her in the air, back parallel to the ground and chest pointed skyward. In the context of physical proficiency and autonomy, this advertisement, and others like it, constructs the ability to put forth a bifurcated bosom as an empowering act for women.

Not only should women worry about the uniboob, according to advertisements, but they should also be concerned with the prominence of their breasts. As stated earlier, the initial intent of the sports bra was to support the breasts by compressing them to the chest. The first sports-bra ad attested to the importance of compression, stating, "Jogbra's unique design holds breasts close to the body" (Jogbra, 1976). Similarly, a 1985 Jogbra ad avowed that the "minimized profile is critical" for participation in sports. The technique of compression, however, seems no longer valued (at least in advertisements), because, with compression, breasts lose their shape and appear smaller. Twenty years after its first advertisement appeared, Jogbra (1996) advocated a different selling point by stating, "Only abs should be flat. . . . Now, a sports bra that respects and defines your natural shape." It seems curious that a natural shape does not simply exist, but that it must be defined. This ad kills two birds with one bra, as it presents readers with idealized messages about both breasts and stomachs. Thus, the ideal breast shape is normalized, and, by extension, so is the ideal body type. The athletic but obviously breasted female body is naturalized, disguising the discipline necessary to achieve that body.

Concern for the shape of one's breasts is also expressed through medicoscientific discourse. An advertisement from Nike (1999) displayed a female figure with her breasts exposed.[7] Superimposed across her body was the question, "After years of exercise, what kind of shape will your breasts be in?" The ad continued, "breasts are held up by non-elastic Cooper's ligaments. And once they stretch, they don't snap back." As such, breasts require Nike's Inner Actives bra to combat this risk. Not only will the Nike bra keep the Cooper's ligaments from stretching, but it will also work without "smashing you down." Other advertisements for sports bras make similar claims. Jogbra (1986) asserted that their "sports bra is scientifically designed to comfortably redistribute breast mass. . . . lessening the gravity pull that tears delicate breast tissue." A sports-bra advertisement from Lily of France (1979) declared that, "running is good for every part of you but two." Therefore, women understand that what might be beneficial for most of their bodies can be a detriment to those parts that signify sexual difference. The advertisements appeal to women's internalization of self-discipline and control while warning that sexual desirability is threatened without their products.

This concern for the shape of one's breasts also indicates that   40
beauty is conferred by a particular age. Young (1990) writes that,
"breasts are the symbol of feminine sexuality, so the 'best' breasts are
like the phallus: high, hard, and pointy" (p. 190). Flattened breasts signify prepubescence—a stage of development in which girls are not yet
fit to be objects of sexual desire. On the other hand, stretched or sag-
ging breasts suggest old age. Like the young girl, the older woman is
also not culturally considered an object of sexual desire. The sports bra,
like other bras, is concerned with promoting a sexuality that most
appeals to the masculine gaze. As an object of consumption, the sports
bra plays on and reinforces hegemonic notions of femininity. Sports-
bra advertising and the repeated publication of Brandi Chastain in her
sports bra represent the dominant icons of consumer culture, including
youth, physical attractiveness, and health (Hargreaves, 1987, p. 150).
These icons are about more than women's breasts—they construct a
bodily ideal for women, as well. Popular representations of sports bras
homogenize and normalize a particular feminine standard, requiring
women to discipline not just their breasts but also their bodies.

BREASTED BODIES

There is a considerable amount of discipline required to achieve the   41
femininity normalized by popular representations of sports bras. The
women in these representations are slender, toned, and fit. Indeed,
writers of both scholarly and popular texts have suggested that this
type of body marks a new version of ideal femininity. M. Ann Hall
(1996) writes, "Popular discourse today, at least in North America,
invokes a normative ideal of female beauty that is slim, strong, sinu-
ous, athletic and healthy" (p. 60; see also, Bordo, 1993; Maguire &
Mansfield, 1998; Markula, 1995; Spitzack, 1990). Race is omitted from
discussions of the culturally constructed ideal of feminine beauty Hall
articulates, but it seems clear that the ideal is also White. I found no
popular representations of sports bras that were associated with
women of color. It also seems safe to assume that the body is coded as
middle to upper class. The Nike Inner Actives bra Chastain wore in the
World Cup retails for $40–50. The average sports bra costs around $30.
In addition, the investment of time and money required to discipline
one's body to work towards this feminine standard is substantial.
Therefore, the beauty ideal is not only gendered, but also raced and
classed as well.

This normative ideal of female beauty has been directly con-   42
nected to discussions of Brandi Chastain. Sullivan's (1999) *Time* magazine article, "Goodbye to Heroin Chic. Now It's Sexy to Be Strong,"

proposed, "perhaps the botters' [soccer players] out-front sexuality will prompt all their come-lately fans—girls and boys both—to reconsider what constitutes healthy, full-bodied femininity" (p. 63). Likewise, the "new aesthetic" Chastain exemplifies "appears to be replacing the traditional dewy paradigm," according to one article in the *Wall Street Journal* ("Comment, 2000, p. A24). Brubach (1996) also speculated on the increasing acceptance of strong female bodies in the 1990s. Brubach, however, suggested that this ideal might be as damaging as other models of femininity, asking, "will the tyranny of the body built for sports be any less punishing—or any healthier—than the tyranny of the body built for fashion?" (p. 48). Like Chernin's (1981) "tyranny of slenderness," involving eating disorders and cultural preoccupations with body size, the discipline required for "the body built for sports" can be damaging to a woman's physical and psychological well being (Park, 1994). The disciplinary practices required for athletic femininity can be tyrannical and the homogenized images of women in their sports bras contribute to powerful forms of docility and normalization.

In *Discipline and Punish* Michael Foucault (1977) theorizes that   43
disciplinary power used by institutions, such as prisons, hospitals, and schools, produces "docile bodies" that are compliant with societal regimes of power. Using the metaphor of Jeremy Benthama's Panopticon, Foucault argues that, in modern society, discipline has been transformed from external force or coercion to internal self-surveillance. Sandra Lee Bartky (1988) argues that Foucault's formulation is "blind" to the ways in which disciplinary practice "turns a female body into a feminine one" (p. 78). Bartky purposes that power emanating from sources such as friends, media, and beauty experts should be considered in the production of docile female bodies.

Scholars have attended to the disciplinary regimes of diet, exer-   44
cise, and sport to interrogate the production of docile bodies (see, for example, Andrews, 1993; Bordo, 1993; Cole, 1994; Johns & Johns, 2000; Spitzack, 1990; Theberge, 1991). Duncan (1994) argues that textual mechanisms in *Shape* magazine result in women's obsessive self-monitoring, furthering the ends of patriarchy and detracting from the empowering possibilities of an active and healthy lifestyle. Eskes, Duncan, and Miller (1998) found that ideologies of empowerment espoused in the rhetoric of women's fitness magazines are "framed in such a way that true health is bypassed for the sake of beauty" (p. 340). Maguire and Mansfield (1998) contend that aerobic exercise "perpetuates the objectification of female bodies, organizing the reshaping of their bodies so that they are (hetero) sexually appealing" (p. 134). Others have argued that the sexualization and objectification of the seemingly transgressive physiques of female bodybuilders recuperate those bodies under the masculine gaze (Balsamo, 1994; MacNeill, 1988). As such,

potentially liberating physical activity instead reinforces patriarchal views of femininity and maintains the gendered subordination of women.

The unidirectional consideration of the production of docility, however, often ignores women's agency (Deveaux, 1994; Hall, 1996). Rather, as Markula (1995) argues in her study of aerobicizers, women do not completely internalize the panoptic power arrangement, but instead actively "question the body ideal and are particularly skeptical about the media presentation of exercising women" (p. 449; see also Collins, 2002; Hall, 1993; Lenskyj, 1994; Lloyd, 1996). Whereas individuals negotiate the meanings of cultural texts, the empowering potential of sport and exercise is jeopardized when those physical activities are cast as a means of achieving dominant and oppressive feminine ideals.   45

The popular representations of sports bras are implicated in the (re)production of these ideals of femininity. For figures such as Brandi Chastain and the women in sports-bra advertisements, female strength, power, and autonomy are often subverted into sexualized attractiveness. Like others, Solomon (2000) posited that athletic female bodies have come to constitute what we culturally consider to be an attractive form of femininity. As Solomon argued, however, "The increasing acceptance of powerful women's bodies has been matched by a frantic attempt at containment. Yes, buff is beautiful—but only as long as its function is to be gawked at by guys." Unrestrained female power disrupts culturally gendered hierarchies. By reformulating that power as (hetero) sexually attractive, these popular mediated representations of sports bras help to restrain it, reining that power in under an objectifying gaze.   46

All this is not to say that the production of particular feminine ideals is only enacted through and by mediated images of sports bras. Though these popular images do ideological work by normalizing and sexualizing a specific type of femininity, it is not a simple case of cause and effect. Bordo (1993) argues that bodies become disciplined through "the practices and bodily habits of everyday life" and not only through images that represent ideal femininity (p. 16). Likewise, Bartky (1988) writes that the "disciplinary power that inscribes femininity on the female body is everywhere and it is nowhere; the disciplinarian is everyone and yet no one in particular" (p. 74). The discipline required to strive for an athletic, feminine ideal should not be seen emanating only from an external, coercive force, such as popular mediated representations. Yet the images of women in their sports bras offer one of the many ways of examining how we continually consider, interpret, construct, perpetuate, and revise our ways of thinking about femininity and female bodies.   47

CONCLUSION

I began this article curious about why there was so much fuss over a   48
sports bra. There is no singular or elementary answer to this question.
Perhaps one of the issues that complicate this analysis is that, as Brandi
Chastain celebrated the World Cup victory in 1999, what she revealed
was much more than a sports bra. To some, Chastain revealed the body of
a female athlete in all its unabashed, muscular glory. To others, Chastain's
divesture was akin to a striptease, revealing a female body proffered for
masculine consumption. A number of onlookers felt Chastain's gesture
was not revealing at all, but rather the way soccer players have traditionally celebrated goals. Other spectators felt that Chastain revealed
her bra—not a piece of sports equipment, but a piece of lingerie that
has traditionally been a source of titillation. Certain individuals read
the moment as a symbol of the progress of women's sports, whereas
there were those who felt saddened that a significant moment in that
progress was cheapened by a bawdy display. A portion of those
witnessing Chastain's celebration understood it as an example of
the commodification of sports and athletic bodies. Others interpreted
the action as a woman calculating to capitalize on the moment in one
of the few venues open to women athletes—that is, marketing her
(hetero) sexuality. In short, what was revealed at the moment Brandi
Chastain removed her soccer jersey was what Michael Messner (1994)
terms the "contested ideological terrain" that has come to characterize
the female athlete and her body.

It is a mistake to think that the iconic sports-bra moments and   49
advertisements mentioned in this article are just about the sports bras.
In some representations, such as those of Brandi Chastain, we must
consider the process by which the sports bra is made visible. A significant portion of the population seemed to lack the frame of reference for
understanding a woman removing her shirt in public, or else their
frames of reference led them to equate the removal with a provocative
gesture. Once the sports bra can be seen publicly, either by disrobing or
by wearing it without a covering shirt, the garment is often sexualized.
Brassieres of all sorts are sexualized, but the sports bra presents an interesting case because it is simultaneously lingerie, sports equipment, and
a fashion statement. In addition, sports bras have traditionally compressed women's breasts for comfort and protection in physical activity. Sports-bra advertisements, however, show women that they can
buy garments that will shape their breasts into ways considered sexually attractive. Finally, popular representations of sports bras offer a
gateway into larger issues about women's bodies. Mediated images of
sports bras homogenize and normalize a particular feminine ideal.

Although this ideal is about strength and fitness, it is packaged in ways that reproduce the traditional gender order. The disciplinary practices that produce these strong and fit bodies are recaptured through sexualized discourse. As such, athletic versions of femininity are not seen as threats, but as particular bodies rendered acceptable to the objectifying gaze.

REFERENCES

Ackerman, E. (1999, July 26). She kicks. She scores. She sells. *U.S. News & World Reports*, p. 42.

Andrews, D.-L. (1993). Desperately seeking Michel: Foucault's genealogy, the body, and critical sport sociology, *Sociology of Sport Journal*, **10**, 148–167.

Andrews, D.L., & Jackson, S.J. (Eds.). (2001). *Sport stars: The cultural politics of sporting celebrity*, London: Routledge.

Barr, A. (2000, June 19). Lucy on the web with sports bras. *Adweek*, p. 6.

Balsamo, A. (1994). Feminist bodybuilding. In S. Birrell & C.L. Cole (Eds.), *Women, sport, and culture* (pp. 341–352). Champaign, IL: Human Kinetics.

Barr, M. (1997, November 11). Women runners full of praise for sports bra. *The Plain Dealer*, p. 4E. Retrieved October 5, 2001, from the LexisNexis database.

Bartky, S.L. (1988). Foucault, femininity, and the modernization of patriarchal power. In I. Diamond & L. Quinby (Eds.), *Feminism and Foucault: Reflections on resistance* (pp. 61–86). Boston: Northeastern University Press.

Bartolomeo, J. (2000, January/February). Sports style: Underwear busts out. *Women's Sport & Fitness*, p. 42.

Bell, G. (2001, July 29). A little All-Star and a lot of spectacle. *The New York Times*, p. 8–10.

Benson, E., & Esten, J. (1996). *Un-mentionables: A brief history of underwear*, New York: Simon & Schuster.

Birrell, S., & McDonald, M.G. (Eds.). (2000). *Reading sport: Critical essays on power and representation*. Boston: Northeastern University Press.

Bordo, S. (1993). *Unbearable weight: Feminism, western culture, and the body*. Berkeley: University of California Press.

Braughman, C. (1995). *Women on ice: Feminist essays on the Tonya Harding/ Nancy Kerrigan spectacle*. New York: Routledge.

Brodeur, N. (1999, August 26). World cup bra incident uplifts girls. *The Seattle Times*, p. B1. Retrieved October 5, 2001, from the LexisNexis database.

Brown, S.-S. (1999, July 18). Nike bra gets good exposure. *Denver Rocky Mountain news*, p. 2S. Retrieved October 5, 2001, from the LexisNexis database.

Brownmiller, S. (1984). *Femininity*. New York: Linden Press/Simon & Schuster.

Brubach, H. (1996, June 23). The athletic esthetic. *New York Times Magazine*, pp. 48; 50–51.

Bruce, T. & Hallinan, C. (2001). Cathy Freeman: The quest for Australian identity. In D.L. Andrews & S.J. Jackson (Eds.), *Sport stars: The cultural politics of sporting celebrity* (pp. 257–270). London: Routledge.

Carter, A. (1992). *Underwear: The fashion history*. New York: Drama.

Champion Jogbra (2000, September). Get in shape. *Women's Sport & Fitness*, p. 62.

Chastain, B. (1999, October 25). A whole new ball game. *Newsweek*, p. 76.

Cherain, K. (1981). *The obsession: Reflections on the tyranny of slenderness*. New York: Harper and Row.

Christopherson, N., Janning, M., & McConnell, E.-D. (2002). Two kicks forward, one kick back: A content analysis of media discourses on the 1999 Women's World Cup soccer championship. *Sociology of Sport Journal*, **19**, 170–188.

Cole, C.L. (1994). Resisting the canon: Feminist cultural studies, sport, and technologies of the body. In S. Birrell & C.L. Cole (Eds.), *Women, sport, and culture* (pp. 5–29), Champaign, IL: Human Kinetics.

Cole, C.L., & Hribar, A. (1995). Celebrity feminism: Nike style, post-Fordism, transcendence, and consumer power. *Sociology of Sport Journal*, **12**, 347–369.

Collins, L.H. (2002). Working out the contradictions: Feminism and aerobics. *Journal of Sport & Social Issues*, **26**, 85–109.

Comment: The fair sex. (2000, May 11). *Wall Street Journal*, p. A24.

Crothers, T. (2000, July 3). Spectacular takeoff. *Sports Illustrated*, pp. 64–67.

Davies, T. (1999, July 26). Brandi's brazen celebration. *Maclean's*, p. 10.

Delaney, A. (1998, March 31). How we got rid of the bloody corsets and other tales of women's sports. *On the Issues: The Progressive Women's Quarterly*. Retrieved September 1, 2002 from *http://www.il.proquest.com/products/pt-product-genderwatch.shtml*

Deveaux, M. (1994). Feminism and empowerment: A critical reading of Foucault. *Feminist Studies*, **20**, 223–247.

Disch, L., & Kane, M.-J. (2000). When a looker is really a bitch: Lisa Olson, sport, and the heterosexual matrix. In S. Birrell & M.-G. McDonald (Eds.), *Reading sport: Critical essays on power and representation* (pp. 108–143). Boston: Northeastern University Press.

Dolbow, S. (2002, January 14). Champion sports bra: Not for jocks. *Brandweek*, p. 9.

Duncan, M.C. (1990). Sports photographs and sexual difference: Images of women and men in the 1984 and 1988 Olympic games. *Sociology of Sport Journal*, **7**, 22–43.

Duncan, M.C. (1994). The politics of women's body images and practices: Foucault, the panopticon, and *Shape* magazine. *Journal of Sport & Social Issues*, **18**, 48–65.

Duquin, M.E. (1989). Fashion and fitness: Images in women's magazine ads. *Arena Review*, **13**, 97–109.

Eisenberg, J. (2001, August 1). Rooney: Cross my heart, wearing a bra "not that bad." *The Palm Beach Post*, p. 8C. Retrieved October 5, 2001, from the LexisNexis database.

Eskes, T.-B., Duncan, M.C., & Miller, E.M. (1998). The discourse of empowerment: Foucault, Marcuse, and women's fitness texts. *Journal of Sport & Social Issues*, **22**, 317–344.

Ewing, E. (1972). *Underwear: A history*. New York: Theatre Arts Books.

Ewing, E. (1978). *Dress and undress: A history of women's underwear*. New York: Drama Book Specialists.

Farrell-Beck, J., & Gau, C. (2002). *Uplift: The bra in America*. Philadelphia: University of Pennsylvania Press.

Fiske, J. (1989). *Television culture*. New York: Methuen.

Foucault, M. (1977). *Discipline and punish: The birth of the prison*. New York: Pantheon Books.

Gardner, C.-F. (2001, July 29). A stripped down showing by stars. *Milwaukee Journal Sentinel*, p. 11C. Retrieved October 5, 2001, from the LexisNexis database.

Gerhart, A. (1999, July 14). Cashing in on world cups. *Washington Post*, p. C01.

Githens, L. (1999, July 27). A show of support. *The Buffalo (New York) News*. Retrieved September 1, 2000, from the LexisNexis database.

Givhan, R. (2001, July 13). Winner takes (off) all. *The Washington Post*. p. C02.

Hall, M.A. (1993). Feminism, theory and the body: a response to Cole. *Journal of Sport & Social Issues*, **17**, 98–105.

Hall, M.A. (1996). *Feminism and sporting bodies*. Champaign, IL: Human Kinetics.

Hall, S. (1980). Encoding/decoding. In S. Hall (Ed.), *Culture, Medical, Language* (pp. 128–138). London: Hutchinson.

Hargreaves, J. (1987). The body, sport and power relations. In J. Horne, D. Jary, & A. Tomlinson (Eds.), *Sport, leisure and social relations* (pp. 139–159). London: Routledge & Kegan Paul.

Hargreaves, J. (1994). *Sporting females: Critical issues in the history and sociology of women's sports*. London: Routledge.

Harvey, R. (1999, December 2). With so much exposure, Brandi can bare her soul. *Los Angeles Times*, p. D2.

Hickey, P. (1999, July 18). Juneau, Habs might be a nice fit. *The Gazette (Montreal, Quebec).* Retrieved October 5, 2001, from the LexisNexis database.

Hiestand, M. (1999, October 28). Moment spurs a movement. *USA Today*, p. 3C.

Hollander, A.L. (1978). *Seeing through clothes.* New York: The Viking Press.

Hummer, S. (2000, September 29). Soccer's fairy-tale story has silver end. *The Atlanta Journal and Constitution*, p. 8E.

Hyman, M. (1999, July 26). The 'babe factor' in women's soccer. *Business Week*, p. 118. Retrieved October 5, 2001, from the ABI/INFORM Global database.

Jackson, S.J. (2001). Gretzky nation: Canada, crisis and Americanization. In D.-L. Andrews & S.J. Jackson (Eds.), *Sport stars: The cultural politics of sporting celebrity* (pp. 164–186). London: Routledge.

Jogbra. (1979, March). No man-made bra can touch it. *WomenSports*, p. 21.

Jogbra. (1985, April). Jogbra: The most important profile in sports history. *Women's Sport & Fitness*, p. 70.

Jogbra. (1986, March). *Women's Sport & Fitness*, p. 9.

Jogbra (1996, May/June). *Women's Sport and Fitness*, p. 49.

Johns, D.P., & Johns, J.-S. (2000). Surveillance, subjectivism, and technologies of power. An analysis of the discursive practice of high-performance sport. *International Review for the Sociology of Sport*, **35**, 219–234.

Jones, G.L. (2000, February 1). Women's team agrees to 'historic' deal. *The Sporting News.* Retrieved June 13, 2002, from *http://tsn.sportingnews.com/voices/grahamel.jones/20000201-p.html*

Jones, G.L. (2001, July 29). Rooney gives full support. *Los Angeles Times*, p. D9.

Kent, M. (2000, August 13). Women's sexual revolution runs into knee-jerk response from male reactionaries. *Scotland on Sunday*, p. T13. Retrieved October 5, 2001, from the LexisNexis database.

Kimball, G. (1999, July 15). Getting tuned into women's soccer. *The Irish Times.* Retrieved October 5, 2001, from the LexisNexis database.

Kimball, G. (2000, July 4). Soccer; a case of overexposure; Chastain still defines Cup win. *The Boston Herald*, p. O60. Retrieved October 5, 2001, from the LexisNexis database.

Leath, V.M., & Lumpkin, A. (1992). An analysis of sportswomen on the covers and in feature articles of *Women's Sports & Fitness Magazine*, 1975–1989. *Journal of Sport & Social Issues*, **16**, 121–126.

Lee, H.M. (1984). Athletics and the bikini girls from Piazza Armerina. *Stadion*, **10**, 45–77.

Lenskyj, H. (1994). Sexuality and femininity in sport contexts: Issues and alternatives. *Journal of Sport & Social Issues*, **18**, 356–376.

Leonard, T. (2001, July 31). Having too much fun at All-Star showcase. *The Record (Bergen County, New Jersey)*, p. S8. Retrieved October 5, 2001, from the LexisNexis database.

Lily of France. (1979, August). Running good for every part of you but two. *Women's Sports*, p. 8.

Lloyd, M. (1996). Feminism, aerobics and the politics of the body. *Body & Society*, **2**, 79–98.

Longman, J. (1999, July 12). Women's world cup: Day in the sun for the girls of summer after a riveting championship run. *New York Times*, p. D1.

Longman, J. (2000). *The girls of summer: The U.S. Women's Soccer Team and how it changed the world*. HarperCollins Publishers.

lucy.com. (2000, September). The uniboob epiphany. *Women's Sport & Fitness*, p. 52.

Macdonald, M. (1995). *Representing women: Myths of femininity in the popular media*. London: Edward Arnold.

MacNeill, M. (1988). Active women, media representations, ideology. In J. Harvey & G. Cantelon (Eds.), *Not just a game: Essays in Canadian sports sociology* (pp. 195–212). Alona, MB: University of Ottawa Press.

Maguire, J. & Mansfield, L. (1998). "No-body's perfect": Women, aerobics, and the body beautiful. *Sociology of Sport of Journal*, **15**, 109–137.

Mahoney, R. (2001, July 29). Donovan reveals skins, skills; Chastain imitators cap All-Star game. *The Washington Post*, p. D10.

Markula, P. (1995). Firm but shapely, fit but sexy, strong but thin: The postmodern aerobicizing female bodies. *Sociology of Sport Journal*, **12**, 424–453.

Markula, P. (2001). Beyond the perfect body: Women's Body Image Distortion in fitness magazine discourse. *Journal of Sport & Social Issues*, **25**, 158–179.

McDonald, M.G., & Birrell, S. (1999). Reading sport critically: A methodology for interrogating power. *Sociology of Sport Journal*, **16**, 283–300.

McKee, S. (2000, July 7). On sports: Joie de soccer. *Wall Street Journal*, p. W4.

Middleton, C. (2000, September 29). Golden goal sinks golden girls. *The Daily Telegraph*, p. 41. Retrieved October 5, 2001, from the LexisNexis database.

Mead, R. (1999, July 26). The talk of the town. *The New Yorker*, p. 25.

Messner, M.A. (1994). Sports and male domination: The female athlete as contested ideological terrain. In S. Birrell, & C.L. Cole (Eds.), *Women, sport and culture* (pp. 65–80). Champaign, IL: Human Kinetics.

More Brandi, please. (2000, September 30). *The San Diego Union-Tribune*, p. 2. Retrieved October 12, 2003, from the LexisNexis database.

Mulvey, L. (1975). Visual pleasure and narrative cinema. *Screen*, **16**(3), 6–18.

Mulvey, L. (1981). Afterthoughts on 'Visual pleasure and narrative cinema' inspired by 'Duel in the Sun' (King Vidor, 1946). *Framework*, **15**, 12–15.

Neporent, L. (1994, February). Fit for a woman. *Women's Sport & Fitness*, pp. 76–83.

Nike (1999, September/October). After years of exercise, what kind of shape will your breasts be in? *Women's Sports & Fitness*, pp. 96–97.

Nyad, D., & Hogan, C.-L. (1998). Women: Empowered by the evolution of sports technology. In A. Bush (Ed.), *Designs for sports: The cult of performance* (pp. 46–67). New York: Princeton Architectural Press.

Park, R.J. (1994). A decade of the body: Researching and writing about the history of health, fitness, exercise and sport, 1983–1993. *Journal of Sport History*, **21**, 59–82.

Payne, S. (1999, July 19). Shirts off to sports bras soccer star's topless turn puts undergarment in spotlight. *The Toronto Sun*. Retrieved October 5, 2001, from the LexisNexis database.

Peck, S. (1999). The bra: Brandi's public peeldown turned the spotlight on the humble sports bra. Retrieved September 20, 2001, from *car/1999/feat_bra1.html" http://www.justforwomen.com/features/year/1999/feat_bra1.html*

Penner, M. (1999, July 11). Bare facts make these two heroes. *Los Angeles Times*, p. D1.

Penner, M. (2000, September 12). Moment's over; now U.S. soccer hero Chastain can get back to game. *Los Angeles Times*, p. D1.

Phillips, J., & Phillips, P. (1993). History from below: Women's underwear and the rise of women's sport. *Journal of Popular Culture*, **27**, 129–148.

Purdie, L. (1988, January/February). Function first. *Women's Sport & Fitness*, p. 63.

Reyburn, W. (1971). *Bust-up*. Englewood Cliffs, NJ: Prentice-Hall, Inc.

Riley, L. (2000, September 21). Bra's support not universal. *The Hartford (Connecticut) Courant*, p. A1. Retrieved October 5, 2001, from the LexisNexis database.

Rozel, L.A. (2002, June 3). Athletes are strapped by sports bra flap. *The Tampa Tribune*. Retrieved August 9, 2002, from the LexisNexis database.

Runner disqualified for illegal bra. (2002, May 31). Retrieved June 3, 2002, from *http://news.findlaw.com/legalnews/sports/index.html*

Saint-Laurent, C. (1966). *A history of ladies underwear*. London: Michael Joseph.

Saporito, B., & Willwerth, J. (1999, July 17). Flat-out fantastic. *Time*, pp. 58–64.

Sharp, D. (1994, September). The women who took the jounce out of jogging. *Health*, p. 25.

Smoron, P. (1999, July 25). A nice Hamm. *Chicago Sun Times*, p. 6. Retrieved October 5, 2001, from the LexisNexis database.

Solomon, A. (2000, April 19–25). Our bodies, ourselves. Retrieved September 12, 2002, from *http://www.villagevoice.com/issues/0016/solomon2.php*

Spencer, N.-E. (2000). Reading between the lines: A discursive analysis of the Billie Jean King vs. Bobby Riggs "Battle of the Sexes." *Sociology of Sport Journal*, **17**, 386–402.

Spitzack, C. (1990). *Confessing excess: Women and the politics of body reduction*. Albany, NY: State University of New York Press.

Sullivan, R. (1999, July 19). Goodbye heroin chic. Now it's sexy to be strong. *Time*, p. 62.

Theberge, N. (1991). Reflections on the body in the sociology of sport. *Quest*, **43**, 148–167.

Tresniowski, A. (1999, July 26). Soccer's happiest feat. *People Magazine*, pp. 54–60.

Vande Berg, L.R. (1998). The sports hero meets mediated celebrityhood. In L.-A. Wenner (Ed.), *MediaSport* (pp. 134–153). London: Routledge.

Wagman, R. (2001, August 9). All-Star sports bra frivolity damages MLS public image. *SoccerTimes*. Retrieved October 5, 2001, from *http://www.soccertimes.com/wagman/2001/aug09.htm*

Wells, M., & Oldenburg, A. (1999, July 13). Sports bra's flash could cash in. *USA Today*, p. 1A.

Whannel, G. (2002). *Media sport stars: Masculinities and moralities*. London: Routledge.

White, P.G., & Gillett, J. (1994). Reading the muscular body: A critical decoding of advertisements in *Flex* magazine. *Sociology of Sport Journal*, **11**, 18–39.

Willis, S. (1990). Working out. *Cultural Studies*, **4**, 1–18.

Yalom, M. (1997). *A history of the breast*. New York: Random House.

Young, I.-M. (1990). *Throwing like a girl and other essays in feminist philosophy and social theory*. Indianapolis: Indiana University Press.

NOTES

[1]For a complete story of the 1999 Women's World Cup, see Longman's (2000) *The Girls of Summer: The U.S. Women's Soccer Team and How It Changed the World*. For an analysis of media discourses surrounding the 1999 World Cup, see Christopherson, Janning, and McConnell (2002).

[2]In this article, I will use the term *objectifying gaze* to refer to the practices of surveillance that construe women as objects of sexual desire. My conceptualization of this term is particularly informed by the work of Laura Mulvey (1975, 1981).

[3]JogBra was sold to Playtex apparel in 1990. JogBra is now a division of Champion Products (Barr, 1997).

[4]It should be noted that Linda Medalen, a female player on the Norwegian national team, also removed her jersey after scoring a goal in an earlier round of the 1999 World Cup, though the act received little media attention.

[5]Public acceptance of a woman in a sports bra without a covering top is not unanimous. For example, in Tampa, Florida, high school officials deemed it "inappropriate" for female runners to wear sports bras without a shirt (Rozel, 2002). An official at a track meet in Wisconsin disqualified a relay team from Stevens Point Area Senior High School because one runner wore a sports bra (Runner Disqualified for Illegal Bra, 2002).

[6]For more on lucy.com's advertising see Baar (2000), p. 6.

[7]This advertisement turned out to be rather controversial. As a result, the advertisement that revealed the model's breasts only appeared in magazines that went to subscription holders. Magazines sold in stores or at newsstands, as well as those in magazines geared toward a younger audience, such as *Seventeen* and *YM*, were altered so that the model's hair hung down over her breasts.

Examining the Text

1. In what ways does Schultz link the practical aspects of the sports bra with its role as an erotic garment? Do you agree with the author's position that it both enables women to participate in sports yet carries with it a certain eroticism? Why, according to Schultz, does the popular media regard the sports bra as an "object of sexual desire, a means of disciplining the breast . . . and disciplining the body?"

2. How does the historical background on the mechanics of brassieres and sports—specifically the various methods women have used to compete athletically, unhindered by their breasts—tie in with current societal perceptions of women's undergarments? What does the response to Chastain publicly exposing her sports bra indicate to you about how the media regard the behavior of women in sports versus male players?

3. Why do you think the media used words like "striptease," "peel-down," "strip-down" and similar terms to describe Chastain's actions in taking off her jersey but referred to the Donovan and Rooney jersey-removals as "ripping off," "whipping off," and "removing"? What does the difference in the descriptions used tell you about gender, power and sexual contexts of language? And why do you think that Ian Bishop, a team-mate of Rooney and Donovan's, chose not to participate in mocking Chastain? What does his response imply about sexual stereotypes?

For Group Discussion

1. As a group, discuss how sexual stereotypes are found in sports. You might begin by listing a range of possible stereotypes, and then go on to discuss the ways in which these stereotypes affect (a) the sport; (b) women's participation in sports in general. What suggestions does the group have to overcome sexual stereotypes of the type identified by Schultz in the article?

2. Re-read the section that begins with the heading, "Tempest in a B-Cup," and discuss whether you believe that, on reflection, Chastain's action in removing her jersey helped or hindered public perceptions about women's sports. Be mindful, that in some cultures, it would be frowned upon (or even illegal) for women to participate in sports. Contrast that to the apparent sexual objectification of women athletes in the United States.

Writing Suggestion

Title IX of the US Civil Rights Act requires schools to provide equal access for girls and boys in school sports and is credited with an upsurge in girls and women participating in a range of athletic activities. Develop a thesis and write an essay discussing the question of whether you think that equality in sports has been achieved. Conversely, you might defend a position asserting that such equality can never be achieved in our society. As you develop your argument, consider all of the ways in which you either agree or disagree with the notion of equality. To provide evidence for your arguments in the body paragraphs of your paper, you might conduct research using the following: the sports section of your daily newspaper, sports coverage on television, sports franchises, gender of coaches, athlete incomes by gender and other sources to inform your essay.

Jack of Smarts: Why the Internet Generation Loves to Play Poker

Justin Peters

Poker has leapt from dimly lit back rooms inhabited by avuncular cigar-chewers to the bright lights of TV broadcast and tech-savvy Generation X-ers weaned on Game Boys and surfing the Internet, according to author Justin Peters. He lays out a poker-*related generation gap in this article first published by the Washington Post. In it, age and perceptions about poker are key elements as the author documents how his own changing attitude to the card game parallels a broader shift that has taken place as a result of Internet poker and the televising of poker tournaments. Peters speculates that poker was declining in interest to the younger generation . . . until the Internet changed that, perhaps forever.*

Peters argues that fear of being perceived as a "novice" kept his generation out of traditional venues of poker games in the past, but that with the advent of anonymous online poker, younger players could participate without any potential embarrassment. The author also attributes the rising popularity of poker to the renewed interest by TV producers who, he says, have figured out a formula for showing poker on television. These combined factors have led to new players entering the professional circuit—and winning big! The author concludes that the qualities essential in a good poker player are aligned with traits that a generation exposed to hours of video games and computer-use already possess. Peters believes that members of his generation are playing poker to such a degree that it has transcended mere novelty into popular entertainment and even parody.

***As you read**, think about how your own perceptions and images of poker players have been formed. For instance, do you recall aged relatives playing poker at holiday times, or yourself playing as a child for candy or play money? Conversely, did televised poker spark your awareness of the game for the first time? How do your memories/perceptions relate to the stereotypes described by Peters? How successful is the author in making his experience relate to your own as a reader?*

Before this year, my only experience with poker was at basketball camp   1
when I was 12. We played during rest periods with Skittles for chips
and about seven different wild cards per hand. Although fun, the game
paled by comparison to other leisure pursuits, such as sleeping, and I
never gave it much thought after that. Yet during the past year, I have
unexpectedly changed my tune. I've joined a weekly card game. I
waste hours surfing online poker sites. I try to drop poker phrases like
"bad beat" and "the nuts" into casual conversation. When I won $140
at the table in February, I spent weeks regaling everybody I knew with
chapter and verse of my victory. Most reacted with raised eyebrows
and condescension, but similarly afflicted friends of mine understood,
greeting the story with measured awe, as if I were Amarillo Slim.

These days poker—specifically Texas hold 'em, the best version of   2
the venerable game—is enjoying an unexpected renaissance among
Americans in general, and twenty-somethings in particular. It is newly
ubiquitous on television: The World Series of Poker, a single event
which took place last May, is replayed on ESPN with obsessive frequency 10 months after it ended. The World Poker Tour, another set of
tournaments located in casinos around the country, got picked up by

the Travel Channel last year. In the fall, Bravo introduced its heavily promoted "Celebrity Poker Showdown" program, betting on viewers being riveted by a fifth-street showdown between Timothy Busfield and Coolio. But perhaps anecdotal evidence speaks louder: Three years ago, when I was a sophomore at Cornell University, there wasn't a game to be had. By the time I graduated, I could choose from several different games every night of the week.

Every generation gambles, but how they gamble says something   3 about the spirit of the age. Why are yuppies-in-the-making suddenly interested in poker, a game most of us grew up associating with either paneled basements and cheap cigars or Rococo Old West saloons filled with bolo-tied card sharps? The answer may be that the popular image of the game has undergone a subtle recasting—one with a great attraction to ironic youngsters like me who find in the game the same slightly glamorous, slightly seedy, go-getter spirit that characterized the Internet boom. It makes sense that today's college-educated young adults, especially young men, choose poker. Strategy oriented, individualistic, and embedded in a nice masculine mythology, poker is the perfect game for the revenge-of-the-nerds generation looking to square their intelligence with their inner maleness.

BOOMTOWNS TO POKER BLOGS

Poker first appeared in the United States in the 1820s, brought to New   4 Orleans by French immigrants who called the game poque. It traveled up the Mississippi River and spread throughout the country, soon becoming an underground national pastime, baseball for the unathletic. As the century turned, poker maintained its popularity, but lost its phenomenon status. Though television shows like "Maverick" in 1957 and the 1971 mini-series "The Gambler" later mythologized the poker players of the good old days—the dandified 1840s gambler, kind to women and merciless to cheaters—no one looked for glory or drama in modern poker anymore. To callow youth like me, the game looked like just another thing that Babbitty men did, like the Rotary club, or golf. People's dads played poker.

And then we started playing poker, too. Like everything else with   5 my generation, technological innovation helped enable our new hobby. By the late '90s and early 2000s, dozens of online casinos had sprung up, allowing the Internet to tap its full potential as a 24-hour gaming paradise. Free from the annoying sanctions of the U.S. Penal Code, these offshore virtual Monte Carlos offered interested parties the opportunity to wager 'round the clock. Especially popular were online poker rooms, where you could play—for money, real or fake—against all comers. For many would-be players, the fear of looking like confused novices in front of a room full of old hands used to keep them from the tables. Now, the online poker rooms provide a convenient place to learn and refine the game at home with no one watching. More recent arrivals are the poker blogs shilling for their favorite sites, swooning over their favorite pros, and telling their stories about the hands that got away.

Televised poker is also a lot better than it used to be. For too long,   6
TV executives were unsure how to treat their poker coverage, cramming it into late-night time slots on cable sports networks. This was odd, as poker belongs in the same dubious semi-sport category as eating contests or spelling bees. Not only did it require no physical prowess, but due to prolonged exposure to tobacco, free drinks, and fluorescent lights, many of the game's finest players appear to be chronic palpitators and arrythmiacs. Little wonder that it never got good ratings on ESPN or the "Wide World of Sports." But with the Travel Channel, formerly the repository of such stinkers as "Busch Gardens Revealed" and "Incredible Vacation Videos," poker met its perfect match. The station has been the prime propagator and beneficiary of the poker craze with its "World Poker Tour" viewing block, which sends viewers casino-hopping around the world to a new poker tournament each week, open to all comers for a modest entrance fee. In its breathless approximation of legitimate sports coverage, the production is hilariously WWFesque in a way that appeals perfectly to ironic 20-somethings: lots of gaudy money shots, a blonde "sideline reporter" who conducts exit interviews with ousted players, and "expert" announcers coming off as campy parodies of real sportscasters, with their nicknaming and jargonese. Well-placed cameras reveal each player's hole cards, allowing viewers at home to revel in omniscience even as they attempt to follow the thought processes of the bettors and sharpen their own skills at home.

Indeed, some of the best self-taught players, variants of 1990s   7
computer nerds, are finding success in the pro poker circuit. The reigning World Series champion is a chubby, eagle-eyed 28-year-old Tennessee accountant with the Dickensian name of Chris Moneymaker. Moneymaker had learned the game just three years earlier and perfected his tricks by playing Internet poker obsessively. The 2003 World Series was his first professional event, and he beat hundreds of long-time professionals, walking away with $2.5 million, and the near-worshipful admiration of millions of delusional amateurs like myself.

BASEBALL FOR THE UNATHLETIC

The myth and aura of the game have perhaps never before been in such   8
perfect accord with the aspirations of a generation. In the post-tech-boom years, the archetype of male success and cool mixes laddish

cockiness and financial acumen. To my friends, blackjack seems like a game for those who trust their fate to chance or byzantine card-counting schemes. Slots are for the old, the overweight, and certain right-wing morality mavens. But poker, you see—for us poker has cache. Most forms of gambling depend on chance, but poker requires skill and it's easy to believe that the player with the strongest will is going to win, leaving weaker minds to will in his wake.

Many of us were introduced to the modern face of poker by the   9
1997 movie Rounders, starring Matt Damon as a debt-ridden poker prodigy, which developed something of a cult status on many college campuses. Rounders popularized the act of reading someone's "tell"— the unique facial or bodily tics that unintentionally reveal his hand. At some games, table banter is nonexistent the players just look at each other, trying in vain to "read" the table's reactions. It's this mental aspect of the game that attracts so many young players. "Before Rounders, I just thought of poker as something they played in saloons in Westerns, and boring five-card draw," says Arthur Wellington, a poker-obsessed student at Lehigh University in Pennsylvania. "[The movie] made me realize there was a lot more to the game than just betting on cards turned over."

My friends and I play every week, sometimes many times a week.   10
A revolving cast of (young, male) characters show up at the games. We are all terrible. Everybody adopts a different persona. I am nearly silent during the game, hoping to project an image of cool rival examination and categorization of everyone else's reactions—a masterful command of the art of the "read". The reality is rather different. Usually I'm just thinking about how hungry I am, or I'm distracted by the TV. But the reality doesn't matter.

One guy, Jesse, is known for buying in, busting out, and repeating   11
the cycle multiple times in the course of one night's action, without giving the matter a second thought. He cheerfully admits that he is down several hundred dollars since he began playing, and he never seems too out of sorts about it, but sometimes I picture him alone, at home, having crises of conscience, staring mournfully at his empty wallet and shaking his head wordlessly.

A few of us have higher ambitions for our game, partly stirred by   12
an increased diet of televised poker. Although my friend Jake Collins had only rarely played before this summer, he is now set on becoming a professional player. I spent several weeks with him this summer in and out of various West Coast motels, where the only consistent televised entertainment we could find was poker tournaments. Thus stoked, Collins is taking a scientific approach to his play, keeping detailed charts and notebooks on his play patterns; despite real progress, he knows he's got a long way to go before he can shoot with the big

guns. He speaks with hushed admiration of professional players' Svengali-like ability to get inside other players' heads: "Those guys are so good."

FIVE-CARD NERDS

Another cult film on college campuses, the recent remake of Ocean's   13
Eleven, pokes fun at the desire of young people like me and my friends to be cool poker players. The opening scene has Brad Pitt's character, a been-around poker hand, coaching a series of Hollywood pretty boys in the finer aspects of the game. Part of the joke is that the actors playing the pretty boys are themselves Hollywood pretty boys (a pre-Punk'd Ashton Kutcher, Joshua Jackson) who don't know much about the game—upon being dealt a hand, Topher Grace gleefully blurts "Fellas! Fellas! Check this! All . . . reds!" Pitt just shakes his head.

You know something is a trend when it's not only being advanced   14
by popular culture, but satirized by it. Neophytes like me imagine that the best players possess the qualities we saw or wanted to see in our father figures: mental toughness, boldness, steadfastness. Plus, the game requires no muscle tone, physical stamina, or quick reflexes–making it a perfect match for a generation that grew up blasting away videogame monsters with the twitch of a thumb and now workdays parked in front of a computer screen. We may not have pecks, but we have the "read."

Examining the Text

1. What's the author's contention about poker appealing to his particular generation? Do you personally identify with his description of his generation? How would you characterize the tone and style of this piece? Do you believe that an older writer who had interviewed poker players of the author's generation could have written with the same tone and style?
2. Re-examine the article to see how the author links the following themes: technology, the generation gap, and issues of manliness. Do you agree with Peters' specific assertions regarding those themes? Could there be other reasons, unexplored in the article, for the apparent rising popularity of poker?
3. Do you think it reasonable for Peters to call the current popularity of poker a "craze," which might suggest a less than lasting appeal? Do you agree or disagree with him? What kind of emotional response does this article give you? Does it resonate with you and/or hold your interest? Why, or why not?

4. Do you believe that the author is right in saying that it's the "mental aspect" of poker that draws in so many younger players? If not, what additional factors might be responsible for poker's new appeal?

For Group Discussion

Survey your class (anonymously, if possible) to discover how many people have played online poker, gone to a casino to play poker, or play regularly for money at friends' homes. As a group discuss the article's central themes ("mental aspect," "fear of embarrassment," "technology") and assess whether those are the reason that poker is drawing in new players. Review the survey results and then revisit the discussion to see if actual poker players in the class were more or less inclined to agree with the author. Discuss additional reasons for the current poker "craze" that group members may have raised during the discussion.

Writing Suggestion

If you're a poker player of the type described in the article, write an essay in which you lay out how you got attracted to playing poker (either online or in card rooms) and what the continued attraction is to playing. Gambling can be addictive; in your essay be sure to explain how you have approached that issue. If you're not a poker player, conduct research to put the rising number of poker players into a broader perspective of other gambling types. How does it compare to horse-betting, roulette, lotteries, and so on? You'll want to also examine the rapid growth of Indian-owned casinos across the nation. In either essay, be sure to examine the question of whether you think the current popularity of poker is harmless, potentially harmful, or neither.

World Games: The U.S. Tries to Colonize Sport

Mike Marqusee

Look at the items you're wearing today. Do you know where your shoes, pants, jacket were manufactured? It's likely they were made in factories as far away as Indonesia, Guatemala, or the Philippines. Fewer consumer items are now made in the U.S. than a decade or two ago, yet choices have expanded and prices have, in many cases, fallen. Consumer goods of U.S. companies are often highly prominent around the world—from Coca-Cola to Nike, Timex to Levi's. In this article, author Mike Marqusee argues that the United States is attempting to corner the market in sports, much as U.S. corporations seek to dominate consumer markets around the globe.

The author is disturbed by what he sees as a troublesome trend: a link between the profit-driven goals of corporations seeking market share around the world and an assault on diverse sporting traditions in Europe, Asia, Africa, and elsewhere. He also believes that there is a connection between this apparent trend and U.S. arrogance over perceptions that its own home-grown sports— basketball, baseball, and "American" grid-iron football—have an wider importance beyond American soil. He concludes that this insidious form of U.S. "colonization," can only be ended through a resistance that transcends national barriers.

As you read, examine the article closely to understand the places in which the author attempts to link the two arenas of sports and economics. Are the two so intertwined as to amount to a form of colonization, as the author claims, or do you see them as separate issues? Do you see parallels in other areas, such as music and film?

The discourse of sport has always been prone to planetary-scale hyperbole, and in some respects the ideology of globalization when applied to sports has only taken old habits to new extremes. What is curious and revealing, however, is the way in which global pretensions are so often mingled with U.S. myopia. And nowhere was this contorted posture, so characteristic of our age, better illustrated than in an issue of *Newsweek* published in October 1999.   1

As part of its breathless celebration of the achievements of the expiring 20th century, the magazine ran a 34-page feature on sporting heroes, entitled "America's Greatest." Here the history of sport in the U.S. was presented as a triumph in which barriers of color and gender prejudice were toppled, along with sporting records, by the efforts of a succession of extraordinary individuals.   2

Amid the predictable exaggerations and omissions, there was one claim in particular that strayed most egregiously from reality. "Sports may be America's most successful export to the world," the editors wrote. "Whatever the world thinks of us, it loves our games. Major League Baseball is increasingly dominated by Latin players, and there is a growing infusion of talent from Japan and South Korea. Basketball is popular on every continent. And in Europe they now play our football along with their own."   3

When I shared this last sentence with students in London, they burst out laughing. What is known in the rest of the world as "American football" is a very minor sport in Europe, viewed by many as a testosterone-fuelled freak show.   4

And while basketball is gaining popularity in parts of Europe,   5
Asia, and Africa, it everywhere lags well behind more established team
sports, just as soccer does in the U.S. In Soweto, you will certainly find
far more Manchester United soccer shirts than Chicago Bulls caps.
Michael Jordan's fame outside his native land rests more on his role as
a shill for the world's biggest sports shoe company than his achievements on the basketball court.

WHOSE WORLD SERIES?

Contrary to the *Newsweek* dictum, sports are actually one of the U.S.'s   6
least successful exports. Other products of American popular culture—
Hollywood films, TV sitcoms, rock-n-roll, rhythm-n-blues, soul, funk,
hip-hop, fashion—have all travelled further and penetrated deeper
into foreign cultures than the games of baseball, American football, or
even basketball.

Indeed, the salient fact about the U.S. sporting culture is that it is   7
shared with so few others. Overseas, the quaint habit of denominating
the finals of the North American baseball competition as a "World
Series" is regarded as an example of typical American arrogance—more
amusing than bombing Third World countries, to be sure, but cut from
the same cloth.

It is not only in preferring their own, home-made sports to gen-   8
uinely world games such as soccer, rugby, cricket, or even field hockey
that Americans plough a furrow of their own. The ways in which sport
is produced and consumed in the U.S. are also distinctive. Despite their
preoccupation with the expression of American national identity through sports, the *Newsweek* editors seem largely unaware of those features
that actually make the U.S. sporting culture distinctive; indeed, to many
foreign observers, downright weird.

Cheerleaders, for example, are a uniquely American phenome-   9
non and attempts to introduce them abroad have enjoyed little success.
Crowds at European or Latin American soccer or South Asian or
Caribbean cricket matches would all find the notion that their response
to events on the field should be mediated by a regiment of scantily-clad
females bizarre in the extreme. Here the songs, chants, jokes, and other
means of expressing partisanship or commenting on the course of the
action emerge from within the crowd itself, often in accordance with
long-established (but continually evolving) popular traditions.

The U.S. also enjoys the dubious honor of being the only country   10
to institutionalize the use of higher education as a nursery for professional sport. When it comes to track and field or swimming, sports in
which America does compete with the world, this practice has given

the U.S. a major advantage, and levelled the playing field with the state-sponsored athletes of the old Soviet bloc. However, *ColorLines* readers will be only too familiar with the corruption and compromise of both educational and sporting values that this long-established American tradition has entailed.

These days athletes from all over the world seek to avail them-   11
selves of the facilities of U.S. higher education. For many Third World sportspersons, a stint at an American university is their only hope of translating raw talent into high-level success and financial reward. In this respect, at least some features of the U.S. sporting culture are now spreading across the globe.

While sporting professionalism was a 19th century British inno-   12
vation, Americans have led the way in the exploitation of sport for commercial purposes. Once upon a time, the idea that a sporting insti-tution like the Brooklyn Dodgers could pull up stakes and move to another locale at the whim of a private owner would have been regarded as an idiosyncratically American phenomenon. Nowadays, the corpo-rate capitalist model pioneered in the U.S. is taking hold nearly everywhere, reshaping ancient sporting traditions and transforming spectator expectations and behavior.

CAPITAL'S BATTERING RAM

Although we do not share a single global sporting culture, we do,   13
increasingly, live under the aegis of a single global sporting industry. This industry is dominated by a corporate elite whose leading mem-bers are only too well known to U.S. sports fans.

Take, for example, cricket in South Asia, a sport with a fan base of   14
many hundreds of millions. The right to exploit this huge audience via television has recently been divided up between Rupert Murdoch's Star TV and Disney's ESPN. The principal sponsors of the Indian and Pakistani cricket teams—whose stars are household names across one-fifth of humanity—are Pepsi and Coca Cola.

Murdoch also has major interests—both as broadcaster and fran-   15
chise owner—in European soccer and Australian and British rugby. In accordance with his oft-stated belief that sport is a "battering ram" for the penetration of national economies, he has teamed up with both the NBA and Manchester United in long-term projects for the development of basketball and soccer in China, capitalism's favorite emerging market.

His partners in these ventures include not only the Chinese govern-   16
ment, but also Mark McCormack's International Management Group (IMG), which has already played a leading role in reshaping professional

golf and tennis. IMG is also the promoter-manager of a series of India-Pakistan cricket clashes held annually in Toronto. While the event is not much of a spectator draw in Canada, the rights to the telecasts beamed back to a rapt South Asian audience are worth a fortune.

When the two teams faced each other on neutral ground in   17
Australia earlier this year, Murdoch and ESPN hyped the contest as "Qayamat"—judgment day. With the military dictatorship in Pakistan and the right-wing Hindu government in India exchanging accusations of terrorism and nuclear threats on a daily basis, the cricket confrontation assumed a grotesquely inflated importance, replete with menacing religious and nationalist overtones. That so many of the big players in the global sporting industry (mainly U.S.-based) now have major vested interests in over-promoting the India-Pakistan cricket rivalry speaks volumes about the distorting and dehumanizing impact of globalization on the culture of sport.

WE BRAND THE WORLD

Everywhere, the vast concentration of wealth that this process engen-   18
ders is transforming long-established competitive patterns and traditional loyalties. Inequalities within and between sports, as well as within and between national sporting cultures, are being exacerbated. In Britain, cricket withers as it finds itself unable to compete with soccer for popular attention; in South Asia, the glamour attached to cricket has marginalized field hockey, once the pride of both India and Pakistan.

The one claim in *Newsweek*'s paean to American sport that has a   19
ring of truth is the assertion that the U.S.'s "most visible symbol has, over the 20th century, evolved from the Stars and Stripes to Coke to the Swoosh." Note the complacency with which the editors appear to regard this disturbing evolution. The duty of representing a nation-state and its culture has been passed from a flag to a mass-manufactured consumer product and then to the symbol of a privately-owned corporation.

Last year at a cricket match in Sri Lanka, I witnessed the power of   20
the swoosh. A poverty-stricken young boy was hanging around outside the gate, unable to afford the price of a ticket but hoping for a glimpse of his heroes. He had no shoes, scrawny legs and dirty, ill-fitting shorts. His tattered tee shirt was hand-decorated with the letters "NIKE" and a big, black swoosh drawn painstakingly with a black marker.

I wanted to say to him what I always feel like saying to young   21
people in Britain or the U.S. who decorate themselves with the swoosh and other corporate logos: they pay Michael Jordan, Andre Agassi, and Tiger Woods millions to wear that thing—how much do they pay you?

At least the young Sri Lankan hadn't actually paid Nike for the privilege of advertising their product—unlike his contemporaries in the West—but the implication was that he would if he could have afforded to. Since he could not, replicating its corporate symbolism was the next best thing, the nearest he could come to joining the global but exclusive club of the consuming classes.

In adorning himself with the swoosh, this sports enthusiast had   22
become part of a vast web that links sweatshop laborers in South and East Asia, kids in the ghettos of North America, the corporate barons of the clothing and footwear industries, the media moguls and marketing gurus, and not least, sports administrators, sports promoters, and professional sports men and women. He had become part of what might be called the media-corporate-sport nexus—a nexus that now links together a substantial portion of the human race, but does so in a highly unequal and exploitative fashion.

THE INCREASING (GLOBAL) SIGNIFICANCE OF SPORT

One of the defining features of an information-based economy is the   23
ever-increasing value attached to "symbolic goods," that is, images and information. A mere 10 percent of the retail value of a Nike shoe is accounted for by the costs of physical production; design, marketing, and profit account for the remainder.

The company spends more on endorsements from stars than it   24
does on the entire army of low-paid workers who actually make the shoes. Remember it was Air Jordans—a product entirely dependent on its association with a sports hero—that placed Nike in pole position in the huge global sports footwear market, now worth more than $16 billion annually.

In this type of economy, sport, which is itself a symbolic good as   25
well as a highly effective carrier of symbolic values of all sorts, assumes increasing social significance and economic weight. But this development is not necessarily to the benefit of sport, sports fans, or society as a whole.

In 1998, global expenditure on sport sponsorship exceeded some   26
$15 billion (a sum that had tripled in a decade and risen by 12 percent in the previous year alone). But the distribution of this enormous investment neatly illustrates the current imbalances in what the apologists of the International Monetary Fund and the World Trade Organization would have us believe is a "global economy." North America accounts for 37.8 percent of the market; Europe 36.4 percent; and Asia 20.8 percent. Africa is left far behind. The recent African soccer championships were followed passionately by a population of nearly one billion, but

since it is a population with a meager disposable income, the competition attracted little sponsorship or media interest. The great African players ply their trade in Europe, just as the top Latin American baseball talent seeks the higher rewards available in the U.S.

Sports sponsorship in Britain now amounts to some $500 million annually—but two-thirds of that sum is consumed by only two sports, soccer and motor racing. Other sports find themselves increasingly disadvantaged in the furious competition for a slice of the cake, and women's sport is left with only the crumbs. A recent survey revealed that 82 percent of British companies involved in sports sponsorship indicated they had "no interest" in women's sport; however, 57 percent of these said they would have an interest if women's sport displayed greater "sex appeal." So, far from busting stereotypes and liberating women's long suppressed sporting potential, the modern marketplace seems to be reproducing the old biases.   27

Along with television rights and sponsorship, the big money in sport derives today from "licensing." For the 1998 soccer World Cup— next to the Olympics, the world's biggest sporting event (in comparison, the Super Bowl is a parochial affair) —FIFA, soccer's governing body, issued 300 licenses to corporations to produce and market more than 400 World Cup-branded products at a total retail value estimated at more than $1.2 billion. The licensing operation was handled for FIFA by the Swiss-based ISL. A top ISL executive explained the logic: "Today the marks of international sports events have become extremely valuable properties; the visible expressions of the link between supporters and events are an effective way of giving products added value."   28

Along with die-hard sports fans in many countries, I continue to believe, perhaps naively, that the "link between supporters and events" ought to be of a different nature. We may occupy diverse national and regional sporting cultures, but we have a common interest in resisting the Murdochs, the ESPNs, and the IMGs—and reclaiming our games.   29

What is happening in global sport reflects a broader crisis in popular culture. Just how popular is it? To what extent are its meanings fashioned among the majority and reflective of their lived experience, and to what extent are they contrived from above and cynically foisted upon a passive public? This crisis isn't something we should regard in a fatalistic manner, bemoaning the loss of a largely mythical sporting innocence from a prone position in front of the boob tube. As events in Seattle reminded us all, the dominant consensus is a fragile one. The colonization of sport, like the corporate appropriation of the Third World gene bank, can be challenged and resisted. But only if sports fans emerge from their nationalist cocoons and begin making links across borders of all kinds.   30

Examining the Text
1. What is the basis for Marqusee's criticism of the *Newsweek* article's claim that "sports may be America's most successful export"? Do you think he succeeds in supporting his contention that *Newsweek* got it wrong? Do you find his arguments persuasive or less than convincing?
2. In what ways does Marqusee associate American arrogance over its attitude towards home-grown sports (baseball, basketball, football) with the power of U.S. corporations to dominate marketing such non-American sports as cricket? How do these actions represent U.S. efforts to "colonize sport"? Is Marqusee's chief complaint more about the domination of certain markets, sporting goods among them, by American companies than about the world of sports?
3. In response to the Swiss-based ISL executive who commented on the value of sport as "a link between supporters and events," Marqusee countered that fans need to reclaim "our games." What do you think he meant by this? Marqusee calls recent events in global sports part of a larger crisis in popular culture that requires a resistance similar to anti-World Trade Organization protests in Seattle several years ago. Short of rioting, what actions can individual sports fans take to arrest this trend in the globalization of sports marketing? In your opinion is the trend even harmful? Is it inevitable? Might it be stopped, if people wanted to take effective measures?

For Group Discussion
Author Marqusee views the emergence of globalized sports marketing as something to be resisted. However, might there be any benefits to this phenomenon? As a group, discuss whether you feel that the marketing of sports and sports paraphernalia has gone too far. For instance, how many people in the room own clothing bearing a sports company logo? How do you feel about being a "billboard" for Nike or Adidas? Discuss the significance of this free advertising in terms of the author's call for change. Do you think it would make a difference if the most popular brands were Asian or European rather than American?

Writing Suggestions
Write a persuasive essay in which you take a position for or against the current trends in "U.S. sporting culture" and the global dominance of American sporting goods companies. In order to provide concrete evidence for your supporting paragraphs, survey your friends and relatives for opinions on this question and conduct Internet research on the global share of U.S. sporting goods companies.

Sports, Stars, and Society

Risk

Paul Roberts

In this piece, Paul Roberts wonders why an increasing number of Americans are choosing "the leisure pursuit of danger," spending their free time climbing slick rocks, steep mountains, and frozen waterfalls; paragliding; whitewater rafting; or even turning moderately dangerous sports such as downhill skiing into life-threatening endeavors such as "extreme skiing."

In this essay, originally published in Psychology Today, *Roberts tries to answer these questions by looking at the psychology of the high-risk takers. And while he does discuss some of the same issues as the* Time *writers do, Roberts emphasizes the individual psychology of thrill seekers more than the larger cultural trends on which Dowell et al. focus. Conventional theories of personality suggest that these people are acting on a "death wish," and indeed, Roberts quotes one climber as saying "What we do for kicks, most people wouldn't do if you held a gun to their heads." But Roberts discusses alternative explanations that offer a more positive view of high-risk activities. As he notes, some researchers suggest that courting peril and undertaking potentially dangerous challenges are actually essential for the progress of societies and for the development of confidence, self-awareness, and a stronger sense of identity in an individual. Although most of his examples are drawn from mountain climbing, Roberts is more broadly concerned with how a proclivity toward risky behavior affects our lives more generally, including such important areas as career choices, marital happiness, and sexual habits.*

As you read, *take note of where Roberts draws on disciplines other than psychology to account for the rise of popularity in high-risk sports. How do anthropology sociology, history, biology, and chemistry add to an understanding of risk taking?*

In the land of seatbelts and safety helmets, the leisure pursuit of danger is a growth industry. Some experts say that courting uncertainty is the only way to protect the inner force America was founded on. Or to define the self. 1

Risky business has never been more popular. Mountain climbing is among America's fastest growing sports. Extreme skiing—in which skiers descend cliff-like runs by dropping from ledge to snow-covered 2 ledge—is drawing wider interest. Sports like paragliding and cliff-parachuting are marching into the recreational mainstream while the adventure-travel business, which often mixes activities like climbing or river rafting with wildlife safaris, has grown into a multimillion-dollar industry. "Forget the beach," declared *Newsweek* last year. "We're hot for mountain biking, river running, climbing, and bungee jumping."

> Thirty-six year-old Derek Hersey knew a thing or two about life on the edge. Where most rock climbers used ropes and other safety gear, the wiry, wise-cracking Brit usually climbed "free solo"—alone, using nothing but climbing shoes, finger chalk, and his wits. As one climbing buddy put it, Hersey went "for the adrenaline and risk," and on May 28, 1993, he got a dose of both. High on the face of Yosemite's Sentinel Rock, Hersey met with rain and, apparently, slick rock. Friends who found the battered body reckon he fell several hundred feet. In the not-too-distant past, students of human behavior might have explained Hersey's fall as death-wish fulfillment. Under conventional personality theories, normal individuals do everything possible to avoid tension and risk.

In fact, as researchers are discovering, the psychology of risk   3
involves far more than a simple "death wish." Studies now indicate that the inclination to take high risks may be hard-wired into the brain, intimately linked to arousal and pleasure mechanisms, and may offer such a thrill that it functions like an addiction. The tendency probably affects one in five people, mostly young males, and declines with age. It may ensure our survival, even spur our evolution as individuals and as a species. Risk taking probably bestowed a crucial evolutionary advantage, inciting the fighting and foraging of the hunter-gatherer.

In mapping out the mechanisms of risk, psychologists hope to do   4
more than explain why people climb mountains. Risk-taking, which one researcher defines as "engaging in any activity with an uncertain outcome," arises in nearly all walks of life. Asking someone on a date, accepting a challenging work assignment, raising a sensitive issue with a spouse or a friend, confronting an abusive boss—all involve uncertain outcomes, and present some level of risk. Understanding the psychology of risk, understanding why some individuals will take chances and others won't, could have important consequences in everything from career counseling to programs for juvenile delinquents.

Researchers don't yet know precisely how a risk taking impulse   5
arises from within or what role is played by environmental factors, from upbringing to the culture at large. And, while some level of risk taking is clearly necessary for survival (try crossing a busy street without it), scientists are divided as to whether, in a modern society, a

"high-risk gene" is still advantageous. Some scientists, like Frank
Farley, Ph.D., a University of Wisconsin psychologist and past president of the American Psychological Association, see a willingness to
take big risks as essential for success. The same inner force that pushed
Derek Hersey, Farley argues, may also explain why some dare to run
for office, launch a corporate raid, or lead a civil rights demonstration.

Yet research has also revealed the darker side of risk taking. High-   6
risk takers are easily bored and may suffer low job satisfaction. Their
craving for stimulation can make them more likely to abuse drugs,
gamble, commit crimes, and be promiscuous. As psychologist Salvadore
Maddi, Ph.D., of the University of California-Davis warns, "high-risk
takers may have a hard time deriving meaning and purpose from
everyday life."

Indeed, this peculiar form of dissatisfaction could help explain   7
the explosion of high-risk sports in America and other post-industrial
Western nations. In unstable cultures, such as those at war or suffering
poverty, people rarely seek out additional thrills. But in a rich and
safety-obsessed country like America, land of guardrails, seat belts,
and personal-injury lawsuits, everyday life may have become too safe,
predictable, and boring for those programmed for risk-taking.

In an unsettling paradox, our culture's emphasis on security and   8
certainty—two defining elements of a "civilized" society—may not
only be fostering the current risk-taking wave, but could spawn riskier
activities in the future. "The safer we try to make life," cautions psychologist Michael Aptor, Ph.D, a visiting professor at Yale and author
of *The Dangerous Edge: The Psychology of Excitement*, "the more people
may take on risks."

UNIQUE WAVELENGTHS

In Icicle Canyon, a towering rocky corridor in the Cascade Mountains   9
of Washington State, this strange interplay between safety and risk is a
common sight. When weather permits, the canyon's formidable walls
swarm with fit-looking men and women, using improbably small
ledges and cracks to hoist themselves upward. For novices, risk can be
kept to a minimum. Beginners' climbs are "top-roped" by a line running from the climber to a fixed cliff-top anchor and back down to a
partner on the ground.

Even so, the novice can quickly experience a very realistic fear—   10
what veterans call "getting gripped." Halfway up one short cliff, a
first-timer in a tee shirt and shorts stabs out beneath a rock overhang.
Unable to find a foothold, the climber peels off the cliff like wet wallpaper and dangles limply from the rope. His partner lowers him back

to safety, where he stands white-faced, like someone emerging from an auto accident. Five minutes later, he is back on the cliff.

It's easy to see why high-risk sports receive so much academic   11
attention. Climbers, for example, score higher on risk-preference tests than nearly all other groups. They show a strong need for intense stimulation and seek it in environments—sheer cliffs or frozen waterfalls—that most humans seem genetically programmed to avoid.

Climbers' own explanations for why they climb illustrate the diffi-   12
culty of separating genetic, environmental, and cognitive components of this or any other behavioral trait. Many say they climb for decidedly conscious reasons: to test limits, to build or maintain self-esteem, to gain self-knowledge. Some regard it as a form of meditation. "Climbing demands absolute concentration," says Barbara, a lithe, 30-ish climber from Washington State. "It's the only time I ever feel in the moment."

Yet even the most contemplative climbers concede that their minds   13
and bodies do operate on a unique wavelength. As Forrest Kennedy, a 32-year-old climber from Georgia, bluntly puts it, "What we do for kicks, most people wouldn't do if you held a gun to their heads."

Many climbers recognize that their commitment to the sport bor-   14
ders on addiction, one that persists after brushes with injury and death. Seattle attorney Jim Wickwire, for example, is probably best known for being on the first American team to summit Pakistan's 28,250-foot K-2, second highest peak in the world and arguably the most challenging. (The movie *K-2* was based on his story.) Yet this handsome, soft-spoken father of five is almost as well known for his obstinacy. On K-2, Wickwire lost several toes to frostbite and half a lung to altitude sickness. A year before, in 1977, he'd seen two climbing partners fall 4,000 feet. In 1981 on Alaska's Mount McKinley, he watched helplessly as another partner froze to death after becoming wedged in an ice crevasse.

Wickwire vowed then never to climb again. But in 1982, he   15
attempted 29,028-foot Mount Everest, the world's tallest peak—and there saw yet another partner plunge 6,000 feet to her death. In 1993, as Wickwire, then 53, prepared for a second Everest attempt, he told a climbing magazine that he'd "stopped questioning why" he still climbed. Today, he seems just as uncertain. "The people who engage in this," Wickwire says, "are probably driven to it in a psychological fashion that they may not even understand themselves."

Until recently, researchers were equally baffled. Psychoana-   16
lytic theory and learning theory relied heavily on the notion of stimulus reduction, which saw all human motivation geared toward eliminating tension. Behaviors that created tension, such as risk taking, were deemed dysfunctional, masking anxieties or feelings of inadequacy.

A CRAVING FOR AROUSAL

Yet as far back as the 1950s, research was hinting at alternative expla-   17
nations. British psychologist Hans J. Eysenck developed a scale to
measure the personality trait of extroversion, now one of the most
consistent predictors of risk taking. Other studies revealed that, contrary to Freud, the brain not only craved arousal, but somehow regulated that arousal at an optimal level. Over the next three decades,
researchers extended these early findings into a host of theories about
risk taking.

Some scientists, like UC-Davis's Maddi and Wisconsin's Farley,   18
concentrate on risk taking primarily as a cognitive or behavioral phenomenon. Maddi sees risk taking as an element of a larger personality
dimension he calls "hardiness," which measures individuals' sense of
control over their environment and their willingness to seek out challenges. Farley regards risk taking more as a whole personality type.
Where other researchers speak of Types A and B personalities, Farley
adds Type T, for thrill-seeking. He breaks Type-T behavior into four
categories: T-mental and T-physical, to distinguish between intellectual
and physical risk taking; and T-positive and T-negative, to distinguish
between productive and destructive risk taking.

A second line of research focuses on risk's biological roots. A pio-   19
neer in these studies is psychologist Marvin Zuckerman at the University
of Delaware. He produced a detailed profile of the high-sensation seeking (HSS) personality. HSS individuals, or "highs," as Zuckerman calls
them, are typically impulsive, uninhibited, social, intend toward liberal
political views. They like high-stimulus activities, such as loud rock
music or pornography or horror movies, yet are rarely satisfied by vicarious thrills. Some level of actual risk—whether physical, social, or legal—
seems necessary. Highs tend to be heavy bettors. They may try many
kinds of drugs and favor sports like skiing or mountain climbing to running or gymnastics. Highs also show a clear aversion to low-sensation
situations, otherwise known as boredom.

High-sensation seeking plays a huge role in relationships. Highs   20
favor friends with interesting or offbeat life-styles, and avoid boring
people. They're also far more sexually permissive, particularly in the
number of sex partners, than lows. Highs favor mates with similar pro-
clivities for stimulation, while lows generally pair off with other lows.
And woe, apparently, to those who break this rule. "The combination
of a high- and a low-sensation seeker," says Zuckerman, "seems to put
the marriage relationship at risk."

Indeed, one benefit of such research is that it can be applied to   21
many areas of everyday life. Those seeking mates, the University of
Wisconsin's Farley says, should focus on those who share their level of

risk taking, particularly in terms of sexual habits. Likewise, thrill seekers should also look for the right level of on-the-job excitement. "If you're a Big T type working on a microchip assembly line, you're going to be miserable," Farley predicts. "But if you're Big T on a big daily newspaper or a police force, where you never know what you'll be doing next, you're probably going to thrive."

Many climbers fit the HSS profile. Many report difficulty keeping   22
full-time jobs, either because the work bores them, or because it interferes with their climbing schedule. Long-term relationships can be problematic, especially where climbers marry nonclimbers, or where one partner begins losing interest in the sport. Nonclimbing partners often complain that their spouses spend too much time away from home, or refuse to commit to projects (children, for example) that might interfere with climbing. Relationships are also strained by the ever-present threat of injury or death. As one Midwestern climber puts it, "the possibility that I might miss dinner, forever, doesn't make things any smoother."

Further, while many climbers are models of clean living, the sport   23
has its share of hard-partiers. Some even boast of making first ascents while high on marijuana or hallucinogens like LSD. Climbers say such drugs enhance or intensity the climbing experience. But studies suggest that the drugs may also mimic the process that pushes climbers in the first place.

WIRED FOR THRILLS

Researchers have long known of physiological differences between   24
high- and low-sensation seekers. According to Zuckerman, the cortical system of a high can handle higher levels of stimulation without overloading and switching to the fight-or-flight response. Psychologist Randy Larsen, Ph.D., at the University of Michigan, has even shown that high-sensation seekers not only tolerate high stimulus but crave it as well.

Larsen calls high-sensation seekers "reducers": Their brains auto-   25
matically dampen the level of incoming stimuli, leaving them with a kind of excitement deficit. (Low-sensation seekers, by contrast, tend to "augment" stimuli, and thus desire less excitement.) Why are some brains wired for excitement? Since 1974, researchers have known that the enzyme monoamine oxidase (MAO) plays a central role in regulating arousal, inhibition, and pleasure. They also found that low levels of MAO correlate with high levels of certain behaviors, including criminality, social activity, and drug abuse. When Zuckerman began testing HSS individuals, they, too, showed unusually low MAO levels.

The enzyme's precise role isn't clear. It regulates levels of at least   26
three important neurotransmitters: norepinephrine, which arouses the
brain in response to stimuli; dopamine, which is involved with the sensation of pleasure in response to arousal; and serotonin, which acts as
a brake on norepinephrine and inhibits arousal. It's possible that high-
sensation seekers have lower base levels of norepinephrine and thus,
can tolerate more stimulation before triggering serotonin's dampen-
ing effect. High-sensation seekers may also have lower levels of
dopamine and are thus in a chronic state of underarousal in the brain's
pleasure centers.

Such individuals may turn to drugs, like cocaine, which mimic   27
dopamine's pleasure reaction. But they may also use intense and novel
stimulation, triggering norepinephrine's arousal reaction and getting
rewarded by the dopamine pleasure reaction. "What you get is a combination of tremendous arousal with tremendous pleasure," Zuckerman
speculates. "And the faster that arousal reaches its peak, the more
intense your pleasure." Just as important, individuals may develop a
tolerance for the pleasure reaction, and thus may need ever higher levels of stimulation—of risk—to achieve the same rush.

Today such an addictive dynamic may seem largely problematic.   28
In prehistoric times it was very likely essential. Dopamine, for example, has known links to various "approach" behaviors: feeding, fighting, foraging, and exploration. Probably, the same mechanism that
gave people like Derek Hersey a rush from climbing also rewarded
their predecessors for the more necessary acts of survival.

Psychologist Aptor suggests that the willingness to take risks,   29
even if expressed by only certain individuals, would have produced
benefits for an entire group. Upon entering a new territory, a tribe
would quickly need to assess the environment's safety in terms of
"which water holes are safe to drink from, which caves are empty of
dangerous animals." Some risk takers would surely die. But, Aptor
points out, "it's better for one person to eat a poisonous fruit than
for everybody."

Climbers are understandably leery of such explanations. They   30
admit that they may be more inclined to take risks than the average
human. But that inclination's ultimate expression, they argue, is largely
a matter of personal volition. "At some level, there is a reason, chemical, mechanical, or whatever, for why we climb. But doesn't that take
the human element out of it, and make us all robots?" grouses Todd
Wells, a 40-year-old climber from Chattanooga. "I climb so I don't
feel like a robot, so I feel like I'm doing something that is motivated
by the self."

Even physiologically oriented scientists like Zuckerman admit the   31
dopamine reaction is only part of the risk-taking picture. Upbringing,

personal experience, socioeconomic status, and learning are also
crucial in determining how that risk-taking impulse is ultimately
expressed.

CULTURE OF ASCENT

Although many climbers report a childhood preference for thrills, their   32
interest in climbing was often shaped externally, either through contact
with older climbers or by reading about great expeditions. Upon entering the sport, novices are often immersed in a tight-knit climbing
subculture, with its own lingo, rules of conduct, and standards of
excellence.

This learned aspect may be the most important element in the for-   33
mation of the high-sensation-seeking personality. While risk-taking
may have arisen from neuro-chemicals and environmental influences,
there is an intellectual or conscious side to it that is now not only distinct from them but is itself a powerful motivator. Working through a
challenging climbing route, for example, generates a powerful sense of
competence that can also provide climbers with a new-found confidence in their everyday life. "There is nothing more empowering than
taking a risk and succeeding," says Farley.

No wonder scaling the face of a cliff is a potent act that can pene-   34
trate to the very essence of self and help reshape it. Many climbers
report using that empowering dynamic to overcome some of their own
inner obstacles. Among these, fear—of heights, of loss of control, of
death—is the most commonly cited.

Richard Gottlieb, 42-year-old climber from New York, is known for   35
climbing frozen waterfalls, one of the riskiest facets of the sport. But as a
kid, he was too scared even to go to summer camp. "Yet there was something in me that wanted to get into some swashbuckling adventure," he
says. Climbing satisfied that impulse while helping him overcome his
fearful nature. Gottlieb believes climbing has helped him cope with his
fear of death: "We open the door, see the Grim Reaper right there, but
instead of just slamming the door, you push him back a few steps."

NEW OUTLETS

Traditional outlets for the risk-taking impulse have been disappearing   36
from everyday life. As civilization steadily minimized natural risks,
Aptor says, and as cultures have sought to maintain their hard-won
stability through repressive laws and stifling social mores, risk takers
have been forced to devise new outlets. In the 20th century, that has

brought about a rise in thrill sports. But Aptor believes the tension between civilization and risk-taking dates back eons. Aptor wonders how much of the British Empire "was built up by people trying to escape the desperately conformist society of Victorian England."

When channeled into sports like climbing, where skill and train-   37
ing can minimize danger, or into starting a new business, risk-taking may continue to be a healthy psychological outlet. It may provide a means to cope with boredom and modern anxieties, to bolster self-esteem. Risk-taking may provide a crucial sense of control in a period where so much of what happens—from crime and auto accidents to environmental disasters and economic downturns—seems almost random.

Unfortunately, the risk-taking impulse doesn't always find such   38
healthy outlets. Many high-sensation seekers don't have the money or the role models for sky-diving or rock-climbing, Zuckerman notes. "In such groups, the main forms of sensation seeking include sex, drugs, heavy drinking, gambling, and reckless driving." Indeed, sensation-seeking may emerge as a critical factor in crime. No surprise, then, that some researchers place the risk-taking personality in the "abnormal" category and regard high-risk-takers almost as an evolutionarily obsolete subspecies. Maddi suggests that well-adjusted people are "good at turning everyday experience into something interesting. My guess is that the safecracker or the mountain climber can't do that as well. They have to do something exciting to get a sense of vitality. It's the only way they have of getting away from the sense that life sucks." Larsen is even blunter: "I think risk-takers are a little sociopathic."

Farley is more optimistic. Even civilized society, he says, holds   39
ample opportunity for constructive risk-taking: investing in a high-stakes business venture, running for political office, taking an unpopular social stand. Farley argues that history's most crucial events are shaped by Big T behavior and Big T individuals, from Boris Yeltsin to Martin Luther King, Jr. The act of emigration, he says, is an intrinsically risky endeavor that selects individuals who are high in sensation-seeking. Consequently, countries built upon immigrant population—America, Canada, Australia—probably have an above-average level of risk-takers. He warns that much of the current effort to minimize risk and risk-taking itself runs the risk of eliminating "a large part of what made this country great in the first place."

For all the societal aspects of this peculiar trait, the ultimate bene-   40
fits may continue to be purely personal. "There's a freshness to the [climbing] experience that clears away the weariness of routine and the complexity of social norms" says Seattle climber Bill Pilling. "Climbing brings you back to a primal place, where values are being created and transformed."

To push away from society's rides and protections, Farley sug-   41
gests, is the only way to get a sense of where "society" ends and "you"
begin. "Taking a risk, stepping away from the guardrails, from the
rules and the status quo, that's when you get a sense of who you are,"
he says. "If you don't stretch, try to push past the frontiers, it's very difficult to know that."

Examining the Text

1. Roberts opens his essay with a paradox that he returns to several
times in the text: that America's preoccupation with safety and security
seems to foster higher levels of risk taking. Do you think that beginning
an essay with a paradox—a seeming contradiction—is a good strategy?
Why or why not? Does Roberts ever "solve" this paradox?
2. In your own words, explain the psychological theory of "stimulus
reduction." How does risk-taking behavior contradict and confound
this theory?
3. Briefly summarize the characteristics of Farley's Type T personality
and Zuckerman's HSS individual. In what ways are these models similar and different? In your opinion, which one offers a more accurate
description of the personalities and motivations of high-risk takers?
4. Consider the two "expert" sources from whom Roberts quotes: psychologists and climbers. Go back through the essay and look at the specific statements made by these experts. To what different uses does
Roberts put them? How do their different kinds of expertise help
Roberts construct his argument?

For Group Discussion

Roberts weighs the benefits and dangers of risk-taking activities, but he
ultimately chooses to remain neutral and impartial. In groups, discuss
your own opinion about whether risk-taking activities have primarily
positive or negative effects on participants. Choose one side of the
question and argue for it as persuasively and logically as you can,
drawing on Roberts' arguments and those of the climbers and psychologists he cites in his essay. As a class, decide which arguments are the
most persuasive.

Writing Suggestion

Even if you're not a high-risk taker—one of Farley's Type T or
Zuckerman's HSS personalities—you've undoubtedly taken a few
risks in your life. Risking is defined in the essay as "engaging in any
activity with an uncertain outcome," such as asking someone for a date or

taking on a new and difficult challenge. Recall a time when you took a risk and assess both the positive and negative effects of this experience. Write an essay in which you describe your experience and evaluate its impact on you. You should draw on Roberts' assessment of the benefits and harms of risk-taking and relate them to your own experience with risk.

Life on the Edge

*William Dowell et al. (*Time *Magazine)*

Fewer Americans are getting together for relaxed games of touch football or slow-pitch softball, and professional team sporting events are no longer attracting the large audiences of the past. Meanwhile, however, participation in high-risk extreme sports is on the rise. Increasing numbers of healthy, seemingly sane men and women are risking life and limb on a Sunday afternoon by jumping from a bridge or cliff or by climbing up a steep, sheer mountain face. In this article, the authors examine the increasing popularity of extreme sports such as BASE jumping, paragliding, and so on, arguing that our current interest in dangerous sports stems from the fact that most Americans are living comfortable, safe lives. We seek out risk because it no longer seeks us—as in past eras when risks came routinely from war, famine, disease, and wild animals. In support of this argument, the authors point out the prevalence of other types of risk-taking behavior, which are common outside of sports, such as playing the stock market or engaging in unprotected sex.

As you read, think about the legitimacy of the authors' argument. Is there necessarily a connection between the popularity of extreme sports and risky behavior in other areas of social life? Is it fair to connect these behaviors to our generally comfortable lives? Can you think of other possible reasons for the rise in risky sporting behavior? Or are you persuaded by the connections these authors make?

"Five . . . four . . . three . . . two . . . one . . . see ya!" And Chance McGuire,   1
25, is airborne off a 650-ft. concrete dam in Northern California. In one second he falls 16 ft., in two seconds 63 ft., and after three seconds and 137 ft. he is flying at 65 m.p.h. He prays that his parachute will open facing away from the dam, that his canopy won't collapse, that his toggles will be handy and that no ill wind will slam him back into the cold concrete. The chute snaps open, the sound ricocheting through the gorge like a gunshot, and McGuire is soaring, carving S-turns into the

air, swooping over a winding creek. When he lands, he is a speck on a path along the creek. He hurriedly packs his chute and then, clearly audible above the rushing water, lets out a war whoop that rises past those mortals still perched on the dam, past the commuters puttering by on the roadway, past even the hawks who circle the ravine. It is a cry of defiance, thanks and victory; he has survived another BASE jump.

McGuire is a practitioner of what he calls the king of all extreme   2
sports. BASE—an acronym for building, antenna, span (bridge), and earth (cliffs)—jumping has one of the sporting world's highest fatality rates: in its 18-year history, 46 participants have been killed. Yet the sport has never been more popular, with more than a thousand jumpers in the U.S. and more seeking to get into it every day. It is an activity without margin for error. If your chute malfunctions, don't bother reaching for a reserve—there isn't time. There are no second chances.

Still, the sport's stark metaphor—a human leaving safety behind   3
to leap into the void—may be a perfect fit with our times. As extreme a risk taker as McGuire seems, we may all have more in common with him than we know or care to admit. Heading into the millennium, America has embarked on a national orgy of thrill seeking and risk taking. The rise of adventure and extreme sports like BASE jumping, snowboarding, ice climbing, skateboarding and paragliding is merely the most vivid manifestation of this new national behavior. Investors once content to buy stocks and hold them quit their day jobs to become day traders, making volatile careers of risk taking. Even our social behavior has tilted toward the treacherous, with unprotected sex on the upswing and hard drugs like heroin the choice of the chic as well as the junkies. In ways many of us take for granted, we engage in risks our parents would have shunned and our grandparents would have dismissed as just plain stupid.

More than 30% of U.S. households own stocks of some form or   4
another, whether in investment accounts, mutual funds or retirement plans, up from 12% just 10 years ago. While an ongoing bull market has lulled us into a sense of security about investing, the reality is we are taking greater risks with our money than any other generation in American history. Many of us even take this a step further, buying "speculative growth," i.e., highly risky Internet and technology stocks, breezily ignoring the potentially precipitous downside.

We change jobs, leaping into the employment void, imagining   5
rich opportunities everywhere. The quit rate, a measure of those who voluntarily left their most recent job, is at 14.5%, the highest in a decade. Even among those schooled in risk management, hotshot M.B.A.s who previously would have headed to Wall Street or Main Street, there is a predilection to spurn Goldman Sachs and Procter & Gamble in order to take a flyer on striking it rich quickly in dot.com

land. "I didn't want someone in 20 years to ask me where I was when the Internet took off," says Greg Schoeny, a recent University of Denver M.B.A. who passed up opportunities with established technology firms like Lucent to work at an Internet start-up called STS Communications. Schoeny is a double-dare sort who also likes to ski in the Rockies' dangerous, unpatrolled backcountry.

A full 30% of this year's Harvard Business School graduates are joining venture-capital or high-tech firms, up from 12% just four years ago. "The extended period of prosperity has encouraged people to behave in ways they didn't behave in other times—the way people spend money, change jobs, the quit rate, day trading, and people really thinking they know more about the market than anyone else," says Peter Bernstein, an economic consultant and author of the best-selling *Against the Gods: The Remarkable Story of Risk*. "It takes a particular kind of environment for all these things to happen." That environment— unprecedented prosperity and almost a decade without a major ground war—may be what causes Americans to express some inveterate need to take risks.

There is a certain logic to it: at the end of a decade of American triumphalism abroad and prosperity at home, we could be seeking to

6

7

Bungee Jumping at the X Games

upsize our personalities, our sense of ourselves. Perhaps we as a people are acting out our success as a nation, in a manner unfelt since the
postwar era.

The rising popularity of extreme sports bespeaks an eagerness on   8
the part of millions of Americans to participate in activities closer to the
metaphorical edge, where danger, skill and fear combine to give weekend warriors and professional athletes alike a sense of pushing out personal boundaries. According to American Sports Data Inc., a consulting
firm, participation in so-called extreme sports is way up. Snowboarding has grown 113% in five years and now boasts nearly 5.5 million
participants. Mountain biking, skateboarding, scuba diving, you name
the adventure sport—the growth curves reveal a nation that loves to
play with danger. Contrast that with activities like baseball, touch football and aerobics, all of which have been in steady decline throughout
the '90s.

The pursuits that are becoming more popular have one thing in   9
common: the perception that they are somehow more challenging than
a game of touch football. "Every human being with two legs, two arms
is going to wonder how fast, how strong, how enduring he or she is,"
says Eric Perlman, a mountaineer and filmmaker specializing in extreme
sports. "We are designed to experiment or die."

And to get hurt. More Americans than ever are injuring them-   10
selves while pushing their personal limits. In 1997 the U.S. Consumer
Products Safety Commission reported that 48,000 Americans were
admitted to hospital emergency rooms with skateboarding-related
injuries. That's 33% more than the previous year. Snowboarding E.R.
visits were up 31%; mountain climbing up 20%. By every statistical
measure available, Americans are participating in and injuring themselves through adventure sports at an unprecedented rate.

Consider Mike Carr, an environmental engineer and paraglider   11
pilot from Denver who last year survived a bad landing that smashed
10 ribs and collapsed his lung. Paraglider pilots use feathery nylon wings
to take off from mountaintops and float on thermal wind currents—a
completely unpredictable ride. Carr also mountain bikes and climbs
rock faces. He walked away from a 1,500-ft. fall in Peru in 1988. After
his recovery, he returned to paragliding. "This has taken over many of
our lives," he explains. "You float like a bird out there. You can go as
high as 18,000 ft. and go for 200 miles. That's magic."

America has always been defined by risk; it may be our predomi-   12
nant national characteristic. It's a country founded by risk takers fed up
with the English Crown and expanded by pioneers—a word that seems
utterly American. Our heritage throws up heroes—Lewis and Clark,
Thomas Edison, Frederick Douglass, Teddy Roosevelt, Henry Ford,
Amelia Earhart—who bucked the odds, taking perilous chances.

Previous generations didn't need to seek out risk; it showed up   13
uninvited and regularly: global wars, childbirth complications, diseases and pandemics from the flu to polio, dangerous products and even
the omnipresent cold war threat of mutually assured destruction. "I just
don't think extreme sports would have been popular in a ground-war
era," says Dan Cady, professor of popular culture at California State
University at Fullerton. "Coming back from a war and getting onto a
skateboard would not seem so extreme."

But for recent generations, many of those traditional risks have   14
been reduced by science, government or legions of personal-injury
lawyers, leaving boomers and Generations X and Y to face less real
risk. Life expectancy has increased. Violent crime is down. You are 57%
less likely to die of heart disease than your parents; smallpox, measles
and polio have virtually been eradicated.

Combat survivors speak of the terror and the excitement of play-   15
ing in a death match. Are we somehow incomplete as people if we do
not taste that terror and excitement on the brink? "People are [taking
risks] because everyday risk is minimized and people want to be challenged," says Joy Marr, 43, an adventure racer who was the only
woman member of a five-person team that finished the 1998 Raid

Tony Hawk

Gauloises, the granddaddy of all adventure races. This is a sport that requires several days of nonstop slogging, climbing, rappelling, rafting and surviving through some of the roughest terrain in the world. Says fellow adventure racer and former Army Ranger Jonathan Senk, 35: "Our society is so surgically sterile. It's almost like our socialization just desensitizes us. Every time I'm out doing this I'm searching my soul. It's the Lewis and Clark gene, to venture out, to find what your limitations are."

That idea of feeling bracingly alive through high-risk endeavor is   16
commonly echoed by athletes, day traders and other risk takers. Indeed, many Silicon Valley entrepreneurs are extreme-sports junkies. Mike McCue, 32, CEO and chairman of Tellme Networks, walked away from millions of dollars at his previous job to get his new company off the ground. It's his third start-up, and each time he has risked every-thing. In his spare time, McCue gets himself off the ground. He's also an avid rock climber. "I like to feel self-reliant and independent," he says. "And when I'm up there, I know if I make a knot wrong, I die."

Even at ground level, the Valley is a preserve of fearless entrepre-   17
neurs. Nirav Tolia passed up $10 million in Yahoo stock options to start epinions.com, a shopping-guide Web site. "I don't know if I would call it living dangerously," he says. "At Yahoo I realized that money was not the driver for me. It's the sense of adventure."

Psychologist Frank Farley of Temple University believes that tak-   18
ing conscious risk involves overcoming our instincts. He points out that no other animal intentionally puts itself in peril. "The human race is particularly risk taking compared with other species," he says. He describes risk takers as the Type T personality, and the U.S. as a Type T nation, as opposed to what Farley considers more risk-averse nations like Japan. He breaks it down further, into Type T physical (extreme athletes) and Type T intellectual (Albert Einstein, Galileo). He warns there is also Type T negative, that is, those who are drawn to delin-quency, crime, experimentation with drugs, unprotected sex, and a whole litany of destructive behaviors.

All these Type Ts are related, and perhaps even different aspects   19
of the same character trait. There is, says Farley, a direct link between Einstein and BASE jumper Chance McGuire. They are different mani-festations of the thrill-seeking component of our characters: Einstein was thrilled by his mental life, and McGuire—well, Chance jumps off buildings.

McGuire, at the moment, is driving from Hollister to another   20
California town, Auburn, where he is planning another BASE jump from a bridge. Riding with him is Adam Fillipino, president of Consolidated Rigging, a company that manufactures parachutes and gear for BASE jumpers. McGuire talks about the leap ahead, about his feelings

when he is at the exit point, and how at that moment, looking down at the ground, what goes through his mind is that this is not something a human being should be doing. But that's exactly what makes him take that leap: that sense of overcoming his inhibitions and winning what he calls the gravity game. "Football is for pansies," says McGuire. "What do you need all those pads for? This sport [BASE jumping] is pushing all the limits. I have a friend who calls it suicide with a kick."

When a BASE jumper dies, other BASE jumpers say he has "gone   21
in," as in gone into the ground or gone into a wall. "I'm sick of people going in," says Fillipino. "In the past year, a friend went in on a sky-dive, another drowned as a result of a BASE jump, another friend went in on a jump, another died in a skydiving-plane crash. You can't escape death, but you don't want to flirt with it either." It may be the need to flirt with death, or at least take extreme chances, that has his business growing at a rate of 50% a year.

The jump today from the Auburn bridge, which Fillipino has   22
done dozens of times, is about as routine as BASE jumping can be. But Fillipino is a veteran with 450 BASE jumps to his credit. For McGuire, who has just 45, every jump is still a challenge. And at dawn, as he gets his gear ready, stuffing his chute and rig into a backpack so it won't be conspicuous as he climbs the trestles beneath the bridge (jumping from this bridge, as from many other public and private structures, is ille-gal), he has entered into a tranquil state, as if he were silently preparing himself for the upcoming risk.

When our Type T traits turn negative, though, there is a disturb-   23
ing, less serene element to America's being the risk nation. One chilling development is the trend of "barebacking," a practice in which gay men have unprotected sex with multiple partners. Jack, an avid propo-nent of barebacking, argues that the risk of becoming HIV positive is outweighed by the rush of latex-free passion—especially in an era when, in his view, protease inhibitors are on the verge of turning AIDS from a fatal disease into a chronic illness. "It's the bad boy in me get-ting off," he admits. "One thing that barebacking allows is a certain amount of control over the risk. In sex, we have the ability to face the risk and look it in the eye."

The Stop AIDS Foundation surveyed some 22,000 gay men in San   24
Francisco between 1994 and 1997, and during this period, the number of men who reported they always used condoms fell from 70% to 61%. "For some gay men, there is a sense of inevitability of becoming infected," says Michael Scarce, 29, a doctoral student in medical sociol-ogy who has been researching the barebacking phenomenon for the past two years. Scarce says that rather than living in fear and wonder-ing when their next HIV test is going to return positive, some men

create an infection ritual. "It really is a lifestyle choice," he says. "It comes down to quality of life vs. quantity of life."

This consequences-be-damned attitude may also be behind some   25
disquieting trends that surfaced in a report issued last week by the Substance Abuse and Mental Health Services Administration stating that the number of Americans entering treatment centers for heroin surged 29% between 1992 and 1997. "I'm seeking the widest possible range of human experience," says a recent Ivy League graduate about his heroin use.

The most notorious example of negative thrill seeking may have   26
been when the Risk Taker in Chief, Bill Clinton, engaged in unprotected sex in the Oval Office. Experts point out that many people were forgiving of Clinton in part because they could identify with his impulsiveness. "Risky behavior has been elevated to new heights," argues Cal State's Cady. "There was never so much value put upon risk as there is now."

The question is, How much is enough? Without some expression   27
of risk, we may never know our limits and therefore who we are as individuals. "If you don't assume a certain amount of risk," says paraglider pilot Wade Ellet, 51, "you're missing a certain amount of life." And it is by taking risks that we may flirt with greatness. "We create technologies, we make new discoveries, but in order to do that, we have to push beyond the set of rules that are governing us at that time," says psychologist Farley.

That's certainly what's driving McGuire and Fillipino as they   28
position themselves on the Auburn bridge. It's dawn again, barely light, and they appear as shadows moving on the catwalk beneath the roadway. As they survey the drop zone, they compute a series of risk assessments. "It's a matter of weighing the variables," Fillipino says, pointing out that the wind, about 15 m.p.h. out of the northwest, has picked up a little more than he would like. Still, it's a clear morning, and they've climbed all the way up here. McGuire is eager to jump. But Fillipino continues to scan the valley below them, the Sacramento River rushing through the gorge.

Then a white parks-department SUV pulls up on an access road   29
that winds alongside the river. Park rangers are a notorious scourge of BASE jumpers, confiscating equipment and prosecuting for trespassing. Fillipino contemplates what would happen if the president of a BASE rig company were busted for an illegal jump. He foresees trouble with his bankers, he imagines the bad publicity his business would garner, and he says he's not going. There are some risks he is simply not willing to take.

Examining the Text

1. What do the authors mean when they state that the "stark metaphor" of BASE jumping "may be a perfect fit with our times" (3)?

2. In contrast to all the risk taking mentioned in this article, as a society we also engage in a lot of risk minimizing. Paradoxically, these efforts to ensure safety may be helping to spawn more thrill-seeking activities. Discuss examples of safety measures and risk minimizing in which we as a culture engage—both on the personal as well as on a political or public level.

3. Explain why the authors state that risk taking is perhaps America's "predominant national characteristic." Do you agree or disagree, and why? If this assertion is true, what are the positive and negative consequences of this characteristic for us as country?

For Group Discussion

While this article focuses on the risky characteristics of extreme sports— and uses this element of these sports to make connections to the larger cultural climate in America—another characteristic of extreme sports is noteworthy: nearly all of the sports discussed in this article are individual in nature. The rock climber, for example, tests her own individual abilities against the challenges posed by nature. Interestingly, the increasing popularity of these individual sports corresponds with the declining interest in playing and watching team sports, as discussed in earlier pieces by Solomon and by Lim and Turco.

Use these ideas to theorize, as a group, about the possible significance of this shift from team to individual sports. Just as the *Time* article makes connections between sports and other cultural phenomena, ultimately using all of it to comment upon human nature as it appears in America today, can you think of other cultural phenomena that might relate to this issue of individualism? Does this lead you to theorize some ideas about where we are or where we seem to be headed?

Writing Suggestion

Write a paper in which you use points from earlier readings in the chapter to expand on the issues raised by Dowell and colleagues in this article. For example, how might the declining interest in team sports, as discussed by Solomon and by Lim and Turco relate to increased interest in risky sports? How might features of Generation Y relate here as well? Are there ways in which Rounds's points on gender in sports might fit into the equation?

Analyzing Sports

Champion of the World

Maya Angelou

Maya Angelou is a well-known poet, novelist, and performer. Born in 1928 and raised in the segregated South, Angelou persevered through countless hardships to become one of the country's most revered authors and cultural leaders. Angelou read her poem, "On the Pulse of Morning," at the 1993 inauguration of President Bill Clinton.

The selection which follows is from Angelou's first volume of autobiography, I Know Why the Caged Bird Sings *(1969). She relates an important recollection from childhood about the night in the 1930s when world heavyweight champion Joe Louis, nicknamed the "Brown Bomber," defended his boxing title against a White contender. Much of Angelou's narrative is made up of the words and feelings of the local Black community gathered in her Uncle Willie's store to listen to the broadcast of that highly publicized match. Angelou shows how her neighbors' hopes and fears and their image of themselves as a people were intimately connected to the fortunes of Louis, one of a very few Black heroes of the day. Her narrative reveals that a "simple" sporting event can be of intense significance for a group of people who see it as a symbol of personal victory or defeat.*

***Before you read**, recall any experience you've had or heard about in which a sporting event took on an emotional power and significance far greater than the event itself would seem to warrant. Whether this event is one that you participated in, watched, or read about, think about how and why sports can have such an intense influence on people's lives.*

The last inch of space was filled, yet people continued to wedge themselves along the walls of the Store. Uncle Willie had turned the radio up to its last notch so that youngsters on the porch wouldn't miss a word. Women sat on kitchen chairs, dining-room chairs, stools, and upturned wooden boxes. Small children and babies perched on every lap available and men leaned on the shelves or on each other. 1

The apprehensive mood was shot through with shafts of gaiety, as a black sky is streaked with lightning. 2

"I ain't worried 'bout this fight. Joe's gonna whip that cracker like it's open season." 3

"He gone whip him till that white boy call him Momma." 4

At last the talking finished and the sing-along songs about razor   5
blades were over and the fight began.

"A quick jab to the head." In the Store the crowd grunted. "A left   6
to the head and a right and another left." One of the listeners cackled
like a hen and was quieted.

"They're in a clinch, Louis is trying to fight his way out."   7

Some bitter comedian on the porch said, "That white man don't   8
mind hugging that niggah now, I betcha."

"The referee is moving in to break them up, but Louis finally   9
pushed the contender away and it's an uppercut to the chin. The contender is hanging on, now he's backing away. Louis catches him with a   10
short left to the jaw."

A tide of murmuring assent poured out the door and into the yard.   11

"Another left and another left. Louis is saving that mighty right ..."
The mutter in the Store had grown into a baby roar and it was pierced
by the clang of a bell and the announcer's "That's the bell for round
three, ladies and gentlemen."

As I pushed my way into the Store I wondered if the announcer   12
gave any thought to the fact that he was addressing as "ladies and gentlemen" all the Negroes around the world who sat sweating and praying, glued to their "Master's voice."

There were only a few calls for RC Colas, Dr. Peppers, and Hires   13
root beer. The real festivities would begin after the fight. Then even the
old Christian ladies who taught their children and tried themselves to
practice turning the other cheek would buy soft drinks, and if the
Brown Bomber's victory was a particularly bloody one they would
order peanut patties and Baby Ruths, also.

Bailey and I laid coins on top of the cash register. Uncle Willie didn't   14
allow us to ring up sales during a fight. It was too noisy and might
shake up the atmosphere. When the gong rang for the next round we
pushed through the near-sacred quiet to the herd of children outside.

"He's got Louis against the ropes and now it's a left to the body   15
and a right to the ribs. Another right to the body, it looks like it was
low ... Yes, ladies and gentlemen, the referee is signaling but the contender keeps raining the blows on Louis. It's another to the body, and it
looks like Louis is going down."

My race groaned. It was our people falling. It was another lynch-   16
ing, yet another Black man hanging on a tree. One more woman
ambushed and raped. A Black boy whipped and maimed. It was
hounds on the trail of a man running through slimy swamps. It was a
white woman slapping her maid for being forgetful.

The men in the Store stood away from the walls and at attention.   17
Women greedily clutched the babes on their laps while on the porch

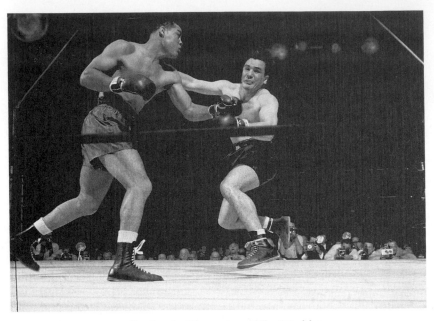

Joe Louis, Champion of the World

the shufflings and smiles, flirtings and pinching of a few minutes
before were gone. This might be the end of the world. If Joe lost we
were back in slavery and beyond help. It would all be true, the accusations that we were lower types of human beings. Only a little higher
than apes. True that we were stupid and ugly and lazy and dirty and,
unlucky and worst of all, that God Himself hated us and ordained us
to be hewers of wood and drawers of water, forever and ever, world
without end.

We didn't breathe. We didn't hope. We waited.   18

"He's off the ropes, ladies and gentlemen. He's moving towards   19
the center of the ring." There was no time to be relieved. The worst
might still happen.

"And now it looks like Joe is mad. He's caught Carnera with a left   20
hook to the head and a right to the head. It's a left jab to the body and
another left to the head. There's a left cross and a right to the head. The
contender's right eye is bleeding and he can't seem to keep his block
up. Louis is penetrating every block. The referee is moving in, but
Louis sends a left to the body and it's an uppercut to the chin and the
contender is dropping. He's on the canvas, ladies and gentlemen."

Babies slid to the floor as women stood up and men leaned   21
toward the radio.

"Here's the referee. He's counting. One, two, three, four, five, six, 22
seven . . . Is the contender trying to get up again?"

All the men in the store shouted, "NO." 23

"—eight, nine, ten." There were a few sounds from the audience, 24
but they seemed to be holding themselves in against tremendous
pressure.

"The fight is all over, ladies and gentlemen. Let's get the micro- 25
phone over to the referee . . . Here he is. He's got the Brown Bomber's
hand, he's holding it up . . . Here he is . . ."

Then the voice, husky and familiar, came to wash over us—"The 26
winnah, and still heavyweight champeen of the world . . . Joe Louis."

Champion of the world. A Black boy. Some Black mother's son. 27

He was the strongest man in the world. People drank Coca-Colas 28
like ambrosia and ate candy bars like Christmas. Some of the men went
behind the Store and poured white lightning in their soft-drink bottles,
and a few of the bigger boys followed them. Those who were not
chased away came back blowing their breath in front of themselves like
proud smokers.

It would take an hour or more before people would leave the 29
Store and head home. Those who lived too far had made arrangements
to stay in town. It wouldn't do for a Black man and his family to be
caught on a lonely country road on a night when Joe Louis had proved
that we were the strongest people in the world.

Examining the Text

1. Unlike the other selections in this chapter which offer fairly objective analyses of sport, Angelou relates a personal recollection. What
conclusions about the influence of sports on culture, and specifically
on African American culture in the 1930s, can you draw from
her story? Has that influence changed significantly over the last
sixty years?

2. In paragraphs 16 and 17 Angelou describes her own thoughts about
the prospect of Louis losing the match. After rereading these paragraphs, what do you think they contribute to the overall meaning and
drama of the story? How are they connected to the final paragraph?

3. What is the effect of the concluding paragraph in the story? How
would Angelou's message be different if she had not ended it this way?

For Group Discussion

Angelou's recollection demonstrates in vivid detail how a sporting
event can take on much larger significance, how people can invest a
great deal of emotion in the performance of an athlete or team. In your
group, list some other specific examples of sporting contests that have
taken on intense emotional significance and meaning for an individual

or a group of fans. As a class, discuss the advantages and disadvantages of the strong influence sports has on its fans.

Writing Suggestion
In her narrative, Angelou describes how Joe Louis was an inspiration and sign of hope for African Americans in the 1930s. Choose another athlete who you think has similarly been an inspiration to his or her fans or has served as a role model. In an essay discuss the qualities that make that person a particularly good model. At the same time, if you think that athlete has negative qualities, you may cite these as well in analyzing how he or she has influenced fans.

Tiger Time: The Wonder of an American Hero

Jay Nordlinger

Surely by now most Americans—whether they care about golf or not—know the basic outlines of Tiger Woods's phenomenal golf career. Nordlinger fills in many of the details of Woods's success: his amazing amateur career was followed by twenty-seven tournament wins by the age of twenty-five—he won the Master's tournament by an unprecedented twelve strokes—and the list goes on. After lauding Woods's golf game, Nordlinger goes on to praise his general demeanor, especially in regard to those who would have Woods serve as a role model for African Americans. According to Nordlinger, Woods' repeated insistence that he's a role model for all kids—not just those who are black—is an admirable and gutsy move.

As you read, think about the impact that a sports figure can have in the culture at large. What kind of impact has Tiger Woods had—both within the world of golf and beyond it? How does his impact compare to that of boxer Joe Louis, as portrayed by Maya Angelou in the last reading?

Sometime last season, I e-mailed a friend of mine, an ex-pro golfer and   1
a keen student of the game. "Are we ready to concede that Tiger is the best ever?" I asked. His answer was slightly ambiguous; I couldn't tell whether he was being sincere or sarcastic. So I asked for a clarification. "Oh, let me be perfectly clear," he replied. "Nicklaus in his heyday couldn't carry Tiger's clubs. Really."

Now, my friend and I were Nicklaus worshipers from way 2 back—we still are. When it comes to Nicklaus, we are dangerously close to violating the First Commandment. So acknowledging the truth about Tiger came hard. Jack Nicklaus—this is gospel in golf—dominated his sport as no other athlete ever dominated any sport. I once began a piece about Nicklaus roughly this way: Boxing folks can talk about Louis versus Ali; baseball people can talk about Cobb and Ruth and Mays (or whomever); tennis people can have a high time about Laver and Sampras; but in golf, there's nothing to discuss.

What's more, no one else was ever supposed to dominate the 3 game. Nicklaus was supposed to be the last giant, the last player ever to make the others quake, the last to win predictably. You see, "parity" had arrived: That was the big buzzword on Tour. There were now thirty, forty—maybe sixty—guys who could win in any given week. Golf instruction—swing science—had equalized things. Advances in equipment had equalized things. Conditioning, nutrition, etc., had equalized things. If a guy won, say, three tournaments in a season, that would be practically a freak, and the fellow would be Player of the Year, for sure. We would never see anything close to Nicklaus again.

Furthermore, his mark of 18 professional majors—twenty majors, 4 if you counted his two U.S. Amateurs (and most of us did, because we loved that round, awesome number)—was an inviolable record. It would stand forever. It was the most unapproachable record in golf.

All of this needs to be remembered, because people forget. I've 5 seen this in my own (not terribly long) lifetime. When I was young, the greatest record in baseball—the one that would live unto eternity—was Lou Gehrig's 2,130 consecutive games. That, all the experts said, was the one mark no one would ever reach. But then, when Cal Ripken closed in on it, they changed. They cheated. Now they said it was Joe D's 56–game hitting streak that was numero uno. Ah, but I remember: I won't forget. Ripken's achievement must not be slighted—everyone said it was impossible.

And now Tiger: the non-golfer will simply have to trust me that 6 no one was supposed to be able to do what Tiger has, in fact, done. His achievements are—or were—unimaginable. The question arises, has Woods won the Grand Slam? I, for one, don't care: he has won something like it—four consecutive majors—and no one else has (forgetting Bobby Jones, in the "premodern" Slam). I vow not to forget—no matter how fuzzy the past becomes—that Woods has accomplished what was proclaimed by one and all unaccomplishable.

How to talk about Tiger Woods? I don't know. Start with this (a 7 cliche, but a useful cliche): when Nicklaus first showed up at the Masters, Bob Jones said, "He plays a game with which I am not familiar." The same has to be said of Woods. Another friend of mine—a pro golfer and a genuine philosophe—made the following, arresting statement: "It's not just that Woods is the best ever to play the game; it is that he is the first ever to play it." Think about that for more than a second or two, and you grow dizzy. What does it mean? It means, I think, that Tiger is the first truly to exploit the possibilities of the game. That he is the first to swing the club as it ought to be swung. That he—this gets a bit mystical—sees a game that others have been blind to, or have caught only glimpses of.

In the last years of his life, I had lessons—and many long 8 conversations—with Bill Strausbaugh Jr., the most decorated teacher in the history of the PGA. "Coach" was one of the wisest men I ever hope to meet in golf, or to meet, period. Speaking of Tiger—this was in 1998, I believe—he said, "That young man has the best golf motion ever." (Coach disdained the word "swing"—he thought it gave his students the wrong idea.) I replied, condescendingly, like an idiot, "Oh, Coach, you must mean that he has one of the best ever. You've seen Hogan, Snead—all of them." He fixed me with a look and said, "No, Jay, I meant what I said: Tiger has the best golf motion ever." I was tremendously impressed by this, because the old are usually afflicted with the vice of nostalgia: no one is ever as good now as then. Thus, in baseball, for example, you hear, "Yeah, Roger Clemens is okay, but Grover Alexander! There was a pitcher!" Right.

Bill Strausbaugh also said, "Tiger has three things: a great golf 9 motion, a great golf mind, and a great golf body. (This last, Coach maintained, is grossly underrated.) He is ideal—I never thought I would see it."

Tiger Woods was a legend before he ever turned pro. He had, I 10 would argue, the greatest amateur career ever. (Bobby Jones idolaters— of whom I am one, from the crib—should just sit still. There is an argument here. And Jones wasn't an "amateur" in our present sense.) In fact, it's unfortunate about Tiger's dazzling pro career that it has been allowed to overshadow, inevitably, his amateur career. Tiger Woods, starting when he was 15 years old, won three straight U.S. Junior Championships and three straight U.S. Amateur Championships. This achievement is positively stupefying. I could try to explain, but, again, I say: trust me.

Tiger was the youngest ever to win the Junior—he was 15. No one 11 had ever won twice, and he would win three times. He was the youngest ever to win the U.S. Amateur—he was 18. He would be the only player ever to win the Am three years in a row. This takes a discipline, a kind of genius, that is hard to fathom. I argued, quite seriously, that if, God forbid, Tiger died before he ever had a chance to tee it up as a pro, he would die as one of the finest players in history. And he would have.

(I should interject here that Tiger—it is almost an afterthought—   12
won the NCAA championship. He attended college—Stanford—for
two years. Condoleezza Rice once told me—she had been provost of
Stanford—that it was a shame that Tiger left school, understandable as
it was, because he "really enjoyed it.")

Then there is Tiger the pro. Once more, how to convey the   13
uniqueness—the impossibility—of it all? Tiger is only 25—and he has
won 27 tournaments, including six majors (nine, if you count the way
we do for Nicklaus). To provide a little comparison, Curtis Strange,
who was the best player in the world for several years, won 17 tournaments, and two majors. At one stage, Woods won six PGA events in a
row: farewell, parity. Indeed, before Woods, it was absurd to say, "I
think so-and-so will win this golf tournament," or even, "So-and-so is
the favorite." Golf is not a football game, in which one team or the
other must win. Tiger has introduced a strange element: predictability.

Let's grapple with some victory margins: in 1997 (at age 21, but   14
that's a different matter), Tiger won the Masters by twelve shots. I once
heard the TV commentator Ken Venturi, in the pre-Tiger era, say of a
guy who was leading some tournament by three shots—three shots—
"He's lapping the field." And he was. When you win the Masters, you
win it by one shot, two shots—three shots, maybe. Often, you're forced
to win it in a sudden-death playoff. Tiger won the 1997 Masters by
twelve shots: he could have made a 15 at the final par 4 and still won—
could have made 16 to play off.

In 2000, he won the U.S. Open, at Pebble Beach, by fifteen shots.   15
He won the British Open, at St. Andrews, by eight shots. (These are all
records, but we can't possibly begin to go into the record book.) I
argued—only half-jokingly, or a third jokingly—that Tiger should retire
then and there, rather as Bobby Jones did, at age 28. What did he have
left to prove? Sure, he had dreamed all his life of breaking Nicklaus's lifetime records, but that was just a matter of longevity, of hanging around,
of staying uninjured, of keeping oneself interested. What is there left to
do after winning the U.S. Open at Pebble (by fifteen) and the British at
St. Andrews (by eight), and in the millennial year of 2000?

Well, you can go on to win a type of Slam, I guess. And Woods is   16
still charging.

Of course, he is more than a golfer: He is an important American,   17
not least because of the racial or ethnic question. There is probably no
one in the country more refreshing, more resolute about race than Tiger
Woods. He is a one-man army against cant and stupidity. One of the
most thrilling television moments I have ever seen occurred at the
Masters, when Tiger was playing as an amateur. Jim Nantz of CBS asked
him one of those softball, standard, perfunctory questions: "Do you
think you have an obligation to be a role model for minority kids?"

Tiger answered, quick as a flash, "No." I almost fell out of my chair. He continued, "I have an obligation to be a role model for all kids."

After Tiger won the Masters in '97, President Clinton asked him,   18
the morning after, to join him the following day, to participate in a Jackie Robinson ceremony at Shea Stadium. Tiger said . . . no, to the President of the United States. The invitation was last-minute, and Tiger was suspicious of its motives. He had long planned a vacation in Mexico with friends, and he wouldn't scrap or alter it. Many people criticized Tiger for this decision; but he told them, essentially, to get lost. Here was a firm, self-confident democratic citizen, not a serf, complying with the ruler's summons. The same mettle Woods shows on the golf course, he shows off it.

A good number of people don't like Tiger's attitude—don't like it   19
at all. Larry King asked him, in 1998, "Do you feel that you're an influence on young blacks?" Tiger answered, calmly, unmovably, "Young children." An annoyed King shot back, "Just 'young children'? Don't you think you've attracted a lot more blacks to the game?" Replied Woods, "Yeah, I think I've attracted minorities to the game, but you know what? Why limit it to just that? I think you should be able to influence people in general, not just one race or social-economic background. Everybody should be in the fold." Again, I almost fell out of my chair. Tiger may be the most pointed universalist in public life.

Even Colin Powell, the current Secretary of State, has gotten   20
snippy with Tiger, or about him. Woods coined a word to describe his racial makeup: "Cablinasian." This is meant to stand for a mixture of Caucasian, black, Indian (American Indian), and Asian. Tiger's dad, a tough, no-nonsense career military man, is (to be disgustingly racial, but this is to make a point) half black, a quarter Chinese, and a quarter Indian; Tiger's mom is half Thai, a quarter Chinese, and a quarter white. Tiger is, in other words, 100 percent, pure American. Back to General Powell. On Meet the Press one Sunday in 1997, Tim Russert asked him (rather in the manner of Orval Faubus, actually), "If you have an ounce of black blood, aren't you black?" Powell responded that, like Tiger, he was of varied background, but "in order to not come up with a very strange word such as Tiger did, I consider myself black American. I'm very proud of it."

Well, despite his distaste for racial baloney, so is Woods: he is nei-   21
ther unaware nor unappreciative of the struggles of black people in this country. After winning the Masters that first time, he paid due homage to black players before him, including Charlie Sifford and Lee Elder (the first black to be allowed to play in the Masters, in 1975).

Yet Woods refuses to spend his life in obeisance to the race gods.   22
At one point, he felt obliged to put out a "Media Statement," the purpose of which was "to explain my heritage." It would be—this is

typical Tiger—"the final and only comment I will make regarding the issue":

> My parents have taught me to always be proud of my ethnic back-
> ground. Please rest assured that is, and always will be, the case . . . On
> my father's side, I am African-American. On my mother's side, I am
> Thai. Truthfully, I feel very fortunate, and EQUALLY PROUD, to be both
> African-American and Asian!
>   The critical and fundamental point is that ethnic background and/or
> composition should NOT make a difference. It does NOT make a differ-
> ence to me. The bottom line is that I am an American . . . and proud of it!
> That is who I am and what I am. Now, with your cooperation, I hope I
> can just be a golfer and a human being.

We're told that we shouldn't need heroes. Well, too bad: we   23
got one.

Not every touring pro has been gracious about Tiger and what he   24
means; envy and resentment run deep. But the Scottish champion
Colin Montgomerie said a lot when he commented recently, "We never
thought this would happen [Tiger's explosion] or that there was even a
chance it would happen. We're fortunate to have the world's best athlete playing our game. We're all not bad. He's just better. He is magnif-
icent in every department."

Yes, in every department. A rare spirit shoots through Tiger. Con-   25
sider a few, disparate things. Every year at Augusta, the Champions
Dinner is held, for which the previous year's winner selects the menu.
In 1998, Tiger—age 22—chose hamburgers and milkshakes: the all-
American meal. After he won the '97 Masters (remember, by a historic
twelve shots), he took a look at the film and announced, "My swing
stinks" (he didn't say "stinks," but I've cleaned it up a little). So he
worked to make it even better—and it may become better yet. Woods is
a perfect combination of the cool, self-contained golfer, a la Ben Hogan
(or Nicklaus, for that matter), and the hot, impassioned golfer, a la
Arnold Palmer, or Seve Ballesteros. And, finally, there is no better interview in sports: he handles himself superbly, and is not above displaying a contempt (usually sly) for dumb questions.

My golf friends and I have made our peace with Tiger, to say the   26
least. Initially, I think we all had a fear of his displacing Nicklaus,
which seemed sacrilegious. It helped, however, that Woods is the
biggest Nicklaus worshiper of all: he venerates him as Nicklaus vener-
ated Jones, and as Nicklaus pledged to follow in Jones's footsteps,
Tiger has pledged to follow in Nicklaus's. Said Nicklaus five years ago,
"There isn't a flaw in [Tiger's] golf or in his makeup. He will win more
majors than Arnold Palmer and me [Arnie was standing next to him]

combined. Somebody is going to dust my records. It might as well be Tiger, because he's such a great kid."

     Oh, it's a thrill to be alive in the Time of Tiger. Whether you give a   27 hoot about golf or not, I ask you—a final time—to trust me: rejoice.

Examining the Text
1. Nordlinger opens this essay with an anecdote about e-mailing a friend. Do you think this is an effective way to begin the article? Why or why not?
2. Explain the concept of parity in professional golf, and discuss how Woods has affected it.
3. In your own words, sum up how Nordlinger characterizes Woods's attitudes toward race. What does Nordlinger admire about this attitude?

For Group Discussion
Discuss why Nordlinger thinks that "whether you give a hoot about golf or not," Tiger Woods gives us reason to "rejoice" (27). Do you agree? Why or why not? Discuss how other sports figures compare to Woods in terms of their influence, their status as role models for youth, their attitudes on race, and their sheer talent and commitment to their sport. Can you and your group come up with other prominent athletes to place alongside Tiger Woods in these ways?

Writing Suggestion
Tiger Woods was born in 1975; thus he's a little too old to fit into Generation Y. Nonetheless, a number of writers have characterized him as an icon for this generation (see, for example "Managing Generation Y" by Bruce Tulgan and Carolyn A. Martin, 2001). Use Lim and Turco's descriptions of Generation Y to write an essay exploring the reasons why Woods works—or doesn't—as an icon or symbol for Generation Y.

Fields of Broken Dreams:
Latinos and Baseball

Marcos Bretón

Major league baseball has turned to the United States' neighbors to the south for talented youngsters who might become the future star hitters and pitchers. Latino players now comprise 25% of both leagues' roster of players, and the majority of them entered the privileged world of professional baseball from poverty. Indeed, some of the league's most famous players, including Sammy Sosa and Miguel Tejada, grew up in neighborhoods without running water, sewers or electricity. For talented youngsters raised in miserable conditions, baseball represents an opportunity to hit a home run for a brighter, more prosperous future. Yet, according to writer Marcos Bretón, major league baseball appears to be exploiting these poor kids by optioning them for considerably smaller sums than American-born players.

Bretón explores what one baseball team official calls the "boatload mentality," in which professional teams will scoop up dozens of youngsters, train them at facilities in the Dominican Republic, bring them to the U.S., but then ultimately reject up to 95% of them. Bretón refers to the unlucky majority as "discarded Latino players" and goes on to describe how many of these young men remain in the U.S. as undocumented immigrants whose lives are "dangerous, destitute and sad."

In the course of his discussion, Bretón traces the growth of baseball in the Caribbean, Mexico, and Central America through U.S. foreign policy. The presence of American troops (and accompanying civilian forces) on foreign soil was often the first exposure to baseball for residents of such countries as Cuba, Nicaragua, Panama, Dominican Republic, Puerto Rica, and others. He sees the spread of baseball as an extension of U.S. military exploitation and domination. The game quickly caught on in Latino countries; talented players of Latino and mixed race subsequently emerged into a talent pool regularly trolled by American baseball teams. By the turn of the 20th century, Latino players offered talent yet posed a problem: how to get around baseball regulations that excluded all but white players from the major league teams. The solution was a piece of paper in which Cuban-born players declared their racial heritage as strictly European and not tinged with African blood.

This article documents the uneasy, unbalanced relationship baseball has with its Latino players. Even those who make it big are not acknowledged as being Latino. Despite their massive contribution to the game, Latinos are still largely invisible to the sports writers and, by association, to the majority of fans, according to the author. Unlike American-born players who may rise through the minor leagues, foreign-born Latino players have the additional disadvantages of a language barrier and cultural isolation to endure as they toil in small towns across the United States.

As you read, *consider the case that Bretón makes against major league baseball, both in contemporary times and historically. How well does Bretón make his point about "broken dreams" without being explicit about it? Do you see this account as being primarily about money or something broader?*

The conversation was with a nationally syndicated sports columnist.　　　1

　　　I said: "Did you know that at the end of the 1999 season, nine out　　2
of the top ten hitters in the American League were Latino or had Latino
roots?"

Silence. . . ."I didn't know that."   3

This ignorance came as no surprise to me after having spent most   4
of 1999 promoting my book *Away Games: The Life and Times of a Latin
Ballplayer*, along with my collaborator José Luis Villegas. Despite an
explosion of exciting new Latinos stars, the story of Latino baseball
players in the major leagues is still grossly underreported.

Even more troubling is the invisibility of the realities behind   5
this story.

Almost all the Latino stars in baseball today—now 25 percent of   6
major league rosters and growing—come from overwhelming poverty,
a reality that Major League Baseball (MLB) avidly exploits. For example: The focal point of my book—Miguel Tejada, shortstop of the Oakland
Athletics—came from a destitute barrio in the Dominican Republic with
no running water and little electricity.

Knowing he had no alternatives, the Athletics acquired Tejada's   7
considerable talent for a mere $2,000. By comparison, Tejada's white
American teammate, Ben Grieve, received a $1.2 million signing bonus.
Similarly, the Texas Rangers acquired Sammy Sosa's services in 1986
for $3,500—the exact amount the Brooklyn Dodgers paid to sign Jackie
Robinson in 1946.

"BOATLOAD MENTALITY"

Every team in Major League Baseball exploits Latino baseball players.   8
Dick Balderson, vice-president of the Colorado Rockies, frankly calls
this the "boatload mentality"—sign a "boatload" of Latinos for little
money and if only a couple make it to the big leagues, teams still come
out ahead. "Instead of signing four [American] guys at $25,000 each,
you sign 20 [Dominican] guys for $5,000 each."

The justification for this "boatload mentality" used by baseball peo-   9
ple is this: Tejada and other budding Latino players are fortunate that MLB
affords them an opportunity to escape the third world poverty they grew
up in. Baseball gives them a way out, a chance to get paid, eat regularly,
sleep in clean beds, and, for the very best, a crack at fame and fortune.

After all, their reasoning goes, isn't Sammy Sosa—a former shoe   10
shine boy like Tejada—a perfect example of the rags-to-riches life only
MLB can confer on Latino kids otherwise bound for the sugar cane
fields or worse?

The answer is yes. And there is a fundamental truth to the notion   11
that baseball was the only way for Sosa and Tejada to pull themselves
and their families out of poverty.

But does that make it right for MLB to sign Latino ballplayers—   12
whose talent is paying huge dividends for big league teams—for next

to nothing? It is, after all, the same justification used by U.S. employers for their pervasive mistreatment and exploitation of Latino immigrant workers.

According to Major League Baseball, 90 to 95 percent of Latino   13
players signed to contracts never reach the big leagues. The vast majority never get a chance to play in the U.S., not even in the minor leagues.
And all but a few of those brought to the U.S. are released without ever
playing major league ball.

Most of these discarded Latino players stay in the U.S. as undoc-   14
umented immigrants rather than return as "failures" to a country that
offers them little future. The lives these young men lead are often dangerous, destitute, and sad. Many go to New York because they have
friends or family in what is the largest concentration of Dominicans in
the United States.

José Santana was a Houston Astros prospect until he was released   15
in 1995. Now he mops floors in a Brooklyn bodega and plays semi-pro
on the weekends, all the while frantically placing calls to an American
agent who once filled his head with dollar signs, but now can't be bothered. Tony McDonald is a former minor league star who had the misfor-
tune of being a third baseman in the Philadelphia Phillies organization at
the same time Hall of Famer Mike Schmidt was in his prime. Today,
McDonald works in a warehouse. These castoffs represent the underside
of the Sammy Sosa story, the rule rather than the exception in the high-
stakes recruitment of ball players from Latin America and the Caribbean.

THE TALENT PLUNDER

Baseball is investing millions in Latin America, sending scouts across   16
the Caribbean basin in search of barefoot boys with quick reflexes,
strong hand-eye coordination, and powerful arms.

Miguel Tejada was one of these boys. Born and raised in a miser-   17
able barrio in the Dominican town of Bani, Tejada's family was dis-
placed by a hurricane when he was three. For the next five years, the
family lived in homeless shelters until settling in a shanty town on the
outskirts of Bani. Tejada was shining shoes by the age of five.

He quit school to work full-time at the age of eleven. His mother   18
died when he was 13. At about the same time, his father left to find
work in another town, leaving Tejada and his older brother to fend
for themselves. For the next four years, Tejada lived a hand-to-mouth
existence.

But it turns out that Miguel had baseball talent, and he was   19
signed by the Oakland Athletics in 1993 when he was 17. He was sent
to a "baseball academy" the Athletics built in a Dominican jungle,

where signees are drilled in baseball fundamentals all day every day. At the academy, Tejada ate balanced meals for the first time in his life. He was given English lessons every night. And he was taught to steel himself for competition.

There were 70 other Miguel Tejadas at his camp alone, all of them   20 from backgrounds similar to his, all with the same intense desire to stand out—not just for the love of the game, but for survival.

And all were signed for almost no money. Most big league teams   21 run academies in the Dominican Republic because it costs a small fraction of what it takes to field minor league teams in the U.S. The best of the best get sent to America. The ones who aren't good enough or "cooperative" enough are sent back to the poverty they've always known. These academies are baseball factories producing big league talent at subminimum wages.

Tejada started his first summer league game on the bench, watching other players the Athletics thought had more talent. Then he got his   22 first at-bat: he hit a home run. Soon, this destitute, uneducated kid was being shipped to the U.S. as a "prospect."

Speaking no English, he put aside intense homesickness to make   23 a name for himself on the field in far-flung towns like Medford, Oregon, Modesto, California, and Huntsville, Alabama.

He came alive only when he was on the field. Off the field, he had   24 few friends, no transportation or understanding of the world around him. Like all Latino minor leaguers, he led a lonely life in the U.S. From 1995 to 1997, Tejada spent his off-field time isolated in his room watching Spanish-language novellas on TV, cooking Spanish rice and beans, and listening to his music.

On the field, he played among American players of far less talent   25 who had signed for far more money than he. With his skills, Tejada would have easily commanded a seven-figure signing bonus were he an American.

A bright young man despite his lack of formal education, Tejada   26 knew exactly where he stood in baseball's hierarchy. He somehow managed not to let it get him down, but other Latinos burn with rage at the inequities they face at the hands of MLB.

When Tejada reached the big leagues in August of 1997, his   27 dream was realized and baseball people could rightly say that the game had given a wonderful life to a kid with no options. But Tejada was the only survivor from the dozens of Dominican kids signed at the same time he was. While those other young men have been forgotten, numerous eager young Latino players have been signed to take their place.

Meanwhile, Tejada has secured his spot in the Athletics infield.   28 He is now a fan favorite with a bright future. And he is coming of age at a time when Latino players like Sammy Sosa, Ivan Rodriguez of the Texas Rangers, and Pedro Martinez of the Boston Red Sox are dominating the game. I call their story "the last great, untold story of baseball."

GUNBOATS AND BASEBALL

Few Americans realize that Tejada's Dominican Republic, the greatest   29
producer of Latino players today, was invaded and occupied by U.S. forces twice in this century and has been bullied and dominated by the U.S. ever since.

It was those invading U.S. forces, and the employees of the big   30
American companies that followed, that taught Latinos the game of baseball. The sport spread from Cuba, to the Dominican Republic, Puerto Rico, Mexico, Venezuela, Panama, Colombia, and Nicaragua as the U.S. flexed its muscles throughout the Western Hemisphere in the 20th century. The way Dominican players like Tejada are recruited is an extension of that history of exploitation.

Latino players have been in the majors since 1902, a full 45 years   31
before Jackie Robinson broke baseball's color barrier. At least 45 Latinos, mostly Cubans, played big league ball between 1902 and 1947, the year of Robinson's historic breakthrough. Some, like Rafael Almeida and Armando Marsans—signed by the Cincinnati Reds in 1911—were forced to sign pieces of paper stating that they were of European and not African descent.

Most of these Latino players had African, European, and indige-   32
nous blood flowing through their veins. Their appearance defied America's narrow, black or white, definition of race. In fact, José Acosta and Jacinto Calvo, both Cubans, pulled an amazing feat—first playing in the old Negro Leagues in 1915 and then "passing" in the segregated big leagues five years later.

Why have they been forgotten?   33

Because many early Latino players, with their "un-American"   34
skin colors, were treated like novelties and slipped under the U.S. racial radar. But the best Latino players, whose African ancestry was evident, were barred from the big leagues, along with legendary Negro Leaguers like Hall of Famer Josh Gibson.

Those who slipped into the big leagues were sworn to lie about   35
their African heritage and barely made a dent in the public consciousness before fading into oblivion. For centuries, the U.S. refused to forthrightly deal with the racism it visited upon African Americans. And Latinos were rendered invisible.

Once Robinson entered the game, all things racial in baseball   36
were overtaken by his story. But historians have never given Robinson

credit for opening the doors of opportunity for the best players Latin America had to offer—men who were black as well as Latino.

"HOT-TEMPERED SHOWBOATS"

Minnie Minoso, Roberto Clemente, Orlando Cepeda, and others took baseball by storm in the 1950s, and changed the game.   37

Chico Carrasquel, a Venezuelan who starred with the Chicago White Sox, transformed the shortstop position into one of artistry and flair in the early 1950s, ushering in today's era of dazzling Latino short-stops. Vic Power, a Puerto Rican, won seven Gold Glove awards at first base in the late 1950s and early 1960s by pioneering the one-handed catch.   38

Because of this and because Power—who was also black—refused to be cowed by Jim Crow segregation, sportswriters coined a new phrase to describe him: "the showboat." Other negative labels soon followed: "moody," "hot-tempered," and, worst of all, "not a team player." These labels were rooted in negative white perceptions of Latinos, labels that took hold and became a burden even the great players had to carry.   39

The now legendary Roberto Clemente, who died in 1972 in a tragic plane crash while rushing emergency aid to earthquake-ravaged Nicaragua, railed at the negative labels placed upon him by reporters in the 1960s and early 1970s. Reporters branded him a "malingerer," an injury faker, and worse. They mocked Clemente's English skills. Unable to deny Clemente's talent, they added the now familiar racist caveat: the "troubled," "angry" star.   40

In a game where mythology and the clever quote spawn legends, Latino players saw their on-field talents ignored because of their inability to communicate with reporters. Even milestones, such as when Cuban shortstop Zoilo Versalles was the first Latino named Most Valuable Player while with the Minnesota Twins in 1965, were scarcely noted.   41

And when Latinos get injured or pass their prime, they are quickly abandoned. "It happens to all of us," said Tony Oliva, a Cuban and the American League batting champion in 1964, 1965, and 1971. "We all get released . . . . To the Americans, we are like some stray dog, like a rudderless ship at sea."   42

READY OR NOT

Sports, it is often said, is a mirror of society.   43

What does baseball tell us about the 40 million Latinos in this country?   44

We can say: it's time their story made it onto the cultural radar　45
screen because—ready or not—Latinos have arrived. We are not just a
black-and-white country anymore.

It's time for this country to come to grips with the harrowing road　46
traveled by Latinos, ballplayers and workers alike, because Latinos are
becoming a major force in baseball and the broader society.

In 1998, Latino players swept the Most Valuable Player awards.　47
And in 1999, eight of the 12 players selected to the Associated Press's
All-Star team were Latino. Sammy Sosa is leading a Latino wave that is
energizing the game, just as African American players did in the 1950s.

But, so far, only Sosa has registered in a meaningful way with the　48
American people—and he had to hit nearly 130 home runs in two years
to do that. As Tejada's story shows, there is much more to baseball's
Latino story than Sammy Sosa.

Whether that story and the exploitation of Latino prospects ever　49
becomes known or debated remains to be seen. Right now, it's MIA on
our sports pages.

Theirs is part of a story that eluded us in the 20th century. Hope-　50
fully, this new century will be different.

Examining the Text

1. In what ways does the article document the assertion that baseball
has done a disservice to Latino players? Do you agree with the author's
contention that the stories of Latino 'ball players are "grossly under-
reported?" Why, or why not?

2. Bretón's article has three broad themes. Identify and assess each
theme carefully and determine if, in your opinion, there is a dominant
theme. What makes it more persuasive? If you don't find any of Bretón's
themes persuasive, explain what you think the article lacks.

3. The article states that "most big league teams run academies in the
Dominican Republic . . . these academies are baseball factories producing big league talent at sub-minimum wages." Compare this to the
assertion that baseball "gives them a way out, a chance to get paid, eat
regularly, sleep in clean beds and, for the very best, a crack at fame and
fortune." Upon reflection, does the former position balance the latter
position? Do you think the author was seeking to balance the two
extremes in the article? Why or why not?

4. In the section headed *Gunboats and Baseball*, Bretón attempts to link U.S.
foreign policy—specifically, its invasions of the Dominican Republic—
with the league's current efforts to exploit Dominican talent. What was
his intent in tying these two disparate concepts together? Do you think
he succeeds in making a case that the current baseball-recruitment practices are in some way a continuation of U.S. military policy of the past?

What other devices does he employ to bolster his general position about current recruitment practices?

5. *Rhetorical question*: Look closely at the technique Bretón employed in setting down his article. What category does it most easily fall into: scientific, persuasive essay, journalism, or personal opinion . . . or a combination of several of these? Did Bretón limit the article's effectiveness by using the chosen technique? By what specific means does he support the central tenet of the article? Do these techniques render the article convincing? If not, what other means might be employed to bolster the article's persuasiveness?

For Group Discussion

Divide your group into two halves. Let one half of the group support the position that, all things considered, the practices discussed in this article are positive because they allow impoverished young men a great opportunity to succeed financially that they would otherwise not have. The other half of the group will take the position that baseball is exploiting poor people and engaging in practices that it would not use if it were dealing with American players. Before the discussion begins, each half should compile a list of key points in support of its position.

Writing Suggestion

Using the Internet and other sources such as newspaper files and libraries, determine if your favorite (or local if you have no favorite) major league baseball team runs an academy in the Dominican Republic or any other foreign country. Find out how your team treats its locally recruited players and compare that to the general outline used by Bretón in his article. Write a persuasive essay in which you either defend your team's practices or condemn them. Be sure to cite as many specifics as possible, such as signing fees for American-born versus foreign players, support for "farm" and "feeder" teams and the number of foreign-born players in your team's roster currently versus ten years ago.

ADDITIONAL SUGGESTIONS FOR WRITING ABOUT SPORTS

1. Using Maya Angelou's "Champion of the World" as a model, write a narrative in which you tell of a past experience with sports, either as a spectator or as a participant, that had a significant effect on your life. Perhaps this experience revealed something about yourself that you didn't realize, helped you to better understand someone else, taught you an important lesson, or corrected a misconception that you had. Or perhaps you're not certain what effect the experience had, and can use this assignment to speculate on its significance.

2. Attend a local sporting event, and bring a notebook and, if possible, a tape recorder or video camera. Observe and take notes about how the people around you behave, what they do and say, what they wear, how they relate to one another, what interests or bores them, when they seem satisfied or disappointed. Note also how their behavior is different from what it would likely be in other contexts. Try to be an impartial observer, simply recording what you see in as much detail as possible.

From your notes, write an extended description of one or several typical spectators, and then draw some conclusions about why people enjoy watching sports. You may also want to discuss the psychological benefits and/or harm that being a spectator might cause.

3. Choose a sport with which you're very familiar, either because you play it or watch it regularly. Reflect on your experience playing or watching this sport, and write down some of your recollections. Think about what you've learned from this sport, and how it has affected other areas of your life.

Then write an essay in which you show how this particular sport has influenced your beliefs, attitudes, and values. Be as specific as possible and try to show precisely how and why the sport has influenced you.

4. Many of the writers in this chapter discuss the impact of professional sports on individuals and on society as a whole. Referring to essays in this chapter, construct your own argument about the influence of professional sports. As a prewriting exercise, make lists of the beneficial and the detrimental influences of professional sports on our society. Try to come up with specific examples to illustrate each of the items on your lists. Working from those lists, develop a persuasive argument about the influence of sports on our society.

Internet Activities

1. Professional athletes are often role models in our society. As a prewriting exercise for this assignment, list some of the reasons why this is so, especially for young people. Also list the ways in which athletes might be good role models, as well as some of the reasons other professionals (for example, teachers or government leaders) might actually be better role models.

Next, visit the links to information about professional athletes, provided at the *Common Culture* Web site, to official and unofficial homepages of individual athletes. After browsing through these links, choose an athlete who you think is either a good or a bad role model. Do further research on this athlete, looking up interviews and articles about him or her in the library. From this information, write a brief biography of the athlete, focusing on the kind of role model he or she is.

2. Professional sports teams are in the business of making money, and the World Wide Web is increasingly becoming a venue for advertising and marketing. It's no surprise, then, that all of the major professional sports teams now have their own Web sites. Go to the *Common Culture* Web site for links that you can follow to visit the homepages of professional teams in baseball, football, men's basketball, women's basketball, and hockey. Choose a Web site for one team and read the site carefully and completely. Make a list of the information that the site offers, including statistics, pictures, news and "inside information," schedules, and so on. Then analyze the ways in which the information offered at the site is intended to promote or "sell" the team. Is the site addressed to current fans of the team, or is it intended to cultivate new fans? How effectively do you believe the Web site is in advertising and marketing the team it represents?

Reading Images

Brandi Chastain, shown in the photo on p. CI-09, is famous for her game-winning shot during the 1999 women's World Cup. But perhaps she is more famous for what happened after the game—in a moment of unbridled joy, she removed her jersey and bounded joyfully on the field in a sports bra, helping to make such apparel some of the most recognizable items of clothing in the country at that moment in pop-cultural history. She received so much notoriety for this single act that Brandi Chastain was moved to create her own Web site in response to the furor. The site, which she calls, "It's Not About the Bra," can be found at *http://www.itsnotaboutthebra.com/*

In an essay, "read" the images in this text and on Brandi's website, to uncover and discuss the sociocultural messages they contain. Look carefully at all elements of the graphics. Discuss possible meanings implicit in the colors and the central images of Chastain. However, don't be content merely to focus on the central images: study the background "negative space" as well, to ascertain how the entire composition combines to create meaning. Note also the juxtaposition of image and text, along with messages contained in the text itself.

If you wish, you may take this discussion a step further by addressing a central issue raised by the pictures: namely, the commodification of sport. Some purists believe that sports are tainted by commercialism. They might therefore point to commercial use of the images that depict Chastain in her Nike sports bra and charge that by capitalizing on this pure moment of sport-centered bliss, the spirit of competition is reduced to a crass attempt to sell. Consider this issue, examining your own feelings about the pros and cons of commercialism in sport, and then develop a thesis that takes a persuasive stance with regard to this issue.

Movies

It's Friday night. You park in an exhaust-filled subterranean garage or a vast asphalt lot surrounding a mall. You make your way into the neon-lit mega-plex, where you and a companion or two pay half a day's salary for tickets, an industrial-size bucket of popcorn, and a couple of ten-gallon sodas. You wind your way through a maze of corridors to the theater of your choice, where a psychedelic montage filling the screen is soon replaced by the first of an interminable series of quick-cutting, MTV-style previews, as you bathe in rolling quadraphonic surround sound. You sink into your space-age plastic seat and kick back, surrendering to the waves of sound and images. . . .

Such is moviegoing in the new millennium. Gone are the nickel matinee and the discount double feature, newsreels, cartoons, and comic short subjects, and the drive-in, where many a pair of teenagers learned human anatomy in the back seat of a Chevy.

The external trappings of the moviegoing experience may have changed, but the reasons people go are still pretty much the same: to get out of the house and escape the routine of their daily lives; to be part of a communal group sharing an experience; to find a romantic setting where conversation is at a minimum; to indulge, for one night, in an orgy of junk food; and, above all, to be entertained and, perhaps, touched emotionally. So strong is the draw of motion pictures that Americans fork over billions of dollars a year on domestic movies alone.

As there are many reasons for going to the movies, so there are many ways of explaining their popularity and studying their influence within the fabric of contemporary culture. From a sociological perspective, movies can reflect, define, or even redefine social norms, and—in the work of politically focused filmmakers such as Michael Moore—depict urgent social problems within the relative safety of the big screen. From a psychological perspective, viewers identify with the character and project their own feelings into the action, giving them a deep emotional connection to a protagonist along with feelings of tension and, ultimately release. From a literary perspective, movies can be interpreted in terms of genres—horror movies, or crime dramas, or menaced-female stories—or in terms of plot, characterization, imagery, and so forth. From an economic perspective, movies may be seen primarily as a consumable product, defined solely by the marketplace. To the cultural critic, this economic influence might seem to be negative, reducing a potentially powerful artistic form to the lowest common denominator. The capitalist observer might see such forces as positive, however, because they encourage the worldwide spread of American cultural values. Finally, from a semiological perspective, movies are ripe with symbolic imagery, from the multiple associations possible in a character's name to the way images are juxtaposed in the editing.

This chapter introduces film criticism arising from several of these views. The first readings focus on the social impacts and implications of film in the new millennium. The second part looks at two controversies: one about a cutting-edge filmmaker, Quentin Tarantino, and one about a recent film that stirred much public reaction, *The Passion of the Christ*. The two controversies are related, since both have film violence as the central issue around which much debate rages. As you think and write about film and the film industry, you may find that you want to pick and choose among these various approaches, incorporating parts of any number of them into your own theoretical analyses.

Film and American Culture

The Way We Are

Sydney Pollack

If anyone knows American moviemaking, it's Sydney Pollack. A director of more than sixteen films—including The Way We Were, Tootsie, Out of Africa, *and* The Firm—*and an occasional actor (Dustin Hoffman's agent in* Tootsie), *Pollack has had an unparalleled opportunity to observe the changing tastes of the American viewing public and the movie industry's response to those changes. In the following article, a transcript of an address Pollack delivered at a conference about the influence of the popular media on American values, Pollack suggests that changes in the moral fabric of our society are responsible for the kinds of movies we see today, not vice versa.*

When he looks at contemporary America, Pollack finds a conspicuous lack of the "kind of scrupulous ethical concern for the sanctity of life" that prevailed in past decades and was reflected in motion pictures of the time, when there were less frequent and less graphic scenes of violence, when characters were esteemed for their humility and personal integrity, and when explicit sexuality was found only in "stag" films, not in mainstream theaters. Many people today, Pollack notes, are nostalgic for the "old values" and believe that movies should encourage the return of these values rather than reflecting current values. Pollack disagrees, however, pointing out that, although screenwriters and directors may want their movies to reflect some moral content, the economics of the industry require first and foremost that movies be entertaining, and therefore, they must appeal to a buying audience whose values may be very different from those of the reformers.

As you read*, consider whether you agree with Pollack's notions of artistic integrity, especially his assertions that a filmmaker's prime goal should be to entertain an audience and that movies simply reflect the surrounding society. Is it possible that, in responding to their audience's changing tastes, filmmakers also "construct" public attitudes towards violence, sexuality, and so forth by pushing their explicitness further and further?*

Six weeks ago, I thought I was going to be happy to be a part of this   1
conference, which shows you how naive I am. The agenda—for me at least—is a mine field. Normally, I spend my time worrying about specific problems and not reflecting, as many of you on these panels do. So I've really thought about this, and I've talked to anyone who would

listen. My colleagues are sick and tired of it, my wife has left for the country and even my agents—and these are people I pay—don't return my phone calls. By turns, I have felt myself stupid, unethical, a philistine, unpatriotic, a panderer, a cultural polluter, and stupid. And I've completely failed to solve your problems, except in one small way. You have delayed by at least six weeks the possibility of my contributing further to the problems you see.

I know your concerns have to do with American values and whether   2
those values are being upheld or assaulted by American entertainment— by what I and others like me do. But which values exactly?

In the thirties, forties, and fifties, six men in the Valley, immi-   3
grants really, ran the movie industry. Our society was vastly different. The language of the movies was a language of shared values. If you put forward a virtuousness on the part of your hero, everybody responded to it.

When Sergeant York, played by Gary Cooper, refused to endorse   4
a breakfast cereal, knowing he'd been asked because he'd won the Medal of Honor, he said: "I ain't proud of what I've done. You don't make money off of killing people. That there is wrong." We expected him to behave that way.

But society's values have changed. That kind of scrupulous, ethi-   5
cal concern for the sanctity of human life doesn't exist in the same way, and that fact is reflected in the movies. There's a nostalgia now for some of the old values, but so many people embrace other expressions of values that it's hard to say these other expressions aren't reality.

Their idea of love, for example, is a different idea of love. It's a much   6
less chaste, much less idealized love than was depicted in the earlier films. We are seeing some sort of return to the ideal of marriage. There was a decade or two when marriage really lost its popularity, and while young people are swinging toward it again, I don't believe one could say that values have not changed significantly since the thirties, forties, and fifties.

Morality, the definitions of virtue, justice, and injustice, the sanc-   7
tity of the individual, have been fairly fluid for American audiences in terms of what they choose to embrace or not embrace.

Take a picture like *Dances With Wolves*. You could not have made   8
it in the thirties or forties. It calls into question every value that existed in traditional Westerns. It may not reflect what everybody thinks now, but it expresses a lot of guilty re-evaluation of what happened in the West, the very things shown in the old Westerns that celebrated the frontier.

If we got the movies to assert or talk about better values, would   9
that fix our society? Well, let me quote Sam Goldwyn. When he was told by his staff how poorly his studio's new—and very expensive—film

was doing, Sam thought a minute, shrugged, and said, "Listen, if they don't want to come, you can't stop them."

Now that's as close to a first principle of Hollywood as I can come. 10 It informs everything that we're here to discuss and it controls every solution that we may propose.

OUT OF HOLLYWOOD

Before they can be anything else, American movies are a product. This 11 is not good or bad, this is what we've got. A very few may become art, but all of them, whatever their ambitions, are first financed as commodities. They're the work of craftsmen and artists, but they're soon offered for sale.

Whether we say that we're "creating a film" or merely "making a 12 movie," the enterprise itself is sufficiently expensive and risky that it cannot be, and it will not be, undertaken without the hope of reward. We have no Medicis here. It takes two distinct entities, the financiers and the makers, to produce movies, and there is a tension between them. Their goals are sometimes similar, but they do different things. Financiers are not in the business of philanthropy. They've got to answer to stockholders.

Of course, the controlling influence in filmmaking hasn't changed 13 in 50 years: it still belongs to the consumer. That's the dilemma and, in my view, what we're finally talking about. What do you do about culture in a society that celebrates the common man but doesn't always like his taste?

If you operate in a democracy and you're market-supported and 14 driven, the spectrum of what you will get is going to be very wide indeed. It will range from trash to gems. There are 53,000 books published in this country every year. How many of them are really good? Tired as I may be of fast-food-recipe, conscienceless, simple-minded books, films, TV, and music, the question remains, who is to be society's moral policeman?

Over the course of their first 30 or 40 years, the movies were a 15 cottage industry, and the morality that was reflected in them was the morality of the early film pioneers. Now, film studios are tiny divisions of multinational corporations, and they feel the pressure for profits that happens in any other repeatable-product business. They look for a formula. Say you get the recipe for a soft drink and perfect it; once customers like it, you just repeat it and it will sell. More fortunes have been lost than made in the movie business pursuing such a formula, but unfortunately today, more junk than anything else is being made pursuing it. And film companies are folding like crazy.

Since we are in the democracy business, we can't tell people what   16
they should or shouldn't hear, or support, or see, so they make their
choices. The market tries to cater to those choices, and we have what
we have.

MAKING FILMS

Are American films bad? A lot of them surely are, and so are a lot of   17
everybody else's, the way a lot of anything produced is bad—breakfast
cereals, music, most chairs, architecture, mail-order shirts. There probably hasn't been a really beautiful rake since the Shakers stopped making
farm implements. But that is no excuse.

I realize that I am a prime suspect here, but I'm not sure that you   18
really understand how odd and unpredictable a business the making of
films actually is. It just doesn't conform to the logic or rules of any
other business. It's always been an uneasy merger of two antithetical
things: some form of art and sheer commerce.

If the people who make films get the money that is invested in   19
them back to the people who finance them, then they'll get to make
more. We know that the business of films is to reach as many people as
possible. That works two ways; it's not just a market discipline. You
have to remember that most of us who are doing this got into it for the
romance, the glory, the applause, the chance to tell stories, even to
learn, but rarely for the money. The more people you reach, the greater
your sense of success. Given the choice, I'd rather make the whole
world cry than 17 intellectuals in a classroom.

But, paradoxically, if you are the actual maker of the film—not   20
the financier—you can't make films and worry about whether they'll
reach a large audience or make money, first, because nobody really
knows a formula for what will make money. If they did, I promise you
we would have heard about it, and studios would not be going broke.
Second, and much more practically, if you spent your time while you
were making the film consciously thinking about what was commercial, then the real mechanism of choice—the mechanism that is your
own unconscious, your own taste and imagination, your fantasy—
would be replaced by constant reference to this formula that we know
doesn't work.

So the only practical approach a filmmaker can take is to make a   21
film that he or she would want to see. This sounds arrogant, but you try
to make a movie for yourself, and you hope that as many people as
possible will like it too. If that happens, it's because you've done something in the telling of the story that makes people care. One of the things
that makes a film distinct from other American business products is

this emotional involvement of the maker. A producer of auto parts can become pretty emotional about a sales slump, but it isn't the same thing. His product hasn't come from his history; it isn't somehow in the image of his life; and it lacks mystery. It is entirely measurable and concrete, which is certainly appropriate in the manufacture of auto parts. I wouldn't want to buy a carburetor from a neurotic, mixed-up auto manufacturer.

Fortunately for those of us in film, no such standards apply. Quite   22
the contrary, in fact. No matter what his conscious intentions are, the best part of what the filmmaker does—the part, when it works, that makes you want to see the film—doesn't come from a rational, consciously controllable process. It comes from somewhere inside the filmmaker's unconscious. It comes from making unlikely connections seem inevitable, from a kind of free association that jumps to odd or surprising places, conclusions that cause delights, something that creates goose pimples or awe.

This conference has suggested a question: While you're actually   23
making the movie, do you think about whether or not it will be doing the world any good? I can't answer it for filmmakers in general. For myself, candidly, no, I don't.

I try to discover and tell the truth and not be dull about it. In that   24
sense, the question has no significance for me. I assume that trying to discover the truth is in itself a good and virtuous aim. By truth I don't mean some grand, pretentious axiom to live by; I just mean the truth of a character from moment to moment. I try to discover and describe things like the motives that are hidden in day-to-day life. And the truth is rarely dull. If I can find it, I will have fulfilled my primary obligation as a filmmaker, which is not to bore the pants off you.

Most of us in this business have enormous sympathy for   25
Scheherazade—we're terrified we're going to be murdered if we're boring. So our first obligation is to not bore people; it isn't to teach.

Most of the time, high-mindedness just leads to pretentious or   26
well-meaning, often very bad, films. Most of the Russian films made under communism were of high quality in terms of craft, but they were soporific because their intent to do good as it was perceived by the state or an all-knowing party committee was too transparent.

I'm sure that you think the person in whose hands the process   27
actually rests, the filmmaker, could exert an enormous amount of control over the film's final worthiness. The question usually goes like this: Should filmmakers pander to the public, or should they try to elevate public taste to something that many at this conference would find more acceptable? Is the job of an American filmmaker to give the public what it wants or what the filmmaker thinks the public should have? This doesn't leave much doubt as to what you think is the right answer.

But framing your question this way not only betrays a misund-   28
erstanding of how the filmmaking process works but also is just plain
wishful thinking about how to improve society. I share your nostalgia
for some of those lost traditional values, but attempting to reinstall
them by arbitrarily putting them into movies when they don't exist in
everyday life will not get people to go to the movies or put those values
back into life. I wish it were that simple.

ENGAGING AN AUDIENCE

This conference is concerned with something called popular culture   29
and its effect on society, but I am concerned with one film at a time and
its effect. You are debating whether movies corrupt our souls or elevate
them, and I'm debating whether a film will touch a soul. As a filmmaker, I never set out to create popular culture, and I don't know a single other filmmaker who does.

Maybe it's tempting to think of Hollywood as some collective   30
behemoth grinding out the same stories and pushing the same values,
but it's not that simple. Hollywood, whatever that means, is Oliver
Stone castigating war in *Born on the Fourth of July* and John Milius celebrating it in *The Wind and the Lion*. It's Walt Disney and Martin
Scorsese. It's Steven Spielberg and Milos Foreman. It's *Amadeus* and
Terminator and hundreds of choices in between.

I don't want to defend Hollywood, because I don't represent   31
Hollywood—I can't, any more than one particular writer can represent
literature or one painter art. For the most part, the impulse toward all art,
entertainment, culture, pop culture, comes from the same place within
the makers of it. The level of talent and the soul, if you'll forgive the
word again, is what finally limits it.

At the risk of telling you more than you need to know about   32
my own work, I make the movies I make because there is in each
film some argument that fascinates me, an issue I want to work
through. I call this a spine or an armature because it functions for
me like an armature in sculpture—something I can cover up and it
will support the whole structure. I can test the scenes against it. For
me, the film, when properly dramatized, adds up to this idea, this
argument.

But there are lots of other ways to go about making a film, and   33
lots of other filmmakers who do it differently. Some filmmakers begin
knowing exactly what they want to say and then craft a vehicle that
contains that statement. Some are interested in pure escape. Here's the
catch. The effectiveness and the success of all our films is determined
by exactly the same standards—unfortunately, not by the particular

validity of their message but by their ability to engage the concentration and emotions of the audience.

Citizen Kane is an attack on acquisition, but that's not why people   34
go to see it. I don't have any idea if the audience that saw *Tootsie*
thought at any conscious level that it could be about a guy who became
a better man for having been a woman; or that *The Way We Were*, a film
I made 20 years ago, may have been about the tension between passion, often of the moment, and wisdom, often part of a longer view; or
that *Out Of Africa* might be about the inability to possess another individual and even the inability of one country to possess another. That's
intellectual and stuffy. I just hope the audiences were entertained.

I may choose the movies I make because there's an issue I want   35
to explore, but the how—the framing of that issue, the process of
finding the best way to explore it—is a much more mysterious, elusive,
and messy process. I can't tell you that I understand it; if I did, I would
have a pep talk with myself and go out and make a terrific movie
every time.

I would not make a film that ethically, or morally, or politically   36
trashed what I believe is fair. But by the same token, I feel an obligation—
and this is more complicated and personal—to do films about arguments.

Orson Welles in
Citizen Kane

I try hard to give each side a strong argument—not because I'm a fair guy but because I believe it's more interesting. Both things are going on.

I do the same thing on every movie I make. I find an argument, a   37
couple of characters I would like to have dinner with, and try to find
the most fascinating way to explore it. I work as hard as I can to tell the
story in the way I'd like to have it told to me.

What is really good is also entertaining and interesting because   38
it's closer to a newer way to look at the truth. You can't do that consciously. You can't start out by saying, "I am now going to make a great
film."

The virtue in making a film, if there is any, is in making it well. If   39
there's any morality that's going to come out, it will develop as you
begin to construct, at every moment you have a choice to make. You
can do it the honest way or you can bend it, and the collection of those
moments of choice is what makes the work good or not good and is
what reveals morality or the lack of it.

I've made 16 films. I've had some enormous successes and I've   40
had some colossal failures, but I can't tell you what the difference is in
terms of what I did.

AN AMERICAN AESTHETIC?

In some circles, American films suffer by comparison with European   41
films precisely because a lot of our movies seem to be the product of little deliberation and much instinct. It's been said of European movies
that essence precedes existence, which is just a fancy way of saying that
European movies exist in order to say something. Certainly one never
doubts with a European film that it's saying something, and often it
just comes right out and says it.

American films work by indirection; they work by action and   42
movement, either internal or external, but almost always movement.
Our films are more narratively driven than others, which has a lot to do
with the American character and the way we look at our lives. We see
ourselves and our lives as being part of a story.

Most of our movies have been pro the underdog, concerned with   43
injustice, relatively anti-authority. There's usually a system—or a
bureaucracy—to triumph over.

More often than not, American movies have been affirmative and   44
hopeful about destiny. They're usually about individuals who control
their own lives and their fate. In Europe, the system was so class-bound
and steeped in tradition that there was no democratization of that
process.

There's no prior education required to assimilate American   45
movies or American culture. American culture is general, as opposed
to the specificity of Japanese or Indian culture. America has the most
easily digestible culture.

Our movies seem artless. The best of them keep us interested   46
without seeming to engage our minds. The very thing that makes
movies so popular here and abroad is one of the primary things that
drives their critics to apoplexy, but seeming artlessness isn't necessarily
mindlessness. There's a deliberate kind of artlessness in American
movies that has come from a discipline or aesthetic long ago imposed
by the marketplace. Our movies began as immigrants' dreams that
would appeal to the dreams of other immigrants, and this aesthetic has
led American films to transcend languages and cultures and communicate to every country in the world.

THE FILMMAKER'S RESPONSIBILITY

It has been suggested to some extent in this conference that I ought to   47
study my own and American filmmakers' responsibilities to the public
and to the world. I realize I have responsibilities as a filmmaker, but I
don't believe that they are as a moralist, a preacher, or a purveyor of
values. I know it's tempting to use filmmaking as such, but utility is a
poor standard to use in art. It's a standard that has been and is still used
by every totalitarian state in the world.

My responsibility is to try to make good films, but "good" is a   48
subjective word. To me at any rate, "good" doesn't necessarily mean
"good for us" in the narrow sense that they must elevate our spirits
and send us out of the theater singing, or even that they must promote
only those values that some think are worth promoting.

Good movies challenge us, they provoke us, they make us angry   49
sometimes. They present points of view we don't agree with. They
force us to clarify our positions in opposition to them, and they do this
best when they provide us with an experience and not a polemic.

Somebody gave the okay to pay for *One Flew Over the Cuckoo's*   50
Nest, Driving Miss Daisy, Stand By Me, Moonstruck, Terms of Endearment,
and *Amadeus,* and despite conventional wisdom that said those films
could not be successful, those decisions paid off handsomely because
there are no rules. Studio executives and other financiers do exceed themselves. They take chances. They have to, and we have to hope that
they'll do it more often.

What we see in movie theaters today is not a simple reflection of   51
today's economics or politics in this country but is a sense of the people
who make the movies, and they vary as individuals vary. So what we

really want is for this very privileged process to be in the best hands possible, but I know of no force that can regulate this except the moral climate and appetites of our society.

What we're exporting now is largely a youth culture. It's full of   52
adolescent values; it's full of adolescent rage, love, rebelliousness, and a desire to shock. If you're unhappy with their taste—and this is a free market—then an appetite has to be created for something better. How do we do that? Well, we're back to square one: the supplier or the consumer, the chicken or the egg? Let's not even ask the question; the answer is both.

Of course filmmakers ought to be encouraged toward excellence,   53
and audiences ought to be encouraged to demand it. How? That's for thinkers and social scientists to figure out. I have no idea. But if I had to play this scene out as an imaginary dialogue, I might say that you must educate the consumer first, and the best places to start are at school and at home. And then you would say that that is my job, that popular entertainment must participate in this education. And I would say, ideally, perhaps, but I do not think that will happen within a system that operates so fundamentally from an economic point of view. On an individual basis, yes, one filmmaker at a time; as an industry, no. An appetite or market will have to exist first.

That's not as bad as it sounds, because in the best of all possible   54
worlds, we do try to satisfy both needs: entertain people and be reasonably intelligent about it. It can be done, and it is done more often than you might think. It's just very difficult.

It's like the two Oxford dons who were sitting at the Boarshead.   55
They were playwrights, grousing because neither one of them could get produced, neither one could get performed. One turned to the other and said, "Oh, the hell with it. Let's just do what Shakespeare did—give them entertainment."

Examining the Text
1. What is Pollack's point in paragraph 8? How does *Dances With Wolves* "call into question every value that existed in traditional Westerns," and how does it reflect a change in society's values? Is *Dances With Wolves* a good example of the kind of movie that critics would say contributes to the decline in American values? Why do you think Pollack mentions it so early in his speech?
2. Pollack says there "probably hasn't been a really beautiful rake since the Shakers stopped making farm implements" (paragraph 17). What does his point say in terms of questioning whether American films are "bad"? Do you find his analogy persuasive?
3. When Pollack asserts that he'd "rather make the whole world cry than 17 intellectuals in a classroom" (19), what is he implying about

his—and other filmmakers'—motivations? Do you think most creative people feel this way?

4. Pollack describes his interest in making "films about arguments" and giving "each side a strong argument" (36). What does he mean? Do you think movies that balance two sides of an "argument" are "more interesting" than those with clear-cut "good guys" and "bad guys"?

For Group Discussion

Pollack himself does not make the kinds of graphically violent movies that critics claim have a negative influence on American society. Nonetheless, he argues that "scrupulous, ethical concern for the sanctity of human life doesn't exist in the same way [it did in the past], and that fact is reflected in the movies." As a group, list examples from current events and recent films that demonstrate this lack of concern for human life. As a class, consider whether, based on these examples, you agree with Pollack that movies only reflect the values of society and do not contribute to their creation.

Writing Suggestion

Rent and watch one or more of Pollack's films (titles other than those mentioned in the headnote include *They Shoot Horses, Don't They?*, *Three Days of the Condor*, and *The Electric Horseman*). In an essay analyze Pollack's work as a reflection of contemporary American life. What themes or messages do you discover beyond his aim to tell a good story? Does he succeed in his stated goal of presenting an "argument"?

The Politics of Moviemaking

Saul Austerlitz

Politics and power have always been fodder for the camera. From the barely veiled depiction of newspaper titan Randolph W. Hearst in Citizen Kane *to the exploration of Richard Nixon's dark scheming in* All the President's Men, *Hollywood has unabashedly looked to real life as the basis of scripted entertainment. More recently, the following* MovieMaker *article contends, political documentaries have enjoyed a renaissance. So, too, have feature films with allegorical themes related to contemporary American political life. In the article, author Saul Austerlitz explores films both direct and documentary, such as Michael Moore's* Fahrenheit 911, *and fictional, such as* Mystic River, *for references to partisan politics.*

While filmmakers like Moore are virulently anti-administration and anti-corporation, even mainstream Hollywood movies in recent years have embraced scripts which, while less overt in their tone and intended message, are still anti-establishment. The article deals mainly with films that appear to question the current administration, and especially its foreign policies. *Only one film,* The Passion of the Christ, *counteracts the so-called New Left's near-monopoly of politically themed movies, according to the author.*

Finally, the article raises the question of whether the public's apparent interest in films with a political bent represents a new direction for cinema audiences, a groundswell of opposition to current governmental policies, an angry outcry by liberal film directors and producers . . . or all of the above. **As you read,** *look for comments the author makes in relation to both the public's perception and filmmakers' responses to the terrorist attacks of September 11, 2001, and uncover any biases the author may have toward these impressions and events.*

Public enemy's Chuck D once famously remarked that hip-hop was 1 like street CNN, informing its listeners of what was *truly* happening in their neighborhoods, their country and around the globe. In the post-September 11th era, when the actions of politicians and the lives of faraway strangers have come to be urgent matters even for those disaffected by, or bored with, politics, the need for an uncensored voice is greater than ever.

It is often said that art is at its most successful when politics is at 2 its most reactionary; that times of political unrest and conservative government often impel artists to do their best work. Hip-hop's role as a funnel for current affairs has largely fallen by the wayside. But in the past three years, a tidal wave of films, from studios and indies worldwide, have filled the gap.

Encompassing everything from Michael Moore's *Fahrenheit 9/11* 3 and Errol Morris' *Fog of War* to Gus Van Sant's *Elephant* and Quentin Tarantino's *Kill Bill*, there has been a recent shift toward engaging with partisan political content among moviemakers, and a willingness among moviegoers to support these films. Part of this is the rebirth of documentaries, which are unashamed to take a political slant. The other segment of this reawakening is the political content that has found its way into mainstream Hollywood moviemaking. Examples range from the overt anti-Bushism of *The Manchurian Candidate* to subtler musings on the instinct toward revenge in Clint Eastwood's *Mystic River.*

Since the astonishing "this-could-only-happen-in-a-movie" twists 4 and turns of the 2000 election, and even more so since the terrorist attacks of September 11th, the U.S. has been a country divided. With the 2004 election upon us, it is increasingly clear that the American electorate is segmented into two equal and increasingly opposite parts. Democrats, still enormously bitter about the election that got away (and about a president who ranks among the most radically conservative in recent memory) have chosen the box office as a shadow ballot, a place for disgruntled liberals to vote with their wallets. *Fahrenheit 9/11* capitalized brilliantly on this, with Moore and the Weinstein brothers marketing the film in such a way that weekend box office numbers served as a stand-in election. Cultural commentators made much of the close relationship between *Fahrenheit* and Mel Gibson's *The Passion of the Christ*, both box office smashes, one for the left and one for the right. But what truly united the two films was the sense of responsibility they engendered in their base audience. Liberals didn't just *want* to see *Fahrenheit 9/11*, they *had* to see it in order to spite President Bush and prove that liberals, far from a dying breed, had the clout to turn a fairly radical anti-administration rant into a blockbuster. With the enormous success of these politically-oriented films, the stunning possibility arises: Will movies play a decisive role in determining the outcome of this year's presidential election? By the time you read this, the answer may be clear.

MOVIES: THE NEW CNN

Film's role as "The New CNN" is best illustrated by the startling surge 5 in interest in documentary films. Cinema's hold on audiences for the last century is often described as a search for escape, a desire to return to the comfort of the womb in the darkness of the movie theater. But it's clear that, today, growing numbers of politically astute filmgoers are choosing to go to the movies to be faced with a clearer version of reality than what they get from their local news. One of the major reasons film is the new CNN is because the old CNN and its competitors, Fox News, MSNBC and the network news programs, have proved so derelict in their duty. In their effort to deliver the news as speedily as possible, television news has presented a highly distorted vision of contemporary reality, one that favors mindless patriotism and quasi-overt support of the Bush administration in lieu of hard-hitting journalism. Those looking for a more carefully drawn portrait of the world have been required to turn to other sources, namely their local art-house theaters. "I think there's much more technology now to do films, to use entertainment as a *platform for advocacy*," says Robin Bronk, editor of the political essay collection "If You Had Five Minutes with the President." "There is an infinite number of outlets for filmmakers now to make their voices heard."

Among documentarians, two primary tacks have been taken in   6
wrestling with the issues of the moment: some, like Moore, tackle them
straight on; others, like Morris, choose allegory and metaphor. Morris'
2003 doc, *The Fog of War*, is a movie-length interview with former Secretary of Defense Robert McNamara. McNamara served in Lyndon
Johnson's cabinet and was widely seen (and reviled) as the architect of
Johnson's strategy for pursuing the war in Vietnam. Morris structures
the film around 13 essential tenets regarding the appropriate pursuit of
war, gleaned from McNamara's musings.

Coming in the immediate aftermath of the American invasion of   7
Iraq, *The Fog of War* was seen by many as an explicit rebuke of the Bush
administration for their blatant disregard of world opinion, their willingness to bend the truth about the aims and effects of the war and for
the Vietnam-like quagmire that Iraq threatened to become. Seeing
McNamara, once a titan of world affairs, admired and despised in
equal measure, now searching for forgiveness, one could not help but
imagine a future Morris film starring Donald Rumsfeld.

INCONSISTENCY AND PASSION:
FAHRENHEIT 9/11 AND *CONTROL ROOM*

Moore's *Fahrenheit* brooked no such trafficking in metaphorical pon-   8
derings. Starting at the beginning, namely election night 2000, it's a
polemic, passionate and messy screed against Bush and his merry gang
of adventurers. It's the anti-CNN, a collection of clips that are shocking
primarily because the American public had not previously seen them.
Moore is less a great moviemaker than a terrific researcher, digging out
diamonds from the rough of the 24-hour news universe. To see Bush in
that Florida classroom on the morning of September 11, so terrifyingly
unsure of how to comport himself, or footage of American soldiers
wounded in Iraq, is to realize the enormous abyss between perception
and reality in contemporary politics.

Fahrenheit 9/11 is an inconsistent film, with certain segments, like   9
that about the Saudi menace, poorly argued and reeking of reckless
conspiracy-mongering. Moore, ever the isolationist defender of the
working-class, blames the Saudis for American troubles in language
that is eerily reminiscent of the "Buy American" anti-identification
with the working class, however, also allows him to see the class-based
nature of the American volunteer army. When a recruit from Moore's
hometown says that parts of Iraq reminded him of Flint, it speaks
volumes about the experiences of the American working poor. The
film finds an icon of contemporary political disillusionment in Lila
Lipscomb, a conservative Michigan homemaker radicalized by the death

of her son in Iraq. Her unalloyed anger at an administration that went to war under false pretenses and sacrificed her son to no purpose made Lipscomb a paragon of liberal fury. At the Democratic National Convention, videos were shown between speeches of lifelong Republicans describing their motivations for leaving the GOP—a sign of the Democrats borrowing Moore's strategies of convincing swing voters that the party of moderation is their own.

Another surprising hit earlier this year, *Control Room*, directed by   10
Jehane Noujaim, tackled the Iraq war and the concomitant media coverage and grossed close to $2 million. Rather than embed with an American military unit, missing the forest for the trees, *Control Room* details the work done by Arabic-language news channel Al Jazeera. Situated in Doha, Qatar, media center of the American Central Command, Al Jazeera reporters did their utmost to deliver a fuller portrayal of the horrors of the facts considerably to deliver a heroic version of Al Jazeera (overlooking their highly skewed reporting on the Israeli-Palestinian conflict and their tasteful look away from the atrocities perpetrated by Hussein's regime). Whether this Al Jazeera is fact or fiction is debatable, but what is remarkable is the overwhelming desire on the part of the viewing public for an unsullied news source, real or otherwise. *Control Room* was a hit because of the thirst for unfiltered truth about Iraq, whatever the truth quotient of the film itself. Noujaim's film was wish fulfillment for an American populace tired of the evasions and distortions of truth, from Ari Fleischer to the New York *Times*.

NOT FAIR AND BALANCED: *OUTFOXED* AND *UNCOVERED*

Producer-Director Robert Greenwald's *Outfoxed* put the lie to the Fox   11
News Channel's claims of "fair and balanced" coverage. Detailing the channel's numerous ties to leading conservatives, and the policy memos outlining the means by which news coverage is skewed to place Republicans in the best possible light, *Outfoxed* was a damning indictment of Fox News in particular, and the cable news media in general. The prolific Greenwald (*see Profile, pg. 92—ed.*) has also released two other films of notable interest in recent months: A newly updated version of the 2000 election doc *Unprecedented* (directed by Joan Selker and Richard Ray Perez) and the Iraq war study *Uncovered*. *Unprecedented* is a frankly partisan accounting of Bush v. Gore detailing Republican machinations to limit the Florida recount and preserve Bush's minuscule statewide lead. *Unprecedented* also presents the surprising thesis that the Gore campaign would have benefited from calling for a statewide

recount; their desire to limit the recount to Democrat-heavy counties
may have cost them the election.

Another crucial subject left primarily untouched by the main-   12
stream media, and told properly by documentary filmmakers, is that of
the Arab-Americans detained by the government after September 11.
Alison Maclean and Tobias Perse's *Persons of Interest* requires only the
barest necessities to tell its story. In a stark, unfurnished room reminiscent of a prison cell, or maybe a torture chamber, a series of witnesses
appear to testify before the camera. In addition to their verbal testi-
monies, which speak of visits in the night, lengthy spans in jail and
families without loved ones, the camera records the testimony of their
bodies. We get their anguish and confusion about what has happened
to them and what continues to happen to them. Maclean and Perse
reveal the flip side of national security's post 9/11 crackdown—its brutal impact on those innocent individuals noted as "persons of interest."
"We wanted to puncture the mendacity around the Justice Department
and the war on terror," says Perse. "They weren't even investigating
most of the people they were arresting."

MURDER AND REVENGE: *KILL BILL* AND *MYSTIC RIVER*

On the fictional side, the events of September 11, Afghanistan and Iraq   13
were reflected through the prism of films about political maneuvering,
violence, revenge and death. Revenge was a constant, from *Kill Bill*'s
Bride to *Mystic River*'s Jimmy to *Man on Fire*'s bitter Secret Service agent
Creasy. *Kill Bill* and *Mystic River* were both baroque fantasies of revenge
on one's sworn enemies, the murderers of one's children—potent
metaphors for the American psyche after the deaths of close to 3,000
people on September 11, 2001. Clint Eastwood's *Mystic River* presented a
more complex, nuanced version of the thirst for revenge, with Sean
Penn's Jimmy deciding, with much hesitation, to kill the man he believes
murdered his daughter, only to discover that he has killed an innocent
man. *Mystic River* reflected the anxiety that the wars in Afghanistan, and
Iraq, were glorified revenge-seeking missions, where the U.S. struck out
blindly at the unseen, misunderstood enemy in the hopes of soothing a
tormented breast. Eastwood does not stint on the anguish of loss,
though; the scene of Jimmy being dragged away by a phalanx of police
officers, flailing wildly while screaming, "Is that my daughter in there?,"
is among the rawest, deepest depictions of grief ever on-screen.

The desire to fight a just war against sworn enemies, and to van-   14
quish them once and for all, was a factor in the enormous appeal of
Jackson's *Lord of the Rings* trilogy. The source material, J.R.R. Tolkien's

novel, was a refighting of World War II in elfish garb, but the film could not help but look to Afghanistan and Iraq for metaphorical resonance. The wars of Middle Earth were tinged with a naïve, boy's-magazine quality, but the trilogy's aura of evocative doom, and the gloom of a world locked in a desperate struggle for the future, resonated deeply.

EXPLORATIONS OF VIOLENCE: *ELEPHANT*

Gus Van Sant's *Elephant*, another exploration of the impulse of violence, fictionalized the events of the Columbine shootings, depicting a day in the life of what appears to be a fairly regularly American high school. The Columbine connection, while obvious, overshadows the film's deeper concern, which is the eruption of violence from within the framework of mundane daily life. The protagonists echoed Dylan Klebold and Eric Harris for many, but with a little tweaking, they could just as easily have been Mohamed Atta and Zacarias Moussaoui— seemingly normal young men who secretly sought revenge on a world that rendered them deeply angry. Cultural critics have often remarked that dreadful events like the Holocaust or the bombing of Hiroshima and Nagasaki cannot be depicted artistically in a head-on fashion; their horrors too deep to be adequately represented.

15

The events of September 11 are impossible to be shown in such a fashion as well, for the above reasons as well as the fact that we have all already seen them depicted as such. To have seen the second lower of the World Trade Center collapse live on television, and to know that one has just witnessed the death of thousands of people is a sensation too overpowering to ever be recreated, no matter how acute the film wizardry. Knowing this, *Elephant* does not attempt to do so, but Van Sant powerfully summons the ordinariness of workaday American life in order to utterly shatter it beyond repair.

16

The image of a world permanently altered is a subtext of Martin Scorsese's historical epic *Gangs of New York*. The bitter gang warfare between the Nativists, led by Daniel Day-Lewis's flag-covered Bill the Butcher, and the Dead Rabbits, led by Leonardo DiCaprio's Amsterdam Vallon. Amsterdam, another revenge-seeker (Bill had killed his father some years prior) leads his gang into a final showdown with the Nativists, and the battle is raging at full blast when, unexpectedly, history erupts. The draft riot 1863, pitting Confederate-tilting New Yorkers against the fatcats seeking to draft them for Union cannon fodder, and against the African-Americans they irrationally blame for the outbreak of war, breakout, and the petty gang warfare is place permanently on hold. *Gangs of New York* powerfully summons the sense of personal concerns subsumed by the tidal wave of history. In the film's unforgettable closing

17

image, Amsterdam, standing in a small cemetery across the water from Manhattan, remarks that "For the rest of time, it would be like no one even knew we were here." Over his dialogue, Scorsese places a fast-forward history of New York, as reflected in its skyline—the buildings growing progressively higher until the World Trade Center emerges as its peak, then the towers disappearing, while the cemetery is simultaneously covered in weeds and growth until it, too, vanishes. This image is simultaneously enormously consoling and powerful, and deeply saddening; it is a comfort to know that even the most jagged wounds are eventually healed by the passage of time, and the amnesiac qualities of history, but it is also distressing beyond words to conceive of a time when the struggles and losses that defined all our lives will be forgotten beyond recall.

ISOLATIONIST ANXIETY: *THE VILLAGE*

Contemporary politics are also about fear—fear of terrorism, fear of   18
what the next day will bring, fear-mongering by savvy politicians. M. Night Shyamalan has always been a moviemaker whose primary concerns are fear and death, so it comes as little surprise that *The Village* is a remarkably contemporary evocation of the climate of isolationist anxiety. His film concerns a small enclave of individuals living in an isolated hamlet surrounded by foreboding woods. The villagers are deathly afraid of the creatures that lurk just outside the boundaries of their community, and have incorporated rules to govern their interaction with them. They fervently believe that if only they can separate themselves fully from the rest of the world, no harm can befall them— a comfortingly false belief similar to that of many Americans, liberal and conservative, after September 11.

Michael Koresky, an editor at *Film Comment*, points out "What   19
Fahrenheit 9/11 proved was that the direct address with politics in film is the only through-road to the American consciousness. Shyamalan's *The Village* is arguably a more complex, more highly allegorical investigation of isolationism and social complacency in the contemporary U.S., and its outright rejection proved that cloaking politics in metaphor sadly no longer suffices in our CNN and Fox News 'reality' TV-burdened, barely literate climate."

CONTEMPORARY POLITICS: *THE MANCHURIAN CANDIDATE*

Demme's remake of the 1964 classic *The Manchurian Candidate* takes on   20
the contemporary political climate through the prism of politics itself. As in the original, a powerful, domineering mother pushes her weakling

son forward as a vice-presidential candidate for her own nefarious purposes. Where the original concerned the Soviet menace, and presented the spectacle of a McCarthyesque, anti-Communist hatemonger revealed to be a Communist shill himself, the 2004 version features a shadowy multi-national corporation, Manchurian Global.

Like a through-the-looking-glass version of Halliburton, Manc-   21
hurian looks to secretly commandeer the wheel of American political discourse, and attempts to do so via a secretly controlled vice-presidential candidate. Once elected, he will be, as one wag points out in the film, "The first bought and paid for vice president of the United States." Using the televisions in practically every scene as a contemporary Greek chorus, *The Manchurian Candidate* presents the specter of a world one step beyond ours, with terrorist attacks a weekly affair, and a government dedicated to fighting shadowy wars across the globe. Liev Schreiber's politician patsy contains echoes of George W. Bush (third-generation political scion, lightweight tool of his political masters) and Dick Cheney (that bought-and-paid-for comment deliberately touches on fears of Cheney's ongoing relationship with the defense gaint Halliburton). Demme's film is resolutely fictional, but freed from the requirement of truth-telling, *The Manchurian Candidate* reaches for deeper truths about the Bush administration's penchant for fear-mongering as a means of maintaining the reins of political discourse.

THE MOVIE THEATER AS CULTURAL MIRROR

In the past four years, politics have moved significantly closer to home.   22
The ability of many Americans to thoroughly tune out politics as irrelevant to their daily existence has evaporated, and this new reality has seeped into the world of cinema as well. A movie, being a collective endeavor, is often an expression of shared hopes and worries and of ideas bubbling underneath the surface of contemporary life. Films have long served as a barometer of American life, reflecting the complex, tangled web of fears and desires angling for superiority. The 2000 election, the events of September 11 and their aftermath, the invasions of Afghanistan and Iraq and the actions of the current administration have all found their way onto American movie screens, in coded, allusive form, as well as through factual documentation. Increasingly, Americans are looking to moviemakers for answers and for direction, in a manner reminiscent of the impact of counterculture films like *Easy Rider* and *Hearts and Minds* on the Vietnam generation. "I do think there's something about the way people are engaging with these films," says Perse. "They want to interact with these films."

The movie theater has become the mirror in which Americans can   23
truly see themselves. What they see, unsurprisingly, is far from simple.
Much of the passionate advocacy found in recent films has been in
anticipation of the upcoming presidential election, generally considered by most observers to be the most important (and bitterly fought)
since 1968. The outcome of that election will place these films into
clearer focus, and establish them as an expression of the groundswell of
populist opposition to the Bush administration, and to the war in Iraq,
or as an ultimately futile and unrepresentative explosion of liberal bit-
terness. Only time—and the ballot box—will tell.

Examining the Text

1. What is the author saying about the role film is playing in the
American public's desire for news? Do you agree with the author's
contention about this new "public information" role of movies? In your
opinion can a given movie, which has a relatively long gestation
period, truly provide a meaningful way of analyzing current events
compared to radio, newspapers, television, and even the Web?

2. The article states that "films have long served as a barometer of
American life . . . " What is meant by that statement? When they depict
actual events, do films focus more on developing the film's story more
than on telling the "truth," in your opinion? Do you believe films do
this to a greater or lesser degree than other media?

3. In what ways does the author suggest that the September 11, 2001
terrorist attacks on New York and Washington DC have influenced
filmmakers and people's interest in film? Do you agree with the
author's views on this issue? Do you believe that the author is correct
in asserting that for many mainstream audience members, attending
movies is no longer about "searching for an escape . . . " (line 5)?

4. What does the author mean when he claims that documentaries are
proving successful because cable and TV news, especially MSNBC,
CNN, and Fox present a "highly distorted vision of contemporary
reality" and are "derelict in their duty"? Do you agree that most
television news is distorted; if so, does this have to do with the speed
at which journalists and producers must operate, as Austerlitz
suggests? What other theories might you posit about distortion in
the news?

5. *Thinking rhetorically*: In several places the author uses the following
phrases as rhetorical devices: *it is said* (line 2); *it's clear that* (line 5);
is often described as (line 5) *was seen by many* (line 7). How would
you characterize such writing, and what do you think is the author's
purpose in using this technique? Do you find it effective or evasive,
and why?

For Group Discussion

Among your group, discuss how many of you have personally sought out films as a way to help answer questions you have about events of major importance (the war in Iraq, corporate scandals, the Presidential election, the media). Did you attend a film to order to complete your understanding or to have your already existing view reinforced by the filmmaker? If the latter, do you think that is a new role for film writers, directors, and producers? Would you make a point of seeing a film that you knew from advanced publicity was contradictory to your view on an issue?

Writing Suggestion

You've just received a commission to write a prose treatment for a new movie about your favorite, under-reported political issue. Your film could focus on animal rights, prayer in schools, Third World aid, bicycle paths, or any other subject near and dear to your heart. Your 500-word treatment has to be detailed enough to convince skeptics that the issue is important and that it will be visually suited to film and win financial backing. Your text should be full of passion for your subject, factually accurate and compelling, yet should explore why you think your subject has not been given a fair airing by the media previously.

The Asian Invasion (of Multiculturalism) in Hollywood

Minh-Ha Pham

Hollywood film representations of Asian immigrants, especially those of Chinese descent, are sometimes branded as stereotypical depictions of submissiveness, shyness, industriousness, and clannishness ... with a few karate chops thrown into the mix. Few Asian-American actors have achieved movie super-stardom, and Asian-American directors are only just beginning to break down the wall beyond art-house success. In the following article from Journal of Popular Film & Television, *writer Minh-Ha Pham examines the historical cultural context of Asians in Hollywood through an analysis of two films,* Rush Hour *(1998), a mainstream movie, and* Crouching Tiger, Hidden Dragon *(2000), a Mandarin-language, Chinese production that received widespread U.S. distribution.*

Pham attempts to fit these films into what the popular media have called "an Asian invasion" of Hollywood following the success of Rush Hour, *which featured Jackie Chan, perhaps Hong Kong's most successful actor in the kung-fu/action genre. Pham examines the underlying messages encoded in these films. Further, he looks at the ways in which they depict race (Rush Hour) and gender (Crouching Tiger)—all within the broader term of multiculturalism. The article initially asks whether Rush Hour challenges stereotypes about Chinese and African-Americans; the film is set in an apparently racially tranquil Los Angeles, though there are tensions between the two protagonists of differing races. The article then moves on to Crouching Tiger, which is set a continent and a two centuries away from California: namely, in rural China, where a variety of tensions between and among the characters are shown with a mythical, surreal-like quality. According to Pham, there are qualities—multicultural values—embedded in Crouching Tiger that transcend the film's era and setting. These portrayed values strike a cultural note with which American audiences easily and naturally resonate: a kind of global sensibility, if you will.*

   As you read, notice the ways in which Pham sets down both historic and cultural details to provide a context for the article's interpretation of the films. Consider also the reasons why it might be important that readers have this background first, before examining the specific film "texts."

When Ang Lee's *Crouching Tiger, Hidden Dragon*, a subtitled, epic   1
Chinese drama, was released to American movie theaters in December
2000, the film marked the peak of what many American film reviewers
and film critics have been calling an "Asian invasion" in Hollywood.
The so-called invasion began when John Woo started filming *Broken
Arrow* in 1995 and gained momentum in 1998 with *Rush Hour*, a
Hollywood-produced film starring Jackie Chan. The invasion continued with *Romeo Must Die* (2000), *Rush Hour 2* (2001), *Kiss of the
Dragon* (2001), and Quentin Tarentino's re-release of Tsui Hark's *Iron
Monkey* (2001). Although Ang Lee is taking a break from the martial
arts genre (at the time of this writing, he had just released *The Hulk*,
starring Australian actor Eric Bana and American actors Nick Nolte
and Jennifer Connelly), the Asian invasion is not quite over. Recently
released were Chow Yunfat's *Bulletproof Monk* (2003) and *Cradle 2
The Grave* (2003) starring Jet Li, Kelly Hu, and rap artist DMX. *Rush
Hour 3* is scheduled for release in 2004.

   Scholars across a range of disciplines are debating what these   2
films say about Hollywood and its audiences, the processes of globalization in Asia and the United States, and the state of the Hong Kong
film industry. Shu-mei Shih, a Chinese studies scholar, argues that
Taiwan's history of colonialism and imperialism has "accidentally and
ironically become a historical benefit" for cultural producers such as

Ang Lee whose knowledge of American culture—an inevitable byproduct of America's cultural hegemony in Taiwan—enables him to translate himself and his work easily to the American mainstream (86). Steve Fore, a film studies scholar, observes that the marketing and editing strategies employed in all of Jackie Chan's films emphasize action at the expense of the plot to ensure increased traffic at the box office. Whereas Fore argues that "universal marketability is the signature of the international blockbuster" (258), Yingjin Zhang, a scholar of comparative literature, argues that these films are neither universal nor translatable. Instead, Zhang suggests that films such as those mentioned above make it possible for us to "screen China in a more meaningful way; not exclusively in a Western theoretical context, nor merely in one of 'authentic' Chinese culture and history, but ultimately in the context of cross-cultural, multiethnic, and transnational aspects of filmmaking, film viewing, and film criticism in the contemporary world" (113). All of these American-based scholars and many others, including those from Europe and Australia, have made important contributions to what Zhang calls the emergence of "Chinese film studies in the West" (43).

Curiously, Asian American studies scholars have been relatively quiet witnesses to the phenomena of Chinese transnational films. Whereas fanzines and online chatrooms reveal that amateur Asian American and Asian film critics have a lot to say about Jackie Chan, Chow Yun-fat, and Ang Lee, there has been little Asian American scholarship to date that investigates the Asian invasion or its impact on Asian American representational politics. One reason for this relative silence might be a point Roger Garcia makes in the introduction to Out of the Shadows: Asians in American Cinema, a catalog published to accompany a retrospective series by the same name at the Fifty-fourth International Film Festival at Locarno, Switzerland. Distinguishing Asian American cinematic representation from the Asian presence of Jet Li and Chow Yun-fat in Hollywood films, Garcia writes:

[3]

> [D]espite developments in the independent realm, and the greater presence of Asian filmmakers in the mainstream industry, the struggle for the representation of the Asian American experience in the media continues. This is different from recognizing an Asian presence on American screens where movies like *Romeo Must Die* or *Crouching Tiger, Hidden Dragon* have brought Chinese heroes and legends to American audiences. Asian America is a distinct and discrete entity—it is not a sub-set of China, Japan or Vietnam, but a constituency that has lived, breathed and contributed to the nation for over a century. It has its own achievements, artists, stories and traditions that have grown separate from its various Asian roots. (19–20)

Garcia's introduction echoes a point Asian American cultural   4
nationalists such as Frank Chin and Jeffery Paul Chan made during the
inaugural moment of Asian American studies in the mid-1970s. Both
Garcia and the Asian American cultural nationalists of the 1970s speak
to the long history of cultural marginalization, legal exclusions, and
social rejection that Asian Americans have had to bear as a consequence of the dominant culture's conflation of Asian Americans' lived
experiences and Hollywood's exoticized representations of Asians.
Such conflation continues today. As Asian American historian Ronald
Takaki puts it, "People come up to me and assume I must know karate.
Most of us haven't studied the martial arts. It's not something we
inherit. Crouching Tiger and other Americanized representations of
Asia aren't so innocent. They reinforce our identity as outsiders and
strangers" (qtd. in Barker).

Takaki's statement is an important reminder that the Asian inva-   5
sion itself is an American construct. Since the mid-1800s, America has
imagined Asia to be a homogenous continent of cultural and economic
marauders whose presence in America had to be quarantined and regulated by immigration exclusion acts, segregation, internment camps,
and auditors. Unlike the other Asian invasions, however, the Asian
invasion of Hollywood is framed by an increasingly popular discourse
of multiculturalism, a discourse that, in Lisa Lowe's words, "levels the
important differences and contradictions within and among racial and
ethnic minority groups according to the discourse of pluralism . . .
while simultaneously masking the existence of exclusions by recuper-
ating dissent, conflict, and otherness through the promise of inclusion"
(86). In the Asian invasion, multiculturalism functions to abate the
paranoia that has traditionally accompanied the other Asian invasion
scares and, at the same time, to re-present and reactivate a particularly
American drama of assimilation and socialization at both the national
and international levels.

Unlike prior renditions of the Asian invasion, Hollywood is not   6
threatened by the increased presence of Asian and Asian American
actors and filmmakers; instead, the so-called Asian invasion enhances
Hollywood's image as a racially inclusive, equal opportunity, global
industry. Moreover, Asian actors and filmmakers are not invading Hollywood as much as they are finally being admitted into Hollywood—
under very specific conditions and for very specific roles. Despite the
increased presence of Asian actors in Hollywood, the struggle for equitable and fair Asian American representation in Hollywood has not
ended. Asian American filmmaker Wayne Wang has noted in several
interviews that the mainstream success of Crouching Tiger, Hidden
Dragon "only helps Kung fu action films," not Asian American films
(qtd. in Kai).

Even so, an Asian American studies analysis of Hollywood's   7
Asian invasion is useful to determine the influence of multicultural discourse on Hollywood's representations of Asians—whether they are
transnational subjects becoming American national subjects, such as
Jackie Chan's character in *Rush Hour*, or national subjects who are
transnationally conceived, such as the characters in *Crouching Tiger*.
Transpacific migrations, in the form of cinematic plots, financial
investments, and on-screen and off-screen labor, are undeniably Asian
American issues because these issues require the field to rethink and
reposition many of its political and social commitments from the
nation to the diaspora. At the same time, the transpacific migrations
within and of Hollywood continue to perpetuate the myth that
any marker of Asianness is synonymous with foreignness. Jackie Chan
and Chow Yun-fat never play Asian Americans and are never in
Asian American films; yet, as Takaki's experience demonstrates, Asian
Americans are often confused with the Asian characters they play.

In *Rush Hour* (1998), a conventionally produced Hollywood film   8
set in post-riot Los Angeles, multiculturalism is represented as a discursive and bodily meeting of the East and West. The movie uses Jackie
Chan's and Chris Tucker's bodies to externalize the differences
between the East and the West as an unavoidable binarism. Where
Chan's Inspector Lee is overly modest and unassuming, Tucker's
Detective Carter is overly boastful and presumptuous; where Lee is
quiet and reserved, Carter is loud and obnoxious; where Lee is asexual,
Carter is sexually aggressive; and where Carter's ability to speak the
street slang of Los Angeles gives him access into the community, Lee's
failed attempts to mimic Carter's slang constantly bar him from Los
Angeles and remind us that Lee is a foreigner. Against the backdrop of
LA's racial tensions, *Rush Hour* offers a reconciliatory multiculturalist
utopia that re-envisions the American topography of race relations.

Unlike *Rush Hour*, the nineteenth-century mythicality of *Crouching*   9
Tiger, Hidden Dragon does not offer a national narrative of racial recon-
ciliation but instead offers a transnational model of global feminism.
Instead of "the fastest hands in the East meeting the biggest mouth in the
West," as articulated in *Rush Hour's* tagline, ancient Chinese masculinist
tradition meets global feminism in *Crouching Tiger, Hidden Dragon*. In
both films, Hollywood's multiculturalisms revitalize an old East meets
West paradigm, which presupposes that the East and the West are always
dialectically opposed in binaries of ancient and modern, exotic and familiar, and feminine and masculine, only to disavow these differences in
melting pot narratives of discursive and bodily assimilation. Using these
two articulations of multiculturalism, both films effectively and prof-
itably hook large American audiences by appealing to neo-liberal, cosmopolitan America, a powerful social, if not political, community.

"THE FASTEST HANDS IN THE EAST MEET THE BIGGEST MOUTH IN THE WEST" MEETS MULTICULTURAL COMMODIFICATION

The tagline New Line Cinema used to advertise *Rush Hour*, "The   10
Fastest Hands in the East Meet the Biggest Mouth in the West," establishes, even at the paratextual level, a multicultural logic that operates throughout the film. The East and the West, personified by Inspector Lee and Detective Carter, are dichotomous entities with distinct characters. At one end of this dichotomy is Inspector Lee, a police detective in the Hong Kong Royal Police Department whose position in the Chinese heritage is established at the beginning of the movie when we see—but do not hear—Lee recovering 5,000-year-old Chinese artifacts stolen by the Juntao criminal organization, a British-run operation. Moving stealthily and quietly across the screen, Lee epitomizes the ninja hero whose greatest asset is his silence.

At the other end of the East–West dichotomy is Detective Carter,   11
an African American police officer with the Los Angeles Police Department. Unlike Lee, who we see before we hear, we hear Carter long before we see him. In our first "meeting" with Carter, he is honking and yelling at other drivers to "get the hell out of [his] way!" Soon, we learn that Carter is on his way to meet an illegal arms dealer, Clive Cod (Chris Penn), whom Carter is trying to arrest. Unlike Lee's capture of the Juntao criminal organization, Carter's arrest is less than effective. Two white police officers who happen to be walking through the parking lot in which Clive and Carter are meeting do not recognize Carter as a police detective and think they are witnessing a real transaction. Even though Carter attempts to signal to them that he is a police detective, they arrest both Carter and Clive. By the time Carter successfully makes his arrest, one police officer is shot, and Clive's car blows up, as does an entire city block. Unlike Lee, who is a credit to his government, Carter is not an esteemed member of the Western heritage or the Los Angeles Police Department. The relationship between the LAPD and the African American community, as American audiences are well aware, has been particularly strained since the videotaped beating of Rodney King and the acquittal of the officers who beat him. Carter's status as an African American man in the LAPD is an uncomfortable one as he reveals to his partner, Tania Johnston (Elizabeth Pena), "My own mama's ashamed of me. She tells everybody I'm a drug dealer." The LAPD appears equally ashamed of Carter.

The central plot of *Rush Hour* begins when Chinese Consul Han's   12
young daughter is kidnapped by the Juntao. The FBI's investigation of the kidnapping is stymied when Han requests that the FBI bring one of Hong Kong's finest, Inspector Lee, into their investigation. To keep

Lee—"the Chunking cop"—away from its investigation, FBI agents Russ and Whitney devise a "bullshit assignment" designed to both humiliate a member of the LAPD as well as protect their case. Carter is immediately given this "bullshit assignment." Throughout the rest of the movie, Lee's mis-placement in the West is matched by Carter's displacement.

Carter's reassignment effectively transforms him from a police   13 officer into a cultural guide (for Lee as well as Hollywood audiences), but Carter's tour does not include Beverly Hills or Santa Monica, locations highlighted in most films set in Los Angeles. Instead, Carter takes Lee to a seedy pool hall, a liquor store, and a jail. Through Carter, Lee meets convicted criminals such as Clive Cod, Carter's shady cousin Luke (Clifton Powell), and an ex-drug dealer (Jason Davis). Carter's itinerary suggests that he is an insider not of the mainstream but of the periphery. The liquor store and the jail, peripheral sites in America, have been particularly condemned by African Americans as sites that cripple African American communities as well as aid in their criminalization. That Carter's tour of Los Angeles focuses on these peripheral sites suggests that, despite his status as an officer, Carter belongs in the liquor store and the jail rather than in the FBI. In addition, Carter's tour introduces Lee to the racial politics of the United States.

There are two "educational" scenes that highlight Lee's foreignness   14 during this introduction. Frustrated because Carter rebuffs all of Lee's attempts to get to Consul Han, Lee turns on Carter's car radio without Carter's permission.

> LEE: The Beach Boys!
> CARTER: Ah, man, hell no! You didn't just touch my goddamn radio!
> LEE: The Beach Boys are great American music.
> CARTER: The Beach Boys are gonna get you a great ass whoopin'. Don't you ever touch a black man's radio, boy! You can do that in China but you can get your ass killed out here, man.

After teaching Lee that "you never touch a black man's radio,"   15 Carter quickly displaces Lee's idea of "great American music" by replacing the Beach Boys with Jay-Z, a commercially successful African American hip hop artist. Like the connection between the 5,000-year-old artifacts that Lee recovers and Lee's heritage, Carter's radio, the only "artifact" he guards and protects, signifies a connection to an African American heritage of which the Beach Boys are not a part.

A second educational opportunity arises when Carter takes Lee to   16 Azteca Billiards for a "shakedown." Following Carter's orders that Lee "follow [his] lead and do what [he does]," Lee imitates Carter by greeting the African American bartender with, "What's up, my nigga?". Lee is, of course, completely unaware that the term carries distinctly different connotations depending on who is speaking. When the bartender asks Lee to repeat himself, Lee assumes, in his ignorance, that the bartender just doesn't understand his English. After repeating the greeting again, this time, more slowly, the bartender responds by grabbing Lee by the collar of his jacket and punching him. A barroom brawl ensues, and Lee is forced to rely on his "fast hands" to compensate for his cultural ignorance. Beside providing Lee with another lesson on racial politics, this scene reiterates the differences between Lee and Carter established paratextually by the tagline. The difference between the East and the West is a difference between the nonspeaking but laboring hands of the East and the expressive and affective culture of the West. Speaking gets Lee into trouble at the pool hall, whereas speaking gets Carter into the pool hall, further establishing the pool hall as a black space. Lee's hands are the only things that save him from his cultural ignorance. After beating up eight or nine men (and apologizing to them profusely), Lee leaves the pool hall with Carter.

Lee's mistakes accentuate his foreignness and reconfirm the distinctions between East and West. At the same time, Lee is able to quickly learn from his mistakes, which minimizes the significance of his foreignness and underscores the myth that Asians learn fast and are assimilable. This is the promise and appeal of multicultural discourse: Racial differences exist but are easily overcome. In this ideal multicultural meeting of East and West, both the East and the West benefit from the meeting. Not only does Lee learn valuable lessons from Carter, Carter learns from Lee as well.   17

From the first moment that Carter and Lee meet, Carter's bigotry against all things Eastern is obvious. He expresses many of the same kinds of stereotypes that all Asians, whether native born or foreign born, in America are subjected to at one time or another. Carter assumes at their first meeting, for example, that Lee cannot speak English. When he meets Lee at the airport, Carter asks in a condescendingly slow and loud tone, "Please tell me you speak English. I'm Detective Carter. Do you speaka any English? Do you understand the words that are coming out of my mouth?!?" When Lee responds only with a smile, Carter says to himself, "I cannot believe this SHIT! First I get a bullshit assignment, now Mr. Ricearoni doesn't even speak American." It is not until a few scenes later when a white cab driver pulls a gun on Carter and Lee that Carter realizes Lee can speak English. Carter's amazement is punctuated by the cliche of a gong that sounds when Carter realizes his mistake.   18

CARTER: All of a sudden you speaking English now, huh?
LEE: A little.

CARTER: A little my ass—you lied to me.

LEE: I didn't say I didn't speak English. You assumed I didn't.

CARTER: Assume I kick your little Beijing ass right now, man.

LEE: I'm not responsible for your assumption.

CARTER: You full of shit, you understand that, you full of shit.

LEE: Not being able to speak is not the same as not speaking. You seem as if you like to talk. I like to let people talk who like to talk. It makes it easier to find out how full of shit they are.

CARTER: What the hell did you just say? [. . .] So I'm the one full of shit, right?

LEE: We're both full of shit.

When Lee tells Carter that he is "not responsible for Carter's assumption," Lee is speaking for all Asian/Americans. Asian/Americans are not responsible for the assumptions African Americans or anyone else has about Asians in America. After explaining that "not being able to speak is not the same as not speaking," Carter is demonstrably shocked at both Lee's ability to speak and his eloquence. Carter's only comeback is to mock Lee's English. The racial tensions might have been elevated by Lee's accusation that Carter is full of shit, but Lee quickly defuses the tensions by sharing the blame for Carter's assumption: "We're both full of shit." After Lee accepts partial responsibility for the racial tensions between them, Lee and Carter are on their way to multicultural harmony. This scene, twenty-seven minutes into the movie, is the first sign that the differences between Lee and Carter—between Asian and African American, between East and West—may not be insurmountable after all. Throughout the last half of the film, Lee and Carter's differences, always racialized, are resolved through the medium of multicultural exchange.   19

In a classic situation of multicultural resolution, Lee and Carter's friendship begins when they share a meal. Carter's initial disdain for the Chinese takeout food Lee offers him reflects his bigotry, but once he discovers that he actually likes the food, he and Lee become friends. In other words, Lee is finally accepted by Carter, a representative of one part of the West, via Chinese takeout.   20

CARTER: Damn, Chin, this is some greasy shit. You ain't got no better food, like some chicken wings, some baby back ribs, some fries or something?

CHIN: Chinese food, no soul food here!

CARTER: I didn't say nothin' 'bout no soul food, I said you got some better food. I don't want that greasy shit. How you gonna sell a big box of grease?

CARTER: Man, what you got me eatin'?

LEE: That's eel.
CARTER: Is it good?
LEE: Very good.
CARTER: What you got?
LEE: Camel's hump.
CARTER: Mmm! Kinda good. Need a little hot sauce but it's
  kinda good though.

Although food is always a cultural and ethnic signifier, the signif- 21
icance of Chinese food is elevated in this movie in which East meets
West. Within the East–West paradigm, Chinese food operates as a sign
for Chinese culture. It is no wonder that a *Newsweek* article claiming
that "Hollywood was destined to discover Hong Kong" is titled
"Chinese Takeout" (Ansen). The allusion to manifest destiny ("destined to discover") speaks volumes about the colonial relationship
structured into the East–West paradigm. The eel and the camel's hump
that Lee "has Carter eating" reify the strangeness of the East. The exotic
East is only made acceptable in the West when it is turned into a consumable commodity, as it is when Carter decides eel is "kinda good"
even if it does "need a little hot sauce." The conflation of Lee and the
Chinese food is what finally makes the West's acceptance of the East
(and Lee) possible. The appreciation of Chinese food suggests at least
one common denominator that connects this biracial odd couple.

Besides food, however, Lee and Carter, or rather Jackie Chan and 22
Chris Tucker, have one more important thing in common: the ways that
the commodification of racial difference influences their representation
as Asian and African American men. The economic strands of multiculturalism are nowhere more revealing in *Rush Hour* than in the consistent manner in which both men are described only in terms of their
fragmented body parts. "The fast hands of the East" carries with it two
well-known stereotypes of Asians as martial artists and laborers. On
one level, the "fast hands of the East" refer to Inspector Lee's martial
arts skills (or one facet of his skills given that Lee uses more than just
fast hands when he is fighting). Because Lee is representative of the
East, we can assume that Lee's martial arts skills are not unique to him
but shared by many in the East as well. As noted by Takaki, there is an
assumption that most Asians know martial arts.

On another level, the "fast hands of the East" refer to a widely 23
circulating stereotype used to exploit the labors of Asian workers globally. Large multinational corporations as well as global sex service
industries (here, I am referring to the fantasies surrounding Oriental
massage parlors) have long targeted Asians for their supposed manual
dexterity. Although Chan is not a "manual laborer" in either of these
senses, the tagline does permit us to redefine the "manual laborer" to

include the martial artist. By emphasizing Chan's hands, the East–West binary employed in the tagline and in the movie operates on a long and broad history of Asian stereotypes in America that recognizes the Asian immigrant not as a fully embodied human being but as a set of laboring hands, the part of the Asian body that traditionally produces the most profit and, therefore, the part that is most vulnerable to exploitation. The meeting of East and West, within a multicultural frame, is beneficial not only for cultural appreciation but for the profits that such a meeting produces for the West. Jackie Chan's laboring hands are, after all, one of the main attractions of the movie.

Similarly, Carter's character is reduced to the site of his (big) mouth. It is not just that Carter is loud and obnoxious, however. Carter's mouth defines him and confines him within stereotypically racialized parameters of blackness. His slang situates him not just in the West but in the streets of the West. The streets, often a euphemism for the ghetto, are a liminal national space, which are both geographically inside but culturally outside the nation. Carter's peripheralized position can be described in similar terms. Carter's mouth, the most playful and privileged site on his black body, registers loudly within the global economy of black male bodies. In his book Yo' Mama's Disfunktional! Robin Kelley has noted that "[i]n a nation with few employment opportunities for African Americans and a white consumer market eager to be entertained by the Other, blacks have historically occupied a central place in the popular culture industry" (41). While Kelley's observation gently references America's long obsession with black bodies that range from Step 'n' Fetchit to Michael Jordan, it is possible to extend this history to Carter's character as well. Carter's mouth is his most entertaining and most obvious feature. Although Carter's character is not defined by the protruding lips that other black bodies historically have been defined by, Carter's mouth does over-reach and over-step social standards of propriety, and it is this over-stepping that makes Carter funny. Without his obnoxious but colorful language, Carter is nothing but an inefficient, bad cop. We like him because he makes us laugh; that is, we like him because he entertains us. Carter's mouth not only produces the most laughter in this film, it also produces the most profits in Hollywood. Just as Inspector Lee's broken English heightens his foreignness and greatly adds to the comic value of the film, Carter's big mouth also marks him as a racial Other, a mark that is absolutely essential to the multicultural and comic value of the movie. Carter is nothing without his mouth, and *Rush Hour* is nothing without Carter. As I have already noted, the importance of this particular body part is underscored when we first meet Carter. Both Carter and Lee represent racialized laboring bodies in Hollywood's global industry; the difference between them is not so

24

much their race but how their race translates as labor in the racially segmented global economy.

Although the racial tensions between Lee and Carter are so central to this film that they often overshadow the plot, these differences are never so important or so substantial that they lead to any real problems, certainly nothing that could compare to the Los Angeles riots in 1992. Although Carter often threatens to "kick Lee's ass," these threats are never realized. Post-riot Los Angeles is rescripted in *Rush Hour* as a multicultural utopia and a capitalist's dream. Thus, the multicultural moral of this biracial odd coupling is that racial differences are never so significant that they cannot be overcome and are never so insignificant that they cannot be turned into a profit.[1] Tables 1–3 show box-office figures for Hollywood blockbusters starring white actors and "Asian invasion" films starring Asian/American actors. "The Tucker–Chan pairing" reifies a multicultural fantasy of racial pluralism: at the same time, such a pairing also displaces this fantasy. That Lee enters America via the cultural routes of African Americans (by the end of the movie, Lee has adopted Carter's taste for music, imitates Carter's dance moves, and uses Carter's slang) suggests that Asian (im)migrants have an alternative means of assimilation, a path that is distinctly non-white. Asian (im)migrants can gain access into the nation—at least into the nation's widening periphery—by approximating blackness (or brownness or redness, for that matter) rather than whiteness. Moreover, their coalition offers

Table 1. Top-Grossing Movies of All Time in the United States

Rank	Title	Total box office (in $US)
1	*Titanic* (1997)	600,743,440
2	*Star Wars* (1977)	460,935,655
3	*Star Wars: Episode 1—The Phantom Menace* (1999)	431,065,444
10	*The Sixth Sense* (1999)	293,501,675
20	*Twister* (1996)	241,700,000
30	*Saving Private Ryan* (1998)	216,119,491
40	*Pearl Harbor* (2001)	198,539,855
50	*Liar, Liar* (1997)	181,395,000
100	*The Jungle Book* (1967)	141,843,000
115	*Godzilla* (1998)	136,142,003
133	*Crouching Tiger, Hidden Dragon* (2000)	128,026,803
150	*Clear and Present Danger* (1994)	121,985,472
200	*Chicken Run* (2000)	106,604,314

Source: Internet Movie Database *http://www.imdb.com*.

Table 2.   Top-Grossing Movies of All Time Worldwide

Rank	Title	Total box office (in $US)
1	*Titanic* (1997)	1,835,300,000
2	*Star Wars: Episode 1—The Phantom Menace* (1999)	922,300,000
3	*Jurassic Park* (1993)	919,700,000
10	*Lost World: Jurassic Park* (1997)	614,300,000
20	*Indiana Jones and the Last Crusade* (1989)	494,700,000
	Twister (1996)	494,700,000
30	*Pretty Woman* (1990)	438,200,000
40	*Gone with the Wind* (1939)	390,500,000
50	*Jurassic Park 3* (2001)	362,100,000
100	*Harry Potter and the Sorcerer's Stone* (2001)	297,200,000
120	*Bambi* (1942)	267,900,000
135	*Hercules* (1997)	250,600,000
150	*Die Hard 2* (1990)	237,500,000

Source: Internet Movie Database *http://www.imdb.com*.
Note: There is no non-English language, non-Hollywood film on this list.

Table 3.   Asian Invasion Financial Statistics

Year released	Title	Budget (in millions $US)	Gross (in millions $US)
1996	*Rumble in the Bronx*	7.5	32
1998	*Rush Hour*	35	141
2000	*Romeo Must Die*	25	56
2000	*Crouching Tiger, Hidden Dragon*	15	128
2001	*Kiss of the Dragon*	25	37
2001	*Rush Hour 2*	90	226
2001	*Iron Monkey**	2	14.7

Source: Internet Movie Database *http://www.imdb.com*.
*Quentin Tarantino's restoration.

them both a way to challenge their marginalization in America. After all, despite Carter and Lee's exclusion from the big FBI investigation, they are ultimately responsible for safely rescuing Consul Han's daughter, Soo-Young.

Because Hollywood films are made not only for American audiences, it is important to note that although there are embedded in *Rush Hour* multicultural "handles" for American audiences to grab onto, these handles are not accessible to all audiences in other parts of the world. For audiences outside of America, Lee and Carter probably do

26

not represent the East and West in the same way that I have represented them. In this sense, the "East" and "West" are historically contingent constructs. Nonetheless, because Lee and Carter are the racial underdogs who successfully challenge two white FBI agents, they represent globally sympathetic figures. The appeal of the underdogs is further increased when Carter remains loyal to his partner even when he has the opportunity to join the ranks of those who once marginalized him. Instead of taking the FBI badge Agents Russ and Whitney offer him, Carter tells them, "Why don't y'all take that badge and shove it up your ass? All up in your ass." All audiences can appreciate Carter's loyalty as well as the momentary power reversal that allows the underdog to tell off his bullies. More important for Hollywood and Hollywood's global audiences, Carter's loyalty to Lee means that we can expect *Rush Hour* sequels as well as *Rush Hour* imitations.

CROUCHING TIGER, HIDDEN DRAGON: MULTICULTURAL BREAKTHROUGH OR BREAKDOWN?

Salman Rushdie, literary author and critic, has argued that the popularity of *Crouching Tiger, Hidden Dragon* signals a major paradigm shift in Hollywood's repertoire as well as in the tastes of American audiences. In an article written for the New York Times, Rushdie claims that the staggering numbers of multicultural moviegoers to *Crouching Tiger*, including Asian Americans, delegitimizes any possible accusations of Orientalism. Instead, he is optimistic that *Crouching Tiger* is evidence of a new and more tolerant American audience. Rushdie calls *Crouching Tiger* a "breakthrough movie that has taught Americans to accept subtitled foreign films" and calls its critics "killjoys." Rushdie goes on to say that "[I]t may just be that the mass audience is ready, at long last, to enjoy rather more diversity in its cultural diet." The success of *Crouching Tiger*—and more broadly, the Asian invasion—demonstrates America's growing multicultural sensibilities. Implicitly, Rushdie's glowing evaluation is also an appraisal of Hollywood, whose multicultural track record has been bleak at best. Thus, *Crouching Tiger* is a breakthrough movie on many levels. Besides teaching Americans to read at the movies, as Rushdie's review suggests, the film is a breakthrough for Asian/American actors in Hollywood as well as a breakthrough for multicultural discourse in Hollywood. Although it is important to investigate whether these breakthroughs will result in any longterm and more consistent changes in the film industry, the answers to these kinds of questions have a frustrating way of falling back on either pessimistic or optimistic speculation depending on one's own

27

stakes in representational cultural politics. Instead, a more useful approach may be to focus on the ways that multiculturalism functions in *Crouching Tiger*. What does multiculturalism do for Hollywood films? What does it do to and for Hollywood audiences?

In the previous section, I argued that *Rush Hour* repositions Los Angeles as a site where multicultural fantasies of racial pluralism are still possible against the backdrop of "real" racial tensions between African Americans and Korean Americans as well as Asian/Americans in general. *Rush Hour* recuperates Los Angeles's recent dystopic past by offering an alternative narrative of multicultural harmony through an altered process of socialization in which new Asian (im)migrants enter the nation culturally via African American-based cultural routes. That is, contemporary Asian roots are cultivated on the grounds of African American routes. By forcing Jackie Chan's character and Chris Tucker's character together in contemporary Los Angeles, *Rush Hour* offers an alternative relationship between Asian/American and African American people in the "post-riot" period.

28

Crouching Tiger is an entirely different kind of Asian invasion film. *Crouching Tiger* is not a traditional Hollywood film. Unlike other major Hollywood blockbusters, *Crouching Tiger*'s budget was a modest $15 million and was filmed entirely in China and in Mandarin. The total cost of production was shared by nine American and Chinese companies, including Sony Pictures Entertainment, Edko Film Limited, which is based in Hong Kong, and Ang Lee's own production company, Good Machine. The eleven companies in charge of distribution for *Crouching Tiger* are headquartered in Germany, Argentina, Canada, Slovenia, Hong Kong, the Netherlands, Spain, France, and the United States. Moreover, Crouching Tiger is set in mythical nineteenth-century China rather than contemporary America or contemporary China. That *Crouching Tiger* is set in the mythical past means that it has no real-life baggage attached to it. Without the boundaries and burdens of recuperation, *Crouching Tiger* is freer to imagine multicultural harmony not between racialized minorities but between ancient Eastern philosophy and modern Western discourse. *Crouching Tiger*'s success is due in large part to the film's ability to offer its audience the best of both the East and the West.

29

Unlike *Rush Hour*, Ang Lee's film lacked a catchy tagline. However, the film's brilliant promotion team more than made up for this lack. As Tom Bernard, co-president of Sony Picture Classics, explains, this movie's success depended on its popularity with diverse communities of film audiences. "We targeted five different groups—the art house crowd, the young, females, action lovers, and the popcorn mainstream" (qtd. in Pappas S2). This broad-based marketing strategy ensures the film's success in mainstream venues. If men aren't interested

30

in the romantic aspects of the film, they will be interested in the special effects and action. If women aren't interested in the martial arts action, they will enjoy this film as a love story or as a profoundly feminist story. Those who have never taken an interest in the low-budget feel of Kung fu films will embrace *Crouching Tiger* as a film that raises the martial arts genre from low- to highbrow. However, because *Crouching Tiger* is an Asian film with Asian actors, to target American audiences, all of the marketing strategies must ultimately appeal to America's desire for cultural diversity. The film has to appeal, in other words, to American multiculturalism.

The multicultural value of *Crouching Tiger* comes from the care-   31
fully controlled way in which racial difference is displayed and con-tained. Sony Picture Classics successfully promoted the foreignness of *Crouching Tiger* while also familiarizing the foreignness, making it palatable for mainstream America's "cultural diet." Following the logic of this marketing "master plan," both Sony's marketing team and Ang Lee have described this movie in terms of its approximation to well-known Western cultural products. Widely circulating descriptions of the movie include "a mix of Jane Austen lovemaking with Bruce Lee butt-kicking" and "a kung fu Titanic" (Pappas). Ang Lee explains the hybridity of the film in this way, "'Family dramas and *Sense and Sensibility* are all about conflict, about family obligations versus free will.' The martial arts form 'externalizes the elements of restraint and exhilara-tion. In a family drama there is a verbal fight. Here you kick butt" (qtd. in Sunshine 83). By invoking *Titanic* and *Sense and Sensibility*, Lee neutralizes the foreignness of *Crouching Tiger* by reframing *Crouching Tiger*'s storyline as a derivative of these Western narratives. *Crouching Tiger*, in the logic of Sony's marketing, is part of a Western tradition of film. As one reviewer describes the movie, "While undeniably exotic to Western eyes, Ang Lee's film is not entirely foreign. The landscapes and costumes speak a universal language, the Taoist acrobatics suggest a refinement of *The Matrix*, and the adventure in the desert conjures up any number of classic westerns" (Johnson 61). Mainstream American audiences, like this film critic, could only link *Crouching Tiger*'s martial arts tradition back to *The Matrix* (1999), a Hollywood-produced, science fiction film starring Keanu Reeves. Although Yuen Wo Ping was involved in both *The Matrix* and *Crouching Tiger*, Lee's decision to use Yuen was based not on his work in *The Matrix* but on his long career directing and choreographing Kung fu films in Hong Kong.

Sony's marketing strategy could not ensure that all American audi-   32
ences would love the movie, but it did succeed in piquing their interest enough to buy a ticket. Box-office figures for *Crouching Tiger* reached record-breaking numbers, with a large boost after the Academy Awards ceremony where it won for Best Foreign Picture. As of this writing,

Crouching Tiger has grossed nearly $150 million in the United States alone, making it the highest grossing foreign language film ever. But why was this "foreign" or Asian film so commercially successful with Hollywood audiences when similar films have enjoyed only art house success? Although Lee claims that he and James Schamus, a writer involved in all of Lee's films, "didn't exactly have [*Crouching Tiger*] in mind for a western audience," Lee does admit that he wanted "to tell a story with a global sense" ("Interview"). This "global sense" is accomplished in large part by making a particularly palatable form of ethnic feminism central to the movie, an ethnic feminism that privileges a globally universal rather than locally and temporally specific kinship among women.

Zhang Ziyi's character, Jen, the young and dangerously talented   33
protagonist of the film, struggles with many kinds of "crouching tigers and hidden dragons," but perhaps her biggest personal struggle is her struggle to define herself as her own woman. If we emphasize Jen's struggles and personal growth, we can add one more Western genre to the descriptions of *Crouching Tiger*, the genre of the bildungsroman. Like so many narratives of this genre, *Crouching Tiger*'s Tom Jonesian protagonist, after unintentionally disrupting the social order in her understandable if misguided desire to create her own identity, learns difficult life lessons and redeems herself by the narrative's end, thereby restoring and reaffirming the dominant social order. That Jen is a young woman with modern feminist ideas only slightly changes the classically masculinist bildungsroman to a superficially feminist narrative in which even the most legendary swordswomen are powerless to escape the traditional male gaze of Li Mu Bai.

Although Lee's film has been positively received by female audi-   34
ences because of the large amount of screen time devoted to highlighting the ability of very talented swordswomen, Lee's female heroines are not unique to the martial arts genre. There is, in fact, a long tradition of nuxia (female knight-errant) films dating back as early as the 1900s, which have their cultural basis in Chinese legends, such as the story of Fa Mu Lan. Describing the basic formula of the nuxia subgenre, Zhang Zhen writes:

> In the nuxia subgenre as a whole, the heroine is usually pushed onto "stage" by default, due to either the absence or enfeebled condition of a male heir in the family. Having assumed the role of the avenger for an unjust death in the family and of the guardian of a community under external threat, the heroine takes up the responsibility and renounces or postpones her sexual desire. (53)

In *Crouching Tiger*, the female heroines are not "pushed onto   35
stage" but actively clear a feminist space in the male-dominated Giang Hu world. Even Jade Fox, the most clearly defined female villain,

seems to be motivated in part by anti-sexist ideals. As she tells Li Mu Bai before their fight, "Your master underestimated us women. Sure, he'd sleep with me, but he would never teach me."

Jade Fox's admonition speaks to the sexism of the Giang Hu 36 world and, at the same time, emphasizes the exceptional skill of Jade Fox, Shu Lien, and Jen, who have had some impact on Giang Hu, however minimal. Nonetheless, these three very talented swordswomen only matter in the film insofar as they affect Li Mu Bai's life. Jade Fox's sexual oppression may justify her rage against Li Mu Bai's master, but because these women are defined so tightly through Li Mu Bai, audiences have little choice but to hate Jade Fox for hurting the more sympathetic Li Mu Bai. Our disgust for her is further heightened by her unappealing physical characteristics. When not undercover as Jen's governess, Jade Fox is always represented as a bitter old hag. She hunches over when she walks, her hair is always stringy and matted, and she is reviled by women and men of all social classes. We may recognize and even empathize with the misogyny of which Jade Fox accuses Li Mu Bai's master, but we cannot side with her.

On the other end of Crouching Tiger's spectrum of female charac- 37 ters is Shu Lien, an older and more traditional nuxia. Shu Lien respects and abides by the social codes that Jade Fox and Jen revile, even when these codes stand in the way of her own self-fulfillment. It is her fidelity not only to her dead fiance and Li Mu Bai but also to Giang Hu's dominant social order that makes Shu Lien so likable. Although she pines for Li Mu Bai, she does so quietly without imposing her personal desires on Li Mu Bai. Thus, the true hero of the film is free to follow his own life's path, even when Li Mu Bai's attachments to the Giang Hu world, his need to avenge his master's death, and his personal desire for an apprentice outweigh his desire for her.

Finally, even Jen, who refused to submit to Li Mu Bai (as an 38 apprentice or sexual partner), ultimately bows down to the world for which he stands when she kneels before Shu Lien in the aftermath of Li Mu Bai's death. This is the moment of feminism's failure. When the most active feminist figure, the young woman who once dreamed of the freedom "to live my own life, to choose whom I love," and the modern woman who embraced her individual rights even at the expense of her communal and family obligations—an archetypically feminist subject—submits to the traditions that Shu Lien lives by, not only has feminism failed, but the social order against which Jen's feminist ideals were in struggle prevails. That Jen kneels for Shu Lien rather than Li Mu Bai or Jade Fox demonstrates the final phase of Jen's development in which she atones for both the death of Li Mu Bai and the sins of her master, Jade Fox. And yet, for many audiences, Jen still represents a modern feminist figure. There are good reasons for this.

Jen's ability to befriend both Shu Lien and Jade Fox, two women   39
who do not share Jen's aristocratic social class, makes her an appealing
global feminist figure. Even Shu Lien, who remains fond of Jen throughout the movie, cannot overlook their social differences, as she tells
Li Mu Bai, "She's an aristocrat's daughter. She's not one of us." Jade Fox
also warns Jen against befriending Shu Lien because "[her] mother
would not want [Jen] consorting with [Shu Lien's] kind." Despite these
warnings, Jen welcomes Shu Lien and begs her, "Don't distance us.
From now on, let's be like sisters." Jen is most recognizable as a feminist
to Hollywood audiences because of her pluralism. Her willingness to
create sisterhood with those unlike her invites female audiences to
relate to Jen despite differences in race, culture, nation, and temporality,
which is perhaps why Elaine Showalter observes that *Crouching Tiger*
"speaks with luminous directness to the aspirations of contemporary
women" (38).

In fact, it is the differences (racial, cultural, class, and temporal)   40
between Jen and female audiences that make her an attractive feminist
figure. A nineteenth-century Chinese woman. Jen is an authentic racial
Other. Her ability to embrace pluralism affirms the value of pluralistic
feminism as not exclusively Western and modern but universal and
global. Jen's character suggests that class boundaries, such as race,
nation, and culture, cannot keep women apart.

Jen's sisterhood evokes a brand of contemporary global feminism   41
in which Western middle-class and upper middle class women claim a
"sisterhood" with women in the Third World. The same erasures of history and culture must be made for this "sisterhood," whose power is
unevenly distributed, to function. Jen's appeal for sisterhood is
unlikely but nevertheless compatible with Rushdie's assessment of the
multiculturality of this film because both multiculturalism and pluralistic feminism offer the possibility of transcending the limitations of
one's own social and geographic position to try on or test an Other's
position. Herein lies the fantasy of multiculturalism: Differences in
race, class, and history are flattened out, making movement across race
and class much less problematic. As multiculturalism homogenizes
difference by making all differences the same, so too does global
feminism, according to Caren Kaplan, "homogenize economic and cultural difference in favor of a universalizable female identity" (50). Jen's
"sisterhood" offers another marker of multiculturalism in this movie
whose box-office success depends on Hollywood's ability to sell itself
and the movie in a global economy in which multicultural products are
valuable commodities.

If we are to understand fully these films in their material and   42
historical context, a critical dialogue between Asian American studies
scholars and the scholars of "Chinese film studies in the West" is

extremely important. Asian Americanists can help articulate the relationships between transnational Chinese cultural producers and Asian
American cultural consumers that the scholars of "Chinese film studies
in the West" have not been able to do. Although non-Asian Americanist
film scholars such as Gina Marchetti have provided important contributions to the study of Chinese films, without a more sustained attention
to Asian American identity politics, the effect of these transnational
films on Asian American audiences is lost.

NOTES

[1]The African American-Asian pairing has proved to be a fairly profitable
formula when it comes to transnational Asian action heroes as evinced most
famously in Bruce Lee's *Enter the Dragon* (1973) and *Romeo Must Die*, starring
Jet Li and Aaliyah. However, the success of Asian/American action heroes, however popular the Asian invasion discourse would have us believe, still does not
compare to the success of white action heroes.

[2]Here, the "post" is both temporal and discursive. Not only is *Rush Hour*
set in the late 1990s, years after the Los Angeles riots, its alternative social
dramatization of real racial tensions demonstrates that, in the period of "post-
riot LA," we are beyond the extreme racial tensions that finally ignited the riots
in 1992.

WORKS CITED

Ansen, David. "Chinese Takeout." Newsweek Feb. 19, 1996: 66–68.
Barker, Olivia. "Eastern Influences Become Icons of Popular Culture."
    USA Today Mar. 22, 2001 *http://www.usatoday.com/life/2001-13-22-
    easterninfluences.htm*.
Crouching Tiger, Hidden Dragon [Wo Hu Cang Long]. Dir. Ang Lee.
    Perf. Chow Yun-fat, Michelle Yeoh, and Zhang Ziyi. Edko Film Ltd.,
    Good Machine, and Sony Pictures Classics, 2000.
Fore, Steve. "Jackie Chan and the Cultural Dynamics of Global Enter-
    tainment." Transnational Chinese Cinemas: Identity, Nationhood,
    Gender. Ed. Sheldon Hsiao-peng Lu. Honolulu: U of Hawai'i P,
    1997. 239–94.
Garcia, Roger. Introduction. Out of the Shadows: Asians in American
    Cinema. Ed. Roger Garcia. Locarno, Switzerland: Festival inter-
    nazionale del film Locarno, 2001. 13–31.
"Interview with Ang Lee and James Schamus." Guardian Unlimited
    Nov. 7, 2000 *http://film.guardian.co.uk/interview/interviewpages/0
    6737,394698,00.html*.

Johnson, Brian D. "In the Mood for Asia." MacLean's Feb. 26, 2001: 60–01.

Kai, Suzanne. "Wayne Wang, Director of Center of the World." Studio LA *http://studiola.rottentomatoes.com/interviews/wayne.wang/center.of.the.world/index2.php*.

Kaplan, Caren. "A World without Boundaries: The Body Shop's Trans/National Geographics." Social Text 43 (Fall 1995): 45–66.

Kelley, Robin D. G. Yo' Mama's Disfunktional! Fighting the Culture Wars in Urban America. Boston: Beacon, 1997.

Lowe, Lisa. Immigrant Acts: On Asian American Cultural Politics. Durham, NC: Duke UP, 1996.

Pappas, Charles, "Improbable Eastern Hit Proves It Can Fly in U.S." Advertising Age Mar. 26, 2001: S2.

Rush Hour. Dir. Brett Ratner. Perf. Jackie Chan and Chris Tucker. New Line Cinema, 1998.

Rushdie, Salman. "Can Hollywood See the Tiger?" New York Times Mar. 9, 2001: A21.

Shih, Shu-mei. "Globalisation and Minoritisation: Ang Lee and the Politics of Flexibility." New Formations 40 (2000): 86–600.

Showalter, Elaine. "Sex Goddess: Portrayals of Women in Motion Pictures." American Prospect 12.9 (May 21, 2001): 38–40.

Sunshine, Linda, Ed. Crouching Tiger, Hidden Dragon: A Portrait of the Ang Lee Film. New York: Newmarket, 2000.

Zhang, Yingjin. Screening China: Critical Interventions, Cinematic Reconfigurations, and the Transnational Imaginary in Contemporary Chinese Cinema. Ann Arbor, Michigan: Center for Chinese Studies at the University of Michigan, 2002.

Zhen, Zhang. "Bodies in the Air: The Magic of Science and the Fate of the Early 'Martial Arts' Film in China." PostScript 20.2–3 (2001): 43–58.

Examining the Text

1. What does the author mean when he states, ". . . the struggle for the representation of the Asian American experience in the media continues. This is different from recognizing an Asian presence on American screens . . . " (line 3) ? What point does the author make about Asian-American films and filmmakers versus imported films from China, Japan, or Vietnam? How are Asians "exoticized" in Hollywood movies, according to the author?

2. What is the central point of author's *Rush Hour* critique? Does the author indicate that this movie will expand the boundaries of intercultural understanding, or might it put forth some other message, whether intentionally or not? Does the author appear to favor one film over the other in terms of its cultural consciousness? By the end of the article, what is the author arguing for?

3. The author details at length an interpretation of *Rush Hour's* tagline: "The fastest hands of the East Meet the Biggest Mouth of the West." Why does the author go to such lengths to explode possible cultural meanings within that brief passage? What thematic points are at the core of this detailed textual analysis?

4. *Thinking rhetorically*: The author of this article spends much time and energy establishing a cultural/historical context for analysis of the two films under consideration.

What specific types of information does he marshal to lend his film analysis an air of credibility? In the end, would you consider this mainly an "informative" article, or one that skews its concrete evidence (or chooses not to present certain evidence) in order to persuade readers toward a certain position—namely, that of the author?

For Group Discussion

As a class, consider the following questions: Does cinema have the power to construct the racial/ethnic opinions of viewers? Further, by addressing head-on certain social issues and representations of ethnic groups, can filmmakers undo stereotypical racial views? If the answer to the latter question is Yes, do film studios therefore have a responsibility to commission films that correct racial stereotypes of the past? Should feature films be largely about entertainment, or can movies both be entertaining and tackle stereotypes, too? Cite any films you have seen that entertained *and* consciously addressed social issues such as race?

Writing Suggestion

Arrange to rent any one of literally thousands of Kung Fu movies available either on DVD or in VHS video format. As you watch the movie, record each time you think a character utters dialog or engages in an activity that is stereotypical or seems to be making assumptions about gender or racial roles. Note also any dialog or action that seems to dispel or fly in the face of racial/gender stereotypes. Using your list, build an essay that agrees with or contradicts central points in Pham's articles on *Rush Hour* and *Crouching Tiger*. Your essay's thesis should address this question: Does the film you examined expand the boundaries of multicultural understanding, or does it conform to and perpetuate existing beliefs? Use your film notes as supporting evidence.

Fight Club: A Ritual Cure for the Spiritual Ailment of American Masculinity

Jethro Rothe-Kushel

Some social observers believe that corporate, consumer life has visited a loss of masculinity upon American males. Absent the hard labor that earlier times required in order to survive, men have lost their strength and toughness. In the process, according to these social critics, society has lost the containment and support of ritualized passages that transition boys into manhood. In this article the author analyzes these broad social issues raised by the movie, Fight Club (1999).

Fight Club stars Edward Norton as Jack, an aimless, contemporary American male who seemingly lives the American dream in a home furnished from a catalog. He meets his alter-ego, Tyler, played by Brad Pitt, a rugged, risk-taking individual who is everything that Jack is not. Together, the two form Fight Club: a kind of men's support group without the drumming circles or manly hugs. The men in Fight Club engage in physical therapy, otherwise known as punches, kicks and brute violence. The club's goal is to help men find their inner hooligan using a modified set of the Marquess of Queensberry rules that normally govern boxing. Naturally, things spin out of control.

In the following article, the author/film critic scans the movie through a sociological lens to find references to masculinity and meaning in the post-industrial, consumer-driven society that is modern America. The author turns to Freud and Jung and other psychoanalysts to understand such concepts as the ego and symbols of masculinity. The problem, Rothe-Kushel concludes, is that Jack and Tyler are confused. Their lack of clarity about what it means to be a man mirrors the confusion in the wider society. By setting up the Fight Club and going to blows to save the soul of their masculinity, the movie's characters reveal a darker side of American culture, where violence, lawlessness, and rage are glorified and, ultimately, seen as redemptive. Tyler is the violent foil to Jack's tenderness, the rage against Jack's tears, the absent father to Jack's solicitous mother.

As you read, notice how the author parallels the film's use of cinematic effects with the ultimate breakdown of the Fight Club into Project Mayhem. The audience sees a disintegration of the film stock—or at least a deliberate diminishment in visual quality—as the concept of seeking violence in search of masculinity begins to unravel. What does the filmmaker want to achieve by tying a plot device to a visual effect?

"Motion Pictures are going to save our civilization from the destruction which has successively overwhelmed every civilization
of the past. They provide what every previous civilization has
lacked—namely a means of relief, happiness, and mental inspiration
to the people at the bottom. Without happiness and inspiration
being accessible to those upon whom the social burden rests most
heavily, there can be no stable social system. Revolutions are born
of misery and despair."
> —Mary Gray Peck, General Federation of Women's Clubs, 1917.

"Hollywood is the nearest thing to "hell on earth" which Satan
has been able thus far to establish in this world. And the influence
of Hollywood is undermining the Christian culture and civilization which our fathers built in this land."
> —Dan Gilbert, Chairman of the Christian Newspaper Men's
> Committee to Investigate the Motion Picture Industry, 1994.

INTRODUCTION

When I first saw *Fight Club* (1999 dir. David Fincher), I had just   1
returned from a workshop in Oregon entitled "Men: Born to Kill?" The
program was a four-day workshop for about thirty men in which we
learned to hold hands and "discharge." It was the first time since
infancy I had been given a forum in which to touch other men and cry
together with no discomfort or judgement. In the privacy of this idyllic
setting, we discussed the ways in which we use women for touch and
to hold us emotionally because we are too afraid to use other men for
this purpose.

As a filmmaker and a man, I had been told *Fight Club* was one of   2
those movies I would like. I tend not to enjoy violent films, but with the
new energy from the workshop I thought I would give it a chance. I was
not sure how I felt about the movie then and I'm not sure now, but I felt.

SYNOPSIS

Directed by David Fincher, written for the screen by Jim Uhls, and   3
based on a novel by Chuck Plahniuk, *Fight Club* was released to Americans
recovering from the Columbine school shootings in the fall of 1999.
From the beginning, the film examines consciousness itself. We hear a
gun cock and watch the sound as an electrical impulse inside the
psychoneurotic center of the protagonist's brain. "The electricity that's
running through it is like photo-electrical stimuli . . . These are fear-
based impulses. We're changing scale the whole time so we're starting

at the size of a dendrite and we pull through the frontal lobe." Our narrator, Jack, is a product of American problems of meaning. America may promise freedom, especially to the white man, but Jack's life is anything but free. He lives in indentured servitude to his corporate copying office job and his IKEA catalogues. He is on a spiritual[1] train straight to nowhere. But when he sees a doctor for a diagnosis of his spiritual death, the doctor assures him, "No, you can't die from insomnia . . . You want to see pain?" mocks the doctor. "Swing by Meyer High on a Tuesday night and see the guys with testicular cancer. Now that's pain!"

The testicular cancer support group gives Jack the kind of emotional attention he needs. Here people "really listen" and he can cry and feel for the first time. The testicular cancer group inspires him to join support groups for lymphoma, tuberculosis, blood parasites, brain parasites, organic brain dementia, and ascending bowel cancer. He becomes a support group addict with a different group each day of the week—all for a condition he does not have. Accustomed to regarding people as packages, he meets a perfect "single-serving friend" who sits next to him on a business flight. Tyler Durden (Brad Pitt) is everything the narrator wishes he could be. Tyler is a walking, talking, cultural commentator. He is cynical, strong, and forthright. This chance encounter with Tyler Durden leads our narrator to his drastic change of "life-style." When the narrator's IKEA-furnished house burns down, he moves in with Tyler Durden. Together, they start Fight Club, a new kind of support group for men that encourages them to sock and punch and tear at each other in order to feel saved. The fights are primal, brutal, and bloody. This is an honorable group with its own codes and ethics. But Fight Club aggression spins out of control into Project Mayhem. When the narrator finally confronts Tyler about the project, he comes to the realization that he is Tyler Durden. The narrator confronts the inner psychological split by placing a gun in his own mouth. He shoots himself to kill off his alter-ego, but it is too late. Project Mayhem ends where it began, at "ground zero," with bombs exploding and corporate skyscrapers crumbling.

CULTURAL AND ARCHETYPAL MYTH

Fight Club comments profoundly on America's problems of meaning (e.g. indentured servitude to capitalism in a land of freedom, violence in a land of justice, consumer Darwinism in a land of community, meaning in a post-modern reality that understands all meaning as a relative cultural construct, etc.). In sociological terms, Jack, a white male, could represent the hierarchical leadership of the American patriarchy. "I was the warm little center that the life of this world crowded around." America seems to love him, but he feels hurt and betrayed by his culture and the dulled-down consumerist dreams he has inherited.

> We're consumers. We're by-products of a
> lifestyle obsession. Murder, crime, poverty
> —these things don't concern me. What
> concerns me is celebrity magazines,
> television with five hundred channels, some
> guy's name on my underwear. Rogaine, Viagra,
> Olestra.

But according to Fincher, "We're designed to be hunters and we're in a society of shopping. There's nothing to kill anymore, there's nothing to fight, nothing to overcome, nothing to explore. In that societal emasculation this everyman is created."[2] Where does Jack go to discuss his problems? What community exists to support him emotionally and spiritually?   6

Seeking guidance, Jack stumbles into a group for men with testicular cancer. He finds that a weekly catharsis between Bob's breasts rids him of his insomnia by allowing him to feel. But this apparent solution produces a new dilemma for Jack-crying men.   7

> BOB
> We're still men.
>
> JACK
> Yes. We're men. Men is what we are.
>
> JACK (V.O.)
> Bob cried. Six months ago, his testicles
> were removed. Then hormone therapy. He
> developed bitch tits because his
> testosterone was too high and his body upped
> the estrogen. That was where my head fit—
> into his sweating tits that hang enormous,
> the way we think of God's as big.

Jack's masculinity has been reduced to undifferentiated tears. But from these tears, he finds "strength." Despite the temporary relief he feels from his catharsis, Jack quickly returns to his initial dilemma: 8

> You are here because the world
> As you know it no longer makes sense.
> You've been raised on television
> To believe we'll all be
> Millionaires and movie gods and

Rock stars—but we won't.
You pray for a different life.[3]

If Jack is not allowed to express his creativity as a "movie god" or   9
"rock star," he can create his own god in the theater of his mind that
will grant him permission to feel in a more lasting way.

Carl Gustav Jung (1875–1961), a disciple of Sigmund Freud,   10
believed that his mentor had neglected the soul and religion in his understanding of human psychology. For this reason, Jung left Freud and spent
years of research in religious iconography and mythical stories. His findings suggest that archetypal stories exist cross-culturally and that each
individual psyche has the potential for two opposing personalities: ego
and shadow. Ego controls the psyche, but when ego is disrupted (through
Tyler's cutting frames into the film) or weakened through sleep loss or an
emotional void (in Jack's case), the shadow creeps in to take control. The
ego is constructed around societal norms and the desire for behavior
which "fits into society." However, Post-Modernity challenges these
social norms as simply one narrative or structure which is no better than
any other structured narrative. The destruction of Jack's ego also parallels
the destruction of American hegemony.

Tyler Durden, Jack's alter-ego creation, forces Jack to create binary   11
oppositions (love/fear, ego/shadow, etc.) which perhaps necessitate
post-modern "queering" for any resolution.

> Howard Teich calls The Solar/Lunar Twin-Ego, "a universal theme that
> is documented in nearly all cultural histories. Rivalrous pairs such as
> Romulus and Remus, Jacob and Esau, may be most familiar to us, but
> examples of amicable solar/lunar Twins abound as well. It is for exam-
> ple, seldom recalled that even our superhero Hercules was born with a
> twin named Iphicles. Together the Twins represent a balanced, complete
> energetic principle of the masculine, partaking of both light and dark
> influences."[4]

It is this "balanced, complete energetic principle of the masculine"   12
which Jack strives to be. Without Tyler, Jack is a spineless, volumeless,
emotionless, placid, and flaccid half-man. Jack's creation of Tyler
Durden allows him to reclaim his masculinity amidst a culture of post-
feminist, cathartic, "self"-help groups.

Eugene Monick, a contemporary of Jung, wrote a recent book enti-   13
tled *Phallos: Sacred Image of the Masculine*, in which he explains a concept
of Phallos which Jung neglected in his research and writings. According
to Monick, masculine identity in the American patriarchy is often taken
for granted as dominant; therefore it is neglected. Monick suggests that
in a post-feminist America, masculine identity may have become a
larger enigma for men than feminine identity for women. He also

explains that in his own practice of analysis more men are coming to therapy to correct a psychological situation in which they "feel something is missing." Men often find themselves in a quandary about their violent and sexual urges and tend either to act on them and feel guilty, or to suppress them and remain unfulfilled. Nothing has been written on the archetypal basis of masculinity since Erich Neumann's *Origins and History of Consciousness* in 1995.[5] Monick explains:

> Phallos is subjective authority for a male, and objective for those who come into contact with him. This is what makes phallus archetypal. No male has to learn phallos. It presents itself to him as a god does.[6]

With his addiction to self-help groups, Jack attends a leukemia group and experiences a guided meditation. When he is told to meet his power animal in one meditation, he finds a penguin in a snowy cave who speaks like a child—a poignant image of Jack's lonely and docile masculinity. In an article entitled "What Men Really Want," Robert Bly captures this over-emphasized docility: 14

> When I look out at my audiences, perhaps half the young males are what I'd call soft. They're lovely, valuable people—I like them— and they're not interested in harming the earth, or starting wars, or working for corporations. There's something favorable toward life in their whole general mood and style of living. But something's wrong. There's not much energy in them. They are life-preserving but not exactly life-giving.[7]

In a culture that's been robbed of its masculine principle, Jack finds himself only accepting his masculinity through tears and the estrogen-enriched breasts of another man who completes him.   15

> JACK (V.O.)
> The big moosie, his eyes already shrink-
> wrapped in tears. Knees together, invisible
> steps.
>
> Bob takes Jack into an embrace.
>
> JACK (V.O.)
> He pancaked down on top of me.
>
> BOB
> Two grown kids . . . and they won't return my
> calls.
>
> JACK (V.O.)
> Strangers with this kind of honesty make me
> go a big rubbery one.

Jack's face is rapt and sincere. Bob stops
talking and breaks into sobbing, putting his
head down on Jack's shoulder and completely
covering Jack's face.

JACK (V.O.)
Then, I was lost in oblivion—dark and
silent and complete.

Jack's body begins to jerk in sobs. He
tightens his arms around Bob.

JACK (V.O.)
This was freedom. Losing all hope was
freedom.

Crying for Jack seems to be one way to address his masculinity   16
and disappointment with a spiritless life. In contemporary America, it
seems that an increasing number of men are turning to tears as a way of
emoting. Bly discusses this catharsis-obsessed American males.

> Often the younger males would begin to talk and within five minutes
> they would be weeping. The amount of grief and anguish in the
> younger males was astounding! The river was deep. . . They had learned
> to be receptive, and it wasn't enough to carry their marriages. In every
> relationship something fierce is needed once in a while; both the man
> and the woman need to have it.[8]

Monick suggests that the fierceness excluded from the masculine   17
crying model comes with the re-integration of the shadow. Monick
devotes the sixth chapter of his book to the shadow of phallus called
chthonic phallus:

> . . . characterized by its grossness, brutality and carelessness. It can be
> characterized by its unmitigated power needs, by a kind of mad driven-
> ness, by the mayhem of war and ruthless competition it occasions. Life
> is replete with examples of its stupid and devastating behavior, 'the man
> eater,' as Jung's mother called it in his childhood dream.[9]

Though Freud and Jung saw the mother as the primary relation-   18
ship for any child, Monick suggests that for a man, religion helps fill
the void neglected by his father. "Psychoanalytic theory, whether
Freudian or Jungian, gives singular primacy to the mother as the basis
of life. This is an error."[10]

The argument could be made that Freud, Jung, and Monick all   19
cater to perhaps outdated gender roles that have no place in a postmodern scholarship where all gender roles are merely conditioned
identities to maintain social control. Judith Butler, among others,

argues that to speak of gender in any way is to speak of mere conceptual binaries that have been mistakenly mapped onto the human body. Perhaps I am stuck in an outdated paradigm that does not take into account the plurality of roles a human can play for a child and the plurality of circumstances in which a child can be raised, but this writer still finds psychological gender theories interesting if not useful.

Monick claims an individuating spirit cannot become complete until it incorporates the shadowed Other—the darker side of masculinity.   20

> The issue of chthonic phallus is important to men who have a strong spiritual component in their lives and/or a dominant solar masculinity. What do they do with the sweaty, hairy, animal phallos represented by Iron John?[11]

Monick suggests that in the ideal nuclear family, the individuating spirit can grow under the guidance of a mother and a father. But like most American families, Jack's family was anything but ideal: 21

> JACK
> My mother would just go into hysterics. My
> Dad . . . Don't know where he is. Only knew
> him for six years. Then, he ran off to a new
> city and married another woman and had more
> kids. Every six years—new
> city, new family. He was setting up
> franchises.
>
> Tyler smiles, snorts, shakes his head.
>
> TYLER
> A generation of men raised by women. Look
> what it's done to you.

With households across the country either consisting of or dominated by women, young men seem to have trouble finding guidance on the integration of the darker sides of masculinity. Monick claims mothers cannot teach their sons about chthonic phallus.   22

> It is not only the mother's desire to keep her son close and compatible with her style of life that damages chthonic phallos. The father participates, as the king did in the fairy tale. The father who has lost the power and raw energy of chthonic phallos would also deny it to the son. In practical terms, this may become manifest in the abrogation of the father's masculine authority, which by default goes to the mother. And often when the father experiences the return of phallic energy, he leaves the domestic scene to act it out. In such cases, the son is left to fend for himself in a maternal—and often hostile-environment, with no male role-model.[12]

With the lack of a male role-model, all that is left for the American   23
boy without a father is the consumer "product." When there is no other
solution, Jack turns to a "modern versatile domestic solution" to fill the
void:

> Jack flips the page of the catalogue to
> reveal a full-page photo of an entire
> kitchen and dining room set.
>
>   JACK (V.O.)
> I would flip and wonder, "What kind of
> dining room set *defines* me as a person?"

Jack wants out of his dead end corporate job and his IKEA fur-   24
nished "life-style." Jack, who does not have enough courage of his
own, creates a shadow that has enough nerve to break free and enough
audacity to become his own true individual. Jack creates Tyler Durden
as a mentoring father figure who will help him integrate his shadow in
relationship with sex and violence and bring Jack closer to the Other.

>   TYLER
> Shut up! Our fathers were our models for
> God.
> And if our fathers bailed, what does that
> tell you about God?

Increasingly American boys are raised by their mothers with a   25
lack of any strong male role-model in their life. Tyler becomes such a
role-model for Jack who paradoxically holds all of Jack's rage and all of
his love simultaneously. The fighting itself becomes an act of love
through which they can relate to one another. However, Tyler Durden,
like Iron John, is only a temporary experience.

> The young prince must go into the forest to live for a time with Iron
> John. A gentleman must know that he is also a beast and know the ap-
> propriate times to become that beast—that is the integration of shadow
> chthonic phallos. The prince must of course emerge from the forest, but
> with his eyes open to the duality of his nature.

The last scene of the film illuminates Jack's final encounter with   26
Tyler. With a gun to Jack's head, Tyler begins the last scene where the
film began.

>   TYLER
> 3 minutes. This is it. Here we are at the
> beginning. Ground zero. Would you like to
> say a few words to mark the occasion?

Jack is at a loss for words, but realizes he no longer craves the   27
destruction Tyler wants. "I don't want this!" But it is too late. Vans
loaded with "blasting gelatin" are set to detonate and destroy urban
phallic skyscrapers in a matter of minutes. Jack realizes the only way to
stop his alter-ego gone awry is to point the gun at himself. Tyler dies
when Jack shoots himself in the mouth, but Jack remains a spirit to bear
witness to "ground zero."[13] The last image of the film is framed as a
vista from within a glass skyscraper. Jack and his lover, Marla Singer,
hold hands at the "theater of mass destruction." Two tall towers crumble to the ground. Premiered years before September eleventh, the film
serves as chilling prophecy even more profound and ripe with cultural
and historical mythic elements than even this author had expected.

FIGHT CLUB AS SACRED

But how can a film with such a dark and violent conclusion be classi-   28
fied as sacred? The French anthropologist, René Girard, suggests that
sacred violence is an inherent component of any well functioning society throughout history. Girard classifies violence into pure and impure
violence. Impure violence is uncontained and lawless and warrants
retaliation from the victim's fellowship. Such violence is ultimately
destructive to the community because its results are interminable.
However, pure violence is contained through a lawful sacrifice in
which the victim and his fellowship understand the death as sacred.
Such a sacrifice satisfies the cultural need for violence while maintaining order and purpose. *Fight Club* becomes such a structure wherein
violence is contained within a particular communal order. It is worth
noting that all participants in *Fight Club* are white males, kings of
American hegemony, who have no scapegoat for their problems but
themselves and the corporations. The sacrificial victim becomes a
scapegoat by which to purge the society of its anger and hatred. The
scapegoat allows the community to project all of its anger onto the victim, thereby eliminating its anger at itself. By sacrificing the scapegoat
the community relinquishes itself from its anger. Girard suggest that
the scapegoat is both fatherless and randomly chosen so that he will
not be avenged after his death. The ideal scapegoat is a king or hero
who has achieved success in the community, but is destroyed by destiny. "God giveth and God taketh. The best of scapegoats is thus a
dethroned idol, a broken idol marginalized from the society he once
ruled. And this is exactly what the action hero is."[14] Tyler Durden is
such an action hero—fatherless as Jack is his only creator, and a model
of the ultimate American idol, popular icon and movie star Brad Pitt
himself. While Tyler Durden becomes a scapegoat for Jack, corporate

buildings become a scapegoat for Tyler as the "Demolitions Committee" of "Project Mayhem." The demolition of Brad Pitt and about seven skyscrapers leaves the viewer with a sense of peace leaving the theater.[15] *Fight Club*, the film, and Fight Club, the cult within the film, becomes the reclamation of American sacred violence.

I would argue *Fight Club* is avante garde sublime art. However, categorizing the film in artistic terms negates the highest measurement of sacredness in America: box-office success. As with most American endeavors that afford some power, the projected image does not come for free. Film is the most costly and time-consuming art form.[16] Production on such a grand and costly scale will both comment on culture and affect culture profoundly. If money is not sacred in America, what is? The American dollar dictates American values, and by that measure, *Fight Club* is irrevocably sacred.

29

FORMATIVE MYTH AND ITS MEDIUM

But what is the impact of this violent myth on the community? The space of the movie theater is a sacred ritual arena that few scholars have analyzed as such. Martin discusses the lack of scholarly work linking film and religion:

30

> Scholars engaged in prevailing modes of film criticism have had almost nothing to say about religion. And scholars who study religion have had almost nothing to say about Hollywood film. Instead of encountering an ongoing and stimulating dialogue about religion and film, I encountered silence.[17]

The viewer experiences a cognitive shift when he steps into the movie theater. *Fight Club* as a cultural artifact has the ability to affect individual and collective consciousness. But how do we measure this effect? In oral traditions, the communication of sacred stories is confined to a specific time and place. However, with a text, cultural effects can be analyzed through critical literary faculties that human consciousness has developed over hundreds of years. The impact of the classic text on its culture is also easily discussed from the privileged temporal position of having a distance of many years with which to measure cultural change. However, discussing the impact of a contemporary film on its community is a much more daunting task for which scholars have only the most archaic tools.

31

The French philosopher, Emmanuel Levinas, suggests that a significant cognitive distinction exists between the experience of reading a text and the experience of viewing an image. The linearity of the textual

32

narrative empowers its consumer in a way that the image does not. The literary text is only reconstructed through the critical faculties of its reader. Thus, the textual consumer is empowered with ultimate control over his or her interpretation. However, the viewer of the image is instantaneously seduced into an uncontrollable holistic experience. The image dominates its viewer, requires a fundamental passivity, and denies the viewer the freedom of interpretation. Levinas has an abhorrence of images. He critiques the artist whose compulsion for expressing truth supercedes the responsibility of the consequences of such an expression. The question remains: does the artist influence the culture or does the culture merely influence the artist? When people remarked that Gertrude Stein did not look like Picasso's portrait, Picasso replied, "She will." In a similar way, when *Fight Club* was first released in 1999, many critics were upset by its violence voicing the concern that the film itself creates a violence that does not exist within the culture. However, five years later, the last image of two buildings crumbling confirms the film's prophetic power as young American men come together to fight a new scapegoat—Islamic fundamentalists.

The visual arts bring us to a safe place where we can experience extreme emotion. Film can have the effect of a formative religious experience more so than the most sublime texts. However, such a film experience is more dangerous; text depends on critical faculties whereas the film requires passive vulnerability.   33

Film belongs in both the critical worlds of text and image. The rapid projection of twenty-four 35mm photographs every second is reconstructed only in the viewer's memory using both narrative critical faculties and image domination. There becomes a temporal quality to the image that allows the mind to re-create a holistic experience. And sound only complicates this ultimately inarticulatable experience.   34

Film can seduce and indoctrinate the viewer urging him or her to confront his or her own emotion. Also, film can have a stronger emotional draw than even theater (assuming the audience chooses to accept the film as a reality) by permitting the viewer to suspend critical judgment. The safety of the movie setting allows the viewer to make himself more vulnerable and be affected in emotionally deeper ways. Consumers move from a "normal" sphere to a sphere in which they allow alternative realities to be presented. In this act, the consumer suspends his or her control of how reality "should" operate. Artaud, the French poet, essayist, playwright, and actor conceptualized cinema as "literally a stimulant or narcotic, acting directly and materially on the mind."[18] Artaud's film work combats the medium, attempting to "tear the image from representation and position it in proximity within the viewer's perception/interpretative sensorium."[19] In his work, Artaud interrupts the narrative itself so the audience can become conscious of   35 its existence. He theorized that "raw cinema" would come from eliminating film's narrative qualities and therefore relying solely on the indoctrination of the image. *Fight Club* moves in this direction.

That the film has its viewers blindly accept a new value structure   36
which undermines and subverts most "normal" values of right and wrong, is a stunning testament to film's ability to create a separate reality within the confines of the theater space.

> That the film promotes this idea and wins our involvement, before completely undermining itself and the exercise, displays a clever, highly manipulative comment on the influence of a film to persuade its viewers into accepting a new set of values . . .[20]

The film's ability to persuade its viewer to accept a moral relativity   37
has some frightening implications:

> It's a modern, cerebral world, and these characters go away and be macho not to re-claim some latent untapped masculinity, but to revel in the absurdity of doing so, and thus the absurdity of being cerebral; the power of its world that ropes us in and that we take for granted has us in chains.[21]

The film which exists apart from conventional reality can provide an   38
extasy—an ex stasis allowing the viewer to be taken outside of the domain of normal consciousness and into a reality that is probably most similar to the passive experience of the unconscious dream mixed with conscious memory. The film exists within the inner life of Jack:

> JACK
> Listen to this. It's an article written in
> first person. "I am Jack's medulla
> oblongata, without me Jack could not
> regulate his heart rate, blood pressure or
> breathing!" There's a whole series of these!
> "I am Jill's nipples". "I am Jack's Colon."

From such statements about the inner body of Jack stem further   39
meditations by Jack about his own inner life: "I am Jack's smirking revenge." "I am Jack's cold sweat." "I am Jack's broken heart."

What may be unique about *Fight Club* is its self-consciousness   40
about its own medium. The breakdown of Jack's ego is manifest through the breakdown of cinematic form itself. *Fight Club* itself is a radical meditation on film form and language.

Tyler appears to Jack about six times before the audience becomes   41
conscious of the encounter. This is accomplished through a technique
that may be truly unique by which Tyler is introduced to single frames
in the film. Ironically, Tyler works as a projectionist who cuts in singular frames of pornography into family films. In the last scene of the film
a single frame of a naked penis is cut into the film just before the crumbling buildings fade to black. The splice acts as a formal reminder of
our journey with "chthonic phallos."

Fight Club also examines the temporal quality of film itself creat-   42
ing a unique stream-of-consciousness experience. Computer concepts
like RAM (random access memory) seem to influence Fincher's understanding of time.

> We take the first forty minutes to literally indoctrinate you in this sub-
> jective psychotic state, the way he thinks, the way he talks about what's
> behind the refrigerator . . . It's gotta move as quick as you can think.
> We've gotta come up with a way that the camera can illustrate things at
> the speed of thought. And that's one of the things that was interesting
> to me, how much can you jump around in time and go: Wait, let me
> back up a little bit more, okay, no, no, this is where this started, this is
> how I met this person. . . . So there's this jumping around in time to
> bring you into the present and then leaping back to go, Let me tell you
> about this other thing. It's almost conversational. It's as erratic in its
> presentation as the narrator is in his thinking. I think maybe the possi-
> bilities of this kind of temporal and freedom points to a future direction
> for movies.[22]

In addition to temporality, Fincher manipulates the medium itself   43
dirtying the film through specific processing. "When we processed it,
we stretched the contrast to make it kind of ugly, a little bit of underex-
posure, a little bit of re-silvering, and using new high-contrast print
stocks and stepping all over it so it has a dirty patina."[23] The processing
of the film is apparently similar to Fincher's last film, *Seven* (1995).
"The blacks become incredibly rich and kind of dirty. We did it on
Seven a little, just to make the prints nice. But it's really in this more for
making it ugly." The deconstruction of the film chemistry itself and
Fincher's homage to his own formal past indicates the layers of complexity that contribute to the experience of the film. Gavin Smith positions *Fight Club* and its form in relation to other contemporary cinema:

> Is *Fight Club* the end of something in cinema, or the beginning? Zeitgeist
> movie or cult item? Whether you find the state-of-the-art cinematic val-
> ues of this current moment liberating or oppressive, radical or specious,
> of lasting significance or entirely transitory, as the little girl in Poltergeist
> says: they're here.

The speed with which film is produced makes a conscious inter- 44
textual dialogue difficult—or at least undermines the ability of the
critic to place himself within a contemporary dialogue about film form.

A performance is only ritualized by its repetition, and only cult 45
viewers naturally watch a movie multiple times. Thus, *Fight Club* as a film
can only become ritualized by its small but growing cult watching public.

AFTER THE THEATER

When an individual steps into a church, how much do they expect of 46
their experience to follow them out? Great art changes our experience
of reality and challenges us to take that experience home with us. Is this
great art?

> TYLER
> 3 minutes. This is it. Here we are at the
> beginning. Ground zero. Would you like to
> say a few words to mark the occasion?

The film effectively holds up a mirror to the male viewer and sug- 47
gests that the real story begins at "ground zero" in "three minutes" as
the film fades out, the end credits begin, and the audience exits the theater. Most of us are confused when we leave a movie theater and enjoy
reveling in the passivity of the experience. However, the film maintains
a moral ambiguity which challenges the viewer to "say a few words to
mark the occasion." One informant says of his experience, "It didn't let
me be a white, middle-class American male, ages 18–24, the most powerful person in the world, and remain comfortable in my seat."[24] During an interview at Yale University, Edward Norton confirmed this
reaction as intentional:

> I hope it rattles people. I hope it dunks very squarely in your lap be-
> cause I think one of the things we strove very specifically to do with this
> was on some levels retain a kind of moral ambivalence or a moral
> ambiguity—not to deliver a neatly wrapped package of meaning into
> your lap. Or in any way that let you walk away from the film like this,
> comfortable in having been told what you should make of it.[25]

But what words can Americans say to "mark the occasion?" 48
Howard Hampton expresses his anger towards an American public
that received the film with no noticeable "kamikaze act[s] of homage":

> ... *Fight Club* generated no noticeably baleful side effects whatsoever.
> Are left-wing critics and right-wing politicians the only ones left who

believe in the potency of "transgression"? What is the world coming to when a movie featuring charismatic performers reveling in anti-social behavior and a host of semi-subliminal advertisements for the joys of chaos can't incite a single unbalanced loner to commit a kamikaze act of homage?[26]

Unfortunately, in the wake of September 11th terrorist attacks,   49 *Fight Club*'s moral aloofness has become less clear. A more courageous cultural critic might argue that the film encouraged Americans to create an alter-ego (Islamic Fundamentalists) which could ignite a new kind of *Fight Club*-war. However, I would not be so courageous.

While the collective effects of the film remain ephemeral, the indi-   50 vidual responses are easier to attain. For example, Alexander Walker of the *London Evening Standard* is quoted as attacking *Fight Club* as "an inadmissible assault on personal decency and on society itself."[27] Kenneth Turan of the *Los Angeles Times* (1999, pg. 1) suggests that, "What's most troubling about this witless mishmash of whiny, infantile philosophizing and bone-crunching violence is the increasing realization that it actually thinks it's saying something of significance. That is a scary notion indeed." Edward Norton challenges dismissing *Fight Club* because of its violence or moral ambiguity.

> My feeling is that it is the responsibility of people making films and people making all art to specifically address dysfunctions in the culture. I think that any culture where the art is not reflecting a really dysfunctional component of the culture, is a culture in denial. And I think that's much more intensely dangerous on lots of levels than considered examinations of those dysfunctions through art is dangerous. I don't believe that it's the chicken and the egg question, I do think there is violence in the culture. I think there always has been violence in our culture in one form or another. I think that it's a very appropriate discussion to ask what are the ways in which the presentations of violence effect us.[28]

After interviewing a dozen American male college students, I feel   51 confident that I have attained some sense of the emotional response it may have warranted from its intended audience (American males age 18–24). Though the sample size was relatively small, the informants included a cross-section of socio-economic and cultural backgrounds. Though the specifics varied, all males interviewed felt something. One informant was "anesthetized":

> I guess I felt shock in response to all this destruction, yet the visual image was so beautiful that I was seduced by it and gave myself over to scopophilic consumption. When I left the theater, I felt numb. I was anesthetized.[29]

Others similarly describe the anesthesia of *Fight Club* as "stress release," "peace," and "liberating."

I felt violated, but not really violated. Like I was tricked into seeing something I shouldn't see. Like taken advantage of. It was a stress release.[30]

It was jarring, I guess, because he shoots himself. But there's a sense of peace in the destruction. He's sitting there holding her hand, and it's just kind of peaceful. It's kind of a defiant peace. It was definitely one of those moments where you're like, 'Whoa! Dude! Like Jesus Christ. I got to think about it.'[31]

Liberating. As unjustified as it was, the buildings were tolerable. You'd expect a feeling of regret for the antagonist to accomplish destruction. But there was a liberating feeling somehow.[32]

Jack, the character, has a similar experience to 'he informants when he finishes his fight.

> JACK (V.O.)
> Fight Club was not about winning or losing.
> It wasn't about words.

The Opponent recovers, throws a headlock on Jack. Jack snakes his arm into a counter headlock. They, wrestling like wild animals. The crowd CHEERS maniacally.

> JACK (V.O.)
> The hysterical shouting was in tongues, like at a Pentecostal church.

The onlookers kneel to stay with the fight, cheering ever louder. The Opponent smashes Jack's head into the floor, over and over.

> JACK
> Stop.

Everyone moves in as the Opponent steps away. They lift Jack to his feet. On the floor is a BLOOD MASK of Jack's face— similar to his TEAR MASK on BOB'S SHIRT, seen earlier.

EXT. BAR - NIGHT

Everyone files out of the bar, sweating, bleeding, smiling.

> JACK (V.O.)
> Nothing was solved. But nothing mattered.
> Afterwards, we all felt saved.

The screening of *Fight Club* itself can become the classic salvation   52
experience for its audience by which an icon (in this case the screen or
television) serves as a scapegoat which asks to become an object onto
which the viewer can manifest his own darkness. The salvation experience in the Greco-Roman tradition of the Cults of Metamorphosis
operates through the re-integration of the self with something lost.
The self is saved through sacred violence from a self-alienation it is
suffering. The same process governs the Christian cross, an object that
materializes and owns human sin. The weight of the human experience is somehow saved, enlightened, or made more peaceful by the
presence of a sullied sacred icon. One informant describes the film as
such an icon:

> I thought it was like destruction, but cathartic destruction. That's
> what people need at times . . . I get frustrated. . . and feel a subcon-
> scious or latent desire to react against it all . . . I don't feel like I have a
> place to vent my destructive behavior. It eats at my conscience . . . I
> also appreciated the scenes where he went to those self-help sessions . . .
> I probably wouldn't do anything like that—go and cry and hug and
> stuff . . . It might help some people, even me, but it didn't influence
> me to do anything like that. When I want to cry, I go to my family at
> home-two older brothers, an older sister, and a mother. My dad's not
> around.[33]

CONCLUSION

Fight Club, the movie, exists to solve the very problems of meaning it   53
poses. It holds a mirror up to young white males and says, "This is who
you are." And the very act of holding up that mirror allows the film to
own a dark part of the culture which cannot be experienced within the
culture.

Fight Club frames America lacking a public venue to integrate   54
the emotional component of white male identity. When there is a
communal or cultural void, history suggests that violence can complete that lack. *Fight Club* exposes the void and offers three solutions:
crying, violence, and movies. *Fight Club* asks the question, what do
you want to do with the Jacks of our country—those unwanted children of America who were raised on cultural action hero myths and
yearn to live those stories? We can send them to support groups to
mourn the impossibility of living this dream, send them to war to
partake in the battle, or send them to experience the "Fight Club" of
American cinema.

AFTERWARD

Since the initial conception and transcription of my argument, I have   55
been given reason to revisit a concern of many critics addressed in an
article by Gary Crowdus: "They felt scenes served only as a mindless
glamorization of brutality, a morally irresponsible portrayal, which they
feared might encourage impressionable young male viewers to set up
their own real-life Fight Clubs in order to beat each other senseless."[34]

Since my interest in *Fight Club* has blossomed, I have been   56
informed on numerous occasions of accounts of real life Fight Clubs
formed in honor of the film. In one Ivy League college, fraternity brothers gather weekly in the name of their "Fight Club." On at least one
occasion they were seen engaged in a ritual taken directly from the
film—pouring lye on each other and burning holes in their brothers'
skin. Another informant confesses:

> I thought it was very confusing. I was definitely surprised by the end-
> ing. I also felt a weird urge to be like the guys in the movie. That is,
> I wanted to be able to participate in that type of violence except that
> I knew that I was too scared to do that. I did not feel brave enough to
> participate in that even though I kind of wanted to. Too afraid of hurting
> myself . . . Although at one point a friend of mine and I started punching
> each other in the head to progressively toughen ourselves. We stopped
> when we thought of what happened to Mohamed Ali. I also know of a
> guy whose frat (not here) had a Fight Club like the one in the movie.[35]

One female college student in Mexico informs me that she   57
engages regularly in "fight club" with her brothers after having
watched the film in which they bruise each other for the fun of it.

One African-American informant who detested the film offers   58
perhaps the most simple and sober solution:

> I thought, "Just great! This is what America needs. Another 'the-
> solution-to-our-deteriorating-white-male-crisis is violence and rebellion
> and stuff.' . . . just replacing one problem with another. The solution is to
> be honest. Admit how you feel. Love. And feel however it is you feel.
> The support groups were weird. I was like, "What's this guy doing?"
> and "What's this all about?" I'm still trying to find a place to feel. I like
> to think that it takes being alone and by yourself a lot of times so you
> can truly hear yourself and find out what truly is the problem that's
> bothering you. I don't want to say that it can't be done with other peo-
> ple, but it's just a very personal thing. To really understand and accept
> what's happing inside you, it takes getting in touch with the part of you
> that people tried to kill even before you could speak —when you knew

you wanted to cry, but they told you that wasn't okay. You had to sublimate that to exist in this world. So the problem is trying to get back into it. But they've had you sublimate it so long, that you don't even know what the problem is any more. The movie didn't solve anything for me. It just re-confirmed my ideas that society is really wrong.[36]

These examples further problematize my claim that *Fight Club* the film does in fact solve the problems it poses—or at least that it does so neatly and non-violently without consequences. Herein lies the moral ambiguity of both my argument and the film that I submit to the reader and future scholars for further reflection. 59

NOTES

[1]For the purposes of this paper, I am defining spiritual as that experience of wholeness or oneness classically found in religion which is relegated in modern America to the confines of the individual.

[2]David Fincher as quoted in Gavin Smith,"Inside out," *Film Comment.* New York; Sep/Oct 1999; Vol. 35, Iss. 5, 58–66.

[3]Jim Uhls, *Fight Club, "The Shooting Script,"* February, 16, 1998.

[4]M. Greene, 2000.

[5]Erich Neumann, Translation by R. F. C. Hull, *The Origins and History of Consciousness* (Mythos Books) (New Jersey: Princeton University Press, 1995).

[6]Eugene Monick, "Studies in Jungian Psychology," *Phallos: Sacred Image of the Masculine,* 9.

[7]Quoted by Keith Thompson in "What Men Really Want: A New Age Interview with Robert Bly," 32.

[8]Bly, 23.

[9]Monick,, 94.

[10]Monick, 96.

[11]Monick, 95.

[12]Monick, 95.

[13]The definition of "ground zero" *http://dictionary.reference.com/* expands on the rich depth of meaning of the term in relation to recent events in America and the film itself:

> **ground zero n**. 1) The target of a projectile, such as a missile or bomb. 2) The site directly below, directly above, or at the point of detonation of a nuclear weapon. 3) The center of rapid or intense development or change: "The neighborhood scarcely existed five years ago, but today it is the ground zero from which designer shops and restaurants radiate" (Robert Clark). 4) The starting point or most basic level: My client didn't like my preliminary designs, so I returned to ground zero.

[14]J. David Slocum, *Violence and American Cinema.* "Passion and Acceleration: Generic Change in the Action Film," by Rikke Schubart. New York: Routledge, 2001, 194.

[15]See section entitled "After The Theater" for a chronicle of peaceful feelings and reactions upon leaving the theater.

[16]This statement is made solely from the rationality of the author. With the possible exception of rare public architecture, I cannot think of an art form that costs many millions of dollars to produce like the Hollywood film.

[17]Joel W. Martin and Conrad E. Ostwalt, Jr., *Screening the Sacred: Religion, Myth, and Ideology in Popular American Film* (Boulder: Westview Press, 1995), p. 2.

[18]Adrian Gargett. *Doppelganger: Exploded States of Consciousness in Fight Club*, http://www.disinfo.com/pages/article/id1497/, 2001, 7.

[19]Gargett, 7.

[20]Adrian McOran-Campbell, "Recent Incarnations: Generation X-Y," *Postmodern Science Fiction and Cyberpunk: The 'New Edge' as Cultural and Evolutionary Leap*. Version of Dissertation submitted for degree-level English Literature (Chester, UK, May 2000), 25.

[21]McOran-Campbel, 26.

[22]Smith, 58.

[23]Smith, 60.

[24]American male college student, personal interview, March 10, 2003.

[25]Edward Norton, Interview printed on *Fight Club* DVD disc 2 "Special Features."

[26]Howard Hampton, "Blood and Gore Wars", *Film Comment* (New York, Nov/Dec 2000, Vol. 36, Iss. 6) 30.

[27]"How to Start a Fight," *Fight Club* DVD, 200, 14.

[28]Edward Norton, Interview printed on *Fight Club* DVD disc 2 "Special Features."

[29]American male college student, interview, March 10, 2003.

[30]American male college student, personal interview, March 10, 2003.

[31]American male college student, personal interview, March 10, 2003.

[32]American male college student, personal interview, March 10, 2003.

[33]American male college student, personal interview, March 12, 2003.

[34]Gary Crowdus, "Getting Exercised over Fight Club," *Cineaste* September 2000 (25:4), 47.

[35]American male college student, personal interview, March 8, 2003.

[36]American male college student, personal interview, March 9, 2003 and March 12, 2003.

BIBLIOGRAPHY

Althusser, Louis. *For Marx*. New York: Vintage Books, 1970.

Arthur, Chris. "Media, Meaning and Method in Religious Studies" in *Rethinking Media, Religion, and Culture*, ed. S. Hoover and K. Lundby. Thousand Oaks, London, New Delhi: Sage, 1996.

Bellah, Robert N. "Civil Religion in America," in *Daedalus*, 1967.

Bryant, M. Darrol. "Cinema, Religion, and Popular Culture", in *Religion in Film*, edited by John R. May and Michael Bird. Knoxville: University of Tennessee Press, 1982.

Cavell, Stanley. *The World Viewed: Reflections on the Ontology of Film.* Cambridge: Harvard University Press, 1979.

Clark, J. Michael. "Faludi, *Fight Club* and Phallic Masculinity: Exploring the Emasculating Economics of Patriarchy," in *Journal of Men's Studies.* 11(1):65–76, 2002.

Crowdus, Gary, "Getting Exercised over *Fight Club*," *Cineaste* September 2000 (25:4), 46–48.

Deacy, Christopher. "Redemption and Film: Cinema as a Contemporary Site of Religious Activity," in *Media Development* XLVII (1), 2000, 50–54.

Deacy, Christopher. "Integration and Rebirth through Confrontation: *Fight Club* and American Beauty as Contemporary Religious Parables," in *Journal of Contemporary Religion.* London: Carfax Publishing, 2002.

Deren, Maya. "Cinematography: The Creative Use of Reality." *Daedalus*, the journal of the American Academy of Arts and Sciences. Boston, Massachusetts: The Visual Arts Today, 1960.

Dreyer, Richard. *Heavenly Bodies: Film Stars and Society.* New York: St. martin's Press, 1986.

Durkheim, Emile. *The Elementary Forms of Religious Life.* New York: The Free Press, 1995.

Eliade, Mircea, *The Sacred and the Profane; the Nature of Religion.* Trans. from the French by Willard R. Trask. New York: Harcourt, Brace, 1959.

Gargett, Adrian. *Doppelganger: Exploded States of Consciousness in Fight Club. http://www.disinfo.com/pages/article/id1497/*, 2001.

Girard, Rene´ (tr. Patrick Gregory). *Violence and the Sacred.* Baltimore, London: John Hopkins, 1977.

Graham, David John. "The Uses of Film in Theology." In Marsh, C. & Ortiz, G., eds. *Explorations in Theology and Film: Movies and Meaning.* Oxford: Blackwell, 1997.

Hampton, Howard. "Blood and Gore Wars," *Film Comment.* New York, Nov/Dec 2000, Vol. 36, Iss. 6.

Hoover, Stewart M. "Media and the Construction of the Religious Public Sphere," in *Rethinking Media, Religion, and Culture*, ed. S. Hoover and K. Lundby. Thousand Oaks: Sage, 1996.

Hoover, Stewart M. "Religion, Media, and the Cultural Center of Gravity." *Religion and Popular Culture: Studies on the Interaction of Worldviews.* Ed. Daniel A. Stout and Judith M. Buddenbaum. Ames, Iowa: Iowa State University Press, 2001.

Hoover, Stewart M. and Shalini S. Venturelli. 'The Category of the Religious: The Blindspot of Contemporary Media Theory?', in *Critical Studies in Mass Communication*, 1996.

Jarvie, Ian Charles. *Movies and Society.* New York: Basic Books, 1970.

Jarvie, Ian Charles. *Towards a Sociology of the Cinema: A Comparative Essay on the Structure and Functioning of a Major Entertainment Industry*. London: Routledge & K. Paul, 1970.

Jowett, Garth. *Film: The Democratic Art*. Boston: Little, Brown, 1976.

Lévi-Strauss, Claude. *Myth and Meaning*. New York: Schoken Books, 1995.

Levinas, Emmanuel. Ed. Seán Hand. *The Levinas Reader*. "Reality and It's Shadow," and "The Transcendence of Words." Malden Massachusetts: Blackwell Publishers, Inc., 1989.

Marsh and Ortiz. *Explorations in Theology and Film: Movies and Meaning*. Malden, MA: Blackwell Publishers, 1997.

Martin, Joel W. and Conrad E. Ostwalt, Jr. *Screening the Sacred: Religion, Myth, and Ideology in Popular American Film*. Boulder, CO: Westview Press, 1995.

Carolyn, Marvin, and David W. Ingle. "Blood Sacrifice and the Nation: Revisiting Civil Religion," in *Journal of the American Academy of Religion*, 1996.

Marx, Karl. *The Marx-Engels Reader*. New York: W. W. Norton & Company, 1978

McOran-Campbell, Adrian. *Postmodern Science Fiction and Cyberpunk: The 'New Edge' as Cultural and Evolutionary Leap*. "Recent Incarnations: Generation X-Y." Version of Dissertation submitted for degree-level English Literature, Chester, UK, May 2000.

Miles, Margaret R. *Seeing and Believing: Religion and Values in the Movies*. Boston: Beacon Press, 1996.

Neumann, Erich. Translation by R. F. C. Hull. *The Origins and History of Consciousness* (Mythos Books). New Jersey: Princeton University Press, 1995.

Nietzsche, Friedrich Wilhelm. 1974. *The Gay Science*. Translated by Walter Kaufmann. New York: Random House.

Palahniuk, Chuck. *Fight Club*. London: Vintage Books, 1997.

Scott, Bernard Brandon. *Hollywood Dreams and Biblical Stories*. Minneapolis, MN: Fortress Press, 1994.

Smith, Gavin. "Inside out," *Film Comment*. New York; Sep/Oct 1999; Vol. 35, Iss. 5, 58–66.

Smith, Warren and Debbie Leslie, *"Fight Club" International Feminist Journal of Politics*.

Steimatsky, Noa. 1998. "Pasolini on Terra Sancta: Towards a Theology of Film." *The Yale Journal of Criticism*.

Tarkovsky, Andrey. 1987. *Sculpting in Time: Reflections on the Cinema*. New York: Knopf.

Turner, Bryan S. *Religion and Social Theory*. Thousand Oaks: SAGE Publications, 1991.

Tremblay, Robert. *Canada: DIS (Hons) IV*, Carleton University, 1999–2000.

Turner, Victor. *The Ritual Process: Structure and Anti-Structure*.

White, David Manning. *Sight, Sound, and Society; Motion Pictures and Television in America*. Boston: Beacon Press, 1968.

Wilson, Charles Reagan. 1995. "The Religion of the Lost Clause: Ritual and Organization of the Southern Civil Religion, 1865–1920," in ed. D. Hackett. *Religion and American Culture: A Reader*. New York and London: Routledge.

Examining the Text

1. In this article, the author argues that American culture has been robbed of its masculine principle? What does he mean by this assertion, and do you agree with his position? Cite specific examples in the text that the author uses to support his contention.

2. Identify the ways in which the author relates the idea of sacredness to the themes in *Fight Club* and movies in general. What does the word "sacred" mean to you; what do you think of the author's use of this word in the context of a film about a bunch of guys beating the holy daylights out of each other?

3. The author initially describes *Fight Club* as "avant-garde sublime art," yet seems to concede that the real measure of a film's value is its box-office success. What do you think the author is implying when he discusses these issues of sacredness and money; what comment might he be making about the preoccupation with money and material value in American society?

4. The author states, "When an individual steps into a church, how much do they expect of their experience to follow them out? Great art changes our experience of reality and challenges us to take that experience home with us. Is this great art?" (line 46). Examine this passage from the article again; in what ways might art change our perceptions and beliefs? Based on your knowledge of the film gleaned from the article, as well as your own experience as a film-goer, does *Fight Club* fall into the category of great art?

5. *Thinking rhetorically*: What sources does the author use to provide evidence for his assertions in this essay? Does the author's use of a variety of sources, ranging from the familiar to the obscure, enhance the clarity and depth of the article? What does the use of such diverse references suggest about the article's intended audience? On a more personal note, do the references increase your own understanding of the article? What risks might be posed when writers quote from sources that are not commonly known and are not explained in the article?

For Group Discussion

In a full-class discussion, engage in a debate over the question: Do men in American society lack rituals that mark their entry into manhood? Do rituals already exist that might support the passage of contemporary

American males into adulthood? Short of organizing mutual-mayhem groups, as happens in the film, what other means can you imagine for boys to become "real" men? Discuss ways in which the enactment of such rituals might support or detract from author Rothe-Kushel's thesis in this piece.

Writing Suggestion

The author of this essay acknowledges that he may be "stuck in an out-dated paradigm that does not take into account the plurality of roles a human can play?" (line 19). Using libraries and the Internet, write an essay that responds to the article from a feminine perspective. Be sure to address both the underlying themes of the movie as well as the text of the article itself. For example, examine carefully the author's contention that households across the country are dominated by women, and that young men are left without adequate models of masculinity. Do you agree that men need male role models or are women equally suited to raising sons who are comfortable and clear about their masculinity?

Tarantino and *The Passion*: A Controversy Casebook

Pulp Fiction

Alan A. Stone

Quentin Tarantino assembles films the way radical Bauhaus architects design homes: both toss aside the conventions of their peers to produce original—and sometimes highly controversial—approaches to their craft. This section of the Popular Film chapter explores the controversy surrounding Tarantino's moviemaking aesthetic. It also presents a second "controversies" section, this one focusing on strong opinions concerning a recent film, The Passion of the Christ*. In both cases, excessive filmic violence serves as a focal point for the authors' reactions and subsequent discussions.*

In the Tarantino section, critics focus on the movies Pulp Fiction *and* Kill Bill*, which—in the opinion of some commentators—put an emphasis not just on depicting the gore of violent acts, but also on suggesting the pervasiveness of violence in modern society. In the following article, originally published in the* Boston Review*, Alan Stone writes that Tarantino includes violence as an essential element of the visual experience in* Pulp Fiction*. Stone compares* Pulp Fiction *to Van Gogh's famous sunflowers painting: an artifact that, in its way, also challenged artistic expression in its time. Stone describes Tarantino's depiction of violence as "stylized" and the film as both a celebration and a satire of popular culture. Indeed, Stone notes, even the title is borrowed from popular culture, pulp fiction being a somewhat derisory description of cheap, monthly short story magazines produced in the thirties and later.*

The Boston Review *article also examines how Tarantino seeks to explore, exploit and expand on the ordinary, juxtaposing seemingly innocuous conversation in unconventional settings, or unexpected characters in conventional settings. His use of both dialog and dramatic situations are highly individualistic; one such example is his use of a British couple, complete with seemingly out-of-place accents, as armed robbers in Los Angeles. In another situation, he has two unsentimental killers talking about differences between American fast-food in Europe and how that compares to the home-grown version in the States.*

Is Tarantino merely out to shock audiences with his new approach to violence? Certainly, other filmmakers have used special effects to creating scenes of carnage caused by bullets, explosions, knives, death rays, chainsaws, samurai swords, piano wire, and bare human hands. But, says Stone, Tarantino is

mindful that some, especially European critics, have called violence in Ameri-
can films a form of pornography. Stone doubts that Tarantino seeks to cross the
threshold of good taste merely to exploit some of the public's taste for
unabashed violence. Instead he sees in Tarantino a filmmaker who deliberately
blurs the line between appeasing a societal depiction of violence and mocking it
at the same time. Furthermore, he finds in Pulp Fiction *no violence against*
women and no nudity. In the end, Stone suggests there is much more to value
in Pulp Fiction, *beneath the visual surface of blood and gore.*

   As you read, *notice how Stone mentions the murder of the young man*
in the second paragraph (line 2) and then returns to this scene in the film
towards the end of the article. Why do you think the author chooses to do this
rather than deal with that particular scene in successive paragraphs? What
effect do you think the author was seeking in emphasizing that particular
scene?

If you take no pleasure in popular culture, with all its manic excesses,   1
then you are likely to be bewildered, even offended, by Quentin
Tarantino's extraordinary film, *Pulp Fiction*. Tarantino unapologetically
enjoys popular culture at the same time that he satirizes it. Unfortunately, he also seems to specialize in violence. Still, taken on its own
terms, *Pulp Fiction* is a rare accomplishment; it opens a new aesthetic
horizon in film. Like Van Gogh's sunflowers, the ordinary suddenly
takes on a striking vibrancy; from the dazzling title colors on, it is easy
to recognize the artist, but almost impossible to imagine how one could
imitate him. Tarantino, a one-time video store clerk, now the hottest
director in Hollywood, has memory banks packed with movies and he
draws on some of the most ordinary to create something brilliantly
original. This is no experimental film of intellectual pretensions and
high-brow obscurantism. *Pulp Fiction* is already building a cult following, even as its mother-fucker language and graphic violence offends
others.

   Violence in film is a serious matter, and for some people an inex-   2
cusable offense. They can see no justification for the scene in which
John Travolta's character accidentally blows a young man's brains out.
Even worse for those concerned about film violence, most of the audience laughed despite the spatter of blood and brain tissue—and with
spontaneous amusement, not the nervous hysteria often heard at horror films. The violence of *Pulp Fiction* is essential to its aesthetic; though
he knew that many would complain, Tarantino meant the audience to
laugh.

   Deliberately violating the conventions of action-violence films,   3
Tarantino reimagines stylized moments of violence and exaggerates

them until they are almost surrealistic. Then he creates dialogue that leads up to the violence and then away from it. When most directors would be building tension and suspense, Tarantino has his killers chatting. When most directors would cut away from the violence, Tarantino stays with the aftermath. And he has achieved something I would have thought impossible; he has made violence humorous by doing it tongue-in-cheek—and the tongue has a stud in it.

Tarantino's film garnered top honors at the Cannes Film Festival   4
but will probably pay for its "punkness" at the Oscars. Its box office success, however, should comfort the many aspiring Hollywood directors who dream of doing something different. But they will not find it easy to follow in Tarantino's tracks. His film is put together with touch, spin, and nuance, and then goes off in your face like a letter bomb.

What Tarantino has crafted in this film can be best appreciated in   5
the performance he has extracted from John Travolta. In 1977, Travolta gave his unforgettable portrayal of the cock-of-the-walk dancer in *Saturday Night Fever*. Far from a natural dancer, he nonetheless gave a heart-winning performance. Ever since then, he has been fighting the battle of the bulge and trying with less and less success to prove that he can act. One might have concluded that he was too old, too fat, and too far over the hill for *Pulp Fiction*. But it turns out that he is brilliantly cast in the film; everything wrong about him is right for this part. In his early-forties he still has a teenager's winning vulnerability. His broad mouth and high cheek bones are now bejowled but there is still a promise of sensuality in that ruined face. His appealing and familiar presence brings just the feel of movie nostalgia Tarantino wanted.

Travolta plays a laid back, get-along kind of guy who is living a   6
depraved and drug-addicted life as a paid killer, but has an astonishingly innocent soul, as do most of Tarantino's low-life characters. This innocence in depravity is *Pulp Fiction*'s central theme. It keeps the film from being an exercise in sado-masochistic perversity; it is the source of its humor and its creative energy.

The film title *Pulp Fiction* harks back to the 30s and 40s when   7
newsstands featured an array of monthly short story magazines. Among the most popular were those about hard-nosed private investigators. Written by such authors as Dashiell Hammet, Raymond Chandler, and James M. Cain, these stories were the forerunners of dark, city crime movies that became *film noir*. Pulp fiction stories typically began in the front of the magazine, competing for the reader's attention, and were then continued in the back. Tarantino, though not old enough to remember this genre of pulp fiction, has put his film together as if he had that structure in mind.

We begin with one short story: a hopped-up British couple   8
(Amanda Plummer and Tim Roth) deciding to rob the coffee shop

where they are having breakfast. Before they do, we turn the page—a dark screen—to the next story of Travolta and Jackson going off to retrieve a mysterious briefcase and to kill some drug dealers who didn't pay off their boss. Then another dark screen—to the childhood of the Bruce Willis character who grows up to be the boxer who refuses to throw the fight. Unlike the old pulp fiction magazines, the triptych of stories eventually comes together as the seemingly disparate plots are interwoven by coincidence and by Tarantino's central theme. Because the film is set in Los Angeles, its anthology structure may of course owe much more to Robert Altman's *Shortcuts* or to his brilliant *Nashville* than to pulp fiction magazines.

But Tarantino's borrowings are no defect. He is winking at his 9 audience; he wants them to be aware of his references. The more they recognize the more they will enjoy the texture of his tapestry. It is because John Travolta carries so much baggage that he is so wonderful in this film. Moreover, everything Tarantino borrows is a cliché that has been given an original spin. *Pulp Fiction* takes the dead genre of *film noir* and gives it new life. Finally, Tarantino's startling humor takes his film beyond anything he has drawn from others.

Tarantino's interweaving of his three stories complicates the lin- 10 ear time structure of each plot. The most surprising result is that the Travolta character is killed only to reappear in the final scene of the movie, which took place earlier and is presented out of sequence. Once you figure out the puzzle, it becomes clear that Tarantino is playing with convention rather than rejecting or deconstructing it. Tarantino's entire film is playful, but he is playing with the imaginary world of film, not with reality itself.

There can be no doubt that the self-taught Tarantino intends to 11 shock his audience. The many scenes of graphic violence testify to that. European film-makers are concerned that violence in American film is pornography that appeals to the lowest common denominator and, like American fast food, is destroying the taste for better things. Some psychologists believe that film and TV violence teach America's young people to be violent, or at the very least, inure them to real-life violence. Perhaps most troubling is the idea that graphic violence, like pornography, exploits an appetite in our basest instincts that degrades rather than edifies. Many people are refusing to see this film and a surprising number of my middle-aged friends report that their teenage children love it but have warned them they will hate the film. These reactions to the violence are too important to be dismissed, but I do not believe that Tarantino has dismissed them. His film exploits violence but as the jury at Cannes recognized he is neither lacking in moral sensibility nor, even though he wallows in popular culture, is he a Philistine.

If violence is a form of pornography, then like pornography it   12
presents the same problem of line-drawing between exploiting our
passions and edifying them. But as our modern courts have recognized, it is necessary to go beyond that simple categorical distinction
and ask whether an admittedly exploitive work of art has redeeming
social value.

When Shakespeare wrote *Hamlet* and *King Lear*, he intended to   13
exploit his audiences' violent passions as well as to edify them. There
is, after all, a great deal of violence, even graphic violence, in *Lear*—
remember "out vile jelly" as Cornwall gouges out Gloucester's eyes on
stage. The greatest works of Western Civilization mock those who
count graphic violence as *ipso facto* unredeemable exploitation.

This is not to say that Tarantino intends to redeem the violence; if   14
anything, he seems to be mocking the arbiters of good taste with his
"wicked" humor. This is most blatant, not in the scenes of violence, but
in the quirky introduction to the Bruce Willis/boxer story. Christopher
Walken, an actor who will be remembered for his Oscar-winning
performance in *Deer Hunter* (a Vietnam war-film), makes a brief
appearance in *Pulp Fiction* as a former Vietnam POW. He has come to
deliver his dead cellmate's gold watch to the young boy who never
knew his father. The Walken character begins to tell the boy what happened to his father in standard heroic pulp fiction rhetoric, but then
veers perversely into a description of the intestinal orifice where the
father hid the watch, and the intestinal disorders that complicated its
concealment.

It is an account that no sane adult would give a child and a scene   15
right out of a graffiti imagination. Other directors are capable of imagining such graffiti, but Tarantino was brash enough to keep it in his
film. Like all toilet graffiti it can be understood as an example of adolescent bad taste and Tarantino knows that. It is "gross," it is inappropriate, it is irreverent, and one can understand why the younger generation would be warning off their fuddy-duddy parents. Yet even this
heavy-handed moment belongs in the film. The scene begins as a
patriotic-die-for-your-country cliché in which the reality of how the
gold watch survived would have been unimagined. Tarantino's script
takes up the challenge of an explanation and as he veers into scatology,
he gives the finger to the false norm of noble death in all such war
clichés. But Tarantino is interested less in making an anti-war gesture
than in doing a send-up of a movie cliché. Similarly, this is not an
anti-violence film. It is a send up of movie violence.

One astute teenage critic remarked that Tarantino learned some-   16
thing from his first film, *Reservoir Dogs*. All the guys in her high school
loved the macho violence but there was not much in this male-oriented
film for her and her female friends. Despite its violence and male

orientation, *Pulp Fiction* has something for the female gender, particularly the scenes between Travolta and Uma Thurman.

This teenage critic and her girl friends especially enjoyed the   17
episode in which the Travolta character is required to entertain the
black crime boss's white wife (Uma Thurman). The previous man
charged with this task had given her a foot massage; the boss took
umbrage and had the massager thrown out of a four-story window.
The Travolta–Thurman episode quickly turns into an over-the-top parody of a blind date. Travolta prepares himself by going to his drug
dealer for a batch of the ultimate hit—a mixture of cocaine and heroin
that only a seasoned addict could tolerate. Travolta mainlines the stuff
the way a nervous guy might take a drink to boost his confidence
before a date. Meanwhile, Uma Thurman is sniffing cocaine, not
because she's uneasy, but because she is a man-eater whetting her
appetite.

Thurman takes Travolta to a dance contest where they do the   18
twist, to the delight of Saturday Night Fever fans. Tarantino's elaborate
set features vintage 50s convertibles as booths, pop culture look-alikes
as servers, top-of-the-charts music, all of it so extravagant in its evocation of nostalgia as to be unreal. The scene is somehow true to the spirit
of *Pulp Fiction*, a film that parodies popular culture without ever condescending to those who take pleasure in it.

The Travolta/Thurman blind date has clever dialogue, the twist   19
is a trip, and the sexual tension escalates as they tango back into her
home at the end of the evening. But while Travolta is in the toilet (it
turns out he is always in the toilet at critical moments) Thurman finds
his drug stash, snorts it, and overdoses. Instead of a sexual conclusion,
the evening ends with a slapstick resuscitation involving a huge
syringe stuck in her sternum. In this funny and surreal scene it
becomes clear that Travolta and his low-life friends are playing overaged adolescents. Indeed the whole film has the spirit, energy, and sensibility of adolescence. No wonder teenagers love it.

Although Tarantino wants to shock us with violence, his film is   20
politically correct. There is no nudity and no violence directed against
women; in fact a man, the crime boss, gets raped and the only essentially evil people in the film are two sadistic honkies straight out of
Deliverance who do the raping. The film celebrates interracial friendship and cultural diversity; there are strong women and strong black
men, and the director swims against the current of class stereotype.

It is the British couple who, out of place in Los Angeles in the very   21
first scene, fill the sound track with British-accented "mother fuckers."
Amanda Plummer, who was born to play Ophelia, does a crazed "Honey
Bunny" to Tim Roth's "Pumpkin." They are two waifs holding hands in
the storm of their strung-outness on drugs and their hare-brained career

of sticking up liquor stores. The juxtaposition of their lost teddy bear attachment to each other with their nervous trigger-finger desperation establishes Tarantino's tone of innocence in depravity. Samuel Jackson, who will best be remembered as the drug-addicted older brother in Spike Lee's *Jungle Fever*, sustains that tone as Travolta's hit-man partner. His presence on the screen is a match for Travolta; he has a face that looks different in every camera angle and he radiates strength. These professional killers engage first in an earnest discussion about the European nomenclature of American fast foods and then a subtle analysis of the sexual significance of the foot massage as they make their way to the apartment where they will kill three men. The Jackson character miraculously eludes a point-blank fusillade of bullets. As they leave, they debate whether he was saved by divine intervention or simple luck. Jackson, who quotes from Ezekiel to spellbinding effect when he kills people, suddenly understands his Biblical text in a quite different way. As it turns out, his life and perhaps—if it is possible for a killer—his soul will be saved by this epiphany.

This theme of redemption is present in each of the three stories. [22] Willis as Butch the boxer rescues his would-be killer, the black crime boss, from the honkey rapists. Butch, who was to be their next victim, has the opportunity to escape, but goes back. Redeemed by this act of solidarity, he is forgiven by the crime boss for not throwing the fight and is sent on his way.

The British couple are also saved. They try to rob Jackson who has [23] ended up in the restaurant where the film began. He has drawn his gun under the table and could easily blow them both away. Instead, in the spirit of justice and honor that prevails among the low-lifes in this film, Jackson does the right thing. He stares the amateur criminals down, letting them take his own money but not the mysterious briefcase that he is dutifully returning to the crime boss. We believe that the strung-out British couple are capable of a killing rampage in the restaurant— Amanda Plummer is a remarkable sight standing on a restaurant table screaming obscenities and waving a Saturday-night special. We also know that the day before Jackson would have killed them without blinking an eye, and that he will have to kill them today if they try to take the boss's briefcase. Instead Jackson sends the couple peacefully out of the restaurant clutching each other and a trash bag filled with stolen money.

But the best scenes involve Jackson and Travolta. When they are [24] not killing, they are like college sophomores, one black, one white— both amateur philosophers eager to share their ideas and experiences. Tarantino's ingenious dialogue humanizes their homicidal partnership. The improbable juxtaposition of their earnest dialogue and the violence is the stylistic twist that allows us to laugh at the spatter of brains and blood in the backseat of their car. Travolta reacts like a teenager unjustly blamed by his buddy for accidentally spilling the beer. And like children of over-indulgent parents, they have no idea how to clean up the mess.

Yes, they seem oblivious to the fact that a person has been killed.   25
In that light their conversation is ludicrous. But this absurd dialogue unexpectedly transforms the meaning of the violence cliché. If Tarantino wanted to defend his film, this is where he could make his strongest arguments. *Pulp Fiction* unmasks the macho myth by making it laughable and deheroicizes the power trip glorified by standard Hollywood violence. But Tarantino is irreverent, not didactic. He goes from Road-Runner cartoon-violence humor in the Bruce Willis segment to whips and chain homosexual rape that silences the laughter. Tarantino will stop at nothing and yet never loses control. He dives into a nightmare and comes up with something funny, taking his audience up and down with him. Though Tarantino thinks his screenplay is funny, and would be disappointed if no one laughed, he doesn't consider *Pulp Fiction* a comedy. He is quite right; but if you don't get the studded tongue-in-cheek humor, you may not like this extraordinary movie.

Examining the Text

1. What do you think the author means when he writes (line 3), "Deliberately violating the conventions of action-violence films, Tarantino reimagines stylized moments of violence and exaggerates them until they are almost surrealistic?" Can you think of instances in which an action movie might have followed these so-called conventions, creating non-stylized depictions of violence? What distinguishes a "stylized" depiction of violence versus a mere straightforward depiction, and what might be the desired effect in creating stylized images of violence?

2. Based on your reading of this article, how do you think the author views Tarantino's use of violence in *Pulp Fiction*? Find sections of the article that support your interpretation of the author's position.

3. The author writes that Tarantino seeks to "shock his audience." By what specific means does the filmmaker achieve this end, in the opinion of Stone? Might Tarantino have other, non-shocking intentions in his depictions of violence? Finally, since film is a visual medium, do you think that violence has to be depicted with blood and gore, or are there other effective ways to portray it?

4. *Thinking rhetorically*: What is the author's thematic intention in the following sentence: "*Pulp Fiction* unmasks the macho myth by making it laughable and deheroicizes the power glorified by standard Hollywood violence." What textual evidence does the author provide to support the author's position of how Tarantino seeks to "deheroicize" *Pulp Fiction*?

Is this assertion logically consistent with the author's contention (in the last paragraph) that Tarantino "delves into a nightmare and comes up with something funny"? In your opinion, does the author succeed in this article's rhetorical purpose: namely to make a strong case that *Pulp Fiction* seeks to demythologize Hollywood violence by making audiences laugh?

For Group Discussion

Some research studies suggest a causal relationship between fictional violence depicted in films and actual violence in American streets and homes. In groups of four or five, discuss whether you think that violence in movies promotes real violence, or whether film violence might have a redeeming role as social commentary or as a healthy outlet for people's natural aggressive impulses. Select one member from your group to represent the "film violence is healthy" position, and one member to represent the anti-violence position. When you reassemble as a full class, have each of those group representatives engage in a debate, attempting to arrive at some consensus regarding the role of film violence in contemporary culture.

Writing Suggestion

Rent the movies *Pulp Fiction* and *A Clockwork Orange*: both films whose violence is not merely gratuitous but rather serves a larger thematic purpose as social commentary . . . at least in the eyes of many critics. Take notes on how violence is depicted in each film, and as you watch, comment also on how the violence affects you personally. Did you look away, especially at first? Did you become immune after a while? After viewing both films, write a comparison/contrast essay in which you examine the thematic role of violence in each film. To substantiate your points, include some research material: film criticism on Tarantino and Kubrick, and/or primary sources in which the filmmakers discuss their own approaches to filmmaking and attitudes toward violence in film.

She'll Kill Bill While You Chill

Thomas de Zengotita

His biographical details are the stuff of legend. Movie-obsessed kid gets job at video store frequented by movie-industry insiders. Kid impresses many with his savvy, energy, and wit. Kid writes script, which finds its way to the right people in Hollywood. Film script gets the nod. Kid (OK, now he's a young adult) makes movie in which he draws on his encyclopedic knowledge of the movies . . . and in many ways seeks to satirize the society in which Hollywood was created. The film is a huge success and vaults our former Kid to filmmaking mega-stardom. That kid, of course, is Quentin Tarantino. In the following article, author Thomas de Zengotita examines the young filmmaker's background, his approach to writing and directing, and his two recent films, Kill Bill *and* Kill Bill II.

De Zengotita states starkly that these two films don't contain any significant content but are, instead, more of a commentary (and a gory one at that) on American society and culture. He says Tarantino movies are full of allusions to society and, more especially, references to popular culture. Everything from pop music to TV to fast food to television sitcoms to street slang to earlier movies is blended in the filmic smoothie that has become Tarantino's hallmark. Through this process he seeks to entertain but at the same time to reach a deeper level, to make an offbeat, acerbic and wise commentary on contemporary American culture. **As you read**, *notice how the author seeks to qualify his own credentials for dissecting Tarantino's movies. What does he mean when he says, ". . . I am just a visiting participant-observer, not even close to being a native Tarantinian"? Watch out for other, similar references. What is the author's goal in using this distancing device? What's your reaction to this?*

> *"One of the most brilliant visual storytelling movies I've seen since the talkies. . . . It is pretty violent, I must say. At a certain point, it was like a Takashi Miike film. It got so fucked up it was funny. At one point, my friend and I, we just started laughing. I was into the seriousness of the story, of course, but in the crucifixion scene, when they turned the cross over, you had to laugh."*
> Quentin Tarantino on *The Passion of the Christ*

Someone should take charge of the word "sensationalism," refer it to an articulated system of beliefs and practices, and put it on the list that includes, say, "socialism" and "Islamic fundamentalism." The implicated ideas and activities are out there, just waiting be formalized. Millions of people dedicate their lives to media-induced sensations, to their pursuit and their creation. Why not make it official? 1

The sensationalist movement is vast and varied and getting more so with every innovation in representational technology. But movies are primal. And when it comes to creating sensations through cinematic depictions of violence, nobody can match Quentin Tarantino. That makes his work an ideal object of reflection for anyone concerned about the psychosocial effects of mediated violence—and I don't mean 2 its influence on sociopaths already on the verge of mayhem, but the much subtler question of what it says about our culture. It's easy to condemn graphic gore when it's schlocky, but what are we to make of depictions that are, on their own terms, masterworks?

"Their own terms" means movie terms. It means the history of   3
movies, all kinds of movies, but especially violent movies—a self-referential world of movies within which Tarantinians dwell.

The Tarantino origin myth (that's not too strong a description)   4
puts this tenth-grade dropout and pop culture addict behind the counter of Video Archives in Manhattan Beach, California, in the late eighties. There he held court for five years, dispensing freely of analysis and opinion to a widening circle of steady customers, some of them with Hollywood connections, many of them in thrall to his astonishing mastery of movie lore—an omnivorous authority that ranged indiscriminately across genres and periods, from early Hitchcock and fifties noir to the French avant-garde and obscure Hong Kong martial arts splatter flicks. Tarantino had seen it all, and remembered it all; that was the incredible thing—credits, music, dialogue, cinematography, editing, sets, plots—everything. And he wove it all into a single hyperenergetic discourse, a comparative tapestry that seemed to render, upon the screen of a single consciousness, the entirety of cinematic experience. No wonder Hollywood players whose acquaintance he made took him seriously when he asked them to consider his early screenplays. This was no schmuck with a script; this was a living library, a walking tribute to all they held dear.

Tarantino became a mythic entity, a cult figure, because he actual-   5
ized a transformation to which his followers aspire. In him, the Ultimate Fan became the Ultimate Auteur. Through *this* video store clerk, the slacker media geek was vindicated, his obsessions justified—his tastes, his slang, his values, his vast comic book collection, his online gaming, his fantasy quests—his whole investment in virtual living was redeemed.

And Tarantino understands this. He remains true to his origins.   6
He may now be acclaimed by the establishment, honored with the chair of the jury at Cannes, but he represents a virtual way of life that postmodern media have made possible in more marginal precincts—though no true Tarantinian would get caught talking seriously about anything as ponderous as postmodernism. Sensationalists are allergic to such abstractions. They are dogmatically anti-intellectual and apolitical. They draw that line around themselves in order to protect their way of life from the uncomprehending disdain they have come to expect from society's grown-ups. And Tarantino makes it easy to defend that line. The intricacy of his plots and the density of his allusions make for a genuine complexity in his work—if not what you

could call (perish the thought) depth. That complexity, so richly apparent to the cognoscenti, is more or less invisible otherwise, and so it sup-
plies sensationalists with a trump. When it comes to Tarantino, they
can truly say that their critics just don't get it.

The complexity of a Tarantino movie is all the more alluring   7
because it lurks beneath a fabulous surface, a sensual pleasure package
for the puzzles and the lore. The riveting cinematography, the blend of
editing and scoring, the pacing, the way the whole composition radiates hyper-real clarity, that distinctive look and feel we also find in
David Lynch movies. This hyper-realism alerts the knowing viewer to
a subversive intent that will lend heft to this feast of surfaces. It
addresses those with the keys to the kingdom, flattering them with a
wink and a nod that only they can detect. It invites them to pore indefinitely over intricacies of plot and timeline, to recline on a web of allusions so extended that even the most knowledgeable fans will never
know if they have reached its end.

And it allows for inexhaustible discussion on websites and blogs.   8

In Tarantino movies the postmodern aesthetic of pastiche, of mix-   9
ing and citing and recycling, reaches its logical limit. His movies are literally about movies (and TV shows and ads and pop music). And not
just indexically. Tarantino resurrects and manipulates tonalities and
styles; entire moods, entire genres are evoked, and the playing never
ends. The spaghetti western score accompanies a chicks-about-to-kick-
butt buildup to a frenetic ninja blowout scene, and there is David
Carradine (echoing his seventies kung fu TV show) as Bill, a villainous
inversion of the original character, but deploying the same affect, fla-
vored with (and undercut by) a hint of sadism that, in turn, contrasts
(in the first (John Ford inspired) scene of Volume II) so ludicrously with
(yet another Carradine echo) the oh-so-authentic flute he still carries.

Even I could go on listing allusions, and I am just a visiting   10
participant-observer, not even close to being a native Tarantinian.

Nor would I want to be. I have better things to do with my time.   11

But of that, more anon.   12

Back to the undercutting contrasts. They are importantly typical   13
of Tarantino's allusive style. He doesn't just cite, this isn't mere
homage; he plays havoc with citations. He can make them fit, even
when they don't—and that's his extraordinary gift, which also conveys
the essential message: *It's all in fun.*

Sensationalism is the ideology of fun in general, but this particu-   14
lar kind of fun is far from innocent. It is designed to put the Tarantinian
one up, always, and to expose those who recoil from the graphic violence as congenitally out of it. If Pai Mei (the martial arts SuperMaster
to whom Bill takes members of his Deadly Viper Assassination Squad
for training) turns out to be the very opposite of the serene sensei we

expect in this role, shouldn't that tell you something? If he turns out to be a spoiled prima donna, irascible, vain, and spiteful, the Tarantinian asks: Don't you see how funny that is? Deadly Viper Assassination Squad? Hello? Shouldn't that tell you something about the attitude here?

Then there are the plot twists and the temporality games. Chapter 1   15
of *Kill Bill I* is called "2," with a little handwritten circle around it. That refers to Uma's to do list, which names the four members of the Deadly Viper Assassination Squad she is out to slaughter—item number five being "Kill Bill," of course. As I recall (I may be wrong), you don't see that list actually being made out until the middle of Vol. II (a whole separate movie, released months later), and *that* movie begins with the massacre that precipitates the whole two-volume story, temporally speaking. I can't detect aesthetic motivation for this juggling. To me it seems designed to keep the web sites buzzing with Tarantinians puzzling out the timeline. But I may be missing something. I probably am.

But the plot twists have effects I can follow. Their shock value is   16
strangely akin to the shock value of the goriest images—like Uma crushing Daryl's fresh plucked eyeball between her bare toes (Uma's feet deserve separate billing in this movie) on the linoleum floor of Budd's trailer (he's dead in the kitchen area, surprised by a black mamba in a suitcase full of money) while Daryl (now minus both eyes, Pai Mei having deftly extracted the first one in a fit of pique during her training year with him, but that's OK because, after it was over, Daryl poisoned Pai Mei's rice bowl and watched him die) thrashes around in the bathroom screaming in agony, bleeding from the hole in her face, ripping down the shower curtain, tearing fixtures from the walls, and, in general, giving new meaning to the expression "blind fury" as the whole scene dissolves into another case of things getting so fucked up that, as a Tarantinian, you just have to laugh—as (refer back to the dash at the top of this paragraph) when Uma finally makes it (at the end of Volume II) to Bill's luxurious Caribbean hideaway and does one of those stealth entry sequences, her priceless Hattori Hanzo sword slung across her back in that cool ninja way, her silver nine millimeter held out from her body in the official two-handed grip, and she pivoting to cover every angle as she springs into one room after the other (having crept suspensefully up to each), intent as a leopard (or a viper) on one thing only (killing Bill, remember?) and then, as she rounds the last doorframe, what does she find but her four-year-old daughter, whom she has never seen because she was born after Uma went into a coma when Bill shot her in the head (and she in a bridal gown, eight months pregnant) at her wedding (rehearsal), where he and the rest of the Deadly Viper Assassination Squad slaughtered the entire wedding

party (Samuel Jackson barely recognizable in a cameo as the piano player) because Uma (code name: Black Mamba) had not only abandoned the Assassination Squad lifestyle, but had abandoned Bill, the father of the very same child, which pissed Bill off big time, but didn't stop him from taking their daughter into his keeping and, lo and behold, there he is now, playing with her, as Uma springs into that last room, and not just playing any old game, by golly, but playing a bang-bang game with a toy plastic space gun (no doubt a very specific one, recognizable to multitudes of Tarantinians), and Bill, all mock innocence, urging Uma, who is beginning to weep at the sight of her child, to join the game, and getting the little girl to bang-bang Uma, then cajoling Uma into doing one of those grip-your-stomach-and-groan-and-pretend-to-die things, because that's what the game requires, and Uma, her deadly purpose melted away (but only temporarily), complies, and after that Uma and Bill put their little girl to bed—and the upshot is: now, *that's* a plot twist.

If you followed all this, you have a sense of how recursively 17 embedded, how freewheeling and precise, a Tarantino movie is. Sort of like Proust—except for one thing.

There is no significant content of any kind. 18

And the question arises: What kind of culture invests so much in 19 something so hollow, hollow by design, hollow as a matter of principle?

A sensationalist culture devoted to fun. 20

But such a culture inevitably runs up against certain limits. There 21 are only so many ways you can produce these shocks and thrills. Tarantino is Tarantino because he found a whole new level of possibility, thanks to his reflexivity. Naïve viewers focus on the gore, but the initiated are accustomed to gore. For them, the violence and the plot twists aren't that different. Both are designed to elicit that I-can't-believe-I'm-seeing-*this* reaction, which is what you get when a how-can-he-top-*that* moment is successfully resolved.

Topping that is what Tarantino does. 22

Finally, there's the dialogue. Actor talk in movie promos is even 23 more hackneyed and formulaic than other forms of puffery, but when actors talk about being in a Tarantino movie, there is a tone of genuine admiration, mixed with bemusement, perhaps, but tinged with awe as well. They know these are not just movies starring them, but movies *about* them, about the world of their concerns, and they feel that world being transformed by this alchemist into something weighty and thick, something that achieves the standing of art without ever leaving the realm of the popular. For these actors, working with Tarantino isn't like starring in a revival of some classic play—that involves the implicit admission that what you normally do is less worthy. No, working with Tarantino means elevating what you normally do. The Ultimate Fan as

Ultimate Auteur serves his actors in the same way he serves his followers. He turns total immersion in movies into a kind of wisdom.

But the actors don't seem conscious of this in so many words.   24
What they dwell on is Tarantino's dialogue, which provides the ultimate in comic contrast, a relentlessly prosaic and naturalistic verbal counterpoint to his cinematic virtuosity. Actors love the dialogue, not only for that contrast but also because it reflects their training—years of method acting, years of improvs. Most representative and most renowned is the discussion in *Pulp Fiction* between John Travolta and Samuel Jackson about how Quarter Pounders have to be called Le Royale in France because of the metric system. The kicker is that they are hit men on their way to massacre a room full of college kids while they are having this conversation. They even pause in the hall to clarify some point about fast food before busting down the door and blazing away.

How do you top *that?*   25

It was typical of Tarantino to praise Gibson's bloody movie while   26
sophisticated people everywhere were condemning it. But it was even more typical of him to find comedy in what the simple minded Gibson meant to be transcendentally serious. The image of Tarantino and his friend chortling in their seats at the crucifixion is irresistible because it distills the issue to its essence. When I first read that description, I was reminded of Abu Ghraib guards, laughing as they tormented their prisoners, and I wondered, for a moment, what's the difference? But no sooner was the question framed than the Tarantinian reply came to me. I could imagine Quentin's face and voice:

The Passion of the Christ is a *movie*, you idiot!

                                                                       27
Ah, well, yes, of course.   28
The Tarantinian is always a step ahead, the Tarantinian is never taken in, the Tarantinian can experience sadomasochistic sensations as intense and various as the master's prodigious talent can contrive—and find forgiveness in the last laugh as well.
                                                                       29
The Tarantinian way guarantees immunity for the perpetually entertained.

Examining the Text
1. The author comments that any deeper meanings to be found in Tarantino movies "lurk beneath a fabulous surface, a sensual pleasure package . . ." What does the author mean by this assertion, and do you agree with it or not?

2. What is meant by the statement: "In Tarantino movies the postmodern aesthetic of pastiche, of mixing and citing and recycling, reaches its logical limit"? Can you find examples in the text where the author cites particular scenes to which his statement would seem to apply? Given the desire of a filmmaker like Tarantino to push boundaries, can there really be a logical limit? Are there limits to what the public will find acceptable in a Hollywood movie?

3. Why do you think actors seem to see participation in a Tarantino film as elevating their craft? Is this a comment on "mainstream" Hollywood films, or the quality of Tarantino's films, or both? Why would actors be "bemused" by working on a Tarantino film?

4. *Thinking rhetorically*: What do you think the author means by "sensationalism" or "sensationalist" in the context of this article's arguments? What is the author's rhetorical intention—in this case, his intended persuasive purpose—in proposing that "sensationalism" belongs in the same category as "socialism" or "Islamic fundamentalism"? Do you feel that his strategy is effective here, or that he's taking a position that's too extreme to be plausible?

For Group Discussion

Consider again the sentiment, ". . . I am just a visiting participant-observer, not even close to being a native Tarantinian." Discuss the qualities that potentially give a person the authority or entitlement to write a film criticism article, or to do any form of art criticism. Must you be a graduate of a university? Should you have a certain amount of experience viewing films, discussing films, reading other people's critiques? Reflecting on various art and film criticism that you've encountered, discuss what has been valuable to you, what hasn't been valuable . . . and what has been downright annoying.

Writing Suggestion

View either or both of the *Kill Bill* films and take notes, then write your own critique of the film(s). In writing critique, keep in mind that film critics routinely refer to other reviewers' articles on the same films (for example, the two Tarantino articles in this reader), and that they draw on any additional knowledge they might have about the writer/director, such as biographical information. Furthermore, since a critique is a personal assessment of a film, feel free to take a very opinionated tone in your own piece. However, if you take this tack, make sure that you support your strong opinions with evidence from research and from the film's text itself.

Nailed

David Denby

Sometimes the most unlikely people, events, and creations become popular in American culture. Usually the surprise is in how something so goofy, silly, or frivolous can appeal to many people: "pet rocks" in the 1970s, Cabbage Patch dolls in the 1980s, the Spice Girls in the 1990s, Beanie Babies at the turn of the millennium. For very different reasons, The Passion of the Christ *is a surprising part of the popular culture of the current decade. This is a movie in which the dialogue is entirely in Aramaic and Latin, a staggeringly violent movie about the Biblical story of Christ's crucifixion. Who would imagine that such a movie would play in mainstream theaters for millions of viewers and would generate a great amount of discussion and debate in the popular media? Equally surprising is that this is a movie directed and financed ($25 million, almost all of it recouped on the first day of the movie's release) by Mel Gibson, an actor who gained stardom as "Mad Max," a post-apocalyptic vigilante.*

The Passion of the Christ *provoked a great deal of controversy when it was released, much of it having to do with the film's extremely graphic and detailed depiction of Jesus' suffering during the final twelve hours of his life. The two articles in this subsection present contrasting views on the violence in the film. We begin with David Denby's review of the movie that appeared in* The New Yorker *magazine. Denby, a longtime* New Yorker *movie critic and the author of two film criticism books, gives Gibson's movie a complete "thumbs-down," describing it as "one of the cruelest movies in the history of the cinema."* **As you read***, pay attention to the evidence Denby provides to support his opinion about the movie; note the points in his argument that you find most persuasive and those that you find relatively weak.*

In "The Passion of the Christ," Mel Gibson shows little interest in cele-   1
brating the electric charge of hope and redemption that Jesus Christ brought into the world. He largely ignores Jesus' heart-stopping elo-quence, his startling ethical radicalism and personal radiance—Christ as a "paragon of vitality and poetic assertion," as John Updike described Jesus' character in his essay "The Gospel According to Saint Matthew." Cecil B. De Mille had his version of Jesus' life, Pier Paolo Pasolini and Martin Scorsese had theirs, and Gibson, of course, is free to skip over the incomparable glories of Jesus' temperament and to devote himself, as he does, to Jesus' pain and martyrdom in the last twelve hours of his life. As a viewer, I am equally free to say that the movie Gibson has made from his personal obsessions is a sickening

death trip, a grimly unilluminating procession of treachery, beatings,
blood, and agony—and to say so without indulging in "anti-Christian
sentiment" (Gibson's term for what his critics are spreading). For two
hours, with only an occasional pause or gentle flashback, we watch,
stupefied, as a handsome, strapping, at times half-naked young man
(James Caviezel) is slowly tortured to death. Gibson is so thoroughly
fixated on the scourging and crushing of Christ, and so meagrely
involved in the spiritual meanings of the final hours, that he falls in
danger of altering Jesus' message of love into one of hate.

And against whom will the audience direct its hate? As Gibson   2
was completing the film, some historians, theologians, and clergymen
accused him of emphasizing the discredited charge that it was the
ancient Jews who were primarily responsible for killing Jesus, a claim
that has served as the traditional justification for the persecution of the
Jews in Europe for nearly two millennia. The critics turn out to have
been right. Gibson is guilty of some serious mischief in his handling of
these issues. But he may have also committed an aggression against
Christian believers. The movie has been hailed as a religious experience by various Catholic and Protestant groups, some of whom, with
an ungodly eye to the commercial realities of film distribution, have
prepurchased blocks of tickets or rented theatres to insure "The Passion" a healthy opening weekend's business. But how, I wonder, will
people become better Christians if they are filled with the guilt,
anguish, or loathing that this movie may create in their souls?

"The Passion" opens at night in the Garden of Gethsemane—a   3
hushed, misty grotto bathed in a purplish disco light. Softly chanting
female voices float on the soundtrack, accompanied by electronic
shrieks and thuds. At first, the movie looks like a graveyard horror
flick, and then, as Jewish temple guards show up bearing torches, like a
faintly tedious art film. The Jews speak in Aramaic, and the Romans
speak in Latin; the movie is subtitled in English. Gibson distances the
dialogue from us, as if Jesus' famous words were only incidental and
the visual spectacle—Gibson's work as a director—were the real point.
Then the beatings begin: Jesus is punched and slapped, struck with
chains, trussed, and dangled over a wall. In the middle of the night, a
hasty trial gets under way before Caiaphas (Mattia Sbragia) and other
Jewish priests. Caiaphas, a cynical, devious, petty dictator, interrogates
Jesus, and then turns him over to the Roman prefect Pontius Pilate
(Hristo Naumov Shopov), who tries again and again to spare Jesus
from the crucifixion that the priests demand. From the movie, we get
the impression that the priests are either merely envious of Jesus'
spiritual power or inherently and inexplicably vicious. And Pilate is
not the bloody governor of history (even Tiberius paused at his crimes
against the Jews) but a civilized and humane leader tormented by the

burdens of power—he holds a soulful discussion with his wife on the nature of truth.

Gibson and his screenwriter, Benedict Fitzgerald, selected and   4
enhanced incidents from the four Gospels and collated them into a single, surpassingly violent narrative—the scourging, for instance, which is mentioned only in a few phrases in Matthew, Mark, and John, is drawn out to the point of excruciation and beyond. History is also treated selectively. The writer Jon Meacham, in a patient and thorough article in *Newsweek*, has detailed the many small ways that Gibson disregarded what historians know of the period, with the effect of assigning greater responsibility to the Jews, and less to the Romans, for Jesus' death. Meacham's central thesis, which is shared by others, is that the priests may have been willing to sacrifice Jesus—whose mass following may have posed a threat to Roman governance—in order to deter Pilate from crushing the Jewish community altogether. It's also possible that the temple élite may have wanted to get rid of the leader of a new sect, but only Pilate had the authority to order a crucifixion—a very public event that was designed to be a warning to potential rebels. Gibson ignores most of the dismaying political context, as well as the likelihood that the Gospel writers, still under Roman rule, had very practical reasons to downplay the Romans' role in the Crucifixion.

It's true that when the Roman soldiers, their faces twisted in glee, go to work on Jesus, they seem even more depraved than the Jews. But, as Gibson knows, history rescued the pagans from eternal blame— eventually, they came to their senses and saw the light. The Emperor Constantine converted in the early fourth century, and Christianized the empire, and the medieval period saw the rise of the Roman Catholic Church. So the Romans' descendants triumphed, while the Jews were cast into darkness and, one might conclude from this movie, deserved what they got. "The Passion," in its confused way, confirms the old justifications for persecuting the Jews, and one somehow doubts that Gibson will make a sequel in which he reminds the audience that in later centuries the Church itself used torture and execution to punish not only Jews but heretics, non-believers, and dissidents.

I realize that the mere mention of historical research could exacer-   5
bate the awkward breach between medieval and modern minds, between literalist belief and the weighing of empirical evidence. "John was an eyewitness," Gibson has said. "Matthew was there." Well, they may have been there, but for decades it's been a commonplace of Biblical scholarship that the Gospels were written forty to seventy years after the death of Jesus, and not by the disciples but by nameless Christians using both written and oral sources. Gibson can brush aside the work of scholars and historians because he has a powerful weapon at hand—the cinema—with which he can create something greater than argument; he can create faith. As a moviemaker, Gibson is not without skill. The sets, which were built in Italy, where the movie was filmed, are far from perfect, but they convey the beauty of Jerusalem's courtyards and archways. Gibson, working with the cinematographer Caleb Deschanel, gives us the ravaged stone face of Calvary, the gray light at the time of the Crucifixion, the leaden pace of the movie's spectacular agonies. Felliniesque tormenters gambol and jeer on the sidelines, and, at times, the whirl of figures around Jesus, both hostile and friendly, seems held in place by a kind of magnetic force. The hounding and suicide of the betrayer Judas is accomplished in a few brusque strokes. Here and there, the movie has a dismal, heavy-souled power.

By contrast with the dispatching of Judas, the lashing and flaying   6
of Jesus goes on forever, prolonged by Gibson's punishing use of slow motion, sometimes with Jesus' face in the foreground, so that we can see him writhe and howl. In the climb up to Calvary, Caviezel, one eye swollen shut, his mouth open in agony, collapses repeatedly in slow motion under the weight of the Cross. Then comes the Crucifixion itself, dramatized with a curious fixation on the technical details—an arm pulled out of its socket, huge nails hammered into hands, with Caviezel jumping after each whack. At that point, I said to myself, "Mel Gibson has lost it," and I was reminded of what other writers have

pointed out—that Gibson, as an actor, has been beaten, mashed, and disembowelled in many of his movies. His obsession with pain, disguised by religious feelings, has now reached a frightening apotheosis.

Mel Gibson is an extremely conservative Catholic who rejects the   7
reforms of the Second Vatican council. He's against complacent, feel-good Christianity, and, judging from his movie, he must despise the grandiose old Hollywood kitsch of "The Robe," "The King of Kings," "The Greatest Story Ever Told," and "Ben-Hur," with their Hallmark twinkling skies, their big stars treading across sacred California sands, and their lamblike Jesus, whose simple presence overwhelms Charlton Heston. But saying that Gibson is sincere doesn't mean he isn't foolish, or worse. He can rightly claim that there's a strain of morbidity running through Christian iconography—one thinks of the reliquaries in Roman churches and the bloody and ravaged Christ in Northern Renaissance and German art, culminating in such works as Matthias Grünewald's 1515 "Isenheim Altarpiece," with its thorned Christ in full torment on the Cross. But the central tradition of Italian Renaissance painting left Christ relatively unscathed; the artists emphasized not the physical suffering of the man but the sacrificial nature of his death and the astonishing mystery of his transformation into godhood—the Resurrection and the triumph over carnality. Gibson instructed Deschanel to make the movie look like the paintings of Caravaggio, but in Caravaggio's own "Flagellation of Christ" the body of Jesus is only slightly marked. Even Goya, who hardly shrank from dismemberment and pain in his work, created a "Crucifixion" with a nearly unblemished Jesus. Crucifixion, as the Romans used it, was meant to make a spectacle out of degradation and suffering—to humiliate the victim through the apparatus of torture. By embracing the Roman pageant so openly, using all the emotional resources of cinema, Gibson has cancelled out the redemptive and transfiguring power of art. And by casting James Caviezel, an actor without charisma here, and then feasting on his physical destruction, he has turned Jesus back into a mere body. The depictions in "The Passion," one of the cruellest movies in the history of the cinema, are akin to the bloody Pop representation of Jesus found in, say, a roadside shrine in Mexico, where the addition of an Aztec sacrificial flourish makes the passion a little more passionate. Such are the traps of literal-mindedness. The great modernist artists, aware of the danger of kitsch and the fascination of sado-masochism, have largely withdrawn into austerity and awed abstraction or into fervent humanism, as in Scorsese's "The Last Temptation of Christ" (1988), which features an existential Jesus sorely tried by the difficulty of the task before him. There are many ways of putting Jesus at risk and making us feel his suffering.

What is most depressing about "The Passion" is the thought that   8
people will take their children to see it. Jesus said, "Suffer the little children to come unto me," not "Let the little children watch me suffer."
How will parents deal with the pain, terror, and anger that children
will doubtless feel as they watch a man flayed and pierced until dead?
The despair of the movie is hard to shrug off, and Gibson's timing
couldn't be more unfortunate: another dose of death-haunted religious
fanaticism is the last thing we need.

Examining the Text

1. Why do you think Denby begins by focusing on what he thinks is *left
out* of Gibson's movie: "the electric charge of hope and redemption that
Jesus Christ brought into the world"; "Jesus' heart-stopping eloquence,
his startling ethical radicalism and personal radiance"? What effect do
these phrases have on you as a reader? How do they position Denby as
a reviewer?

2. According to Denby, what effect does Gibson's use of Aramaic and
Latin have on viewers? Do you agree with his central thematic position
on this point?

3. What connections does Denby suggest between Mel Gibson's acting
career and the movie? What connections does he suggest between
Gibson's personal religious beliefs and the movie? In your opinion, are
these connections valid, based on your knowledge of the actor and his
film roles, and your understanding of *The Passion of the Christ*?

4. *Thinking rhetorically*: Reread the final paragraph of the article. What
strategies is Denby using here to bring his review to a powerful close?
What do you see as the strengths and/or weaknesses of this paragraph
as a conclusion for the review?

For Group Discussion

As you read in the introduction, this article first appeared as a movie
review in *The New Yorker* magazine, right around the time that *The Passion of the Christ* was coming out in theaters. In a small group, discuss
what goals you think Denby had for this review. Do you think his
intention was to discourage people from seeing the movie? Or was he
more concerned with shaping the opinions of people who had already
seen the movie? In general, what do you think are the key functions
and purposes of movie reviews as a genre? Discuss with the others in
your group how each of you uses movie reviews—if you use them at
all—to shape your movie viewing choices.

Writing Suggestion
In paragraphs 2 and 5, Denby introduces the ideas of historians and Biblical scholars in the debate over who was responsible for Jesus' death. Why do you think Denby does this, and what function does it serve in his movie review to compare Gibson's movie to the work of historians and scholars? Do some additional library and internet research into this question, and then write an essay that either supports or disproves Denby's evidence-driven assertions, based on the additional facts that you uncovered.

Gibson's Sublime Passion: In Defense of the Violence

William Irwin

The article that follows takes a very different stand than Denby's review does on the violence in The Passion of The Christ. *As you can see from the subtitle of this article, William Irwin offers a kind of apology for the violence in Gibson's film, countering Denby's claims that* The Passion *is "one of the cruelest movies in the history of the cinema." Indeed, Irwin argues that although the movie is difficult to watch and is neither "beautiful" nor "tragic," the violence in it is justified because it is a necessary part of Gibson's attempt to give viewers of his movie an experience of the sublime.*

The thesis of this article rests on understanding comprehensively the concept of "the sublime." Irwin defines this term in the article, along with several other key philosophical terms such as beauty and tragedy. In his explanations, he draws on quotations from philosophers such as Aristotle and Kant, illustrating their ideas with examples drawn from popular contemporary movies. Although Irwin focuses on The Passion of the Christ, *his ideas about violence and his philosophical approach to movies is more broadly applicable; for instance, he briefly comments on the violence in Tarantino's films drawing some interesting contrasts to points made in earlier articles in this chapter.*

Irwin has a great deal of experience making connections between popular culture and philosophy. He is an Associate Professor of Philosophy at King's College, Pennsylvania and the Editor of Seinfeld and Philosophy *(2000),* The Simpsons and Philosophy *(2001),* The Matrix and Philosophy *(2002), and* More Matrix and Philosophy *(2005). Clearly, Irwin would argue that philosophy can be used to help us understand popular culture, especially film and TV.* **As you read**, *then, consider the strategies that Irwin uses to make fairly daunting philosophical concepts easier for the reader to understand. In particular, note the sometimes informal and conversational style of*

Irwin's writing. Try to pay attention to the way that Irwin writes and whether his style helps you get a better understanding of the content of his argument.

———————

The Passion has spurred much controversy and debate, but nearly all   1
people agree that the film is difficult to watch. The violence, the blood,
the gore for some people make it too painful to watch.

So why do we willingly watch works of art that bring pain with   2
pleasure? Aesthetics, the branch of philosophy concerned with the
study of art, helps us answer this question, which has concerned
philosophers since Aristotle (384–322 B.C.). To address this question
and justify Gibson's depiction of violence let's consider *The Passion* in
terms of three important categories: beauty, tragedy, and the sublime.

THE BEAUTIFUL AND THE MORAL

Whatever beauty is, no one could rightfully call Mel Gibson's   3
The Passion of the Christ beautiful. Nor could anyone deny that
Michelangelo's Vatican *Pietà* is beautiful. Admittedly, the subject mat-
ters of the sculpture and film are different, but there is a *Pietà* allusion in
The Passion, as we see the bloody Jesus in the arms of a weary Mary at
the foot of the cross.

Immanuel Kant (1724–1804) aside, most philosophers recognize   4
that beauty is contextual, that knowing about the artwork and its subject matter bears on how we evaluate it. Michelangelo's *Pietà* is sad,
delicate, and displays a cherry-blossom beauty, but it does not inspire
thought and moral reflection. In fact the beauty of the *Pietà* distracts us
from its subject matter. We do not feel moved to reflection on the suffering of Jesus and Mary. Rather we behold a sight unlike anything we
have seen before, and we marvel at the artistic accomplishment.

When the beautiful connects us to the moral it tends to do so   5
mistakenly, getting it wrong or getting it right only by accident. Still a
common and psychologically persuasive notion, the ancient Greek
kalos-kagathon, the beautiful good, implies that the beautiful is morally
good and the morally good is beautiful. But experience tells us that the
beautiful is generally appreciated for itself, and when it begins to steer
us towards moral judgment we need to be careful. As a beautiful face
can distract us from a person's moral substance or lack thereof, so can a
beautiful artwork. Knowing the subject of the artwork may heighten
our appreciation for the artwork's beauty, but its beauty is unlikely to
heighten our appreciation for its subject. Viewing the *Pietà* we are far
less inspired to devotion than we are awed at the artistic achievement.

In fact, the beauty of Michelangelo's *Pietà* is inappropriate for the   6
sad scene it depicts. Better would have been to free a Madonna and
child from the rock prison, using the same technique on the same piece
of marble. But Michelangelo had his commission, had his subject matter, and had his marching orders from a paying patron. By contrast,
Gibson had his own vision and put his own money behind *The Passion*.
This is not to say he created a greater work of art than did Michelangelo,
but that he was financially free to match subject and expression more
appropriately.

THE CHOICE OF VIOLENCE

Could *The Passion* have been beautiful? Quentin Tarantino has been   7
wrongly acclaimed for the "exquisite and elegant violence" in films
such as *Kill Bill* and *Pulp Fiction*. While the choreographed, sword-
wielding violence of *Kill Bill* is spectacular, it is not beautiful and it conveys no moral truth. The crass violence of *Pulp Fiction* conveys moral
truth, that redemption is possible, but lacks beauty. Gibson's choice to
show the violence to tell the story of the passion precludes it being
beautiful, especially if it is to succeed in directing us to moral truth.
Contra Keats, truth is not beauty, nor beauty truth. *Quid est veritas?* It
sometimes ain't pretty.

"It's too violent, too much blood and gore. I couldn't stand to   8
watch it." So goes one common complaint about Gibson's *Passion*. For
many Christians, *The Passion* fails to highlight the parts of Jesus' min-
istry that they believe are most important, his message of love and
peace. The film could have been different. The violence and suffering
was a choice of emphasis, not a necessity.

But Gibson did not choose to tell the story of Jesus' entire min-   9
istry with special emphasis on his passion. He chose to tell the story of
the passion. So how *should* he have told that story? It is, after all, a
"cruci-fiction." Aware that "cross" and "crucifixion" connote torture in
Latin, what should we expect? Torture at the hands of Roman soldiers
was far worse than what counts as torture at the hands of wayward
American soldiers. So *ecce homo*, behold the man, through the sheer
horror of his flogging, scourged as he is, bathed in a bouquet of blood,
crowned with thorns, and made to carry his cross to the place of execution. This is the "bloody Christ" of *The Passion*, not the "buddy Christ"
of *Dogma*.

Some complain and conjecture that the actual scourging and flog-   10
ging could not have been as severe as Gibson portrays them. Perhaps.
But Scripture says that Simon carried the cross, so we can safely
assume the scourging was sufficient to leave Jesus unable to carry it.

And undoubtedly the inner agony and humiliation of the actual crucifixion were far worse than anything that film images can convey. In any
case, to witness in person the bloody scourging would have been far
worse than merely watching it on screen, even if the screen version
surpassed the reality.

    A director's choices of emphasis and perspective inevitably dis-   11
please some. You can't make everybody happy and you shouldn't even
try. For example, Holocaust films no matter how finely done find critics. Steven Spielberg's *Schindler's List* portrays the utter inhumanity of
the concentration camps, but some complain it makes a hero of Oscar
Schindler. Perhaps he was a hero, but does his heroism deserve such
attention? Shouldn't Spielberg have focused attention elsewhere?
Roberto Benigni's *Life Is Beautiful* is a story of boundless hope, a triumph of the spirit, a testament to resilience, but it was criticized as
"Holocaust lite." Yes, Benigni and Spielberg could have made different
choices, could have made different films. But the films they made are
gifts to be appreciated for what they are, not to be rejected for what
they could have been.

    Viewers who reject *The Passion* for Gibson's choice of emphasis   12
include in large numbers those who imagine Jesus as much like Barney
the Dinosaur singing, "I love you/you love me/let's be friends/in
Galilee." They choose to focus on the message of love, passing the passion, going directly to the resurrection. Of course this is not a fair
description of *all* people who reject *The Passion*, and that *is* one way to
tell the story. But it is not the way Gibson chose. If Jesus did not suffer
for our sins and rise from the dead, then he was simply a philosopher.
But Christianity holds that he was much more.

    Gibson's choice to graphically portray the violence of *The Passion*   13
makes the film difficult to watch, and this is just the point.

WHAT? A TRAGEDY?

Plato (428–348 B.C.) spoke against Greek tragedies and Homeric epics,   14
finding they gave false depictions of the gods and aroused fear and
pity, emotions one should avoid. Plato was right: violence can inflame
"the passions." As a boy, I came out of *Rocky III* throwing punches
in the air, looking to take on all comers in the parking lot. As a man,
I came out of *Troy* feeling like Achilles, wanting to slay my enemies.
Curiously, though, the violence of *The Passion* has no effect of that kind.
It is not the "guns, lots of guns" and Kung Fu fighting of *The Matrix*. It
does not incite one to violence. If anything, it leaves one numb. Plato
was quick to banish the tragic poets from his ideal Republic. We should
not be so quick to pan *The Passion*.

As Aristotle asked of the Greek tragedies of his day, so we may   15
ask of *The Passion*: why would anyone want to watch such suffering
anyway? Aristotle agreed with Plato that these works of art aroused
fear and pity, but unlike Plato, Aristotle found this beneficial. Watching
the tragedies produces a *catharsis*, a cleansing of these feelings and
emotions. In fact, this cathartic effect is part of Aristotle's classic definition of tragedy.

> Tragedy, then, is a representation of an action which is serious, complete,
> and of a certain magnitude—in language which is garnished in various
> forms in its different parts in the mode of dramatic enactment, not narra-
> tive—and through the arousal of pity and fear effecting the *katharsis* of
> such emotions (1449b 24–29).

So is *The Passion* a tragedy? Not in any sense that Aristotle would   16
recognize, not in the way *Antigone* and *Oedipus Rex* are tragedies, not in
the way *Hamlet* and *King Lear* are tragedies, not at all. Consider more of
what Aristotle has to say. On the proper subject matter for tragedy, he
says "the poet's task is to speak not of events which have occurred, but
of the kind of events which *could* occur, and are possible by the standards of probability or necessity" (1451a 38–40). *The Passion* purports to
tell the story of events that no matter how wildly improbable *did* occur.
Aristotle argues that certain plot types are inappropriate for tragedy.
Most importantly for our purposes, "good men should not be shown
passing from prosperity to affliction, for this is neither fearful nor piti-
ful but repulsive" (1452b 34–35). And "repulsive" is precisely how
some viewers find *The Passion*. Certainly it is not cleansing, cathartic.
Describing the proper type of main character for tragedy Aristotle says,
"such a man is one who is not preeminent in virtue and justice, and one
who falls into affliction not because of evil and wickedness, but
because of a certain fallibility (*hamartia*)" (1453a 7–9). Tragedies end in
death due to the fallibility of the main character. Certainly a flawless
Christ cannot take such a fall.

SUBLIMITY IN THE DIVINE

So if we don't benefit from a tragic catharsis, why do we watch   17
The Passion? Why do some of us actually enjoy it? Simply watching it is
easy enough to explain. The film is a pop cultural phenomenon, a
"must see." Explaining why some of us actually enjoyed the film is
tougher. Perhaps the experience is sublime? But what is "the sublime"?
Peter Schjedahl claims that the sublime is a "hopelessly jumbled

philosophical notion that has had more than two centuries to start meaning something cogent and hasn't succeeded yet" (in Danto 2003, p. 148). Although he overstates the case, Schjedahl appropriately highlights the confusion and chaos surrounding the idea of the sublime. Nonetheless I'd like to suggest that we can use the sublime and *The Passion* to make sense of one another.

In discussing the sublime Edmund Burke (1729–1797) points us to accounts of divine encounter in Scripture.   18

> But the scripture alone can supply ideas answerable to the majesty of this subject. In the scripture, wherever God is represented as appearing or speaking, everything terrible in nature is called up to heighten the awe and solemnity of the divine presence. The psalms, and the prophetical books, are crowded with instances of this kind. *The earth shook,* (says the psalmist), *the heavens also dropped at the presence of the Lord* (112).

The sublime, like God, is fearful, but we are not afraid of it. So what is the sublime? While early modern views on the sublime associated it with awe-inspiring, terrifying natural objects such as jagged cliffs shrouded in mist, more recent views have applied the sublime to art, helping to answer Aristotle's perennial question: why would we voluntarily look at art that produces unpleasant emotions? Well, why would an eighty-year old man jump out of an airplane? Why would a fourteen-year old girl ride the roller coaster repeatedly? Because a thrill, a heightened sense of life, is concomitant with the fear.   19

Musing on movies, and revising the theories of Kant and Burke, Cynthia Freeland finds four features in the sublime. First, it involves conflict between feelings of pain and pleasure, what Burke called "rapturous terror." Second, something about the sublime object is "great" and astonishing, what Longinus (c. 213–272 AD) called the "bold and grand"—the sublime object is vast, powerful, and overwhelming. Third, the sublime "evokes ineffable and painful feelings through which a transformation occurs into pleasure and cognition." And fourth, the sublime prompts moral reflection (Freeland 1999, pp. 66–69).   20

While all four of Freeland's features are presented as necessary for an experience of the sublime, not every example of the cinematic sublime is an entire film. Scenes and parts of movies can be sublime. And commonly one or more of the features can be found without the others, in which case the film or scene does not produce an experience of the sublime.   21

The first feature, the conflict or commingling of pain and pleasure, distinguishes the sublime from the beautiful. According to Kant, there is restful contemplation in the beautiful whereas there is "mental movement" or even a "vibration" in the sublime (Freeland 1999, 70). The   22 experience of beauty is an escape from reality, whereas the experience of the sublime is a heightened, if contrived, confrontation with reality. *The Silence of the Lambs*, like most horror movies, elicits a conflict of pain and pleasure, though not an experience of the sublime. *The Passion* produces emotional conflict throughout. As Jesus is brutally beaten we want to cover our eyes, to be shielded from the pain, yet we take pleasure in knowing that the final victory will be his. Nonbelievers can also have this experience as long as they know the story from Scripture.

The second feature—greatness, power, vastness, and an overwhelm-   23
ing quality—is familiar in film. Think of *The Matrix* and Neo's awakening in a gooey pink pod to see himself one among countless others in the field of human batteries. The truth is almost too much to take. Think of *Troy* and the "thousand ships" gradually revealed as the camera pans to wider and wider shots. While *The Matrix* and *Troy* have sublime scenes, *The Passion* is powerful and overwhelming practically throughout. The mistreatment of the God-man is too much to take, with the indignities of being slapped, shackled, and spit upon. But even those who do not believe Jesus is God find the flogging, scourging, and fall-ridden way of the cross too much to bear. In a surreal scene one Roman soldier gives a lesson to another in "how it's done," oblivious to the suffering of the man whose flesh he impales with nine-inch nails. We just cringe.

Consider too the grotesque in *The Passion*: powerful, overwhelm-   24
ing, tough to stomach. Taking license with scriptural narrative, Gibson shows us the devil incarnate as an androgynous hooded figure and slithering serpent. We have no sympathy for this devil. Rather, the figure's sinister voice and appearance arouse disgust and fear, so close to Christ as it comes. As if the gore of the flogging were not enough, we see Satan as spectator, hideous child in his arms, wicked words from his forked tongue. Judas, too, is treated to the grotesque as madness descends on him. Children lose their innocence for virulence and chase him like the Furies to his suicidal end. Too much, it is all too much to bear.

The third feature, that the sublime "evokes ineffable and painful   25
feelings through which a transformation occurs into pleasure and cognition," links us to the suffering of Jesus. The sublime is related to the mystical via the ineffable, that to which we cannot give words. As Eric Bronson notes, mystics often journey through great pain to reach a higher truth that the rational mind cannot comprehend and language cannot express. The experience of the mystic is ineffable, and likewise the portrayal of the suffering of Jesus engenders an ineffable response in the viewer. Sharing vicariously in the pain of Jesus, the viewer is led to the pleasure of realizing that all is not lost. Quite the contrary, everything is gained.

Thought itself is pleasurable. "All people by nature desire to   26
know," is the first line of Aristotle's *Metaphysics*. We seek through

thought the satisfaction of knowledge, true-justified-belief. Exercise of the mind, no less than the body, though sometimes painful in the process, is pleasurable in its product. There are films that are not sublime, though they keep us wondering and reward us with knowledge in the end, such as *The Usual Suspects* and *Snatch*. Not all knowledge is of the kind that comes at the cost of transformative suffering.

The fourth feature—the prompting of moral reflection—is the most important of all. According to Freeland, a gap or disruption in the very medium of representation evokes a deep moral response from the viewer (2004, p. 27). Whereas we rest contentedly in contemplating beauty in art, the disquiet characteristic of contemplating the cinematic sublime makes us aware it is a movie we're watching. We are pushed from sympathetic emotional reactions to deep reflective cognitions, from feelings to thoughts. Our very will to shatter the illusion of the fiction of the film becomes Gibson's tool for directing our thought. According to Kant, beauty is not in the eye of the beholder but in the object, not in our subjective belief that the *Pietà* is beautiful but in the *Pietà* itself. By contrast, according to Kant, the sublime is in us—it is our experience. For Kant this makes the sublime no less objective. What we judge as sublime we implicitly believe others too should judge as sublime. Lots of movies, even cartoons like *The Lion King*, prompt moral reflections, sometimes even by disrupting the medium. But the disruption in *The Passion* purposefully engenders the sublime. 27

Consider the use of Aramaic and Latin. Whatever else may be said, these languages heighten our sense of the sublime by adding to the strange and foreign quality of our experience, making us intellectually aware that this is not the familiar version of the story from memory or imagination. The subtitles engage us cognitively in a way we would not otherwise be engaged. All viewers, aside from the scarce few who know both Latin and Aramaic, get the film with subtitles and need them to follow the dialogue. The subtitles rupture the film and lead us from the emotional to the cognitive, from feeling to thought. 28

The visceral emotional reaction to the violence, pain, suffering, gore, and grotesque overwhelms us in such a way as to compel moral reflection. And although the film may guide us towards certain moral conclusions, we need not accept them. 29

IT WASN'T SUBLIME FOR ME

Surely not everyone who has seen *The Passion* has found it sublime. Some will even agree that the film has all four of Freeland's features and yet insist that they did not experience *The Passion* as sublime. Fair enough. Does that mean that Freeland's account is mistaken? Not 30 necessarily. Does that mean that sublimity is relative, that *The Passion* can be sublime for you but not for me? Not necessarily.

Watching a film safely in the theater, like watching a stormy sea   31
safely on land, allows for an experience of the sublime. The awful and terrible sight we would run from hiding our eyes becomes the object of fascination, as pain mysteriously mingles with pleasure. Kant believed the sublime puts us in touch with a truth about ourselves, that our rational nature and free will make us superior to the sublime objects of nature, like tornadoes and tidal waves, which have the power to crush us. As Kant says, "And we like to call these objects sublime because they raise the soul's fortitude above its usual middle range and allow us to discover in ourselves an ability to resist which is of a quite different kind, and which gives us the courage [to believe] that we could be a match for nature's seeming omnipotence" (120).

Still, not everyone likes to watch tornadoes and tidal waves, feel-   32
ing fearful even at an objectively safe distance. Such a person misses out on the experience of the sublime. The tornado is perfectly capable of affording the experience of the sublime, but fear stands in the way. As Kant notes, "Just as we cannot pass judgment on the beautiful if we are seized by inclination and appetite, so we cannot pass judgment at all on the sublime in nature if we are afraid" (120). I suspect something similar occurs in the case of *some* devout Christians viewing *The Passion*. Despite the objective safety, despite knowing "it's just a movie," fear stands in the way of experiencing the sublime of *The Passion*. We can no more insist that such people watch the film again to experience the sublime than we can insist that someone watch the thunderstorm approaching. But in both cases the experience of the sublime awaits those who leave fear at the gates.

THE VIOLENCE DEFENDED

To conclude, the expectations and desires we bring to a work of art   33
shape our reactions to it. A movie director must make choices concerning how to film and tell a story, and when the story is already well known the director's choices will inevitably disappoint some. A beautiful movie would have been an ill-suited form of expression for the passion of Jesus. To be true to the subject matter Gibson was forced to make a movie that would be difficult to watch. Thus we considered the perennial philosophical question: Why do we willingly watch works of art that bring pain with pleasure? In the case of tragedies it may be that Aristotle is right, that we experience a cleansing, a catharsis. But as we saw, the story of the passion cannot be told as a tragedy. So are the controversial blood and violence of *The Passion* simply gratuitous? No,

they are justified by Gibson's attempt to deliver an experience of the sublime.

BIBLIOGRAPHY

Aristotle, Poetics (Stephen Halliwell trans.) London: Duckworth, 1986.
Edmund Burke, A Philosophical Enquiry into the Origins of our Ideas of the Sublime and Beautiful and Other Pre-Revolutionary Writings, ed. David Womersley London: Penguin Books, 1998.
Peg Zeglin Brand, ed., Beauty Matters. Bloomington and Indianapolis, IN: Indiana University Press, 2000.
Arthur C. Danto, The Abuse of Beauty: Aesthetics and the Concept of Art. Chicago: Open Court, 2003.
Cynthia Freeland, "The Sublime in Cinema," in Carl Plantinga and Greg M. Smith, eds., Passionate Views: Film, Cognition, and Emotion. Baltimore, MD: Johns Hopkins University Press, 1999, pp. 65–83.
Cynthia Freeland, "Piercing Our Inaccessible, Inmost Parts," in Chris Townsend, ed., The Art of Bill Viola. London: Thames and Hudson, 2004, pp. 24–45.
Immanuel Kant, Critique of Judgment (Werner S. Pluhar trans.) Indianapolis: Hackett Publishing Company, 1987.
Longinus, On the Sublime, James A. Arieti and Crossett trans. New York: Mellen Press, 1985.
Plato, Republic (G.M.S. Grube trans.) Indianapolis: Hackett Publishing Company, 1992, especially books II, III, and X.

Examining the Text
1. According to Irwin, what are the key differences between Gibson's *The Passion* and Michelangelo's *Pietà*? Using this comparison, what points does Irwin try to prove about the nature of beauty?
2. How does the author explain the notion of tragedy in this piece, and what examples/evidence does he bring to bear on this explanation? In what ways does *The Passion* fail to qualify as a tragedy, in his opinion? Do you agree or disagree with Irwin's point here?
3. Briefly restate the four features of the sublime that Irwin discusses. In what ways does each feature apply to Gibson's movie?
4. *Thinking rhetorically*: This question is intended to parallel the "Thinking rhetorically" question for David Denby's article on *The Passion*: namely, what is the function of Irwin's final paragraph? Do you think it is a strong conclusion for the article; why or why not? If not, what additional rhetorical strategies might the author have employed to drive home his thematic point in this piece? How does his concluding strategy differ from Denby's?

For Group Discussion

In his discussion of the sublime, Irwin relies on Cynthia Freeland's four-part definition of that elusive and much-discussed term. Reread paragraph 20, in which Irwin briefly summarizes Freeland's four key features. Then, as a group, choose one of these four and reread the section of the article where Irwin discusses that feature at greater length. (It would be very helpful to have someone in the group read the aloud.) Try to define that feature in your own words, and to apply it to another example—perhaps to another movie or to another experience you've had that does or doesn't fit the criteria. As a group, be prepared to report back to the class about the particular feature of the sublime that you discussed.

Writing Suggestion

Write an essay in which you compare and contrast Irwin's and Denby's arguments about *The Passion of the Christ*. We suggest that you begin this task in a somewhat unusual way: write down opposing or contradictory quotations from each article. For instance, Denby describes the movie as "a grimly unilluminating procession of treachery, beatings, blood, and agony"; Irwin, on the contrary, says that "A beautiful movie would have been an ill-suited form of expression for the passion of Jesus." Denby mentions "the guilt, anguish, or loathing that this movie may create" in the souls of viewers; Irwin writes that "The visceral emotional reaction to the violence, pain, suffering, gore, and grotesque overwhelms us in such a way as to compel moral reflection." Writing down quotations from each article will help you identify exactly where Denby and Irwin disagree. Once you've come up with a list of clear points of disagreement, consider whether there are any points that the two authors agree on (aside from the fact that the movie is violent, that is). Finally, write your essay focusing on the key points of comparison and contrast between the articles. You might consider concluding the essay by stating which article you found more persuasive; give reasons, of course, to support your opinion.

ADDITIONAL SUGGESTIONS FOR WRITING ABOUT MOVIES

1. In this chapter, we presented several articles that focus on a central filmic theme, namely violence. In your own interpretative essay, compare and contrast several movies dealing with a different central theme or issue. For instance, you might compare several films about the Vietnam War, or about the lives of the current generation of "Twentysomethings," or about inner-city gangs, or about parent–child relationships. Choose movies that interest you and, ideally, that you can see again. You might want to structure your essay as an argument aimed at convincing your readers that one movie is in some way "better" than the others. Or you might use your comparison of the movies to draw some larger point about popular culture and the images it presents to us.

2. In a research or "I-search" essay, consider the complex relationship between film and social morality. Do you believe that films such as *Fight Club* and *Pulp Fiction* tend to encourage audience identification with the villain and help sanction violent behavior . . . or is there a more "sublime" dimension to film violence, as suggested by some of the authors in this chapter? In your research, explore what other experts say about the relationship between real and fictional violence. Can you find specific current events that support your arguments?

3. In a speculative essay, explore why audiences crave movies of a certain genre: futuristic techno-thrillers, movies based on television sit-coms and cartoons, chase movies, menaced-female dramas, psychotic-killer stories, romantic comedies, supernatural comedies, and so forth. Choose a type of movie familiar to you so that you can offer as many specific examples as possible. In approaching this assignment, try to answer some of these questions: What is the "fun" of seeing this type of movie? What sort of "psychic relief" does it deliver? Are there specific types of people who are likely to enjoy the genre more than others? Does the genre serve any function for society? In what ways do movies in this genre affect us, changing our thoughts or feelings after we've seen them?

Internet Activities

1. These days, anyone with a Web site has the power to post a movie review. Choose several online reviews—written by both professional movie critics and "regular" moviegoers such as yourself—for a movie you've seen (some options are available on the *Common Culture* Web site). Write an essay in which you note the primary differences between the reviews done by professionals and those done by the regular fan(s). What aspects of the film do the professionals focus on? Are they the same as those of the regular fan or do they vary? Does one group emphasize certain elements, such as the emotions encouraged by the film, the acting, or the cinematography? Which of the reviews most closely reflects your opinion of the movie? Why do you think these reviews are the ones with which you best identify?

2. Visit a Web site for a new film you're interested in seeing and write a review of the site (some options are available on the *Common Culture* Web site). What is offered on the Web site that a potential audience wouldn't get from any other form of media? What do you like best about the Web site? What would you change? Describe the advantages of having a Web site for a new film. Are there any disadvantages? How do you feel movie Web sites will influence which movies we want to watch?

Reading Images

The drawing on page 608 accompanied Denby's review of *The Passion of the Christ* when it was first published in *The New Yorker*. As you can see, it depicts Mel Gibson on a cross with blood being spattered on him. After rereading the section in Chapter 1 about how to analyze images, take notes about the particular features of this image and come to a conclusion about the message that this image is intended to convey. Then in an essay, explain your analysis of the image. Also include in the essay a discussion of how the image functions in the context of the movie review. That is, does it convey exactly the same point as Denby's review, or does it emphasize certain ideas in the review and ignore others? You might conclude your essay by discussing what effect the image had on you as a reader, and whether another type of image (for instance, a still from the movie itself) would have been more or less effective.

For Further Reading: A Common Culture Bibliography

CHAPTER 2: ADVERTISING

Barthel, Diane. *Putting on Appearances: Gender and Advertising*. Philadelphia, PA: Temple University Press, 1988.

Berger, Arthur Asa. *Ads, Fads, and Consumer Culture: Advertising's Impact on American Character and Society*. Lanham, MD: Rowman & Littlefield, 2000.

Cortese, Anthony Joseph Paul. *Provocateur: Images of Women and Minorities in Advertising*. Lanham, MD: Rowman & Littlefield Publishers, 1999.

Ewen, Stuart and Elizabeth Ewen. *Channels of Desire: Mass Images and the Shaping of American Consciousness*. 2nd edition. Minneapolis, MN: University of Minnesota Press, 1992.

Fowles, Jib. *Advertising and Popular Culture*. Thousand Oaks, CA: Sage, 1996.

Fox, Roy. *Mediaspeak: Three American Voices*. Westport, CT: Praeger, 2001.

Kilbourne, Jean, director. *Still Killing Us Softly*. Cambridge, MA: Cambridge Documentary Films, 1992 Videocassette.

—. *Deadly Persuasion: Why Women and Girls Must Fight the Addictive Power of Advertising*. New York: Free Press, 1999.

Klein, Naomi. *No Logo: No Space, No Choice, No Jobs*. New York: Picador, 2002.

Lasn, Kalle. *Culture Jam: The Uncooling of America*. New York: Eagle Brook, 1999.

Mitchell, Arthur. *The Nine American Lifestyles: Who We Are and Where We're Going*. New York: Warner Books, 1983.

O'Shaughnessy, John. *The Marketing Power of Emotion*. Oxford: Oxford University Press, 2003.

Parkin, Katherine. *Food is Love: Advertising and Gender Roles in Modern America*. Pennsylvania: University of Pennsylvania Press, 2006.

Quart, Alissa. *Branded: The Buying and Selling of Teenagers*. New York: Basic Books, 2004.

Sivulka, Juliann. *Soap, Sex, and Cigarettes: A Cultural History of American Advertising*. Belmont, CA: Wadsworth, 1998.

Schor, Juliet. *Born to Buy: The Commercialized Child and the New Consumer Culture*. New York: Scribner, 2004.

Twitchell, James. *Twenty Ads That Shook the World: The Century's Most Groundbreaking Advertising and How it Changed Us All*. New York: Crown Publishers, 2000.

CHAPTER 3: TELEVISION

Abt, Vicki and Leonard Mustazza. *Coming After Oprah: Cultural Fallout in the Age of the TV Talk Show*. Bowling Green, OH: Bowling Green State University Popular Press, 1997.

Alberti, John (Ed.). *Leaving Springfield: The Simpsons and the Possibility of Oppositional Culture*. Detroit, MI: Wayne State University Press, 2004.

Andrejevic, Mark. *Reality TV: The Work of Being Watched*. Lanham, MD: Rowman & Littlefield Publishers, 2003.

Batten, Frank with Jeffrey L. Cruikshank. *The Weather Channel: The Improbably Rise of a Media Phenomenon*. Boston, MA: Harvard Business School Press, 2002.

Cantor, Paul A. *Gilligan Unbound: Pop Culture in the Age of Globalization*. Lanham, MD: Rowman & Littlefield, 2001.

Gitlin, Todd. *Inside Prime Time*. 2nd edition. New York: Pantheon, 1994.

Gray, Jonathan. *Watching with The Simpsons: Television, Parody, and Intertextuality*. New York: Routledge, 2005.

Hartley, John. *Uses of Television*. London: Routledge, 1999.

Holmes, Su and Jermyn, Deborah (Eds.). *Understanding Reality Television*. London: Routledge, 2004.

Johnson, Steven. *Everything Bad is Good For You: How Today's Popular Culture is Actually Making Us Smarter*. New York: Riverhead, 2005.

Mander, Jerry. *Four Arguments for the Elimination of Television*. New York: Morrow, 1978.

Miller, Mark Crispin. *Boxed In: The Culture of TV*. Evanston, IL: Northwestern University Press, 1988.

Morreale, Joanne (Ed.). *Critiquing the Sitcom: A Reader*. Syracuse, NY: Syracuse University Press, 2003.

Murray, Susan and Ouellette, Laurie (Eds.). *Reality TV: Remaking Television Culture*. New York: New York University Press, 2004.

Newcomb, Horace. *Television: The Critical View*. New York: Oxford University Press, 2000.

O'Neill, John. *Plato's Cave: Television and Its Discontents*. Cresskill, NJ: Hampton Press, 2002.

Oppenheimer, Jerry. *Seinfeld: The Making of an American Idol*. New York: HarperCollins, 2002.

Postman, Neil. *Amusing Ourselves to Death*. New York: Penguin Books, 1985.

Spiegel, Lynn and Olsson, Jan (Eds.). *Television After TV: Essays on a Medium in Transition*. Durham, NC: Duke University Press, 2004.

Williams, Raymond. *Television: Technology and Cultural Form*. New York: Schocken Books, 1975.

CHAPTER 4: POPULAR MUSIC

Appell, Glenn and David F. Hemphill. *American Popular Music: A Multicultural History*. New York: Wadsworth Publishing, 2005.

Baraka, Amiri. *Blues People: Negro Music in White America*. New York: Harper, 1999.

Chang, Kevin and Wayne Chen. *Reggae Routes: The Story of Jamaican Music*. Philadelphia: Temple University Press, 1998.

Chuck D. and Yusaf Jah. *Fight the Power: Rap, Race, and Reality*. New York: Delacorte Press, 1997.

Cloonan, Martin and Reebee Garofalo. *Policing Pop*. Philadelphia: Temple University Press, 2003.

Colegrave, Stephen and Chris Sullivan. *Punk: The Definitive Record of a Revolution*. Boston: Thunder's Mouth Press, 2001.

Costello, Mark and David Foster Wallace. *Signifying Rappers: Rap and Race in the Urban Present*. New York: Ecco Press, 1997.

Dickerson, James. *Women On Top: The Quiet Revolution That's Rocking the American Music Industry.* New York: Billboard Books, 1999.

Forman, Murray. *The 'Hood Comes First: Race, Space, and Place in Rap and Hip-Hop.* Middletown: Wesleyan University Press, 2002.

George, Nelson. *Hip Hop America.* New York: Viking Press, 1998.

Goodman, Fred. "La explosion pop Latino." *Rolling Stone,* n812 (May 13, 1999): 21.

Jones, Quincey and the Editors of *Vibe* Magazine. *Tupac Amaru Shakur 1971–1996.* Pittsburgh: Three Rivers Press, 1998.

Joyner, David Lee. *American Popular Music.* New York: McGraw-Hill, 2002.

Krasilovsky, M. William, Sidney Shemel and John M. Gross. *This Business of Music: The Definitive Guide to the Music Industry.* New York: Billboard Books, 2003.

Krims, Adam. *Rap Music and the Poetics of Identity.* Cambridge University Press, 2003.

Marcus, Greil. *Mystery Train: Images of America in Rock 'N' Roll Music.* New York: Plume, 1997.

Marcus, Greil. *In the Fascist Bathroom: Punk in Pop Music, 1977–1992.* Cambridge, MA: Harvard University Press, 1999.

McNeil, Legs and Gillian McCain. *Please Kill Me: The Uncensored Oral History of Punk.* New York: Penguin, 1997.

Moore, Allan F. *Analyzing Popular Music.* Boston: Cambridge University Press, 2003.

Neal, Mark Anthony. *Soul Babies: Black Popular Culture and the Post-Soul Aesthetic.* New York: Routledge, 2002.

Perkins, William Eric. *Droppin' Science: Critical Essays on Rap Music and Hip Hop Culture.* Philadelphia: Temple Univ Press, 1996.

Posner, Gerald L. *Motown: Money, Power, Sex, and Music.* New York: Random House, 2002.

Potter, Russell A. *Spectacular Vernaculars: Hip-Hop and the Politics of Postmodernism.* New York: State Univ of New York Press, 1995.

Queen Latifah. *Ladies First: Revelations from a Strong Woman.* New York: William Morrow & Company, 1999.

Reynolds, Simon. *Generation Ecstasy: Into the World of Techno and Rave Culture.* New York: Little Brown & Company, 1998.

Savage, Jon. *England's Dreaming: Anarchy, Sex Pistols, Punk Rock, and Beyond.* New York: St. Martin's Press, 2002.

Sicko, Dan. *Techno Rebels: The Renegades of Electronic Funk.* New York: Billboard Books, 1999.

Starr, Larry. *American Popular Music: From Minstrelsy to MTV.* Oxford: Oxford University Press, 2002.

Ward, Brian. *Just My Soul Responding: Rhythm and Blues, Black Consciousness, and Race Relations.* Berkeley: University of California Press, 1998.

CHAPTER 5: TECHNOLOGY

Beck, John and Wade, Mitchell. *Got Game: How the Gamer Generation is Reshaping Business Forever.* Boston, MA: Harvard Business School Press, 2004.

Blood, Rebecca. *We've Got Blog: How Weblogs are Changing Our Culture.* New York: Perseus Books, 2002.

Chayko, Mary. *Connecting: How We Form Social Bonds and Communities in the Internet Age.* Albany, NY: State University of New York Press, 2002.

Fornas, Johan (Ed.) *Digital Borderlands: Cultural Studies of Identity and Interactivity on the Internet.* New York: Peter Lang, 2002.

Gee, James Paul. *What Video Games Have to Teach Us About Learning and Literacy*. New York: Palgrave Macmillan, 2003.

Gergen, Kenneth. *The Saturated Self: Dilemmas of Identity in Contemporary Life*. New York: Basic Books, 2000.

Holloway, Sarah L. and Gill Valentine. *Cyberkids: Children in the Information Age*. London: Routledge, 2003.

Kline, David. *Blog!: How the Newest Media Revolution is Changing Politics, Business, and Culture*. New York: CDS Books, 2005.

O'Brien, Barbara. *Blogging America: Political Discourse in a Digital Nation*. New York: William James and Company, 2004.

Poole, Steven. *Trigger Happy: Videogames and the Entertainment Revolution*. New York: Arcade Publishing, 2000.

Postman, Neil. *Technopoly: The Surrender of Culture to Technology*. New York: Vintage Books, 1993.

Rheingold, Howard. *The Virtual Community: Homesteading on the Electronic Frontier*. Reading, MA: Addison-Wesley, 1993.

Smolan, Rick and Jennifer Erwitt (Eds.). *24 Hours in Cyberspace: Photographed on One Day by 150 of the World's Leading Photojournalists*. QUE Macmillan: Against All Odds Productions, 1996.

Wolf, Mark (Ed.). *The Medium of the Video Game*. Austin, TX: University of Texas Press, 2002.

Wolf, Mark and Perron, Bernard. *The Video Game Theory Reader*. London, Routledge, 2003.

CHAPTER 6: SPORTS

Bellin, Andy. *Poker Nation: A High-Stakes, Low-Life Adventure into the Heart of a Gambling Country*. New York: Harper, 2003.

Boyle, Raymond and Richard Haynes. *Power Play: Sport, the Media and Popular Culture*. New York: Longman, 2000.

Bloom, John and Michael Nevin Willard. *Sports Matters: Race, Recreation, and Culture*. New York: NYU Press, 2002.

Cahn, Susan K. *Coming on Strong: Gender and Sexuality in Twentieth-Century American Sports*. New York: Macmillan, 1994.

Coakley, Jay J. *Sport in Society: Issues and Controversies*. Boston: Irwin/McGraw-Hill, 1998.

Crawford, Garry. *Consuming Sport; Fans, Sport and Culture*. New York: Routledge, 2004.

David, Paulo. *Human Rights in Youth Sport*. New York: Routledge, 2004.

Eitzen, D. Stanley. *Fair and Foul: Beyond the Myths and Paradoxes of Sport*. New York: Rowman & Littlefield, 2006.

Gerdy, John R. *Sports: The All-American Addiction*. Mississippi: University Press of Mississippi, 2002.

Leifer, Eric Matheson. *Making the Majors: The Transformation of Team Sports in America*. Cambridge: Harvard University Press, 1995.

Lupica, Mike. *Mad as Hell: How Sports Got Away From the Fans—and How We Get it Back*. New York: Putnam, 1996.

Miller, Toby. *Sportsex*. Philadelphia: Temple University Press, 2002.

Munslow, Alun (Foreword) and Murray G. Phillips (Editor). *Deconstructing Sport History: A Postmodern Analysis*. New York: State University of New York Press, 2006.

Nelson, Mariah Burton. *The Stronger Women Get, the More Men Love Football: Sexism and the American Culture of Sports*. New York: Harcourt Brace, 1994.

Platt, Larry. *New Jack Jocks: Rebels, Race, and the American Athlete*. Philadelphia: Temple University Press, 2002.

Quirk, James P. and Rodney Fort. *Hard Ball: The Abuse of Power in Pro Team Sports*. Princeton: Princeton University Press, 1999.

Rinehart, Robert E. and Synthia Sydnor. *To the Extreme: Alternative Sports, Inside and Out*. New York: State University of New York Press, 2003.

Sugden, John and Alan Tomlinson. *A Critical Sociology of Sport*. New York: Routledge, 2002.

Vlasich. James A. (Editor). *Horsehide, Pigskin, Oval Tracks And Apple Pie: Essays on Sport And American Culture*. McFarland & Company, 2005.

Weyland, Jocko. *The Answer Is Never: A Skateboarder's History of the World*. New York: Grove Press, 2002.

Wilcox, Ralph C. et al. *Sporting Dystopias: The Making and Meaning of Urban Sport Cultures*. New York: State University of New York Press, 2003.

CHAPTER 7: MOVIES

Benshoff, Harry M. and Sean Griffin. *America on Film: Representing Race, Class, Gender, and Sexuality at the Movies*. New York: Blackwell, 2003.

Bernard Jami. *Quentin Tarantino: The Man and His Movies*. New York: Harper Perennial, 1996.

Charyn, Jerome. *Raised by Wolves: The Turbulent Art and Times of Quentin Tarantino*. New York: Thunder's Mouth Press, 2006.

Denzin, Norman K. *Images of Postmodern Society: Social Theory and Contemporary Cinema*. New York: Sage Publications, 2001.

Dixon, Wheeler Winston. *Straight: Constructions of Heterosexuality in the Cinema*. New York: State University of New York Press, 2003.

Dunne, John Gregory. *Monster: Living Off the Big Screen*. New York: Random House, 1997.

Dunne, Michael. *Intertextual Encounters in American Fiction, Film, and Popular Culture*. Bowling Green: Popular Press, 2001.

Fredriksen, Paula (Editor). *On The Passion of the Christ: Exploring the Issues Raised by the Controversial Movie*. Berkeley: University of California Press, 2006.

Gabler, Neal. *Life, the Movie: How Entertainment Conquered Reality*. New York: Knopf, 1998.

Grundmann, Roy. *Andy Warhol's Blow Job: Culture and the Moving Image*. Philadelphia: Temple University Press, 2003.

Haberski, Raymond J. *It's Only a Movie!: Films and Critics in American Culture*. Louisville: University Press of Kentucky, 2001.

Lopate, Phillip. *Totally, Tenderly, Tragically: Essays and Criticism from a Lifelong Love Affair with the Movies*. New York: Anchor Books, 1998.

Martinez, Gerald. *What It Is . . . What It Was! The Black Film Explosion of the '70s in Words and Pictures*. New York: Hyperion, 1998.

May, Larry. *The Big Tomorrow: Hollywood and the Politics of the American Way*. Chicago: University of Chicago Press, 2002.

Muller, Eddie. *Dark City: The Lost World of Film Noir*. St. Martin's Press, 1998.

Naremore, James. *More Than Night: Film Noir in Its Contexts*. Berkeley: University of California Press, 1998.

Natoli, Joseph P. *Memory's Orbit: Film and Culture, 1999–2000.* New York: State University of New York Press, 2003.

Rueschmann, Eva. *Moving Pictures, Migrating Identities.* Mississippi: University Press of Mississippi, 2003.

Skal, David. *The Monster Show: A Cultural History of Horror.* Boston: Faber & Faber, 2001.

Skal, David J. *Screams of Reason: Mad Science in Modern Culture.* New York: W.W. Norton & Company, 1998.

Slotkin, Richard. *Gunfighter Nation: The Myth of the Frontier in Twentieth-Century America.* Norman: University of Oklahoma Press, 1998.

Tarkovsky, Andrey. *Sculpting in Time: Reflections on the Cinema.* Austin: University of Texas Press, 1989.

Trice, Ashton D. and Samuel A. Holland. *Heroes, Antiheroes and Dolts: Portrayals of Masculinity in American Popular Films 1921–1999.* New York: McFarland & Company, 2001.

Acknowledgments

TEXT CREDITS

p. 158 Harry Waters, "Life According to TV" from *Newsweek* (December 6, 1982). Copyright © 1982 by Newsweek, Inc. All rights reserved. Reprinted with permission.

p. 169 Steven Johnson, "Watching TV Makes You Smarter" from *Everything Bad is Good for You*. Originally published in *The New York Times Magazine* (April 24, 2005). Copyright © 2005 by Steven Johnson. Reprinted with the permission of Riverhead Books, an imprint of Penguin Group (USA) Inc.

p. 193 Robert Samuels, "Keeping It Real: Why We Like to Watch Reality Dating Television Shows." Reprinted with the permission of the author.

p. 201 Paul A. Cantor, "The Simpsons: Atomistic Politics and the Nuclear Family" from *Political Theory* 27, no. 6 (December 1999): 734. Copyright © 1999 by Sage Publications, Inc. Reprinted with the permission of the publisher.

p. 219 Lisa Frank, "The Evolution of the Seven Deadly Sins: From God to the Simpsons" from *Journal of Popular Culture* 35, no 1 (Summer 2001). Reprinted with the permission of Blackwell Publishers, Ltd.

p. 237 Rachel E. Sullivan, "Rap and Race: It's Got a Nice Beat, But What About the Message?" from *Journal of Black Studies* 33, no. 5 (May 2003). Copyright © 2003 by Sage Publications, Inc. Reprinted with the permission of the publisher.

p. 252 Evelyn Jamilah, "The Miseducation of Hip-Hop" from *Black Issues in Higher Education* 17 (December 7, 2000). Copyright © 2000. Reprinted by permission.

p. 261 Vincent Stephens, "Pop Goes the Rapper: A Close Reading of Eminem's Genderphobia" from *Popular Music* 24/1 (2005). Copyright © 2005. Reprinted with the permission of Cambridge University Press.

p. 284 Gary Burns, "Marilyn Manson and the Apt Pupils of Littleton" from *Popular Music and Society* 2, no. 3 (Fall 1999). Reprinted with the permission of the author and Taylor & Francis Ltd., *http://www.tandf.co.uk/journals*

p. 286 James Brooke, excerpt from "Teachers of Colorado's Gunmen Alerted Parents" from *The New York Times* (May 11, 1999): A14. Copyright © 1999 by The New York Times Company. Reprinted with permission.

p. 291 John Seabrook, "The Money Note: Can the Record Business Be Saved?" from *The New Yorker* 79:18 (July 2003). Copyright © 2003 by John Seabrook. Reprinted with the permission of the author.

p. 316 Alex Ross, "I Hate Classical Music" from *The New Yorker* 80:1 (February 2004). Copyright © 2004 by Alex Ross. Reprinted with the permission of the author.

p. 339 Robert Samuels, "Breaking Down Borders: How Technology Transforms the Private and Public Realms." Reprinted with the permission of the author.

p. 343 John Perry Barlow, "Cyberhood vs. Neighborhood" from *Utne Reader* 58 (March–April 1995). Reprinted with the permission of the author.

p. 351 Christine Rosen, "Our Cell Phones, Ourselves" from *The New Atlantis: A Journal of Technology and Society* (Summer 2004), *www.thenewatlantis.com/archive/6/rosen.htm*. Copyright © 2004. Reprinted with the permission of the publishers.

p. 372 Steve Jones, "Let the Games Begin: Gaming Technology and Entertainment among College Students," Pew Internet and American Life Project. *www.pewinternet.org/pdfs/PIP_College_Gaming_Reports.pdf*. Reprinted with permission.

p. 385 Brian Cowlishaw, "Playing War: The Emerging Trend of Real Virtual Combat in Current Video Games" from *Magazine Americana: The American Popular Culture Online Magazine* (January 2005). *www.americanpopularculture.com/archive/emerging/real_virtual_combat.htm*. Reprinted with permission.

p. 399 Rebecca Blood, "Weblogs: A History and Perspective" from *Rebecca's Pocket* (September 7, 2000). Copyright © 2000 by Rebecca Blood. Reprinted with permission.

p. 407 John Hiler, "Borg Journalism" (April 1, 2002), from *www.microcontentnews.com/articles/borgjournalism.htm*. Reprinted with the permission of John Hiler.

p. 421 Peter Cary, Randy Dotinga and Avery Comarow, "Fixing Kids' Sports" from *U.S. New & World Report* 126, No. 20 (June 7, 2004). Copyright © 2004. Reprinted with permission.

p. 432 "Baby, You're the Greatest" from *ESPN Magazine* (February 14, 2005). Copyright © 2005. Reprinted with the permission of ESPN Magazine.

p. 440 Jaime Schultz, "Discipline and Push-Up: Female Bodies, Feminism, and Sexuality in Popular Representations of Sports Bras" from *Sociology of Sport Journal* 1 (June 2004). Copyright © 2004 by Human Kinetics Publishers, Inc. Reprinted with the permission of the author and Human Kinetics (Champaign, IL).

p. 467 Justin Peters, "Jack of Smarts: Why the Internet Generation Loves to Play Poker" from *The Washington Monthly* 36, No. 5 (May 2004). Copyright © 2004 by Washington Monthly Publishing, LLC. Reprinted with the permission of *The Washington Monthly*, 733 15th Street, NW, Suite 520, Washington, DC 20005.

p. 473 Tram Nguyen, "World Games: The U.S. Tries to Colonize Sport" from *ColorLines* 3, No. 1 (March 2, 2005). Copyright © 2005. Reprinted with the permission of the author and *Color Lines*.

p. 481 Paul Roberts, "Risk" from *Psychology Today* 27, No. 6 (November–December 1994). Copyright © 1994 by Sussex Publishers, Inc. Reprinted with the permission of Psychology Today Magazine.

p. 491 William Dowell and the Editors of Time Magazine, "Life on the Edge" from *Time* 154, no. 10 (September 6, 1999). Copyright © 1999 by Time, Inc. Reprinted with permission.

p. 500 Maya Angelou, "Champion of the World" from *I Know Why the Caged Bird Sings*. Copyright © 1969 by Maya Angelou. Reprinted with the permission of Random House, Inc.

p. 504 Jay Nordlinger, "Tiger Time: The Wonder of an American Hero" from *National Review* 53, no. 8 (April 30, 2001). Copyright © 2001. Reprinted with the permission of United Media.

p. 510 Marcos Bréton, "Fields of Broken Dreams: Latinos and Baseball" from *ColorLines* 3, No. 1 (January 24, 2005). Reprinted with the permission of the author and *ColorLines*.

PHOTOGRAPH AND ILLUSTRATION CREDITS

Chapter 1:   p. 1 Dan Krauss/AP Wide World Photos

Chapter 2:   p. 47 Timex Corporation; p. 56 Adbusters, Inc.; p. 114 The Mary Boone Gallery, New York

Chapter 3:   p. 144 The New Yorker Magazine, Inc./The Cartoon Bank; p. 168 Santa Barbara News-Press; p. 218 Twentieth Century Fox/Neal Peters Collection

Chapter 4:   p. 235 The Lord Group; p. 287 AP Wide World Photos; Photograph from Lord, Dentsu & Partners/NY. Copyright © 1993 TKD Electronics Corporation.

Chapter 5:   p. 337 Victor Habbick Visions/Photo Researchers, Inc.; p. 352 Joseph Farris, CartoonArts International/Cartoonists & Writers Syndicate

Chapter 6:   p. 419 Mark J. Terrill/AP Wide World Photos; p. 493 AP Wide World Photos; p. 495 John Storey/Getty Images/Time Life Pictures; p. 502 AP Wide World Photos

Chapter 7:   p. 521 Universal City Studios, Inc./Photofest; p. 529 Getty Images, Inc./Hulton Archive Photos; p. 608 Gerald Scarfe Limited

Color insert: p. CI-1 (top) Aaron Goodman; (bottom) Kimmy McCann; "Conversion Barbie", c. 2001 Kimmy McCann, Artist. Private Collection: Ms. Taea Calcut. p. CI-2 (top) Adbusters, Inc.; (bottom) Tom Allison and Chris Gomien/Carl Solway Gallery; p. CI-3 Frank Trapper/Corbis Sygma; p. CI-4 DMI/TimePix; Getty Image/Time Life Pictures; p. CI-5 Picture Desk, Inc./Kobal Collection; p. CI-6 Picture Desk, Inc./Kobal Collection; p. CI-7 Mike Blake/Corbis/Reuters America LLC; p. CI-8 Picture Desk, Inc./Kobal Collection. Photographer: Phillipe Antonello/Icon Productions.

Index by Author and Title

Index by Academic Discipline

Index by Rhetorical Mode